ISBN 978-1-330-65421-7
PIBN 10087970

This book is a reproduction of an important historical work. Forgotten Books uses
state-of-the-art technology to digitally reconstruct the work, preserving the original format
whilst repairing imperfections present in the aged copy. In rare cases, an imperfection in
the original, such as a blemish or missing page, may be replicated in our edition. We do,
however, repair the vast majority of imperfections successfully; any imperfections that
remain are intentionally left to preserve the state of such historical works.

1 MONTH OF
FREE
READING

at
www.ForgottenBooks.com

By purchasing this book you are eligible for one month membership to ForgottenBooks.com, giving you unlimited access to our entire collection of over 700,000 titles via our web site and mobile apps.

To claim your free month visit:
www.forgottenbooks.com/free87970

Similar Books Are Available from
www.forgottenbooks.com

Revd George Ross

the kind regards of

William Laurie

4th March
1878

LINDORES ABBEY

AND ITS

𝔅urgh of 𝔑ewburgh.

PRINTED BY CRAWFORD AND M'CABE

FOR

EDMONSTON & DOUGLAS

EDINBURGH.

LONDON, - - - - HAMILTON, ADAMS, & CO.

CAMBRIDGE, - - - MACMILLAN & CO.

GLASGOW, - - - - JAMES MACLEHOSE.

MUGDRUM CROSS

NORTH SIDE

LINDORES ABBE

AND ITS

THEIR HISTORY AND ANNALS

BY

ALEXANDER LAING, F.S.A. Scot.

Mankind
By empires and by races metes its life,
And each to each bequeaths its legacy
Of lore and wisdom.

W. Davy Watson.

Edinburgh
EDMONSTON AND DOUGLAS

MDCCCLXXVI

PREFACE.

———◦×◦———

THE following pages are the fruit of leisure hours in the intervals of business. They have extended to a greater length than I contemplated, and yet they do not embrace all that I originally intended. The more closely I studied our ancient records, the more I felt that ' the early life of a community contains the seeds of its greatness or of its decay,' and that no mere narrative could convey half so vivid an impression of the state of society in the past, as the contemporary records of the words and deeds of the men and women who died and suffered at the time.

These considerations induced me to make lengthened extracts from local records, which may prove dry and uninteresting to the cursory reader, but are nevertheless the foundations of true history. These records bring to light customs and modes of procedure, which filled a large place in the public mind, and in the daily life, of the times to which they relate; but which are now utterly unknown. I regret that in printing some of the earliest of these extracts, I should have fallen into the error of using *z* for *y*, and *ye* for *the;* these are now generally admitted to be corruptions of the forms of the old letters ȝ and þ, which are equivalent to *y* and *th* respectively.

The length to which these extracts have extended, has induced me to leave out biographical sketches of men born in Newburgh, or connected with the neighbourhood, who acquired distinction in their respective spheres; narratives of adventures and escapes incident to a seafaring population, and events illustrative of social life in bygone times. These sketches, if health and leisure permit, may form the subject of a separate publication. I much wish, also, that I could find leisure to prepare a history of Abernethy; more especially as, in a hurriedly written lecture delivered some years since, and afterwards published, I made some statements, which I would now alter.

In the preparation of the present volume I have received much kindness from David Laing, Esq., LL.D., of the Signet Library, in affording me information, and in putting manuscripts, from his ample stores, at my disposal. I owe a like acknowledgment to John Stuart, Esq., LL.D., for his uniform help and encouragement. To Thomas Dickson, Esq., Curator of the Historical Department of the Register House, for much and constant aid in collating manuscripts, and furnishing information otherwise inaccessible. To Andrew Jervise, Esq. of Brechin, for counsel and assistance, and for the sketches of Stob Cross, and of the window of the ruined chapel at Ayton; engravings of which appear among the illustrations of this volume. To all these gentlemen my warmest thanks are due. My best thanks are also due to J. D. Marwick, Esq., Town-Clerk of Glasgow; Arthur Mitchell, Esq., M.D., Edinburgh; to Joseph Anderson, Esq., of the Museum of Antiquities, Edinburgh; to Thomas Ross, Esq., Architect, Edinburgh, for the ground-plan and drawings of Lindores Abbey; and to John Young, Esq., C.E., and Architect, Perth, for the ground-plan and section of the Fort on Clachard Craig. I have also to express my sincere thanks to the Magistrates and Town-Council of Newburgh, and to the Ministers and Kirk-Sessions of the parishes of Newburgh and Abdie, for the ready access they have afforded me to the records under their charge. I beg also to express my obligations and thanks to the Right Reverend Dr Wordsworth, Bishop of St Andrews, for the elucidation of an ancient ecclesiastical practice otherwise unexplained. To William Tullis, Esq., Rothes, Markinch, for notices of the ancient topography of that parish. To my aunt, Mrs Charlotte Anderson, for reminiscences of old customs. To Mr John Cameron, schoolmaster of Abdie, for the etymology of names of places in the neighbourhood ; though it is right to state, that he is not answerable for all the derivations from Gaelic that have been given in the following pages.

My especial thanks are due to George Wilson, Esq., S.S.C., Edinburgh, for the ready access he has afforded me to the Mugdrum archives. To John Berry, Esq. of Tayfield and Inverdovat ; Andrew Walker Buist, Esq. of Berryhill ; and Major F. W. Balfour of Fernie, for putting their old charters and writs at my service. To Sir Patrick Murray Threipland, Bart., for information regarding the ancient possessions of the Earls of Newburgh. I beg also to express my obligations to Thomas Barclay, Esq., Sheriff-Clerk of Fife ; Walter Malcolm, Esq., North Berwick ; and to William A. Taylor, Esq., Cupar-Fife. To William Ballingall, Esq., Engraver, Edinburgh, for the use of the blocks of the engravings of Abdie Old Church, and of the view from Cross Macduff ; and for the care and pains which he has bestowed on the engravings which illustrate this volume. Also to William Proudfoot, Esq., Perth, for the drawing of the moulding of the door-way in the nave of the Abbey Church ; and to the Council of the Society of Antiquaries of Scotland, for the use of the electrotype of the carved stone ball and blocks of the engravings of the *Bos primigenius* belonging to the Society.

The list of plants in the Appendix is perhaps more

copious than it should have been in a book devoted to antiquities; but I was specially desirous of making it as full as possible, and of giving the exact *habitats* of the plants growing in the neighbourhood, in the hope that the youth of both sexes may be induced to study those beautiful creations of God, and partake of the ever-increasing enjoyment which the study of any department of His works never fails to afford. I have been enabled to supplement this list by the kindness of John Sadler, Esq. of the Royal Botanic Gardens, Edinburgh, in supplying me with a note of the plants gathered by Professor Balfour's class, on an excursion to Loch Lindores and Marie's Craig, in 1873. I have also to thank Charles Howie, Esq. of Largo, for additions to the list.

In conclusion, I have to express my obligations to James A. Smith, Esq., London, for researches made expressly in the British Museum, and for assistance in compiling the Index appended. I tender my best thanks to him and to all others who have assisted me from the beginning, without whose ever-ready help this volume would have been much more imperfect than it is.

NEWBURGH-ON-TAY, 21st *March* 1876.

Inscription

ON THE SEAL REFERRED TO AT PAGE 67, WHICH IS NOT THAT OF
ABBOT THOMAS AS THERE STATED, BUT THE COMMON
SEAL OF LINDORES ABBEY.

✠ Sigillum Sante Marie Virginis de Lundore.

CONTENTS.

——◦◦—

CHAPTER I.

PREHISTORIC.

Ancient canoes found in the bed of the Tay, opposite Lindores Abbey—
Skull of a *Bos primigenius* discovered at Mugdrum—Still entire—Its size—
Primeval Circular huts—Traces of early cultivation—Raised terraces—Hill
forts—Entrenched fort on Clachard—Carved stone ball found there,

CHAPTER II.

THE ROMAN INVASION.

Appearance of the natives of Britain at that era—The Horesti inhabited Fife
Cohort of them served on the Rhine—Tutelary *genius* raised by them—Still
preserved—Roman army in Fife, ...

CHAPTER III.

CELT AND TEUTON.

Early occupation of Fife by the Celtic race—Evidence of this in the oldest
names of places—Instances adduced—Remarkable prevalence of the prefix
Pit in the neighbourhood of Abernethy—Early immigration of Frisians—
Danish names and terms common in neighbourhood—Idiom peculiar to South
Jutland prevalent in Newburgh, ...

CHAPTER IV.

PAGAN RELIGIONS.

The religion of the Celtic people 'Druidical'—Its tenets—Scandinavians
worshippers of Odin and Thor—Their funeral rites—Buried their chiefs on
heights—Origin of term 'Law,' applied to hills—Ancient relics found at
Norrie's Law—Cotemporary description of a burial of a chieftain—Similar
rites among ancient Aryans, ...

CHAPTER IX.

ABBOTS GUIDO, JOHN, THOMAS, JOHN, AND NICHOLAS.

CHAPTER X.

EDWARD AND WALLACE.

CHAPTER XI.

ABBOTS ADAM, WILLIAM OF ANGUS, ROGER, AND JOHN STEELE.
THE DUKE OF ROTHESAY.

CHAPTER XII.

PRE-REFORMATION MARTYRS. ABBOTS JAMES, JOHN, AND ANDREW CAVERS.

CHAPTER XIII.

ABBOTS HENRY, JOHN PHILIP, AND JOHN LESLIE. PATRICK HAMILTON, MARTYR.

CHAPTER XIV.

THE COMMENDATOR.

CHAPTER XV.

THE BURGH OF NEWBURGH.

CHAPTER XIX.

WITCHCRAFT.

CHAPTER XX.

PAROCHIAL ANNALS.

CHAPTER XXI.

FROM THE REVOLUTION TO THE 'PORTY-PIVE.'

CHAPTER XXII.

ECCLESIASTICAL AND MAGISTERIAL RULE.

CHAPTER XXIII.

INDUSTRIAL PURSUITS.

CHAPTER XXIV.

SCULPTURED STONE AT LINDORES, MUGDRUM CROSS; AND CROSS MACDUFF.

CHAPTER XXV.

DENMILN CASTLE.

CHAPTER XXVI.

OLD CUSTOMS AND FOLKLORE.

APPENDIX.

——✳——

ILLUSTRATIONS.

———✳———

CHAPTER I.

PREHISTORIC.[1]

What aspect bore the man who roved or fled,
First of his tribe to this fair vale
What hopes came with him?'

Wordsworth.

MODERN investigation has, in comparatively recent times, endeavoured to make up for the lack of written history, by the study of the structure of language, and by a scientific examination of the relics of the past. Students of language affirm that the affinity of nations, now far apart, is as clearly proved by the science of philology, as any fact in modern history; and modern archæology, by the inductive examination of existing remains, has unquestionably thrown light on the occupations and condition of those who fashioned and used the rude implements, that have from time to time been discovered.

It needs no evidence to prove that the men who navigated our shores and rivers, in canoes hollowed out of single trees, had made but little progress in the constructive arts. About sixty years ago two canoes, so made, were found in the bed of the Tay, opposite

---

[1] Portions of this, and of the immediately succeeding chapters, have already appeared as a contribution to Mr Ballingall's 'Shores of Fife.'

A

Lindores Abbey, the largest was twenty-eight feet long, and was quite entire.[1]

Another relic, telling of a condition and aspect of country widely different from the present, was discovered in the neighbourhood of Newburgh, in the end of the last century. In draining what was called the Session Loch, at Mugdrum, the skull of a 'Great Ox,' *Bos primigenius*, or *Urus*, was found. So huge was this skull, that even in that unscientific age the people flocked to see it. Dr Fleming, in his 'History of British Animals,' records that it was 27½ inches in length.[2] He says nothing of the kind of strata in which it was found, for geologists to build deductions on; but the cutting was carried through a great ridge of sand and river gravel, and the head was discovered at a considerable depth below the surface. The *Urus* was little inferior to the elephant in size; one skull measured by Cuvier gave the proportions of the animal to be 12 feet in length and 6½ in height. Other skeletons have been found of much greater magnitude, affording indubitable evidence of the gigantic size of these wild denizens of the ancient Scottish forests.

The wild ox was a favourite object of the chase among our barbarian forefathers, and it was counted a great feat for a young man to bring home the horns of a *Urus*; they edged the finest of these horns with silver, and used them as drinking cups at great festal gatherings.[3] It is believed that the Urus existed in the

---

[1] These canoes were taken out of the Cruive bank opposite Lindores Abbey. They were cut up and used for lintels in the erection of granaries at the west shore of Newburgh. The largest canoe ever found in Scotland was 36 feet long and 4 feet wide,—it was discovered at Carron.—Wilson's *Prehist. Ann.*, Ed. 1851., p. 32. Out of a list of about fifty ancient canoes, recorded as having been discovered in the west of Europe, only three are mentioned as larger than the largest found in the Cruive bank. There is one which was found in the Rhône, preserved in the museum at Lyons, 41 feet long.—Figuier's *Primitive Man*, p. 17.

[2] Wilson's *Prehist. Ann.*, p. 23, Ed. 1851.

[3] The representation of hunting scenes, on so many of the 'Sculptured Stones of Scotland,' of which Mugdrum Cross is an instance, is enduring evidence of the importance of the chase among our forefathers.

forests of Central Europe down to the beginning or middle of the sixteenth century; but when these wild oxen ceased to exist in Britain is nowhere recorded. Julius Cæsar, in speaking of them, says, 'Even when taken young they could not be tamed, and never were domesticated.' 'Their swiftness,' he adds, 'was as great as their strength, and they often attacked both man and beast.'[1]

It is obvious that an animal so huge and fierce required an extensive range for concealment and pasturage, and that the country at that period must have been for the most part a dense primeval forest.

In a district so thoroughly cultivated as Fife, most of the traces of primitive occupation have been obliterated by the plough, but on the southern shoulder of the hill immediately behind Newburgh, a little west from Ormiston, may still be seen the foundation of one of those primeval circular huts, of which numerous clusters remain, where they happen to be out of the range of cultivation. The floor of the hut measures thirty feet in diameter, and, like almost all of the kind that have been discovered, the doorway faces the south. There seems no reason to doubt that this is the remains

---

[1] Their strength and fierceness are forcibly set forth in the book of Job (xxxix. 9, 10), where, speaking of the Unicorn or *Reem*, which has been identified with the Urus, it is asked,

> ' Will the unicorn be willing to serve thee,
> Or abide by thy crib ?
> Canst thou bind the unicorn with his band in the furrow ?
> Or will he harrow the valleys after thee ? '

W. Boyd Dawkins quoted Wood's *Bible Annals*, p. 128. Smith's *Dict. of the Bible, Reem*. The wild cattle protected at Chillingham and other places in the country, are, in the opinion of scientific men, the descendants of a smaller breed than the *Bos primigenius.*—*Proceedings of Society of Antiquaries*, Vol. IX. p. 587-674.

' It is worthy of mention, that when new magistrates are elected in the Swiss Canton of Uri, which, it is understood, derives its name from the Urus, two ancient and gigantic horns are carried in solemn procession before the newly elected magistrates.'—Wood's *Bible Animals*, p. 127.

of one of those kind of huts, having a tapering roof of straw or wattles, which Julius Cæsar found the inhabitants of the southern portion of the island occupying at the time of his invasion (B.C. 55).[1] In its immediate neighbourhood we have evidence that its occupants had advanced beyond the nomadic state, and were in the enjoyment of the comforts derived from the cultivation of the soil. Close by, where there are patches of soil of that rich dry kind to be found on the shelves of the trap formation, are still to be seen several short, narrow, high-raised ridges, evidently the remains of primitive agriculture. Close at hand there are also yet to be seen traces of a small square fold for cattle, so well chosen, that in stormy weather the flocks still seek shelter in and around it. There is of very necessity much obscurity regarding primitive agriculture,—the silent on-goings of peace taking less hold on the imagination or memory, than the feats of war, and they are therefore left unrecorded. But beyond all doubt, there are in many places 'marks of cultivation at a height above where any farmer would now think of ploughing or sowing.'[2] One explanation of this may be found in the fact, that the low lands, at that early period, were either in a state of morass, utterly unfit for bearing grain, or overgrown with wood. As usual, when the people meet with any work of antiquity which they do not understand, they attribute it to supernatural agency,—this elevated tillage is accordingly known, in many parts of the country, as *elf furrows*. The very small patches, however, which exhibit evidence of cultivation, show how circumscribed were the agricultural operations in these early times, and how dependent the

---

[1] *See* Wilson's *Prehistoric Annals*, chap. iv., for an interesting account of these primitive dwellings; also '*Proceedings of the Society of Antiquaries*,' Vol. VI., pp. 402–410, for an equally interesting account of groups of them at Balnabroch, in the parish of Kirkmichael, Strathardle, by John Stuart, LL.D., Secy. of the Society of Antiq. There are traces of the foundation of a smaller hut, 20 feet in diameter, adjacent to the one mentioned in the text.

[2] Cosmo Innes, *Pro. of Soc. of Ant.*, Vol. V., p. 203; Sinclair's *Statist. Acct.*, Vol. II., p. 582.

population must have been on their cattle, and perhaps in no less a degree, on the chase, for sustenance.[1]

The remains of the dire necessities of war are, however, more prominent than those of the arts of peace. On the Black Cairn, the highest point of the Ochils behind Newburgh, there is one of those rude stone entrenchments named in Irish Gaelic, *Cathair*, encircling the summit which are found on so many isolated heights throughout Scotland. It is of the rudest description, consisting merely of loose stones, no earthwork having apparently ever been cast up. It exhibits no trace of vitrification, and there

---

[1] The numerous terraces which are found on hillsides in Scotland are believed, with good reason, to have been thrown up for the cultivation of grain; and it is obvious, that this mode of treating the soil must have had the same effect as draining in modern times, making the ground thrown up not only deeper but drier, and fitter for bearing crops.

'There are few hills,' says the writer of the Old Statistical Account (of Buittle), ' in this part of Galloway where cultivation is at all practicable, that do not bear distinct marks of the plough. The depth of the furrows too plainly declare that this tillage has not been casual, or merely experimental, but frequent and successive.'—Vol. XVII., p. 115. There is an exhaustive paper on the subject in the first Vol. of *Proceedings of the Society of Antiquaries*, p. 127, by Robert Chambers.

This mode of cultivation on terraces seems to have been prevalent in all countries. Mr Disraeli says, ' The wide plains of the Holy Land are as fertile and as fair as in old days,—it is the hill culture that has been destroyed, and that is the culture on which Judea mainly depended. Its hills were terraced gardens, vineyards, and groves of olive trees.' In the Malay Archipelago this mode of cultivation is universally adopted by the natives in that extensive group of islands.

On the hill above Strathmiglo there is a series of terraces marked on the Ordnance map, which were evidently for cultivation. But all the existing terraces were not for that purpose,—some, such as the series on the north side of the height behind Markinch, were undoubtedly formed for public spectacles,— the fact of the field which they overlook being still known by the name of the *Playfield*, corroborates this, and shows that they were used for the exhibition of those ' miracle plays ' which formed such a marked feature in the amusements of the people in mediæval times. ' Few towns of note were without such places, That of Cupar was on the Castle Hill.'—Hugo Arnot's *Hist. of Edinburgh*. Thousands of all grades of society, from royalty downwards, assembled to witness these spectacles.

is not the slightest defensive skill displayed beyond the mere raising of a rampart. On Norman's Law, in the adjoining parish of Abdie, there is the hill fort of Dunmore (the *Great Fort*), of the same description, but much more extensive. It, however, displays considerable advance in the art of fortification, the entrance having bastions for defence, though the ramparts are equally rude in their construction, being merely rubble stones thrown together. The frequent notices of the burning of these hill-forts shows that there were dwellings within the circuit of the entrenchments, and in 'many of them vestiges of circular foundations may yet be seen, as at the Catherthuns, in Strathmore;'[1] but no traces of dwellings are visible within the fort on Dunmore, or on the Black Cairn. The circular huts within these rude forts, were frail tenements, similar to the one already described, and they constituted the dwellings of the Caledonians, down at least to the sixth century.[2] This is corroborated by numerous passages in the Irish records. A writer well acquainted with the subject says, 'In the seventh century those *duns* and *raths* were the abodes of kings and chieftains, and that within the security of the entrenchments there were dwellings for a considerable population.'[3]

Since the plantation on the Black Cairn has grown up, the entrenchment around it has become moss-covered, and it is now scarcely known; but in the last generation it was familiarly known by the name of 'The Ring' (as the White Catherthun in Strathmore is to this day); and it is so designated (A.D. 1457) in the charter by the Abbot of Lindores, which confirms the

---

[1] *Book of Deer.* Preface, p. lvii.

[2] *Ibid.* The Celtic word *Cathair*, denotes a class of forts formed of uncemented stone walls, and is the same as the British *Kaer.—Book of Deer*, p. clv. This seems the origin of the name Blackcairn. 'The primary meaning of the Celtic word *dun*, is, strong or firm.'—*Joyce*, p. 266. And as fortified places were almost invariably thrown up by the native tribes on hills, the Celtic *Dun* forms a prefix to numerous hills in Scotland.

[3] O'Donovan, quoted by Joyce.—*Irish Names*, p. 257.

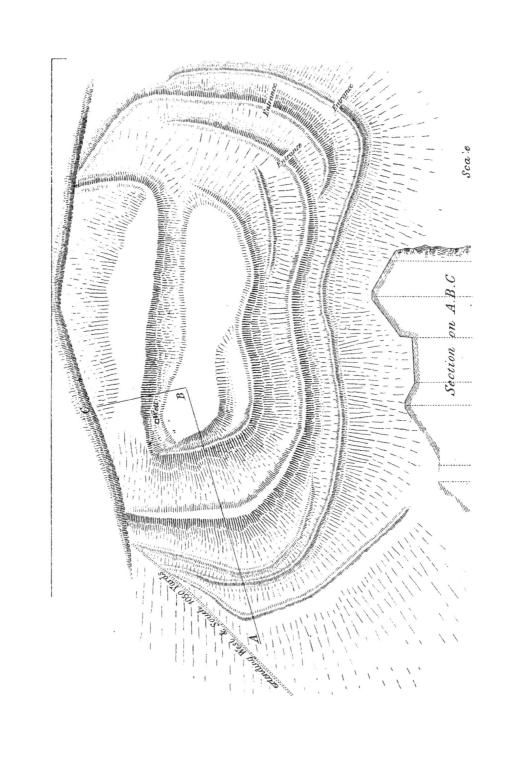

Section on A.B.C

Scale

possession of it to the burgesses of Newburgh, to whom it still belongs.[1]

On the picturesque craig of Clachard, almost overhanging Lindores Abbey, there is a stronghold, displaying in its construction a great advance over the ruder defensive works of the Black Cairn and Norman's Law. The entrenchments are skilfully adapted to the nature of the ground, the most assailable points having a succession of ramparts of great strength. On the west side there are six ramparts in succession, some of them from five to six feet in height, and of proportionate thickness. They are now covered with a beautiful sward, but internally are made up of earth and stones,—many of the latter being free-stones brought from the valley beneath, and must have been carried up with great labour, the ascent being very precipitous in that direction. Like most forts of the kind, the pasturage within the entrenchments is nutritious, and capable of sustaining a considerable number of cattle on an emergency.[2] The magnitude and extent of the defensive works of Clachard bear unmistakeable evidence of the condition of insecurity which prevailed at the time of their construction; and their substantial character testifies that this insecurity was not of a passing nature, but seems to indicate a condition of tribal warfare, which it was necessary at all times to be prepared for.[3]

---

[1] *Chartulary of Lindores*, p. 6.

[2] In other forts of the same kind there is almost invariably a well, but in that of Clachard there is none. What is called the '*Bluidy Well*,' which the rising generation look on with mysterious awe, as the place where the combatants washed their swords after a battle, is merely a hollow in the rock, which retains rain water having a reddish tinge imparted to it by the nature of the rock.

[3] Sir James Balfour, in his notes, says, 'that hard adjoining Denmill there is a great rock, on the top of which stood a strong castle, double trenched, which,' he says, 'was levelled with the ground by the Romans under Martius, commander of the Thracian Cohorts, under the Emperor Commodus; the ruins of the trenches may yet be seen.'—Sibbald's *Fife*, p. 70. This refers to Clachard, which is close by Denmiln, but the slightest inspection of the ground within the entrenchments

In confirmation of this insecurity there still exists the remains of an enclosure for keeping the cattle of the inmates of the fort within range of their sight. Beginning at the outer entrenchment of the fort, a dyke can be distinctly traced fully one-third of a mile up the side of the sloping hill to the west, but before it reaches the sky-line it turns abruptly to the south, and extends a considerable way in that direction. The remains of this dyke on the south side are completely obliterated by the plough, but when the circuit was complete it must have enclosed a large space, sufficient for the sustenance of a very considerable herd. This enclosing dyke appears to have been formed of earth where available, and of stones and earth at other places. There can be no doubt of the object of this extensive and laborious work, as similar enclosures have been noticed in the neighbourhood of hill-forts of a like description. The line chosen is admirably adapted for the purpose intended, as no spoiler could approach the range of the wall without being distinctly seen against the sky by the watchers in the fort.[1]

The remains of art found in these forts are an indication of the period of their construction. Judging from the only relic of the kind that has been found at Clachard—a carved stone ball, the use of which antiquarians are not agreed upon—the origin of the fort is thrown back to a very remote period. This ball, which unfortunately has been lost sight of, was one of the kind that antiquaries have named corn-crushers, though there is little probability of their ever having been used for such a purpose; the

---

shows, that *the castle* must have been constructed of wood, and consumed by fire. See *antea*, which, as Mr Hill Burton says, ' is to be inferred from the numerous burnings of these forts.' See also *Book of Deer*, p. cxlviii., wherein we are informed, ' Edward Bruce burned Rathmore in Ireland,' a similarly constructed fort, so late as A.D. 1315.

[1] For the information of the curious, it may be mentioned, that the dyke is very observable in a line south from the top of the Whitecraig,—a range of stones standing on end may still be seen there. The dyke runs 690 yards west from Clachard, and can be traced 360 yards south.

elaborate ornamentation on some that have been found positively forbidding such a conjecture. The ball found at Clachard was of hard sandstone, and about the size of an orange, elaborately carved in relief, leaves being represented as springing from the stalk and covering the lower half of the sphere. These balls may have been used in some game or amusement, the ornamentation serving to indicate their ownership; but it has been conjectured with a greater degree of probability, that they were attached to a thong, and used in the chase

or in war exactly as the savage races of South America use their *bolas* at the present day.[1] The annexed engraving of one of these balls, found in the parish of Towie, Aberdeenshire, and preserved in the Antiquarian Museum, Edinburgh, is a good example of the exquisite workmanship expended on these mysterious implements.[2]

---

[1] Evan's *Ancient Stone Implements of Great Britain*, pp. 377, 379. The ball referred to in the text passed into the hands of the Rev. Dr Anderson of Newburgh, but was not found in his collection after his death. A massive finger-ring of gold was found at Clachard when the railway was being made. The letters cut upon it are so rude that they have all the appearance of being Runic. An impression of the seal was sent to Professor Stephens of Copenhagen, who has given his opinion that the ring is mediæval, and that the inscription is I. H. S.,—the initial letters of Jesus Hominis Salvator. The ring is in the Perth Museum.

[2] Proceedings of the Society of Antiquaries, Vol. III., p. 439.

Note.—Since the foregoing was in the press, an exhaustive paper on the ' Ancient Cattle of Scotland,' by J. A. Smith, M.D., has appeared. From it we learn that the skull of the Urus mentioned at p 2 was found imbedded in marl, and that it is preserved in the Museum of the New College, Edinburgh. The circumference of the base of the cores of the horns is 14 inches.—*Proceedings of Society of Antiquaries*, Vol. IX., pp., 587-674.

CHAPTER II.

THE ROMAN INVASION.

' An iron race, who bent or broke
  Surrounding nations to their sway !
  From Rome branch out to distant lands,
  Roads, straight as the arrow to the mark,
  Which still remain on mountain heights,
  Memorials of unswerving aims and power
  On strong foundations laid.
  Upon these roads, for war prepared,
  Followed the apostles of the Cross,
  Proclaiming "Peace on earth, goodwill to men!"
  Bringing a light so strong and pure,
  That men may see that "God is love." '

Anon.

WITH the advent of the Romans we come upon the domain of written history. At the time of the invasion of Scotland under Agricola, A.D. 80–85, the inhabitants were known as Caledonians. This name disappeared, and they became known as Picts. Dr John Stuart, in his work on the *Sculptured Stones of Scotland*, says, 'We learn it was the custom of the Britons to stain their bodies before the Roman settlement.' Herodian (who flourished in the middle of the third century) says, 'They puncture their bodies with pictured forms of every sort of animal.' Thomas Innes (the learned author of the *Critical Essay on the Ancient Inhabitants of Scotland*, 1729), supposes that those of them (the Britons) in the south, under the Roman sway, having given up the custom, the term 'Picti'—the painted—came to be applied to those in the north, who 'continued the practice towards the end of the third century.'[1] The *Historia Britonum*, a work composed in the course of the seventh or eighth centuries, says:

> ' From their tatooing their fair skins
> Were they called Picti.'

The appearance, therefore, which our forefathers presented to the Roman invaders, must have been not very dissimilar to that which the natives of New Zealand presented to the Europeans who first landed among them.

We learn from Bede, who wrote in the beginning of the eighth century, that the Picts inhabited the country north of the Forth:[3] they therefore occupied this portion of the country. The Romans named the Pictish tribe, which inhabited what is now called Fife, and the lower portion of Strathearn, Horesti.[4] Using them as they used the inhabitants of the other countries they subdued, and as we have used the native tribes of India, they drafted the youth of the Horesti into their army, and sent them to distant countries, away from kindred and patriotic influences, to fight the battles of the empire.[5] Cohorts of Horesti, serving under the Romans, have been traced to the banks of the Rhine,—relics of their occupation having recently been found

---

[1] *Sculpd. Stones of Scotd.*, Vol. II., p. 124, and p. iv.

[2] *Chron. of the Picts and Scots*, p. 33. Thomas Innes further says, 'The Roman name was continued by the Welsh, Saxon, and Irish in their different forms; the last using the word *Cruithneach*, from *Cruith*, which signifies forms or figures, such as the Picts used to paint or make upon themselves.'—*Sculptured Stones of Scotland*, Vol. II., p. iv.

[3] *Ecc. History*, Bk. IV., cap. 26.

[4] Sibbald's *Fife*, p. 39. Some writers are of opinion that the Horesti occupied the district north of the Tay, but Chalmers, in his *Caledonia*, fixes their seat in Fife and Strathearn.

[5] 'According to the *Notitia*, the fourth *ala*, or wing, of Britons, were stationed in Egypt. The twenty-sixth cohort of Britons occurs in Armenia. A body of the 'Invincible Younger Britons' were stationed in Spain, and one of the 'Elder Britons' in Illyricum. The 'Younger British Slingers' are found among the Palatine Auxiliaries. Other bodies of Britons are found in Gaul, Italy, and

seven miles above Coblentz, on the site of a Roman military station at Niederbieber, two miles north from Neuwied, on the right bank of that river.   Among the remains found there, and deposited in the museum of Neuwied, is a tablet having an

inscription on it, bearing that it was a votive offering raised by Opfius Ibkiomarius to the tutelary genius of the *numerus* or company of Britons of the tribe of Horesti, stationed there.[1]   This interesting monument, as will be seen from the subjoined engraving, copied from a photograph taken from the original, is surmounted the figure of a *genius* holding a *cornucopia* in one hand and a *patera* in the other.[2]   The tablet bears the following inscription :

IDVSOCTO BG IINIo
HORNBRITTONVM
A·IBKIOMARIVSOPFI
VSPOSITTVMQVINTA
NIISIS POSNT V H M.

Filling up the usual conventional contractions, the inscription reads as follows :—'Idus Octobris Genio Horestorum Numeri Brittonum, A. Ibkiomarius Opfius Posuit Titulum Quintanences Posuerunt Votum Hoc Monumentum. The numerous consonants in the name of the votive offerer carries strong internal evidence of his Celtic origin.   From other relics discovered at the same military station, it would

---

other countries.'—Wright's *Celt, Roman and Saxon*, p. 104.   There is a strong probability that some of the soldiers of these cohorts may have listened to the first preachers of the Gospel; but as the Roman troops remained long at distant stations, they may never have had the opportunity of returning to tell the good tidings' they had heard.

[1] Roach Smith's *Collectanea*, Vol. II., pp. 133-4.

[2] The monument is 2¼ feet in height.

appear that the *numerus* of the Horesti must have occupied it for a considerable period in the time of the Emperor Gordian, who reigned from A.D. 238 to 251.[1]

Though the Romans managed to enlist some of the natives of this district, their occupation of it was of too uneasy a nature to permit them to settle down into peaceful communities, and latterly the attacks of the natives were incessant.[2] The Roman historians are unanimous in stating that, during their whole occupation of this portion of the northern province, the native tribes 'were ever ready to avail themselves of the slightest appearance of insecurity or of intermitted watchfulness.' In a night attack, supposed to have been near Lochore, Tacitus records that the Roman troops were so dismayed, that they begged their commander to retire beyond the Forth, rather than be driven back with disgrace.[3] And on the final retirement of the Romans, the Picts 'crossed the sea (the Firth of Forth was anciently called the Scottish sea), broke into the borders, overran every place within reach, and like men mowing down ripe corn, bore down all before them.'[4] The Roman invasion had this good effect, that it compelled the discordant tribes to unite for their common defence. Tacitus, the historian of these events, says, 'Though beaten, the Caledonians did not give up any of their arrogancy; transporting their wives and children to places of safety beyond the reach of the Roman arms, they armed their youth, and, uniting in solemn sacrifices to their gods, established and confirmed their conspiracy.' This union was a great gain to the Caledonians, independently altogether of the knowledge of arts which they would necessarily acquire by coming in contact with a highly civilised people.

---

[1] Roach Smith's *Collectanea*, Vol. II., pp. 134-4.
[2] *Scotland under her Early Kings*, Vol. I., p. 2.
[3] *Tacitus*, cap. 30.
[4] *Bede*, Bk. I., cap. 12.

CHAPTER III.

'Another language spreads from coast to coast ;
Only perchance some melancholy stream
And some indignant hills old names preserve.'

Wordsworth.

THE race who first owned land in the 'Kingdom of Fife,' were undoubtedly of Celtic origin.[1] This is apparent from the fact, that the oldest settlements, as well as the prominent features of the country, bear names in *Gaelic*, in most cases descriptive of

---

[1] The 'Kingdom of Fife' is not a modern appellation. Wynton, in his 'Cronykil,' written about A.D. 1380, calls Fife a 'Kynrick,' or Kingdom. In the tract of the Scots of Dalriada, *Chronicles of the Picts and Scots*, p. 316, the follow ing words occur, 'the men of Fife in the sovereignty.' The first mention we have of Fife is in the verses ascribed to St Columba

'Seven children of Cruthne
Divided Alban into seven divisions.
Cait, Ce, Cirig a warlike clan,
Fib, Fidach, Fotla, Fortren.'

Ib., p. 25.

'This legend means simply that the territory occupied by the Cruthne (see p. 11, note) consisted of seven provinces bearing these names. Fib is obviously Fife. Fotla appears in the name Athfodla, the old form of the word corrupted into Athole; Cait, Caithness; Circin is found in Maghcircin (the meadow or plain of Circin), now corrupted into the Mearns.'—*Ib.*, Pref., p. ciii. Doncad, Earl of *Fib*, appears as a witness to the confirmation of the freedom of the church of Deer, A.D., 1124-1153.—*National MS. of Scotland*, p. ii. Robertson, in his most valuable work, *Scotland under her Early Kings*, gives the name of Fib, or Fibh, as 'the Forest,' Vol. I., p. 32. *Fib*, in the speech of South Jütland, is

their situation or appearance ;[1] and upon good grounds it may be affirmed, that *Gaelic* continued to be the spoken language of this district up to the end of the twelfth century.[2] It is noticeable,

---

pronounced almost exactly the same as the modern Fife.—Atkinson's *Cleveland Glossary*, p. 76.

[1] The following are some of the oldest names in the neighbourhood :

Mugdrum, anciently Mukedrum—Gaelic, *Muc-druim*—the sow's ridge. It is worthy of note, that one of the compartments of Mugdrum Cross represents a boar hunt.

Ballinbriech, Bal-an-breac, Town of Trouts. It is still celebrated as a salmon-fishing station.

Pitcairly, anciently Petcarlingis.

Lumbennie, *Lom*-bare, *beannan*, the diminutive of *bein*, a height—'The bare little height.'

The Bo' Park—the Cattle Park.

Clach-ard-Craig—The Craig of the High Stone. This name is, or rather was, eminently descriptive. Before the railway was formed, there was a projecting portion of the rock showing two sides of a square, upwards of ninety feet in height and about twenty-five feet on the side, known as the 'High Post.' It rose in one columnar mass from the base to the summit of the craig ; the other two sides closely adjoined the rock, but the pillar was so much disjoined that it was thrown down by one charge of gunpowder inserted at its base. There was a legend attached, on the never-wanting authority of Thomas the Rhymer (the predictions attributed to him being generally annunciations of improbabilities), that it was to stand till it fell on a white horse that never was born ; and strangely enough, as if in literal fulfilment of the prophecy, the grand pillar stood till it fell before the 'majestical white horse' of steam. When it became known that the 'High Post' was to be thrown down, several thousand people assembled to witness its downfall. On the afternoon of Wednesday, the 3d June 1846, all being prepared, the match was applied, and in a few seconds the mighty mass rose majestically from its base, and then slowly fell over in one unbroken column. The pillar leaned towards the east, and almost overhung the old public road ; and many who had looked up to it with awe from their youth wished that it could have been spared. Dr Anderson, then minister of Newburgh, made application for its perpetuation, but his application was unsuccessful, and 'The High Stone of the Craig' is now only a name.

[2] Robertson's *Scotland under her Early Kings*, Vol. II., p. 143. There is an indication that Gaelic continued to be spoken in this neighbourhood after the foundation of the abbey (A.D. 1178). On the hill-side above Newburgh there is a spring still called 'The Monk's Well.' A course, evidently an artificial one, led the water to the abbey   This course was called the 'Rood-linn-burn,' or the

however, that in the immediate neighbourhood of Newburgh, there is evidence of an immigration, and early settlement, of Teutonic or Scandinavian tribes. The term '*Law*' is applied to many of the heights in the neighbourhood. '*Haugh*,' a purely Norwegian term for an alluvial level close by a river, occurs ; and the suffix *son*, so characteristic of the same language, prevails largely in the names of the oldest families of the town, as far back as the Burgh Records extend.[1] There is, besides, a very peculiar idiom in every day use in Newburgh, which can be traced to South Jütland, and which could only have originated at a remote period.[2] This idiom and nomenclature corroborates the view so ably stated by Mr W. F. Skene, that an immigration of Frisian tribes began early in the latter half of the fourth century, and planted themselves along the estuaries of the Tay and Forth.[3]

The fact of an immigration, and settlement by a people speaking another tongue, is the more evident from the contrast afforded

---

Holywell burn. The inference is, that the monks appropriated the spring—an excellent one—which arose on their own ground, for the use of the abbey ; and the name, part of which is Gaelic, was given to the course they dug for it, in the vernacular of the time. The burn was covered up about twenty-five years ago, and its name is fast being forgotten.

[1] In addition to the names mentioned in the text, the following occur : '*Wodrife*,' anciently *Vodrufe*, the name of the burgh lands, which is referred to *Vidr*, an old Teutonic word for a wood or forest ; *Goat*, a trench, or gully, where water runs out—hence 'Katies-goat,' a deep open watercourse near the abbey, now covered over. *Toft*, etc. Further inland 'The *Boose*' and '*Weddersby*' occur ; the first is pure Danish for 'The Cattle Stalls,' and the latter, *Wedder* or *Veder*, a man's name, still common in Norway, and *By* a town.—See *Worsae's Danes in Scotland*.

[2] For instance, it is quite common to say, in answer to the question, 'Where is he ?' Doon ae close, ae face ae brae, ae barn, ae house, etc.,—that is, down the close, on the face of the brae, in the barn, in the house,—as the case may be. A Danish writer, speaking of this form of speech, says : 'The most striking peculiarity of the South Jütland dialect is the *e* or *ae*, which is used prepositively, and is the same in all genders and numbers,—as e *By*, e *Barn*, e *hele hus.*—Atkinson's *Cleveland Glossary*, pp. xxiii, xxiv.

[3] *Pro. of Soc. of Ant.*, Vol. IV., p. 169.

by the names of places in and around Abernethy, only three miles distant. In the neighbourhood of that ancient Pictish seat, most of the holdings (and they are very much subdivided), and even some of the tenements in the town bear Celtic names, testifying unmistakeably to its being the centre of a numerous and settled Celtic population.[1]

[1] The following names of places are copied from Lord Douglas's *Abernethy Vassalage* of 1846 :—Abernethy, Innernethy, Aberargie, Culfargie, Carey, Cordon, Ballochmiln, Balgonie, Drummore, Remore, Drumhead, Colzie. Gattaway, Tarduff, Potie, Muckley, Carpow, Wester Clunie, Balnacreuch, Balehyrewell (corrupted into Broadwell), Pitfersie, Drums of Pitfersie, Pitgrunzie, Pitindie, Pitmedden, Pittenbroigh (one of the tenements of the town is described as having belonged to the prebend of Pittenbroigh), Pitcuran, Pitcarrick, Pitblae, Pitlour, etc. Such a number of places having the prefix *Pit*, mostly situated within a short distance of one another, shows that they were, as they still are, small holdings, and that the meaning ascribed to the term by Mr W. F. Skene is the correct one. He says, 'The old form of *Pit* or *Pitten*, as appears from the *Book of Deer*, is *Pette*, and it seems to mean a portion of land, as it is conjoined with proper names, as Pette Mac-Garnait, Pette Malduib. But it also appears connected with Gaelic specific terms, as *Pette an Mulenn*, the Pette of the Mill; and in a charter of the Chartulary of St Andrews of the Church of Migvie, the *terra ecclesiæ* (the church land) is said to be called Pettentaggart—'an taggart' being the Gaelic form of the expression 'of the priest.'—Skene's *Four Ancient Books of Wales*, Vol. I., p. 157.

CHAPTER IV.

PAGAN RELIGIONS.

'Once, while the name Jehovah, was a sound
Within the circuit of this sea-girt isle
Unheard, the savage nations bowed the head
To Gods delighting in remorseless deeds.'

Wordsworth.

THE religion of the Celtic population was Druidical. Of the nature of its tenets we have only the accounts of strangers, for the priests never committed them to writing, though they knew and practised that art. They transmitted their system through their successors by oral tradition, perhaps to throw a greater air of mystery around their rites and ceremonies, and to inspire the people with awe for their decisions. It is said that they taught 'there was only one God, that the souls of men did not perish with their bodies, and after death men were rewarded according to the life they led on earth. Those who had chosen the evil instead of the good, returned after death to the state of evil, and were condemned to an inferior grade of animal life, low in proportion to the debasement whereto they had reduced themselves.'[1] There is, however, much uncertainty regarding their doctrines; but, it is certain, that they practised most cruel rites. 'When any calamity befell the people they sacrificed human victims, and they pretended they could discover by the manner in which the victim fell, events which were to come.'[2]

It is in this latter character of practising magical arts, that the

---

[1] Southey's *Book of the Church*, p. 4.   [2] *Ib.*

Druids are represented by the Christian missionaries who first came in contact with them. The 'Historia Britonum' says—

'Necromancy and idolatry, illusion

.   .   .   .   .

By them were taught
The honouring *Sredhs* and omens,
Choice of weather, lucky times,
The watching of the voice of birds
They practised without disguise.' [1]

The same authority informs us that they taught 'bright poems.' Their vocation of bards gave them great influence over the people, for in those early times when books were not, the man that could celebrate, in glowing verse and rapturous music, the deeds of their ancestors, found willing listeners, whom he moulded to his will. The terrible powers of life and death, which Druidical priests wielded as controllers of all religious rites and ceremonies, and as judges of every cause, whether civil or sacred, rendered their authority irresistible. When their mandate went forth, their nearest and dearest dared not afford them relief. 'The wretched outcast' was 'from the gift of fire and food cut off,' and

'From every sympathy that man bestowed.' [2]

An excommunication so terrible, that humanity could not endure it and live, and from which the 'mercy and love' of the Gospel was a double deliverance.

The Scandinavian immigrants worshipped other gods. The lateness of the conversion of the Northern Nations to Christianity, somewhere about the beginning of the eleventh century, and the preservation of their ancient *Sagas*, embodying many of their heathen beliefs, have helped to keep the nature of their old faith more clearly before us. There is therefore no uncertainty as to the character of their religion, or of the gods they worshipped.

---

[1] *The Chronicles of the Picts and Scots*, p. 42.   [2] Wordsworth.

Three of them, Odin, or Woden, Thor, and Freya, have stamped their names on three days of the week. The entrance to the everlasting pleasures of Valhalla was through battle and bloodshed, and the souls of all who were slain in battle were received into Odin's palace, their highest heaven. There they passed their time in the continual enjoyment of fighting, of cutting each other to pieces, and drinking out of the skulls of their enemies, reviving next morning from death for the renewal of their bloody orgies.

Their funeral rites were in accordance with these beliefs. When a warrior died he was buried in his armour, or with his arms beside him, to be ready for the occupations of Valhalla.[1] A very significant passage, confirmatory of this practise, occurs in an Icelandic Saga, written in the tenth century, when men worshipped Woden and Thor. 'Now Gisli made ready to bury Vestein in his howe (mound or height), and they meant to bury him on the sand-hill which looks down on the tarn. . . . . And when they had heaped up the howe, and were going to lay the body in it, Thorgrim the priest goes up to Gisli and says, "'Tis the custom brother-in-law to bind the hell-shoon on men so that they may walk on them to Valhalla, and I will do that by Vestein."'[2]

---

[1] The silver armour discovered in the mound on Norrie's Law, in the parish of Largo, about the year 1817, is a notable instance of the practice mentioned in the text. Twenty years after the discovery, when the knowledge of it transpired, investigation was made by the late Dr George Buist, who took an active interest in all that related to the history and natural history of the county, and from all that he could learn, there must have been about 400 ounces of pure bullion. All that escaped the melting-pot were a few fragments, which Mrs Durham, formerly of Largo, now of Polton, has generously presented to the Museum of the Society of Antiquaries of Scotland. The value of these fragments is enhanced by the circumstance of their having engraved upon them, the same mysterious symbols which are carved on the ancient sculptured stones found on the east coast of Scotland —See Wilson's *Prehist. Annals*, p. 511-515.

[2] *Gisli, the Outlaw*, p. 44.

In these old Sagas there are not wanting glimpses of still more horrid rites ; and more than dim hints are given that slaves and domestic animals were sacrificed on the occasion of their lord's death, and buried with them in the same grave-mound, that they might accompany him to the unseen world. In one of these Sagas, Brynhild, when drawing near her death, says to her husband, 'and now I pray thee Gunnar one last boon— let make a great bale on the plain meads for all of us, for me and for Sigurd, and for those who were slain with him, and let that be covered with cloth dyed red by the folk of the Gauls, and burn me thereon on one side of the King of the Huns (Sigurd, for whom in dying she avowed her love), and on the other those men of mine, two at the head and two at the feet, and two hawks withal, and even so is all shared equally, and lay there betwixt us a drawn sword, as in the other days when we twain stepped into one bed together, and then may we have the name of man and wife, nor shall the door swing at the heel of him. Nor shall that be a niggard company if there follow him those five bond-women, and eight bond-men whom my father gave me, and those burn there withal who were slain with Sigurd.' [1]

In the Anglo-Saxon poem of 'Beowulf,' the dying hero gives still more minute directions for the celebration of his obsequies. 'Make,' he says, enjoining his companions and followers,

'According to the deeds of your friend,
on the place of the funeral pyle,
the lofty barrow
large and famous.'

---

[1] *The Story of the Volsungs and Niblungs.* Ed. 1870, p. 127. The horrid custom of sacrificing slaves to accompany their master to the next world still survives, and seems to have been as wide as the human race. ' Among the savage Kayans of Borneo, slaves are killed in order that they may follow the deceased and attend upon him. Before they are killed, the relations who surround them, enjoin them to take great care of their master when they join him.'—Taylor's *Primitive Culture*, Vol. I., p. 414.

They accordingly raised a mighty funeral pile to burn his corpse; it was

> 'hung round with helmets
> with boards of war [*shields*]
> and with bright byrnies [*breast-defences*]
> as he had requested.
> Then the heroes weeping,
> laid down in the midst
> the famous chieftain,
> their dear lord.
> Then began on the hills
> the warriors to awake
> the mightiest of funeral fires.'

After the fire had done its work, the companions of the departed chief proceeded to raise above his remains

> ' A mound over the sea ;
> it was high and broad,
> by the sailors over the waves
> to be seen afar.
> And they built up
> during ten days
> the beacon of the war-renowned.
> They surrounded it with a wall
> in the most honourable manner
> that wise men
> could desire.
> They put into the mound
> rings and bright gems.
>
> .   .   .
>
> they suffered the earth to hold
> the treasure of warriors,
> gold on the sand,
> where it yet remains.'

' When the mound was completed the war-chiefs rode round it, chanting the praises of their departed king.'[1]

---

[1] Wright's ' *Celt, Roman and Saxon*, pp. 400-1.

In these lines we have a vivid picture of the ceremonies observed on funereal occasions among the Teutonic races; they also throw light on the origin of the grave-mounds that are found scattered over Britain, and the building up by the devoted followers of the departed warrior—

> ' during ten days
> the beacon of the war renowned,'

sufficiently accounts for the many large *tumuli*, or grave-mounds, which still remain. The dying request which the hero makes to his people, throws still further light on these interesting memorials.

> ' Command the war-chiefs
> to make a mound,
> bright after the funeral fire
> upon the nose of the promontory,
> which shall for a memorial
> to my people
> rise high aloft
> on Hronesness;
> that the sea-sailors
> may afterwards call it
> Beowulf's barrow,
> when the Brentings
> over the darkness of the floods
> shall sail afar.' [1]

---

[1] Wright's *Celt, Roman and Saxon*, p. 404.

It may appear somewhat irrelevant, but it is most interesting to learn, that ages before the date of the poem quoted in the text, our forefathers, ere they left their original home in Central Asia, practised the same ceremonies at the burial of their dead. Max Müller has recently translated from the Sanscrit, *Hymns from the Vedas;* poems that can be proved to have been written upwards of three thousand years ago. One of these describes the mode in which the funeral ceremonies were performed, and they correspond, in a marked manner, with those mentioned in the text. Baron Bunsen, in his work on *God in History,* says: ' A serious and spiritual view of the world, and the noble dignity of the proud Aryan heroes (from whom our forefathers and the Greeks, Romans,

We have in this injunction an explanation of the reason why the term *Law* (*hlæw*), which originally signified a heaped up mound,

---

Hindoos, etc., etc., are descended) is displayed in the hymns relating to the dead, and used on the occasion of their incremation.'

On the funeral pile of the deceased, his widow and bow are placed; the latter is taken down and broken while reciting these words:

> ' The bow I take from the hand of the dead,
> To be our defence, our glory and shield;
> Do thou lie there, we remain here as heroes,
> And in all battles we smite down our foes.'

But before this is done, the brother, or foster-son, or old servant, leads the widow down from the pile, saying:

> ' Rise up, O woman, to the world of life!
> Thou sleep'st beside a corpse—come down.''

When the pile was lighted, the following address to the spirit of the departed (of which we quote a portion) was recited:

> 'Depart, depart, along those ancient paths,
> By which our fathers have gone home to rest;
> The god Varuna (*Uranos*) shalt thou now behold,
> And Yama (the sun-god or sky-god) the two kings who take our gifts.
>
> Go to thy loving mother, home to earth,
> With wide-spread arms and blessing-bringing hands
> She takes the pious to her kindly breast,
> As 'twere a maiden's bosom soft as wool,
> And holds thee safe from danger's threatening edge.
> Open thy arms, O earth, do him no harm,
> Receive him gently with a loving kiss,
> And wrap him round, O earth, as when a babe
> His mother in her garment folds to rest.

---

[1] It is most pleasing to notice that we have here ' a direct contradiction to the horrible custom which the Brahmans upheld so long, in defiance of the expostulation of a Christian government, on the plea that the burning of widows was commanded by the Vedas.'

is applied to so many heights on the east coast of Britain, and of which Norman's Law (or the Northman's Law), in the north of

---

After the obsequies were ended, the chief officiating priest turned to the living and said :

> ' Travel your course, rejoice in length of days,
> Ye who are here marching in due array ;
> Your living Lord who offers you good increase,
> He, the Creator, grant you long to live.'

At the close of the ceremony the mourners return in procession home to the village. On the following day the household sit around a fire outside the house, singing of the deeds of the ancients, on into the silent night.

Then the leader of the chorus admonishes the relations.

Be pure and pious, all ye who have joined in this sacrifice, that your way may not go down to the house of death, but that you may enjoy length of days, and abundance of cattle and of treasures.

After this he pours libations over a stone, repeating, amongst others, this prayer in the ears of the family :

> ' As days succeed days, changing seasons with seasons,
> Lo give, O Creator, these here to live, that the younger
> May not leave their parents desolate.'

The priest then says to the women who now approach—

> ' Not widows they, no, proud of noble husbands,
> First to the altar let the mothers come
> In fair attire, and with no grief or tears.'

Then turning to the men, he says :

> ' The torrent flows away ; bestir yourselves,
> Rise up, and go your ways, ye comrades.
> Let us now leave this mourning company,
> And all go forth to new and joyous strife.'

And the whole concludes with the chanting of the following words :—

> ' To-day they led the ox around, they stirred up the
> bright fire, they brought to God a sacrifice of praises
> and thanksgiving. Who shall dare to lay hands on them ?'

Vol. I., pp. 309-312.

Fife, and Largo Law in the south, are prominent examples. Both of them meet the requirements of the dying warrior's wish, and are distinctly 'seen afar, by the sailors over the waves.' [1]

Posthumous honours were only reserved for those who distinguished themselves by their bravery, and fell in battle. Those who died of sickness or old age, were reckoned cowardly and vile, and were consigned to the goddess Hel, who dwelt in a region of eternal frost, where bitter cold, remorse, famine, and hunger, were their portion.[2] To avoid this terrible fate, men threw themselves from precipices, and rushed on death. This latter alternative was in course of time avoided by a subterfuge. When in a later age a warrior died a 'straw death,'—as death on a bed, from disease or age, was contemptuously called, he received, before life was extinct, the scratch of a spear—Odin's mark—to wipe away the reproach, and that he might have a passport to Valhalla.[3]

A religion which so directly inculcated battle and bloodshed, while it fostered some noble qualities, necessarily begat indiffer-

---

[1] In Abdie parish, besides Norman's Law, there is also the Green Law, a conical height near Collessie, on which there is unmistakeable evidence of inhumation. In Newburgh parish we had 'The Greenlaw,' on which the Madras School is now built. Upwards of forty years ago skulls and other portions of human skeletons were found in it. When the 'Law' was being levelled for the erection of the school, instructions were given to preserve carefully any remains, —and some fragments of human bones and of metal were found, but the latter were so much corroded that their original form was utterly undistinguishable. There is on the *Kaim*, or ridge, between Inchrye and Lindores Loch, a conical mound called 'the Watchman's Tower,' traditionally said to have been used as a place of outlook in Covenanting times, to guard against surprisal during field-worship; but it has all the marks of an ancient barrow, or burial-mound, and is identical with some that have been opened in England (at Bartlow, Essex); figured in *Ferguson's Rude Stone Monuments*, p. 83. That the 'Watchman's Tower' is not what its modern name implies, is apparent from the fact that it does not command a view of the approaches all round, which a height a few yards distant does.

[2] Southey's *Book of the Church*, p. 42.

[3] Taylor's *Primitive Culture*, Vol. II., p. 82.

ence to human life; and there are grounds for believing that fathers sacrificed their children for the most trivial reasons. In the Saga of ' Gisli the Outlaw' of Iceland, we read : 'They landed just beyond the farm where Hallstein offered up his son, that a large tree of sixty feet might be thrown up by the sea, and there are still to be seen the pillars of his high seat, which he made out of that tree.'[1] It is certain that these fierce warriors enjoyed positive delight in the sufferings which they inflicted. They gave Olver the Norwegian, the nickname of Barnakall, or Preserver of Bairns, in contempt, because he abolished, in his company of Vikings, the custom of tossing infants on their pikes for amusement, until their helpless victims died.[2]

---

[1] Gisli the Outlaw, p. 87.   [2] Southey's *Book of the Church*, p. 45.

CHAPTER V.

COLUMBA AND HIS FOLLOWERS.

'How beautiful upon the mountains
Are the feet of him that bringeth good tidings, that publisheth peace;
That bringeth good tidings of good, that publisheth salvation.'

Isa. lii. 7.

THE first successful efforts that were made to christianize our heathen forefathers were undoubtedly those of St Ninian and St Columba. The one preached the Gospel to the southern Picts (A.D. 398–432), and the other to the northern (A.D. 562). They were both of royal descent; but the nobleness of their labours in the cause of truth, has added a lustre to their names, which no ancestry, however noble or illustrious, could have conferred. More ample details of the life and labours of St Columba have been preserved than those of St Ninian; and the narrative of his life bears testimony to the greatness of the labours undergone, and the perils encountered by the early missionaries of the Gospel in Scotland. They dared the dangers of the northern seas in frail boats of skins, penetrating, in these slender and diminutive vessels, to the Orkney, Shetland, and Faroe Islands, and even to distant Iceland;[1] and centuries afterwards, 'when the Norwegians went first to Iceland, they found no traces of civilization there, but the crosses, bells, and books of the monks of Iona.'[2]

---

[1] '*Currachs,*' as these frail boats are named, made of a framework of light wood, covered with tarred canvas, are still used by the Clare fishermen in Galway Bay. From their extreme buoyancy, they dance lightly over the waves, and they are quite safe even in rough weather, when dexterously managed by an experienced boatman.'—*West of Ireland and its Cities,* p. 53, A.D. 1863.

[2] Innes' *Scotland in the Middle Ages,* p. 101.

Bede has left a beautiful picture of the self-denying and successful labours of Aedan, a disciple of Columba, among the heathen
inhabitants of Northumbria (A.D. 635). Besides bringing them
to the knowledge of the truth, he exemplified his religion in his
life, and realized to the letter the picture of a faithful pastor,
drawn in a later age:

> 'This noble ensample to his shepe he gaf,
> That first he wrought and afterwards he taught.
> Out of the Gospel he the wordes caught,
> And this figure he added yet therto,
> That if gold ruste, what shuld iren do?'[1]

'It was,' says the venerable historian, 'the highest commendation of his doctrine, that he taught no otherwise than he and
his followers lived; he neither sought nor loved anything of this
world for its own sake, but delighted in distributing among the
poor what was given him by the rich. Wherever in his journeyings he met either rich or poor, he invited them, if unbelievers, to
embrace the Gospel; if they were believers, he strengthened their
faith, and stirred them up, by example and exhortation, to charity
and good works. If he received money, he used it in ransoming
such as were unjustly sold for slaves; and many of these he
taught and sent them forth to preach the Gospel.'[2]

The disciples of Columba continued for centuries to keep alive
the knowledge of the truth, and to shed abroad the light of religion in Scotland.[3] 'The number of places to which his name and

---

[1] Chaucer's *Poore Persone.*

[2] Bede, Bk. 3. cap. 5. Aedan died on 31st August A.D. 651. It may beguile
the tedium of the wind-bound mariner at Holy Island to remember, that within
its little cemetery was laid the dust of him who first brought the light of Revelation to the neighbouring land.

[3] In comparatively recent times, the successors of Columba came to be known
as Culdees. As much controversy has arisen regarding their name and tenets,
the opinion of Dr Reeves, as given in his work on *The Culdees of the British
Islands*, is subjoined,—a work so exhaustive, that it must for ever set at rest all
controversy on the subject. 'The devotion and self-denial which characterized

that of his followers are attached, bear witness to the zeal and success of their labours.'[1] But unhappily it can be said of them, as of too many others, that if they were 'pure in the spring, they were miry in the stream.' When we come upon the domain of written record, we find that their zeal had died out, and 'in many instances, the entire religious character of their monasteries had perished, except in name.'[2] The offices of the Church had become hereditary; the son succeeding the father without any regard to spiritual fitness for the charge, till at last even the semblance of religion was thrown aside, and laymen assumed the office of abbot, and kept possession of the lands which had been bequeathed to the Church. No stronger evidence of the thorough declension of the clergy, and of the corruption of society, could be adduced than the fact, that the Lord's Day was not merely neglected, it

---

monastic life upon its introduction into the Latin Church, procured for those who adopted it the special designation of *Servus Dei* (servant of God), which, in process of time, acquired a technical application, so that *Servus Dei* and Monachus (Monk) became convertible terms,'—p. 119. 'Familiarized, therefore, to the expression *Servus Dei*, it is only reasonable to suppose that the Irish would adopt, in their discourse, and find a conventional equivalent for it in the language of their country. To this origin we may safely refer the creation of the Celtic compound *Cele-de* (two Irish words; or, in the Scottish Gaelic, *Gille-de*, signifying servant of God), which, in its employment, possessed all the latitude of its model, and in the lapse of ages underwent all the modifications or limitations of meaning which the changes of time and circumstances, or local usage, produced in the class to whom the epithet was applied,'—p. 120. 'When at last *Cele-de* does become a distinctive term, it is only so as contrasting those who clung to the old conventual observances of the country,'—p. 121. Besides, it may be added, the old priests who spoke the Celtic language, would come to be known by the Celtic appellation, in contradistinction to the Saxon preachers introduced by Queen Margaret. As regards their tenets, Dr Reeves continues: 'During the range of time in which the term is on record, we discover the greatest diversity in its application,—sometimes borne by hermits, sometimes by conventuals; in one situation implying the condition of celibacy, in another understood of married men; here denoting regulars, there seculars,'—diversities great enough surely, to show the futility of attempting to liken them to any existing ecclesiastical institution.

[1] Innes' *Scotland in the Middle Ages*, p. 108.   [2] Reeves' *Culdees*, p 147.

was disregarded; and the toil-worn serf was obliged to labour without intermission all the days of the week.[1]

The declension of zeal and true piety from the time when Columba and his followers multiplied copies of the Scriptures, and when men flocked to Iona for instruction, is painfully apparent. The entire absence of native manuscripts, with a single exception, up to the foundation of the abbeys in the twelfth century, unless the violent character of the proceedings at the Reformation in part accounts for it, shows, more especially when the rich stores of Irish manuscripts of the same period is kept in mind, how totally learning and zeal for the propagation of the truth had died out, and how deeply the priesthood had sunk into ignorance and apathy. The work therefore of Queen Margaret was in reality a Reformation, though it might have been wiser to have endeavoured to revive the ancient spirit within the existing institutions, instead of establishing a new order in their place. Still, her object was to disseminate true religion, and to bring the blessings of civilization to her husband's people; and in her days no instrument was reckoned so effectual for this purpose, as the monastic institutions, then springing up in renewed favour all over Europe.

'However,' said Cosmo Innes, 'it may have become the fashion in later times to censure or ridicule the sudden and magnificent endowment of a Church, the poor natives of Scotland of the twelfth century, had no cause to regret it. Before, they had nothing of the freedom of savage life, none of the picturesqueness of feudal society. For ages they had enjoyed no settled government. Crushed by oppression, without security of life or property, knowing nothing of the law but its heavy gripe, alternately plundering and plundered, neglecting agriculture, and suffering the penalty of famine and disease, the churches venerated by their forefathers had gone to ruin, and religion was for the most part degraded and despised. At such a time it was

---

[1] *Statuta Ec. Scot.*, p. xxiii.

undoubtedly one great step in improvement to throw a vast mass
of property into the hands of that class whose duty and interest
alike inculcated peace, and who had interest and power to command it. Repose was the one thing most wanted, and the
people found it under the protection of the crozier.'[1]

The foundation of an abbey, therefore, in those days, was a
work not of piety merely, but of patriotism. Around it grew up
the arts of peace, and it was a blessing to the neighbourhood in
which it was placed. Agriculture flourished, learning was fostered and protected,—there and there only were the Holy Scriptures copied and multiplied. The studious and peaceful found
there a refuge from the seething turbulence without, and the poor
and the miserable sought and found relief and consolation at its
gates.

The awakening which took place in the era of the Crusades
had much to do with the revival of religion at the time. A lofty
spirit was evoked, men threw themselves and their substance
with unselfish devotion into the cause of God, and churches were
endowed and monasteries founded. A new order of architecture
was developed, which for sublimity and grandeur has never been
surpassed, and which still testifies to the loftiness of the aspira-
tions and the grandeur of the conceptions of the men of those
times.

The numerous magnificent abbeys and churches that arose in
those days, show the wide-spread enthusiasm that prevailed; and
when we look on even the little that is left to us in Scotland of
the stately structures that they raised; how meanly, with a few
princely exceptions, does the stunted benevolence of modern
times contrast with the lofty and magnanimous liberality of
theirs?

---

[1] *Scotland in the Middle Ages*, p. 113.

CHAPTER VI.

DAVID, EARL OF HUNTINGDON.

'He halsed and kissed his dearest dame, that was as sweet as May,
And said, 'Now lady of my heart, attend the words I say.
'Tis I have vow'd a pilgrimage unto a distant shrine,
And I must seek Saint Thomas-land, and leave the land that's mine.'

Scott.

DAVID, Earl of Huntingdon, the founder of Lindores Abbey, was born, *circa*, A.D. 1144.[1] He was the youngest son of Prince Henry, son of David I.[2] According to Fordun, our earliest historian, he founded Lindores in the same year (1178) that his brother, William the Lion, founded the Abbey of Aberbrothick. Hector Boece, in his 'Chronicles of Scotland,' gives the following account of its origin: 'King Richard (Cœur de Lion) after his coronation, full of curage and spirits, gaderit ane strong army to pas in the Holy Land; and maid peace with all nichtbouris, that na troubill suld follow in his realm in his absence. Afore his journey he randerit Berwik, Roxburgh, and Striveling to King William;

---

[1] Fordun. Bk. V., cap. 33.
[2] The following exhibits the descent of the Earl of Huntingdon:—

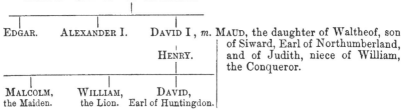

MALCOLM CANMORE *m.* MARGARET.

EDGAR.   ALEXANDER I.   DAVID I, *m.* MAUD, the daughter of Waltheof, son of Siward, Earl of Northumberland, and of Judith, niece of William, the Conqueror.

HENRY.

MALCOLM,   WILLIAM,   DAVID,
the Maiden.   the Lion.   Earl of Huntingdon.

C

with sa mekil of Northumberland as wes tane fra him afore in his
last battal at Anwick. · He gaf ouer all the landis of Cumberland
and Huntingtown, undir thir conditionis: "The munitionis and
strenthis thairof sall remane undir his capitanis; and the remanent
landis thairof to be inhabit be the Scottis. Attoure to have the
more benevolence of the Scottis, he dischargit the residew of King
Williamis ranson, except X.M. (10,000) poundis to support his
weris. And quhen King William had resavit all his landis and
castellis on this maner, he maid his brother David, Erle of Huntingtown, and send him with V.M. (5000) men, to support King Richard
in his weris. Nocht long after King Richard come with mony
nobil men, dukis, erlis, baronis to Massilia (Marseilles), ane port
of Provence, quhare he pullit up salis, with ane hundreth and fifty
schippis to pass to Jerusalem." . . . . "And when he had
deliverit the Ile of Cypre (Cyprus) to Cristin pepil, he pullit up
salis to meet King Philip (of France) at Achon."[1] . . . . "The
sege continewit lang time at this town, throw great defence that
the Sarrayenis maid with the samin   At last King Philip
fell in sic infirmitie that he was constranit to return in France.
Nochtheless King Richard determinit, nocht to depart fra the sege
of Achon, quhill the same were expugnat. In the mene time
hapnit ane Scot, namet Oliver to be in the said town; for he was
banist afore out of Scotland, and fled to the Sarayenis, and be
lang conversatioun with thaim he had their perfite language, nane
of them knowing quhat he wes. This Oliver was thair sodjour in
ane tour of this town, quhare na trinschis nor out wallis wer
beyond the samin. He happinit be aventure to se amang the
wache of Erle David of Huntington, ane of his kinsmen namet
John Durward, with quhome he was lang time afore acquentit;
and incontinent he cryit on him be name, desiring under assurance
to commoun with him. Efter certané commoning, this Oliver set
ane hour to geif entres to Erle David with all his army, in the
town, sa that Erle David wald restore him to his land and heritage

---

[1] Judges i. 31.

1367244

in Scotland. The houre set, Erle David came with ane gret power of men, to the toure afore rehersit, quhare he gat enteres with his army; and incontinent, with gret noyis and clamoure he came throw the town, to the gret slauchter of all pepill foundin in it. King Richard seand, on the morrow, the Scottis standart on the wallis enterit in the town, and within a short time after brocht ane gret castell to rewine." . . . "At last quhen King Richard had destroyit this town of Achon, and was returnand in Italy, ane suddand tempest severit his navy, throu quhilk he was destituit of freindis, and finaly, be treasoun of certane evill cristin men, he was brocht to Hary, Emprioure. The schip that Erle David was intil, be rageand tempest was sa broken, that many of thaim quhilkis was in her perist, and he narrowly eschapit with his life. Efter this he was tane be the inhabitantis of this land, and brocht to Alexandria, quhare he was haldin lang in preson, quhill he at last was coft be marchandis of Venice, and brocht to Constantinople. Nocht lang efter he was brocht to Venis, quhare he was redemit be marchandis of Ingland and brocht to Flanderis; and thair he pullit up salis to returne in Scotland; quhen he was littill departet fra the land, he was drevin be unmercifull tempest nocht far fra Norroway and Schetland, with incredibill dangeir. Finaly quhen he had maid ane voit to big ane kirk in honore of the Virgine Mary gif he was fortunate to eschape the dangeir of seis,—he arrivit in Tay, beside Dunde, not far fra Sanct Nicholas chapell, but ony rudder or tackill, and gaif thankis to God and the Blissit Virgine for delivering him fra sic extreme perill. The place quhare he arrivit was callit Allectum; but after his cumming it changit name, and was callit Dunde,[1] quhilk signifys in our language the Gift of God. King William heirand the returning of his brother, quhome he belevit mony yeiris deceissit, come with maist diligence to Dunde and embrasit him; syne gaif thankis to God and the Blissit

---

[1] It is scarcely necessary to say that this origin of the name of Dundee is one of those fanciful derivations frequently found in old writers. The origin of the name must unquestionably be looked for in the spoken language of the country.

Virgin Mary, that deliverit his brothir fra sa mony dangeris. Efter this, he gart maik generall processionis throw the realme, to geif thankis to God for the happy returning of his brother."

'Sic thingis done, ane conventioun was maid at Dunde, in the quhilk license was gevin to Erle David to big ane abbay in quhat place he plesit of Scotland, and to dotat it with landis and rentis at his pleseir. King William gaif mony privileges to Dunde, quhilk induris to thir dayis. David nocht refusing the benevolence of his brothir, biggit ane abbay callit Lundoris, efter the ordour of St Benedict.'[1]

Such is the romantic story of Boece, who unquestionably had access to documents which are now lost; but his accuracy is not to be entirely relied on, and, unfortunately, his narration is unsupported by any other testimony.   Sir Walter Scott has accepted it as true, and has made the Earl of Huntingdon the hero of the 'Talisman;' placing him in circumstances, however, which, unfortunately for the verisimilitude of the romance, are contradicted by the Earl's real history.   Fordun, who lived a century earlier than Boece, and within a century and a half of the Earl's death, makes no mention of a voyage to Palestine, or of any escape from shipwreck.[2]   He merely states that William, after his release from captivity (A.D. 1175), gave to his brother David 'the Earldom of Huntingdon, to be held of him; likewise the Earldom of Garvioch, the town of Dunde, the town of Inverbervie, and the lordship of Langforgonde, together with many other lands.'[3]

---

[1] Bellenden's *Boece*, Bk. 13, cap. 7.

[2] On the other hand, Fordun, at the date of Malcolm the Maiden's accession to the throne (A D. 1153), states, 'that his brother William was abroad, fighting for the Church against the heretics' (Albigenses).   This statement is most improbable, as William at that time could not have been more than twelve years old.

[3] *Hist. of Scot.*, Fordun's *Annals*, chap. xxx.   This bestowal of William, in 1175, seems to be a re-investiture, as it is distinctly stated that the Earldoms of Huntingdon and the Garioch was conferred on David at the time of his brother Malcolm's accession to the throne, A.D. 1153.—*Fordun*, Vol II., p. 249.   Besides the estates mentioned, Fordun elsewhere specifies Londoris and Inchmartin as forming part of the Earl's possessions.—Vol. II. p. 42.—*a Goodall.*

In addition to this silence on the part of Fordun, it tends to throw a doubt on Boece's narrative, that the Foundation Charter of Lindores makes no mention of any such escape from ship-wreck. The Charter sets forth explicitly, that Earl David had founded the Abbey ' for the honour of God and of the Virgin Mary, for the honour of the Apostle St Andrew, and of all the Saints; and for the weal of the soul of his grandfather King David, of the soul of his father Earl Henry, of his mother Ada, of his brother King Malcolm, of his brother King William, and his Queen Arme-garde, and of all his ancestors, and for the safety of his own soul, and of that of his wife Matilda, of that of his son David, and of all his descendants, and of all his brothers and sisters.' Seeing that the Earl is so particular in naming those for whose safety he cared for, it is only reasonable to conjecture, that had any vow, or special deliverance, been the moving cause to the pious act, it would have been mentioned. We have an instance of this in ' the chartulary of Lindores ' (Charter No. V.), where Duncan, Earl of Fife, specially gives the Church of Auchtermuchty to the abbey ' out of gratitude for his escape from death at the battle of Durham (17th Oct. 1346), and for his subsequent deliverance from captivity.

Besides this silence on the part of the charter, a difficulty has been found in the circumstance, that the Earl had scarcely time to proceed to Palestine, and be present at the siege of Acre (the Achon of Boece) between the date of his marriage and that of the fall of that town. He married Matilda, daughter of the Earl of Chester, on the 26th August 1190, and Acre fell on the 12th July 1191.[1] Richard, whom he is said to have accompanied, did not leave Sicily till October 1190.[2] The Earl had therefore two months to come up with the King, and it was quite in accordance with the spirit of the age, to leave a newly wedded wife for the deliverance of the Holy Land.

There is, however, a difficulty in reconciling the foundation of

---

[1] Robertson's *Early Kings*, Vol. II., page 10—*note*.
[2] Fuller's *Holy War*, p. 137.

the abbey in the year A.D. 1178, not merely with the narrative of
Boece, but with the date of the charter. It needs no evidence to
prove that a shipwreck in A.D. 1191, could not have been the
moving cause to a foundation in A.D. 1178. But the charter itself
bears internal evidence that it was not executed earlier than A.D.
1196.[1] Another circumstance tending to throw doubt on the
foundation having been so early as 1178, is the fact, stated by
Fordun himself, that Guido, the first abbot, 'ruled the monastery
for nearly twenty eight years from its foundation.'[2] Guido died
in A.D. 1219, this brings down the date to A.D. 1191, and gives
more consistency to Boece's story. But so far as relates to that
portion of his narrative, that 'his brother belevit him many years
afore decessit,' the Earl's entire absence could not have been more
than three years and a few months; for, as already stated, his mar
riage took place in August 1190, and he was present at the siege of
Nottingham in the early part of the year 1194.[3]

The Honor of Huntingdon, so often mentioned in the history of
the time, came originally into the royal family of Scotland by the
marriage of Prince David, afterwards David I., with Maud, daughter of Waltheof, son of Siward, Earl of Northumberland (a name
which the pen of genius has placed on imperishable record[4]), and
of Judith, niece of the Conqueror. Waltheof received with Judith,
the Earldoms of Northampton and Huntingdon, but on the accusation of treason, he was beheaded at Winchester, and his vast
estates confiscated. The Conqueror gave Waltheof's only daughter
in marriage to Simon St Liz, a Norman nobleman, and bestowed
on him, as her dowry, a large part of her father's possessions. St
Liz built the Castle of Fotheringhay, somewhere about the end of

---

[1] The late Joseph Robertson assigns it to 1202-6.—*Collections on the Shires of
Banff and Aberdeen*, p. 246. It is with extreme diffidence that I venture to differ
from Dr Robertson; but this date would place it after the confirmation by the
Pope, in A.D. 1198.

[2] Vol. II., p. 34.

[3] Robertson's *Scotland under her Early Kings*, Vol. I., p. 397.

[4] *See* 'Macbeth.'

the eleventh or the beginning of the twelfth century, and on his death David I., then Prince of Scotland, married his widow, and acquired her large possessions; these he transmitted to his descendants, and eventually his grandson David, the founder of Lindores, succeeded to the Honor and estates.[1]

Earl David, was not, however, allowed to remain in undisturbed possession of the Honor of Huntingdon. In the year 1213, in the troublous times of King John of England, he was required to give up the Castle of Fotheringhay to the Crown. The Earl refused to comply, but the Sheriff of the county was directed to raise the *posse comitatus* with the townsmen of Northampton, and by force of arms to compel him to surrender it. The castle was strongly situated on a steep projecting ridge having the river Nene in front, and a wide deep moat surrounding the other sides.

It must therefore have been a very strong force that compelled the Earl to give up his proud Norman keep.[2] He seems to have spent some happy years of his life there, in the enjoyment of the society of his grand-children. Devoirguilla, the daughter of his eldest daughter Margaret, lived so much with him, that she was known as the Lady of Fotheringhay, and it was there that John Baliol wooed and won her as his bride.[3] It was a strange link in fortune that brought his ill-fated descendant, Mary Stuart, after so many changes in the place of her imprisonment, to die there. The ancient story of domestic happiness is forgotten, and all interest in the now bare mound is centred in the tragic fate of her, who, after long years of sorrow, there 'reposed her head upon the block.'[4] The Earl appears shortly afterwards to have

---

[1] Bridges' *Northamptonshire*, Vol. I., pp. 394–5. [2] *Ib.*

[3] Macdowall's *Hist. of Dumfries*, p. 39.

[4] Wordsworth. Not a vestige of the walls of Fotheringhay Castle remains, excepting a large block of firmly compacted *rubble*, which appears to have tumbled from the height to the edge of the river. An impression prevails, that James I. ordered the castle to be razed, to efface the remembrance of his mother's execution,—this is a mistake. On the 3d April 1625 it was surveyed and described. 'Soon after this it seems to have been consigned to pillage and ruin,

re-acquired Fotheringhay, for, on his death, it fell to his son John, surnamed the Scot, and after him to his grand-daughters Devoirguilla and Christian. The moiety which fell to Devoirguilla passed to her son John Baliol, the unfortunate occupant of the Scottish throne ; and on his rupture with Edward, it became the property of the English crown.[1] During the time it was in the possession of the Baliols they endowed an 'Ermytage' with a messuage of land to provide for a chaplain, under the neighbouring Abbey of Sawtrey, to perform divine services there on Monday, Wednesday, and Friday, in every week, for the soul of John Baliol, and the souls of his ancestors, the Kings of Scotland.[2] Devoirguilla founded the Abbey of 'The Sweet Heart,' in Dumfriesshire, that her husband's heart might rest there ; and there she was laid beside him. The services at the Ermytage have long since ceased, and the Abbey of 'the Sweet Heart' is ruined and desolate, but the memory of the rude Galloway chieftain's daughter will be fresh and green so long as her grand foundation of Baliol College, Oxford, continues to fulfil the purposes of the pious foundress.

> ' Who from out an age of wildness,
> Lawless force, unbridled crime,
> Reached forth wise hands in mildness
> Helpful to the coming time.'[3]

---

for Sir Robert Cotton, the well-known antiquary, purchased the hall in which the Queen of Scots was beheaded, and removed it to Connington Park, Huntingdonshire. The last remains of the walls of the castle were used for the purpose of repairing the navigation of the river Nene.'—Bonney's *Hist. Notices of Fotheringhay*, p. 31. The parish church, which is at a very short distance from the ruins of the castle, is a noble structure; the tower is visible for many miles up the valley of the Nene, and forms a prominent object in the landscape. Several members of the Royal Family of England are buried within its walls, and the fact that it is unchanged since long before the days of Mary, throws an additional interest around it. A.D. 1868.

[1] Bonney's *Hist. Notices of Fotheringhay*, pp. 18–20.
[2] Bridges' *Northamptonshire*, Vol. II., p. 450.
[3] Shairp's *Kilmahoe*, p. 154.

After the Earl of Huntingdon's expulsion from Fotheringhay, he seems to have removed to Yardley, now Yardley-Hastings, about eight miles north-east from Northampton. Yardley-Castle stood on a height overlooking the noble domain of Yardley-Chase, which stretches out for miles in front of it. A portion of an ancient building, with the roof entire, known by the people in the neighbourhood, as 'The Court Parlour,' still remains; but, though of great antiquity, it is very questionable whether it formed a part of the castle in which the Earl lived. The style of the building does not indicate so early a date as the beginning of the thirteenth century. There can, however, be little or no doubt, that the massive Norman tower of the parish church, which stands close by, is as old as the time of the founder of Lindores Abbey, and it remains an interesting link between the present and the past. Under its shadow the Earl spent his last days, and there he died.[1]

The Earl of Huntingdon bore an active and prominent part in the affairs of his time, and the incidents recorded of him prove him to have been of a chivalrous spirit and of devoted loyalty. When his brother William the Lion, by his fool-hardy chivalry, was taken at Alnwick, and carried captive in the train of Henry II. of England to France, the Earl of Huntingdon exerted himself for the restoration of his brother's freedom, and ever afterwards stood at his side against all the assailants of his throne. On the release of Richard Cœur de Lion, from his Austrian dungeon, he was the first to declare in his favour, and take up arms on his behalf; and on the occasion of Richard's coronation, he was honoured to bear one of the swords of state, incidents manifesting a friendship

---

[1] Yardley Church itself is of the early-pointed style, and is of a later date than the tower. The porch door is of a most antique description, and has all the appearance of being coeval with the church,—there is a small wicket in it, closed by a most antique latch, and the door itself is secured by a bolt drawn from a recess in the wall, the same as may be observed in the abbeys of the period. In the aisle there is a rude piscina and an almry, almost identical in design with those in Lindores Abbey (1868).

which tends to give support to the story of Boece, and which may have been cemented on the fields of Palestine.[1]

The last occasions on which the Earl appeared in public life, was at the coronation of his nephew, Alexander II., A.D. 1214, and at the funeral of his brother, the deceased King. Though bowed down with years and infirmities, he hastened to Scone, and loyally assisted at all the ceremonials of the coronation, which was celebrated with more than accustomed splendour, and then accompanied by the young King, turned to discharge his duty to the dead. At the bridge of Perth he met the funeral cortege of his departed brother, proceeding in solemn state, on its way to the then newly erected pile of Arbroath Abbey, which King William had selected as his burial place.[2] Accompanied by most of the nobility of Scotland, they buried the chivalrous monarch before the high altar of his own great foundation.[3]

The Earl did not long survive his brother. After a lingering illness he died at Jerdelay, now Yardley-Hastings, in Northamptonshire, on Monday, the 17th June, A.D. 1219. It was often

---

[1] Robertson's *Scotland under her Early Kings*, Vol. I., p. 397. Richard's restoration of the independence of Scotland, which had been extorted by Henry II. as part of the price of William the Lion's freedom, produced the happiest effects. 'There was,' says Fordun, 'so hearty a union and so great a friendship, that the two peoples were reckoned as one . . . . The English could roam scathless through Scotland as they pleased, and the Scots could do so throughout England, though laden with gold or any ware whatever.'—*Hist. of Scotland*, Fordun, Vol. II., p. 271. This friendship, perhaps, tended to induce the prompt aid given by the Earl of Huntingdon in Richard's behalf. A facsimile of the treaty of the Restoration of the independence of the kingdom, is given in the First Part of the National Manuscripts of Scotland, No. 46.

[2] *Hist. of Scotland*, Fordun, Vol. II., p. 276.

[3] Innes' *Sketches of Early Scottish History*. With touching minuteness the old chronicler tells, that when the aged Earl, verging on his eightieth year, met the body of his departed brother, he alighted from his horse 'at the head of Perth bridge, took upon his shoulder one arm of the bier, and, with the other Earls, devoutly carried the body as far as the boundary, where a cross was ordered to be set up;' and afterwards, at the entombment, broke down in sorrow, as the grave closed over his brother's remains.'—*Fordun*, Vol. II., p. 276.

his expressed desire ' that his body should be taken down to his own monastery of Lindores, but by the advice of some' (the great distance probably prompting the advice) ' he was taken down to the neighbouring Abbey of Sawtrey, and was buried there in state on the following day.' Of this abbey, founded and endowed by his ancestral connection the son of Simon St Liz, not a vestige remains above ground, and its very name is forgotten in the neighbourhood. The Earl's last resting-place has, therefore, fared worse than his foundation of Lindores, which he fixed on as the burial place of his offspring, and where the coffins of two of his infant children rest in the choir of the Abbey Church, in the very spot where they were laid, nearly seven hundred years ago. [1]

The Earl of Huntingdon left one son and four daughters. John, his son, surnamed the Scot, was (it was alleged) poisoned by his wife, a daughter of Llewellyn, Prince of Wales; he died at Dernhall without issue, and was buried in the Chapter House of Chester Cathedral.[2] On the failure of the line of William the Lion, by the death of the Maiden of Norway (A.D. 1290), the right

---

[1] *Hist. of Scot.*, Fordun, Vol. II., p. 277. Sawtrey Abbey was situated in the parish of Sawtrey Judith, in the county of Huntingdon, in a level expanse, about four miles south-west from Holm Station, on the Great Northern Railway. The field in which it stood is known by the name of the 'Abbey Park.' The unevenness of the surface testifies to a considerable extent of foundations beneath, but the antiquary looks in vain for a single stone remaining above ground. In a straw-shed, forming part of the farm buildings, however, may be seen standing on end, four stone coffins, which were dug out of the 'Abbey-field' a few years ago. They are hewn out of solid blocks of white sandstone; one of them is more elaborate than the others, having a circular niche hewn out for the head; but there is no inscription or symbol on any of them, to indicate whether they were the resting places of warriors or ecclesiastics. Surely these receptacles of the dead are deserving of more reverential usage, and of a safer place for their preservation. 'Sir Richard Cromwell, one of the visitors of monasteries, great grandfather of Oliver Cromwell, received Sawtrey Abbey, besides six other religious houses, from Henry VIII.'—Blunt's *History of the Reformation.*

[2] Robertson's *Early Kings*, Vol. II., p. 32; *Records of Bruces and Cummings.*

of succession to the throne opened to the descendants of the daughters of his brother David. The contests which ensued have inscribed such a glorious page in the history of Scotland, and are so well known, that it is scarcely necessary to say, that Robert Bruce, the grandson of Isabella, the Earl of Huntingdon's second daughter, eventually obtained possession of the Scottish crown, and his descendants have ever since occupied the throne.

The annexed engraving is a *fac simile* of the seal of the Earl of Huntingdon, appended to a charter in the office of the Duchy of Lancaster:—

The completed legend reads as follows:

SIGILL DAVID COMITIS FRATRIS REGIS SCOCIE.

CHAPTER VII.

' Behold a stately fane ! by pious builders
  Raised of old, for worship of Jehovah.
  Within its long-withdrawing aisles
  Attendant monks in slow procession go,
  Chanting the praise of Him who died upon Cross.
  On festal days the people crowd its sacred courts,
  And join in that triumphant hymn of praise,
  To "God, the Father," and to "Christ, the King of Glory !"
  Which still swells the heart of gladden'd worshippers,
  And sends them home renewed in vigour for their daily life.'

Anon.

LINDORES ABBEY was founded and endowed for monks of the Tironensian or Reformed class of the Benedictine order. The Benedictines derived their name from Benedict (an Italian monk), who founded a monastery (A.D. 528), in which ' he proclaimed the rule, which became the model for all subsequent rules, and which the restorers of discipline after it had decayed, were always seeking to bring back.' 'What he did was to lead men away from their farms and their merchandise, that they might become the teachers of the nations and the assertors of a spiritual and divine foundation for the culture of Western Europe.' 'Idleness,' he said, ' is the enemy of the soul. Therefore at certain times the brethren must be occupied in the labours of the hands, and again at certain times in divine study. We think that both ends may be accomplished by this arrangement. From Easter to the Calends of October, let them go out in the morning, and from the first hour till nearly the fourth hour, let them labour for the procuring of that which is necessary.[1] Again, from the fourth hour to the sixth, let them be at leisure for reading. Rising from the table at the sixth hour, let them have an interval of rest upon their beds; or, if any one should wish to read, let him so read that he may not disturb his neighbour. At the ninth hour let them again work till the evening, if the necessity of the place, or their poverty require it, and let them gather the fruits of the earth, seeing that those are true monks who live by the labour of their hands, as our fathers and apostles did. But let all things be done moderately, and in measure on account of those that are feeble. From the Calends of October till the beginning of Lent, let them be at leisure for reading till the second hour, then from the third to the ninth hour, let all labour at the work which is enjoined them. In the days of Lent, let them be at leisure for their readings, from the early morning to the third hour, from thence to the eleventh hour, let them do the work which is enjoined them.'[2] An eyewitness of the labours of the monks, writing more than eight hundred years ago, says—'You might see the abbot, when the office was done in the church, carrying the seed-corn on his shoulder, and a rake and mattock in his hand, going forth to the field. The monks were busy with labour all day; they cleaned the land from thorns and brambles; others brought dung on their shoulders. They hoed, they sowed, no one ate his bread in idleness, and at each hour of prayer they assembled for services at the church. But,' he adds, 'what is most carefully to be attended to is, that the things without which the soul cannot be saved shall be maintained inviolate; I mean faith, contempt of the world, charity, purity, humility, patience, obedience, sorrow for

---

[1] The first hour is six o'clock A.M.—the same as the mode of computation in the New Testament.

[2] Quoted in F. D. Maurice's *Learning and Working*, pp. 50–2. The members of the Reformed Order of Benedictines were obliged to perform their devotions seven times in the twenty-four hours; the whole circle of which had reference to the passion and death of our Lord. When they went out they were obliged to walk two and two together.

faults committed, and then humble confession, frequent prayer, fitting silence (meditation), and such like. Where these are preserved then most rightly may the rule of St Benedict and the order of the monastic life be said to be kept.'[1]

It is obvious that so long as the rules of the founder were acted up to, the corruptions incident to indolence could not overtake the brotherhood of the monastery; but history tells too surely that sloth and indulgence, vices which seclusion from the world are apt to engender, gradually crept in, and undermined the bright ideal which the early founders had set up.

Even in the worst of times, however, there are never wanting some spirits desirous of bringing back to the institutions under which they have grown up, the purity of more pristine times. Bernard of Abbeville, a monk of the Benedictine order, dissatisfied with the practices which he saw prevailing around him, retired to the woods of Tiron, in France, and in the year 1109, laid the foundation of the monastery which has given the name to the Reformed class which he instituted. The task which he set before himself was the revival of the original spirit of the order of St Benedict. Deviating from the letter, he adhered to the spirit of the original founder, by enlarging the sphere of industrial labours in the monastery. All who joined the brotherhood were compelled to practise whatever handicraft they knew. A Tironensian monastery, therefore, was an assemblage of masons, carpenters, smiths, carvers, painters, and husbandmen.[2] Besides these there were brethren, whose special duty it was to educate and instruct the young,[3] and the numerous rare and medicinal plants which still flourish round their old abodes, show that they practised the healing art in common with the rest of the monastic orders.

The discipline of the Benedictines exhibiting religion, not in acts of devotion merely, but in the business of every-day life, had

---

[1] Lanfranc, quoted in *Life of St Anselm*, Church, pp. 29–45.

[2] Morton's *Monastic Annals of Teviotdale*, p. 77.

[3] Joseph Robertson. *Spald. Christ. Mis.*, Vol. V., pp. 73, 74.

a greater and more direct influence in a rude age (or in any age), than a life divided between devotional exercises and contemplation. This was the error of the Cistertians, forgetful of the great truth, that 'in the theatre of the world, God and angels only can be lookers on.' They held it sinful to converse with each other, except upon religious subjects, not realizing that it is the spirit of our conversation, and not the words, which constitutes its guilt or innocence. The consequence of their dismal system was, that they invented a language of pantomimic signs to express their bodily wants.[1]

One of the great necessities of that age, when more than half the land was lying waste, was the encouragement of peaceful industry. At the time of the rise of the monastic system, labour in the fields was accounted beneath the dignity of free men; it was work for serfs only. The rule of the Benedictine monks, many of whom at the outset were of exalted rank, binding them to work with their hands, rescued labour from this degradation, and was the first application of free-labour to the cultivation of the soil. It was therefore of importance to have a body of free men in a neighbourhood, setting the much-needed example, and who had leisure to continue their operations undisturbed by the violent and harassing services of war. That the exertions and example of the founder of the Reformed order of Benedictines (Tironensians) were successful in evoking this spirit and setting this example, is evident from the numerous munificent foundations that philanthropists (as they would be called in our days) raised and endowed for carrying on the good work. It is said that David I., the grand-father of the founder of Lindores Abbey,

---

[1] Two of the lists of signs, or dictionaries, of the Cistercians referred to in the text, are printed in the collected edition of Leibnitz's works.—E. B. Tylor's *Researches into the Early History of Mankind*, p. 40. In consequence of the evil effects of this seclusion from the world, many of the Cistercian monasteries were closed before the Reformation. About A.D. 1440 the Cistercians were extruded from Pluscardine Abbey, and Benedictines introduced in their place.—*Records of the Monastery of Kinloss*, p. xl.

went to France to satisfy himself, how far the reports of their success were true. All over Europe wise princes encouraged them as the best promoters of civilization.[1] Around the monasteries, the turbulent warriors by whom they were surrounded, saw the effects of settled industry, in richly cultivated fields, marshes drained, wastes reclaimed, abundant crops, and in improvements promoted; and the poor experienced the blessing of living under masters whose interests lay in the maintenance of peace.

In addition to these benefits, posterity is under another great obligation to the monks for the preservation of the writings of antiquity. The *Scriptorium*, or writing-room of the abbey, was a quiet, but busy scene ; it was the printing-press of those days, and from it emanated all the light of the knowledge that was then in the world. The patient monks there multiplied copies of the word of God,[2] and, as a relaxation, perhaps, gave a spare hour to the great works of the ancient classics, which they thus 'saved for all posterity.' There also they penned those chronicles which have proved such precious bequests to history.

---

[1] Southey's *Book of the Church*, p. 59.

[2] 'In the thirteenth century a copy of the Bible cost from £40 to £60 for the writing only, for it took an expert copyist about ten months labour to make one.'—Smiles' *Huguenots*, pp. 1, 2. Estimated by the price of grain, the cost of a Bible was enormous. 'In 1388 barley was commuted in Norfolk at twenty pence the quarter, *English Gilds*.'—*Old English Text Society*, p. 123.

D

CHAPTER VIII.

> ' A house of prayer and penitence—dedicate
> Hundreds of years ago to God, and Her
> Who bore the Son of Man!   An abbey fair
> As ever lifted reverentially
> The solemn quiet of its stately roof
> Beneath the moon and stars.'
>
> *Wilson.*

LINDORES ABBEY was dedicated to the Virgin Mary and to St
Andrew the Apostle. Its ruins stand on a gentle rise, almost
close by the Tay, about a quarter of a mile east from the town
of Newburgh. The site is of great fertility, and commands a
prospect of exceeding beauty.

> ' The Tay roll'd down from Highland hills
> There rests his waves, after so rude a race,
> In the fair Carse of Gowrie.'

The Sidlaws rise beyond the long rich level of the Carse, on
the north; the Ochils, in picturesque crags, rise close behind the
abbey on the south; and the broken outline of the giant Grampians on the west, closes in a scene which, for loveliness and
grandeur, is scarcely equalled in Scotland.

Sir Robert Sibbald, in his 'History of Fife,' says, 'almost con-
tiguous to Newburgh East, and anciently within Earnside-wood,
are the ruins and seat of the Abbacy of Lundoris, a right sweet
situation, and of most rich soil; witness the vastly big old pear
trees there.' In addition to the fertility of the soil, it had two
prime requisites for a monastery, wood and running water. The

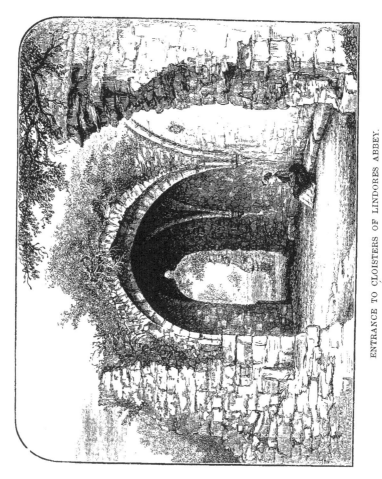

ENTRANCE TO CLOISTERS OF LINDORES ABBEY.

water that issues from Loch Lindores flowed past the abbey garden, and turned the abbey mill; and Earnside-wood afforded abundance of fuel close at hand. The 'vastly big old pear trees' still survive to attest the fertility of the soil; one of them is believed to be the largest pear tree in Scotland; it measures within two inches of eighteen feet in circumference, round the trunk one foot from the ground; is of proportionate height, has a spread of branches of fifty-three feet from side to side, and is still in bearing, yielding large crops.

Boece, speaking of Lindores Abbey, says, 'Ane thing is thair richt marvellous—na man is hurt in that abbay with eddiris. Thir eddiris lyis in the middis of ane vale circulit with wood and rinnand water, throw quilk thay burgeon with mair plenteous nowmer than evir was sene in ony ither parts. Howbeit na man gets skaith thairof, for we have sene young barnis play amang thaim but (without) danger or hurt following.'[1] Sir James Balfour gives a very graphic account of the same phenomenon. 'This place,' he says, 'was wearie (very) famous of old for the hudge number of serpentis in it, without stinges creeping about mens bodies without harming of them at all.'

'The wearie (very) sleeping chalmers of the monkis being full of them. How they ingendered heir in suche aboundance, and how they wair destroyed, tak a memorandum of ane abbot of this place (as he himself callis it), wreittin in his awin Legir booke as it is extant by me.

'Memorandum that in the zeir of our Lordis Nativitie 1316, this place was sore affrayed with hudge swarmes of *Stintes* aderes that bred in a great heap of draff that had layand at the great entrie that luikes to the towne of Newburgh, and that for many zeiris; we war fred (freed) of them by the help of the Blissed Virgine Marie, our glorious patroness in the zeir 1330 '—the pious monk guilelessly adding—' having tormentit them with both watter and fyre.'[2]

---

[1] *Hist.*, chap. 7.   [2] *Balfour MSS.*, Advocates' Library.

What Boece recounts as a marvel akin to the miraculous, is a simple fact in the natural history of the collared snake, which is perfectly harmless, having no poison fangs; it is very common in moist places in England, and the low damp ground near to the abbey seems to have suited the nature and habits of the animal.[1] The same ignorance of natural history attributed Divine protection, under similar circumstances, in other parts. It is recorded of St Godric of Finchale, near Durham, 1099–1128, that he allowed swarms of these snakes, attracted by the warmth, to lie by the fire of his cell on winter nights, and that he caressed and handled them with impunity. The people, believing them poisonous, attributed their harmlessness to miraculous interference in the saint's behalf. [2]

Most of the buildings of the abbey were erected under the superintendence of Guido, the first abbot, who was previously prior of Kelso.[2] The ruins still testify that the buildings were spacious and magnificent, but there is not one entire portion remaining. The church was 195 feet in length, and the transepts were 110 feet from north to south. The most perfect portion of the abbey remaining is the groined arch of the porch which formed the entrance to the abbey through the cloister court. The ruins have recently been cleared of superincumbent rubbish, and the ground plan, and style of the buildings, are now clearly seen; they belong to the 'Early English,' or 'first pointed style,'

---

[1] The snake referred to is the *Natrix Torquata,* or collared snake; it measures three to four feet in length, and feeds on frogs, field-mice, etc. It is generally found in woods in the neighbourhood of moist places.

[2] Kingsley's *Hermits,* p. 310. Sir James Balfour, in the same manuscript, adds, 'Boetius wreittis that if any venemous or poysonable creature be brought thither it will not live, and that this place can nourische non suche' 'wche (which) indeed is a great mistaking, Daylie experience proveing the contrair to be true.' A popular belief akin to this prevails, that the black soil around Lindores Abbey was originally brought from Ireland.

[3] Fordun—*a Goodal,* Bk. 9, cap. 27; *Liber de Melros,* p. 35.

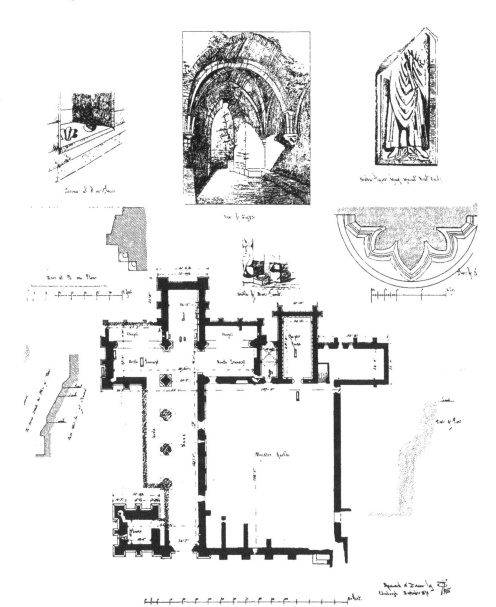

which prevailed in Scotland at the period of their erection.[1] But none of the graceful shafts of the piers of the arches, or the mullions of the windows, which characterize that style, remain entire. The abbey was chiefly built of red sandstone, from the Founder's 'quarry of Hyrneside,' to which he gave 'his monks of Lundoris' a perpetual right to take as many stones as they required for the use of their house.[2] The pillars and ornamental parts of the building, were, however, mostly of gray sandstone, brought from a distance.

Lindores Abbey was most munificently endowed; the Founder not only laid his Scottish, but his English estates, under contribution for its support; he bestowed on it 'the church Londoris and all the lands belonging to it; the church of Dunde and every thing pertaining to it,' and the churches of Fentrith (Fintray), Inverurin, with the chapel of Munkegin (Inverurie and Monkegie), Durnach (Logie-Dornoch), Prame (Premnay), Radmuriel, Inchmabanin (Insch), Culsamuel (Culsalmond), and Kelalcmund (Kennethmont), in his Earldom of Garioch.[3] Besides these churches, the Bull of Pope Innocent III., dated 19th April 1198, confirming the privileges of the abbey, specially mentions 'the church of Mothel, in the bishopric of Stratheren,' and the churches of 'Cuningroue and Wissinden, in the bishopric of Lincoln,' as pertaining to Lindores Abbey.[4] No record has appeared showing who bestowed the ancient Culdee Church of Mothel, now Muthil, on Lindores; but the monks continued to draw revenues from the lands of 'Ardoche, Bennie and Eister Feddellis,' all formerly within the parish of Muthil, down to the suppression of the monastery; and those of Wester Feddellis were held under the burden of conveying two

---

[1] See Plan, p. 52.

[2] Chartulary of Lindores, p. 24. The quarry, which is now covered up, was of old red sandstone,—it was about a mile east from the abbey, on the farm of Parkhill. The track of a small canal for conveying the stones to the abbey was said to be discernible in recent times.

[3] Chartulary of Lindores, p. 38.   [4] Ib., p. 40.

horse-loads of herring from Glasgow to the abbey yearly.[1] A subsequent opportunity will be afforded for further notice of the other
Scottish endowments ; but as the English churches are not again
mentioned in the abbey charters, it may be proper here to state
that, unless Cuningroue is Cotgrave in Nottinghamshire, it cannot
be identified with any existing church. No doubt however exists
of Whisendine in Rutlandshire, being the Wissinden of the charter. It existed in Saxon times ; immediately after the Conquest it
was held by Earl Waltheof; in the time of the survey it was
the property of his widow Judith,[2] and through this ancestral
connection the church came into the possession of the Abbey of
Lindores. ' It is curious to find in the reign of Edward I. (1272–
1307), the advowson or patronage of the church was in the Monastery of Lindores. Sir John Swinburne, Knt.,[3] and Friar John
of Lindores, as procurators for that monastery, presented to it,
but in the succeeding reign it was alienated to the prior and
convent of Sempringham in Lincolnshire.'[4] The breaking out of
the war of Independence, consequent on Edward's attempted
subjugation of Scotland, sufficiently accounts for the abbey being
deprived of its property in England. The Church of Whisendine
is a fine old structure, and one portion of it, at least, is coeval with
the time when it belonged to Lindores Abbey ; its lofty and massive tower forms a conspicuous object over a wide extent of
beautifully undulating country.[5]

---

[1] *Perth Retours*, No. 504.

[2] Brewer's *Beauties of Eng. and Wales*, Vol. II., p. 2.

[3] Sir John de Swynbourne was frequently employed on church matters about
this time. In the year 1295, in the reign of John Baliol, he was joint-collector
of the revenues of the Bishopric of St Andrews, ' the bishop at that time being
in foreign parts, and against the peace of the king.'—*Hist. Doc. Scotland*, 1286 ;
1306, Vol. II., p. 17.

[4] Brewer's *Beauties of England*, Vol. II., p. 2.

[5] Mr Scott, son of Sir Gilbert Scott, the eminent architect, who had the
charge of the restoration of Whisendine Church (1868), ' is of opinion that the
north transept, which still stands, was built about A.D. 1220.' Most of the church

The charter by which the Earl of Huntingdon conveyed all these churches to the Monastery of Lindores, was certainly executed before A.D. 1198, and it is in it that the town of Dundee is first mentioned in authentic record. For some reason which does not appear, unless the territory on which the town is built was a special appanage of the Crown, Dundee is almost invariably styled in ancient records 'the Royal Town' (*regiam villam*). There are many stories in Boece and other writers, of a romantic character, regarding the Earl of Huntingdon's connection with Dundee ; of his landing there after his return from the Holy Land, and of his building a church in the town ; but, unfortunately, there are no authentic records to support them. The one thing certain is, that there was a church in Dundee in the end of the twelfth century, which the Earl bestowed on his new foundation of Lindores.

Though there is no direct mention of Dundee in any more ancient record, it must have been, from the fertility of the neighbourhood and its admirable position as a port, a place of importance from very early times. Considering too, its proximity to Invergowrie, one of the early centres of Christianity of Scotland, there is every probability of there having been a church in the town from a time almost coeval with the first introduction of the Gospel into eastern Scotland. Whether it was such an ancient church, that is mentioned in the charter to Lindores, or whether it was, as tradition has it, a church built by the Earl of Huntingdon in gratitude for his escape, is uncertain ; no portion of the ancient structure remains. What constituted the most ancient portion of the mother church of Dundee was wholly destroyed by fire in 1841, and all that is left is the grand old square tower ('one of the noblest in Great Britain') which has been so

---

has been rebuilt, but the whole building bears the marks of venerable antiquity. In the north aisle there is a series of life-sized grotesque human figures in oak, forming brackets for the support of the rafters of the open roof. There is no such grand old parish church in Scotland.

munificently restored, but which certainly is not older than the middle of the fourteenth century.[1]

'The first recorded pastor of Dundee was William of Kerneil, A.D. 1214.'[2] About A.D. 1220, Gregory, Bishop of Brechin, in a license or decree preserved in the chartulary of Lindores Abbey, confirms the right of the monks of that abbey to the church and chapels of Dundee; the mention of these latter, for the first time, affords evidence of an increasing population. In the license, Gregory, as Bishop of the diocese, consents to the appointment of a vicar by the monks of Lindores, to perform the duties of the church, on condition that they pay him a stipend of ten pounds sterling; a large allowance, considering the value of money at the time, and an additional collateral evidence of the growing importance of the town. In the same document the Bishop gave the monks permission to plant schools in the parish.[3] This is one of the earliest notices of schools in Scotland; the very earliest is contained in a charter of Ethelred, Abbot of Dunkeld, and Earl of Fife, son of Queen Margaret and Malcolm Canmore, by which he bestows the lands of Admore (Auchmore on the Leven) on the Culdees of Lochleven, A.D. 1093—1107, to which Berbeadh, 'Rector of the schools of Abernethy,' is one of the witnesses.[4]

The ancient Pictish capital has, therefore, the precedence; but the permission given to the monks to plant schools in Dundee in the beginning of the thirteenth century, confirms the statement, that they set apart one or more of their number for the important duty of educating the young, and testifies to the pleasing fact, that they had not then forgotten that the great purpose of their princely foundation was the education and elevation of the people.[5]

---

[1] Gilbert Scott's *Report*.
[2] Jervise's *Memorials of Angus and Mearns*, p. 181.
[3] *Chartulary of Lindores*, p. 17.
[4] Reeve's *Culdees of the British Islands*, pp. 245, 6.
[5] Joseph Robertson, *Miscell. Spald. Club*, Vol. V., p. 68.

These provisions were ratified by Pope Gregory IX., on the 17th April 1239.[1]

On the appointment by the monks of Lindores of Mr William Mydford, as vicar of Dundee, instead of allowing him a fixed stipend, the monks, apparently to be freed from the trouble of an accounting for the baptismal and burial fees, and to avoid all disputes about these casual payments, agreed to allow the Vicar to uplift the whole altarage in name of vicarage, both parties leaving it to the Bishop of the Diocese to fix how much should be rendered to the Abbot and convent as their share of these fees, as Rectors of the parish. The Bishop decided that the Vicar should pay them ten merks sterling at Pasch.[2] The Vicar felt himself aggrieved by this decision, and appealed to the Pope, alleging that it did not leave him 'a suitable portion for the due performance of the sacred duties of his office.' He, however, did not follow up his appeal, and on a petition by the Abbot and convent, Pope Alexander IV. confirmed the Bishop's decision by a Bull, dated 17th April 1256, in which, for the first time, the name 'the church of St Mary of Dundee,' is mentioned.[3]

The Vicar, however, would not submit, and the Abbot and his brethren again appealed to the Pope, who granted 'letters, empowering the Prior of (the Isle of) May, and the Provost of the church of St Mary of St Andrews to enforce the decree. After a lengthened litigation, the Vicar agreed to submit to the decision of the Bishop of Dunblane and other prelates, who, at a meeting held in the chapter house of Arbroath (20th September 1256), gave sentence against him; the monks agreeing to forego a large portion of the interest and expenses for the sake of restoring harmony, and bringing the dispute to an amicable conclusion.[4] To make sure that this portion of the revenues of the church should not be encroached upon, the monks obtained (11th February 1257) a decree from the Pope exempting their

---

[1] *Chartulary of Lindores*, p. 18.   [2] *Ib.*, p. 10.
[3] *Ib.*, p. 13.   [4] *Ib.*, p. 14.

share from the diocesan burdens, which the Vicar was bound to bear.[1]

These details may be reckoned too minute, but the whole transaction is a noticeable instance of the injurious effects of the abstraction of the revenues of a parish church from their primary and legitimate uses. It was a weak point in the abbey system, and entailed the appointment of a Vicar at a diminished stipend with consequent diminished influence.[2] The absorption of the revenues of so many parish churches by the abbeys, tended ultimately to swell the discontent against monasteries, which ended in their suppression.

The revenue derived from the various churches and estates belonging to the abbey, was estimated for the purpose of taxation in the year 1275 by the Roman Legate at i mvjc. lxvj. li. xiij. s. iiij. d. It is difficult to arrive at the relative value of money at that period; but when it is borne in mind that a cow could be bought for five shillings, sheep at tenpence a head, and that a chalder of oatmeal cost exactly a pound Scots[3] (twenty pence sterling), it will be seen that the wealth at the disposal of the monks was very great, and rightly expended, capable of exercising a most beneficial influence.[4] This was of importance, as there is reason to believe that the monasteries were productive of greater benefit in a social, than in a strictly religious point of view.

---

[1] *Chartulary of Lindores*, p. 16.

[2] 'When the revenues of a church or parish fell to the lot of a monastery, it became the duty of that monastery to perform the religious services of the parish. But inasmuch as the monastery was a corporate body, they appointed one, whom they denominated their *vicar*, to discharge those offices for them.'— F. W. *Robertson*. Sermons, Third Series, p. 101.

[3] Tytler, Vol. I., p. 280.

[4] Preface to the 'Statuta Ecclesiæ Scoticæ,' by the late Joseph Robertson, p. cciii. A work full of condensed information and of great research. Its very excellency adds poignancy to the sorrow for the early death of the author. It gives an idea of the relative wealth of the abbey, to learn from the same source that Arbroath Abbey was valued at £4000, Balmerino at £533, 6s. 8d., and the Ministry at Scotland Well at £83, 6s. 8d.

The monks, in their corporate capacity, undoubtedly exercised a beneficial influence, by carrying the spirit of religion through all their social relations, and by exhibiting to their turbulent neighbours the benefits arising from peaceful avocations. Bringing with them a knowledge of the most approved modes of cultivation; the luxuriant crops of their fields, and the rich fruits of their gardens soon became standing evidence of what undisturbed industry could effect. They were the pioneers of improvement, and were the first to adopt every discovery calculated to increase the productiveness of the soil, of which, from their intercourse with their brethren, both at home and abroad, they had the earliest intelligence. To this source can be traced the excellence of the fruit, especially of many of the admirable varieties of pears, for which the orchards of Newburgh are so justly celebrated.[1]

There is every reason to believe too, that the monks were the first to introduce the grinding of corn by machinery into this neighbourhood, and that before their time the handmill, or quern, was

---

[1] The names of many of these kinds of pears bear witness to their foreign origin. In a treatise on Fruit Trees, printed in Paris, A.D. 1548, the following notice of the Bon-Chreton (Good Christian) pear occurs :—'They are,' the author says, ' of surpassing sweetness, and so tender and juicy that they dissolve in the mouth ; they sometimes grow to the weight of a pound, and bear every year;' a description which is still applicable. The author says, that ' the Bon-Chreton was first brought from Campania, near Naples, in the time of Charles VIII. (A.D. 1494). The Bergamot pears,' he says, 'are much to be commended ; they began to be cultivated in our recollection (i.e. before 1548), and are juicy and excellent in flavour.' For the use of this rare volume, which is of beautiful type, the writer is indebted to Mr Milne of Hill Park. It is interesting to learn the origin of trees, which are flourishing in our orchards, and which, after an interval of nearly four hundred years from their first production from the seed, are still propagated by grafting. There are several very old Bon-Chreton and Bergamot trees in the orchards of Newburgh, still bearing large crops. From the frequent mention made of vineyards in old records, there is reason to believe that the monks were also successful in growing grapes. In Lord Douglas' *Vassalage of Abernethy* (A.D. 1846) there is a feu in the neighbourhood of that ancient ecclesiastical seat designated ' The Vineyard.'

the sole mode by which meal was ground.　In 1284, in the reign of Alexander III., it was enacted that na man sall presume to grind quheit, maishlock (mixed grain), or rye with hands-mylne, except he be compelled be storm, or be lack of mills, quhilk sould grind the samen.　Gif a man grinds at hand mylnes he sall gif the threttein measure as multer; and gif onie man contraveins this our prohibition he sall tyne his land mylnes perpetuallie.' [1] This enactment was obviously for the purpose of promoting the erection of mills wrought by machinery and driven by water, which was rightly deemed an important invention, deserving encouragement.　The domestication of bees, which was early attempted, was also actively encouraged and promoted by the clergy.　The foundation charter of the abbey (*circa* 1196 or 7), which conveys 'The church and lands of Londors,' makes no mention of a mill; but two years later, the confirmation by the Pope expressly specifies 'the mill of Londors,' as part of the

---

[1] Wilson's *Prehistoric Annals*, Ed. 1851, p. 150. In the outlying islands of the Hebrides the primitive hand-mill is still, or at least very recently was, in use. In the year 1847, Captain Dall (a native of Newburgh, now of Chicago, United States), after a walk of fourteen miles in the island of Lewis, in the early morning, felt the need of something to satisfy his hunger. He asked the master of a house on the shore for something to eat till he could reach his vessel, which lay some miles out in the bay. The latter said he had no bread, but he would soon get it. He immediately spoke a few words in Gaelic to two young women, who went to a barley stack, and took out three sheaves, which they threshed by beating them with a stick each. They winnowed the grain by tossing it up in the wind to drive away the chaff; they afterwards put it in a pot on the fire till it was sufficiently dried, and then cooling it in the open air for a few minutes, they set down with a hand-mill, or *quern*, between them, exemplifying the verse, 'two shall be grinding at the mill, the one shall be taken and the other left.' The pure meal gradually came forth, and in little more than an hour the anxious waiter on the operations was presented with a barley bannock, which his previous fast made doubly sweet. Still later—in 1851—Mr Ross of Bachilton, while on an agricultural tour in Ireland, saw, in the wilds of Connemara, the same primitive operations, and had an oaten cake given to him in less than two hours.

monks' property; the legitimate inference being, that it had been erected by them in the interval.[1]

The farms, which are still found throughout the country in the neighbourhood of old abbeys, named 'The Grange,' were the farm-steadings where the monks carried on their farming operations, and where the grain and cattle derived from their more distant possessions were stored and housed. Around the 'Grange' were clustered numerous cottages for the labourers and their families, and the whole was under the charge of a monk, or lay brother, named from his office—'The Granger.' From details afforded by Cosmo Innes, in his valuable *Sketches of Early Scotch History*, we learn that 'the situation of cottars was far above the class now known by that name.' At Kelso each of "the Grange" cottars occupied from one to nine acres of land, and a class above them, the *husbandi*, or husbandmen, possessed small farms of twenty-six acres each. The latter kept two oxen, and six of them united their twelve oxen to draw the ponderous plough of those days. They paid their rent in money and services, and it is worthy of notice, that no service was imposed on women, except harvest work.'[2]

---

[1] The original 'mill of Londors,' appears to have stood in the Den of Lindores, exactly where a fall could be obtained with least labour. The foundations of an old mill were removed from that spot within the last few years.

[2] Small holdings continued in this neighbourhood till the end of the last century. Descriptive of a state of society utterly past away, it is worthy of being recorded that, in the memory of some yet alive (A.D. 1871) there were resident in the hamlet of Kinloch, in the parish of Collessie, upwards of fifty men, young and old, where there is now only one cottage. Each cottar of the hamlet rented as much land as maintained a horse and two kye; a class above these had as much land as maintained two horses and several kye,—these larger holders were called by the others 'The Tenants.' The same gradation apparently continuing as in the abbey Granges. In such hamlets and homesteads were brought up, in rough comfort, a healthful population, who were a tower of strength in the hour of their country's need; and from the larger, but still small homesteads, arose a great proportion of the students of the Scottish Universities in the preceding century, many of whom rose to distinction, and brought honour to their country. It may be that the physical comforts of ploughmen are now much superior to

The Grange of Lindores exhibits in its outward features many of the characteristics of primitive times—around the steading are still to be seen straw-thatched cottages with straw-bound chimneys, each, with its patch of garden, standing in most picturesque irregularity, and showing, in some degree, the appearance of a Grange of the olden time.

In these Granges there arose a peaceful population of free

---

those of the small tenants of former days, and it is evident that the increasing application of machinery to the cultivation of the soil, which has tended so much to the improvement of agriculture, renders the management of small farms more and more difficult. Still their extinction has a depressing effect on the ploughman ; it blots hope out of his horizon, and widens that chasm which separates the employer and employed, already too wide, and is one of the most undesirable features in the social condition of modern times.

Connected with one of these small hamlets, that of Lochend, in the parish of Abdie, is an incident which throws light on the condition and mode of life of students in the end of last century, and it is so creditable to one who afterwards rose to distinction, that it deserves to be recorded. In the end of the year 1776, a student from Cairn, a small farm in the parish of Muthil, Strathearn, plodding his way on foot to St Andrews, was overtaken by a snow-storm a little beyond the village of Lindores. The storm raged so furiously that he was in imminent peril of his life ; struggling on through the drift, darkness came on, and he was all but exhausted, when he caught a glimpse of light from a cottage window, to which he fought his way. The inmates, awakened by his knocking, at once arose and bestowed on the stranger the attention which he required, and the comforts which their humble dwelling afforded. This student was John Barclay, afterwards the famous anatomist. Forty-six years afterwards, when in the height of his fame, having ascertained from a young man belonging to Newburgh, who attended his lectures in 1822, that the worthy couple who had sheltered him were alive, he sent by this student (David H. Lyell, M.D.) a set of silver teaspoons to the wife, and a silver snuff-box to the husband, the latter bearing the appropriate inscription, ' To James Wilson from Dr Barclay.' ' I was a stranger and ye took me in.' The box is in the possession of Mr William Wilson, draper, Newburgh, grand-nephew of James Wilson ; the spoons were parted among the female relatives, and are carefully preserved as heirlooms, precious for their associations. The brothers Bethune, who dwelt for many years in the same hamlet where the illustrious professor found shelter, have made the incident the subject of a pleasing tale. It appeared among the *Tales of the Borders*, under the title of the ' Bewildered Student.'—Vol. III., pp. 90–98.

THE GRANGE OF LINDORES.

labourers engaged in the cultivation of the soil, but the records of the abbeys show that the monks had descended from their high original, and must bear the opprobrium of keeping serfs to assist in field labours.[1] Still the monastic movement accelerated the death of serfdom. The monks, in common with all men at that time, recognised slavery as an existing fact, but in principle their doctrines were hostile to its continuance; their very union as a brotherhood acted as a protest against it. 'They taught that all men were the children of one father, and brothers of one family,' and as this teaching of the church prevailed, the condition of the slave was ameliorated. The terrible power of life and death, which masters exercised by law over slaves in the old Roman world, disappeared before the mild spirit of Christianity. It may be that labour by freemen was found to be more economical than that by bondmen. Evidence of this is not wanting in the manumission of serfs by churchmen, for an annual payment instead of constant enforced labour. About the year 1340 the monks of Dunfermline granted freedom to *their men* of Tweedale on payment of an ox of two years old, or four shillings yearly.[2] Little by little the shackles of the serf, and the rigours of slavery, were re-

---

[1] Records of the genealogy of serfs were kept, that they might be reclaimed, in case they attempted to escape. In the *Chartulary of Dunfermline Abbey*, there is a record of the residences of serfs belonging to that abbey, which is locally interesting, as it mentions the names of farms in this neighbourhood where their serfs resided: 'Galf (Galfrid) of Dunberauch at Dunberauch (Dumbarrow in the parish of Abernethy); Cristin, the son of Ada, at Wester Urchard (in the parish of Strathmiglo); Oenene Freberner at Hicher-mokedi (Auchtermuchty); Patrick his brother, at Renkelouch (Rankeilour, in the parish of Collessie); Maurice Colms at Pettynkyr.' It adds touching interest to this list to find, that the monks were equally careful in recording the place of death and burial of their bondmen. Under the head, 'Genealogy of Maurice Sutherlin,' the following occurs: 'Alwin Cambrun, son of William Fleming, died at Tolibrench, and was buried *(jacet)* in the churchyard *(cimiterio)* of Markynchs; Eugene his son, died at Kynglassie, and was buried there.'—*Registrum de Dumfermelyn*, pp. 220, 221.

[2] *Regist. de Dunfermelyn*, p. 192; Innes' *Sketches of Early Scotch Hist.*, p. 144.

laxed ; the monks practically showing that all men were brethren, by admitting slaves into their brotherhood, whose bonds fell from them at the abbey door.[1]

The encouragement too, which the monks gave to the erection of burghs in the neighbourhood of their abbeys, tended to the same result. In these communities there arose an industrial population, whose activity and energy accumulated wealth, and whose freedom and increasing influence gradually led to the extinction of the bondage of serfdom, and to the personal liberty which now prevails.

---

[1] Sigersen's *History of the Land Tenures of Ireland.*

CHAPTER IX.

'Watch and be firm! for soul-subduing vice,
　Heart-killing luxury, on your steps await
　To sap your hardy virtue, and abate
　Your love of Him upon whose forehead sate
　The crown of thorns; whose life-blood flowed, the price
　Of your redemption.'

Wordsworth.

CONSIDERING the length of time the monks occupied the abbey, the amount of wealth at their disposal, and the powerful territorial influence they exercised, it is curious that not a single tradition of them, either good or bad, survives in the neighbourhood, save one that has passed into a proverb. A recalcitrant bell-ringer of the abbey threw up his place, under the impression that his services could not be dispensed with; but he had not gone far, when, hearing the bells ringing as usual, he was fain to admit, 'The bells o' the abbey will aye be gotten rung.'[1]

---

[1] The name for *shortbread* in Newburgh is so exclusively local, that, combined with its origin, it seems to be a relic of proximity to the abbey, and of 'Abbey times.' It is invariably designated 'Pentie.' Various explanations have been given of the name,—that the bread was originally made in the form of a pen tagon,—that it was used at the feast of Pentecost; but these are mere conjec tures. The true etymology is from the name *pain-demayn*. The editor of the *Book of Days* (Vol. I., p. 119) says, 'This word has given considerable trouble to commentators, but which means no more than ' bread of our Lord,' from the figures of our Saviour, or the Virgin Mary, impressed upon each round flat loaf, as is still the usage in Belgium with respect to certain rich cakes much

E

There are however in the chartulary of the abbey, records extending over a period of more than three hundred and fifty years, from which can be gleaned something of its internal, as well as its external history. From the foundation charter, we learn that the first bequest to the abbey, was, 'the Church of Londors,' and the lands belonging to it; the Church of 'Dunde,' and the Churches in the Garioch. The church and lands of Londors are described as formerly belonging to Master *(Magister)* Thomas; this appellation denotes an ecclesiastic, and there can be little doubt that the Church of Londors, now Abdie, in which the old cleric ministered, was of Culdee origin, and one of the early religious settlements of the country. It was dedicated to St Magridin, whose name appeared on Cross Macduff.[1] The

---

esteemed there.' Other writers simply assert that it was the name for the finest bread. *Pentie* is clearly the two first syllables of the name *pain-de*-mayn. Dunbar, in his poem of 'The Freires of Berwick,' more than once alludes to this kind of bread as a great dainty, but in doing so, instead of retaining the French *pain*, he names it '*bread* of mane.' Presumably this bread, like shortbread, was unleavened,—which latter was used for communion purposes in St Michael's Church, Dumfries, up to the year 1864, in all probability because of unbroken custom from pre-Reformation times.

[1] W. F. Skene, *Pro. of Soc. of Ant.*, Vol. IV., p. 318. The parish church of Flisk was dedicated to the same saint, and in that parish there is a hill known as St Muggan's Seat. There are several names of places in the neighbourhood of Abdie Church indicative of antiquity, as the Lecturer's Inch, the Priest's Burn, the Teind Knowe; and at the foot of Lindores bank, St Andrew's Well, now covered up. There were also at a little distance from Abdie Church two upright stones, known as *The Lickerstanes*, whose origin and use are both alike lost in antiquity. They consisted of unhewn boulders about three feet high, somewhat square on the sides and flat on the top. They stood like pillars, one on each side of the footpath leading from the Den of Lindores to the churchyard, just where the path met the road from the Grange to Lindores. They were removed about the beginning of the present century, and it is said were applied to some utilitarian purpose in effecting some repairs on the out-buildings of the manse. Stones bearing the same name are found in other places in Scotland, and invariably on the side of the road leading from the outskirts of the parish to the churchyard. There are Lickerstanes in

ABDIE OLD CHURCH

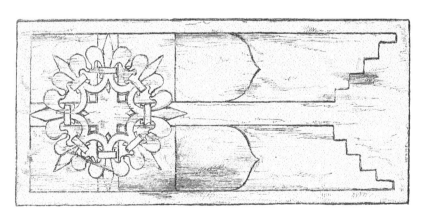

TOMBSTONE IN CHANCEL

etymology of the name Londors tends to throw back the origin of the church to an early period. *Lon*, or *Lun*, in which way the first syllable continued to be spelt down to the middle of the last century, is the Gaelic equivalent for the Welsh *Llan*, which signifies a church, and *dwr* from the same language, signifying water, which, anglicised *Lundore*, is the earliest form of the name, and is thus spelt on the seal of Abbot Thomas, who died in A.D. 1273. Neither of these terms is common in Scotland, and the fact that the Gaelic *dobhar*, water (pronounced dore), has long been obsolete, goes to show that the old Church of Lundores is very ancient. The name, ' The Church by the Water,' is admirably descriptive ; the little knoll which constitutes the churchyard almost jutting into the Loch.[1]   In Abdie Church there was an altar dedicated to

---

the parish of Abernethy, and there was a Lickerstane in the parish of Falkland, but it has been removed; the place is, however, known by the name of ' Lickerstane.' There was also a ' Likkerstane' in the neighbourhood of Pittenweem. *Fife Retours*, 508. In a record of the marches of the lands of Kirkness, as bestowed on the Culdees of Lochleven by Macbeth and his Queen Gruoch, preserved in the Register of the Priory of St Andrews (p. 1), entered certainly not later than the middle of the fourteenth century, ' a heap of stones called in the vulgar tongue *lykyrstyne*' (' *unum acervum lapidum qui dicitur in vulgari* lykyrstyne'), is specially mentioned as one of the points of the march or boundary. This notice proves the antiquity of the name, but unfortunately there is nothing on record to show the purpose for which these stones were erected. Tradition however is uniform that the corpse carried to burial was laid on them, and that the priest there met the funeral procession, and began the service for the burial of the dead. From this traditionally assumed reading of the service, it has been conjectured by some, that the name is derived from the Latin word *Lector*, signifying a reader; but the oldest orthography, coupled with the fact that it is expressly said to be known in the vulgar tongue as the Lykyrstyne, goes to prove that the name is derived from the old English or Saxon word *lic* or *lych*, a corpse, hence *Lychstane*, and that these stones were connected with the burial of the dead. The covered gateway to many of the old churchyards of England is uniformly known as the Lychgate, because the funeral service begins there. The seal of the town of Lichfield shows a field strewn with corpses.

[1] Mr W. F. Skene, in his most valuable notes to the *Four Ancient Books of Wales*, says : ' A curious illustration of two different terms, lying side by side,

St Ninian, the apostle of the Southern Picts, still further showing its connection with the Early Scottish Church.

The abbey, though built at a distance of two miles from the original church, was within the *parochia*, and therefore rightly named Londors ; the monks wisely endeavouring to transfer the hallowed associations which had grown up around the ancient church to their new erection. Even so late as the middle of the last century, the lands around the mansion house of Lindores were named, in legal documents, ' Auld Lundores.' [2]

' It was, doubtless, from his brother, William the Lion, that Earl David received the grant of Lindores.' [3]   This property was extensive and of great value ; it embraced within its limits at least the modern farms of Grange of Lindorés, Berryhill, Ormiston, Lindores, Lindores Abbey, Craigmill, and the Burgh Lands of Newburgh, a stretch of about four miles in length, and upwards of two miles in breadth, of fine upland pasture, and of rich and diversified arable soil.

The name of the parish, Londors, occurs in a list of churches in the Deanery of Fife, in the eleventh year of the reign of William the Lion (1176).[4] ' In the modern name of Abdie, it seems not improbable that we are to recognise *Abthen* or *Abden*, the terms by which the lands belonging to our early monasteries came to be

---

which are derived from the same word, undergoing different changes, will be found in Forfarshire, where the term *Llan*, for a church, appears, as in Luntrethin. It is a phonetic law between Latin and Celtic, that words beginning in the former with *pl*, are, in the latter *ll*. The word *Planum* in Latin, signifying any cultivated spot, in contradistinction from a desert spot, and which, according to Duncange, came to signify *Cimiterium*, becomes in Celtic, Llan, the old meaning of which was a fertile spot as well as a church.'—P. 159. The topography of Wales abounds with places beginning with Llan, and among them is Llandore, near Swansea.

² Abbot Thomas's seal is engraved on the frontispiece of the *Liber Sancte Marie de Lundoris*.

³ Preface to *The Sculptured Stones of Scotland*.

⁴ Sibbald's *Fife*, p. 207.

designated.'[1] The first time that the name 'Ebedyn' occurs, is in a list of churches dedicated by Bishop David de Bernhame, A.D. 1242.[2] It next appears as 'Vicaria de Ebde' in Boiamund's Tax Roll of Scottish Church Benefices ; a roll that was made up in the year 1275, for the purpose of imposing a tax of a tenth part of their revenues for the support of a Crusade.[3] That the old Church of Londors was all but despoiled of its revenues for the endowment of the abbey, is apparent from the fact, that it is the only church in the deanery returned in Boiamund's Roll as beneath the tax ; benefices having less annual revenue than forty merks being exempt. In the same Roll, the rectory of Flisk, a much smaller parish, the revenue is put down at one hundred pounds ; facts which corroborate what is said in a previous page, of the depreciation of the revenues of vicarages.

The change in the name of the parish seems to have been brought about by the absorption of the old name by the abbey, while popularly the old church came to be known by the designation of the lands which formerly belonged to it, *Abthen*, *Abden*, Abdie. The roofless old church (used for the last time on the 11th November 1827), which forms such a picturesque object on the margin of Loch Lindores, does not however date back to Culdee times. In a writing of the thirteenth century, on a fly-leaf of a volume preserved in the Imperial Library, Paris, it is recorded that the consecration of 'Ebedyn' Church by David de Bernhame, Bishop of St Andrews, took place on the 5th day of September A.D. 1242, a date which corresponds with the style of its architecture.[4]

---

[1] *Sculp. Stones of Scot.*, Vol. II., Preface.

[2] *Stat. Ec. Scot.*, Appendix to Preface, pp. cciii–ccc.

[3] *Ib.*, p. ccciv.

[4] *Ib.*, p. ccc ; *Old Church Architecture*, pp. 57, 58. After the old church of Abdie ceased to be used as a place of worship, there was found in digging a grave in the chancel, a tombstone having a cross of a beautiful floreated design incised upon it. The style indicates an origin not later than the

The monks of Lindores had not been long in their new abode, when their generous benefactor bestowed on them the island called 'Redinche' (Reedinch),[1] now Mugdrum Island, with the whole of the fishings around it, excepting 'his own yhare at Colcrick.' The charter which conveys this grant was confirmed by the Pope in 1198, and it contains one of the earliest notices of fishing by yares in Scotland. Colcrick seems to have been a valuable fishing station, as a few years later (1198–1237), David de Haya of Errol bestows on the monks of Lindores, the third share of the drawings of his nets on the sandbank of Glasbannyn (now Clash-bennie) opposite Colcrick, 'saving,' however, 'his fixed or stake net fishings and their waters.'[3] With the exception of 'a carucate'

---

fourteenth century. This interesting relic, of which an illustration is given, is carefully protected within the chancel of the old church. There is also in the chancel a recumbent figure of a woman with her hands folded across her breast; it is of sandstone. Formerly this statue lay unprotected in the churchyard, and it is much defaced.

[1] So named from the immense extent of Reeds, *Phragmites Communis*, which grow around it, an exceedingly graceful plant, of sometimes 10 to 11 feet in height. It was formerly used exclusively for thatching. On this point Sir James Balfour (M.S. Advocates' Library) says 'thairwith they thack houssis quhos induring with the smallest supplie will near out-brave ane hundreth years.' The reeds are now bought up for the manufacture of paper, A.D. 1873.

[2] *Bk. of Lindores Charter*, No. 4.

[3] Shortly afterwards David de Haya granted to the monks of Coupar in Angus, to whom the family of Errol were great benefactors 'the right to draw a net betwixt Lornyn, and Randulf de Haya's march,' which also must have been near the fishing of Colcrick. The charter which conveys this privilege contains a reminiscence of an interesting phase of religious life, which is worthy of notice; besides the right of fishing it bestows on the monks of Coupar 'the hermitage which Gillimichael the hermit possessed, and the three acres of land lying beside it.' It is interesting to know that the farm on which the hermitage stood retains the name of the old recluse, and is still called 'Inchmichael.'— *Spalding Club Miscel.*, Vol. II., p. 307. That the spot where the hermit dwelt was the residence of man from very early times, appears from the fact that when the railway though the Carse of Gowrie was being made, a very consider-able number of stone implements were found in a gravel mound on the farm, none of which, it is to be feared, passed into any public collection. One of

of land in Neutile, another in Pert (Perth), and the Church of Mothel,[1] the only other property conferred on the abbey in the lifetime of the founder, seems to have been ' a toft' in each of the ' burghs of Berevic, Strivelin, Karel, Pertht, Forfare, Munros, and Aberdene,' by his brother William the Lion.[2]

The frequent appearance of Guido, the first abbot, as a witness to various charters, shows that he took an active part in public life. He attended a council of the church held by Cardinal John of Salerno, at Perth, in December 1201. None of its enactments have come down to us, except that 'no priest who had been ordained on the Lord's day should continue to officiate at the altar.[3] This

---

them, a stone cruse or lamp, is in the possession of Mr Davie of St Fillans Hotel, Loch Earn. It has no ornamentation whatever, but is of the same shape, though more rude, than the stone lamps used at this day in the Faroe Islands, one of which figured in Warings ' *Stone Monuments, etc., of Remote Ages*, Pl. 5, p. 41,' was presented to the Society of Antiquaries of Scotland by Sir W. C. Trevelyan.

Clashbennie, celebrated for its fossils, is named ' Egclisbannyn,' in the Errol Charters, the name indicating that there had been a church there.—*Spalding Club Miscellany*, Vol. II., p. 308. *Colcrick* cannot now be identified. The fishing stations in the estuary of the Tay shift with the shifting of the sands, and their names change accordingly. But further up the river the same names have continued for centuries. In A.D. 1178–1180, William the Lion bestowed on Arbroath Abbey, ' one net upon his water of Pert (Perth) called the " Stoc." In 1431 the monks of the Priory of the Isle of May claimed from the monks of Scone the tithes of four fishings, viz., ' Sleples and Elpenslau, and Chingil, and Inchesiryth, within the bounds of the parish of Rind (Rhynd).' All these fishings, with the exception of Elpenslau, are still known by the same names.—*Arbroath Chartulary*, p. 11. *Records of Priory of Isle of May*, p. 30. The rent of the ' Stoc ' fishing for the season of 1873 was £550 sterling.

[1] Bull of Pope Innocent, *Book of Lindores*, p. 39. The *Caruca*, so often met with in old records, meant a team of eight oxen, supposed to be required for the tillage of a ploughland, which was subdivided accordingly into eight ' ox-gangs,' or *Bovata*. From a charter of William the Lion, we gather that a ploughgate, or carucate of land, in Scotland, contained 104 acres.—E. W. Robertson's *Essays*, pp. 89, 133.

[2] *Ib.*, p. 9.   [3] *Stat. Ec. Scot.*, p. xl.

enactment arose out of the example set by the primitive church on the occasion of Barnabas and Saul being ordained to preach the Gospel to the Gentiles. It is recorded (Acts xiii. v. 3), that ' when they had fasted and prayed, and laid their hands on them, they sent them away.' In conformity with this example, fasting was deemed an essential element in the act of ordination ; and as the Lord's day was a joyful festival (because commemorative of the resurrection), on which fasting was strictly forbidden, ordinations taking place on that day were wanting in this scriptural requirement, and were therefore declared invalid. The abbot was also a member of the Council held at Perth in A.D. 1212, convoked by the Bishops of St Andrews and of Glasgow, under the authority of Pope Innocent III., for the purpose of sanctioning a Crusade for the relief of Jerusalem. Great privileges and encouragements were held out as inducements to join the Crusade, and multitudes took up the Cross, but few of the rich or great embarked in the enterprise.[1] It was given as a reason for this backwardness, that many of the rich had previously earned a promise of paradise in reward for their services against the Albigenses, and, as has bitingly been remarked, ' perhaps they feared being put in possession thereof too soon, by losing their lives in that service.'[2]

The next incident in the History of Lindores is of a character calculated to give weight to the accusation of those who charge abbeys with being fostering places of luxury and self-indulgence. Sir James Balfour, in his ' Annals,' says, ' In the zeire 1217, Guallo, the Pope's Legat, comes to Scotland, excommunicats K. Alexander II., and hes quhole nobility and gentrey, and interdicts the kingdom from the usse of aney religious exercise, and solemnly with book and bell, cursses all of quhat-sumever degree or quality that had carried armes against K. John of England, now Pope's wassal and feodatary, wich interdiction lasted from Februarij 1217, to Februarij 1218, a quhole zeire; about wich tyme the Prior of

---

[1] *Stat. Ec. Scot.*, p. xlii.   [2] Fuller's *Holy War*. p. 156.

Dursome (Durham), and the Dean of York came to Scotland, being sent by the English legat, making their progress from Berwick to Aberdein, and absolved the kingdom from Guallo's cursse and interdictione; and in return home to England, being lodged in the Abbey of Londors, the Prior of Durseme was burnt to death in his chalmer, wich took fyre in the night by chance ' (his chamberlain being very drunk) and he fast asleep.'[1]   The curse which the prior and his colleague came to remove, was pronounced because of the assistance rendered by King Alexander to the Barons of England, when they extorted the famous Magna Charta from King John.[2]   Sir James Balfour is in error in stating that the Prior of Durham died at Lindores.   He was able to proceed on his journey homeward; but he suffered so much from the effects of the fire, that his health was seriously affected, and it was with difficulty that he got as far as the Priory of Coldingham, where he became much worse, and died on the 13th May 1218.[3]

The ceremony of excommunication was performed with awful solemnity, and it required more than ordinary firmness and enlightenment to be able to brave the terrible sentence.   While the dread words were being pronounced, bells were solemnly tolled, and the Cross inverted, 'By the authority of Almighty God the King was cursed in soul and body, in his going out and in his coming in, sleeping and waking, day and night, at every hour and in all places.   None were to compassionate him in his sufferings, and none to relieve him in his sickness.'   Torches prepared for the purpose were cast down and trampled out, symbolical of the awful adjuration, ' unless he repent may his light be put out before Him who liveth for ever and ever.'[4]   ' No priest dare officiate in public or private, save only, that baptism was allowed

---

[1] *Annals*, Vol. I., p. 41.   [2] Robertson's *Early Kings*, Vol. II., p. 2.

[3] 'The prior, Thomas de Melsonby, was a man of refined taste, and some of the finest parts of Durham cathedral owe their origin to him.'—Hunter's *History of the Priory of Coldingham.*

[4] Southey's *Book of the Church*, p. 115; Morton's *Monastic Annals of Teviotdale*, p. 84.

to infants, and confession to those at the point of death.   The
dead were deprived of Christian burial.'[1]

> ' The church by mandate shadowing forth the power
> She arrogates o'er heaven's eternal door,
> Closes the gate of every sacred place.
> .   Bells are dumb ;
> Ditches are graves—funereal rites denied.
> And in the churchyard he must take his bride
> Who dares be wedded.'[2]

Alexander was personally released from this sentence on his
submission to the Pope ; but the churches were not opened or his
people absolved, until they had contributed largely to the officiating cardinal. This functionary's behaviour and extortions were
so oppressive, that they roused the Scottish clergy into a combined
determination to send deputies to Rome to complain of his conduct ; but though Guallo was obliged to disgorge part of his exactions, the spoil, it is said, was shared between himself and his
master. The Scottish deputies were therefore obliged to be
content with a Bull from the Pope, confirming the privileges and
future independence of the Church of Scotland.[3]

It was during these troublous times that the life of Guido, the
first Abbot of Lindores, was drawing to a close ; and, singularly
enough, his spirit passed away on the same day that the Earl of
Huntingdon, the founder of the abbey, breathed his last in
England. They both died on Monday, the 17th June 1219.
The historian, in recording the abbot's death, says, ' he ruled
the monastery with firmness, and left behind him twenty-six

---

[1] Southey, *Bk. of the Church*, p. 117.   [2] Wordsworth.
[3] Spottiswoode's *History of the Church of Scotland*, Vol. I., p. 85. A fac-
simile of the Bull is given in the first part of *The National Manuscripts of Scot
land*, No. 47. The late Joseph Robertson says, ' its writing may be regarded as
one of the triumphs of the Roman chancery.' Guallo built the church of Sant
Andrea, still extant at Vercelli in Piedmont, his native country, with the money
he levied in England and Scotland.—Robertson's *Early Kings*, Vol. II., p. 8,
note.

monks in it, instructed in the ordinances of religion. In his last moments he exhorted them all to mutual charity, and with his head leaning on the hand of one of the brethren, his countenance shadowing forth inward peace, he fell asleep in the Lord.'[1] Of Guido's successor, John, almost nothing is known, excepting that he was a monk in the abbey before his promotion.[2] He must have held the office of abbot at least twenty-five years; for, on the 28th April 1244, he was a witness in the Cathedral Church of Aberdeen, to a Charter conveying the Church of Bourdyn (Bourtie) to the Church and Canons of St Andrews.[3]

John was succeeded by Thomas, of whom it is recorded, that he was remarkable for the holiness of his life, *vir magnæ sanctitatis.*[4] He and the prior of the abbey were appointed by Pope Alexander IV., A.D. 1257, to settle a dispute between the monks of Reading, in Berkshire, as superiors of the priory of the Isle of May, regarding a tenement in North Berwick. 'After a litigation involving much argument, labour and expense,' they pronounced their decision ' in the Conventual Church of St Andrews, on Monday after the feast of St Luke the Evangelist (18th October), in the year A.D. 1261.[5]

In the time of Thomas, or that of his predecessor, Roger de Quincy, Earl of Winchester, and Constable of Scotland, bestowed on the monks of Lindores, the right of taking ' two hundred cart loads of brushwood or heather *(bruere);* and as many peats as they require for the use of their house, from that peatery which is called Menegre, in the moor of Kindelouch, none else having right to dig peats there without their permission ; together with an acre of land to dry their peats on, and two acres on which

---

[1] Fordun, Vol. II., p. 34, and Bk. IX., cap. 27.

[2] Fordun—*a Goodal*, Bk. IX., cap. 27.

[3] *Collect. of Aberdeen, etc.*, Spald. Club, p. 565. He appears as second witness to the charter to the Earldom of Fife, granted at Perth by Alexander II., on the 21st March 1225.—*Nat. MS. of Scotland*, Part I., No. 50.

[4] Fordun, Bk. X., cap. 33.

[5] *Records of the Priory of May*, pp. xxii.–xxvii.

to store their peats and heather, with pasturage for ten ewes and two kye for the use of the keeper of their fuel on the moor.'[1]

The family of De Quincy, from whom the monks acquired the right to the moor of Kinloch, appears in Scottish history for three generations, and then suddenly, by the failure of heirs male, the name became extinct in Scotland.[2] Their appearance and rise in Scotland is accounted for by their close relationship to the Royal Family, their direct ancestor, Seher De Quincy, having married Maud St Liz, the daughter by her first marriage of Queen Maud, wife of David I. Robert De Quincy, the first of the name that occurs on record in Scotland, married Orabile, Countess of Mar, daughter and heiress of Nes, the son of William, owner of the lands of Locres (Leuchars) in Fife, and of Duglyn (Deuglie), in Perthshire.[3] Through his marriage with this rich heiress, Robert De Quincy acquired these properties, besides other estates in Scotland, of which that of ' Kindelouch ' appears to have been among the number.[4]

It may be affirmed, almost with certainty, that we owe to the

---

[1] *Chartulary of Lindores*, p. 41.

[2] Thomas De Quincey, the well-known author, claimed to be a cadet of this family.

[3] *Chartulary of Cambuskenneth*, pp. 91–93.

[4] Charter records carry back evidence of the ownership of the properties of Leuchars and Deuglie to a very early period, certainly to the beginning of the twelfth century, if not even earlier. From the *Chartulary of Cambuskenneth* we learn that Seher De Quincy, Earl of Winchester, sitting in his court at Locres, *circa*, 1207, bestowed on the Church St Mary of Striveling, afterwards Cambuskenneth, the lands of Duglyn, all as they were marched by the same bounds as when they were held by his grandfather Nes, the son of William.—*Cambuskenneth Chartulary*, pp. 91–93. At a subsequent period, ' between 1210 and 1219, Earl Seher, with consent of his son Roger, bestowed on the canons of St Andrews three merks of silver yearly from his mill of Lochres, for the weal of the souls of his grandfather and grandmother, of his father, Robert De Quinci, and his mother Orabile.' Before this, ' about the year 1180, Nes, the son of William, and Orabile, his daughter and heir, gave the church of Losresch in Fife, to the canons of St Andrews.'—*Antiquities of Aberdeen and Banff*, Vol. IV., p. 692. This latter appears to be the modern Lathrisk.

De Quincys the fine old Church of Leuchars. Symone de Quinci, evidently a cadet of the family, who had two *clerics* under him, was parson *(persona)* of Louchres, *circa* 1210–1219,[1] and the enriched details of the beautiful romanesque style of the church corresponds with the architecture of the period during which they held their courts at Leuchars, as lords of the estate;[2] reasons which may be held as conclusive on the point.

Seher De Quincy, the son of Robert and Orabile, succeeded to , his mother's làrge estates. He was created Earl of Winchester in 1207, and was one of the celebrated twenty-five barons who were appointed to enforce the observance of Magna Charta. In accordance with the spirit of the age, he set out on a crusade, and took part in the siege of Damietta in 1219. He died shortly afterwards in the Holy Land, on a pilgrimage to Jerusalem.[3] He was succeeded in his honours and estates by his son Roger, who married Helen, the eldest daughter of Alan Fitz Roland, Lord of Galloway, and by her, besides acquiring large accessions to his estates, he became Constable of Scotland.[4]

Between the years 1235 and 1264, Roger De Quincy, Earl of Winchester, and Constable of Scotland, 'from motives of piety,' conferred on the Abbot and Convent of Lindores, in addition to the grant of the moor of Kindelouch, the further favour of the patronage and revenues of the Church of Cullessy; a right which was confirmed by Pope Nicholas IV., on the 13th December 1288, on condition that a suitable portion of the revenues be reserved for a perpetual Vicar.[5]

Roger De Quincy died in 1264, and his vast estates in Scotland descended to three daughters, who, by marriage, carried them into the families of Comyn, De Ferrars, and De La Zouche, whose

---

[1] *Reg. Priory of St Andrew's*, pp. 254–257.
[2] *Characteristics of Old Church Architecture*, pp. 11–13.
[3] *Historic Peerage of England*, by Sir Harris Nicolas, p. 515.
[4] *Scotland under her Early Kings*, Vol. II., p. 25.
[5] *Historical Documents of Scotland*, Vol. I., p. 60.

representatives forfeited the whole, by espousing the cause of Baliol in the Wars of the Succession.[1]

The privilege which Roger De Quincy bestowed on the Monks of Lindores, of digging peats in the moss of Kinloch, was one of great value, as, even in districts where coal now abounds, peat at that period, and for long afterwards, formed the common fuel of the country.[2] 'Æneas Sylvius, afterwards Pope Pius II., records the wonder with which he beheld, in the year 1435, not far from Edinburgh, coal which he took for stones,' 'joyfully received as alms by the half-naked beggars who stood shivering at the church doors.'[3] The abundance of brushwood over the whole country supplied ready fuel, and it is natural to suppose coal would only be extensively dug for after the wood was exhausted. The 'Moor of Kindeloch,' after the Earl granted it to the abbey, was known as the *Monks' moss*.[4] It is curious also to notice, that the far-off grant of an English nobleman has given its name to the neighbouring railway station of Ladybank, now so familiar to travellers through Fife. Lindores Abbey was dedicated to the Virgin Mary, and in honour of her the monks fondly named their newly acquired possession, 'Our Lady's Bog;' latterly it was known as Ladybog, and shortly before the station was erected, Ladybank.

The charter to the moss contains names, now obsolete, of places in the neighbourhood. One of these names Thors-ton, is indicative of Norse origin, while the existing names of Orkie, Kettle (Ketil is a name of frequent occurrence in Iceland), Weddersby, and the Boose, all in the same neighbourhood, point to an early and somewhat extensive Danish settlement.

The Monastery of Lindores had the honour of a visit from Alexander III., on the 14th March 1265. The King was accompanied by Alexander Comyn, Earl of Buchan, Justiciar of Scot-

---

[1] *Notes and Queries*, 4th S., Vol. X., p. 366.
[2] Innes's *Sketches of Early Scot. His.*, pp. 101-131, and note, p. 132.
[3] *Stat. Ec. Scot.*, pp. 93, 94.   [4] Sibbald's *Fife*, p. 385.

land, and William, Earl of Mar, Great Chamberlain. The presence of these officials make it all but certain, that Alexander was on one of those annual circuits for the administration of justice, for which he is so justly celebrated. It is said of him :—

> ' The Lawch he gert be kepyd welle,
> In all his Kynryk ilka dele.[1]

At that period the abbeys, then in their first new splendour, afforded accommodation superior to that of the castles of the nobles. The numerous Royal Charters dated from monasteries, show that the Sovereigns, in their journeys through the country, very frequently took up their abode in them, where, during their temporary sojourn, in addition to the comfort of the abbey, they had the advantage of meeting and conversing with the best educated men of the time. Not unfrequently, however, the monks received substantial favours in return for their hospitality. On the occasion of his visit to Lindores, the King repaid his hosts by bestowing on them the privileges of a ' Free Forest ' over their woods of Lundoris.[2] ' Forest,' in charter language, ' signifies a range having certain legal privileges for the preservation of game.'[3] The penalty for infringing these rights is fixed by the charter at ten pounds ; a heavy fine when estimated by its equivalent in grain, and shows the value that was set upon the privilege conferred by the Royal Charter.[4]

Thomas, the third abbot, died A.D. 1273, and was succeeded by John the Prior, who died the following year, and was buried in Kelso. Previous to John's appointment as abbot, he and the

---

[1] Wyntoun, Bk. VII., c. x.   [2] *Bk. of Lindores Chart.*, No. 9.
[3] *Liber-de-Melros*, Pref., p. xv.
[4] Wyntoun says, in the time of King Alexander III.
> ' A Bolle of aits pennys foure
> Of Scottis mone past noucht oure ;
> A Bolle of Bere awcht or ten
> In comowne prys sawld wes then.'

Bk. VII., cap. x.

Abbot of Dunfermline, and two bishops, were selected by the clergy of Scotland to represent them in London, before the Papal Legate, who had been peremptorily refused admission into the kingdom by Alexander III. The representatives of the clergy showed themselves worthy of the trust confided to them; they withstood the demands of the Legate, resolutely withholding their sanction, and refusing obedience to canons which he procured, affecting the privileges and liberties of the Church of Scotland.[1]

It was either in the time of John, or that of his successor, that the monks solicited permission from the Pope to wear caps or bonnets, while engaged in celebrating the solemn festivals of the church, and in processions. The Pope acceded to their request, 'because the coldness of the climate of Scotland' rendered many of them unable to celebrate the divine services of the monastery; but during the 'reading of the Gospels, and the elevation of the body of our Lord Jesus Christ,' he strictly enjoined that the heads of all be uncovered and due reverence be paid.[2]

The successor of John, the trusted representative of his brethren, was Nicholas, the cellarer of the abbey.[3] 'The cellarer ought,' says the rule of the Benedictine Abbey of Bec in Normandy, 'to be the father of the whole congregation, to have the

---

[1] Tytler, Vol. I., p. 19.

[2] *Book of Lindores*, p. 24. The monks had to take other precautions against cold. 'Having daily to recite long offices in cold churches, at early hours of the morning, they found it expedient to adopt long coats of skins as part of their choir costume. These were called 'pelliceæ' (Latin, *pellis*, a skin). In 1200 A.D., a Synod at London restricted the Black Monks and Nuns (Benedictines) to lamb, cat, and fox skin,' to restrain luxury in dress.—*Contemp. Review*, Vol. I., p. 267. As these 'pellisses,' from continued use, became unsightly, the monks began to wear linen tunics over them while celebrating divine service; these were called *super-pelliccæ*, hence surplice. In the inventory of articles given in *Liber Sancte Marie de Lundores*, belonging to the abbey, A.D. 1530, it is worthy of note, that only the permitted kind of skins are enumerated amongst them, 'V quhyt cat skyns w^t diuss (divers) furryngs of hwds and brok blak cla^t.' P. 33.

[3] Fordun—*a Goodal*, Bk. X., cap. 34.

care both of these in health, and also, and especially of the sick brethren.'[1]   It is not known how long Nicholas held the office of abbot, neither is anything known of his history or administration; he appears as a witness to a charter conveying the lands of Galuflat to Nichol de Haya of Errol;[2] and also to a charter of Patrick, Earl of Dunbar, relieving the monks of the Isle of May from the payment of a cow for their lands in Lambermor (Lammermuir.)[3]

While Nicholas was abbot, Prince Alexander, the son of Alexander III., and heir to the throne, for some reason which is not recorded, came to Lindores Abbey, and after a lingering illness died there.   Only a few months before, his marriage had been celebrated with great splendour.   This marriage was the subject of great rejoicing throughout Scotland, as it gave promise of the removal of the possibility of a disputed succession.   These hopes were rudely dashed by the tidings of his illness, and the old chroniclers can scarcely find words to express the sorrow and gloom which overspread the land.   It is on record that the Prince was filled with forebodings of the dangers to which Scotland would be exposed by his death, and 'upon the night before he died, he talked wildly about an approaching contest with his uncle (Edward I.), and suddenly exclaimed, ' Before to-morrow's sun rise the sun of Scotland will have set.'[4]

' In after years of misery and woe, those who stood around his death-bed, and listened to his words of warning, deemed that he had been inspired in his dying hours with prophetic visions of the future.'[5]   He died on the feast of St Agnes (21st January 1283–4), in the twentieth year of his age, and was buried among his ancestors, in the Abbey Church of Dunfermline.

---

[1] *St Anselm, R. W. Church*, p. 65.

[2] *Spald. Club Mis.*, Vol. II., p. 310.

[3] *Records of Priory of May*, p. 13.

[4] *Chronicon de Lanercost*, p. 111 ; Fordun, Bk. X., cap. 37.

[5] Robertson's *Early Kings*, Vol. II., p. 116.

There are some letters of Prince Alexander addressed to his uncle Edward I., preserved in the Tower of London. They throw no light on contemporary history, but they are of interest, as showing the friendly feelings which subsisted between the two countries at the time.[1]

The calamitous death of Alexander III. filled the cup of Scotland's sorrow. The prosperity which the country had enjoyed under him, was quenched in strife and bloodshed, in the memorable struggle which ensued on the failure of direct heirs to the throne, and centuries elapsed ere the country regained the prosperity which it had attained in his days.

> ' Scotland menyd[2] hym ful sare,
> For wnder hym all his Legis ware
> In honore Qwyetè, and Pes.'[3]

The change from this happy and prosperous condition, to the long years of misery and bloodshed which ensued, gives a touching pathos to the oldest of all the extant songs of Scotland; and which ' wes made of hym.'

> Quhen Alysander our Kyng was dede,
> That Scotland led in luive and le
> Away was sons of ale and brede,
> Of wyne and wax, of gamyn and gle.
>
> ' Our gold wes changyd into lede
> Cryst, borne in-to virgynte,
> Succour Scotland and remede
> That stad is in perplextye.'[4]

---

[1] A fac-simile of one of the Prince's letters is given in the first volume of the *National MS. of Scotland* (No. 65). The monkish chronicler, in recording the statement in the text, says: ' I have received this relation from those who stood by his bedside at death,—one of them was a soldier, and the Prince's tutor (magister), and the other a rector of a church and his chaplain (sacerdos).'— *Chronicon de Lanercost,* p. 37.

[2] Moaned—mourned. *Mein,* to grieve or pity, is still in use in Fife.

[3] Wyntoun, Vol. I., p. 399.   [4] *Ib.*

CHAPTER X.

EDWARD AND WALLACE.

'Powers depart,
Possessions vanish, and opinions change;
But by the storms of circumstance unshaken,
And subject neither to eclipse nor wane
Duty exists.'

Wordsworth.

THE fears the lamented Prince expressed of his uncle's ambitious designs, were strikingly fulfilled in the very place where they were uttered. On the 23d July 1291, Edward I. came to Lindores Abbey, and it is recorded that John, the Abbot, Sir William of Fenton, and Sir Simon of Freschele (Fraser), 'touched the Host, kissed the Gospels,' and swore upon the great altar of the Abbey Church, allegiance to Edward.[1]

Two years later John Baliol visited Lindores Abbey, accompanied by his officers of state, John Comin, Earl of Buchan, Constable of Scotland, Alexander de Baliol, chamberlain, and other attendants. The result of this visit is preserved in a charter granted by Baliol in favour of Nicholas de Haya of Errol, erecting the lands of 'Errol, Inchesirech, Kilspinedi, Dronlawe, Pethponti, Gaskengrai, and of Fossewy in free warren.' The seals of the noblemen named were attached to the charter at Lindores, on the 1st August 1294, the second year of Baliol's unhappy reign.[2] Warrens (from *wahren*, German to preserve) seem mainly to have

---

[1] *Ragman's Rolls*, p. 16.   [2] *Spald. Club Missl.*, Vol. II., p. 313.

been for the preservation of rabbits. Contrary to what might have been expected, rabbits were very scarce in the thirteenth and fourteen centuries, their flesh was esteemed a delicacy, and the right to protect them was regarded as a most valuable privilege.[1]

In the year 1296, Lindores Abbey had the questionable honour of another visit from Edward I. Baliol had just completed his humiliation, by resigning the crown into Edward's hands, and there, as at every place where he stopped in his progress through the kingdom, Edward compelled all classes to assemble and swear allegiance to him. He remained for this purpose at Lindores longer than usual. The record of his journey, which is interesting from its local allusions, tells us, that ' on Monday (6th August) he was at Dunde; on Tuesday at Baligerny, the red castle; on Wednesday at Perth; on Thursday at the Abbey of Lundores; and there he remained the Friday, St Laurence's day (10th August). On Saturday he was at the city of St Andrews, a castle, and a good town; on Sunday at Markinch, where are only the Minster and three houses,[2] on Monday he was at the Abbey of Dunfermline, where nearly all the kings of Scotland lie,'[3] and, it is added, ' he

---

[1] *Roger's History of Agriculture, quoted Edin. Review*, No. 257, p. 52.

[2] The ' Minster,' as the writer of King Edward's itinerary designates Markinch Church, has been replaced by a modern structure, but the Minster Tower still stands. It is ' pure Norman, one of five of the same character to be found in Scotland,' and is anterior to the time of Edward. The author of ' Characteristics of Old Church Architecture,' whose opinion we have quoted, says, ' the tower at Markinch is a good and nearly perfect specimen ' of its kind. Topping the dome-vaulted roof, ' there was originally a low pyramidal stone capping, surmounted by a rod and weather-cock; but in 1807, this characteristic feature was removed to make way for the present incongruous structure,' pp. 20, 21.

[3] The tombs and monuments of the ancient Scottish Kings, and the monuments which were raised to the memory of warriors and statesmen, of whom Scotsmen are now justly proud, have all, with scarcely one exception, been utterly demolished. Not a vestige of the Royal tombs at Dunfermline remains, excepting several very small fragments of the tomb of King Robert Bruce, preserved in the collection of Mr Paton of Dunfermline, to whom the country is indebted for the preservation of many relics of historic value. These fragments, which are of

conquered the realm of Scotland, and searched it, as is above written, within twenty-one weeks withat any more.'[1]

It was on this occasion that Edward carried off the Coronation Stone from Scone. Lists of those who swore fealty to Edward in the Parliament held by him at Berwick, a few weeks later, are still preserved among the English archives, and the number of names recorded shows the extent of the humiliation effected; amongst others Thomas, Abbot of Lundores, Adam of Lumbyny, Patrick of Dundemor (Dunmore), William of Latheresk (Lathrisk), Henry of Monimel in this neighbourhood, are ingloriously enrolled.[2]

Edward's triumph was of short duration. Within a year of his 'conquest' of the country, a spirit of opposition manifested itself, which he was never able afterwards effectually to quell. The leader in this movement was the illustrious hero, William Wallace, whose name, an English poet has truly said, 'is found, like a wild flower, over all his dear country.'[3] Burning with indignation at

---

pure white marble, exhibit most elaborate workmanship, and show, from the small fractions of carving that remain, that the monument must have been of an exquisitely beautiful Gothic design. No Scotsman but must now regret that fanaticism should have been allowed to wreak its rage on a monument which would now be of such great historic value. Even the massive slab of mountain-lime-stone which formed the base on which stood the tomb of Queen Margaret, in what was the Lady Chapel of Dunfermline Abbey Church, has not escaped. Though about twelve inches in thickness it has been split asunder: neither the sanctity of the grave, nor the saintly character of the Queen, proved any protection. It is a strange anomaly, and much to be deplored, that a race so proud of their country and of its history, should have demolished the monuments of the men who made the country great. The tomb of Aymer de Valence, the brave opponent of Wallace at the battle of Black Earnside, of exquisite design and workmanship, is still preserved, with religious care, in Westminster Abbey.

[1] *Hist. Documents, Scotland*, Vol. II., pp. 30, 31.

[2] *Ragman Rolls*, p. 116–144.

[3] Wordsworth *Prelude*. This holds good in the Highlands as well as the Lowlands. The twin Lomonds in Fife, whose tops are seen from the Highlands, peering over lesser heights, are known by the Highlanders, as *Cuispairn Bhallist*, 'Wallace's Marks' at quoits, a lasting memorial of the honour in which the name of the Scottish hero is held.

the utter humiliation of his country, Wallace gathered around him a band of kindred spirits, and within a few months wrenched stronghold after stronghold from Edward's hands.[1] Unsupported by the great or powerful, who, with few exceptions, had sworn fealty to Edward,[2] the success of Wallace and his compatriots is the more surprising, and proves the depth of patriotism which is to be found among the people, and the power

'Which a brave people into light can bring,
For freedom combating.'[3]

One of the battles of the war of independence took place in the

---

[1] Wyntoun, Vol., II. p. 120.

[2] For the nobles it ought in justice to be stated, that Edward had contrived to obtain possession of the eldest sons of the most powerful and influential, and he held them as hostages for the *good conduct* of their fathers.

[3] Wordsworth. Under the year 1300, Sir James Balfour in his 'Aunals,' gives an account of a great battle fought on the north-western declivity of Cairneyhall hill, near the margin of Loch Lindores. He says, 'In this zeire John Comyne the Governour defait the English armey two several times, and the same zeir K. Edward sent a great armey to Fyffe, and miserably wastit the same. The Governour sent Sir John Fraser with 4000 men in their reire quho often cut them short, and in Junij in a battell neir the Castell of Lindores, assisted by Sir William Wallace ouerthrew them quyte, and killed their Generall Sr John Pseworth. This battle is called Dillicarrew Field (*Dal-a-cairidh*, dh silent, Gaelic, the Field of the Carey; signifying a mound at a bend of a river requiring protection from the encroachments of the stream), quherein 3000 Englishe were killed and 500 takin prissoners. The Scots lost not above 300, in respecte the woods and passages of the montans and quagmires were weill knowen to them, only Sir John Syntone, Sir Thomas Lochore, and Sir John Balfour, Shriffe of Fyffe, wer woundit and hurte.' The Castle of Lindores mentioned by Sir James stood on the summit of the high ridge at the east-end of Lindores village. Boece records that ' Edward I. of England came and relieved the Castle of Loch-indore (Loch Lindores), with 4000 souldiers, and then destroyed and overcam Fyff ' (Book XIV). About seventy years ago, portions of the foundations of the castle were excavated, and in doing so, a small apartment, in which was a shelved recess, was discovered. On the shelves lay what seemed folded cloth, which, on exposure, soon dissolved and disappeared. The site of the castle is known by the villagers as ' Macduff.'

neighbourhood of Lindores Abbey, within the limits of the 'Forest of Irnsyde,' and hence it is known by the name of the 'Battle of Black Irnsyde,' or Earnside. Later historians find difficulty in reconciling the date assigned to this battle (12th June 1298), with other facts in Wallace's history; but Blair, in his 'Relationes' (believed to have been written A.D. 1327) distinctly states, that 'on the 12th June 1298, the guardian of the kingdom (Wallace) vanquished the English in battle at Ironside in Fife, with their general and leader Aymer de Valence, Earl of Pembroke.'[1]

Blind Harry, the minstrel, in his account of the battle, says, that Wallace and a hundred of his followers were surrounded by superior numbers, in the wood of Black Irnsyde and

---

[1] P. 7. The name 'Black Irnsyde,' has given rise to various conjectures to account for its origin, as it is the Tay which flows past the scene of the fight, the Earn being merged in the Tay about four miles further up. It has been attempted to account for the name by supposing that the Earn, in some long past age, flowed in a separate channel, and met the Tay much farther down, and therefore the 'Forest' or 'Wood' was on the Earn side. But there can be little doubt the name is derived from *Fearn*, the Gaelic term for the alder tree, which is still retained in *arn*, the Scottish appellation of the alder. The then marshy condition of the low grounds, which are of considerable extent, would be peculiarly favourable for the growth of this kind of tree; and the sloping sides of the adjoining 'Forest' would, in consequence, be called Earn or Arnside, the latter approaching nearer in pronunciation to the most ancient form of the name. In the district of Aldearn in Moray, there is a place named Earnside, so named from the Earn or Alder burn which runs through it. Near Hexham there is a place also of the same name. The river Earn itself seems to derive its name from the same root. The term appears in Fernie and Collairnie—*Cul-earnie*—in this neighbourhood.

Sir James Balfour, who died A.D. 1657, describes the Forest of Earnside as 'scarce ane myle in length of bramble and hazel-nut trees, intermixed with some few oaks, was of old great and beautiful, and four miles in length and three in breadth.' In the end of the last century some parts of the ground had much the appearance described by Sir James, but it is now, with the exception of a small portion of hill, all in a state of high cultivation, and not a single tree or shrub remains.

were cut off from all communication with their friends ; his words are—

> ' To Fyfe he (Wallace) past, to wesy[1] that countre,
> Bot wrangwarnyt off Inglissmen was he.
> Schyr Jhon Sewart quhen thai wer passyt by,
> Fra the Ochell he sped him haistely ;
> Upon Wallace folowit in all his mycht,
> In Abernethy tuk luging that first nycht.
> Apon the morn, with fiftene hundredth men,
> Till Black Irnsyde his gydis couth them ken.
> Thar Wallace was, and mycht no message send
> Till sanct Jhonstoun, to mak this jornay kend.'[2]

They had therefore no resource left but to fight for their lives, for Wallace was expressly excluded from all terms of amnesty by Edward. Hastily throwing up a stockade of trees and wattles, they so intrenched themselves that their foes could not approach them, excepting to almost certain death.

> ' A rowm was left, quhar part in frount mycht fayr,
> Quha entrit in, agayn yeid nevir mar.'

Thus set at bay, their assailants ceased their attack; in the interval the ministrel tells us that Wallace bravely ventured out for water to refresh his wounded followers, who ' bled full mekill blud, and feblyt fast for want of fud.'

> ' Other refut (refreshment) as than he wyst of nayn,
> A littil strand he fand that ran hym by ;
> Of cler watter he brocht haboundandly,
> And drank him selff, syn said with sober mud,[3]
> "The wyn of Frans me thocht nocht halff so gud " ' [4]

Tidings of the jeopardy of Wallace and his followers having spread, five hundred of his countrymen hasted to their rescue.

---

[1] Wesy—*visè*.   [2] Bk. IX., lines 779–788.   [3] Bk. IX., lines 974–978.

[4] The ' littil strand ' still runs ' clear,' not far from what was once the site of the small homestead of Mount Halie Butts. The field is still known by that name.

Thus reinforced, and their enemies having also received aid, the fight was renewed and bravely contested, but after a fierce and determined struggle the Scots remained masters of the field. Sir John Graham was wounded, and Duncan of Balfour, Sheriff of Fife, was killed in the battle.[1]

The name of ' Wallace's Den,' that immemorially attached to a deep gully on the farm of Parkhill, which has disappeared in the course of agricultural improvement, affords a certain amount of presumptive evidence of the site of the battle. This den was a little to the eastward of Lindores Abbey, and so near that its inmates could not fail to hear the noise of the fight. The wearied warriors, after their desperate struggle, repaired to the abbey for refreshment and rest.

> ' Wallace, Crawfurd, and with them gud Guthrè,
> Rychard Wallace had long beyn in mellè,
> And Longaweill in to Lindoris baid still;
> Fastyt thai had to lang agayn thar will.
> Wallange thai maid thar St(e)wart for to be ;
> Off meit and drynk thai fand aboundandle,
> The Priour fled, and durst na reknyng bid ;
> He was befor apon the tothir syde.'[2]

The arched gateway by which the warriors entered Lindores Abbey still stands,[3] and surely, it is pardonable to hold in veneration the ground once known to have been trodden by one, whose heroism and unselfish devotion, have indissolubly linked his name with the annals of his country, and the affections of the people.[4]

---

[1] Blair's *Relationes*, pp. 7–76.

[2] *Harry the Minstrel*, Bk. IX., lines 1117–1124.　　[3] See Frontispiece.

[4] On another occasion, in an early period of his career, Wallace, accompanied by his mother, came from Kilspindie, in the Carse of Gowrie, by Lindores. The words of the Blind Minstrel are—

> ' Besyd Londoris the ferrye our thai past,
> Syn thro the Ochell sped thaim wondyr fast.'

The remains of an ancient pier may still be seen at ebb tide, at the mouth of the Pow of Lindores, which undoubtedly was the landing-place for the abbey.

Wallace went down to death with his country undelivered,
but—

> 'The greatest gift the hero leaves his race
> Is to have been a hero.'[1]

It is an imperishable bequest. The patriotism of Wallace has
infused a spirit of heroism into the hearts of the humblest of his
countrymen, which has roused them to deeds of daring in the
hour of their country's need; and his noble struggle still forms the
subject of conversation at many a lowly fireside. But his fame is
so exclusively linked in the popular mind with warlike feats, that
it throws light on his character, and shows the true source of his
courage to know that when his neck was laid bare for the executioner's axe, there fell from his bosom a copy of the Psalms of
David, the gift of his mother, and the companion of all his
wanderings.

---

[1] *The Spanish Gipsy*, p. 153.

CHAPTER XI.

ABBOTS ADAM, WILLIAM OF ANGUS, ROGER AND JOHN STEELE.
DUKE OF ROTHESAY.

> A ! fredome is a noble thing !
> Fredom mayss (makes) man to haiff liking ;
> Fredome all solace to man giffis :
> He levys at ess that frely levys !
> A noble heart may haiff nane ess
> Na ellys nocht that may him pless
> Giff fredome failyhe ; for fre liking
> Is yharnyt our all other thing.
> Na he, that ay hass levyt fre,
> May nocht knaw weill the propyrtè,
> The angyr, na the wrechyt dome,
> That is cowplit to foule thyrldome,
> But gyff he had assayit it,
> Than all perquer he suld it wyt ;
> And suld think fredome mar to pryss.
> Than all the gold in warld that is.'
>
> *The Bruce, Barbour.*

WITHIN six months after the execution of Wallace, Robert Bruce asserted his claim to the throne of Scotland. Those who rallied around him in his all but desperate enterprise, were few in number, and with one or two exceptions, were not of high position or rank. One of these exceptions was Sir Gilbert de Hay of Errol, and through him the Abbey of Lindores has the honour of being connected with the deliverance of the country from usurped domination. Sir James Balfour, in his *Annals*, records, 'This zeire (1306) there was a mutuall endenture made betwix Sr Gilbert Haye of Erol and Sr Neill Campbell of Lochaw, and Sr Alexander Setton, knights, at the Abbey of Londors, to defend the King Robert Bruce and hes crowne to the last of ther bloodes and fortunes; upon the sealling of the said indenture they solemnly toke the sacrament at St Mariés altar in the said Abbey Church.'[1] This vow involved a contest with the overwhelming power of England, but it was nobly fulfilled. The three compatriots adhered to Bruce with unswerving devotion, and were his inseparable companions in all his reverses and wanderings. Sir Gilbert had the honour of leading a thousand horse at the final victory of Bannockburn, a victory, which a true-hearted Englishman has said, was 'one of the greatest blessings which ever befell England, while that of Strongbow, in Ireland, has savoured of a curse.'[2] The knight of Errol was one of the most devoted of Bruce's followers,[3] and for his faithful and valiant services the grateful monarch bestowed on him the office of High Constable of Scotland, an honour which his descendants still enjoy.[4] It ought not to be forgotten too, that he was one of the thirty-eight barons who subscribed the memorable letter to the Pope in Arbroath Abbey, on the 6th April 1320, in which they manfully declared that if his Holiness continued to show favour to England at the expense of Scotland, ' he would be answerable to the Most High for all the blood, loss of souls, and other calamities that would follow,' and, while one hundred of them remained alive, they would fight for the liberty and independence of their country.'[5] The brave old knight died A.D. 1330, and was laid among his ancestors in the Abbey of Cupar, in Angus, where, however, not a vestige of any of their tombs remains.[6]

Sir Neil Campbell was the grandson of Gillespic Campbell, who was a witness to the charter of the erection of Newburgh into a burgh by Alexander III., and son of Sir Colin Campbell of Lochow, known as Macalan-More, ancestors of the family of Argyle.

---

[1] Vol. I., p. 89.   [2] Dr Arnold.   [3] Fordun, Bk. XII., cap. 11.
[4] Spald. Club Mis., Vol. II., p. 211.
[5] Hill Burton, Hist. of Scot., Vol. II., pp. 404-6.
[6] Douglas' Peerage, Wood—Errol.

' Sir Neil swore fealty to Edward I., A.D. 1296, but afterwards he joined Bruce, and adhered to him in prosperity and adversity. He fought by his side in almost every encounter, from the defeat of Methven to the victory of Bannockburn.' Bruce valued his services so highly, that he gave him his sister, Lady Mary, in marriage, and dowered her with the estates forfeited bv David of Strathbogie, Earl of Atholl.[1]

Sir Alexander Seton of Seton came of a race that fought bravely and suffered much for the independence of Scotland. He signed the famous letter to the Pope, and his whole career shows how faithfully he fulfilled the vow he had made. Alexander, supposed to be his eldest son, was killed in opposing the landing of Edward Baliol near Kinghorn (6th August 1332). His second son Thomas, a comely and noble looking youth, a hostage in the lands of Edward III. for the surrender of Berwick if not relieved, was hanged before the gate of that town, so near that his father the governor, could witness his son's execution ; but with unswerving patriotism Sir Alexander refused to save his son by the betrayal of his trust ; and he saw his third son William drowned in a gallant attack on the English fleet, near Berwick.[2] The fate of Seton's sons brings painfully before us the heroic sacrifices by which the independence of the country was maintained.

On the 6th November 1314 the Abbot of Londors, four months after the battle of Bannockburn, appears in the Parliament summoned by King Robert Bruce at Cambuskenneth Abbey. He affixed his seal to the statute then enacted, holding and declaring that all who did not come into ' the peace of the king ' and acknowledge him as their sovereign, would be held as traitors and their estates confiscated.[3] If the abbot was Thomas who swore fealty to Edward in 1296, as there is every reason to believe, the overwhelming power of Edward, and the violence and

---

[1] Douglas' *Peerage*, Wood's Ed.—*Argyle*.
[2] Tytler, Vol. I., p. 171; Douglas' *Peerage*, Wood's Ed.—*Seton of Winton*.
[3] *Scott's Poems*, Ed. 1857, Vol. X., p. 347.

divisions which prevailed formed a better apology, and a more valid excuse for his change than the thinly disguised ambition of modern politicians. Thomas was succeeded by Abbot Adam, whose name appears as a witness at Dundemor (Dunmore, erroneously Dunmuir), to a charter in 1331 of John of Dundemor, conveying to the monks of Balmerino the right to the water which runs through the lands of Dunberauch (Dumbarry) in the parish of Abernethy, for the use of their mill of Petgornach.[1] He also appears as a witness to a charter of David II., A.D. 1342.[2]

In Abbot Adam's time, Sir David de Lindsay of Crawford, another of the sturdy barons who signed the famous letter to the Pope, retired to Lindores Abbey, and spent the last of his days in the quiet of its retirement. 'He was the tried friend of Bruce, who bestowed on him a hereditary annual-rent of one hundred merks, then a very large sum, from the great customs of Dundee.[3] He was intrusted at one time with the custody of Berwick Castle, and at another with that of Edinburgh; and it is specially mentioned by Wyntoun, in praise of his orderly and prudent conduct while in that office,

'Intil his time with the countrie
Na riot, na na strife made he.'

Towards the close of his career I find, says his distinguished descendant and biographer, Lord Lindsay, 'him mortifying, as it was then called, two marks annually out of the lands of "Pethfour," near Cairnie, in the parish of St Madoes, for the maintenance of a wax-light, to be kept burning though all future time, at the tomb where the Lady Mary, his late wife, lay buried, and where he hoped to be laid beside her, in the choir of the Abbey Church of Lundors, for the benefit of both their souls.' The charter making this provision is dated at the monastery on the 19th November 1355.[4]

---

[1] *Book of Balmerino*, pp. 40, 41.　　　[2] *Bk. of Lindores*, p. iv.
[3] *Lives of the Lindsays*, Vol. I., p. 48.
[4] *Ib.* Vol. I., pp. 49, 50; *Chartulary of Lindores*, Charter No. VI.

Much religious importance was attached to the burning of wax-lights at the tomb of the deceased in mediæval times.   What the rich were able to procure for themselves, the poor united their contributions to provide for one another.   In the same century as the bequest of Sir David, the numerous gilds of craftsmen established at that period in England, made this one of the special objects of their fraternities.   One of the rules of the ' Gild of St Katerine in the Cite of Londone, which is founden in the Churche of Saint Botulf with-oute Aldrichesgate,' A.D. 1389, is in these words : ' Gif it so bifalle that a symple brother dye, that may nought finde himselve no light, than the V tapres of the weight of XX li of wex schul be mad newe, and set aboute the body, and the torches also ; and when any brother is ded, that he have the torches redy to bryng hym withe to cherche gif ned be.'[1]

Lady Mary, the wife of Sir David Lindsay, for whom posthumous provision for lights was made, was descended from the Lay Abbots of Abernethy, a family whose origin is lost in antiquity.   The first who appears in record is ' Orm, the son of Hugh,' styled of 'Abernithi,' about A.D. 1160, and Lawrence, the son of Orm, about 1230.   Sir Alexander of Abernethy, the fourth in descent from Lawrence,[2] dying without male heirs, the great Lordship of Abernethy was divided between his two daughters, of whom Lady Mary was the younger.[3]   She married Sir Andrew

---

[1] *English Gilds*, p. 8.   The great weight of the wax-lights provided at deaths and funerals, accounts for the numerous bequests and fines payable in wax.   A stone candlestick, apparently for these great wax-lights, was found in a window of the nave of Lindores Abbey, *in proprio situ.*

[2] *Spalding Club Misc.*, Vol. V., p. 63.

[3] Lady Margaret of Abernethy, the eldest daughter of Sir Alexander of Abernethy, married John Stewart, Earl of Angus—(*Hist. Rec. of the Fam. of Leslie*, Vol. I., pp. 18–37),—and her descendant, the Countess of Home, is still feudal superior of the lands around Abernethy.   These lands formed part of the great lordship of Abernethy, and were originally bestowed on the Church by Nectan, King of the Picts, ' perhaps as early as the sixth century, in the time when Columba was yet alive.'—(Innes' *Scotland in the Middle*

de Leslie (A.D. 1312), and her eldest son by this marriage succeeded to her estates; and through him the family of Leslie, now represented by the Countess of Rothes, acquired, besides other possessions, the barony of Ballinbriech. On the death of her first husband, Lady Mary married Sir David Lindsay of Crawford,[1] who in all probability, in accordance with his own wish, was buried in the choir of Lindores Abbey Church, beside his wife.

During the incumbency of Adam as abbot, Duncan, Earl of Fife, out of gratitude for his escape from death at the battle of Durham, and subsequent deliverance from captivity, bestowed on the monastery of 'Lyndores' the Church of 'Uchtermukedy' (Auchtermuchty), and the lands which have pertained to it from of old.' The incapacity and folly of David II. provoked a war with England, which ended in his defeat at Durham in 1346. The Scottish nobles loyally threw themselves around their king, and bravely defended him. Thirty of them, among whom was David de la Haye of Errol, the Constable of Scotland, were slain

---

Ages, p. 108),—certainly not later than the beginning of the eighth century. The territory around Abernethy given to the church by Nectan, *ad diem judicii*, is the first grant of land on record in Scotland, and therefore it is all the more interesting to endeavour to trace its boundaries and extent. It is defined as lying within these bounds: ' A lapide in Apurfeirt usque ad lapidem juxta Ceirfuill id est Lethfoss, et inde in altum usque ad Athan'—(*Chronicles of the Picts and Scots*, p. 6),—that is, from the stone in Apurfeirt (conjectured to be the modern Aberargie), to the stone near Ceirfuill (Carpow), thence to the height or watershed of the Ochils, and along as far as Athan, which, in Gaelic, signifies a little ford. The stone at Apurfeirt has not been identified, though diligent search has been made for it; but there can be little doubt that the large fragment of rock or boulder which still forms the upper march between the lands of Carpow and Clunie, called, from its being split in two, 'The Cloven Stone,' is the stone 'nigh Ceirfuill,' mentioned in the ancient grant of the Pictish King, and that the ford over the Farg at Greenend of Aberargie, is 'the Athan' of the record. Assuming these boundaries to be correct, of which there is every probability, the lands extended from the river Farg to Carpow on the east, and from the Earn to the watershed of the Ochils on the south, comprising a goodly territory of about four miles long by three miles broad.

[1] *Hist. Rec. of the Fam. of Leslie*, Vol. I., p. 23.

at his feet; but notwithstanding their gallant defence, the King was taken prisoner, and with his captive nobles, was marched in triumph through London, amid great rejoicings of the citizens, escorted by 20,000 soldiers, and imprisoned in the Tower.[1]

The charter conveying the Church of Auchtermuchty to the Lindores Abbey, which expressly sets forth the motives of the Earl's pious dedication, was executed at the abbey on the 17th March 1350-1.[2] Robert, the Steward of Scotland, afterwards King Robert II., was one of the witnesses, and Laurence Bell, Provost of the Collegiate Church of Abernethy, another.[3] In virtue of this charter feu-duties are still collected from the lands which belonged to the Church of 'Uchtermukedy,' by the proprietor of Lindores Abbey.

William of Angus succeeded Adam as abbot. His name appears as a witness to a charter by Thomas, Earl of Mar, of lands in his Lordship of the Garioch, A.D. 1355-7, and it also appears in a charter in favour of David Aberkirder, conveying annual rents from various properties in the town of 'Dunde' by the abbot and convent until the sum of forty merks sterling, which he had advanced for the use of the monastery, was repaid. This charter was confirmed by Robert III. on the 23d March 1392-3, but no date is given in the charter itself, and it therefore affords no clue to the length of time William of Angus continued abbot.[4] He was one of the clerical members of the Parliament summoned to meet at Scone on the 27th September 1367, to consider the condition of the kingdom.[5] The infatuation and misrule of David II. had brought the country almost to the verge of ruin; internal dissensions and war hindered the cultivation of the soil, famine and pestilence ensued, and the people were brought to a condition of wretchedness that exceeds belief. To such straits were they reduced, that they greedily devoured (*more porcorum*, like swine,

---

[1] Tytler, Vol. I., p. 192.   [2] *Book of Lindores*, p. 43.

[3] *Spald. Club, Collections of Aberdeen, etc.*, pp. 537, 8.

[4] *Bk. of Lindores*, p. 48.   [5] Tytler, Vol. I., p. 376.

are the words of the old chronicler), any herbs or nuts they could pick up in the fields or woods.[1] Besides these privations, an eminent ecclesiastic, writing a few years later, says, ' slaughters, robberies, fire-raisings, and other crimes passed unpunished, and outlawed justice was banished the realm.'[2]

Two years earlier (on the 3d August 1365) David II. visited Lindores, and during his stay confirmed the charter of Sir David Lindsay, previously referred to.[3] On a subsequent occasion the King celebrated Christmas in the abbey, and, in keeping with his character, and perhaps his necessities, left his expenses unpaid. David de Barclay, Sheriff of Fife, who had advanced the amount for the Royal festivities, was refunded by the Chamberlain of Scotland after the king's death.[4]

It was no easy matter to supply the wants of the cavalcades that attended dignitaries and official personages in those days. It is recorded that David II., A.D. 1343, travelled with forty attendants, and his Queen with sixty, all on horseback ; such large numbers, in the entire absence of wheel-carriages, being in great part necessary for carrying about whatever was requisite on the journey. The same authority records that Alexander Lesley had seventy in his retinue.[5] The whole of these composing such a numerous train, and their horses, were generally quartered in the abbeys, and on the neighbouring farmers and parochial clergy ; the farmers being bound by the terms on which they held their lands, to provide the required accommodation, and to maintain a specified number of travellers for a fixed number of nights in the course of a year.[6]

---

[1] Fordun, Bk. XIII., cap. 39.   [2] Preface, *Stat. Ec. Scot.*, p. 78.

[3] *Bk. of Lindores*, p. 45.   [4] *Ib.*, p. vi.

[5] *Transactions of the Soc. of Antiq. of Scotland*, Vol. I., p. 278.

[6] This obligation on the part of the farmers, in virtue of which, and other obligations, they held their lands, was called *Can* and *Cuiart*, or tribute and free quarters, or visitation. The word *Can* or *Kain* still survives as the name for payment in kind, which is yet a condition of some leases. The terms are of great antiquity.—*See* Robertson's *Scotland under her Early Kings*, Vol. I., p. 10, *et passim.*

The custom of travelling at free quarters had its origin in primitive times; but in an altered and more complex state of society, it became vexatious and burdensome, and laws had to be enacted for its regulation,- and for the prevention of abuses attending it. In the reign of David II. it was enacted,—'Gif anie cum tc the Kings Court' (the greater Barons were bound to attend these courts every forty days), he sall not waist the lands perteining to the King, Bischops, or others, with ane great and superflous multitude in his compaine.'

'*Item*, Quhen they cum at even before nicht to anie man's house in their way, they sall desire herberie fra him, and thereafter quhen their men or companie, at his command, are distribute severallie in sundrie houses, to be lodged conforme to the use of the cuntrie, they sall not desire meat nor drink violentlie fra their hosts aboue their power.'   On the other hand,—'Gif any of them quha be the ordinance of the Lord of the ground is commanded to receauve them in herberie, casts furth or ejects any ane of them to the dore, and causes him to fast without the house, he sall give to his maister ane kow.'   'The King likewaies commands that within his realm for charities cause, convenient and lauchful hospitalitie sall be keiped. And that all hostile waisting and destruction be violence sall be utterly extinguished, and that na man presume to use it in time cumming.'[1]

These regulations form a picture from real life, and bring before us an extinct condition of society, as vividly as the fossil remains exhumed by geologists reveal the former condition of the earth. They show that privileges so vague and undefined as travelling at free quarters implies (depending so much on individual character and mere caprice), were necessarily productive of constant disputes and oppression; a state of matters which was happily exchanged for fixed and determinate payments.   It was in virtue of this change that the expenses of the Royal festivities at Lindores had to be refunded.

The next abbot to William of Angus of whom we have any

---

[1] *Regiam Majest. Stat. of David II.*, chap. XI.

record, is Abbot Roger. His name does not occur in any of the recovered charters of the abbey, and it is omitted in the list of abbots by the Editor of the Chartulary of Lindores. He appears as a witness to a charter ' by Sir Andrew Leslie of that Ilk,'—the grandson of Lady Mary Abernethy, in favour of Sir Hugh Barclay of Kilnairn (*query* Culairnie), of 24 merks yearly out of the barony of Ballinbriech.' This charter, from internal evidence, must have been granted between A.D. 1373 and 1381.[1]

John Steele, who previously held the office of Prior of Coldingham, is the next who appears in record as Abbot of Lindores.[2] It was probably in his time that the unfortunate Duke of Rothesay, the eldest son of Robert III. and the first who bore the title, was buried in Lindores Abbey. The touching narrative of the circumstances attending the death of the unhappy Prince, by Sir Walter Scott, in the ' Fair Maid of Perth,' has made his miserable fate familiar to all, and yet it may be doubted if the genius of Scott has added anything more truly affecting than the simple words of the chronicler. Sir James Balfour, in his Annals under A.D. 1401–2, says, ' King Robert being now old and decrepit, hering the deboshit liffe and demeanour of his eldest sone David, Duck of Rothesay, Earl of Carrick, sends his two trustie counsellouris Sr William Lindesay of Rossie, Sr John Ramorney, knights, with letters to the gover-nor, the Duck of Albany, commanding him to apprehend the said Duck, and imprison him till he was sensible of his guilt carriage, and promissed to amend. He was taken betwix Nydin and Strathtyrin, and led captive to St Andrews, but shortly thereafter removed to the Castell of Falkland, quher he was committed to the custody of two of the Duck of Albanye's ruffians, John Selkirke and John Wright, quho handled him so roughly that he deyed on the 7th Aprile, as they gave out, of a dissentery, but the truth was, that through extream hunger and famine he eat of his awen fingers.'[3] The place where the Prince came to this fearful end,

---

[1] *Hist. Records of the Family of Leslie*, Vol. I., p. 25.
[2] *Fordun Bk. XI.*, cap. 24.—*Note.*   [3] *Annals*, Vol. I., p. 139.

could not have been that which is pointed out in the garden of the palace of Falkland, for it was not then built, but in the dungeon under the western tower of the old castle of the Earls of Fife, to which the buildings of the palace have since been added.   Tradition tells, that a woman passing near the place of his confinement, heard his moaning cries, and with true womanly compassion, assuaged his hunger by milk from her own breasts.   She afterwards managed to minister to his necessities, by slipping thin cakes into his dungeon; but her visits were discovered, and the unhappy Prince was left to his terrible fate.   He was not, however, unlamented.   In conformity with the beliefs of the age, King Robert made provision for the weal of his son's soul.   ' A chaplain of St Salvator, in the parish Church of Dundee, had five pounds from the customs of Dundee allowed yearly in exchequer to pray for the soul of the Duke of Rothesay.   Besides this, the chaplain had the third part of the lands of the Milton of Cragy, and of the lands of Westfield, by grant of Patrick of Inverpeffer;' a grant which was confirmed by the father of the unhappy Prince.[1]

The accusation recorded by Sir James Balfour against Rothesay is unfortunately not without foundation; but it is worthy of special notice, that Wyntoun, who was cotemporary with the Prince, speaks of him in terms of high commendation.   In the passage cited from Wyntoun below, he dwells with such apparent delight on his many engaging qualities, his courteous disposition, his taste for literature,—rare in those days,—and on his manly appearance, that his description bears the impress of having been written from personal knowledge of the ill-fated Prince.   It is noticeable that Wyntoun, evidently from prudential motives, omits all notice of the cause of the Prince's death.   He says—

> ' All before as ye herd done,
> Oure Lorde the Kingis eldest sone
> Suete and virtuous, yong and fair
> And his nearest lauchful Ayr,

---

[1] Report by Cosmo Innes, *in causa*—'The Presby. agt. the Magistrates of Dundee, 1855.

Honest, habil and avenand [1]
Oure Lord, oure Prince in all pleasand.
Cunnand in to Letterature [1]
A seymly persone in stature,
Schir Davy Duke of Rothesay,
Of March the sevyn and twentyd day
Yauld his saule til his Creatoure
His cors til halowit sepulture,
In Lundores his body lyis,
His spirite until Paradys.' [2]

Everything that is recorded of the Prince, whatever may have been his faults, shows that he was above deceit, and that he scorned all that was base and treacherous. His chivalrous resolution not to betray the unprincipled ruffian who proposed to him the assassination of his uncle Albany, and which was no doubt the proximate cause of his own death, places his character in an honourable light, and goes far to justify the commendation which Wyntoun bestows upon him.

The stone coffin which lies in the extreme end of the north transept, has traditionally been pointed out as the one in which the unfortunate Prince was buried; chiefly, perhaps, from the circumstance that it was, until comparatively recent years, the only coffin that was discovered in the abbey. The exact place in the church where he was buried is not recorded, and is not known,—no inscription having been found on any of the tombs in the abbey, but the presumption is, that a Prince of the blood royal, and the heir to the throne, was buried within the chancel.

---

[1] *Habil*, strong; *avenand*, from the Latin *a venio*, approachable, courteous; *cunnand*, learned.

[2] *Cronykil*, Vol. II., p. 397.

CHAPTER XII.

PRE-REFORMATION MARTYRS.

ABBOTS JAMES, JOHN, AND ANDREW CAVERS.   EARL OF DOUGLAS.

> ' Bodies fall by wild sword law,
> But who would force the soul, tilts with a straw
> Against a champion cased in adamant.'
>
> *Wordsworth.*

THE translation of the Bible by Wickliffe in the end of the four-teenth century (A.D. 1380–1389), and the spread of his writings impugning the errors, and assailing the corruptions of the Church, excited a spirit of inquiry which begat many earnest disciples. Among these was James Resby, an English priest who came to Scotland to propagate the doctrines of the Reformer. This open aggression on the received faith aroused opposition. Resby was apprehended and arraigned before a council held at Perth (A.D. 1407) under Laurence, official of Lindores, Inquisitor of here-tical pravity for Scotland. After trial he was condemned as a heretic, and burnt at the stake. Lindores Abbey has therefore the unenviable distinction of being connected, through its official, with the death of the first martyr for the reformed religion in Scotland.[1]

---

[1] ' Laurence of Lindores was Abbot of Scone in 1411, and was the first Pro-fessor of Law in the newly erected University of St Andrews.   In July 1432, when elected Dean of the Faculty of Arts, he is styled Rector of Creich, Master

Tradition tells us that Resby was extremely tall, spare, of commanding aspect, and with an eye which burned with earnestness and enthusiasm. Even the monk who records the fact of his martyrdom, and who bore him no good will as a heretic, was constrained to admit that 'he was held in the highest reputation by the people for the simplicity of his preaching;' but, he added, 'his teaching contained most dangerous doctrines.' The first of these 'dangerous doctrines' was, 'that the Pope is not the vicar of Christ;' and the second, 'that no one is Pope or vicar of Christ except he be holy. He held,' continues the monkish chronicler, 'forty doctrines of a similar or worse character, derived from John Wykliff, an arch-heretic, condemned at London in England.' Wherever Resby went he courageously maintained the truth of his opinions; and the crowds which assembled to hear the unwonted doctrines, listened with eager and wrapt attention to the impassioned eloquence with which he urged on his hearers the truths which he inculcated. The courage of this remarkable man stands out in bold relief against the surrounding darkness, and occupies a loftier and more intrepid sphere than the Reformers whose names fill a much wider page at the consummation of the Reformation.

In Resby's days the adherents of the opinions he advocated were few, and for the most part concealed, acquiring their knowledge of these opinions from the writings of Wickliffe, circulated in manuscript, secretly from hand to hand. The whole power of the Church, and of the Governor, Albany (who had already persecuted, and 'all Lollards haitit'), was arrayed against them. At the era of the Reformation the corruption of the Church had increased, and the vices of the clergy had been unsparingly lashed

---

of Arts, Licentiate of Theology, Inquisitor for Scotland, etc. This office of Dean be held till his death (1437)'—Laing's *Knox History of the Reformation*, Vol. I., p. 497. He is said to have written a work entitled, *Examen Haereticorum Lollardorum; or, Examination of Lollard Heretics*: whom it is added, 'he drove out of the whole kingdom.'—*Liber de Scon*, p. xii.

by writings both in prose and verse. Printed copies of these writings and of the Bible in the vulgar tongue, revealing the wide divergence of the lives and teachings of too many of the clergy from the divine precepts, were circulated throughout the land, and both in Church and State the Reformers at that era had powerful favourers of their opinions, both secret and avowed. Resby had no such friendly supporters, and nothing short of a martyr's spirit could have dared the risk that he encountered. The success of his preaching roused the vigilance of the able Inquisitor for Scotland, and it is recorded that 'the writings (the forty *theses* which Resby maintained), and the author, he refuted and consigned to the fire and reduced to ashes.'[1] No pen, friendly or unfriendly, has told us of the last moments, or recorded the last utterances of the brave Englishman; but his submission to an agonizing martyrdom testifies more strongly than any words, to the depth of his convictions and the strength of his faith.

Notwithstanding the terrible fate of the proto-martyr of the Reformation, the opinions of the Lollards continued to spread, and stringent repressive measures were adopted to meet them. Masters of Art of St Andrews were called upon to take oath that they did not hold these opinions, and that they would withstand them (A.D. 1416), and in 1425 the Scottish Parliament passed an Act having the same end in view.[2] But there have been in every age of the Church men to whom truth is dearer than life, and undeterred by the perils which awaited him, Paul Crawar, a Bohemian physician, came to Scotland to make known what he held to be

---

[1] Fordun-a-Goodall, Bk. CXV. cap. XX. Bower, in his continuation of Fordun, devotes a whole chapter to Laurence of Lindores' refutation of Resby's doctrines. The whole narrative is curious; it shows that texts which are now quoted in support of the Reformed opinions were then quoted against them; and, as is too often the case in controversy, denunciation is made to do the duty of argument.

[2] Grubb's *Ec. History of Scotland*, Vol. I., p. 365.

the truth.   The old chronicler says, 'It was reported he was sent by the Pragensian heretics of Bohemia, whose impious opinions infected Scotland too much at that time, and was recommended by them as excelling in the art of medicine.   Crawar was thoroughly conversant with sacred learning, and most apt in quoting the Holy Scriptures in support of his opinions; but though he pertinaciously held to the opinions of Prague and Wickliffe, he was confuted by that venerable man, Laurence of Lindores.'   He was brought to trial in St Andrews on 23d July 1433, was found guilty, condemned as an obstinate heretic, and, like his precursor, burnt at the stake.[1]

A sentence so inhuman shows us how far the best are apt to go astray whenever charity ceases to regulate our actions.   Laurence of Lindores was not only a man of great learning, but also, we are told, of 'great sanctity,' and yet we see his zeal for truth led him to acts which charity forbids.   It may temper our judgment to remember, that toleration was not understood, certainly was not practised until within very recent times.   The coronation oath of Scotland 'bound the King and his successors to do their utmost to root out of their kingdom and dominions all whom the Church should denounce as heretics.'   This was exacted by the Pope in 1329 as the price for permitting the Bishops of St Andrews to anoint and crown the kings; a new feature in the investiture of the kings of Scotland, who formerly were merely set upon 'the Lia Fail, or Stone of Destiny,' at Scone, and proclaimed as King without being anointed.   The oath (says the late Joseph Robertson), with this persecuting clause, 'outlived both the Reformation and the Revolution.   It might have been cited to justify the doom of Wishart to the flames and of Knox to the galleys, yet Knox would have aggravated its terms, and they were ratified by the Parliament which established the Protestant religion.   They might have been used to vindicate the severities of the reigns

---

[1] Fordun, Bk. XVI., cap. 20.

of King Charles II. and King James VII., yet the convention which adopted the claim of Right stamped them with its deliberate approval.'[1] In contemplating all this, well may we say with the poet—

> ' Whate'er we look on, at our side
> Be charity—to bid us think,
> And feel if we would know.' [2]

Laurence of Lindores appears in a far more estimable light as the encourager of learning. He was one of the originators of St Andrews University ; and so zealous was he for the spread of knowledge, that he taught the students for some years without remuneration. It would not be just to him therefore, or to the men of that age, to forget that we are indebted to them for most of the universities of Europe. Those of St Andrews, Glasgow, and Aberdeen, in our own country, were all founded before the Reformation.[3]

Abbot James, whose name does not occur in the list of abbots given by the editor of the ' *Liber Sancti Marie de Lundoris,*' succeeded John Steele. In the Brechin Chartulary (A.D. 1443) he is styled James of Rossy.[4] In his time the Convent of Lindores

---

[1] Joseph Robertson *Pref. to Stat. Ec. Scotland*, p. 48-49. William III. refused to take the oath, saying, ' I will not lay myself under any obligation to be a persecutor.' He only agreed to take it on being publicly assured that 'neither the words of the oath nor the laws of Scotland laid him under any such obligation. The Union happily relieved all following Princes from a cruel and impossible obligation, by substituting a more merciful declaration.'—Joseph Robertson, Preface to *Concilia Scotia*, p. xlix. And yet so slow was the growth of religious liberty and real toleration, "I have," says the same author, "before me an able and laborious dissertation on the Absurdity and Perfidy of all authoritative Toleration," published at Glasgow in 1780 by John Brown of Haddington, the most popular Nonconformist divine in Scotland of his day.' *Ib*, p. xlviii.

[2] Wordsworth.

[3] Spottiswoode, *His.*, Vol. I., p. 113.　　　　　　　　　　[4] P. 389.

entered into an arrangement with the provost and burgesses of
Dundee, by which the latter took upon themselves the construction
and reparation of the choir of their parish church.   The monks, as
having right to the rectorial tithes, were bound to maintain the
fabric of the choir, agreeing, on their part, to allow the burgesses
five merks yearly out of tenements belonging to them in Dundee.
This agreement was made in Dundee in presence of the Bishop of
Brechin (10th March 1442-3), and the annual rent was resigned
by Sir John Scrymgeour, constable of Dundee and bailie of the
Monastery of Lindores, in the hands of William de Strathachyne,
the provost, for behoof of the burgesses.[1]

From the express mention of the erection of the choir in this
document, it seems almost certain that the East Church (anciently
the choir) which was burnt down in 1841, was erected immediately
subsequent to the ratification of this agreement.

Nothing further is known of Abbot James, excepting that he
was one of the clergy who met at Edinburgh (28th June 1445), and
signed the transumpt of the Bull of Pope Gregory XI. disallowing
the claim of the Crown to the personal estate of deceased Bishops. [2]
The ground on which this claim of the Crown was preferred, seems
to have been on the principle, 'that what was acquired through
the Church should abide with the Church,' and therefore could not
be bequeathed to relatives.   James was succeeded by an Abbot
named John, in whose time James II. confirmed the right of
the abbey to the lands of Parkhill, and renewed the privileges of
the 'Forest of Irnside' (A.D. 1452).[3]   In the year 1457 John
granted a charter confirming the ancient privileges of the burgesses of Newburgh, and a few months later he granted, in their
favour, a charter to the lands of Vodrufe (Wodrife) and the hill
adjacent; which lands still form part of the property of the burgh
of Newburgh.[4]

---

[1] *Reg. Episc. Brechinen*, p. 90.   [2] Pref. *Stat. Ec. Scot.*, p. cciv.
[3] *Lib. de Lundores*, p. 18.   [4] *Ib*, pp. 3-7.

In the chartulary of the abbey there is preserved a letter by the same abbot, which displays a commendable anxiety for the becoming celebration of divine worship.   The abbot had, no doubt, seen and felt that slovenly or hurried reading impairs the effect of the simplicity and grandeur of the Scriptures, and that imperfect psalmody fails to raise worshippers to adoration.   To remedy this evil he offered a reward to any of the brethren who read the service most devoutly, and by the cultivation of sacred music, led the praises of the congregation most effectively.[1]   This offer exhibits on the part of the abbot anxiety to correct what was evidently a prevailing evil, and a desire to infuse a more solemn and more earnest spirit into the daily worship of the brethren.   This effort on the part of the abbot met the hearty approval of the bishop of the diocese, Patrick Graham, whose zeal for the reform of abuses brought him much molestation and suffering.   Bishop Graham was the son of Lord Graham, by his wife Mary, daughter of King Robert III., and the lending the weight of his authority to the abbot's praiseworthy effort, is in keeping with all that is known of his character and history.   He was the first that was raised to the dignity of archbishop, in Scotland.   This appointment was not a mere personal elevation, it gave power to him and all succeeding archbishops to summon a council of the Church without the intervention of the Pope.   'So long as they had no Metropolitan, the Scottish clergy could meet in council only by authority of the Pope, exercised by a Legate in Scotland, or transmitted by a rescript from Rome.'[2]   Notwithstanding this important advantage to the Church, Bishop Graham's elevation to the archiepiscopal throne, coupled with his express desire for the reform of abuses, gave offence to many of the influential clergy, and at their instigation a Papal Nuncio was sent to investigate the charges which they had laid against him.   This functionary found that the archbishop had blasphemed the Holy See, that he had

---

[1] *Lib. de Lundores*, p. 23.   [2] *Conciliæ Scotiæ*.   Pref. p. xxvi.

said he 'was chosen of God to reform the Church,' and that he had revoked indulgences granted by the Pope, affirming that they had been granted for filthy lucre. For these offences he was denuded of all holy orders, and condemned to captivity within the walls of a monastery for life. 'His first prison was Inchcolm, in the Firth of Forth; then Dunfermline, and latterly Lochleven.'[1] Worn out by suffering, his reason at last gave way —he died in St Serfs Inch, and was buried in the ancient priory of that island. No stone marks his grave, and so completely has the hand of the spoiler passed over that venerable seat of religion and learning, that neither grave nor graveyard are now discernible.[2]

The efforts of the abbot to infuse a higher and more devout spirit into his monastery were not without cause, for existing records show that the corruption of the monastic orders in Scotland had become general at this period. The Bishop of Ross, the last Abbot of Lindores, whom no one will accuse of unfriendliness to the Church of Rome, writing in the year 1571, fixes the year 1473 as the time when 'the Abbayis came to secular abusis, the Abbotis and Priouris being promovit furth of the Court, quha levit courtlyk secularlye and voluptuouslye, and then ceissit all religious and godly myndis and deidis, quhairwith the secularis and temporal men beand sklanderit with thair evill example, fell fra devotion and godlyness to the warkis of wickednes, quhairof daylie mekil evill did increase.'[3]

The worst accusation ever made against the clergy by their enemies finds ample confirmation in the records of their own

---

[1] Pref. *Stat. Ec. Scot.*, pp. 115, 116.

[2] It is to be regretted that the ruins of this most ancient seat of religion are not excavated, and the ground plan traced out; the probability is, that tombstones, and other remains of great antiquity would be found, similar to those which the excavation of the Kirkheugh, St Andrews, has brought to light.

[3] Pref. *Stat. Ec. Scot.*, p. 90.

councils at this period, and in the canons passed for the suppression of evils which many of them deplored.[1] These records reveal a condition of almost incredible licentiousness, and they more than justify the unsparing denunciations of Lindsay, or all that Wordsworth has more mildly, but not less truly said, of monastic voluptuousness. James I. immediately after his long captivity in England, addressed a letter (A.D. 1424-5) to the Abbots and Priors of the Benedictine and Augustinian monasteries in Scotland, 'exhorting them in the bowels of the Lord Jesus Christ to shake off their torpor and sloth, and set themselves to work to restore their fallen discipline and rekindle their decaying fervour.'[2] Forty years later the exhortation was repeated by his grandson James III.

Many among the clergy deplored the corruptions which prevailed, and strove to correct them. 'They bewailed with grief and indignation that rich livings with the cure of thousands of souls were held by boys, by infants even; by men imbecile in mind, hardened in ignorance, old in wickedness and vice,'[3] but these evils continued unabated. Unfortunately the death of most of the leading noblemen at the disastrous defeat of Flodden, deprived the young king (James V.) of councillors from the lay estate, and gave the clergy a predominance in the councils of the nation, which has left its mark to the present day.

Andrew Cavers succeeded John as abbot. Nothing is known of his family connections, but he must have been a person of influence, as twenty years later he was appointed by James IV. keeper of Linlithgow Palace, a situation generally bestowed on those in favour with the reigning sovereign.[4] He must have succeeded to

---

[1] Pref. *Stat. Ec. Scot.*, p. 149, 158-205.

[2] *Ib.*, p. 99. [3] *Ib.*, p. ccvi.

[4] *Reg. Privy Seal*, Vol. I., fol. 97, A.D. 1498. Sir Robert Melville of Murdocairney, afterwards Lord Melville of Monimail, was appointed by Queen Mary keeper of Linlithgow Palace in 1566-7.—*Spottiswoode Miscellany*, Vol. I., p. 359.

the Abbacy of Lindores not later than 1476, for on the 8th April of that year, he granted a life-tack of the lands of Eglismagwl (now Exmagirdle in the parish of Dron) to George Muncrefe of Tyber-mollocke.'[1] With the lands he had also the teind sheaves, altarages and small tithes of the Church of Eglismagwl, together with the mill and the multures of it,' the stipulated rent was forty merks Scots and four dozen of capons 'fat and well fed,' at Christmas and Pasch (Easter), or twelve pennies, equal to one penny sterling, for every capon. Three years later Abbot Andrew grants another life-tack of the fourth part of the 'town of Grange' to Dionisius Cameris (Chalmers) and his son William, excluding the tofts possessed by David Kernour, Andrew Hall, and Symon the granary-keeper, and reserving the right of pasturage for sixty wedders annually. The yearly rent was sixteen pounds thirteen shillings and four pence Scots, services used and wont, and one well-fed pig, two dozen capons, and two dozen hens, commutable at eight shillings, eight pence, and four pence Scots, each respectively. These particulars are interesting as showing the relative value of agricultural pro-duce at that period.

In Abbot Andrew's time, James, ninth Earl of Douglas, sixth Duke of Turenne, spent the last years of his chequered life in Lindores Abbey. Goaded into rebellion by the base assassination of his brother by James II., Douglas nailed a placard to the door of the Parliament House, renouncing his allegiance. He declared war against the king, and so great was the number of adherents he brought into the field, that it trembled in the balance whether the family of Douglas or the Stewarts were to occupy the throne ; but the Earl was routed ; he was obliged to take refuge in England, and his immense possessions were confiscated. On the 4th August 1455, the Scottish Parliament passed an Act, ' that nane receipt James Douglas,' and on the 18th March 1481, another Act was passed ' for resisting of the traitour James Douglas.' Douglas continued

---

[1] *Lib. Sancte Marie le Lindores*, p. 19.

in open hostility, and embraced every favourable opportunity of attacking the Scottish king. In a hostile incursion which he made into Scotland in the year 1484, he was wounded near Lochmaben, and, after thirty years of weary struggle to retrieve his fallen fortunes, surrendered to Kirkpatrick of Closeburn. Kirkpatrick, it is said, 'loved the Earl entirely in his heart; he conveyed him out of the field, and kept him in a poor cottage until he had spoken with the King. The King granted him the Earl's life and gave him as reward the lands of Kirkmichael in Dumfriesshire.'[1] It is said when James saw the venerable aspect and grey hairs of him who had so long troubled him and his house, he was touched with pity for his misfortunes, and with true kingly compassion frankly and at once forgave him. The sole punishment inflicted, if it was a punishment to the war-worn chieftain, was that he must quit the world and spend the remainder of his life in Lindores Abbey. It is said when the aged Earl heard his sentence, he turned to those behind him, and with a bitter smile, used the proverb, ' He that can do no better must needs be a monk.' But after the bitterness of exile endured for thirty years, the quiet seclusion of Lindores would afford him that peace and rest to which he had been so long a stranger. Adversity had not been without its uses to him; it taught him resignation, and the value of the blessings of order and peace. In the end of the reign of James III., Douglas was solicited by the malcontents of the nobility, no doubt with the promise of restoration to his honours and estates, to come forth and espouse their cause against the King; but he resolutely refused, and did all he could to dissuade them from their rebellion; he wrote to the chiefs of his kindred, and urged them loyally to adhere to their allegiance. The King also solicited him to come out and lend him the support of his name and presence, but he playfully answered —hoarding being one of the accusations against James—' You have kept me and your black box too long under lock and key

---

[1] Hume's *Douglas and Angus.*

H

to be of any use to you.' After five years' residence in Lindores Abbey, he died there on the 15th April 1488, and in him, the ninth Earl, ended the first branch of the ancient house of Douglas.

It is not said where the Earl was buried; but in an arched niche in the south end of the transept, there was found, when the ruins were being cleared out, a small fragment of sculptured stone, which, it is thought, formed part of the armorial bearings of the house of Douglas.[1]

In the year 1490 (March 2) the Abbot and Convent of Lindores founded an altar in the Church of St John the Baptist, Perth,[2] in honour of St Blasius, and endowed it with ten pounds fifteen shillings yearly out of the abbey property in Perth.[3] The erection of altars to special saints was a popular mode of promoting religion at that period. St Blasius, Bishop of Sebaste, in Armenia, was patron saint of the wool-combers; he suffered martyrdom in the year 316, and his festival is held on the 3d February.[4] The founding of an altar to him in Perth would seem to indicate that there was a considerable number of the fraternity of wool-combers in the 'Fair City' at that time.

Eight years later, in the year 1498, Andrew Cavers, Abbot of Lindores, provided, by an endowment of thirteen shillings and fourpence yearly, to pay the chaplains and choristers of St John's Church, Perth, for the celebration of the service for the dead on the 3d November yearly.[5] Subsequent to this endowment he purchased for the convent the half of the lands of Pitcaithly, from John Oliphant of Dron. There is no record of this purchase in the chartulary of the abbey, but it was confirmed by James IV., by a charter under the Great Seal, on

---

[1] Douglas's *Peerage*, Wood's Ed., Douglas, Vol. I., pp. 431-2.

[2] The fine interior of St John's Church, Perth, is completely marred by the unsightly pews with which it is crowded.

[3] *Book of Perth*, p. 64.

[4] Butler's *Lives of the Saints*, Vol. II., p. 31-2.

[5] *Book of Perth*, p. 74.

the 6th November, A.D. 1500.[1] Andrew Cavers must have died sometime between 17th October 1502 and the 20th March 1503-4, for, in the chartulary of Lindores there is recorded an obligation by him to Andrew Charters of Cuthilgurdi, and Alexander Tyrie, and Robert Clerk or Wobster, burgesses of Perth, for one hundred and twenty pounds Scots, of the first mentioned date; and another for one hundred and fifteen pounds ten shillings of the latter date, by Henry, Abbot of Lindores, who succeeded him, to John Quhitsum, burgess of Perth. These obligations were simply bills of exchange, though more lengthy than the forms now in use. The first was payable forty days after sight of the 'acquittance' of the factor for the Abbey in Zealand or Flanders. In one of the obligations recorded (A.D. 1502), Stephen Orme, in all likelihood one of the Ormes of Mugdrum, and afterwards one of the bailies of Newburgh, is named as the abbey factor abroad, and the amount remitted was clearly in payment of goods purchased there for the use of the monastery.[2] There is no mention made of the kind of goods purchased by Stephen Orme, but in the 'ledger of Andrew Halliburton,' at that time conservator of the privileges of the Scottish nation in the Netherlands,[3] there is a voluminous record of the imports and exports of church dignitaries, as well as of merchants, and the details show that every article requiring skill in handicraft had to be brought from abroad. In the account of the Dean of Dunkeld (1501-2), there are some interesting particulars recorded. He had sent to 'Bruges' 15 barrels of salmon from his fishings in the Tay; they were disposed of in 'Lyill' (Lisle) 'for 14 li fre mony,' it being particularly recorded that 'off thir 15 br thar was 2 rottin and castyn in the water at Lyill.' The Dean received in exchange vardone [tapestry], pendens [curtains], hats, wearing apparel of various kinds, and besides articles of household furniture, 'an imoch for which 3 li 13 sh. was paid, and 2 bukis that

---

[1] *Reg. Mag. Sig. Lib.*, 13 No. 416.
[2] See appendix No. IV. for abstract of charter.　　[3] *Bk. of Lindores*, p. 26-29.

Master Patrick Panter sent hym cost 1 li.'[1]   Unfortunately the conservator, with thorough commercial brevity, does not mention the names of the books, otherwise we might have had some insight into the Dean's predilections, and the literature that was then current.[2]

---

[1] *Ledger of Andrew Halliburton*, p. 254.

[2] Patrick Panter, or, as he spells his name, Paniter, was one of the most accomplished scholars of his time.   It was while he was prosecuting his studies abroad that he executed the literary commission mentioned in the text, for the Dean of Dunkeld.   After he returned to Scotland, he was appointed Rector of the Church of Fetteresso, then to the Preceptory of the Church of Brechin, and subsequently he was appointed Abbot of Cambuskenneth.   He acted as Secretary of State in the reigns of James IV. and V.   The letters written by him in that capacity to foreign princes, were published (A.D. 1722) under the title of Epistolæ Regum Scotorum, and are distinguished both for their elegance and their ability. It is recorded of Abbot Patrick Panter, that ' had his life been prolonged he intended to have undertaken the task of reforming the abuses which prevailed at Cambuskenneth, as in other monasteries, and of restoring it to its primitive zeal in the cultivation of piety and letters and purity of manners.'   On this point it is worthy of note, that several of the monks of Cambuskenneth embraced the principles, and became preachers, of the doctrines of the Reformation, which is the more remarkable, as Patrick Panter's successor was a strenuous advocate and upholder of the principles of the Roman Church.   Abbot Patrick Panter died in Paris in 1519, at an early age.—*Chartulary of Cambuskenneth*, p. lxxxviii. Lorimer's *Precursors of Knox*, pp. 169-176.

CHAPTER XIII.

ABBOTS HENRY, JOHN PHILP, AND JOHN LESLIE.
PATRICK HAMILTON MARTYR.

'Unbounded is the might of martyrdom.'

Wordsworth.

THE successor of Andrew Cavers to the abbacy was Henry, whose
surname does not appear. He held the office of abbot from 1502
or 3 to the year 1527–8. In his time the lands and possessions
of the abbey were erected into a regality, under the name of the
'Regality of Lindoris.'[1] This concession conferred on the abbot
exclusive criminal jurisdiction, and, as the name implies, almost
regal power over all within the territories of the abbey. An Act
was passed in the reign of James II., obviously for the purpose of
restricting the extension of these excessive powers, which enacted
that no regality be erected without the express sanction of Parliament. Yet to such an extent were these privileges conferred,
'that no inconsiderable portion of the kingdom' was absorbed by
them, 'and when contrasted with what retained the name of
royalty, may justly be regarded as having stripped the Crown of
the better half of its highest prerogative.'[2] The regality of
Lindores was erected in the reign of James IV. (A.D. 1510), and
was confirmed by Parliament a few months after the fatal field
of Flodden; the weakness of the Crown at that disastrous period,
from the death of so many of the ablest lay advisers among the

---

[1] *Reg. Mag. Sig.*, Lib. 18, p. 47.
[2] *Report on Municipal Corporations, Scotland*, 1835, p. 20.

nobility, affording a favourable opportunity for the furtherance of ambitious aims.

Newburgh was the head burgh of the Legality of Lindores, and at its Cross proclamations affecting the whole Regality were made, and in its Tolbooth 'sumoundis were maid aganis any person dwelling' within the Regality.

On the alienation of the abbey estates by the lay proprietor, Lord Lundores, an Act was passed in the reign of James VI. (A.D. 1621) in favour of William Forbes of Craigiewar, 'erecting all the lands within the parochines of Christiskirk, Premnay and others,' into a burgh of barony, under the name of the 'Barony of Lo- gyffintrey.' The same Act declares the barony to be separated 'from the Regality of Lundoris;' and enacted that the 'Courts of the barony be held by the said William Forbes at the Haltoun of ffintrey.' It was further enacted, that all dwelling within the barony 'na wayis be haldin to compeir in na courtis of the said Regalitie of Lundoris haldin at Newburgh in tyme cuming, and that na exe- cutiounes or proclamatiounes be usit aganis them att the said Mercat Croce of Newburtᵗ. But the samyn to be done at Haltoun of ffyntrey   as the samyn wes done, or micht haif been in tyme bygane att the said Croce and in the said Tolbuith of Newburgh.'[1] The privilege of regality conferred on Lindores Abbey was swept away on the abolition of heritable jurisdictions in the reign of George II.

Abbot Henry, on account of the infirmities of age, resigned in favour of a successor named John, in March 1522, reserving to himself the revenue of the benefice, an arrangement which was sanctioned by the Pope.[2] Though Henry resigned the administra- tion of the abbey to his coadjutor and successor, he continued to exercise the judicial functions appertaining to the office of abbot. In this capacity he took part in the trial of Patrick Hamilton, and signed his condemnation. Hamilton, though styled Abbot of Ferne

[1] *Scots Acts*, Vol. IV., p. 685.
[2] Knox's *Hist. of the Reformation*, Vol. II., p. 599.   David Laing—*Notes.*

(Ross-shire), was not in holy orders. While only a youth, he was, according to the corrupt practice of the time, appointed commendator or titular abbot of that abbacy. His father, Sir Patrick Hamilton of Kincavel, in Linlithgowshire, was one of the bravest and most chivalrous knights of his time. Lindsay of Pitscottie says of him, 'he was a right noble and valiant man all his days.' By his mother, Patrick Hamilton the younger was great grandson of James II. When little more than fourteen years of age he went to Paris to attend the university there, and was distinguished among his fellow students for his abilities, and for his love of the newly-revived Greek and Latin literature, which had begun to exercise a powerful influence on the students of that period. Hamilton subsequently returned to St Andrews for the prosecution of his theological studies, where he seems to have been on terms of friendship with the authorities of the Church, as they gratified his musical tastes, by allowing a musical composition of his to be performed in the cathedral service.[1] The introduction of the English translation of the Bible, and of the writings of Luther, into St Andrews, concealed in great numbers in bales of goods, showed that there were secret students of them in that city. The number of monks of the Augustinian Priory of St Andrews, and of the same order at Cambuskenneth, who embraced the doctrines of the Reformation, shows that they were of those who studied the Bible and the writings of the Reformers.[2] Hamilton was suspected, and summoned to answer for his opinions; but not being then nerved for the fight, he fled to Germany. He met there William Tyndale, the translator of the Bible, and John Frith, both destined to die as martyrs at the stake; he also attended the prelections, and listened to the burning eloquence of Luther, and the milder teaching of Melancthon. Inflamed by their zeal, and fired with a martyr's spirit, he returned to Scotland within less than twelve months of his flight, and openly and unflinchingly proclaimed what he believed to be the truth. Invited from his native county to St

---

[1] Lorimer's *Life of Hamilton*, p. 59.   [2] *Ib.*, pp. 163–172.

Andrews, he was allowed, for weeks to declare his opinions, but at last, on the 29th February 1528-9, he was arraigned in the cathedral church to answer for the doctrines he taught, and face to face with his judges before the multitude assembled in its crowded aisles, he boldly maintained his opinions. 'Brother!' he said to his accuser, 'I have never read in the Scripture of God of such a place as purgatory, nor yet believe I that there is anything that may purge the souls of men but the blood of Christ Jesus, which ransom standeth in no earthly thing, nor in soul-mass, nor in *dirigie*, nor in gold nor in silver, but only by repentance of sins and faith in the blood of Christ Jesus.'[1]

Sentence of condemnation was pronounced against him; and the same afternoon, with unpitying haste, he was marched, guarded, for fear of rescue, by several thousand armed men, from the cathedral to the place of execution, at the gate of St Salvador's College, and burnt at the stake;—his sufferings were long and agonizing, and his last audible words were—'How long, Lord, shall darkness overwhelm this kingdom? How long wilt Thou suffer the tyranny of men? Lord Jesus receive my spirit!'[2] It may well be asked, How long? Immediately after the principles of the Reformation were established by the legislature, an Act was passed by the Scottish Parliament (24th August 1560), ordaining that 'if any say mass or hear mass, they were to be punished with confiscation and imprisonment for the first offence, banishment for the second, and death for the third offence.' 'Such strangers,' is the indignant comment of Principal Robertson, 'were men at that time to the spirit of toleration and to the laws of humanity,—and with such indecent haste did the very persons who had just escaped the rigour of ecclesiastical tyranny proceed to imitate those examples of inhumanity, of which they themselves had so justly complained.'[3]

---

[1] Pitscottie, *Hist.*, pp. 133, 134.

[2] Lorimer's *Life of Patrick Hamilton*, p. 154.

[4] Pref. *Stat. Ec. Scot.*, pp. clxiii.-iv. 'More than fifty years afterwards' (says Joseph Robertson), 'another Scottish historian and divine had to give an account of the same statute. If the friends of religious liberty, of Christian charity,

The martyrdom of Hamilton had the very opposite effect from what his persecutors intended, his youth, his illustrious descent, his noble defence, and his constancy in death, made a powerful impression on the public mind, and within fifteen years of his martyrdom, 'the Parliament of Scotland enacted (15th March 1543), that it should be lawful to all men to have and to read Holy Scripture, both in the New and Old Testament in the vulgar tongue.'[1]

> 'The sacred Book,
> In dusty sequestration wrapt too long,
> Assumes the accents of our native tongue;
> And he who guides the plough or wields the crook
> With understanding spirit now may look
> Upon her records, listen to her song,
> And sift her laws—much wondering that the wrong
> Which Faith had suffered, heaven could calmly brook.'[2]

Previous to the passing of this law, however, John, Abbot of Lindores, was called to sit in judgment, with other church digni taries, in the cloisters of St Andrews, on Sir John Borthwick (28th May 1540), for, among other charges, having the New Testament in English in his possession, and for circulating heretical books.[3] Borthwick knowing what awaited him, fled to England; but he was condemned in absence and burnt in effigy. He was employed by Henry VIII., in important services with Protestant sovereigns abroad, and lived to return to St Andrews, where he obtained a reversal of his sentence, and died there in peace.[4]

John, the successor of Henry, was a monk and presbyter at the

---

should regret that he has no word of rebuke for such sanguinary intolerance, they must at least acknowledge the pious care with which he seeks to conceal it from his readers.' 'On the 24th August the Parliament abolished the Papal jurisdiction, prohibited, *under certain penalties*, the celebration of mass, and rescinded all the laws formerly made in support of the Roman Catholic Church, and against the Reformed faith.'—Dr M'Crie's *Life of Knox*, p. 162—Edit. 1857.

[1] Pref. *Stat. Ec. Scot.*, p. cxli.   [2] Wordsworth.
[3] Pref. *Stat. Ec. Scot.*, p. cxli.
[4] Knox's *Hist.*, Vol. I., pp. 533-4; Keith's *Hist.*, Vol. I., pp. 337-341.

time he undertook the administration of the abbey. His surname appears to have been Philp. In a charter granted by him as abbot, on the 2d March 1564, in favour of James Philp of Ormestoun, he describes the latter as 'his beloved cousin,' a designation which may be held conclusive on the point. The frequency of the occurrence of the surname of Philp in the records of Newburgh in the preceding century, tends also to show that he was a native of the neighbourhood.[1] He is spoken of as an excellent and tried man, and must have been a person of some importance, as he was coadjutor and administrator of the Abbey of Kelso during the minority of Lord James Stewart (natural son of James V.), the commendator. In 1540, and in subsequent years, he had a seat in Parliament; in 1544 he was one of the Lords of Session,[2] and in 1549 he sat as Abbot in the General Convention and Provincial Council of the Church, held at Edinburgh in the refectory of the Blackfriars. At this council a great number of canons were enacted, having for their object the reform of the lives and manners of the clergy. 'Heretical books, especially poems and ballads against the church or clergy, were to be diligently sought after and burned.'[3] Though not named, there can be no doubt that the poems of Sir David Lindsay are here aimed at; his scathing satire and unsparing exposure of the vicious lives of too many of the clergy, exercised a most powerful influence on public opinion and on the progress of the reformation.

Various events occurred about this period which tend to show that the opinions of the Reformers were gaining ground. From a report of the English ambassador to his master Henry VIII., we learn that in 1543, destructive attacks were made on the abbeys by the populace. It is unfortunate that we have not the ambassador's own announcement of them, but only a memor-

---

[1] An abstract of this charter is given in the Appendix. In 1481, Sir James Philp was curate of Ibdy (Abdie); and in 1615 John Philp was clerk of the Regality of Lindores.

[2] Knox's *Hist.*, Vol. I., p. 392; Vol. II., p. 599.—D. Laing's *Notes*.

[3] Pref. *Stat. Ec. Scot.*, pp. cxlvii-cl.

andum of its substance in these terms: 'Sir Ralph Sadler (the ambassador) shows that the work began at Dundee by destroying the houses both of the Black and Gray Friars; that afterwards the Abbey of Lindores was sacked by a company of good Christians, as they were called, who turned the monks out of doors.'[1]

Notwithstanding this violent warning of the Dundee reformers, the clergy persisted in repelling the new doctrines by force, instead of meeting them by argument. In April 1558 the prelates, among whom was John, Abbot of Lindores, summoned Walter Miln, the aged parish priest of Lunan in Angus, before them for heresy, and condemned him to death. The sympathies of the people were with the old man, when he exclaimed from the flames, 'I trust in God I am the last that shall suffer death in Scotland for this cause.'[2] A prayer which was happily fulfilled.

The ejection of the monks from Lindores Abbey in 1543, which the English ambassador has recorded, was only temporary. In a letter of John Knox, dated the 23d June 1559, he says, 'we' (the Protestants who had united together under the name of the Congregation) 'came to the Abbey of Lindores, a place of Black monkes, distant from St Andrewis twelve myles, we reformed them, their altars overthrew we, their idols, vestments of idolatrie, and mass books we burnt in their presence, and commanded them to cast away their monkish habits.'[3] The moderation displayed

---

[1] Hill Burton's *Hist. of Scotland*, Vol. III., p. 453.

[2] Tytler, Vol. III., p. 86.

[3] M'Crie's *Life of Knox*, Vol. II., p. 383—Ed. 1814. The following note affords some idea of the destruction of manuscripts at the period of the Reformation. In A.D. 1549, John Bale, a vigorous anti-Romanist, but a man of learning, writing on this subject, says: 'I know a merchant-man, which shall at this time be nameless, that bought the contents of two noble libraries (of English monasteries) for forty shillings price,—a shame it is to be spoken! This stuff hath he occupied instead of gray paper by the space of more than these ten years, and yet he hath store enough for as many years to come.'—Blunt's *History of the Reformation*, p. 388. Every student of history knows that many of these manuscripts were beautifully illuminated, and were worthy of preservation as works of art.

at Lindores is in marked contrast with what happened at St Andrews only eight days before, where the monasteries were ruthlessly destroyed.[1] Perhaps the forbearance was shown because the abbot was believed to have a leaning to the principles of the reformers; this much is certain, that the Queen Regent gave intimation that he should not receive any part of his living in the north from the churches belonging to the abbey in the Garioch, because he had 'submitted himself to the Congregation, and had put some reformation to his place.'[2] Of the nature and extent of the reformation introduced we are left in ignorance, but the probability is, that the second book of Edward VI. was adopted in the daily services of the abbey, as it is known that it was used in Scotland for some years after the Reformation.[3] That the prayers introduced into the service of the abbey at this juncture were Protestant in their character, is evident from the fact, that the Queen Regent subsequently ' dischargit the common prayeris, and foirbad to gif ony portion to sic as war the principall young men quha redde thame.'[4] In August 1560 John, Abbot of Lindores, sat in the convention which sanctioned the Confession of Faith, and assented to it; those prelates who did so were to enjoy the revenues of their benefices during their life, on condition that they upheld in the churches belonging to their abbeys the ministry and ministers under the new order of things.[5]

---

[1] M'Crie's *Life of Knox*, Vol. I., p. 270.

[2] Knox's *Hist.*, Vol. II., p. 291.

Keith's *Hist.*, Vol. III., p. 100.—*Note.* On this point the editors of *The Book of Common Order of the Church of Scotland*, say: In 1557 the Scottish Protestant Lords in Council resolved as follows, that 'the Common Prayers be read weekly on Sunday and other festival days, publicly in the parish kirks, with the lessons of the Old and New Testaments, conform to the Order of the Book of Common Prayers.' The Book of Common Prayers, thus authorized, was the Second Book of King Edward VI., and it was in use accordingly, to some extent, till it was superseded by the Book of Geneva.'—P. xiii.

[4] Knox's *Hist. of the Reformation*, Vol. I., p. 392.

[5] Keith's *Hist.*, Vol. III., p. 24.

He resigned the abbacy in favour of John Leslie, on the 24th February 1566, ' but as commendator of Lindores he is named as having been present at the General Assembly, 25th June 1566, and probably did not long survive.'

John Leslie, the last Abbot of Lindores, occupies a more conspicuous place in history than any of his predecessors. His father, Gavin Leslie, Rector of Kingussie, in Badenoch, and Judge Official or Commissary of the Diocese of Moray, was one of the family of Leslie of Cults, a branch of the Leslies of Balquhain, who, in their turn, were an offshot of the Leslies of Leslie, now represented by the Countess of Rothes. John Leslie, being the son of a priest, was illegitimate, for which a dispensation from the Pope was afterwards received, to enable him to enter into holy orders. He was born on the 29th September 1527, and received his education in King's College, Aberdeen, where he took the degree of Master of Arts. In 1550 he was appointed canon of the cathedral church of Aberdeen and Ellon, the emoluments from this preferment enabling him to prosecute his studies abroad. He studied divinity and languages in Paris, devoting himself especially to Greek and Hebrew. He afterwards went to Poitiers, where, for nearly four years he studied civil and canon law. In Toulouse, where he resided for some time, he took the degree of Doctor of Laws, and for a year read lectures on Canon Law, in that University.

In April 1554, Leslie returned to his native country, where his learning and ability soon obtained for him many preferments. He was appointed Professor of Civil Law in the University of Aberdeen; and in the year 1558 the bishop and chapter of that diocese chose him for their official, a situation which required a knowledge of both Canon and Civil Law, and for which he was eminently fitted by his studies and training. Previous to this, however, he became parson of Oyne (a title by which he is frequently designated in the history of the time) and Morthlack, and prebendary of the cathedral of Aberdeen. But these preferments were not to last; the Reformation was shortly afterwards accomplished, and he and

others were summoned to Edinburgh (January 1561), to give an
account of their faith and opinions. In April of the same year he
was despatched to France by the Roman Catholic noblemen of the
north of Scotland, to endeavour to prepossess Mary in their favour.
He returned to Scotland in the same vessel with the young
Queen, when she came to take possession of the Scottish throne,
and ever afterwards adhered to her with unshaken fidelity. Mary
appointed him one of her Privy Council, and in 1564 he took his
seat as one of the Lords of Session. On the 24th February 1566,
her Majesty bestowed on him the Abbacy of Lindores *in commendam.* Subsequently he was appointed Bishop of Ross, and by
a Papal dispensation was allowed to hold both appointments.
Leslie was present in the palace of Holyrood on that fatal evening when Riccio was murdered. From his known partiality for
the Queen he was looked upon with disfavour by her opponents,
and was exposed to some risk on that occasion. In a contemporary record it is said, that 'Atholle had leave of the Kinge
(Darnley), with Flyske, and Landores (who was lately called
Lyslaye, the parson of Oyne), to go where they wolde, and were
convoid out of the courte.'[1]

After Mary's flight to England, Bishop Leslie followed her, and
never afterwards returned to reside in Scotland. During the
whole of his after life he was indefatigable in the Queen's behalf,
and one of the most zealous defenders of her rights and reputation.
For his complicity in her proposed marriage with Norfolk, he was
sent as a prisoner first to the Isle of Ely, and afterwards to
the Tower, where he suffered great hardships.[2] In his imprison-

---

[1] Knox's *Hist.*, Vol. II., p. 601.—*Appendix.*

[2] On a stone in the *splay* of a window of the cell in the Bloody Tower,
where Bishop Leslie was confined, there is a Latin inscription hewn by him in
Roman capitals, with his name and date appended. Both the inscription and
the beading by which it is surrounded, are neatly cut; it measures $8\frac{1}{2}$ by 6 inches.
The letters are for the most part legible, but the inscription has been destroyed
in several places by the sharp cut of a plasterer's trowel, and it is in consequence

ment he wrote his *Piae Consolationes*, which he was permitted to send to his unfortunate sovereign, who derived comfort and support from them, and in the weary hours of her lengthened captivity endeavoured to turn his pious lucubrations into French verse.

After a long imprisonment it was put in the Bishop's option either to return to Scotland or to go to France,—he chose the latter alternative. During his exile he wrote his History of Scotland, which was published in Rome in 1578, whence he had gone on a mission at the request of the Queen. On the day before her execution, Mary wrote to Philip, King of Spain, beseeching him to show kindness to the Bishop of Ross for his faithful and devoted services to her. The Queen's dying request met with a ready response, and the faithful prelate was provided for in his declining years. His labours and sufferings on behalf of his Royal mistress had, however, so seriously impaired his health, that he was compelled to give up the active duties of the preferment to which the King of Spain had promoted him, and he retired to the monastery of the order of St Augustine at Gertrudenberg, about two miles from Brussels, where he spent the remainder of his days in tranquillity. He died there in June 1596, in the seventieth year of his age, and was buried in the monastery under a monument erected

---

not easily deciphered. The following is an accurate copy of the inscription as it now appears. The obliterated letters are indicated by dots:

E. EGO . RO PATRI. INCIPE TOT MALA
E. TIBI .. E DE.. . NS ME . IN SAT EST
A. PATRIÆ REQVIE.. . T.STA SVB PRINCIP
PACE FRVANTVR AGO VIGILA ME .. HIBENT
VT. RERE. PRÆSTAS IN .. SPE G..ERE SIBI
QV.. VIDE.T GR.TV. S.. MIHI V..E TVVM
CV. PLACVERIN. DOMINO VIÆ HOMINIS
INIMICOS EIVS C.NVERTET .. PACEM
JO. EPS ROSSE. SCOT.S.
1572.

to his memory by his nephew John Leslie, bearing the following inscription—

'SOLA VIRTUS.'

Joannes Leslaeus, Episcopus Rossensis, Scotus, ex illustri familia Leslaeorum, omnis generis scientiarum cultissimus, Orator ad Regem Gall. Fransciscam II. Consiliarius Mariae, P.M. Scotorum Reginae, Catholicae religionis propugnator, post immensis pro avita fide labores, presertim in Regno Scotiae restituenda, post defensam in Anglia Mariam Reginam post varies summa cum laude gesta, tranquillisime excessit Bruxel prid. Kalend, Junii, A.D. MDXCVI Aetatis suæ 70.

'Avunculo grato ne superesset ingratus, Joannes Leslaeus Nepos, haeres moestus posuit et pro eodem anniversarium p. p., fundavit in hoc coenobio Gertrudenbérguensi prid. Kal. Junii celebrandum Natatum Locum et Diem scimus, sepulchri nescimus.'[1]

It is said that during Bishop Leslie's administration of Lindores Abbey he obtained a royal mandate, and took an active part in regard to the confirmation of various feu-fermes of lands pertaining to the abbey.[2] This statement receives confirmation from the

---

[1] Irving's *Scottish Writers*, pp. 122-146; Knox's *Hist.*, Laing's *Annot.*, Vol. II., pp. 600-1; *Hist. Rec. of Family of Leslie*, Vol. III., pp. 402-406. Besides the works previously mentioned, the Bishop of Ross published ' A Defence of Mary, Queen of Scotland ; and that the Regiment of Women is conformable to the Law of God and Nature, 1569.' ' A Discourse conteyning a Perfect Account given to the most vertuous and excellent Princesse Marie, Queen of Scots, and her nobility.' He wrote also in the vernacular, a ' History of Scotland from the death of James I., 1436 to 1561,' which was only published in 1830, from a manuscript belonging to the Earl of Leven and Melville. The Bishop wrote also some smaller works, chiefly in defence of his royal mistress. In the library of King's College, Aberdeen, there is a portrait of Bishop Leslie, in excellent preservation. There is a relic of the Bishop in the possession of Dr John Stuart, consisting of a volume of the works of a German divine, Wecelius, whose writings were much esteemed by those who were in favour of reformation, but did not wish to break with Rome.—*Rec. of the Monastery of Kinloss*, p. lv.

[2] Knox's *Hist. of the Reformation*, Vol. II., p. 601.—*Note*.

fact that John Leslie of New Leslie, son of Andrew Leslie and Janet Leslie, daughter of the Bishop, was served heir to his father in the lands of 'Insch, Chrystiskirk, Eddirleck,' and other lands in Aberdeenshire, which formerly were the property of Lindores Abbey.[1] Previous to this, however, William Leslie, grandfather of John Leslie, of New Leslie, had acquired in feu the lands of Insch and Chrystiskirk,' by his wife Margaret Cowie (rather Calvie), daughter of James Calvie of Newburgh, in Lindores.'[2]

---

[1] *Retour—Aberdeen*, No. 178.

[2] *Historical Records of the Family of Leslie*, Vol. III., p. 342. The family of Calvie was long resident in Newburgh, and seem to have been of considerable position and influence. On the 23d March 1589, John Calvie was served heir to his grandfather, John Calvie, in seven acres and a half of arable land, with the third part of the 'Almeriecruik;' and on the 23d October 1644, John Calvie was served heir to his great-grandfather, John Calvie, in fifteen and a half burgage crofts within the regality of Lindores—(*Fife Retours*),—a very large extent of burgage property to be in the hands of one person.

CHAPTER XIV

THE COMMENDATOR.

' Ryse ! say'd ye King richt blythe, and here
For brave discharge off thye devoir,
Thye guerdon taik—this hand so fair
And Baronye off fayre Lundore.'

M.S. of Elizabeth Leslie, a descendant of Lord Lindores.

AFTER the departure of the Bishop of Ross with his Royal mistress, Patrick Leslie of Pitcairlie, seconds on of Andrew, fourth Earl of Rothes, was appointed Commendator of Lindores.[1] As a layman he could only hold the abbey *in commendam,* or in trust, hence the title of Commendator. Many of the abbeys at that period, and even before the Reformation, were disposed of in this manner. From the record of a 'confirmation of a pension granted by Patrick, Commendator of the Abbey of Lundores to Johne Bonar, lawfull sone to umquhill William Bonar of Rossey, 13 December 1569,'[2] we learn that Patrick Leslie must have received this valuable appointment some time before that date. In addition to this substantial benefit, the King (James VI.) shortly afterwards conferred the honour of knighthood upon him.

How long after the Reformation the monks continued to occupy their old abode, is nowhere recorded. Judging from the complaints they made, their position seems to have been most unen-

---

[1] A notice of the pedigree of the family of Leslie of Lindores is given in the Appendix No. I.

[2] Presentation of Benefices, 1569.

viable, and the pittance allowed them most grudgingly paid by the lay-proprietors who obtained possession of the abbey estates.[1] That there was just cause for the complaints of the monks, is corroborated by the difficulty the Reformed ministers had in obtaining the stipends voted to them. Zealous reformers, who, Knox tells us, 'had greedilie grippit the possessiounis of the kirk,' would scarcely disgorge as much as would suffice for their maintenance. From the zeal manifested in promoting the Reformation, it may seem as if all were animated by a sincere desire for the cause of pure religion; but the after-lives of too many of the laymen, who took an active part in it, showed that a desire for power, and the hope of obtaining a share of the property of the Church, lay at the bottom of their zeal. They used, as men still use, the convictions and passions of others to help themselves to power; they readily assented to the suppression of the dignitaries of the Church, and depressed the clergy, that there might be less chance of powerful claimants re-appearing to demand restitution of the properties which they had obtained. 'Thair was none,' says Knox, 'within the realme, more unmerciful to the poore ministeris than wer thei which had greatest rentis of the Churches.'[2]

In December 1561, the Privy Council decreed that the holders of ecclesiastical benefices should give up one-third of the revenues derived from them for the public service, and for the maintenance of the ministers of the Reformed Church. In furtherance of this decree, they were required to produce, within a specified time, rentals of their various benefices, and collectors were appointed by government to uplift the rents of the abbeys. Many of these 'Rentals' have been preserved, and they form a valuable record of the possessions of the Church. That of Lindores, now published for the first time, is more minute than any hitherto published of it, and is specially interesting, as showing the localities of the extensive possessions of the abbey, and the rental in those days of many well known properties. From the circumstances of the third part of the revenues being appropriated,

---

[1] Keith Hist., Vol. I., p. 389. [2] Knox Hist., Vol. II., p. 128, 129.

these accounts are known by the name of the 'Assumption of Thirds.'[1]

By an Act of Parliament passed in the reign of James VI., in the year 1584, ' The haill thrid of the quheit of Lindores, three chalders, four bolles, three peckes; out of the third of the beir, saxe chalders, nine bolles ane firlot; out of the thrid of the meal, four chalders, XI. bolles, three firlotes two peckes' were assigned for keeping the Castle of Edinburgh, 'one of the four chief strengths of the Realme, maist necessar to be keepit.' Payment from lands which belonged to the Abbey of Lindores, in this neighbourhood, is still made to the Crown in virtue of this Act of Parliament, and is known by the name of Castle Rents. About this period the dismantling of the abbey seems to have begun. On the 21st April 1585, the Town Council of Edinburgh purchased the abbey clock. The following is the entry in the city records sanctioning the purchase—'Vigesimo primo Aprilis 1585. The same day, &c., Ordainis Nicoll Uddert, dene of gild to refound and pay to Henry Nisbet bailzie the soum of fyftie fyve pund debursit be bym for the pryce of the knok of Lindores, and the same sall be allowit to the said dene of gild in his comptis, and the said dene of gild to intromett with the said knok and to be comptabill for the sam.' Unfortunately the entry does not mention to whom the price was paid, and its silence regarding any bell is conclusive that no bell was sold at that time. Sir James Balfour, in his manuscript collections preserved in the Advocates' Library, says, 'They' (the monks) 'had ancientlie in this abbay 4 great bellis, Michael and Raphael, Mary bell and Gabriell, of which Mary bell was of silver, the gift of ther first founder.' The 'Mary Bell' was

---

[1] The rental of Lindores Abbey, referred to in the text, is in the hand-writing of Mr John Nicolson, collector-clerk, and is attested by him; the original was submitted to David Laing, LL.D., and, from internal as well as other evidence, he is of opinion that it was drawn up about the year 1580. It belongs to the present proprietor of Lindores Abbey, Edmund P. Balfour Hay, Esq., and by his kind permission is now published with notes in the Appendix No. II.

of too valuable material to escape being speedily commuted into coin ; but what became of it and the others is not recorded.

On 5th November 1587, Patrick Leslie granted a tack of the teind sheaves of the parish of Dudhope to James Scrymgeour of Dudhope, constable of Dundee, and John Scrymgeour his son, for their lives and nineteen years after their decease. It runs in these terms—'Be it known till all men, Patrick, be permission of God, Commendator of Lundores, with express consent and assent of our convent of the said abey, the weill proffit and utilitie thereof

and considerit after lang advisement and mature delibera- tion, and for certain great sum of silver defressit and payit to us in name of grassum, be ane honourable man James Scrymgeour, of Dudhope, constable of Dundee, to be warit and applyit towards ye reparation of our Abbey Kirk of Lundores.' [1] Of the applica- tion of this ' great sum of silver' to the reparation of the Abbey Church, grave doubts may be entertained ; the probability is, that the tack sets forth what should have been done, rather than what was done.

The Commendator seems to have been too needy to spend ' the great sum of silver' for such a purpose, and he was ad- venturous enough to run some risk to acquire more. In 1599 he and a set of gentlemen, chiefly belonging to Fife, associated themselves together as adventurers, ' to take possession of the islands of Lewis and Harris, which had been confiscated by go- vernment, in consequence of the turbulence of the chiefs. The islanders attacked the settlement of these colonisers, killed most of their people, took the leaders prisoners, and only released them eight months after, on promise that they should never return.' [2]

Shortly after the Commendator's return from this luckless expedition, James VI. bestowed on him the lands of Lindores ; and on 15th November 1600, Parliament ' ratifies and apprevis and confermes the infeftment of feu-ferme grantit be his mat[ie]

---

[1] From the original deed in the possession of Miss Graham of Duntrune.
[2] Chambers's *Annals*, Vol. I., p. 308-9.

to Patrick Leslie of Pitcarlie his airis maill and assignais.' On
Christmas day 1600, James created him Lord of Parliament, by the
title of Lord Lundores, to him and all his heirs male.' This was
confirmed by Parliament on the 11th July 1606. Doubts have
been expressed as to whether it was the Commendator or his son
that was created Lord Lundores; but the following extract from
the Act of Parliament mentioned, seems to show conclusively that
it was the Commendator who first enjoyed that honour. The
grounds of the erection being 'the mony gude trew, thankfull and
profitable services mony ways done to his mat^{te} be Patrik, now
Lord of Lundoris, sumtyme Commendator thereof. And to
the effect above-written, our said soverane Lord and estattis
forsaidis dissolvis, suppresses, extinguishes and abolisches the
foirsaid abbey and monasterie of Lundoris, Memorie and name
thairof, with the haill ordouris, institutiones and foundationes of
the sam^n simpliciter and forevir.' And so closed the magnificent
foundation of David, Earl of Huntingdon.

In reviewing the history of Lindores Abbey, it ought to be
borne in mind, that the object of the institution of monasteries
was to accomplish a social regeneration rather than a strictly religious one. At the period of their great revival in the eleventh and
twelfth centuries, such asylums where peaceful men could exhibit
the benefits of undisturbed industry, were real blessings in the land.
But when law and order began to prevail, and right was stronger
than might, their purpose had been achieved and their vocation
had ceased. The very amelioration which the monasteries had so
powerfully helped to produce, was an argument for their being no
longer required. It would have been true wisdom to have
devoted them to a purpose calculated to meet the requirements
of the age. Unfortunately, the noble piles which the munificence
of their pious founders had reared, were not spared, as they ought
to have been, for places of education for the youth of coming
generations. Within their walls young men might have been
trained to the highest mental culture of the time, and sent forth
to meet the ever varying phases of error, and do battle for the

truth. Even in the first fervour of the Reformation, such a purpose was pointed out for them, and their preservation enjoined ; but unfortunately the corruption of the monasteries had brought them into such bad odour, that the excited populace wrecked their rage on what ought to have been spared.[1]

There is no entire portion of Lindores Abbey remaining; and until within the last few years, so completely were the ruins hidden under mounds of their own rubbish, that even the most experienced in ecclesiastical structures, could with difficulty make out the ground plan of the building. The ruins were so completely overgrown with trees and shrubs, and the place was in such a state of utter desolation and neglect, that it was known in the neighbourhood solely by the name of 'The Wilderness.' This is now all changed ; the rubbish has been cleared away down to the basement, the plan of the building is distinctly seen, and the stumps of pillars which have been uncovered, exhibit the graceful form and the clustered shafts of the early English or First-pointed style. The solidity and the gracefulness of their design remain to attest the grandeur of the original building. About twenty-five years ago, the foundations of a range of pillars, to the height of several feet, running along the north side of the nave, were laid bare by the partial removal of the rubbish by which they had been concealed. They were of the same elegant design as those fragments which remain; but very shortly after their discovery

---

[1] 'If,' says a living scholar, 'a more generous and fairer treatment had been extended to the Church and the Universities at the time of the Reformation, there might have been in Scotland, as there is in England, adequate rewards for learning, of which at present there are next to none. Will it be believed, that apart from Oxford and Cambridge, there are two public schools in England, the annual income of either of which exceeds that, not of one, but of all the Scottish Universities.'—*Professor Geddes*, '*Address to the University of Aberdeen*, Oct. 1869.' Cardinal Wolsey, several years before the Reformation in England, carried out a wise reform of the monastic system ; and with a statesmanlike appreciation of the wants of the times, appropriated the revenues of twelve small monasteries (providing for the inmates at the same time) for the endowment of Christ Church College, Oxford.—Blount *Hist. of Reformation in England*, Vol. I., p. 69.

they were ruthlessly removed.   Part of the walls of the chancel,
to a considerable height, are still standing, but they are thoroughly
stripped of all ashlar and ornamental work, and not a vestige of
the mullions of any of the windows remains, excepting in broken
fragments found among the rubbish.   The walls of the great
western tower, to the height of about eight feet, remain in better
preservation than almost any other portion of the abbey.   The
buttresses are of immense thickness, and show that the tower
must originally have been of great strength.[1]   But the most perfect portion of the abbey remaining is the groined arch of the principal entrance leading into the cloister-court, of which an illustration from a photograph is given; the cloister walls, like almost
every portion of the building, have been thoroughly peeled, and
only the skeleton remains.

That grand old structures were destroyed at the outburst of
the Reformation, history attests; but the demolition of most of
them was the work of a later age.   Unoccupied and neglected,
the abbeys especially became quarries for the neighbourhood,
until, in some instances, scarcely one stone remained above another.
The work of spoliation has gone on so gradually, that it has generally escaped observation and record; but in the charter chest of
Newburgh, there is preserved a record of an appropriation and destruction of such an extensive character, that the heirs of the per-
petrator had to refund the then proprietor, Alexander, Lord Lundores.   Slates, timber, stones, hewn and unhewn, were carried off
for the erection of a house in Newburgh, the mouldings of the
doors and windows of which still bear witness from whence they

---

[1] The great western tower appears to have an exact counterpart of the
existing square tower of the parish church of Brechin, only more massive. About
twenty years ago, a portion of a spiral stair, leading to the top of the tower, was
discovered, but shortly afterwards the whole (excepting two) of the steps were
removed. A heavy iron key of antique shape, was found at the same time, but
it also has disappeared. When the floor of the tower was recently being
cleared, several stone and iron cannon balls were found among the rubbish.

were obtained.[1] On the 18th April 1743, the following occurs in
the records of the kirk session of Newburgh :—' To James Bissatt
for bringing the free stone from the Abby for John Black's House
00. 03. 00 ;' an entry which shows that the abbey was used and
recognised as the quarry for the neighbourhood.

A demolition so sordid and so unsparing had but scant respect
even for the tombs of the departed. The niches, where elaborate
monuments stood, are distinctly visible, but the monuments themselves have been ruthlessly destroyed, and not a fragment remains.
Nine stone coffins have been discovered in Lindores Abbey from
time to time ; the lid which covered the coffin at the door of
the chapter house, has the figure of an ecclesiastic sculptured
upon it.[2] Another had a small incised cross on the lid ; but none
of the coffins bore any inscription to indicate who was buried in
them. It is recorded that Lady Mary Lindsay was buried in the
chancel ; but the exact spot, where the wayward and unfortunate
Duke of Rothesay was laid, is unknown. It is not a little remark-

---

[1] In the deed referred to in the text, the following occurs, ' Moreover dureing
the time above mentioned ' (before Alexander Lord Lundores got his right to the
estate fully established), ' and on pretence of having a right and warrand from the
said factor on said estate, as said is. He, the said,   did also demolish
and take down the principall part of the mansion house of Lundores, carried off
the whole slates, lofts, jests, and timber thereof, and a great many stones therefrom, both hewn and unhewn, and made use of the same for building a house
    in Newburgh, and a maltbarn in the toune of Grange of Lindores.' The
same deed conveys the road from the east port to the foot of the gardens to the
community, and is signed by Lord Lundores, at Newburgh, on 25th May 1741.

In the front wall of a house on the south side of the street of Newburgh there
is a stone, doubtless from the abbey, representing a Bear chained to a ragged
staff, sculptured upon it ; above this is apparently a mitre, surmounted by the
head of a pastoral staff. The Bear chained to a ragged staff, George Seton,
Esq., the learned author of ' The Law and Practice of Heraldry in Scotland,'
informs me, is the well-known badge of the Beauchamps, Earls of Warwick ;
but what connection any member of that family, either ecclesiastically or otherwise, had with Lindores Abbey, nowhere appears.

[2] An engraving of this lid, copied from a drawing by Mr Thomas Ross, architect,
Edinburgh, is given with the ground plan of the abbey, p. 52.

able, that of all who were buried in the abbey, the coffins of two infants lying in front of the high altar, in the exact spot where they were found, and perhaps the very first who were buried within the walls of the abbey, certainly upwards of six hundred and seventy years ago, are the only two that can be identified.[1] Fordun, our earliest historian, tells us that the Earl of Huntingdon selected his own foundation of Lindores as the burial place of his offspring, and that an infant son of the Earl, named Robert, was buried there, amid the lamentations of the people of England as well as of Scotland.[2] It gives a deeper significance to the little

---

[1] The two small coffins are hewn out of solid red sandstone; they measured respectively 27½ and 30½ inches in length; when discovered in 1846, infants' bones were found in them.

[2] Fordun, Vol. II., p. 277. When the work of clearing out the ruins was progressing, an opening, rudely built up by the side of an almry in the side chapel of the north transept, was discovered. On removing this rude mason-work, two piscinæ were discovered side by side, one round and the other fluted, both as fresh and clean as when newly hewn. The mason-work which concealed them bore no mark of a tradesman's hands, but had all the appearance of having been executed for the purpose of concealing the sacred receptacles, and preserving them from sacrilegious uses. It is worthy of remark, that there are two piscinæ exactly similar to those found in Lindores, in the ancient church of Yardley-Hastings, where the Earl of Huntingdon died. Another piscina has since been discovered in the south transept.

With the exception of three very small fragments, no stone with any inscription has been found. One of these fragments has part of the figure of an ecclesiastic, and the letters J. A. L. (conjectured to be the initials of John, Abbot of Lindores) incised upon it. The inscriptions are so fragmentary and so defaced, that they have not been deciphered. In the year 1839, a massive gold signet ring 'was turned up by the plough immediately north of the abbey wall. It was richly chased, and in as perfect condition as if new from the jewellers. It was of more than usual circumference, passing with ease over the thumb-joint of a powerful man. The signet, which was about the size of a fourpenny-piece, was an amethyst, having a head of Janus cut on it in intaglio. There was an inscription in black letter round the ring, which was not very legible, but the words "Johannes" and "Sacer" were made out.'—*Leighton's History of Fife*, Vol. II., p. 169. There were three Abbots of Lindores of the name of John, but as John Leslie was only Commendator, it is not likely that he ever resided at the abbey. The probability is, that the ring belonged to Abbot John, who renewed

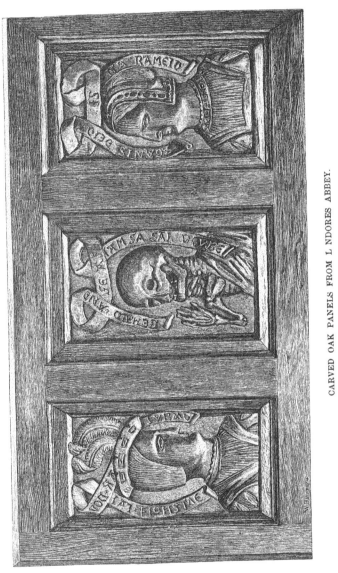

CARVED OAK PANELS FROM LINDORES ABBEY.

coffins to know, that had the infants who were buried in them lived, the course of history would, in all probability, have been changed; their descendants would have been heirs to the throne of Scotland, and Edward I. would have had no pretence on which to found his claims to the Scottish crown.

Kings, warriors, statesmen, who have borne a conspicuous part in history, have trod the courts of the Abbey of Lindores. These are desolate and ruined; but the place where brave men have trod, where brave words have been spoken, and where, for centuries, men worshipped and praised God, can never become, in the eyes of thoughtful men, mere common ground.

---

the charters to the burgesses of Newburgh in 1457, in which case it was nearly 400 years old when found. The person who found the ring left the neighbour-hood shortly afterwards for another part of the country, and if it is still extant, it has in all likelihood passed into hands ignorant of its history. More recently fragments of a chalice of Venetian glass, of beautiful design and workmanship, was found among the lime-rubbish of the ruins. About the same time portions of a latticed window, containing seven or eight *lozens*, with the leaden casing entire, were also discovered. The glass is of coarse quality, thick and opaque; only one or two of the *lozens* have anything like staining or colour upon them. Several small square floor tiles have been found, they are of a dim red hue; on some of them a pattern in cream-colour can be traced. Besides these fragmentary remains, there are three carved oak pannels in the possession of Mr Paton of Dunfermline, which, he was assured, came out of Lindores Abbey. Mr Shepherd of Strathmiglo, from whom Mr Paton acquired these relics, was a man of probity; and when it is considered how comparatively recent the spoliation of the abbey, mentioned in a preceding page, took place, there is nothing improbable in such relics being preserved. The pannels bear all the marks of antiquity, as the engraving given shows. The style of the carvings is the same as the Stirling heads; the form of the letters on the scrolls are ancient, and the words are pure Scottish. They read as follows: 'QUHAT DOTH LAT FLEIIS ME—AS I AM SA SAL YOU BE—AGANIS DEID IS NA REMEID.' The centre pannel measures 9½ inches by 15½, the other two are one inch narrower.

CHAPTER XV

THE BURGH OF NEWBURGH.

Yet more ; around these Abbeys gathered towns
Safe from the feudal castle's haughty frowns ·
Peaceful abodes, where Justice might uphold
Her scales with even hand, and culture mould
The heart of pity, train the mind in care
For rules of life, sound as the time could bear.'

Wordsworth.

IN these days of perfect freedom, where there is scarcely any restriction to our personal liberty, save that we shall do no wrong
to our neighbour, it is scarcely possible to realize the condition
of society when charters were first granted to burghs in Scotland,
or of the necessities which called them forth. Men owned men,
as men own cattle, with this difference, that the former could not
be removed from the soil. The over lord, or ' baron, was supreme
criminal judge within his own barony, and possessed the power
of life and death, and of imprisonment within his own dungeon,'[1]
and it too often happened that the authority of the crown was
powerless to prevent these excessive privileges being exercised
without hardship and caprice.

It helps us to comprehend the condition of society more vividly, to have before us, as it were, the very documents which
completed the purchase of the freedom of a serf and his children,
and to look upon the very warrant that was issued for the capture
of a run-away bondman.

In that most valuable publication, the ' National Manuscripts of

---

[1] Tytler, Vol. I., p. 251.

Scotland,' there are fac-similes of such warrants, and of deeds of sale of serfs, in the reign of Alexander II. (1247). Osulf the Red, and his son Walter, are sold for ten merks. The freedom of Reginald the provost, and his children, is bought ' for twenty merks of sterlings, so that he and his wife and children and all descending from them, may go, return, and stay wherever they please, like other freemen.[1] Later still, in the reign of David II. (A.D. 1369), Brice Wych had conveyed to him the lands of Balloch in Kinross-shire, together with the *bondagiis et nativis*, natives or serfs, on that land.[2]

It was therefore a boon of no common order when men were permitted to unite together in free communities, and to govern themselves. It would be a mistake, however, to imagine that the burgesses were originally of the trading class; the very name *Burg herrs* (*herr*—Lord or Sir—*German*) implies that they were men capable of defending the burg, or fortified place, raised for defence against invaders. Under their protection, and that of the castle which they defended, the trading -class sought shelter for the prosecution of their industry and the sale of their merchandise. It was then as now, commerce and the industries of peace flourished where the strong arm was ready to defend them. Gradually these communities became thriving centres of trade. Enlightened monarchs encouraged them as sources of national wealth, and as a means of promoting the prosperity of the country.

It would therefore be erroneous to suppose that the granting of a charter called trading communities into existence; it found them existing, associated together for mutual help. The history of the early Gilds brings out this latter point most clearly, and it is refreshing to find that these gilds set up something higher than personal gain as the main object of their union. Besides regulating trade, their laws proceed on the assumption that men and women are brothers and sisters, brethren and sistern as they call

---

[1] Part I., *National MS. of Scotland*, p. 31.
[2] Robertson's *Index to Charters*, 85-201.

them. It is evident, however, that these laws having merely the sanction of mutual agreement, could only bind those who chose to continue members of the associated community ; but the granting of a charter immediately invested these internal regulations with the force of law, from which there was no escape, and the obtaining of a charter was therefore a great step in social and political progress.

The churchmen were not slow to encourage these rising communities, and they granted or secured charters, conferring the privileges of burghs on the towns which had arisen in the neighbourhood of their abbeys and cathedrals. Many of the most important cities in the kingdom owe their origin to this connection. The monks of Lindores, in the year 1266, obtained from Alexander III. a charter, erecting 'their town, which is called the new burgh,' into a free burgh. The following is a translation of the charter, 'Alexander, by the grace of God, king of the Scots, to all good men of his whole land, Greeting, know that we, from affection have given, granted, and by this our present charter have confirmed to the religious men, the Abbot and Convent of Lundoris, that they and their successors may have forever their town, which is called New-Burgh, nigh the monastery of Lundoris, a free burgh, and a market in the same, any day in March, with the liberties of burgh and market. Saving in all things the liberties of our burghs. Witnesses, William, Earl of Mar, chamberlain, John of Lambertoun, John of Lyndes, John de Hay and Gillascope Cambell and William Biseth, witnesses, at Stirling, the 4th day of March in the 17th year of our reign' (A.D. 1266).[1] The clause saving 'the liberties of our burghs,' was inserted to protect the rights of royal burghs, some of which, such as Perth, had privileges of trading over extensive districts.

---

[1] William, Earl of Mar, the ninth of that name, was one of the most eminent statesmen of the time in Scotland. Gillascope Cambell is the first of the family of Argyle whose name appears in charter record ; and the charter to Newburgh is the first and only charter in which it occurs.

[2] *Lib. de Lundores*, p. 8.

Such is the first charter of ' the New Burgh of Lindores,' which, notwithstanding its apparently modern name, is of no mean antiquity. It may seem strange that a charter was needed to confer the right of holding a market, when all that is now required is to advertise that a fair is to be held; but fairs at that time were the subjects of special privileges. The fair was a day of perfect liberty, even the fugitive bondman was free from arrest on that day, and though his owner met him in the fair, he dared neither ' chace nor take him.'[1] From the moment that ' the pece of the fair was cryit thar sal na man be takyn, na attachyt within that ilk fair, bot gif he breck the pece of that fair, towart it cummande or within it duelland, or fra thir passand, bot gif he was the king's traytour, or gif he war suilke a mysdour that gyrth of halykyrk an nocht to sauffe hym.' None but the outlaw, the traitor or malefactor of the deepest dye, could be taken during its continuance.[2] It was therefore a day of licence, all the more prized that liberty was at other times so much restricted. In the Saga of ' Grettir the Strong' (A.D. 1029), there is an incident recorded, which is so illustrative of the sacredness in which ' the Peace' was held after it was openly proclaimed, and shows so unmistakeably where this germ of freedom arose, that it is here inserted—Grettir had long been outlawed, and for safety was obliged to live concealed. But he longed to go to the usual spring-tide gathering for the annual sports. Disguised, he sat among the spectators, till they prayed him, a stranger, ' to wrestle with some one.' He said, ' well, if ye are so fain ye must handsel' ('promise, sanctioned by the clasping of hands') ' me peace here at the *Thing*, and until such time as I come back to my home.' They all sprang up and said that so would they do indeed. One of those present then proclaimed ' the peace.' ' Herewith I establish peace betwixt all men and this same guest, who sits here, and so is named; that is to say, all men of rule, and goodly bonders, and all men young and fit to bear arms,

---

[1] *Leges Burgorum*, 88.
[2] *Ib.*, No. 86; and Robertson's *Early Kings*, Vol. I., p. 304.

and all other men of the country side of Heron-ness *Thing* whence-soever any may have come here, of men named or unnamed. Let us handsel safety and full peace to that unknown new-comer, yclept Guest, by name for game, wrestling and all glee, for abiding here and going home, whether he has need to fare over water, or over land, or over ferry; safety shall he have, in all steads named and unnamed, ever so long as he needs for his coming home whole, under faith holden.' When Grettir threw off his disguise they saw the dreaded outlaw before them, and 'they gazed on one another,' enraged that they had been duped. Grettir taunted them and said,

'Round about lay head to head
For belike they heard my name,
And must balance peace and shame.'

Then spake Hialti the son of Thord, 'So shall it not be, we shall hold to our peace and troth given though we have been beguiled, for I will not men shall have such a deed to follow after, if we depart from that peace that we ourselves have settled and hand-selled. All thanked him therefor, and deemed that he had done as a great chief.'[1]

As soon too as the 'Peace of the Fair' was proclaimed, the special privileges of the burghers were in abeyance, and the humblest trader who exposed his goods in the market was on an equality with them for the time; a regulation which purchasers would value, as it broke in upon the monopoly which at other times prevailed. So jealously were the liberties of the Fair guarded, that if any stranger trader broke the laws or 'Peace of the Fair,' he was tried and punished, not by the magistrates of the burgh, but with the true Norse principles of justice, in a temporary court of 'his peers,' the community for the time being of the Fair. It was also provided, 'gif a mute (a plea in court) be raisyt betwene a burges and a marchand, it sall be endyt wythin the third flud of

---

[1] *Grettir the Strong*, pp. 212-216.

the sea.'[1] The latter provision is one of which modern litigants would be only too glad to have the advantage.

It will, however, give a better idea of the privileges of burghs, and of the rights and duties of burgesses, to quote some of the laws which regulated them. These laws (*Leges Burgorum*) date as far back as the reign of David I. (1124-1153), whose enlightened policy did so much to promote the prosperity of the kingdom.

One of the first of the 'laws of the burghs' exhibits the burgess in a very different capacity from that of a peaceful trader. It secures to him the right of combat for the settlement of disputes. A defender, instead of submitting his case to the judgment of an assize, could demand that it be tried by single combat between himself and the pursuer.[2] However incredible it may now appear, our forefathers deemed trial by single combat an appeal to the justice of God. They reckoned the advantages of superior strength, and dexterity in the use of arms of no account, in the firm belief that the righteous cause would prevail. In narrating the preparation for a trial by single combat, Sir Walter Scott makes one of the characters of his story of 'The Talisman,' say, 'What if he should lose the day?' 'It is impossible,' is the immediate reply, 'his opponent is guilty.' From this barbarous mode of deciding the justice of his cause, a burgess when 'passit elde' (above sixty years old), could only be excused from fighting his challenger 'by the athis of xii men suilk as himself.'[3]

According to an old authority, a man who lawfully declined battle, 'is oblissed to acquit and charge himself be the judgement of God; that is be hote iron if he be a frieman, or be water if he be ane husbandman,' apparently proceeding on the assumption that hot iron could not burn, or water drown, the innocent.[4]

---

[1] *Leges Burgorum*, Nos. 54 and 6; Robertson's *Scotland under her Early Kings*, Vol. I., p. 304.

[2] *Leges Burgorum*, No. 13.   [3] *Ib.*, No. 22.

[4] *Regiam Majestatim*, Book IV., cap. III. Trial by the ordeal of hot iron is still practised in Hindostan. In 1873 the Rao of Kurapore caused one of his subjects to prove his innocence of an offence with which he was charged, by

A second law declares that 'na man may be the kyngis burges, but gif he may do service to the kyng.'[1] The service here meant military service, in which the burgess was bound to appear armed, and to follow the king's host into battle.

By the statute of James I., cap. 123, A.D. 1429, it was enacted that 'every burgess having fifty pounds in gudes sall be armed like a gentleman, and a burgess with twenty pounds in gudes, with hat, habergeon, sword and buckler, bow, shaif [of arrows] and knife. And he that is na bowman have a gude axe and sure weapons.' By statute James II., cap. 64, A.D. 1457, it was enacted that 'a pair of bowbutts be set up in every parioch and schuting be usyt, and that ilk man withyn fiftie and past twelve schute six schottes at the least under pain of two pennies, to be given to them that comes to the bow marke to drink, and this from Pasch to All-hallowemes,' i.e. from about April to the end of October.

The place known as The Butts, at the west end of the north gardens, marks the place where archery was practised in Newburgh.

Burgesses were also bound to hold watch and ward during the night, and from every house, that of widows excepted, 'thar sal ane wachman be haldyn to cum furth, when the wakstaff gais fra dure to dure wha sall be of eylde, and sall gang till his wach, with tua wapings at the ryngyng of the curfeu, and sall wach till the dawyng of the daye.'[2] Another law provided that 'gif a burges be attachyt ututh the brugh for det, or ony mysgilt, his nichtburis sal pas to borrow hym [become bail for him] in their own proper dyspence.'[3] A provision which shows they were leagued together for mutual defence, and supports the correct-

---

holding a red-hot ploughshare in both his hands, after four or five *pepul* leaves tied over with thread had been placed in them. The accused had to repeat the following words with his face towards the sun :—'Thou sun-god, if I am guilty of the crime, punish me; if not, let me escape unscathed from the ordeal.' —*Bombay Gazette.*

[1] *Leges Burgorum,* No. 49.

[2] *Ib.,* No. 81. This primitive custom continued in Stirling down to the year 1855.—*Scotland, Social and Domestic*—Dr C. Rogers, p. 45.

[3] *Leges Burgorum,* No. 51.

ness of the meaning ascribed to the name burgh. 'The word broch,' both in England and lowland Scotland, meant one who pledged himself for another, or became bail for him. The 'brough' or 'burgh' was, therefore, a community united together in a common lot or cause, pledges and securities for each other.'[1]

All, however, who dwelt in the burgh were not on the same footing. None could enjoy the rights and privileges of a burgess, unless he was owner of a rood of land within it. On this point it has been said the burgesses 'were old free landed proprietors, partly of the neighbouring estate, but chiefly of land within the territory of the towns themselves. Most of them carried on trade, some probably also handicrafts. But the possession of town-land is the distinguishing mark of these earliest burghers. To this possession alone was full citizenship everywhere attached in the first movements of civic life.'[2] Those who were not burgesses appear to have been as summarily dealt with as they were elsewhere. If, for instance, 'ony kemstaris [wool-combers] levis the burgh to dwell with uplandys men,' it did not matter whether it was for better wages or better treatment, they might at once be 'takyn and prysonit,' on the ground that there was 'sufficient worke to occupie thaim within burgh.'[3] Such was the primitive mode in which our forefathers dealt with strikes in their days.

Absolute freedom, however, attached to the burgess. In Royal Burghs every new-made burgess swore fealty to the king, to the bailies, and to the community of which he was admitted a burgess. He was amenable to no other authority. If attacked and carried before another court, he could claim 'hys awen cros and market;' in other words, he could demand to be tried before the court of his own burgh by his fellow-burgesses. This boon was too valuable to be left unclaimed, and continued in force until the abolition of heritable jurisdictions, in the reign of George II. Another element of freedom pertained to burghs. If a

---

[1] Burton's *History of Scotland*, Vol. II., p. 170.
[2] *English Gilds*, p. xciii. [3] *Leges Burgorum*, No. 103.

thryll[1] or bondman came into a burgh, and possessed a burgage
property for twelvemonths and a day, he was thenceforth free.
This important privilege runs in these words—'Gif oney mannis
thryll barounis or knychtis cummys to burgh and byis a borowage,
and duellis in his borowage a twelfmoneth and a day foroutyn
challange of his lorde, or of his bailye he sall evir mare be fre as a
burges within that kingis burgh, and joyse the fredoume of that
burgh.'[2]

Privileges so valuable were justly prized and jealously guarded.
'In evir ilk burgh of the Kynrick of Scotland, the mare or alder-
man of that ilk burgh sall ger xii of the lelest burges and of the
wysast of the burgh swer be thair gret athe, that all the lawys
and the usyt custumys lauchfully thai sall yeme and maintene
efter thar powar.'[3]

The burgh of Newburgh was not at first a Royal Burgh. It
held under the Abbot of Lindores. Its courts were opened in his
name, and the burgesses were bound to do the abbot service; just
as in Royal Burghs, the courts were opened in the king's name,
and the burgesses were bound to do the king military service.
In a list in the chartulary of Lindores, headed, 'John Chalmaris
acowmpt of ye geir he hes in keipping in O^r Chalm^r and wardrop
xvij.^{o} Aug^{ti} Anno Do^i Mill^o v^o xxx^o the following occurs :—'Item

---

[1] Thyrll, afterwards Thrall, was originally one who had his ear drilled or bored
in token of servitude. In Exodus, chap. xxi. ver. 6, we read, 'Then his master
shall bring him unto the judges; he shall also bring him to the door, or unto the
door-post; and his master shall bore his ear through with an awl; and he shall
serve him for ever.' An older English version has the latter clause, 'Thirlie his
eare with an awl.' In England the ears of serfs were publicly bored at the
church door.—Ellis's *Old English Poets*—Richardson *Dictionary*, *voce* Thrall.
Churchyards seem to have been the recognised place for deciding questions
affecting thralls or serfs. On the 12th May 1340, Sir David of Wemyss, sheriff
of Fyff, and an assize, assembled in the churchyard (*cimiterio*) of the parish
church of Katel, decided that 'Alan, son of the deceased Constantine, and his two
sons, Richard and Alan, were the bondmen of the Abbot of Dunfermelyn.
Registrum de Dunfermelyn, p. 261.

[2] *Leges Burgorum*, No. 15.   [3] *Ibid.*, No. 112.

twa bowss w^t hare & glw [gloves]. Item ix French halberts. It. vi Scotts halberts. It. x aksis [Lochaber axes]. It. ix ged-ward staves [Jedburgh staves]. It. xvij. speirs & ane bagāll heft.'[1] Arms evidently kept in store for the abbot's *men*.[2]

The charter of Alexander erecting the burgh is in very general terms, no constitution being prescribed. It depended therefore entirely on the abbot and convent what privileges were conferred on the new-made burgesses. They appear to have immediately conveyed to them the town *rudes* and the lands of Wodrife, and to have granted them ample freedom in the management of their own affairs. From the preamble of the charter executed by the abbot and convent in favour of the burgesses in 1457,[3] a transla-tion of which is given in the appendix, it appears that the original charter and the muniments of the burgh had been lost or destroyed during the devastating wars which commenced with the struggle for independence; and at the earnest and continued entreaties of the burgesses for a renewal of their writs, the monks granted the renewal charter, which is still preserved. It confirms the rights of the burgesses to their tenements by all their ancient marches; grants them the privilege of using and enjoying the 'Laws of the Burghs,' of electing their own magistrates, of holding courts, of punishing transgressors, of banishing the unworthy, and con-firms them in the exercise of their rights and liberties, as freely as any burgh of the same kind in the kingdom.

A notarial transcript of the charters in favour of the burgesses, was made by John Wyntoun, who designs himself presbyter of the diocese of St Andrews, Bachelor in Decrees, and notary public. The preamble sets forth that the abbot and convent in chapter

---

[1] *Chartulary of Lindores*, p. 32. *See* Appendix No. IV.

[2] The whole list is curious, embracing almost every article necessary for household use. Among other articles, 'ane clairschew' (Gaelic, *Clarsach*), or harp is mentioned. The names of many of the articles indicate a foreign origin, affording another proof how dependent Scotland was at that time on foreign countries for articles requiring skill and design in their manufacture.

[3] *Chartulary of Lindores*, pp. 3, 4.

assembled, received the burgesses in the chapter house of the abbey, on the 13th July 1457, and produced the abbey duplicates of the charters, which the notary, in his official capacity, declared were entire and undefaced. The notary having read first the one conferring the privileges, and the other the lands of the burgh, to the burgesses ; and afterwards explained them in the vulgar tongue, they acknowledged them to be the real charters, and the transcript which had been previously prepared was then formally ratified. This transcript is preserved in the archives of New-burgh ; and it has this additional interest attached to it, that it contains the names of the monks and of the owners of the burgh lands at the time. From it we learn that the burgesses did not acquire the lands of Wodrife in 1457, as is commonly supposed, but had held them previously, most probably from a time almost coeval with the charter of Alexander III., A.D. 1266.[1]

---

[1] The names of the monks, and of the owners of the burgh lands mentioned in the charter, and also a translation of the charter to the burgh lands, are inserted in the appendix. There are several verbal inaccuracies in the copy of the charter printed in *Liber Marie de Lundoris.* In the twelfth line, *stat* is printed for *scatet* (bursts forth), the latter word describes the rising or bursting out of the spring most accurately. In the fifteenth line *juxta crag* is printed instead of *Myl* crag, the name by which the crag is still known. With two exceptions, the lands forming the boundary of the burgh are still known by the names men-tioned in the charter. The first of these names is the lands of St Katharine, now known by the name of the 'White Park,' and the other is the Brodland, now obsolete. The 'Horn and the Ring of the Blakarne' are also now unknown by these names, but in the preceding generation they were familiar terms. The 'Horn' is the projecting craig on the north-east of the Blackcairn, and the 'Ring' is the entrenchment encircling the summit of the hill described in a pre-vious page. The next point in the line of march is the South-running well. At the perambulation, or redding of the marches of the burgh, the head of the last-admitted burgess has, from time immemorial, been 'washed' at this well, and is generally made the occasion of fun and frolic. Superstitious virtues used to be attached to the waters of a spring whose stream runs southwards. In the year 1623, Thomas Greave was tried before the High Court of Justiciary for, among other offences, 'cureing be sorcerie and witchcraft, and making of certain croces and singes (signs) off David Chalmer in Lethame, and be causeing wasche his sark in ane south-rynnand watter, and thairefter putting it upone him, quhairby he

James VI. by royal charter confirmed (25th November 1593) to the community their right to the lands of Wodrife and hill adjacent; and on 29th January 1631, Charles I. not only con-

---

ressauit his helthe.' 'Item, at Martimes 1621, Elspeth Thomesone, sister of John Thomesone, portioner of Pitwar, being visseit with ane grevous seiknes, the said Thomas promeist to cure hir thairof.' For this purpose he and her two brothers walked during the night from Corachie to Burley, a distance of twelve miles, in absolute silence the whole way. 'And at the ffurde be-eist Burley, in ane south-rynning watter, he thair wusche hir sark . . . and cuming hame with the sark, pat the samyn upon hir, and cureit hir of hir seiknes.'—Pitcairn's *Criminal Trials*, Vol. III., pp. 555-557. From time out of mind the family of Hume-Byers have possessed a charm called the 'Black Penny.' When any cattle are afflicted with madness, the Black Penny is dipped in a well, the water of which runs towards the south (this is indispensable). Sufficient water is then drawn and given to the animals infected. Popular belief still formally upholds the value of this remedy (1866).—Henderson's *Folk Lore of the Northern Counties of England and the Borders*, p. 132. It is more than probable that the 'washing' the head of the new-made burgess at the South-running well of the Blackcairn had its origin in a similar superstitious belief. There are several names on the line of the boundary of the burgh, which, though not mentioned in the charter, are of such manifest antiquity that they deserve notice. Craigsparrow is a corruption of the Gaelic Craig-beàrnach (*ch* is silent in pronunciation), the craig with gaps or clefts, a feature which distinguishes it. Dovan's Den is nearly an accurate pronunciation of the Gaelic *Domhain*, signifying deep—the 'Deep Den.' Both of these names evince that marked perception of the features of natural scenery which pervades Gaelic nomenclature. In the same neighbourhood there is a rock called Craig Sheach, which is, as nearly as possible, the pronunciation of *Craig Sithich*, the Gaelic for 'The Craig of the Fairies,'—the sole remaining relic of the belief in the 'peaceful folk' in this neighbourhood. The level summit of the craig, before the wood grew up around it, commanded a prospect which rivalled in beauty the poet's dreams of Fairyland. The Hare Slack is a hollow at the east end of Craigsparrow; or, to use its proper name, *Craig-bearnach* (Craig-bèarney), the word '*harz*,' derived from Armoric, means a bound or limit, and the 'Hare Slack' marks the limit of the burgh lands, and the jurisdiction of the magistrates at that point. There are numerous places throughout Scotland having the prefix 'Hare,' or 'Hore.' 'The Harestane marks the boundary or limit betwixt the parishes of St Vigeans and Carmyllie.'—A. Jervise, *Pro. of Soc. of Antiq.*, Vol. IV., p. 498. There were 'Harey Stanes' in the parish of Collessie, which at one time must have marked the boundary of some barony or estate. They have been removed within the memory of the present generation.

firmed their rights to these lands, but also to their tenements in the burgh, and to all their privileges, used and wont, of electing magistrates and serjeands, holding courts, punishing and banishing offenders, and of proclaiming a free fair within the burgh yearly on the day of St Katharine the virgin, to continue for two days.

Before the first generation of burgesses had passed away, they had a dispute with their lords superior; the burgesses objecting to pay a merk yearly for every brew-house with an acre of land within the burgh. The case was deemed of so much importance, that a jury of barons, free-holders, and others worthy of trust (*dignos fide*) was summoned by Sir Robert of Keth, Mareschal of Scotland, Justiciar benorth the Forth, to decide the point at issue; and it has been cited to show that trial by jury was in use in Scotland at that period (A.D. 1309). The court met in the chapter-house of Lindores on the Thursday before the feast of St Peter (29th June), and besides the jury, there were present on the occasion,—the Bishop of St Andrews, Thomas de Ranulph, lieutenant from the Forth to Orkney; the Abbot of Arbroath, at that time Chancellor of Scotland, the Official of St Andrews, Sir Michael of Wemyss, knight, and John of Dundemore, all of whom appended their seals to the award of the jury. The decision and the names of the jury are recorded in the chartulary of the abbey, and from it we learn, among other circumstances, that Robert of Perth and William the baker, obtained permission from the Justiciar to appear and speak for all their neighbours in Newburgh.[1] The

---

[1] Robert of Keth acted as joint-Justiciar 'between the Forth and the Mountains,' under Edward I. A writ, still preserved, for the payment of his salary of 40 marks, was issued on 25th October 1305.—*His. Doc*. of Scotland*, Vol. II., p. 492. Sir Robert afterwards espoused the fortunes of Bruce, who, in reward for his faithful services, bestowed on him large possessions. In virtue of his office of Great Mareschal of Scotland, he led the horse at Bannockburn, and by his prowess eminently contributed to the success of the day. He signed the famous letter to the Pope. In the humiliating reign of David II., he fell, with many of his kindred, at the disastrous battle of Dupplin, 12th August 1332.

representatives of the burgh challenged Adam Gray, one of the jurors, because he was frequently employed in the abbot's service; their objection was sustained, but the assize decided that the burgesses were justly bound to pay the ferme which they had appealed against.[1]

The wars and devastations which had destroyed the charters seem also to have been fatal to the other records of Newburgh. With the exception of the charter to the lands of Wodrife and hill adjoining, the earliest record preserved is a court book beginning A.D. 1457 and ending 1480. It consists of 109 leaves of narrow folio, and contains a record of judicial proceedings before the magistrates, embracing also the proceedings at the head courts, and transfers of property in the burgh. Unfortunately the individuals who recorded these proceedings seem to have been for the most part very imperfectly educated. The spelling is much more inaccurate than that ordinarily met with in the writings of the period, partaking more of a phonetic character than of a regular rule, and the penmanship is so bad that it is difficult to decipher.

The period embraced by this court book extends from the last years of the reign of James II., to nearly the end of that of James III.; but not once is there the slightest allusion to any

---

[1] *Chartulary of Lindores*, pp. 11-13. An abstract of the case, and the names of the jury, are given in the appendix. The Bishop of St Andrews mentioned as being present was William Lamberton. He was one of the small band of patriots who joined the standard of Bruce when he threw down the gauntlet to Edward I. About two years before the meeting of the jury at Lindores Abbey, he was taken prisoner (immediately after the battle of Methven), and being found in armour, he was carried in fetters to England, and imprisoned in Winchester Castle. Edward was much exasperated against him, and petitioned the Pope to depose him, as he had supplied Bruce not only with money, but men, from the estates belonging to the bishopric. His sacred functions alone saved him from being executed. While a prisoner in Winchester he was allowed for his daily expenses 6d., for one man-servant to attend him 3d., one boy ½d., and a chaplain to say mass daily 1½d. It was Bishop Lamberton who completed the Cathedral of St Andrews. He died A D. 1328.—Keith's *Bishops*, p. 22.

matter of general history, or even to laws affecting trade, or the internal government of the country. There are, however, many notices illustrative of burghal life, and in the following pages selections have been made of those that throw light on the condition of society, or on the customs and forms of procedure of the period.

CHAPTER XVI.

THE BURGH COURT, A.D. 1457-1480.

' Within the narrow bounds of home
  Their cares were fixed. But all the more
They prized their chartered-freedom,
  And with jealous hold maintained
The precious gift; that justice might prevail
  And law and order reign supreme.'

Anon.

IN the end of the fifteenth century manufacturing pursuits were at a low ebb in Scotland. With the exception of small quantities of coarse woollen cloths called 'Scottis gray,' and 'Pabyllis [Peebles] quhit,' almost the only other articles exported were,— wool, hides, salmon, and, occasionally, some native furs, or other raw produce. The imports from the Netherlands (to which the foreign trade of Scotland at that period was almost exclusively confined) embraced every article beyond the commonest necessaries of life, in quantities now to be found in every country town, but which had then to be specially commissioned from abroad. In the 'Ledger of Andrew Halyburton, Conservator of the Privileges of the Scotch nation in the Netherlands (1492–1503),' there is preserved a most valuable record of the exports and imports of the period, and a careful examination of it shows that manufacturing pursuits were then in a backward state in Scotland. When cloth had to be dyed of some prized colour it could not be done at home. Under date March 1502, the following entry occurs, 'Item lyttit [dyed] a stek [piece] of this cloth red in Medilburgh,

and sent it him again in the barg of Dundye.'[1]   The necessity for
this transaction is the more remarkable, as dyeing was a household
art, which has only fallen into disuse in the present century; and
more especially, as the making of tartan in the Highlands required
a knowledge of dyeing shades of varying brightness.   In the
same account, however, there is a charge for '4 pipis tassyl'
(*Dipsacus Fullolum*), which shows that the native manufacturers
had attained and practised the art of dressing woollen cloths.
But everything requiring skill in its manufacture, 'pottis, pannys,
yetlin (cast-iron utensils), paper, canvas, bedsteads, and when elaborate workmanship was required, tombstones had to be brought
from abroad.[2]   Even so late as the year 1724, the following entry
occurs in the Council Records of Newburgh : ' October 21st, Sicklyk
it was moved to rectiffie the weights and to cause bring them
from abrod of brasse mettall, from ane stan to ane halfe pound.'
    In the unskilled condition of home manufactures, the main de-
pendence of the inhabitants of small burghs was in the cultivation
of the burgh lands. That the burgesses of Newburgh were humble
tradesmen, having no foreign dealings, unless Stephen Orme, the
abbey factor, be reckoned an exception, is apparent from the fact
that the abbot and monks of Lindores had, in the beginning of
the sixteenth century, to employ burgesses of Perth and of Aberdeen
to purchase goods for them abroad.   It is not to be wondered at,
therefore, that the Burgh Records of Newburgh, in the end of the
fifteenth century, should almost exclusively be taken up with
judicial proceedings affecting the internal affairs of the burgh,
and with enactments for the management of their common-good
lands, on the produce and pasturage of which they mainly depended for subsistence.
    It serves still further to show the humble position that New-
burgh occupied in the trading and commercial world in the end
of the sixteenth century, to know that the convention of Royal
Burghs, which at that time apportioned the taxation leviable from

---

[1] *Halyburton's Ledger*, p. 275.   [2] *Ib.*, pp. 161-163, 215-270.

the trading community, laid a tax of five pounds thirteen shillings on Abernethy, a burgh of barony in 1579,[1] and it was not until 1613 that Newburgh was deemed of sufficient importance to be worth taxation. On the 15th of September of that year, the following entry occurs in the records of the proceedings of the Convention: 'The quhilk day, the saids commissionars of burrowes, understanding that the burghs of Falkland and Newburgh, and certane other burghs ar frie regall burrowes, and injoyes all the liberties of frie regall burrowes, and as zitt ar nether enrolled with the remanent frie regall burrowes of this realme nor beirs anye portabell chairges with them; thairfore they ordeane James Winrahame thair agent to caus summond the said burghs to compeir before thame the next generall conventione of burrows to be haldin at the burgh of Kirkcaldie, to the effect they may inroll themselfis with the saidis remanent burrowes and beir all portabell chairges with thame accordinglie, and the agent to produce his diligence heiranent the nixt general convention.'[2] Notwithstanding this resolution, Newburgh does not appear even to have been 'enrolled,' or to have sent a representative to the Convention of Royal Burghs; a circumstance which still further corroborates the un-importance of its trade at that period.

The following selections have been extracted from the oldest volume of the Burgh Records of Newburgh, as calculated to throw light on the occupations and social condition of burghal society four hundred years ago.

It may be premised, that the Chapel of St Katherine, in which the burgh courts were held, stood on the site of the present parish church.

> 'Ye burrow curt of ye Newburgh haldyn in ye chapel of Sant Katryn ye xxiii day of Januar ye yeir of god MCCCCLIX yeirs be henry of Kynglassy & John of Kynhard balzies of ye said

---

[1] *Records of Convention of Royal Burghs*, A.D. 1295-1597, p. 93.
[2] *Ib.*, 1597-1614, p. 432.

burgh ye quhylk day ye soytts callit ye curt affirmyt ye
absens ar patent.'

'Ye quhylk day Alex^r Robertson was in amerciate for he
wrangwyssly hylde fra hary of Kynglassy ye balze xx sh
of usual monay of Scotland qu^h ye assyis fand ye said Alex^r
awand be his awn grantyn.'

'New assise ipo [imprimo] Stevyn phylp, John Thomson,
John of Wemes, James lyndsay, John blak, John souzour,
David Anderson, John of hawkston, John Phylp, Smy^t
nicol of bat, James Cordon, Symon Cawart, John Jolly.'

'Ye qu^k day it west fundyn be ye assyis yat Wat of ross
wranguessly analzit part of ye wodrif wytout lyfe.

The expression 'ye soytts callit,' signifies that the names of
the *soytours*, or vassals who were bound to attend the court of their
over-lord, had been called over. In the case of a burgh court,
every burgess was bound to attend, and if absent without a lawful excuse was fined. Every 'Soytour was oblished to make
aith that he sall leallelie pronounce lauchful and trew sentence
according to the knowledge given him be God.' Skene, from
whom this quotation is made, says, 'the office was verie profitable for furthering of justice.'[1] The law regulating the 'assise'
has already been quoted. The absence of surnames, both in the
case of the bailies, and in some of the members of the assize,
shows that they had not become universal at that period; but we
have in the list an indication of how a class of surnames arose, as
in a subsequent generation the descendants of John of Wemes and
John of Hawkston would in all likelihood be known simply by the
names of Wemyss and Hawkston, now Haxton.

'Ye quhylk day, 23 April 1460, app^t [appeared] in plain
curt befor ye balzie and ye communytie Wylzeam gren-
horn and his wyf batht togydd^r on y^r awin fre wyll and

---

[1] *De Verborum Significatione.*

resyngit fra ym in ye balzeis hands John Kynhard, twa
ruds of land lyand on ye suth half of ye stret betweyn ye
lands of rob^t Smytht ayres on ye est part and ye lands of
Scher patrik of Kyrk Chapellan on ye west part in ye
favour of John Andyrson, inhabitant of Kynhard and ye
said Wylzeam and his wyf Marion swoyr ye gret bodily
atht finally yat yai suld hald al thyngs spokyn and
poyntyt anent ye said resyngnacion ferm and stabyll and
wad nar revok word yrof na yit nan by on y^r behalf, and
y^r upon ye said John rasyt an instrument.'

'Ye quhylk day Henry of Kynglassy & John of Kynhard
balyeis of ye said burth comyng toggdder after nwyn
wytht ye officiaris and nyburs, and gaf seissyng frely and
frankly of ii rudes of land ('liand as above') tyl ane
worthy man John Anderson and tyl his wyf jonet and
y^r ayrs executors and assygneis as use of burgth befor y^r
wytnes John Thomson, Symon bell.'

The foregoing is an example of the mode of transferring
heritable subjects in those days. It had its advantages; taking
place before witnesses in open day, and on the ground, in a small
community, a transfer of property thus made was known to all.

23 April 1460, 'ye qu^k day Thomas Sclater amerciate for he
wrangyssly brak ye arestment mad be ye officiars of ye
burgth for ye lords mayll.'

This refers to the *maill* or feu-ferme which every owner of
a rood or croft of land in the burgh was bound to pay to the
abbot and convent of Lindores, in terms of the charter of the
burgh, and in virtue of which they held their crofts. The
words of the charter are, 'rendering to us and our successors
yearly in firm burgage six pennies of current money for every
rood of land at terms used and wont.' Had the 'maills' which
are now payable to the schoolmaster, been specified in grain,

the amount exigible from each croft would have now been very considerable.

> '13 June 1460, 'ye qu^k it was ordand and assentit be ye comunytie of ye burgh yat nan suld be resavyt in hospitalite in hevy schaht of nytburs onder ye pain of viij. s.'

It was one of the 'Laws of the Burghs' that 'na man wonnande in burgh aw to herbery ony strangear in his house langar than a nycht, bot gif he becum borch for hym as a lauchfull man.'[1] That is, cautioner, pledge or surety, for him. This was the more necessary, as the king's chamberlain, when he held his justice-air, or circuit court, made special inquiry whether any strangers were harboured in the burgh,[2] obviously for the purpose of seeing that none who had fled from justice were concealed.

> 4 June 1461. 'It And^u lambert hath put hym in the balzeis wyl for ye wrangous passyng to ye lordes curt.'

This was a direct infringement of the rights of a burgess, and a surrender of the valuable privilege of being tried by his peers. One of the laws of the burghs provided that if a burgess 'be summonde to apper in the kyngis (or Lord Superior's Court) he aw to cum thar and essoinye hym be the court of the burgh befor his bailze, he sall do full rycht.'[3] And another provided that 'he aw and sall be demyt be his peris in burgh be law of burgh.'[4] These privileges were most properly jealously guarded, and the infringement of them summarily punished. So late as the year 1725, Harie Coupar, dyster, was summoned before the magistrates of Newburgh 'for going to another court contrair to the Acts of the brough, and compeiring and acknowledging he did goe by the court ;' he was fined in the sum of four pounds Scots.

---

[1] *Leges Burgorum*, 85.
[2] *Ancient Laws of the Burghs*, p. 122.
[3] *Leges Burgorum*, No. 56.
[4] *Leges Burgorum*, No. 7.

Sederunt 22 June 1463. 'It: ye samyn day John of Rossy,
James Cordinar, Nycoll of Bat, John Wylson ilk ane
amerciamet for ye wrangess brekyn of ye statutes of y^e
Wedurouf and y^t wes gewyn for dom be ye deliverās of
a syss: It: all ye nithburres has statuit y^t na schep cu^m
w^t in ye Wydrouf quhil ye corne be of ye grund and
ilka ma^n suld hald on his awyn grys a kow or a horss in
tedyr, and gyff yai war foundyn loss ye pownd-lan sould
be iiij. d.

The *pownd-lan* here mentioned is the *pund* or poind for tres-
passing on a neighbour's ground and destroying his crops. Burgh
land, indeed much of the land of the country was held in run-rig,
and disputes arising from trespass were endless. In a subsequent
period of the history of the burgh, we shall have occasion to
notice the measures that were adopted for the prevention of
encroachments, and for the protection of the rights and crops of
individuals.

'It: ye sam day John blak and Symon Cullward wes mayd
ffrends in ye chapell, and Symon Cullward sould pay
betwix y^t and Wytsonday nixt to cum, a pownd of wax
and John black a haff a pownd to Sant Katt^n.'

2 June 1466, 'ye q^lk day apr^t John ye ramsay son and ayr
to ye lard of Clatt and of ye lords behalf Abbot of
lundors and mad ye balzeis requist to rasave angus
paterson in fawar tyl a n'bour and gyf bym cast of ye
lands w^t ye ptinents ye q^lk Jonet Kay gaff in fawars to
ye Thom rogerson in fawars of ye forsaid angus and ye
forsaid balzeis and comunite grantit to rasawf hym thank-
fully for ye lords cause.'

'1466, 14 January, Stewyn phylp and William Smitht
balzheis, alswa ye samyn day Thom rogerson askit at ye
balzheis gyf he had lawborows of ye lard of Mugdrowm

and he ordand y^r w^t & he tuk wytness of ye   .
*and of Sir Andrew Lesly and Davy Lesly.'

The Leslies of Ballinbriech held numerous properties all round the neighbourhood, and though no residence is mentioned in connection with the names of the two witnesses adduced, the probability is, that they were members of that family.

> 'Ye xvii. day of ye moneth of October [1466] yir p-sons hav fund pfyt and spedfull and has enactit for to set ye Wodriffe for vii. yeir to xx. ten^{ts} for lx. b of beir and ye Threpland for v. yeir for iii. b. to ye common pfyt and xx. akars of ye hyl abowt ye fyndcraig and ye blakcarn, ye first yher mail fre and for ye iv. yher tak ii.s ye akr.'
> 'Henry Smyth, John Anderson, Bailies.'

The 'Threpland' lay to the west of the town, but from the complete alteration of the boundaries of the fields the name is now obsolete. The word *threp* or *throp* in old English, signifies 'The meeting of the cross roads.'[1] There are many places in Scotland of the same name, and from it the surname of Threipland is, without doubt, derived. On the 1st August 1259 Thomas, Abbot of Lundoris, concluded a composition with Richard, Bishop of Aberdeen, regarding 'the land which is called *threpland*, between the land of Bondynton and the burn of Gethyn.'[2] The 'Fyndcraig' [Fincraig] from the Gaelic *Fion*, white, fair, or beautiful, still retains its name.

> Sed^t. 26 August 1467. 'Alswa ye curt akwardit y^t yar be na lawt^s in ye chapell and na thyng intill it bot godds service and it y^t it is in it be deludit w^t in lawefull day under ye pain of viij^d.'

---

[1] Edmunds' *Traces of History in Names of Places*, p. 269.
[2] *Registrum Aberdonense*, Vol. I., p. 26.

The foregoing decree is not without its lessons in the present day; it shows that our fathers felt that the employment of the house of God for the transactions of daily life had a tendency, by the power of association, to weaken the solemnity of the meeting between God and His creatures therein, and decreed accordingly.

> Sed^t. 13 January 1467. 'ye quylk day Stephyn Phylp grantit y^t he wess burgess of Edinburth, be ye tenor of ye comyssi^n ye q^k he pnt in ye curt.'

The frequent mention of persons of the name of Philp in the Burgh Records shows that they were an influential family at this period, in the town and neighbourhood. A century later the last person who exercised authority as resident Abbot of Lindores, was, there is reason to conclude, named John Philp.

> 10 Feby. 1467. 'John of Kynhard and Thomas Rogson, bailies. John of Rossy ye ar amerciate forspekyn i^n ye curt w^t optenyt lyff, and y^t wess gyffen for duym.'

> '20 July 1468, John of Kynhard & Thomas Rogerson bal-zeis, ye s̄ day Thomas Rogerson accusit Stewyn phylp for ye wrangus accusyn of ye ballze ī to ye lords curt ye q^k suld be cureckit be his newburhs, alswa ye sayd Stewyn was accus^t y^t wrangusly he hayd brocekyn ye hath and ye obligato^n y^t he had mayd to ye cōite off ye town, and he declynyt ye balze, and sayd he wayd not be cureckyt be hym. It: ye balze charth ye serjandys lay yar wandys on hym, and chargh hym to reman in ye towbuthe tyl he shwth a ransuably caws why he declynyt his balze, and he sayd he wald pass furth w^t all ye charghiis off law ande he wuld not obey to balze, no serjands nadyr.'

The 'wandys' of the serjeants here referred to were part of the equipment of serjeand. By Act of Parliament, James I.,

1426, 'it was statute and ordained that ilk officiar of the kingis, as maire, or kingis serjand and Barrone serjand sall not pass in the countrie nor Barrone serjand in the Barronie, but ane horne and his wand, and that sall be in this manner. The kingis officiar sall have an horne and ilk ane a read wand of three quarters of ane zairde lang at the least, and the officiars of the regalitie ane wand of the samin length, the ane end reade and the other end quhite, and an horne quhair he passes within the Regalitie. The Barron serjand ane horne and ane quhite wand of ane elne lang. The serjand of the Burgh ane read wand allanerlie like the Kingis officiar, and as oft as he beis fundin without his wand in the Burgh hee sall pay aucht shillings unforgiven to the king.'

The title of serjeant is not now used in connection with officers of burghs, but at the time of the translation of the authorized version of the Bible, they were so designated. Acts chap. xvi. ver. 35. 'And when it was day, the magistrates sent the serjeants, saying, Let those men go.'

> Sed. 5 Oct. 1468 'ye quhylk day, John Aytkyn wess mayd burges w^n ye plein curt and mayd ye hath yar-to and to pay xxx^d to ye repairs off ye cors.'

The cross which John Aytkyn became bound by oath to repair was, it is much to be regretted, destroyed when the present parish church was erected. It was a slender pillar of grey freestone, about eight feet high, somewhat of an oval shape, and about nine inches in diameter. It stood on a pedestal of the same material, fixed to the eastern corner of a range of small houses, which stood in front of the old church, and which were generally occupied as fleshers' shops. The stone composing the cross was of a friable nature, and had several iron bands around it to hold it together, and to keep it in its place. The last time it was officially used was on the accession of George IV., when the then chief magistrate, John Adamson, stood on the pedestal and read aloud to the assembled people the edict of the proclamation.

4 July 1469. 'It: ye sam day Willzam Cuk was mayde burgess ī ye chapell of Sanc Katⁿ ī plain curt, and ye sayde Willzam gyff ī Alexander Mytchyson ye ballzheis hand and buk ffor x shˢ for his fredom o ye ton.'

23d Oct. 1471. John of Kynhard & Alexander Mytchyson ballzeis. 'It: ye sam day Alexander Mitchyson ffand a bourtht yᵗ John of Kyhard sowlld be nay ballzhe on ffawt ye crafft yᵗ he owssis.'

The 'craft' which John of Kynhard used is not stated, but by the 'Laws of the Burghs' 'Nane provost, bailye nor beddel, sall bake brede, na brew ale to sell wythin thair awin propir house durand the time that thai stand in office.'[1] The obvious reason being that the magistrates were bound by statute to see that both ale and bread were of proper weight and quality.

Besides this, however, the regulation manifests the tendency that gradually prevailed, especially in the larger burghs, that merchant-burgesses only, to the exclusion of burgesses exercising a handicraft, be eligible to the magisterial dignity. Originally all burgesses were eligible, but gradually when men began to employ others, those so employed were excluded from the magistracy.[2]

8 Jany. 1471. 'It: ye sam day Alexander Mytchyson was chosyn tresurer for to kyp ye cōites guds of Newburtht.'

Sed. 10 March 1472. 'Alswa ye sam day Archbalt off Carney was mayd burges in ye plein [curt] be ye ballyhies and cōte, and ye forsayd Archbalt bownde be his hand to kyth yᵗ ye cosell am [erciate].'
Alswa ye sam day, Rytchart ramsay was mayd freman in ye plein curt be ye balzheis and ye cōte and Rychart

---

[1] *Leges Burgorum*, No. 59.　　[2] *English Gilds*, p. cxv.

ramsay to pay iiij sh. off sylar betwix is and Wytsonday next, for to cū to ye comⁿ pfth.'

In the two foregoing entries there is a distinction indicated between a burgess and a freeman, the freeman being called upon to pay the highest sum for his privilege ; but in what the difference consisted there is no evidence in the record to show, though there are several entries of the same kind in the volume from which the extracts are taken. The probability is, the freeman was admitted to the privilege of trade within the burgh, without having burgage property, or being liable to the use and wont services of a burgess. This conjecture is confirmed by the fact, ' that handicraftsmen, who were not full citizens, had to buy from the lords of the town the right of carrying on trade, and had to purchase, by various burdens and imposts, the privilege of using the market-places and other institutions established for buying and selling.'[1]

Sed. 16 June 1473.   ' Stevyn Phylp and David Scot balzeis. It : ye sam day James Cuk was mayde a burges and ffreman iⁿ ye plein curt beffor ye balzeis and ye cōtie.'

'It : ye sam day Robyn of hill, you are amerciate for wranouis, stroblans off ye serjands and ye town and y^t was gyffn ffor dowm.'

Sed. 14 Sepr. 1473.   ' It : ye sam day in plein curt cper^t mast^r John of Wintown and resingit iiij. sh. and vi^d off annowell rent in ye hands of Alexander Mychysson ballze, and ye fforsayde land lyand in ye nourth p^t off ye burth between ye land of Sr James phylp on ye est p^t, and John Joly on ye west p^t and ye iiij. sh. to be pay^t to Sant Katⁿ effter ye dewsess his ayre and ye vjd. to be gyffyn in ya day off commendatoⁿ of souls for hym and his gude deurss,

---

[1] *English Gilds*, p. cxv.

and ye chapellan on ye eyn off his obit, to say placebo and dgy, and on ye moryn a mess ppetually to be down.'

'*Placebo Domino*' is the first antiphon or alternate chant in the evening service of the 'Office for Dead,' in the Roman Catholic Church. *Dirige, Domine Deus meus* are the first words of the first antiphon in the morning service in the same office. The first word of this latter antiphon is the origin of the name *Dirgie* or *Dergie*, given to the feast still customary in some parts of Scotland after a funeral. The remaining portion of the *Placebo* consists of the first nine verses of the 116th Psalm—the whole of the 120th, 121st, 130th, 138th, the Magnificat and prayers. The first part of the *Dirige* consists of the 5th, 6th, and 7th Psalms, and selections from the 7th and 10th chapters of the Book of Job, and prayers.

The title of *Sir*, given to James Phylp, who was curate of Abdie, we learn from the valuable annotations by David Laing to Knox's *History of the Reformation*, was usually applied to priests at this period, in England as well as Scotland. He says, 'This title appears to have been given to persons in priest's orders, who had taken their bachelor's degree, but was not an academical title in itself. Those priests who received the appointment of chaplains, were chiefly persons who, either from want of means or influence, had not been able to prosecute their studies the full time at the University to obtain the higher rank of Master of Arts; and therefore the title *Sir* was given them, but simply to mark the absence of that academic rank which was long held in great respect, and led to the practice both among clergy and laity until the close of the seventeenth century, of signing Master before their names.'[1] The foregoing note explains why the title 'Sir' is constantly applied to the chaplains of St Katharine's, in the subsequent pages. As most clergymen, up to nearly the middle of the last century, passed the degree of Master of Arts, they were uniformly addressed by the title of Master. Gradually the title

---

[1] *Knox's History of the Reformation*, Vol. I., pp. 555-6.—*Note.*

was given to those who had no claim to it, and on its being given,
as is now the case indiscriminately, the appellation of Reverend,
as applied to clergymen, came into use in Scotland.

20th Oct. 1473. 'It: ye samyn day John of Kynhard enti^t
in ye plein curt befoir ye balzheis, Alexander Mytcyson
and Henry Chalm^{rs}, in protestation for Master Thomas
Newman and his resignation in his hand and mayde
rasuygnation of iiij. rudes of land in ye hand of Alexander
Mychyson, lyand on the north p^t of ye gayt of ye Newburtht, betwin the land of Ad^e Cheap on ye west p^t, to
gyff erytabyll stat, and sysyn of to James Newman
and tyll his ayres and ye forsayd James Newman was
sworen and mayde ye g eytht at to be loyll and trow to
ye kyng and to ye Abbot of lowndors and ye convent,
and to ye ballyheis and cōte of ye Newburtht, and fowrth
wytht ye forsayd James was mayd burges and ye freman
in ye curt.'

33 Novr 1473. 'ye burrow curt off ye Newburth haldyn in ye
chapell off Sant Katⁿ wyt ye sayd burth haldyn be ye
wordy man y^t is to say Alexander Mychyon and Henry
Chalm^{rs} ballzheis.'
In ye sam day appert my lord Lundors [the abbot] in ye
plein curt, and myd ītymat^{on} to ye cōte ; y^t he had chosⁿ
Henry Chalm^r till a neud^r off^{ce} to hym, and he may not
beyr ye off^{ce} of balzhery as ffor is yheir.'

2 March 1473. 'It: ye sam day ye balzheis sitt^d ī ye chapell
of Sant Katⁿ, Alexander Mychyson and John Crysty and
ye cōsell. John Phylp eld^r aper^t befoir yham and sayd
he ffor thowt ye grewancyss y^t he hayd grew^d ye balzheis
fforsayd and ye newburhs and fourtwy^t ye balzheis gard
ye fforsayd John Phylp pas to ye dowr and yay war
awyssit and gard call hym ī again, and ramytit him and

fforgyff him hall things by-gayn and fourthwy^t ye fforsayd
John Phylp mayde resignato^n ī ye hand of John Cristy,
balzhe hall ye land and ye gudes it he hayd ī ye fawr of
Sr James his sown be staff and battown to gyff hym
houssis ī bourth and ye fforsayd Sr James ramytit his
gudes and say he wald kyep and sowpli hym and his
wyff and his bairnys wth his gudes, and ye fforsayd John
was rastor^t tyll his landes and his ffredom agayn, and next-
to-cum curt nay plaī̄t nay mayr pot ye fforsayd Sr James
till on an an anoyr c̄sent ī ye burh as ows is ī ye burtht.'

The staff and baton here spoken of 'were the symbols of resignation by a vassal. When a vassal resigned his feu into the
hands of his superior, either for the purpose of remaining perman-
ently with him, or for the purpose of being transferred to a third
party (or in favorem, as it was called), it was done originally by
the delivery of a pen, but afterwards, and for many centuries, of
staff and baton.'

    25 January 1474. 'ye samyn day Jhon Chyld and yliza-
       byth his wiff entrit in plein curt and rasyngit ye rud off
       land in ye balyzeis hands to giff sturt to Jhon of Rossy
       his fay^r als for as he gaff it befor till hym; and ye forsaid
       Jhon sall giff to his doch^r yis saymy^n day iiij. mks off
       usual monie off Scotland, and be ye Witsonday cū xii
       moneths oy^r. iiij. mks.

This transaction gives an idea of the value of a croft in Newburgh at that period; a merk Scots being equal to 1s. 1½d. of
the present currency. It also gives an indication of the adoption
of a surname, the son having taken the name of Chyld, while the
father is known by the name of the place of his birth or abode.

    26 April 1475. 'ye saymy day John of Covintre lard of Mug-
       drum, cperit befor ye baylze and askit y^t na ma^n suld

rassett na set houss, na harb^r to nay folk y^t tuk his gudes und^r paȳ off law loss yai wald rastor.'

The Law of the Burghs[1] under which the laird of Mugdrum made his demand, continued to be put in force in Newburgh down to a comparatively recent period, as is shown by numerous entries in the court books of the burgh, of which examples will be given subsequently.

> 5 May 1475. William Graundiston resigned two roods of land into the hands of the bailies to give 'possession to ye sup^{ors} Den Wylza^m dissart, Den Wylya^m halywell and Den John of Balfour in fawours and in naym of ye convent of Lundors before ya witness Master Thomas Rossy, Mast^r John of Wemyss, Jamys Anderson, Henry Lawson, Wilyu^m . . . . Jamys litiljohn w^t oyr^s.' [Den or Dean was the ordinary appellation of a monk.]

> 26 July 1475. 'ye saymȳ day ye haill curt was wardyt by ye gret ayth, and al ye curt fand speidful and ordynit y^t ye hyll suld be broky^n betwix ye est march by Inchmalow and ye Sely Stan quhar ye cōssell ffynds mast spedfull.'

The foregoing extract is chiefly interesting for the reminiscences of Celtic topography which it contains; both of the names mentioned are descriptive, as Celtic names generally are, and both of them are extinct. *Maladh*, Gaelic, pronounced Malaw, signifies the brow of a hill. Inchmalow would therefore be an inch in the midst of some spongy place on the brow of the hill above the Woodrife. The 'Sely-stane' was a huge block of sandstone that lay on the shoulder of the hill north of the Fincraig; it was broken up about fifty years ago by one of the tenants of the land, like many other

---

[1] *Leges Burgorum*, No. 85.

relics of the past, to make way for agricultural improvements. *Sealladh*, Gaelic, pronounced Sely, signifies a view, and it was well-named, for from the place where it lay there is a most extended prospect of the valleys of the Tay and Earn from their junction to the distant Grampians. The site of the stone completely over-looks Cross Macduff, and no one could have approached the latter unobserved by a watcher there. Assuming the cross to have been a *Girth* or Sanctuary, there may have been some connection between it and the ' Selystane.'

> 1ˢᵗ October 1476. 'ye borow hed curt of ye Newburth haldyn by Stevyn Phylp.'
> ' ye saym day was chossyn balzeis be ye grit ayth wyᵗ cōsent off ye haill nythburs, yᵗ is to say Alexander Mychyson and Michell of Inch.'
> ' ye saym day ye haill curt wardit be ye gret ayth yᵗ yai wald defend ye comⁿ lands off ye toⁿ wᵗ yʳ body and yʳ gudes.'
> ' ye saym day ye haill curt akit be ye grit ayth quhat sum-ever nythburs at war not and wald not byd wᵗ ye balzeis and cōte suld be expellit fᵃ all fredom and pfts of ye toⁿ for yer and day.'

A court or mote was held in burghs every fortnight, where justice was administered, burgesses admitted, and property trans-ferred, and at which every resident burgess was bound to appear. Besides these, there were three head courts held in the course of the year, at which every burgess whether resident or non-resident was bound to attend under a heavy penalty. ' It is for to wyᵗ that three hevyd mutis are thruch the yhere that behofis ilke burges for to be at. That is to wyt the first eftyr the feast of Sanct Michael, the tother next efter Yoill, the thrid eftyr Pasch.[1] The enjoined appearance at these courts is a remnant of

---

[1] *Leges Burgorum*, No. 40.

the obligation of the burgesses to undertake military service when called upon to do so. The preceding entry at a Michaelmas Head Court seems to have been an occasion when these services were likely to be required. Unfortunately, the cause is not stated, but the circumstances of the burgesses being called upon to stand by the magistrates, at the risk of ' their body and gudes,' shows that the rights and privileges of the burgh were believed to be in jeopardy.

These Head Courts continued to be held in Newburgh down to the middle of the last century, but latterly they became so only in name. Had they continued as originally instituted, many of the evils attending the *close system* would have been mitigated, as all matters affecting the interests of the community would have had the advantage of public discussion, and anything savouring of malversation would have been exposed.

It will be noticed in the preceding entry, that the magistrates were elected with the consent of ' ye haill nythburs.' This is the more remarkable, as seven years before (A.D. 1469), by an Act passed 5 Par. James III., cap. 29, the election, which was formerly in the hands of the burgesses, was put into the hands of the existing councillors, who had each the right of nominating a burgess, from among which, and the old council, the new council alone could be elected. The pretext for passing this Act was the ' great contention zeirly in chusing of the baillies and other officiares, throw multitude and clamour of commounes.' This mode of election, justly styled the *close system*, continued in force until the year 1833, when the election was put into the hands of the ten pound householders. This latter enactment, in its turn, has been repealed, and after four hundred years, the privileges of which the burgesses were denuded has been restored by the enactment of 1868.

> 1 Octr 1476. ' ye say^m day ye baylze Stevyn phylp chargit Henry Baxter to forbeyr all freman occupayssions off ye town, for ye dissobeying and sclandering off ye assise,

quhill ye thym he hed maid amends to ye assise and ye town.'

11 Decr 1476. 'ye saym day Stevyn rodger was delivt^t to ye hesp and ye stapill off his fay^{rs} la⁻ds be ye baylze Stewyn phylp and ye officiars, before ye witness Jamys Anderson, D^d. Anderson, Henry Lawson, Nycholl of bayt, John Phylp, and w^t o^{yrs} sundry.

'Hasp and staple was the old form of entering an heir in burgage subjects. The bailie, the town clerk, and the heir went to the property, when the claimant preferred his claim and sub-stantiated it by witnesses. When the bailie was satisfied, he declared the claimant to be the heir, and directed him to take hold of the hasp and staple of the door, as a symbol of possession. The heir then entered the house, and shut and bolted himself in. On coming out, the town clerk made a notarial record of the whole transaction, known as an instrument of cognition and sasine. This and similar forms of entering heirs in burghs was abrogated in 1847. Hasp and staple were the symbols appli-cable to houses, earth and stone to land, clap and happer to mills, net and coble to fishings, a sheaf of corn to parsonage teinds, a psalm book and the keys of the church to patronage, and the books of the court to jurisdictions.' The use of symbols in the transference of property had its origin in times when written records were unknown,—a sod cut from a field and laid on the altar before witnesses, was a proof that the field was conveyed to, and was thenceforth the property of the church.

16 July 1477. 'ye say day And^o. Kyd burges off ye tun off Sant and^{rs} cperit ī pla curt befor ye baylzeis and askit lawborrowis of John of Moncreiff, lard of that ilk and his ptȳs of ye kyngs behawff or ye abbot and con-vent, as he y^t dreidit ye said lard and his ptȳs.'

5 Feby^r 1477. 'ye saӯ day ye baylze Michell of Inch
coperit befor ye baylze Alexander Michyson and ye cosell
and askit amends off ye stroblanss of D^d. blyt stroblyt ye
said balze Michell in his office.'

'Ye say^m day ye cosell ordand y^t D^d. bly^t suld oyss na
fremans lawb^r. quhil ye tym y^t he cō and pffert amends
to ye balze and ye cōite.'

18 Feb. 1477. 'ye say^m day ye haill curt ordand y^t ye
cōssell suld com and gad^r on Sant Mathow day [a mistake
for St Matthias day, 24th February, St Matthew's day
21st Sep^t. being too late to let land for cultivation] next
to cum tyll sit and distrybow ye lands at ar vacand in ye
baylzeis' hands till ye nythburs, or at ar mast speidful tyll
ye pffit of ye thon.'

17 June 1478. 'ye saymy day John Malcomson eld^r and
Henry Thomson were taychit be ye offcārs in ye curt, be
in ye lords curt next eft pasch for bludweit, and John
Stob was borth for ye said Henry and John under pan be
his awon hand.'

The apprehension of these offenders in the Bailie Court was
not only in conformity with the burgh charter, but in strict accordance with the 'Laws of the Burghs.' By the former, the Abbot
of Lindores reserved power to hold three Head Courts in the burgh
yearly, for the trial of offences excluded from the magistrates'
jurisdiction, at which the burgesses were bound to appear to do
homage to him as his vassals; and by the latter it was expressly
declared that 'in burgh sall nocht be herde bludewyt na yet stokisdynt, na merchet[1] na hereyelde, na nane suilk maner of thyng.'

---

[1] With regard to *Merchet*, it is startling to find that a uniform tradition (to
which names are attached) prevails in this neighbourhood, that the exaction was
not commuted; but all evidence goes to show that it was merely a fine paid on
the marriage of a vassal's daughter to the superior.

Bludewyte, as the name implies, was an offence to the effusion of blood. *Stokisdynt* meant a stroke with a baton or stick. *Merchet*, the tax or fine paid by a vassal on the marriage of his daughter beyond the bounds of the barony.[1] *Hereyelde*, that paid to the superior on the death of a vassal, usually the best horse or cow.

> Sed^t 3 Novr 1479. 'ye saym day ye haill c̄sell grantit y^t ony off ya^m y^t wer warnyt to cum to ye cossell and cum not, and he had not a lawfull excowaze suld pay halff a gallowne of ayll.'
>
> 'ye v day of ye moneth off November, ye yerh off owr lord MCCCC seventy and ix yers, ya bayllzeis and c̄sell quenit and gaderit into ye chapell of Sanc Katrin wy^t in ye sayd burgh and be ye gret aiytht sworne ye said balzeis, and c̄sell ackyt and decret y^t quhatsover frema^n y^t rass in ony action in c̄trar off ye sayd balzies an c̄sell but consent off ye heall comunitie suld tyne all fredomys in ye burgh as for y^t yer.'

> Sed^t. 23 Jany. 1479, John Thomson and Henry Chalm^r balzeis. It: ye sam day Thom^s Wenton, yew ar amerciate ffor ye wrangess borth y^t yow fand upon wat of lethyn and y^t was gyfyn for dowm.'
>
> 'It: ye sam day ye cōite fand speydfull y^t inhab^t. off ye hyll suld com to Sanc Kat^n chapell upon Sanc Bdes day [St Brides, 1st February] yarefter and pay yar mayll, or quhat-suer y^t comys not y^t day, his takks sall be vakant and nan denyand in acts, and quhat neyburths y^t comys on ye morn sall hayff his wyt ye consent ye comunite.'

'The common-gude, or property of Scottish burghs, was, until the middle of the sixteenth century, let to the burgesses on short

---

[1] E. W. Robertson, *Historical Essays*, p. liii.

leases and advantageous terms.   To be deprived of their " takks"
was, therefore, equivalent to excluding them from any share in
the revenue of the corporation, and which, in the absence of
manufactures and commerce was to deprive them of their main
dependence and support.' [1]

---

[1] *Analecta Scotica*, Vol. II., p. 294, *note.*—Joseph Robertson.

CHAPTER XVII.

ST KATHARINE'S CHAPEL.

Well may the villagers rejoice !
Nor heat nor cold, nor weary ways,
Will be a hindrance to the voice
That would unite in prayer and praise ;
More duly shall wild-wandering youth
Receive the curb of sacred truth,
Shall tottering age, bent earthward, hear
The promise with uplifted ear ;
And all shall welcome the new ray
Imparted to their Sabbath day.

Heaven prosper it ! may peace and love
And hope, and consolation, fall,
Through its meek influence, from above
And penetrate the hearts of all,
All who around the hallowed Fane
Shall sojourn in this fair domain.'

Wordsworth.

FROM the year 1480 to 1697, the court books of Newburgh have unfortunately disappeared. For two hundred and seventeen years, therefore, embracing the momentous period of the Reformation, there is no continuous record to elucidate the history of the town, or to throw light on the condition of society. In the Advocates' Library, Edinburgh, there is a protocol book of John Kilgour, town clerk of Newburgh, containing entries from 1584 to 1589 ; and another of John Philip, clerk of the regality of Lindores, extending from 1611 to 1626.[1] Both of these books

---

[1] *Proceedings of the Soc. of Antiq. of Scotland*, Vol. II., p. 532.

seem to have been preserved by the care of Sir James Balfour of Denmiln, but they do not contain records of any special interest. Fortunately, since the year 1697, an unbroken series of volumes, containing full records of proceedings in the Burgh courts, has been preserved. There are also a considerable number of charters and other documents in the archives of Newburgh, extending from the year 1470 to the dawn of the Reformation. From one of these we learn that St Katharine's chapel, whose name stands at the head of this chapter, was erected in the year 1508; others record endowments for its support. Not the least interesting of the documents preserved is a decision by John, Lord Glammys, A.D. 1493, at that time Justiciar of Scotland, of a dispute between the Abbot of Lindores and the burgesses regarding their respective rights and privileges. Eight tags for the seals of the Justiciar and his councillors are attached to the parchment, but the seals are entirely worn away. As many points are touched upon in this decision, which are entirely obsolete, it is here printed entire.

> ' At Lundoris the ffyffteine day of the moneth of Januarr the yere of God a thousand four hundreth nynte and thre yeris. We Johnne Lord Glammys with the avys and consale of master Wilyam Scott of Flaw-crag, Alexander Seton of Parbroath, Alexander Spens of Pettyncreff, James of Drummond, John of Rettra, Patryk of Wellis, and Wilyam Quhitbron to me consalouris be me in that part specially chosyn to conclude deliver and finaly determyn in all actionis, debatis, contraversiis, harmys, iniuris, complenzeit and allegit be ane venerabill fader Andro, be the permissione of God Abbot of Lundoris and convent of the samyn, allegit to be done to thaim be thare men, tenentis burgis and comunite of thare burgh of the Newburgh twiching the paying of thare feu-ferm of the landis of the Wodruff and the hill with the comon mett and for common service and homage to be done to thaim

be the said comunite for the saidis landis, and anentis the
making of out men burges but licens of the said abbot
and convent, contrare thare enfefftment and for the procurin of out men to cum to the said burgh in the suple of
thair oppynion aganis thair awin enefftment, contraire the
lawis of the burgh and actis of parleament, and anentis
the bludwitis that happynnis in the said burgh, quihilkis
the knawlag punissioun and profite thereof pertenys to
the said abbot and convent as is allegit, and als upon the
inordinate procedings of the electione of the officeris of the
said burgh at this last Michalmes allegit be the said
abbot and convent to be done be the said communite
contrare the kingis lawis and actis of parleament, and als
anentis the breking oppyning and off takinge of the lokkis
of thair common kyst and out taking thareof of the
sele charteris, and otheris diners writtis and moneth put
in the keping thare in deposit to the vtilite of the said
burgh, and upon diners contemptionis and dysobeysans
allegiit to be done be the said communite to the said
abbot and convent thare superiors, and anent the resav-
inge and in haldinge of certane personis beand convictit
be ane assis in the last chammerlane ayr and bannyst
thareffter the said burgh for thare demeritis, anentis the
forsaidis poyntis of complaynt the forsaid hale convent
with ane consent and assent in the affermyt justice-ayr
of the regalitie of Lundoris haldin and begvn be me in the
said Newburgh, the xiiiith day of the moneth and yere
beforesaid purly and simply referryt compromittit and
oblist thaim for thaim and thare successouris to vnderly
do and fulfyll the decrete ordinans deliverans and consale
of vs the said Johne Lord Glammys and personis forsaid
of consale till vs chosyn, in all and sindrye the forsaidis
actionis and poyntis, and to mak and tak reformation and
correctione into quhat wys and maner sene to vs mast
expedient, for the gude of pece gude rewl, concord and

cherite, and to be haid betuix the saidis partyis in tym
cummyng, quhar throw we procedand in the forsaid
thingis the forsaid day and place athir of the partyis and
thare desiris thare petitionis charteris writts witnessyngis
be vs at length resavyt and vnderstandin, we beand weil
and riply avisit, hafand God before E pronuncis decretis
deliverys ordanis and for finale consale gevis, that the
said communite sall pay and deliver to the said abbot
and convent, thare vitale and ferme aucht be thaim to the
said abbay of the foresaid landis of the Wodruff, and the
hill with the samyn met and mesure that Willyam Quhitbron brocht with him fra the lafe of the kings burowis,
and delyuerit be hym in the chamerlane ayr of the Newbrugh, haldin be Schir Alexander Guthre, ay and quhill
the measure and stand devisit and ordanit be the com-
missaris of four burowis be affermyt be the parleament to
haf cours vniversale throw all the realme, and than with
that stand the said fermys to be mett and payit to the said
abbot and convent; as twichinge the poyntis of homage
and service we ordane the said homage to be maid be the
said communite to the said abbot and convent effter the
form of thare enefftment, and for common service the
declaracion tharof and fasson we continew to the next
parleament with consent of bath the partys but preuidice
of ony party; and as to the makinge of burges we ordane
that na outman be maid burges but consent of the said
abbot and convent, according to thare enefftment, and as
to the procurin and purchessing of out-folkis bringing
thaim to the burgh in the oppressioune of thar nychtbouris
or in contrar the lord and his priuilege, we ordane the
actis of parleament maid in syk casis to be obseruit and
kepit in all poyntis; as to the actione of blude, we ordane
that the said communite nor thare officeris vs nor intromett
with na actione of blude quhilk is nocht specifyit in thar
enefftment; and to the electione of the officeris that in

tym cummyng the day affixit in the kingis lawis of burrowis tharapon be obseruit and kepit ; and as twiching
the electioune of George Nicholson balze we fynd and
ordanes that all process led in courtis and be him lauchfully done to be of avale, and because he was chosyn
balze after the day lymit in the law, we ordane hym to
cess in the executioune of the said office quhill new
electioune proceid and in the said electioune that na fors
be leid, na yit na outman to hafe voce therein, na yit na
burges maid as for this new electioune, bot fra thin furth
to hafe voce and jos all priulege as afferis of law, and als
at the said day of the electioune that the common kyst,
commoun charteris, sele and bukis, moneth, and all
other thingis beand in the said kyst be brocht hale lokkyt
as it was of befor, and the communite to dispone thereupon as is sene speidfull to thaim, and gyff thar be ony
vnganand persons resett in the burgh that has been convictit or beis convictit be ane assys and banyst the tovne,
that thai persons incontinent at the tym of this election
be removit the tovne and the resettowris punist as efferis
apon law, and as to the displeser contempcione and disobey-
sans allegyit to be done to the said abbot and his convent
be the said communite, we ordane the said communite now
in-continent that thai sall syt doune apon thar kneis in presens of vs barheid besekand the said abbot and convent sa
far as thai haff offendyt ony faultis maid be thaim in tymes
bigane to remytt and forgiff and in tym cumming to be
to the said abbot and convent humill and obedient leil
trew men and tenandis as thai suld be to thare lord, and
apon thare gude bering, he to be gude lord to thaim and
this to all thaim that efferis or may affer suthfastly. This
our deliuerans we mak it knawin be thir our present
lettres. In witnes of the quhilk thing we haff set to our
selis at the abbey of Lundoris with the subscriptions of
our awin handis yer day and place aboon written befor

thir witnes master David Setoune personne of Federkarne, Thomas Fresale, son and apperand ayr to Lord Fresale, David Narn of Sandfurd, Sir Johne Lyndesay vicar of creych and notar public, with divers otheris. Willelmas Quhitbron, *manu propria.*

The size of the measure of the barley payable by the burgesses to the abbey, as feu-ferme for the Wodriff lands formed an important point in the dispute. The court of the Four Burghs referred to in the decision (at that period Edinburgh, Stirling, Lanark, and Linlithgow), which had the regulation of all matters affecting trade, had not been able to bring about the desirable result of a uniform standard. 'The innumerable variations of Tron, or public weight in Scotland, was in consequence a source of constant irritation and of endless disputes.'[1]

The justice of the abbot's complaint regarding the non-payment of feu-ferme, and the refusal of homage and common service by the burgesses was manifest. By the charter of the burgh which converted them from merely precarious tenants into proprietors of their tofts and crofts, and conferred upon them the common-good lands, which latter they held as a trust estate, strictly unalienable, they were bound to pay the feu-ferme specified, and to do homage and common service. The charter also expressly prohibited the bailies from making *out-men* burgesses, without the consent of the abbot,—and the harbouring of banished persons was expressly against the law. The inordinate proceedings complained of, as having taken place at the election of the magistrates are not specified. Judging from a decision in a dispute about eight years later by Patrick Wellis, provost of Perth, and a jury, preserved among the archives of Newburgh, there is reason to think that the abbot was endeavouring to exercise an undue control over the election. At the same time the burgesses seemed to have attempted to evade the obligations of the burgh

---

[1] E. W. Robertson's *Historical Essays*, p. 68.

charter. Five years after the passing of the act introducing the close system, it was enacted that in burghs 'there sall be four of the auld councell of the yeir before chosen yeirly to the new councell, . . . to sit with them for that yeir, and have powr with them to do justice.'[1]

The abbot claimed the right of nominating these four persons, and, that from them the council should choose the two bailies for the year. The object of the enactment was to prevent the complete and sudden displacement of the council; but the abbot's claim was clearly a usurpation, and the only justification that can be pled for it, is the circumstance that the bailies were the collectors of the abbot's revenue arising from the burgh maills and fines of court, which were paid to him as superior of the burgh. The abbot had therefore a special pecuniary interest in the character of the persons elected.[2]

The decision of the provost of Perth and his fellow-arbiters, which is inserted in the appendix, is in many respects interesting. Much of the ill-feeling and 'rancour' which it discloses as having prevailed between the Abbot of Lindores and his vassals in Newburgh arose from the inbringing of out-men and investing them with the privileges of burgesses, and giving them a voice in the affairs of the burgh. This was a direct infringement of the charter under which the burgesses held their property and privileges. These had been conferred upon them by the abbot on the express condition that 'the baillies counsale and communite quhen thai [are] requirit to the kingis weris sall pas in cumpany with the said abbotis ballie and remane under his baner all the tyme tharof, becaus thai haif maid sewte to the saidis abbot and convent, and haldis thar landis of hym in homage and service.'[3]

---

[1] Act James III., par. 7, cap. 57, 1474.

[2] *Ballivi* was the title given to the officers who collected the revenues referred to, hence the title of 'Bailie.' In royal burghs 'the bailie was originally appointed by the Crown.'—*Report on Municipal Corporations*, p. 13.

[3] Appendix No. VI.

The right to erect a burgh on their lands conferred by the royal charter, enabled the abbot to acquire a greater number of vassals than he could otherwise have obtained, and was justly esteemed an important privilege, as it called into existence a body of resident vassals at hand and ready whenever required. The bestowal of the rights of burgesses on non-resident or out-men was therefore a direct frustration of the purposes for which the abbot bestowed the lands and privileges ' on his men of Newburgh,' as he could only have a very slender hold on those living at a distance, and could not depend on them coming to his banner when required. Besides this, the increasing wealth and trade of the burghs had given them increased weight in the state ; it, therefore, became a source of power and influence for a neighbouring proprietor to hold the office of chief magistrate of a burgh, a power which was not unfrequently exercised adversely to the interests of the superior. To prevent this power passing into the hands of ambitious individuals living out of and having no direct interest in the welfare of the burgh, an Act was passed in the reign of James IV. expressly against this 'maistership,' as it was called, declaring that none could hold the office of provost or bailie unless they were merchants dwelling therein,[1]—a principle which then as now has this great recommendation, that it places the governing power in the hands of those whose interests are interwoven with the prosperity of the burgh over which they preside.

In a different phase of burgal life, when it became the interest of the burgesses to maintain their trading privileges, they protested against what in a previous age the abbot had objected to. On the 14th April 1529 the Convention of Royal Burghs ' Ordinit that all thame that ar maid burges within the burgh that vsis bying and selling of merchandeis that tha cum and duell within the burgh and hald stob and stack within 40 dais nixt heirefter and that oppin proclamatioun be maid at the merket croces of every burght, that all sic burges cum within the said burght and

---

[1] Par. 6, cap. 80, 1503.

SEAL OF CHAPTER OF LINDORES ABBEY.

mak thar habitatioun and dwelling within the said 40 dais under the pane of tinsaill of thar fredom.'[1]

Similar enactments 'to put remeid and ordour to burgessis, fremen, nocht duelland nor beirand commoun chairgis within thair brughis' continued to be made for a long series of years.[2]

A glimpse is given of the mode of transferring property by a charter dated 18th October 1470. The preamble states that the bailies and community were assembled in the chapel of St Katharine at the sound of the bell, to witness the transfer to a co-burgess named John Vallange of a piece of land 'which from old times belonged to the chapel,' on the condition of payment of eight shillings yearly for the maintenance of the chaplain. An abstract of this and the other charters in Newburgh charter-chest are given in the appendix.[3]

The next charter, dated the 20th August 1478, exhibits the abbot and monks in a pleasing light. By it they convey a rood of land in the burgh to their old quarrier, David Hathinton, for his faithful services.

The charter in favour of the old quarrier is the only one among the archives of Newburgh which has the seal of the chapter of the abbey remaining; it is so exquisitely cut that an engraving of it is given. The obverse, as will be seen from the engraving, bears the legend: 'S. CAPITVLI ECCLIE SCE MARIE ET SCI ANDREE DE LUNDORS.' The Virgin and Child are represented beneath an elaborate canopy; on their right is the representative figure of an abbot, in an attitude of adoration, with a scroll above his head bearing the words 'AVE MARIA.' On the left of the Virgin and child is a group of monks, also in the attitude of adoration, having a scroll above them inscribed with the words 'SALVE SCE PARENS.' The reverse, of which an engraving is given in the 'Supplemental Catalogue of Scottish Seals,' by Henry Laing (Plate XIII., Fig. 4), represents St

---

[1] *Records of Convention of Royal Burghs*—1295-1597, p. 510.
[2] Ib., 1597-1614, p. 11.   [3] Appendix No. VII.

Andrew being nailed to a cross (of the form known by his name);
a half-length figure of a monk appears beneath, with his hands
raised in the attitude of prayer, and on the right, a group of
people are represented as if listening to the dying words of the
saint; this side bears the legend, 'BIDUO PENDENS IN CRUCE
BEATUS ANDREAS DOCEBAT POPULUM.' The head of
the abbot and of several of the monks on the obverse side are so
artistically cut, and the features and expression are so distinct,
that in all probability they are portraits of persons known at the
time. The matrix of another seal of Lindores Abbey was exhibited
to the Society of Antiquaries of London by Mr Brereton, their
secretary, on the 11th May 1797, and an engraving of it is given
in the Archælogia of that Society. The Virgin, with the infant
Saviour in her lap, is represented holding an olive branch in her
right hand, and the Abbey of Lindores in her left. The inscription
runs thus: 'SIGILLUM SANCTE MARIE ET SCI ANDRE
DE LUNDO.' The matrix, which was of bone, and formed a
seal of an oval shape, was broken when exhibited, but part of the
next letter was visible, leaving no doubt of its being the fount of
a very old seal of Lindores Abbey.[1] The matrix is not in the
Museum of the Society of Antiquaries of London, and it is not
known what has become of it.

The record of the monks' care for their old servant, bears out
the character which they had for being considerate to their tenants
and dependants. After the Reformation, when the lands belonging to the abbey passed from the hands of the monks, the 'kindly
tenants,' whose tenures had come down from father to son under
their sway, had to be protected from the avidity of the new proprietors by special enactments of the Parliament.

A charter (dated 25th May 1481) brings before us the bequest
of 'John Wynton, Presbyter of St Andrews and burgess of Newburgh.' He bequeaths to his brother Thomas and his children,
whom failing, to the abbot and convent of Lindores, his tenement

---

[1] *Archæologia of the Soc. of Antiq. of London*, pp. 196-8.

in Newburgh under the burden of two shillings yearly for the maintenance of lights and other ornaments of the blessed virgin St Katharine, and three shillings to be distributed in bread to the poor at the sight and discretion of the chaplain of St Katharine's altar annually, by the hands of the owner of the tenement for ever.' To insure the continuance of the bequest, the donor imposes a penalty of twenty pounds on the owner of the property in case of his failure to comply with these conditions, one half to go 'to the fabric of the chapel of the said burgh,' and the other half to go to 'the common purse of the town.' Unfortunately, with two exceptions, there are no distinctive names attached in the title deeds to any of the tenements of Newburgh; the croft which the monks bestowed on their faithful servant in his old age, as well as to that of the pious priest who took such stringent means to secure the continuance of his benevolent bequest, cannot now therefore be identified. In the parish church of Westham, Essex, bread is distributed to the poor every Lord's day, after the conclusion of the service, from a similar bequest, and a like charity is dispensed in many parish churches in England.

One tenement is named 'The Prince's House,' and another adjoining the Town House on the east, 'The Smiddy Stoop.' This latter name is an evidence of connection with the 'Low Counties,' *stoop* in Dutch signifying an open porch. Why the other was named 'The Prince's House' there is no tradition to show.

The next document in the order of date is an Instrument of Sasine, dated the 5th April 1508. The formalities of infeftment by the delivery of earth and stone were gone through by one of the bailies in presence of Andrew Cavers, abbot, styled in the Sasine, 'pensionary of Londoris,' and in this document the fact is recorded that the chapel which served as the parish church until it was taken down in 1832, to make room for the present church, was then being erected. In a subsequent deed, abbot Andrew Cavers is named as the founder of the new chapel, which was simply a narrow oblong edifice, built chiefly of red sandstone, and roofed

with gray slate; it had no architectural ornament whatever, excepting a very unpretending belfry on the western gable. Had
no chapel existed in the town, the probability is that the nave of
Lindores Abbey Church would have been kept up for the use of
the people of Newburgh, as the nave of abbey churches was invariably set apart for the use of the parishioners, the monks retaining the choir for their own especial use. This arrangement accounts for the preservation of the nave of many of the old churches,
and for the demolition of the choir, as at Brechin and elsewhere;
the choirs ceasing to be used after the expulsion of the monks at
the Reformation. The older chapel, to which reference is so often
made in the oldest Burgh Court Book of Newburgh, and which
must have been of considerable antiquity, was dedicated to St
Katharine, but the new one was dedicated in addition to St
Duthac and St Mary Magdalene; of the latter saint it is unne-
cessary to speak.

St Katharine was a young lady of Alexandria, of illustrious
descent, who, in the twenty-second year of her age suffered
martyrdom in the time of a terrible persecution, A.D. 306, under
Galerius Valerius Maximinus, who rose, from being a shepherd
lad in Illyria, through the various grades of the army, to be co-
Emperor of Rome, and reigned over Syria, Egypt, and Asia Minor.
He was a brutal and profligate tyrant and a furious persecutor of
the Christians.[1] The purity of the lives of converts to Christianity
stood out in such marked contrast with the unbridled licentiousness of those around them, in that most licentious age, that it was
sufficient to arouse suspicion that they belonged to the hated sect.
The high-born St Katharine was suspected, and it is narrated of
her, that when confronted with her persecutors, she unflinchingly
avowed herself a Christian, though she knew that tortures and
death awaited the confession. So eloquently, it is said, did she
defend herself and her faith in her Saviour, that she baffled her
opponents and put them to silence; but the persecutor's argument

---

[1] Baring Gould's *Lives of the Saints*, Vol. I., p. 257.

'the heretic must suffer that heresy be stayed,' was at hand, and the young martyr was condemned to suffer death by rolling over her body a wheel set with sharpened spikes. Her learning and devotion has made her the patron saint of philosophers, and the manner of her martyrdom has given the name of 'St Katharine's Wheel' to the round windows in Gothic cathedrals. Her festival was celebrated on the 25th November. A fair used to be held in Newburgh yearly on that day; but so utterly had St Katharine and her 'faith unto death' been forgotten, that latterly it was known by the name of 'the Haggis Market.' The modern name apparently arising from the abundance of this national dish consequent on the slaughter of sheep bought in the fair for winter provision. The market, in the beginning of the present century, was frequented by pedlars of respectability and of comparative wealth, who in character might have stood for the type of Wordsworth's 'honoured Pedlar' of 'The Excursion.'[1] It long continued to be a great annual gathering, and was the occasion for the inhabitants supplying themselves with clothing and articles of household use. One huckster, the last representative of her class, exhibited her wares in 1869, but since then the Fair has sunk into entire neglect.

St Duthac, more properly Dubthach, was a very popular saint in Scotland at the time of the erection of the chapel in Newburgh. He flourished in the north of Scotland in the beginning of the twelfth century.[2] So great was the trust reposed in the sacredness of his principal shrine at Tain, that the queen of Robert Bruce, in the time of her husband's greatest extremity (A.D. 1306), forsook the strong castle of Kildrummy for the greater security of St Duthac's shrine; but the sanctuary was violated, and the queen and her companions were basely given up to Edward I. St Duthac continued to retain his popularity for centuries. 'In the year 1505 James IV. went on a pilgrimage to Tain to St Duthac's shrine, and on his way he lodged in the Abbot of Lindores' country house at Fintray. From the records of the king's pilgrimage, we can realize

---

[1] See appendix, No. VIII. [2] Reeve's Adamnan's *Life of St Columba*, p. 401.

the curious union of devotion and dissipation which characterized
a pilgrimage of that age.' An organ was carried to Tain and back
for the celebration of divine worship ; alms were bestowed on the
poor, and in strange contrast with a religious pilgrimage, payments
were made ' to the maddins of Forres that dansit to the king.'[1]

It was only, however, in accordance with his tastes that James
IV. caused the organ to be carried to Tain and back. He was
passionately fond of poetry and of music. He had musical instru
ments brought from abroad, and whenever the king went in his
journeyings through the country, the accounts of the Lord High
Treasurer teem with records of payments to minstrels and musi-
cians of all kinds—' to harpers, fithelars and lutaris.' One of these
'Lundoris the lutare,' who, in that age when surnames were
mostly given from the place of birth or residence, was in all probability either a native or resident of Lundores, received ' at the
kingis command xiiij"[s], on the x Julij 1496.' 'Lundoris and
numerous other menstrallis,' received gratuities as their Pasch
reward in March following. Another local musician received a
similar reward from the king. On ' the fift day of Maij 1497, the
brokin-bakket fitular of Sanctandris was paid ixs.' Previous to
this, in 1489, the king commanded the large sum of x li. to be
paid ' to Wilyeam Sangster of Lythgow for a sang buke,' a
collection .that would now be invaluable. James was more than
a lover of music, he was a munificent patron of the fine arts and
an encourager of genius. He was the friend of Dunbar, who stands
in the front rank of Scottish poets ; and the rude but patriotic
rhymes of Blind Harry, the minstrel, were frequently rewarded
by the king.[2] These entries are interesting as showing the
encouragement that was given to poetry and music at the time.

---

[1] *Records of the Priory of May*, preface, p. xlviii. Dissipation as great prevailed in the third decade of the present century at out-door *preachings* on communion occasions in Scotland, till it was happily lashed out of existence by the
well-known satire of Burns.

[2] *The Ballads of Scotland*, Aytoun, Vol. I., pp. lxxx–lxxxvi. *Poems of Scottish
Kings*, Chalmers, pp. 118, 119.

Modern burgesses can only form a very inadequate conception of the homage paid to patron saints of parish churches in pre-reformation times. The yearly festival was not only an occasion of imposing solemnity, but of great rejoicing, and it was the gatherings on these occasions that was the origin of the various fairs throughout the country; traders and those who had anything to sell taking advantage of the crowds that assembled to vend their wares and produce. When the saint's day came round the magistrates, accompanied by the burgesses and burgh officials walked in procession with the insignia of office to the church for worship. In the larger burghs the different *crafts* joined the procession, with banners and the symbols of their patron saint, each vying with the other who would make the most imposing display. The commemoration was the great day of the year in the burgh, and the evening was given over to hilarity and festivity.

The rules of the medieval gilds affords a glimpse of the proceedings on these annual festivals. In the city of Bristol 'On Seynt Kateryns even the maire and shireff and their brethren to walk to Seynt Kateryns Chapel, there to hire [hear] even-song, and from even-song unto the Kateryn halle' for social enjoyment. 'In a religious and social gild, established A.D. 1355, it was ordained that 'all the sisteryn of the gild shall follow the virgin, and afterwards the bretheren; and each of them shall carry a wax light weighing half a pound, and they shall go two and two, slowly pacing to the church, and when they have got there . . . all the sisteren and bretheren shall offer their wax lights together with one penny each. All this being solemnly done, they shall go home again with gladness.'[1]

---

[1] The freemasons are the only body who keep up these customs in this country. There were gilds of almost every kind of *craft*, having for their object social, charitable, and religious purposes, in the rules of many of them there were, like the freemasons, special statutes for securing secrecy.—*Early English Gilds*, pp. 422; 149 55, 58, 61, etc.

Repeated attempts were made in many places by the people after, the Reformation, to celebrate their accustomed festivals, but eventually they were suppressed. Even yet there is a passion for pageantry on the part of the people, and any procession that has an historical character about it, attracts great crowds.

The burgesses of Newburgh manifested commendable liberality in endowing their new chapel, and many of them burdened their properties with an annual payment for the maintenance of the ordinances of religion. This is the origin of the altarage money, which is still payable to the minister of the parish. On the 5th June 1508, Sir John Malcomson, one of the chaplains of 'the new church of Newburgh,' is infeft in two roods of land resigned by James Chawmere, with consent of Thomas Chawmere, his apparent heir, in favour of the chaplain of St Katharine and his successors, 'for praying for the donor, his heirs, ancestors;' and with a broad charity, 'for the souls of those to whom the roods may belong.' Three years later (25th February 1510-11), 'Michael Anderson and John Kawe bailyies of the burcht of Newburcht bewest Lundoris,' constitute their 'weill-belovit nychbour James Philpe,' their procurator for the resignation of two roods of land in excambion 'for four shillings yearly to be tane up be us, or our successouris, factoris, assignais, or chaplainis of our kirk.' On the 24th September 1511, Sir John Malcomson, the chaplain, receives infeftment by the delivery of pennies, of a tenement, in exchange for an annual; the only thing noteworthy in the document is that the infeftment took place ' at the monastery of Londoris near the stone dial at the eleven of the forenoon or thereby.'

An Instrument of Sasine, dated 19th August 1513, brings the old faith more vividly before us than any previously brought under notice. 'Sir John Malcumsone, chaplain of the altar of St Dionysius founded within the monastery of Londoris, is infeft in an annual of five shillings, leviable from a tenement in the town, which belonged to Archibald Carno, in favour of the blessed virgin

St Katrine, and of the chaplain ministering in the church, founded within the burgh, for perpetual prayers for himself, his father, mother, and for Andrew Cavers, formerly Abbot of Londoris, the founder of the church.' 'There were several saints of the name Dionysius, among them Dionysius the Areopagite,' but the most illustrious of the name, and the one most likely to have been commemorated at Lindores, was Archbishop of Alexandria. His writings were highly esteemed by the early church, and in the time of a violent persecution he was rescued from martyrdom by the peasantry of his diocese. He died in the year of our Lord 265. The bailie put several pennies in 'the hands of the image of the virgin St Katrine' (which must have been carried to the ground for the purpose), in token that the annual was 'in all time coming to be levied in the name of her image.' We are left in ignorance as to the nature of this image, but frequently they were of considerable material value. One belonging to the Cathedral of Aberdeen, delivered to John Leslie, Parson of Oyne, and last Abbot of Lindores, contained 114 ounces of silver. The seal of John Kawe, the officiating bailie, was attached to the sasine, but it is entirely worn off.

In these provisions 'for perpetual prayers' for the dead we have an expression of that 'tender pity which is of no avail' for the loved departed.

> ' From this sad source have sprung
> Rites that console the spirit under grief,
> Which ill can brook more rational relief ·
> Hence prayers are shaped amiss, and dirges sung
> For souls whose doom is fixed.' [1]

The endowment of the new chapel having been provided for by the liberality of the burgesses, a commission was granted by the Archbishop of St Andrews for its dedication, and for the consecration of the burying-ground attached to it. The original document,

---

[1] Wordsworth, *Eccles. Sonnets*, Part I., No. XX.

which is the earliest written on paper among the public records of Newburgh, had the large seal of the archbishop affixed, but the same fate has attended it as has befallen most of the other seals of the collection, it is entirely worn off. The following is a translation of the commission :—

> Andrew by divine mercy Archbishop of St Andrews, primate of the whole kingdom of Scotland, legate by virtue of his position, and legate with the power and authority of a legate from the Lateran, throughout the whole foresaid kingdom, and perpetual commendator of the monastery of Dunfermline to our beloved brother James, by the Grace of God and the Apostolical see, Bishop of Dunblane, salvation and mutual love in the Lord. As our beloved clerk Mr Henry Quhit, Canon of the Church of Morray has shown to us by his petition that he has in honour of the Saints, St Michael the Archangel, St Andrew the apostle, Nicholas and the blessed virgin and Martyr Katharine endowed a certain church or chapel founded and built in the burgh of Newburgh near the monastery of Lundores with certain lands and annual rents for the support of a chaplain therein who shall celebrate divine service in all time coming. Wherefore he has forthwith humbly petitioned us for the better celebration of divine worship, and that the devotion of the people therein may be increased, that we should deign to dedicate, or cause to be dedicated the said Chapel or Church founded and endowed as foresaid. We therefore considering this request to be just and agreeable to reason, and wishing to accede to the just desires of the petitioners by the tenour of these presents commit and impart to you our brother foresaid our lawful power and authority of dedicating and erecting into a church or chapel for ever the said chapel founded and endowed as foresaid, the ceremonies and solemnities being observed which of right ought to be observed in the dedication of

Churches, and inquest first being held concerning the said foundation and endowment and other circumstances requisite, and provided that the parish church be not defrauded of its privileges and rights, so that in the same church or chapel, and its alloted cemetery free sepulture may in future be had for all who choose or wish to have sepulture there, and of doing, carrying out and exercising all other things which to the dedication of a Church or Chapel of this sort are known to belong. Given under our round seal at our city of St Andrews, the second day of the month of April in the year one thousand five hundred and sixteen.

By the foresaid most reverend Archbishop and legate,

JO. SANCHAR.

On the 12th April 1522, Isabella Hadingtone conveys a rood of land in Newburgh to the bailies and council and community under the yearly burden of nine shillings to her and her heirs, and of twelve pence to the altar of St John in the monastery of Lindores; if the bailies cease or refuse to pay these sums, her heirs are to resume possession of the property. On 15th January 1522-3, Alison Tod resigns a rood of land 'in favour of the blessed virgin St Katrine and her church for the weal of her own soul and the souls of her forbears.' On the 10th February 1522–3, James Tode conveys a rood of land 'to God and all the saints, the blessed virgin Mary, and especially the church of the blessed virgin Katrine within the town of Newburgh near Londoris, for the welfare of his own soul and the souls of his father and mother,' under burden of a payment of five shillings yearly by the abbot and convent of Londoris to the altar of St Ninian in the church of Ebde.' St Ninian, to whom the altar was dedicated, has been already referred to as the apostle of the Southern Picts; portions of the walls of his church of Candida Casa, built in the fourth century, near Whithorn in Galloway, are, on not very satisfactory evidence, conjectured by some still to be seen.

In a Sasine, dated the 18th June 1526, the interesting `fact is recorded that there was a school in Newburgh at that period. The narrative sets forth that the formalities of infeftment were gone through, besides other witnesses, 'before all the scholars of the school.' In every monastery there is reason to believe that one or more of the monks were set apart to teach the young,[1] and it is not likely that Lindores was an exception; but the notice in the Sasine is the earliest mention of an educational institution in Newburgh.

The latest document preserved in the charter chest of Newburgh preceding the Reformation, is a charter dated 20th June 1542; it is remarkable for the firm trust in the old faith which it displays, at the very time when that faith was being so vehemently attacked. By this charter Michael Tod, one of the burgesses of Newburgh, conveys two roods of land to the bailies and burgesses 'patrons of the chaplaincy of St Katrine, founded by their predecessors within the new church of the burgh, and to Sir John Richartson *alias* Cuk, chaplain, and his successors for money dispensed to him in his urgent necessity, by the bailies and chaplain, for the augmentation of the stipend of the chaplaincy, and for prayers in behalf of the souls of the founders of the monastery of Lundoris, superiors of the burgh of Newburgh, and for the souls of the venerable father John, the present abbot, and his successors in the monastery, and for the souls of his own father and mother, of his ancestors and descendants, and for the souls of all the faithful defunct for ever.' This deed was executed at Newburgh in presence of ' the honourable and venerable masters Robert Lowson and John Philp, Sir Alexander Richartson, and James Philp. It is not without significance that this, the latest deed preceding the Reformation, preserved in the collection, displays so great anxiety for the continuance of prayers for the dead, at the very time that their efficacy was being so keenly canvassed. The very comprehensiveness of its injunctions, embracing so much within its scope,

---

[1] *Miscell. Spalding Club*, Vol. V., Append. to Pref., p. 72, Joseph Robertson.

and at the same time being so specific in its directions, show that a sense of insecurity was aroused by the attacks which within a brief period triumphed in the Reformation. The last document bearing on the internal history of Newburgh in connection with Lindores Abbey, is an obligation by Patrick, commendator of Lindores, conveying the customs of the burgh (which belonged to him as successor to the abbacy) to the bailies and community of Newburgh, because they had at his desire consented to the resignation of the burgh in favour of Patrick Leslie his eldest son. This document, which is preserved among the archives of Newburgh, is signed by the commendator, and it completes the entire severance of the burgh from the dominion of the abbey.

CHAPTER XVIII.

ECCLESIASTICAL DISCIPLINE.

'Meet is it changes should control
Our being, lest we rust in ease.
We all are changed by still degrees,
All but the basis of the soul.'

Tennyson.

THE ecclesiastical records of the parish of Newburgh, which have
been preserved from the year 1652 downwards, furnish vivid
pictures of the social life of our forefathers; the value of which
are enhanced by the circumstance that Ecclesiastical Courts at
that period took cognizance of offences which are now entirely
beyond their sphere. Unfortunately the volume containing the
proceedings of the kirk session from the erection of the parish
in 1622 to the year 1652, extending to upwards of six hundred
pages, has disappeared.

What now constitutes the parish of Newburgh, with the exception of Mugdrum, Pitcairly, and Easter Lumbenny, which belonged
to Abernethy, originally formed part of the parish of Abdie. Previous to its disjunction from Abdie, a visitation of the parish was
held by the Presbytery of Cupar, the following record of which
has been preserved in the Books of the Synod of Fife.

'The visitation of the Kirk of Ebdie holden at Newburgh 2
September 1611.'

'Efter invocation of Godis holy name and doctrine,' 'Mr Jhone
Caldcleuch, minister, is found to teach in the kirk of Ebdie
anes upon the sabboth in winter and twys in summer.
He is appointed to tak to him an ordinar text, and or-

dained that ilk saboth after-noon ane portion of the people sal be catechised either in the kirk of Ebdie or Newburgh as the sessione sall find meitt, and as the people may most commodiously resort; and for this effect thei ar ordenit to devyd the parochyne in convenient portions. The minister removed' [out of the court while his conduct was being judged], 'wes allowed in doctrine, but it was regraitted that he did not kyth himself forward and zealous in censuring and punishing offenders, quhilk being for want of ane commission, they are ordained with all diligence to purchase ane commissioune to the minister, the guidmen of Denmuir, Woodmlyne and Denmylne, the bailyies of Newburgh and James Leslie.'

The commission to be purchased appears to have been a delegation by the Court of High Commission, erected in each of the provinces of the church, granting authority to call before them all persons accused of scandalous offences in life and religion, and with power to enforce their sentences by fine and imprisonment. The powers usurped by these courts were both arbitrary and illegal, never having received the sanction of Parliament, and were often made instruments of oppression.[1] The territorial distinction of 'Guidmen,' applied to such as held their lands of a subject, though they were large, and their superior very noble, only those who held their lands of the prince were called lairds.[2]

'Saboth.—The Sabboth day keiped be giffing the Satterday to the tenantis, except in my Lord of Rothes his boundis, quhilk James Leslie, oversier of my Lordis turnes in theis boundis promised to sie amendit.'

'It appears to have been the custom of farm labourers under

---

[1] Grub's *Ecclesiastical History*, Vol. II., p. 291.
[2] Sir George Mackenzie's *Works*, Vol. II., p. 583.

the designation of cottars, or tenants, to receive from the proprietor or tacksman, a portion of ground in lieu of wages, which they cultivated for their own use. As their time was devoted to their master during the week, Sunday was the only day they had for labouring their own land. The ordinance of the Synod was to prevent the breach of the Sabbath, by obtaining for them a week day (Saturday) for that purpose.' This was a praiseworthy effort. Previous to the Reformation, Saturday afternoon, and the eve of every festival, were observed as a holiday, on which no work was done. The Craft Gilds in England had regulations enjoining this. The following rule of the Fullers of London, 1297, is one instance out of many of the same kind, 'None of them [the brethren] shall work after dinner on Saturdays, nor on any .days which they ought to keep as festivals according to the law of the church.'[1] The forbidding of work on Saturday afternoon, and the eve of festivals, was common to all countries, and had its origin in a custom of the Roman Catholic Church, to solemnize the eve of festivals and Sundays by religious services. This boon of leisure to attend to domestic and other duties was lost at the Reformation, and it is only within the last ten years that workmen have regained their lost holiday.[2] The records of the visitation continues as follows :—

'Na non-communicants. Alexander Philp excommunicat for the slaughter of . Durie.'
'Na disabedientis to discipline. Na Papistes, or resettaris (*i.e.* of papists.)'
' The Kirk of Ebdie is reported to be in good caice. It was regraitted that the towne of Newburgh, containing four hundredth communicantis, or thairby, is so far distant from thair paroche kirk, that they can not, without gryt difficultie resort thairto, and in winter it is altogether impossible. Mairover the inhabitantis declared themselvas willing to

---

[1] *English Gilds*, p. 180. [2] *Ib.*, p. cxxxi.

bestow and contribute for the sustentation of ane minister according to thair power. The work wes thocht verie guid, if thair may be ane settled ministrie at their awin Kirk within the town of Newburgh. But in respect of my Lord Lundores his minoritie, seeing no present dealing may be had it is continowed to be alwayes remembritt when ocasion sal be offred.'

Scole. It is found that thai have ane commoune Scole taught by Mr James Leslie, scolmaister, who past his cours of philosophie in St Salvatouris Colleg in St Androis. Being removed was allowed. His stipend is paid as followis, viz., be the toune of Newburgh xl. libis, be the minister xx. merkis, by my Lord of Lundoris xx. merkis. It is ordanit that ilk pleuch of the pariochine sall pay xiiis. iiij^d. yeirlie to the scolmaister according to commoune ordour, quhilk the gentilmen and parochinaris present promised thankfullie to do their awin pairtis, and likewayes the bailzies of Newburgh thankfull payment alsweill of bygannis as in all time cuming.'

Kirk-dykes. 'Item they ar ordained to big thair kirk dykes according to the Act of Parliament.'

In the reign of James VI. it was enacted, that the Parochinaris repair the kirk yard dykes with stone and mortar, to the height of two ells, with sufficient stiles and entries.'[1]

'Mylnes. Item the minister is ordained ilk Saboth to tak exact tryall if any milnes gang thairon, and to convein the transgressouris befoir thair commissionaris, and to convict them in 20^s. penaltie.'

'Provisionne. The minister possesses mans and gleib and is resident thairupon. And hes for provisionne 10 bolles 2 firlottis quheit, 24 bollis beir, 15 bollis 2 firlottis meill

---

[1] Parliament 21, cap. 1.

and 38 merkis money, and that out of the thrids of Lundoris, the vicarage being erected.'

' Register.   The minister is censured and rebuiked because
he has nocht ane register of the defunctis, and ordained
to have ane with all formalities.'

' Byble.   They are ordained to buy ane common byble.   Item
to gather almes for the poor in the tyme that they sing the
psalme.' [1]

In consequence of the distance of the inhabitants of Newburgh
from their then parish church of Abdie, and the impassable state
of the roads thither in winter, the proposition which was made in
1611 to erect the town of Newburgh into a separate parish was
carried out eleven years afterwards, and the old chapel of the
town was made the parish church.   The following is the deliverance of the Synod on the occasion :—

' Synod Holden at S[t]. Androis, 1st October 1622.   Plantation
of Ebdie and Newburgh, in the presence of Mrs Andrew
Murray and James Leslie.

The day foirsaid, anent the supplication proposed by the
inhabitants the brugh of Newbrughe.   That quhairas
they, and the remanent persons of the paroche of Ebdie,
with the speciell advyce consent and assent of the patrons
having power of the presentation of ane minister to the
said kirk of Ebdie, efter the departure of umquhill Mr
Jhone Caldcleuch last minister to the said kirk, for sundrie
grave and wechtie considerations moving them thairunto,
specified at lenth in thare foirsaid supplication, have with
ane comoun and uniforme consent thoucht meet and expedient for the speciell wiell, profite and commoditie, both
of the saids inhabitants the said brugh of Newburghe, and
parochiners of the said kirk of Ebdie, that the saids

---

[1] *Selections from the Minutes of the Synod of Fife*, p. 31.

parochins heirafter sal be devydit and separat in maner following, viz., That the place of Lundors and the inhabitants of the said brugh of Newburgh sal be designed and apoynted to resort ordinarlie to the kirk alreadie buildit within the said brugh, and the remanent persons of the paroche of Ebdie for ordinar hearing of God's word preached, and participation of the sacrament theirin. And for that effect, twa sufficient ministers sal be provydit for serving the cuir at the saids twa kirks severalie in al tym cumming, upon such reasonable and competent conditions as efferis,—and thairfoir did crave that my Lord Archbishop and his present synod suld give and declair their approbation, and consent to the division and separation of the saids twa kirks in maner foirsaid, and to the admission of Mr Andrew Murray to be actual minister of the said paroche kirk of Ebdie, and Mr James Leslie to be actual minister of the said kirk within the said burgh of Newbrughe, conform to both their presentations grantit to them theiranent. Quhairupon the Archbishop and the present Assemblie having dewlie ponderit and considerit the expediencie and necessitie of the said division and separation; as also, the people and commoditie quhilk may redound theirby to the haill parochiners of both parochis *respective*, did ratifie, approve and allowe the said separation in all poynts. And my Lord Archbishop having receaved sufficient testimonie of the sufficiencie and qualification of the saids Mrs Andrew Murray and James Leslie for the work of the holy ministrie, did proceid to their admission to the cuir at the kirks above designed, and gave unto them the imposition of hands according to the ordour.'[1]

This arrangement was ratified by Parliament on the 28th

---

[1] *Selections from the Minutes of the Synod of Fife*, p. 97.

June 1633. The following is a copy of the Act passed on this occasion: —

> ' Our Soverane Lord and thrie estates of this present Parliament hes ratifiet and approvine. And be the tenner heirof ratifies and approues the separatioune and disunion of the kirkes of Ebdie and Newburgh within the Shirefdome of ffyfe maid be speciall consent of the patrone gentlemen of the parochines heretors. And all vther pairties haveand enteris for the tyme possest be tua ministers, Ratifiet be act of Synodall assemblie. And Act of the Lords Commissioners for the surranders and teinds alredie. And als the maintenance and provisione of the kirk and parochine of Newburgh convenit aggreit vpon alreadie or to be modifiet heireftir. And ordaines the samyne kirk of Newburgh and parochine thairof To be ane severall kirk and parochin be itself In all tvme coming seperat from the said kirk of Ebdie.'[1]

Mr Andrew Murray, mentioned in the deliverance of the Synod of St Andrews, was minister of Abdie. He received the honour of knighthood at the coronation of Charles I. on the 18th of June 1633; and subsequently, the Marquis of Hamilton, the Lord Chief Commissioner, 'having reported that Sir Andrew had been service able in allaying the heats and differences of the Assembly of 1638,'[2] the king raised him to the peerage by the title of Lord Balvaird. Balvaird, from which Sir Andrew took his title, formed part of the barony of Arngask, his ancestral property; and it still belongs to his descendant, the Earl of Mansfield. The old castle of Balvaird is situated in an opening among the hills on the east side of Glenfarg; it is unique in having a court and offices still extant around it, and is worthy of care and preservation. Lord Balvaird died

---

[1] *Selections from the Minutes of the Synod of Fife*, pp. 102–3.
[2] Scott's *Fasti Eccles Scot.*, Vol. II., p. 2.

at the early age of forty-seven. He was succeeded as minister of Abdie by Mr Alexander Balfour, son of Sir Michael Balfour of Denmilu.

Mr James Leslie, also mentioned in the deliverance of the Synod, was the first minister of the newly-erected parish of New-burgh. He was schoolmaster of Newburgh from the 2d September 1611 until his ordination as minister on the 1st October 1622.

After the disjunction of Newburgh from the parish of Abdie, the following extract shows that the community of Newburgh had brought themselves under spiritual censure, which, in these days, involved serious civil consequences.

> '1647, March 11, Quheras it is reported by Mr Lawrence Olyphant, minister at Newburgh that most pairt of the elders and inhabitants of the paroche of Newburgh had conversed with Andrew Andersone who was excommuni-cate three yeir since in the said paroche, the Presbyterie being deeply affected with the said miscarriage, and con-sidering how much of that kynd abounds in the land whiles so many are excommunicate doe refer the matter to the consideration of the Provinciall Assemblye, that a solide course may be taken, both for punishing this so haynous ane offence, and for preventing the lyk in tym comeing, and discharge Mr Lawrence to give the commu-nion whil the Provincial be past.'[1]

The following is the deliverance of 'the Provincial Assembly on the subject held at Dunfermline on the 6th April 1647.'

> '*Parioch* of *Newburgh*. Anent a reference to the Presbyterie of Couper. What shal be the censure of the most part of the paroche of Newbrough for conversing with Andro Anderson, ane excommunicate persone? The Assemblie

---

[1] *Selections from the Minutes of the Presbyteries of St Andrews and Cupar*, p. 109.

ordains that they be cited before the Presbyterie, that thei may receive thair sentence viz[t]., that the severall elders known to have conversed with the said excommunicated persone, shall make their public repentance in the face of the Congregatione, upon a Lord's day. Lykwayes the Assemblie ordains a solemn fast and humiliation to be kept that day, that the rest of the parochinaris foirsaid may mourne for so great ane offence.'[1]

In obedience to the injunction of the Synod, the Presbytery met at Newburgh on the 13th May 1647, and pronounced the following decision :—

At Newburgh 13th May 1647—Elders of Newburgh their confessione and censure.
' The quhilk day the presbyterie held at Newburgh for exe- cution of the ordinance made the last day at Cupar. And after sermon made be Mr John Durie and incalling on the name of God, Mr James Wedderburne, Moderator, for the tyme, asked Mr Lawrence Olyphant whether or not he had made intimatione of the appoyntment of the Presbyterie made the last day ? answered he had done the same, and gave in the names of the elders who eate and drank with Andrew Andersone excommunicate viz. David Wentone, John Laying, Thomas Andersone, Patrick Birrell ; Johne Low, Mr David Fairfull, and Patrick Ramsay, and Andrew Andersone his father, who prayed with his sone excom- municate. The foirsaid persones being particularlie in- terrogate be the Moderator declaired, they drank with him. As also the said Mr Lawrence gave in the names of thes who confessed they did take him by the hand, but did not drink with him viz. John Philp ; Patrick Beatt, John Birrell. The Moderator shewing to the saids Elders the

---

[1] Selections from the Minutes of the Synod of Fife, p. 151.

greatnes of ther sine with the foirsaid excommunicate persone, appoynted Mr Lawrence Olyphant to intimate out of pulpit next Sabboth, a day of humiliatione to be keepit on Sunday come aucht dayes therafter, be the whole parish of Newburgh, that all and everie one of them may be humbled for so great a sine. And in particular the foirsaid elders ar appoynted to sit befor the said pulpit the said day, and everie one of them particularie to acknowledge thir syne in conversing with the foirsaid excommunicate persone, and Andrew Andersone for praying with him. And therafter the said Lawrence is appoynted to receive them. All which is done according to Act of Synod made thereanent.'[1]

'June 24, Mr Lawrence Olyphant declaired that Andro Anderson, elder, had satisfied the kirk according to the ordinance of the presbyterie, for praying with his sone excommunicate.'[2]

None of the foregoing extracts specify the offence of which the unhappy person, who was the cause of all this trouble, was guilty, but whatever it was, the proceedings show the iron rule under which the people were held in those days by their ecclesiastical superiors. It is difficult to conceive how ministers of the gospel of 'Peace and goodwill,' could arrive at the conclusion that a father should not pray with a wayward and erring son, or how the people could stifle their natural affections, and submit to such a tyrannous sentence; but there is too much reason to believe that the people were at one with their ecclesiastical rulers, and that the spirit which dictated the decision was the same as that which lighted the fires of the Inquisition in a preceding age.

That the clergy, however, had a hard task in reforming the manners of the people, is evident from the records of presbyteries

---

[1] *Selection from the Minutes of the Synod of Fife*, p. 112.   [2] *Ib.*, p. 116.

and kirk sessions, which teem with details of licentiousness and abuse. The following in regard to the violation of the Lord's day cannot fail to strike with surprise readers who are accustomed to believe in the strictness of our forefathers in holy things, and who are now in the enjoyment of the quietness of a country Sabbath.

> '9th April 1641. Hyring of shearers on the Sabbath.' 'Anent the fearfull and inordinat abuse of the Sabbath day at Cupar, and divers other partis by mercatis of men and women offering themselves to be hyred for the harvest everie yeir, with such obstinate boldness that it cannot be restrained, recommended to this synod by the ministeris and magistratis of this burgh. It was thoght meit by the whole synod, that it should be earnestlie represented to Parliament for the civill restraint.'

> 'August 6, 1649, this day we received a letter from the Presbvterie of Perth, desyring our concurrence for taking away the scandalous and sinful fying of shearers on the Sabboth day at Abernethy. The Presbyterie ordeines the same to be discharged publickly out of pulpit, and that ther be no fying of shearers upon the Lords' day at Aber-nethy, nor Couper, nor any wher else within our bounds.'

There are, however, frequent records of a more pleasing cha-racter. The following is a notice of a contribution by the churches in the presbytery of Cupar for the people of Argyle, who seem to have come under some heavy calamity, and is one of those many benevolent acts to which the church was so often minis-trant. The minister of Newburgh had been entrusted with the transmission of the fund collected, and at a meeting of presbytery held on the 9th March 1648, he presented a discharge signed by Sir James Stewart as follows :—

'I, James Stewart, merchant of Edinburgh, grauts me to have

ressauit from Mr Laurence Olyphant, minister of Newburgh, in the Presbyterie of Cuper, the soume of six hundreth four scoir and fourtene libs as the collection above specifeit for the distressed people of Argyle, quherof I discharge the said Mr Laurence in name of the said presbyterie, by wertue of ane warrant of the Generall Assembly ordaineing me to receave the severall contributions. Witness my hand at Edinburgh, the 19 of Feb. 1648. J. Stewart.'[1]

The following case of delinquency is from the same record :—

'May 9 1650, James Dury, in the paroche of Newburgh being called, compeirs, and was declared be the minister, to have been out of the Kirk eight sabaoths, and becauce he would no ways give satisfaction, by submitting to the discipline of the Kirk he is recommended to the civile Magistrate to be put in firmance till he fand sufficient caution to give satissfaction to the order of the kirk.'

The following incident connected with Cromwell's invasion is of local interest. After the battle of Dunbar, which was fought on the 3d September 1650, and in which Cromwell was so completely victorious, Charles II. quitted Dumfermline, and assembled a Parliament at Perth, which sat there from the 13th to 31st March 1652. The king endeavoured to retrieve his fallen fortunes by raising troops to join the remains of General Lesly's army near Stirling, and by sending forward supplies. The following order, preserved in Sir James Balfour's Annals, brings before us a commissariat very different from the requirements of modern armies :—

'1651, Saterday 15 March. His Matie and parlt ordaines the Com: of Warre of Fyffe to prowyde horsse for carrinng 700 bolls meal from Newbrughe to Stirling with all possible diligence.'[2]

---

[1] *Selections from the Minutes of the Presbyteries of St Andrews and Cupar*, p. 119.
[2] Balfour's *Annals*, Vol. IV., p. 264.

Cromwell crossed the Forth and over-ran Fife. Charles led his troops southward to be defeated at Worcester, only to return nearly ten years afterwards. General Lesly was the youngest son of Patrick, first Lord Lindores, well known as one of the ablest commanders of his time.

The following extracts are from the records of the kirk session of Newburgh—

> 'This act apointed by the Session to be reg^te the Tennor qrof follows '—
> The q^lk day Patrick Pecock and Thomas Anderson, baillzies sittand in judgement w^t the Counsel and neighbours frequentlie convenit inacts statuts and ordanis yt no heretor or possessor of the borrow ruds of the burgh sall sett any house to strangers incomers to the burgh unles they be tryed be honest people and have sufficient testimonialls from qure they cam or else livd w^t in . . . seven yeires without sclander, under the penaltie of four lib Scottis to be payit be the setter of the house and fourtie shillings be taken, or tennant of the house TOTIES QUOTIES wtout leave askit.' Extract by me, David Fairful, Clerk.'

> '1652 March 21, The whilk day Mr Laurence Oliphant payed to the Session of ye Kirk of Newburgh sextein libs: usual money of this realm, twa yeiris annual-rent off twa hundred merkes money foirsaid left to the kirk of Newburgh be umquhyll Patrick Philp sumtime burges.'

> 'Apryle 11. The Minister advertysed the people for thair better information in the knowledge off the groundis off the Christian religion he was to have every sabbath afternoon catachetical doctrine.'

April 25, 1652. The Minister intimated ane voluntar contribution to be collected for the supplie of sojouris officiaris and gentillmen imprisoned in Tinmonth and about Newcastle.'

The prisoners for whom this contribution was made undoubtedly belonged to the army which Charles II., when he failed to dislodge Cromwell's forces from Fife, led into England, and was defeated at Worcester in September preceding the date of collection. Charles himself, it will be remembered, only escaping by concealment, and by the aid of faithful adherents.[1]

'May 9. The Minister declaired from the pulpit that thair was ane ordinance sett down be the session, that who sall be deprehended taking sneizing, clatering, making tumult, trouble or din, cuting, carving · the comunion tables, or playing at the bowlls, casting bullets or trying ony pastyme upon the sabbath day shall testyfie thair repentance befoir the pulpit in presens of the people, and pay ane pecuniall soum according to the determination of the session.'

'1652, June 20. The comunion should have been celebrated this day but the coming to the towne of three hundereth Inglishmen impeded both people and pastor. Communion God willing was to be celebrated next Sabbath.'

The 'three hundereth Inglishmen' were part of the forces of Cromwell.

'August 28 1652. This day the Presbyterie againe takeing to ther consideration the vyle and horrid murther committed by John Heburne of Atheirstane, in killing James Laing, servant to the Laird of Rankilour Makgill, younger,

---

1 Grub's *Ec. Hist.*, Vol. III., p. 156.

as is confessed by the said Laird of Atherstane in his letter written to the Presbyterie,—the Presbyterie, after due and grave deliberation anent the said matter, and considering the many weighty aggravating circumstances of that murther, doe, for the atrocity of that fact ordane the said John Heburne of Atherstane to be summarlie excommunicated by Mr Alexander Balfour in the Kirk of Ebdy, in the quhilk parish the said murther was committed, as the said Laird of Atherstane was travailing by the way, upon the next Lord's day being the 31 of August.[1]

'1652 Sep. 5. The whilk day compeired Sir Robert Crichtoun in name and behalf of Ludovick Leslie of Mugdrum desyring the Session [of Newburgh] that they wuld apoint some seat in the church, or desyne some pairt in the church for him and his familie to sett up ane seat intill, since the lands was annexed to the parochine of Newburgh and had no seat designed for that familie to sitt in. As also compeired George Orme desyring the foresaid session they wald declair the seat belonging to the lands he had boght, to be appropriated to him and his familie.'

Ludovic Leslie was fourth son of Patrick, first Lord Lindores. He commanded a regiment of Scots in the Swedish army, and served with great distinction under the famous Gustavus Adolphus. His younger and more celebrated brother David, afterwards Lord Newark, was an officer in the same service.[2]   Shortly after his return Colonel Ludovick Leslie bought the 'Reid Inch' [Mugdrum Island] from William Oliphant of Balgonie (10 June 1647), and afterwards the estate of Mugdrum from George Orme, whose family had possessed Mugdrum for several generations.   This

---

[1] *Selections from the Minutes of the Presbytery of St Andrews and Cupar*, p. 165.
[2] Chambers's *Domestic Annals*, Vol. II., pp. 56-57.

latter transaction explains why both of them made application for seats in the church at the sametime. Colonel Ludovick Leslie was Governor of Berwick in 1648, then a most important trust, and was alive as late as 1663–4, as he resold the Reid Inch and Mugdrum to William Arnot, brother of James Arnot of Wood-milne, in the beginning of that year.[1]

> 1653 Januar 9. The Session taking to thair consideration sundrie women of this parochine orderlie contracted three several Sabbaths orderlie proclaimed within the kirk of Newburgh concerning thair promiss of marriage w^t thair future husbands. The saids weomen goeth to other Kirks to perfyt and accomplish thair promise of marriage, whairby ye poor of this parochin are prejudged, the selleris of aill, bread, flesh and other victuals are damnified. Thairfor ye Session with ane assent and voice hes ordained whosoever off that, . our awen minister being present in health able ane willing to perfyt thair promise of marriage y^t they shall goe to ony other church for the effect foirsaid they shall pay ten merkes usuall money of this realme.'

This entry speaks volumes for the marriage festivities at that time, and shows that bridal had not lost its original signification of *bride-ale* in those days. It would appear that before proclamation of marriage was made in the church, both bride and bridegroom were obliged to lodge a pledge in the hands of the session, which was redelivered to them on the consummation of their marriage. These pledges are the origin of the term *wedding*, applied to a marriage. ' The wedding was the civil contract, deriving its name from the *weds*, pledges or securities that passed between the bridegroom and the parents or guardians of the bride. The giving away represented the final completion of the marriage

---

[1] *Mugdrum Charters.*

after the necessary arrangements had been concluded; and upon this occasion, according to an ancient regulation, a priest was to be present in order to sanctify the legal union by his blessing.'[1] The following entries are instances of this custom:—

> ' 1653 Januar 16. Robert Sorroh his pledge viz. 4 lib rede-livered.'
> ' Alison Maire hir gold ring redelivered.'

The next entry shows not only an open disregard of the Lord's day, but an irreverence for the dead which it is difficult to conceive in a people who clung with tenacity to the desire of being buried in the graves of their ancestors.

> ' 16 Januar 1653. The maister maid intimation from ye pulpit, that na person play at ye football, or use ony gams or pastyme in ye kirkyard upon ye Sabbath day, whilk give they doe they shal be conjured be ye session.'[2]

> ' 1653 Januar 16, Qlk day Sir James Balfour, Kn^t de-syred the Session to concur with him to ye expulsion of some notorious thieves remaining in the towne of New-burgh.' On the 6th March following, the session agreed

---

[1] E. W. Robertson's *Historical Essays*, p. 173.

[2] The same disregard for the graves and memorials of the dead, coupled with a longing for being buried in the graves of their forefathers prevails in Ireland. In 1863 the funeral procession of a small farmer was met on its way to Clonmac-noise; it had come upwards of twenty miles, attended by a large concourse of neighbours, yet in that churchyard were to be seen beautifully sculptured stones of extreme antiquity ruthlessly smashed, destroyed, it was said, by *burying parties* to make room for a grave. It is worthy of note that in the west of Ireland, in the churchyard of Kilmacduagh, the graves are covered with small stones, although there is abundance of grassy sod at hand. This is apparently a relic of the primi-tive custom of burying under a cairn. One grave was so covered while the writer was in the churchyard.

to the learned knight's request, and " concludit " y[t] all the honest men of the town convein together,' on the following Wednesday for that purpose.

' Feb. 27. It is concluded y[t] Patrick Ramsay put out Robert Gourlay and his familie from his toft befoir ye sext day of March next, or else the said Patrick Ramsay be put off ye Session upon ye said sext day of March 1653.'

' Apryl 17, given to Middletoun's trumpeter   6s.

Middleton, was John, first Earl of that name ; sprung from a family owning a small estate in Kincardineshire, he had entered life as a pikeman in Hepburn's regiment in France, but soon was called to take a part in the civil wars in his own country. Serving first the English Parliament and Scottish Estates, and afterwards proving an active and vigorous partisan of the king, he was elevated to the Scottish Peerage after the Restoration for his loyal services.[1] At the battle of Worcester he was taken captive, severely wounded, and as soon as he was in a condition to be removed, was imprisoned in the Tower. Cromwell was greatly incensed against him, and designed to have him tried for his life, but he contrived to make his escape. Middleton afterwards returned to Scotland to receive the command of the Royalist army, and it was when he held that appointment that the kirk session of Newburgh displayed their loyalty and their generosity to his trumpeter.[2]

1653, August 3. The Qlk day ye session being conveined for ye reconciling persons at variance befoir ye giving of the communion. Compeired William Blyth younger and Elspeth Ballingall, the said William being inquyred if he was content to be reconciled with Elspeth Ballingall,

---

[1] *Chambers's Domestic Annals*, Vol. II., p. 364.
[2] *Peerage of Scotland*, Wood's Ed.—Middleton.

answered he was. The said Elspeth being inquyred if she was content to be reconciled with William Blyth, she answered not. Qrupon the Session did resolve to admitt the said William to the participation of the sacrament in respect of his willingness to be reconciled with the said Elspeth, and to dischairge the said Elspeth from coming to the Lord's Table in respect of her refusing to be reconciled. Which being intimat to the foirsaid persons, Elspeth Blyth replyed these wordis, if so be Wm Blyth go tak his comunion, 'The muckle divell stand up betwixt him and it.' For this outrageous speech she was summoned to appear before the session, where boldly justifying her conduct, she was cited to appear before the Presbytery, and again and again before the Session, till on the 29 March 1654, it is recorded that 'Elspeth Ballingall apeared befoir ye pulpit and gave evidence of hir repentance.'

CHAPTER XIX.

WITCHCRAFT.

'Superstition rears her baleful form,
  And o'er the landscape casts her dismal shade.
  Strong men shrink with fear, and quail,
  Frenzied by the dread of powers unseen ;
  And on accusations vague as their own fears,
  Doom, to torture and to death,
  Victims of a people's blinded rage.'

Anon.

'Old nature here (she pointed where there stood
  An aged lady in a heavy mood),
  Doth break her staff, denying human race
  To come of her, things born to her disgrace.
  The dove, the dove, the swan doth love the swan
  Nought so relentless unto man as man.'

Drummond.

THE belief in witchcraft, or the supposed possession and exercise of superhuman powers, the most recent writer on the subject says, 'is part and parcel of savage life.'[1] It is universal as the human race, and is the protest of humanity against mere materialism. The belief in the exercise of invisible power filled men with dread, and this dread was all the more terrible from its vagueness. A man under the influence of superstitious fears, saw the working of unhallowed power at every occurrence in life ; at a birth, at death, at home, and on the road, and more especially when any calamity happened. Entertaining not the slightest doubt of the possession

---

[1] E. B. Taylor's *Primitive Culture*, Vol. I., p. 125–6.

of supernatural and unhallowed powers, men wreaked their vengeance on those who, they believed, exercised them. This belief 'sat like a night-mare on public opinion throughout Europe from the 13th to the 17th centuries.' Penal statutes were passed in consequence, which is all the more astonishing, as 'laws of Charlemagne (A.D. 768--800) are actually directed against such as shall put men or women to death on a charge of witchcraft; and in the 11th century ecclesiastical influence discouraged the superstitious belief in sorcery. But a reaction set in, ' mainly due,' it is said, by those who have investigated the subject 'to the spirit of religious persecution which arose in the Roman Church in the 13th century,'[1] and it continued, as the popular persecution of witches, both in England and in Scotland testify, down the opening years of the 18th century.

In Scotland an Act was passed by Parliament four years after the Reformation, dooming all to death who used or sought the aid of ' witchcraft, sorceries or necromancie,' the Act ' to be put in execution by Sheriffs, Stewarts and Baillies with all rigour.'[2] Under this Act an unrecorded number of human beings were brought to trial and suffered death in Scotland. The justiciary records, and those of the kirk sessions, teem with trials and examinations. Were the accusations contained in the latter all published, they would exhibit an appalling list of helpless old women living in constant apprehension of death, either under the forms of law, or by a violent outbreak of popular fury; and society, haunted by a dread of unseen powers, which modern opinion could only faintly realize. The following judicial declaration before the Presbytery of Cupar is one, out of many records, that show how firmly these delusions had taken possession of the popular mind.

' 1649, September 13. Margaret Boyd declares that her good-

---

[1] E. B. Taylor's *Primitive Culture under the Roman Church*, Vol. I., p. 125-6.
[2] Mary, Par. 9, cap. 73.

man Robert Brown, wente to deathe with it, that Elspeth Seith and other two did ryde him to deathe; which he declared before the ministers wyfe, Mr James Sibbald, schoolmaster and David Stennous, elder.'[1]

Grizzel Gairdner, a widow, belonging to Newburgh, was one of the victims of the terrible delusion. She was tried before the High Court of Justiciary in Edinburgh, for 'laying on of seikness upon men, women, bairnis and bestiall.' The belief at that period was universal that witches possessed the power of laying on, or transferring sickness. It was firmly believed that 'they could sicken one at will, and could restore him to health; they could hold his malady in suspense, or lay it dormant, to be excited or let loose as occasion should require; or they could transfer it immediately from one animated being to another.'[2] The record of Grizzel Gairdner's trial brings out very strongly these beliefs, and the terrible delusions which brought so many innocent victims to a cruel and untimely end. The following account of her trial is extracted partly from Pitcairn's *Criminal Trials*, and partly from the original records :—

'A.D. 1610, Sep: 7. The quhilk day Grissell Gairdner, relict of vmqle Johnne Baird burges of Newburgh being enterit vpone, pannell dilaitit, accuset and persewit be dittay at the instance of Mr Robert Foullis, advocat, substitute to Sir Thomas Hamiltoun of Bynnie, knight and advocat to our soverane lord for his hienes enteres, and at the instance of Alexander Wentoun, in Newburgh for himself and as informer to our soverane lordis advocat off the crymes vnderwritten; in the first for onlaying be witchcraft and Inchantment of ane grevons diseas and seiknes vpone the said Alex[r] Wentoun; quhairin he lay in a feirfull madnes and furie the space of ten oulkis togidder; and in end, for af-taking

---

[1] *Selections from the Minutes of the Presbyteries of St Andrews and Cupar*, p. 148.
[2] Dalyell's *Darker Superstitions of Scotland*, p. 103.

of the said diseas and grevons seiknes af him be certane directiones gevin, and utheris practizes vset be hir for his recoverie; committit be hir in the moneth of februare last bypast. Item for her devillisch sorcerie and witchcraft practizet be hir In laying on the lyk feirfull diseas and vnknawin seiknes upone William Andersone, wricht in Newburgh for certane allegit Iniureis done be him to Andro baird hir sone. In the quhilk grevous seiknes he continewit the space of ten dayis togidder, tormentit in maist feirfull maner; and af-taking of the same seiknes be hir be repeiting thryse of certane woirdis, quhilk scho termet prayeris. And sicklyk for bewitching of ane kow perteining to the said William, quhairthrow the haill milk that scho thairefter gaif was bluid and worsam; committed be hir devilrie and inchantment in the monethe of May last by-past. Item for the bewitching, be her devillrie and Inchantment of James Andersone sone to Margaret Balfour in Newburcht, in onlaying of ane grevons seiknes and diseas upon him; quharof in ane grit ffurie and madnes, within foure dayis eftir onlaying thairof, he decessit; and thairthrow for airt and part of his murthour and deid committed be hir in the zeir of God jm vjc and fyve years. Item for ane cowmone and notorious witche and abusear of the people, be laying on of seiknes upone men, wemen, bairnes and bestiall, and be geving of drinkis and useing of uther vngodlie practizes for aftaking of the saidis seiknessis and diseasis, and be consulting with the Devill and seiking of responssis fra him at all tymes this fourtene or fyftene zeir byane, for effectuating of hir devillisch Inventiones. Quhilk being red to hir and scho judiciallie accuset tharupoun denyit the samyn altogidder to be of veritie. The Justice [Sir William Heart] tharfoir referrit the samyn crymes to the knawlege of the persones of assyse following. William Ramsay, burges of Newburgh, chancellor; Robert Ballingall, thair; Robert Allan, thair; George Henderson, thair; James Cuik, thair; John Allan, thair; John Lambhird, thair; John Potter, thair; Andro Andersoun, thair; William Smyth, thair; David Baveradge, thair; Johne Blithe, thair; Henrie Pitcairne, thair; Henrie Tod, in

Burnesyde; David Blithe in Ormestoun and William Ballingall, portioner of Berriehill.'

It will be observed that contrary to the modern practice, the assize were summoned from the locality to which the accused belonged. Mr John Russell, her advocate, raised objections 'to Stevin Philp because he was sib' to the pursuer; 'to Robert Allane because he was thridis of kin' to one of those said to have been injured by the accused, and to George Henderson ' because the pannel had lettres of lauborrus against him.' James Durie was repellit be the Justice because he admitted ' that he buir the pannell na guid will.'

'The advocat desyres for forder information to the assyse of the pannellis giltiness of the haill crymes lybellit, that the minis- teris declaration anent hir lyfe, tred and conversatioun, as also David Orme bailzie of Newburghtis ayth and declaratioun of that part of the dittay concerning Andersones wyfe and bairnis be ressavit.

'Mr Russell, procurator for the pannell, objected to their de- claratiouns being received, "except thai war insert as persewaris in the summondis." And the pannell protestit that the declara- tioun to be maid be Mr John Cauldcleuche, minister in this matter quherupon scho is dilaitit be nawayis respectit, or advertit vnto be the assyse.'

'Mr John Cauldcleuche, minister, being sworn maist solemnlie be the Justice, deponis that a fourtene zeir syne this Grissell gairdner was than suspect to be ane wicket woman and ane sorcerer, and be the depositiones of the witches execute for sorcerie and witchcraft at Abernethie, Falkland and Newburcht scho was reput to be ane manifest witch; bot becaus ther was na precedent fand qualifeit aganis hir, the presbiterie thairfoir delayit hir tryell and accusatioun. And as concerning hir lyfe and conversatioun sen syne scho hes bene suspectit to be ane verrie evill woman; and for hir privat revenge aganis sic as scho buir ony malice vnto, hes uset devillisch and vngodlie measirs be sorcerie and incantatioun to lay on divers grevons diseass on thame; and speciallie on the persones set doun in her Indytement; quhair throw the cuntrie and parochin quherin scho dwellis hes bene gritlie sclanderit in suffering sic ane persone vnpuneist, ffor the quhilk caus the presbiterie eftir tryell of the former offences done be hir alsweill to the persones contenit in hir dittay, as vpon dyuers vtheris that ar nocht nominat therin, directit the deponer as thair moderatour to notifie the treuth of the premissis to the counsell, that sum ordour mycht be tane anent hir tryell and punishment.'

After accusation of the accused, 'of new agane in their presenis,' the jury 'removet altogidder furth of Court to the assyse house quhar thai be pluralitie of voitis elected and choisit the said William Ramsay, burges of Newburgh, chancellor of the said assyse. Ressonit and votit upone the haill pointis of the dittay above specifeit. And being ryplie and at length advisit thairwith. Reenterit agane in Court quhair thai for the maist part be the mouth of the said chancellor in presens of the said Justice pro-nuncit and declairit the said Grissell to be fylet culpable and convictit of the haill crymes above mentionat; ffor the quhilk caus the said Justice be the mouth of Alex^r Kennydie, dempster of Court, ffand pronuncet and declairit the said Grissell to be fylet culpable and convictit, and decernit and ordanit hir to be tane to the castell hill of Edinburgh, and thair to be wirreit at ane staik quhill scho be deid, and thereftir hir body to be brunt in ashes, and all hir moveabill guidis and geir to be escheit and inbrocht to our souerane lordis use, as convict of the saidis crymes; quhilk was pronunced for dome.'[1]

The following extracts from the Records of the Presbytery of St Andrews, where two natural marks on the person of a woman accused of witchcraft, were gravely held as convincing proof of her guilt, is a glaring instance of the popular delusion, and of the superstitious dread under which the whole population laboured.

---

[1] Pitcairn's *Criminal Trials*, Vol. III., pp. 95–98.

'1644 August 21. Roch not to be enlarged: Compeired befor the Presbyterie, James Richiesone, baillie of Pittenweeme and James Airth, clerk therof, requyring the advyce of the Presbyterie, anent one Christian Roch incarcerate there for a witch upon thrie severall dilations of thrie confessing witches, quho have all suffered; as also, a *fama clamosa* for the space of twentie yeirs, and since her incarceration, they have found, by the search of the hangman, two markes; whether or not they might enlarge her upon the earnest dealing of her husband quho is useing all means for obtaineing heirof. The Presbyterie, having taken the matter to their serious consideration thoght the foresaid presumptions so pregnant that they could not bot advyse not to enlarge her till farther tryale.'[1]

In the minutes of the proceedings of the kirk session of Newburgh, there is a record of the examination of a woman, named Katharine Key, on a charge of witchcraft, and 'for cursing the minister.' An imprecation from a reputed witch at that period was heard with dread, and was believed to be followed by certain fulfilment; Katharine Key was therefore brought to trial, and but for a concurrence of circumstances favourable to her, she would have suffered the same or a worse fate than Grissell Gairdner, for many were burnt alive under the same accusation. No apology is offered for the length to which the account of these trials extends, as authentic records are really the history of the period.

'1653 Sep. 4. Katharine Key appointed to be summond against Sunday next for cursing of ye minister because of debarring her from the communion.'

'Sep. 11, Compeired Katharine Key denyed that she cursed the minister, but that she cursed these who were cause the minister debarred her, nevertheles it was declaired by several y^t hard sitting in the Session y^t it wes the minister she cursed and y^t

---

[1] *Selections from the Minutes of the Presbyteries of St Andrews and Cupar*, p. 22.

openly throughout the streitt, and upon her bair knees.' 'The whilk also ye minister gave in against her severall pointis y^t had come to his hearing which he desyred might be put to tryel.'

'1· That being refused of milk from Christian Orme, or some other in David Orme's house, the kow gave nothing but bluid, and being sent for to sie the kow, she clapped the kow and said the kow will be weil, and theirafter the kow became weil.

'2. That John Philp having ane kow new calved, that ye said Katharine .Key came in and took furthe ane peitt fyre and y^r after the kow became so sick that none expected she would have lived, and the said Katharine being sent for to sie the kow, she clapped the kow, and said the kow will be weill enough and she amendit.'

'3. That the minister and his wyfe haveing purpose to take ane chyld of theiris from ye sd Katharine which she had in nursing, the chyld wold sucke none womans breast, being only ane quarter old, bot being brought back againe to the said Katharine presently sucked her breast.'

'4. That theirafter the chyld was spayned she cam to see the chyld and wold have the bairne in her armes, and yrafter the bairne murned and gratt in the nyght and almost the daytyme, also that nothing could stay her untill she died, nevertheles befoir her coming to sie her, and her embracing of her took as weill w^t the spaining and rested as weill as any bairne could doe.

'5. That she is of ane evil brutte and fame and so wes her mother befoir her.

'The Session summonds Katharine Key personally present to compeir against Sunday next to answer to the afoirsaid pointis, and ordainis the beddell to summond the witnesses against afoirs^d day.'

The charges embodied with so much minuteness in the foregoing deliverance, now appear so trivial and childish, that they only provoke a smile; but at the time they were recorded they were a terrible reality, fraught with serious consequences to the accused; life or an agonising death depending on the issue. The accusation contained in the fifth charge of the indictment, that 'her mother befoir her was of evil bruit and fame,' was of momentous import; judge, jury, and people firmly believing that occult powers descended by blood from mother to child.

'Sept. 18, Compeired Katharine Key to answer to the pointis given in against her, as also the witness being called compeired Christian Orme, Katharine Gaddes for the proving of the first point.'

'The said Katharine wes inquyred if she had ony thing to object against the afoirsd witnes, who answered not. The witness were sworn to declair the veritie. Christian Orme depones, that she had ane kow sick and y^t Katharine Key bad her gett ane handfull of rough bear and syth it to her and y^t she did no more.'

'Katharine Gaddes depones that Christian Orme had ane sick kow denyeth the rest. The rest of the witness being called compeired not, ordained to be summond against Sepr 25, and Katharine Key ordained to be present against the said day.'

'Sepr 25, Compeired Katharine Key and Marg^t Philp for the proving of the second point, the said Marg^t was sworn to declair the veritie. Marg^t Philp declairis that her father had ane sick kow but denyes the rest, the rest of ye witness compeired not,—ordained to be summoned against Tuesday next.'

'The aforesaid day Katharine Key is challenged upon these wordis who meitting Patrick Beitt, younger and George Millar upon the way said, 'their goes the kirkmen, the divell take the pack of you;' being enquyred if she spak such speechis denyed the samyn. Patrick Beatt and George Millar ordained to be summond for the proof of them against Sunday next.'

'Octr 2, Compeired Katharine Key, being inquyred if she had any thing to object against the witness, answered not. All of them being sworne depones as followis—David Smyth depones that Christian Orme had ane sick kow but denyes the rest.'

Agnes Stirk being examined anent the third poynt, depones that the bairne did suck her bot would not suck upon ane Sunday after noone.'

P

'Katharine M'Larane being examined anent the third poynt depones y^t ye bairne would suck none until y^t she was had to Kathrine Key.'

'Christian Freebairne being examined depones y^t she hard ye bairne greitt very sore often tymes, but could not tell the reason of it.'

'Kathrine and Margarett Layngs being examined declairis as Christian Freebairne that they hard the bairn greitt sore baith day and night but could not tell the reason of it. Marg^t Peacock declaires sicklyke.'

Kathrine M'Larane examined upon the 4 points declairis that the bairn restett weill enough befoir Kathrine Key cam to see her bot gratt ever after untill her dying day.'

'Kathrine Key was called upon, and Patrick Beatt younger, and George Millar to witness the truth of the wordis spokin be Kathrine Key, to wit, 'Their goes the kirkmen the divell take the pack of you.' Kathrine Key being inquyred if she had any thing to object against the afoirsaid witnes, answered not,—they being sworn depones as followis—Patrick Beatt being examined, depones he hard Kathrine Key speak the wordis lybellit. George Millar being examined depones he hard Kathrine Key speak the wordis lybellit.'

'The session taking to their consideration the afoirsaid pro cess, in respect Janet Andersone one of the witness wes sick; Annas Philp anoy^r of the witness was resyding in Falkland; Margarett W^{m}Sone was in Edinburgh, found that the afoirsd proces wes not fully tryed, y^{r}foir delayed to determine yrin untill it wes more fully tryed be the witness to be examined. Kathrine Key called upon and was shewed her be the minister y^t her process was not as yett fully closed. But y^t advertisement sould be given unto her q^n she sould compeir againe to heir sentence.'

'1654. 19 March. The qlk day ye session taking to consideratioun the afoirsaid process of Kathrine Key which had layn so long over for further tryel and finding y^t y^r was no further lyt to be had in ye afoirsd particulars, the process being read over be ye minister as it is now extracted the whole Elderis in ane voyce declaired y^t it was ye very process as it was led on against Kathrine Key, and y^{r}foir they thought good y^t ye afoirsd sould be referred to the presb: Lykas in one voyce they did refer the samyn to be judged and censured according as they found her fault deserve, and summond Kathrine Key to appear befoir ye presb: to be holden at Cupar ye 23 of yis instant.'

'May 3, 1655, Mr David Orme reports, that he, with Mr Alexander Bàlfour, had delt with Katharin Key and found her sensible of hir guiltinesse of cursing hir minister. The minister is appointed to intimat to the parish if any had anything concerning witchcraft to object, that they come to the sessioun, and give it in; and if nothing be found of that kynd, she shall declare hir repentance in the publict place of repentance for cursing.'[1]

'3d Junii Kathrin Key compeired befoir ye session having been befoir the presb: the minister declaird he was appointed be the presb: to intimatt out of the pulpitt anent Kathrin Key if any person had any thing to lay to her charge anent witchcraft, or relating yrto they sould compeir befoir ye session, and yrafter she to be admitted to her repentance for cursing the minister and session if nothing anent the former came in against hir.'

'10 Junii ye session sitting, ye beddell was desyred to call at ye church door if y^t yr wer any yt had any thing to say against Kathrin Key they sould compeir, he having called 3 severall tymes, and none compeiring ye session appoints her to compeir on the publict place of repentance ye next Saboth, for cursing the minister and Session.'

'24 Junii. This day Kathrin Key appeared in the place of publict repentance for cursing ye minister and session, she declaird her griefe for ye same. No dittay being anent her for witchcraft as so is.'

It is more than probable that the accused was thus leniently

---

[1] *Selections from the Minutes of the Presbytery of St Andrews and Cupar*, p. 170.

dealt with, from the salutary influence of the English judges appointed by Cromwell at this very period to administer the law in Scotland; they having expressed their determination to inquire into the tortures that were used to extort confession from the unhappy victims of popular superstition.[1] All 'the witches' in Newburgh did not, however, escape so easily. In 'Lamont's Diary,' under date November 1661, it is recorded, 'This month, the two weoman in the Newbrought that were apprehended above a yeire agoe for burning Mr Lawrence Oliphant, minister of Newbrough's, his house, were hanged at Cuper in Fyffe, being found guilty by the cyse; also they were accused for witchcraft, because delated by some of ther owne nighbours in the towne, who wer brunt a littell befoir this execution; but ther weomen did confesse nether, bot still pleaded innocence as frie both of burning the house and of witchcraft.' A little further on he says, '1661, This yeire ther were divers persons both men and women apprehended for witch-craft in Lowthian and Edinborough, and sundrys of them brunt; also *some* were taken in Newbrough in Fyffe and brunt likewyse.'[2]

The following extract from the records of the Presbytery of St Andrews, is another proof of the very great number of victims that were executed at the time that the persecutions for witch-craft was at its height.

'1643 October 18. *Attend burning of witches.* Mr Robert Blair, Mr Colein Adams, Mr Robert Traill and Mr James Wood are appointed to goe to Craill on Fryday, and attend the execution of some witches, and to give ther advyce to the judges concerning the dilations of others, if they may be apprehended and tried.'[3]

Such is the indefinite way in which the judicial murder is spoken of. After accusation before the kirk session, the second step in the process seems to have been to hand the accused over

---

[1] Chambers's *Domestic Annals*, Vol. II., p. 219.   [2] Lamont's *Diary*, p. 178-9.
[3] *Selections from the Minutes of the Presbyteries of St Andrews and Cupar*, p. 16.

to the civil authorities for further examination, and for torture to extort confession. 'The whole proceeding was of a most cruel description, and often the worst sufferings of the accused took place before trial, when, dragged from home by an infuriated mob, tortured to extort confession, and half starved in gaol. A wretch, called John Kincaid, acted as pricker of witches, that is, he professed to ascertain, by inserting pins in the flesh, whether they were truly witches or not, the affirmation being given when he pricked a place insensible to pain. Often they were hung up by the two thumbs, till nature being exhausted, they were fain to make acknowledgment of impossible facts.'[1]

Such also was the process by which, and the trivial charges on which fellow-men and women were deprived of life in the cruellest of all forms for an imaginary crime. We too often pass over such a narration without a thought, but if we could, in imagination, call up the actual realities of the scene, we should see a crowd of approving spectators, surrounding a poor unhappy woman writhing and shrieking in agony, until death released her at one and the sametime from her torturers and her sufferings.

It is scarcely possible to conceive that men professing to believe in the message of 'peace on earth and goodwill towards men,' could subject their fellow-men to such atrocious treatment. It can only be accounted for on the supposition that the whole population was seized with a frenzy, which deprived them of the use of their better reason. For it was not the work of one, two, or three arch-criminals, such as are met with in history, but of the whole population, who, it is recorded, many times wreaked their vengeance on those whom they thought ought not to have escaped judicial condemnation.

So late as the year 1705, a poor woman of Pittenween, accused of witchcraft, was let off by the authorities of that town; but she was seized by the inhabitants, dragged along the street by the heels, and put to death under circumstances of savage cruelty.[2]

---

[1] Chambers's *Domestic Annals*, Vol. II., p 278.   [2] *Ib*, Vol. III., p. 301

The persecution of witches raged fiercely also in Roman Catholic countries. About the year 1524, one thousand were burnt in the diocese of Como in Italy in one year, besides numberless deaths in other places. But in countries where the spirit of Puritanism was dominant, the persecution seems to have been fiercest. In Geneva about five hundred were burnt in three months,[1] and it was under what is called the second Reformation (1638), that the persecution attained its greatest height in this country.[2] In Fife alone, in the year 1643, thirty women were put to death for witchcraft. So many executions in one county indicates an appalling number of victims throughout Scotland at that era.[3]

Happily all that remains in this neighbourhood to remind us of the terrible infatuation is the name (fast becoming obsolete) of 'The Witch Wells,' where it is probable the unhappy victims belonging to the parish of Newburgh suffered.[4]

---

[1] Hadyn's *Dictionary of Dates.—Witchcraft.*

[2] *Selections from the Minutes of the Presbyteries of St Andrews and Cupar*, pp. 3, 12, 107–130—*et passim.*

[3] Chambers's *Domestic Annnals*, Vol. II., p. 149–154, *et passim.*

[4] The 'Witch Wells' were near the farthest off house on the Wodrife Road. There was also 'The Witch Tree,' on the side of the old road beyond Clatchard, now covered over by the line of railway, under whose branches it was firmly believed witches held their nocturnal meetings.

CHAPTER XX.

' Watch what main-currents draw the years ;
Cut prejudice against the grain,
But gentle words are always gain :
Regard the weakness of thy peers.'

Tennyson.

THE Kirk Session Records of Scotland teem with vivid pictures of many phases of the social condition of the country in the seventeenth and early part of the eighteenth centuries; and it only requires that selections be made and published, to show the value and importance of these Records. The following excerpts are from the minutes of the Kirk Sessions of Abdie and Newburgh :—

'1653 Octob: 9, The Sessioune wes apointed to meitt upon the 12th of October for provision to ane Schoolmaister.'

'16th Their was alleadged against Patrick Beatt younger yt he had drawn leather furth of ye pott upon ane Sabboth day being clerk to the Sessioune in the tyme, he wes inquyred if he had done such a thing, ansuered yt he had never done the lyke.' Evidence being led on several successive Sundays. On the 30th 'James Bell depones yt he [Patrick Beatt] took neither hyd nor half ane hyd, but ane speild of ane hyd, and caried it to the house and yt he bought it from him.' 'The Session finds the offence proved and ordains that both Patrick Beatt and James Bell sould declair their repentance befoir ye pulpit for ye

samyn;' and on the 4 Decr they compeired in presence
of ye congregation befoir ye pulpitt and confessed ye
breach of ye Saboth w^t y^r griefe for ye same.'

' 6 November. Given out to buy coals and peatis for ye Schoolm^r
his use befoir his coming which the Sessioun gave frely
and would not have repayment yrof 3 lib. 12/^s.'

' 27 November. The elderis appointed to visit y^r quarteris for
putting children to ye scool.'

At a subsequent date the following entry occurs on the same
subject —

' Decemb: 9 1666. The same day the Sessioune condiscended
and concluded that the schoolmaster should receive from
them yearlie the soume of fyftie merks as part of his stipend
payable be them to him in all tyme comeing.'

These entries are worthy of special note. It was this super-
vision and encouragement on the part of the church that made
education so general in Scotland.

' 27 Novr. Mr Andrew Tailyesier, Scoolm^r produced ane
testimoniall from Forgoundeny for himself and Christian
boswell his spous which wes accepted as being every way
sufficient.' On the ' 4 December ye Sessioun laid it upon
Gavin Adamson to dischairge Agnes Graham from keiping
any scoole.' The object of this enactment being to maintain one efficient parish school where all classes could obtain good education.

' 1654–12 Feb, payed for Andrew Homes sones qr^ter payment
to ye scoolm^r wh began ye 28 Novr 1653, and wes to end
ye 28 Feb. 1654–13/^s 4^d.'

' 2 Aprylis. Given for ye mort cloath to a blewgown .   10/^s

The privileged class of ' Blue-gowns,' to one of whom the last
rites of humanity are here recorded as having been paid, has been
rendered so famous by Scott's delineation of ' Edie Ochiltree,' that

it is scarcely necessary to say anything of their habits and character. The order having been abolished in 1833, their once familiar forms have long disappeared, and their dress and appearance are totally unknown to the present generation. It may not be out of place therefore, to mention that the Blue-gowns consisted of a number of old men (chiefly soldiers past service), corresponding with the number of years that the reigning king was old. They were called ' the King's Bedesmen,' from the old English worde *bede*, to pray ; their original function being to pray for the king. Each of these bedesmen received annually, a long blue coat or gown, reaching almost to the heels, with a large round pewter badge worn on the left breast, inscribed with the wearer's name, and the words—'Pass and Repass.' This badge was the warrant for their right to solicit alms, all laws against beggars and vagrants notwithstanding.

The old laws against beggars were most stringent and severe. In the reign of James I., A.D. 1424, all betwixt ' fourteene and three score ten yeires,' were prohibited from begging without tokens (of permission) ' under the paine of burning on the cheike, and banishing of the countrie.' [1] A still more severe law was passed in the reign of James VI., A.D. 1579, ' for the suppressing of strang and idle beggrs,' who are ' to bee committed in waird in the commoun prison, stokkes, or irons. . . And gif they happen to be convicted, to be adjudged to be scourged, and burnt throw the eare with ane hot irone.   . Except sum honest and responsall man will of his charitie be contented to act himself befoir the Judge to take and keip the offender in his service for ane haill yeir nixt following   but gif hee be founden to be fallen againe in his idle and vagabond trade of life, then being apprehended of new, he sall be adjudged and suffer the paines of death as a thief.' [2]   From all these severities the favoured ' Blue-gowns ' were exempt. They had their stated rounds, and were received with a consideration which was seldom accorded to the common

---

[1] James I., Par. 1, cap. 25.   [2] James VI., Par. 6, cap. 74.

beggar. The accustomed dole to the 'Blue-gown' was bestowed with feelings of willingness that did good both to giver and receiver. The severe laws quoted were enacted because of the increasing 'multitude of maisterful and strang beggers.' They are in marked contrast to the more merciful enactments of an earlier period. In the reign of David II. (A.D. 1329–1370) it was 'Statute anent pure and weak folk that all they quha are destitute, and wants the help of all men sall be under the King's procuration and protection within his realme. And gif anie man grants and affirmes that he violentlie without law or judgement, hes taken anie thing fra the pure folk, he sall restore that quhilk he tuke, and for ane mends sall pay aucht kye to the King.'

Before the introduction of the Poor Law Amendment Act the country was over-run with beggars. Some of the parish poor made stated weekly rounds with a meal pock around their neck to receive the invariable dole of a handful of oatmeal. It was not uncommon for a dozen or more strangers to solicit alms daily; and down to a comparatively recent period there were some compassionate residenters in the country who provided sleeping-places in their premises, and a supper of oatmeal porridge, for these vagrant poor. They told their stories at the kitchen fire, and were seldom guilty of any misdemeanour—kindly treatment begetting kindly feeling. It is recorded in 'The Blair Adam Book' by Sir Adam Ferguson, that when Sir Walter Scott came to visit Cross Macduff he was victimised by one of this wandering fraternity. Sir Adam, who was present, gives the following jocular account of the incident :—' On the arrival of the party at the west-end of Newburgh, Sir Walter, with his right hand in his waistcoat pocket in pursuit of a sixpenny piece, asked a very old and infirm man, who approached leaning on his staff, 'if he knew anything of Macduff's Cross?' The old one said he could tell him ''a aboot it.' ' Upon which Sir Walter put the sixpence in his hand,

---

[1] *Regiam Majestatem*, David II., cap. XIII.

which it no sooner reached, than the old man sprang up in the air like a youth of sixteen, and twisting his staff (poising it horizontally on the tips of his fingers) round his head, commenced a circular dance, or saraband, accompanied by a wild jargon of a song; and nothing else could be got out of him.' The old man who was a stranger and knew nothing of the Cross, was quite overjoyed at the success of his trick, and would have been still more so, had he been capable of comprehending that he had overreached the Great Minstrel of the Border. There are many who remember the old man ; he had been a soldier in his youth, and was known in the towns he visited by the refrain of the song, ' Neet, Nat Nindie !' which he repeated when performing the evolutions described by the worthy baronet. Sir Walter's discomfiture seems, from Sir Adam's description of the scene, to have been a subject of merriment, at what he calls ' the ambulatory repast' partaken of by the party at Cross Macduff. Sir Walter's poem of ' Macduff's Cross,' which was the result of this visit, contains lines and passages of great beauty.

> ' 2 Aprylis. A bill given in be Helen Paterson ag^t John Clunie her husband read, and ye said Johne apointed to be s^{md} and ye said Helen to be present.'
>
> ' 16, John Clunie compeired and acknowledged ye pointis of ye bill given ^{agst} him be his wife, as also he s^d he my^t doe with his wife y^t he pleased, as also to break her back if he lykit.' ' Qlk ye Sessioun taking to y^r consideration and because they had not had the lyk befoir ^{ym} at any tym preceding referris ye samen to ye presb:'
>
> 14 May qlk day ye Sessioun ordained y^t John Clunie nor his wife sould have no house in the toune because they were frequentlie troubled w^t y^m, and if any sould sett them ane house to y^r perrill be it.'
>
> 16 July, Janet Adisone, Euphan Blyth and Alison Blyth having been sum^d for ye scandalous cariage in scolding and flyting w^t oy^r apeard befoir ye Sessioune.'

'Andro Williamson compeired to declair ye truth y[t] he hard, —depones he hard Limer and witch between Janet Adison and Euphan Blyth, as also y[t] Alison Blyth cam runing in and took amends of Jenet Adisone at her own handis.'

'Q[r] upon ye Sessioune apoints Euphan Blyth, and Jenet Adison to appear befoir ye pulpit for satisfaction and Alison Blyth to goe to ye pillar for repentance.'

Alison Blyth, however, subsequently appeared before the session, 'and desyred she my[t] be received befoir ye pulpit and promised to give somq[t] to ye poor.'

There is nothing in the record to show the difference between appearing before the pulpit and on the pillar. That the latter was the most distasteful is evident from the offer made by Alison Blyth; this is corroborated by a verse of a song which long continued popular :—

> ' And she maun mount the pillar,
> And that's the way that they maun goe,
> For puir folk hae nae siller.'

'26 July, given to a poore lass . . . 2/[s].'

' 6 Aug: The Session apointed such as were absent from ye comunion to be sum[d].'

'26 ye Elderis wer apointed to visit ye toune ye tym of sermon.'

After a violent case of ' scolding and flyting,' of which instances occur in almost every page, the following significant entry appears :—

' This day ye Sessioun apointed y[t] ane pair of brancks sould be mad for offenders.'

' The branks consisted of an iron frame for enclosing the

head, from which projected a spike, so as to enter the mouth and prevent speech.'[1]

Those sentenced to make public repentance were obliged to appear clothed in sackcloth. So late as the 18th August 1747, the following entry occurs in Newburgh Session Records :—

> 'To 4 yards sakine to be a sake goun   1   0   0
>   Augt. 22. To the making of the sack goun 0 12   0.'
> '3 Sep: 1654. This day ye searchers of ye toun reported they fand these persons drinking ye tyme of afternoon sermon, to wit Patrick Scott, James Bennettie, Robert Scott and David Jacksone, in Henrie Mairs house.'
> '8 Octob: This day ye minister read to ye sessioun James Philp his letter will givin a thousand pounds to ye'
> [the rest wanting] but the following entry shows that the bequest was for behoof of the poor, '3 Decemb. 1654. The minister was to wrett James Balfour, anent the thousand pound left by James Philp to ye toune of New- burgh poore.'

James Balfour here mentioned was the learned Knight of Denmilne, so well known for his antiquarian tastes and zeal in collecting ancient records. The following extracts, curious for the light which they throw on the customs and charges in law pro- ceedings in the 17th century, show also that the zealous antiquary was not allowed to pursue his studies undisturbed by pecuniary anxieties.

> '4 Martii 1655—Given out this day for ye extracting of the decreit against James Balfour befoir ye sreff   16/s 8d
> 'Item for decerning 10/s 8d
> 'Ite to ye judge for decerning and sentence money, and to ye

---

[1] Chambers's *Domestic Annals*, Vol. I., p. 47.

clerk for extracting of ye s^d decreit, and drink money to
ye clerks man .   .   .   13 lib: 13/^{s} 4^d.
'Ite for procu^r fie .   .   .   .   .   48/^{s}.
'Ite for the mans charges who went in   .   . 20/^{s}.
'18 Mai: given out to raise letters of horning against James
Balfour, and for ye charging of him   .   . 4 lib.
'22 Ap: given to ye beddell to goe to falkcoland to sie if the
letteris against James Balfour be put in execution 6/^{s}.'
'20 May Alexander Clunie being sum^d pro 3° to compeir befoir
ye presb: on Thursday last, compeired not, ye minister declared he wes apointed by the presb: to sum him out of
pulpitt.'

The ordinary mode of summoning was citation by the beadle;
but in cases of persistent contumacy, after three warnings by that
official, the accused was summoned by name by the minister from
the pulpit, in face of the congregation.

Sam day, 'Given to John Dempster for his drink q^n he wes
slokin ye lym and mixing it w^t sand .   6/^{s}.'
'27 May. The Sessioun continued Patrick Beat and his wife
and Alexander Clunie because of the English being in
Church.'
'This day Sir James Balfour produced a band sub^t be himself
and witness, of the sonme of ane thousand poundis and
wes assigned to the soume of ane thousand poundis w^t
wes left to the Sessioune be James Philp deceased conform
to his testament.'
'1 July. This day the Sessioun concludit in one voyce y^t
every partie to be married sall consigne 8 lib. of pledge
in money, or else pledge double aught pund.'
'15 July. The Fast intimat to be next Lords day and the
causes read.'

The causes are not stated, but 'a severe frost which set in

early in the year, and continued to the middle of April, to the interruption of all farm work, was undoubtedly the cause.[1] A lengthened frost in spring was a serious calamity, from the want of food for bestial, neither clover nor turnips being then cultivated in the fields in Scotland.[2]

' 29 July. This day ye Minister declared in face of Sessioun to Janet Donaldson y^t she wes apointed by the presb: to stand 3 severall Saboths at the Kirk door barfoot and after to go to ye publict place of repentance, and pay her penaltie.'

' 1656, May 11. This day the collection for the brunt landis in Edinburgh, apointed to be intimat be this day fifteen days.' The sum collected was ' 5 lib. 10/^{s}' but it was 'made up out of the box to 6 lib.'

' 20 July. This day compeired Euphan Williamson being sum^d was challenged for breach of Sabboth in laying out cloathes on the Sabboth day, having confessed the samyn, she was ordained by the Sessioun to appear befoir the pulpit to signifie her repentance y^{r}foir on Setterday next being sermon of preparation to ye communion then to be.'

' 23 July. This day Patrick Lyell and James Wilson being sum^d for y^r variance on with anoy^r, and Elderis having dealt with y^m for agriement, yett notwithstanding they persisted in y^r malice on towards another, having compeired befoir ye Sessioun they wer willing to agrie, and in tokin yrof, took oy^r by the hand and promised after y^t not to wrong on anoy^r.'

' 9 November. Given to buy a sand glass for the use of the church.'

' 1657, 3 May. This day Maister Andro Tailyesier, Scoolmaister did demitt his charge, desyrng the Sessioun to

---

[1] Chambers's *Domestic Annals*, Vol. II., p. 234.
[2] *Ib.*, Vol. III., p. 418.

provyde themselves of a scoolmaister against Whitsunday
next ensuing 1657, because he wes purposed to remove at
the said term, and nothing was objected at that tyme
against his removall.'

'17 May. Given to the Collector of the contribution of the
brunt landis of Northampton . . . . . . 18/ˢ.'

'August 23. Whilk day the Sessioun appointed ane meeting
to be for ane schoolmaster, and Intimation to be made
from the pulpit ye next Lord's day for that effect.'

'Decemb: 6, Whilk day the minister recommended to the
Elders what bairnes are within their respective quarters
that they may be put to the comon school of the parishe,
otherwayes they will be complained upon, and ordained
that Agnes Graham be desired to forbear from teaching
any lasses in tyme coming.'

On the 13th December of the same year (1657) a case is
recorded of no special interest except in the mention of terms
that are now entirely disused. John Bickerton is spoken of as a
worker of '*uvirings*,' and John and William Williamson are designated by their trade of '*braboners;*' which signifies menders of
old shoes, and is the origin of the surname of Brabner or Brebner.
'*Uviring*' from '*uver*,' upper, is evidently a coverlet, the weaving
of which, in woollen only, ceased to be practised in Newburgh
towards the end of the first quarter of the present century.

'1658, April 25, Whilk day the Sessione did conclud that in
tymes coming, becaus of ye disorder that was committed
befor the minister came to the pulpit, that there should
be some verses of ane psalme be sung betwixt ye second
and third bell afternoon, and intimation thereof made ye
next Lord's day.'

The enjoining of the praise of God 'befor the minister came
to the pulpit,' is so different from the modern form of worship,

that a few words explanatory of former usages will not be out of place. This portion of public worship was presided over by the Reader. The duties of this official are very clearly set forth by the authors of the 'Introduction to the Book or Common Order.' 'The Bell having rung an hour before, was rung the second time at 8 o'clock for the Reader's Service. The congregation then assembled and engaged for a little in private devotion. So reverential were they, that it was the custom for the people entering the church to uncover their heads, and to put up a short prayer to God, some kneeling some standing. The Reader took his place at the 'lectern,' read the Common Prayers, and in some churches the Decalogue and the Creed. He then gave out large portions of the Psalter, the singing of which was concluded with the *Gloria Patri*, and next read chapters of Scripture from the Old and New Testaments, going through, in order, any book that was begun, as required by the First Book of Discipline. After an hour thus spent, the bell rang the third time, and the minister entered the pulpit,' and conducted the remainder of the service according to the usage of the time. The afternoon service was begun by the Reader in the same way. These usages continued with more or less uniformity down to A.D. 1638 or 1640.[1]

Subsequent to the date mentioned, the duties of the Reader in the time of Episcopacy are particularly defined in the following extract from the records of the Synod of Aberdeen:—'21st October, 1662. It is enacted by the Lord Bishope with consent of the bretherine of the Synod that [there] shall be readers of the scriptures in everie congregatione, and the reader shall begin with a sett forme of prayer, especially with the Lord's prayer. Thereafter they ar to read some psalms with some chapteris of the Old Testament, thereafter they ar to rehearse the Apostolick creed publicklie, and in rehearsing of it stand up, afterwardis that they read some chapteris of the New Testament according to the appointment of the respective ministers; and last of all they are

---

[1] *Book of Common Order*, Edition 1868, pp. xxxiii., iv.

to rehearse the Ten Commandments publicklie.' An English clergyman, chaplain to a Scotch regiment, who published an account of his visit in 1715 says, 'the precentor about half an hour before the preacher comes, reads two or three chapters to the Congregation of what part of the Scripture he pleases, or as the minister gives him directions.' [1]

> 'May 16. Mr Johne Bayne of Pitcairlie compeired befor the Session, and gave in a supplication for a place for a dask. that the tenants of Pitcairly and Easter Lumbeny, may have an opportunity of hearing the Word as they had befor these lands were annexed to the parish.'

The seats in churches at this period were moveable, and were provided by those who sat in them; this continued to be the custom down to the middle of the last century.

The following notice of the allotment of 'Stances' in New-burgh church at a subsequent date, shows this usage :—

> 1686. Feb. the 15. The Minister, Hereters and Elders mett for settling the scatts in the Kirk   it was agreed that the Kirk be peüed be west the pulpit, and that the communitie should choose four men and the Session other four for settling the same pews. The seatts wer settled as follows:
>
> Sir Michael Balfour of Denmylne his seat being nixt the pulpit on the west side, was lifted and sett befor Bailie Wenton his seatt forgainst the pulpit, ther to stand in time coming.
>
> 'The former stance of the said seat ordained to the Laird Rossie, younger.
>
> 'Next to said stance ane double pew for Alex^r. Spence of Berrieholl, James Todd, etc.' Other allotments follow.

---

[1] *Selections from the Records of the Synod of Aberdeen*, pp. lxvii., 262.

'1689, July the 29. It. to the men that caried the Commūnion
   tables into the kirk   00. 02. 08.'

'Oct. 31 1658. Whilk day, intimatione made from the pulpit
   anent ane solemne fast to be keeped the next Lord's day
   befor ye comunion be celebrated or administered.'

The foregoing notice of a Fast on the Sabbath is one which
frequently occurs in the Session Records at this period. The
practice of fasting on the Lord's day, contrary to the usage of the
early Christian church, which held that day as a joyful festival,
commemorative of the resurrection of our Lord, was made the
subject of biting verses, published at the time, of which the following is a part:—

> ' From fasting one the Lord's auen day,—
> Fasting without wairand, I say.
>
> .   .   .   .   .   .
> Almighty God deliver us.' [1]

1659 Junij 12. The same day Robert Blyth compeared befor
   the Sessione in sackcloath, having been at the presbyterie
   and gotten his last Intimation, qrfor he was appointed
   to goe to the publict place of repentance, and sit other
   three Sabbath dayes, and the third Sunday to be received.'

Robert Blyth had previously appeared before the congregation twenty-four several Sabbaths for his offence. This lengthened
period of public penitence was inflicted, because, as an official of
the church, he had brought scandal on religion.

'July 1. 1660. Intimation was made from the pulpit, anent
   ane day of thanksgiving to be on Thursday next for the

---

[1] Maidment's *Scot. Pasquils*, p. 51.

Kingis Majesties [Charles II.] preservation and safe returne to his wonted liberties.'

Aug* 12. The same day M* Jhone Bayne of Pitcairlie's came to the Sessioune and did accept of the office of ane elder.'

Mr John Bayne was a Writer to the Signet, and acquired the lands of Pitcairly by a decreet of apprising of the Lords of Session, from John, fourth Lord of Lindores, having made large advances to that nobleman. He appears to have been a learned and able man.[1] In the Kirk Session Records of Newburgh (18th July 1687) there is a notice of a legacy by him to the poor of the parish of one hundred pounds Scots. He died on the 28th January 1681, and was buried in the Greyfriars Churchyard, Edinburgh, where there is a monument to his memory, bearing the following inscription :—

MEMORIÆ DOCTISSIMI VIRI MAGISTRI JOANNIS BAYNE DE PITCARLIE, SIGNETO REGIO SCRIBÆ INSIGNI EUPHEMJA AIKMAN, EJUS VIDUA, SIBIQ. UTRIUSQ. ET CONJUGIS COGNATIS, MONUMENTUM HOC ERIGI. CURAVIT. OBIIT, QUINTO CALENDAS FBRUARII MDCLXXXI ÆTATIS SUÆ LX.

The monument also bears the following inscription :—

SACRED TO THE MEMORY OF JAMES CATHCART ESQUIRE OF CARBIESTON AND PITCAIRLIE, WHO WAS INTERRED HERE 25 MARCH 1795.[2]

'Novemb 18 1661. Whilk day compeired Jhone Kirk and desired libertie from the Sessione to be contracted with another woman than Hellene Scott whom he had alreadie contracted.'

---

[1] In 1658 J. Bayne acted as Receiver General for Oliver Cromwell in Scotland. *Hist. Records of the Family of Leslie*, Vol. II., p. 109. In all likelihood this was John Bayne of Pitcairly.

[2] *Epitaphs and Monumental Inscriptions, Greyfriars.* Brown, p. 66.

'Decemb. 9. The said Hellene being thrise cited and not compeirand, the Sessione after deliberatione gave libertie to the said Jhone Kirk to goe on in purpose of marriage with another woman.'

'Novemb 15 1663. Quhilk day Intimatione was again made from pulpit . . . and after sermone, the Sessionne being conveined in their ordinar place of meeting, they caused their beddell againe call at the kirk door, to see if there were any person, or persons that had anything to object against Barbara Andersone, Alesone Andersone, and Jennet Ballingall, daughters to the said Barbara, relating to witchcraft, and they should be heard, and for sa meikle as non did compeir haveing relevant reasones, the minister and Elders takeing the matter to serious consideratione, it was votted whether or no the sd persones might be admitted to the ordinances, they all unanimouslie aggried that in tyme comeing they may be admitted to ordinances.'

'Junii 30 1664. The presbyterie appointed Mr Lawrence Olyphant to baptise Jhone Burrell his child he holding up the same, and finding sufficient cautione and giveing bond for a hundred pounds Scotts money that he sall mak declaratione of his repentance in the church of Newburgh.'

'Martij 12 1665. Collected no almes because there was no preaching in respect of the unseasonableness of the weather.'

In Lamont's Diary it is recorded under the year 1665. 'About the beginning of Januar ther fell mutch snow and the frost began six days before ; this storm continued till near the middle of March or thereby, and some snow was sein after the 1 Aprill in some places, so that some begane to say their would hardly be any seid tyme this yeire, bot it pleased the Lord out of his gratious goodness on a sudden to send seasonable weather for the seid tyme, so that in many places the oatte seide was sooner done this yeire than many yeiris formerly, for the long frost made the ground very frie, and the whole husbandmen, for the most pairt they never saw the ground easier to labour. This yeire ther dyed many sheipe in many places of Fyffe. . . . And this storm blasted mutch broome in many places, as also whinns in divers pairts.'[1]

> 'Junij 4 1665, Quhilk day Intimation was made from the pulpit, anent a solemne fast to be upon wedensday the seventh day of this Instant, and the causes of the fast were publicly read out of the pulpit to wit. That God of his mercie would bless and preserve our Kingis majesties navall forces by sea.'

The people were so alarmed by the dread of invasion that 'the Towns on the north shore of the Firth of Forth had daily and nightly watches for their defence in case they should be surprised by the Hollanders.'[2] Lamont, in mentioning the Fast says, 'Within two or 3 dayes after, newes came that the two fleitts viz.: the English and Dutch had engaged. June the 3 and 4 and that the English had carried the day, and that six of the Dutch Admiralls were taken and some of them brunt, and that only one of the admiralls had escaped namely, Ebertsone with 43 vessels to the Texell. Also 24 more vessels taken and brunt, with about 9 or 10 thousand men taken, as both printed and wretten peapers affirmed, and only one vessell called the Charitie lost to the English, with about 400 men, and some noblemen and others of note.'[3]

> '1665 Sep[r] 10, Intimation was made be ye minister, anent a solemn fast and humiliation to be upon the threttrine day of this ins[t], being Weddensday, whilk was indicted and

---

[1] Lamont's *Diary*, p. 224.   [2] Chambers's *Domestic Annals*, Vol. II., p. 302.
[3] Lamont's *Diary*, p. 226.

commanded be ye counsell. 1ˢᵗ That it would please God of his infinit mercie to remove the plague of the pestilence from ye citie of Lundon and ye suburbis yʳ about. 2ᵈˡⁱᵉ that it would please God to preserve and keep Scotland from that fearfull plague of pestilence; and thirdlie that it would please God to send fair and seasonable weather for collecting and ingathering of the fruites of the ground for the sustentation of man and beast.'

Januarij 27: 1667. Quhilk day there was debursed to the glassen wright for glassen windowes and for repairing the samen . . . . . . 9 libs.

'August 9 1668. Quhilk day Intimation was made anent the celebration of the holie supper of the Lord, to be upon the next Lords' day, and of ane sermon of preparatione to be upon Saturneday befor the Sabbath.'

This was in the time of Episcopacy, under which no public Fast appears to have been appointed previous to the communion.

April 25 1669. Quhilk day the Sessione has condiscendet, that there shal be a voluntar collectione to be next Lords day, for to help George Leslie that he might be cutt of the stone, and the people were exhorted to extend thair charitie yrunto.'

Whatever may have been the cause, there seems to have been a prevalence of this disease in Scotland. Thirty years later a 'chirurgeon' advertised that he had 'cutted nine score persons, without the death of any except five.'[1] Still later there are entries in the Session Records, which show that children were afflicted with this painful disease. In the Books of Abdie Kirk Session the following occurs viz.:—

---

[1] Chambers's *Domestic Annals*, Vol. III., p. 260.

'1720, Oct. 16.   To Michael Hog to help to bear the expenses
   of cutting his child of the gravel.   ·   06   14   06
'1721 April 27.   To the physician to help to
   pay for it   02   08   00
And on the '15th Novr 1739' the following
   appears in Newburgh Kirk Session books.
   'To a poor lad with the stone gravel.'   .   00   04   00

'1670–8 day of May.   The quhilk day the minister did intimat to the congregation that George pattillo and Agnes
   mitchell wer excommunicat, and accordingly advertised
   them, that non of them should have anie felowship with
   them.'
   Sicklyke he intimat William Scot, one of the paroch of
   Dunino was fugitive from the discipline of the church, and
   therefor ordained if any knew of him to give notice.'
'Collected the 29 day of May 9 lib.' which collection was
   given to repaire the breach by fire at Coupar, the   .   .   .
   day of Apprile 1669.'
'1671, 19 day of Feb.   The same day the discharge for the
   supplie of those who wer distressed by fire in Kilmarnock
   and put in the box.'
   The eleventh of Aprill 1672.   The quhilk day the presbyterie
   mett at Newburgh for admission of Mr Robert Bayne to
   the function of the bolie ministrie in the said paroch,
   which was don accordingly in decency and ordour according to the practise of this church, the heritors and elders
   of the paroch being conveined of purpose to countenance
   his admission.'
'1673, 25 May.   The same day the Session and heritors did
   condescend and ordaine, that the two old bells should be
   carried to Kirkcaldie with all convenient dilligence, that
   they might be converked thence to Holland or some other
   convenient pleace for makeing them in a new, and that ther

should be an 100 weight mor added to the sds bells, and
that the bellkony should be fitly repared for careing a bell
of such a quantity as is afforesaid.'

' 28 Decemb. Whilk day David Blyth compeared and gave 4 lib,
and 8d. In part of payment of 10 merks for David Win-
touns buriall in the Church.'

The custom of burying in churches began at an early period.
The author of the extremely curious tract, entitled, 'The Blame
of Kirk-buriall Tending to Perswade Cemiteriall Civilitie,' published in 1606, says, 'So soon as the Kirk-ground came by the
opinion of holy prerogative for souls helpe, the opportunity and
privilege was both sought and boght to ly there,' and he de-
nounces those who practise 'Kirk-buriall,' in quaint and vigorous
language.[1] Shortly after the Reformation, on the 24th October
1576, the General Assembly had proposed to them the question,
'Qwither if burialls sould be in the Kirk or not? Ansuerit, Not;
and that ye contraveiners be suspendit from ye benefites of the
Kirk, quhill they make publick repentance.' On the 6th August
1588, the Assembly passed another ordinance, containing among
other enactments the following: 'The minister that gives his
consent [to burials in his church] and discharges not his conscience
in opponeing them therto salbe suspendit from his function of the
ministrie.' [2]

The desire to be buried in the graves of their forefathers was
stronger than the fear of these ordinances, and there are instances
on record of burials in churches having been effected by main
force.[3] The customary way, however, notwithstanding the pro-
hibitory ordinances of the Assembly, was, as in the case cited from
Newburgh Kirk Session Records, to purchase permission. An
interesting instance of this mode occurs in Perth Session Records,
under date ' Saturday, February 25 1657. Whilk day the Minister

---

[1] *The Blame of Kirk-buriall,* Chap. XIII.
[2] *The Book of the Universall Kirk of Scotland,* pp. 378, 733.   [3] *Ib.* 272.

and Elders convened in the Revestry immediately after morning prayers, the minister propounded that Lady Stormonth earnestly desired license to bury umquhil Dame Margaret Crighton, Lady Balmanno, her mother in the east end of the kirk beside the corpes of umquhil the Earl of Gowry: And that she would pay to the hospital the sum of one hundred pounds money for her buriall leave.' The session consented, and the money was paid to the hospital.[1]

'1674, 9th August. As also it being intimated to the Sessione that the Boatmen haveing passed over the water on the Lords day and broken the Sabbath, should be summoned against the nixt day to answer for the breach of the same.'

'30 Aug[t]. given to ane stranger on the said day called Dame Geils Moncrief, 4 merks according to the Bishop's order.'

'7th March 1675. On which day the minister intimated from the pulpit that the Sacrament of the Lords' Supper should be celebrated the next Lords' day, and for that effect that he would examine those of the Landert after the afternoon sermon, and those in the towne on monday and tuesday, as also that they should have for better preparatione sermon on Saterday.'

'1675 Sep: 18. The qlk day given to Henrie Arnott for carieng a crippell woeman to Abernethie   00 02 00.'

The practice of leading blind, and carrying cripple beggars from house to house, by one neighbour to that of his next neighbour, is fresh in the remembrance of many still alive. The mode of carrying the cripple was on a hand-barrow, and it continued down to the introduction of the Poor Law Amendment Act.

'1675 Dec[r] 18. No collection because ther came feu people, it being a very foule day.'

---

[1] *Blame of Kirk-buriall*, Editor's Preface, p. viii.

'The winter of 1675–6 being singularly mild, was followed by a favourable spring, and there consequently was an abundant harvest. The characteristic mutability of our climate was, however, shown immediately after. There was drought in latter autumn, and about the 18th of December the temperature fell to an extraordinary degree, the most aged people never remembered the like. The birds fell down frae the air dead, the rats in numbers found dead; all liquors froze, even the strongest ale, and the distilled waters of apothecaries in warm rooms froze in whole and the glasses broke.' [1]

> 'The qlk day ther was intimation made conforme to the act of synod of an collection for the Relief of the Captives in Asia.'
> '1678, Feb. 12.—A Collection for the distressed merchants of Monros being intimated the forgoing Sabbath was collected, which is 18. s. and delivered.'
> 'Feb 26. The same day given out of the box 4 lib. 6. s. as the charitie alloūed be the session for the reliefe of the christians taken prisoners with the Turks.
> '1679, May 18. Sicklike Intimatione was made from the ˙pūlpit for tūo Collections for repairing ye harbours of Eeymouth and Piterhead.'
> 'June ye 8. Collect for Piterhead . . . 16/ˢ.'
> 'Augᵗ 23. Sicklike yis day the Collectione for Eeymouth, was augmented and sent to the receiver, being three pounds scots . . . . . . 3 lib:
> '1680, August ye fourth—the familie of Lundores was catechised.'
> 'This day given to a poor man called John Boigie, who had been tennant in Buspie, and his goods all wasted by the malefice of a Witch as his testificat bears . 4/ˢ.'
> 'Sepᵗʳ·1, given to Alexʳ Innes ane Indigent Gentleman in ye

---

[1] Chambers's *Domestic Annals*, Vol. I., p. 373.

paroch of Tannadice in Angus, who had formerly been in
ye Kings troupe and now reduced, resolves to plenish a
roome   .   .   .   .   12/ˢ.'

The expression 'to plenish a roome' is now obsolete in the
sense in which it is used in the foregoing extract; it then signified
to stock land for its cultivation. On the 10th September 1657, Mr
David Orme, minister of Monimail was accused of neglecting his
duty 'by labouring of land;' he admitted 'that he had land in
his own hand in Newburgh, and that he was a conjunct tutor
and curator for two pupills in the parish of Collessy, his sister's
children, who had neither father nor mother, and that he had
furnished some cornes for *plenishing ther rowme*. The Presbytery
advyse him to set that land, and to acquite himselfe of those bur-
dines of that tutory and curatory to the other unqlle by the father's
syde.'[1]

> Oct. 17. The same day ther was an Intimatione from ye
> pulpit of ane thanksgiving sermon to be ye nixt Lord's
> day for ye good harvest weather, ye people exhorted to
> yr dutie.'
> 'Nov. 8. Given to ane Indigent Gentelman Thomas Garne,
> who had sometime been in Claverish troūp and being sick
> was in necessitie   .   .   .   .   00. 13. 04.
> '1681, June ye 26, Sicklike ane intimation from the pulpit,
> the Counsels order ordaining a fast for the long drought
> to be on Wednesday following, the twentie ninth the
> sᵈ fast was keept and sermon tūo dyetts.'

'From March up to this date [24th June] there was a cold
drought, which at length inspired so much dread of famine and
consequent pestilence, that a fast was proclaimed throughout the
kingdom for deprecating God's wrath and obtaining rain. The

---

[1] *Selections from the Minutes of the Presbyteries of St Andrews and Cupar*, p 180.

evil was generally regarded as an effect of the great comet of the past winter, 'and certainly,' says Fountainhall, 'it may drain the moisture from the earth and influence the weather, but there is a higher hand of Providence above all these signs, pointing out to us our luxury, abuse of plenty, and other crying sins.' He adds, 'God thought fit to prevent our applications and addresses, and on 24 June and following days sent plentiful showers.' [1]

> '1681 July ye 10. This day Intimatione was made and the order read for ane voluntary Contribution for the Captives amongst ye Turks belonging to Pittenweem.'

On the 12th March following a collection was made for 'James Johnston in Burntisland under the Turks slaverie.' Many others of a similar kind appear in Newburgh Kirk Session Records. The Algerine corsairs were the scourge and terror of sailors in the seventeenth century; but the collections which were made for the redemption of their captives, proved the very temptation which induced them to set out on their piratical expeditions. Just as vessels leave our shores on voyages of legitimate commerce, these pirates yearly set out for the capture of Christian sailors, feeling certain that they would reap a rich reward in the collections that would be made for the redemption of those who had the misfortune to fall into their hands. The sufferings of these captives were well calculated to call forth the sympathy of the compassionate. In 1637 one unfortunate man presented a petition to the Privy Council 'setting forth his pitiful estate among the Turks in Algiers. He had been forced to carry water on his back through the town with an iron chain about his leg and round his middle . . . and no food but four unce of bread daily as black as tar, while obliged to endure forty or three score of stripes with ane rope of four inches great upon his naked body, sometimes on his naked back, and sometimes on his belly. When the ship is to go to sea he must

---

[1] Chambers's *Domestic Annals*, Vol. II., p. 426.

go perforce and sustein the like misery there,—and all because he will not renunce his faith in Christ, and become ane Turk. His cruel maisters having offered to liberate him for twelve hundred merks, the Privy Council recommended his case to the charity of his fellow countrymen, and appointed David Corsaw in Dysart, the captive's uncle to administer the money for his relief.'[1] On the 23d April 1739 the following harrowing entry occurs in the Records of the Kirk Session of Newburgh. Given 'to a poor man that had his Tongue cutt out among the Algerins . 0. 06. 00.'

This nefarious traffic was never effectually checked until Admiral Lord Exmouth bombarded Algiers in 1816; he completely destroyed the Algerine fleet, and demanded and obtained the immediate release of every Christian captive in the territory. The strong hand of war in this case, as in many others, being not only true policy but true mercy.

> 'On the 29th October 1682. The Minister advertysed ye Heritors to ammend the kirk before ye winter come on, but it was not done.' On the 19th February following, 'it was appointed that the Minister should represent ye ruinous conditione of ye fabrick of ye Church, which hath been formerly maintained upon ye poors money, to my Lord Archbishop.'

Thirty years subsequent to the foregoing representation, the Reverend Thomas Morer, Chaplain to a Scotch Regiment, published [1715] 'A Short Account of Scotland.' Speaking of the churches in the north, he says:—' In the country they are very poor and mean covered, no better than their ordinary cottages . . . but in the burghs and cities they are bricked and tiled and well enough furnished with galleries and other conveniences.'[2]

---

[1] Chambers's *Domestic Annals*, Vol. II., p. 93.
[2] *Quoted Selections from the Records of the Kirk Sessions of the Presbytery of Aberdeen*, *Spald Club*, App. p. lxvii.

1683, feb: 25. This day Mr James Smart, reader, delivered up ye key of the box, but refused to fill up ye Sessione book or give any satisfactione for the offence done, but went out in a contemptible maner, was therefore referred to ye presbyterie.'

'Appryll ye 8. The s^d day an act was read for ane voluntar contributione for ye building ane bridge upon ye water of Leven near Dumbartone to be collect next Lords' day.

'15th collecte for ye sd Bridge . . . 01. 13. 4.'

'August the 5. Allison Mair and Janet Williamsone being summonded befor the Sessione for mutuall scolding, the said Allison calling Janet Williamsone's daughter-in-law ane thief for stealing ane psalm book, the other replying with cursing and prophanatione of the name of God, that by his name she would throw a stone at her head; both persons compeired are found guiltie of scolding and swearing, and so lyable to the penalties contained in the acts of the Sessione viz., the said Allison Mair in two shillings sterling being a relapse, and to appear before the Congregatione and make public satisfactione, or else to the cockstool or joigs, and sicklike the fors^d Mair having defamed the sd Janet Williamsone's daughter-in-law with thift is also found lyable according to the former acts, in four pounds scotts and to go to the cockstool.'

The 'joigs' of Newburgh were fixed to the porch which formed the entrance to the churchyard. They disappeared when the 'Porch' was taken down for the erection of the new church. They were comparatively slender, and had the appearance of being much worn. There is a much more perfect specimen of this instrument of punishment, with padlock attached, fixed to the Round Tower of Abernethy, at the entrance to the churchyard of that parish.

'1683, August the 26. Collect 8/^{s} 4^d· which was given to

> John Dempster as drink money when he was working on
> the kirk.'
> 'Septr the 9th collect 12/^{s} 8^d· being the thanksgiving day for
> the discoverie of the conspiracie against his Majestie.'

The conspiracy here referred to was what is usually called the
Rye House Plot, part of the design, it was alleged, being the assassination of Charles II. and the Duke of York, to secure the
succession of the Duke of Monmouth to the throne, in preference
to the Duke of York, afterwards James II. Many thought the
Plot was a sham, simulated for political intrigue, and in consequence some ministers would not read the proclamation from the
pulpit.

> 'Sept: 16th Qlk day the Minister intimated from the pulpit ane
> collectione to be collected the nixt Sabbath for helping the
> bridge of Aberdeen.' Collect 13/^{s} 2^d·
> '1684, May the 4 qlk day ther was ane proclamatione read
> anent ane solemne fast for the long storm in winter, and
> the great disdaine of the ordinances, to be keept on wed-
> ensday nixt.'

The frost began in November preceding, 'and lasted with
great severity till March, with storms and snow now and then.
The rivers at Dundee, Borrowstounness, and other places, where
the sea ebbs and flows, did freeze, which hath not been observed
in the memory of man before, and thereby the cattle, especially
the sheep, were reduced to great want.' . . . 'This frost
prevailed equally in England and Ireland, producing ice on the
Thames below Gravesend.'[1]

In the year 1685 Newburgh was visited with a calamitous fire
which destroyed eighteen houses, and rendered upwards of thirty
families houseless, they therefore required the aid which the

---

[1] Chambers's *Domestic Annals*, Vol. II., p. 454.

previous pages show they had bestowed on the inhabitants of Edinburgh, Northampton, and other places, when they had been overtaken by a similar calamity. Insurance against fire being unknown in those days, the sufferers had nothing to fall back upon but the compassion of the public, and in their distress, they presented a petition to the Lords of the Privy Council, beseeching them to give authority for a voluntary contribution being made on their behalf, in the parish churches of the neighbouring shires. 'The Council acceded to the prayer of the petition, and passed an Act accordingly, which is here given from one of the printed copies circulated at the time.'

On obtaining this Act, a petition was presented to the Provost and Council of 'Edinburgh, beseeching that they would sanction a contribution in the churches within their jurisdiction; and on the identical petition which was presented to the Council, the words, '17 Feb^ry 1686 grants ye desyre,' are written.

ACT
FOR A VOLUNTAR CONTRIBUTION IN FAVORS OF THE DISTRESSED INHABITANTS OF NEWBURGH.

At Edinburgh the twentieth eight day of January one thousand six hundred and eighty six years, anent a Petition presented by the poor and distressed People and Inhabitants of the burgh of Newburgh in Fife shewing, that where it having pleased God upon the fifteenth day of Apryl last, to visit the Petitioners with an accidentall fyre, which burnt down seventeen or eighteen large Tenements, all for the most part lofted, and thacked with Reed which contained about thirty families and upwards; Each Tenement having all office houses relating thereto, Thacked and Lofted as said is, and burnt all that was therein; whereby, through the suddenness of the fyre, and the greatnes of the wind, burned all that was therein, and nothing is left unto them but what may come by the

R

Charitable supply of well disposed and compassionat Christians : as a Testificat under the neighbouring Gentlemens hands doeth testify. And it alwise having been the Councils laudable custome upon the occasion of such distresse and misery, to interpose their authority for a Voluntar Contribution towards the repairing of the losse of such sufferers as the Petitioners are. And therefore, Humbly Supplicating, that the Council would out of the bowels of pity and compassion Consider the distressed condition of the Petitioners and grant Order for a voluntar contribution for repairing them of their said Loss, in such places as their Lordships shall think fit, since thereby they, and all good Christians, will be encouraged to help others whose Lot it may fall to be in their condition. The Lords of His Majesties Privy Council, having heard and considered the foresaid Petition Do hereby give Order and Warrand for a Voluntar Contribution to be collected for repairing the Petitioners Loss and Dammage, furth of the Shires of Fife and Kinross, Perth, Angus and Mid Lothian ; and Recommended to the most Reverend the Arch-bishops, and Right Reverend, the Bishops, in their respective Diocesses, to cause Intimation to be made hereof by the ministers in their several Paroches, upon a Sabbath forenoon, after Divine Service ; And Appoints Mr George Arnot, Brother-german to James Arnot of Wood-milne, to be Collector of the foresaid voluntar Contribution, in regard he hath found sufficient Caution, to make the same forth-coming, according to the Petitioners their several losses and damages, and to make compt and reckoning accordingly to the Council when required. Extracted by me—

WILL. PATERSON, *Cler sti Concilii.*

Edinburgh, Printed by the Heir of Andrew Anderson, Printer to His most Sacred Majesty, Anno Dom : 1686.

1685 Sepr the 20. The Minister from the pulpit exhorted the parishioners to be charitable against the next Sabbath for these that had suffered losse by the fire in the Towne, to be collected both forenoon and afternoon.'

'Sep^t the 27th, Collect 7 lib. 11/^{s} 4^d. for the fors^d sufferers.' 'The s^d collectione was given to Mr George Arnott to go about the Collection for the s^d sufferers.

'1685 Oct: 11 Qlk day ther was ane act read for the celebratione of his Maties happie birth day [James II.] to be keepit upon Wedensday nixt and so furth yearly.'

'Octr the 18th, Collect 15/^{s} 8^d. of the which given to John Smart Beddell for his extraordinary pains on the Kings birth day . . . . . 00 06 08.'

'Decr the 27. The sd day ther was ane act read for ane voluntar contribution for Balbirnie Bridge.' On the 9th Oct 1687, there was collected and delivered 17 02 00.'

The largeness of the collection shows the importance attached to the erection of a bridge on the direct road to Edinburgh.

'1686 May the 9th. Qlk day the Minister and Elders condescended that Mr James Smart their schoolmaister should have in time comeing, for teaching the poor thretteen shillings and four pennies for each of them.'

'May the 29th, Given out to [a] distressed Gentlewoeman called Elizabeth Nairn, recommended to us by the Archbishop who as her testificat bears was robbed of her goods, and her husband deadly wounded 00 12 00.'

'It to two sick men going to the Lady Pitfirrane to be cured of the sicknes . 00 06 00.'

Lady Pitfirrane, whose maiden name was Anna Murray, was, at the date of the mention of her name in the Records of the Kirk Session of Newburgh, the widow of Sir James Halket of Pitfirrane, Bart. By her father, Mr Robert Murray, she was descended from the family of Tullibardine, and by her mother Jane Drummond, from the family of Drummond, Earl of Perth. Her father was appointed by James VI. preceptor to his second son, afterwards the unhappy Charles I., and subsequently became Provost of Eton College.

The parents of Anna Murray superintended the education of their daughter with pious care, and bestowed on her a higher culture than was usual for women in that age. Charles I. entrusted her with the education of two of his children, the Duke of Gloucester and the Princess Elizabeth; a task which she was well qualified to fulfil. Her cultivated mind, and the deep religious feeling which was the pervading principle of her life, made her eminently fitted for forming the minds of the pupils committed to her charge. The hard fate of the Princess Elizabeth required all the consolation which religion and a religious education could confer. She suffered in her father's sufferings, and untended and alone was found dead on the floor of her prison in Carisbrook Castle, with her head resting on a Bible, open at the text, 'Come unto me all ye that labour and are heavy laden, and I will give you rest.' Queen Victoria, with true womanly feeling, has caused a monument, commemorative of the Princess' death, to be erected in Newport Church (Isle of Wight), where the unhappy Princess was buried. The monument, which is of pure white marble and of exquisite design, represents the Princess as she was found in her cell; with this difference, the bars of her prison are represented as broken, the body captive but the spirit at liberty.

Anna Murray long survived her young pupil. Throughout her life she devoted herself to the then popular study of theology, and has left behind her many manuscript volumes of meditations on scriptural subjects. But her religion did not consist in mere meditation; from her very early years she gave herself to the study of 'Physick,' that she might be able to alleviate the sufferings of the poor. In this work she was eminently successful. It is recorded of her, that after the disastrous battle of Dunbar, coming accidentally to Kinross, 'she and her women dressed about thrie score poor wounded soldiers,' many of whose wounds were in a sad festering condition from neglect. With compassionate forethought she had provided herself with things necessary for this purpose, having anticipated occasion for their employment. Lines addressed to Florence Nightingale, whose devotion to the relief of the suffering and diseased has added lustre to womanhood, may be truthfully applied to Anna Murray, 'Lady Pitfirrane.'

> ' O sweet Lady ! thou indeed,
> Where thy saintly virtues shine
> Dost exalt thy Christian creed,
> By those holy works of thine.' [1]

Lady Halket spared no pains to add to her knowledge in medical science, both by converse and by study of the best works on the subject, until her skill became so highly appreciated, that invalids of rank, both at home and from abroad, sought her opinion and advice. She was a woman of unaffected simplicity of character and kindliness of disposition, ever ready to give the benefit of her skill to all who applied to her ; and it was this trait in her character which induced the two sick men, who were aided by the kirk session of Newburgh, 'to go to Lady Pitfirrane.'

Lady Halket bore four children to her husband, all of whom died young, except a son named Robert, born in 1660. In February 1674 she went with him to St Andrews to enter him to the college, ' offering him up to God and begging the conduct of His good Spirit to lead him and bless him in his studies, and preserve him from all evil ; resolving if she lived to see him safely returned, after the finishing of his Courses to make some Donative to the College, in token of her gratitude to God.' On the completion of Robert's college career, 'she caused a Communion-cup be made of very good workmanship for the Church of St Leonard, out of thankfulness for her son having returned with good testimony.' This votive offering was sent to Dr Skein, then Provost of the old

---

[1] P. G. Hamerton, *Isles of Loch Awe.*

college, who had been her son's regent. It is still preserved, and
bears the following inscription : 'THIS CUP IS DEDICATED TO THE
USE OF THE HOLY TABLE IN ST LEONARD'S CHURCH ST ANDREWS,
BY A DEVOUT WIDOW AS A FREE-WILL OFFERING FOR THE RETURN
OF PRAYER UPON THE XIII DAY OF APRIL MDCLXXXI.' This son,
the object of so much motherly care, entered the army, and died
on the continent in 1693. His mother survived him several years,
and died in 1699, at the advanced age of seventy-seven, esteemed
and lamented both by rich and poor. In the words of her biographer : ' She was one whose conversation was in Heaven, whose
thoughts and desires were ever towards God; whose dayley exercise was to dispose and fit herself for the blessed society above,
by daily growing in grace, in holiness and charity, and in eminent
humility,—which was the ornament of all her other virtues.' [1]

The writings which Lady Halket has left behind her, extend to
upwards of twenty-one volumes of manuscript, and consist chiefly
of meditations on passages of Scripture. Two only of her treatises
have been published. One of these, ' The Mother's Will to the Un-
born Child,' she wrote under the impression that she would
not survive the delivery of her first-born child. This work was
published in Edinburgh in 1788. In 1701 a small quarto volume
was published (also in Edinburgh), containing ' Meditations on the
25th Psalm,' and other treatises. An interesting biography of
Lady Halket is prefixed to this work, from which this notice of
her life has been mainly derived. The ' Meditations ' and the ' Instructions for Youth,' contained in the same volume, are pervaded
by devout and fervent feeling, and testifiy to her having been an
able and thoughtful student of Scripture. The ' Instructions '
abound with good sense, and are well worthy of being republished.

Lady Halket was strongly attached to the Royal family. When
resident in London she materially aided in the escape of James,
Duke of York (in his youth), at the time of his father's great

---

[1] *Memoir of Lady Halket*, 1701. Chambers's *Scottish Biography*, Vol. II., p. 560.

troubles.   In her old age she had the misery of seeing him, by his own folly, again a fugitive and an exile.

> '1686 Septr the 5th John Tod, Bailie, on of the Elders de-lated John Smart, Beddell and Hew Patrick for talking loud in the Kirkyard about ther ordinar discourse in time of Divine Service, and the minister and Elders ordained them to stand before the paroch the nixt Lords day and satisfie for ther fault.'   They both appear, confess their fault, and 'crave Gods pardon.'
>
> '1686 Sep. the 19.   The Minister and Elders hearing that ther were severall abuses comitted in the time of Divine Service, ordained for the time cumeing that some of the Elders should go through the Town for the prevention of the sd abuses.'
>
> '1688 Feb the 12th, qlk day the minister mad intimatione that a thanksgiven sermon for the Queen's being with child was to be keept the next Lords day, don accordingly.'
>
> ' June the 28, thanksgiving sermon for the young Prince was observed.'

The young prince, afterwards known as the Pretender, the father of Prince Charles Edward Stuart, was born on the 10th June.

> 'Sep the qlk day ane proclamatione was read against the vending and importing of seditious books and pamphlets.'
>
> 'Sepr the 23 ane proclamation was read appointing the Randezvous of the militia Regiments and calling out the Heritors.'
>
> 'Sep the 30.   Ane advertisement was given to the Heritors anent the out-reak of the foot militia.'
>
> On Oct 7th an advertisement was read calling on 'the Heri-tors to attend the Kings Host at Burntisland on Wednes-day next.'   And on the 21st October the heritors of Fife

and Kinross-shire were warned to meet at Kirkcaldy on the 22d 'for his majestys speciall service.'

The frequency of these proclamations at this period show, with unmistakable distinctness, the apprehension with which James and his ministers regarded the aspect of the times; apprehensions, which events in a few days proved to have been only too well founded. William, Prince of Orange, landed in Torbay on the 5th November 1688, and on the 13th December following James abdicated the throne by flight.

CHAPTER XXI.

FROM THE REVOLUTION TO THE 'FORTY-FIVE.'

'The old order changeth, yielding place to new.'

Tennyson.

IN the beginning of the year 1689 a Convention of Estates was assembled for the settlement of the Crown. The following entry regarding it appears in Newburgh Kirk Session Records :—

> '1689 Feb. 24. Qlk day ther was an order read for a meeting of the Shyre for choicing the Commissioners to the Convention the fourteenth day of s^d moneth' [March].

This convention passed an act enjoining that 'all ministers of the Gospel within the Kingdom publickly pray for King William and Queen Mary, as King and Queen of this Realm, and to read this proclamation publickly from their pulpits under the pain of being deprived and losing their benefices.'[1] The minister of Newburgh, Mr William Grant, who was a native of Morayshire, refused to read the proclamation, conscientiously adhering to his own convictions, and thereby incurred the certainty of deprivation. The last time he appears to have officiated in the pulpit of Newburgh was on the 2d September 1689. He was deprived on the Tuesday following. Though he would not renounce his allegiance to James, he made public intimation from the pulpit, as enjoined by the convention, that, 'a thanksgiving sermon was to be keeped on Tuesday next [9 May 1689] for our preservation from Popery;' and, it is recorded, 'it was observed.' Mr Grant con-

---

[1] *Acts of Estates of Scots*, Cap. 16.

tinned to reside in Newburgh for upwards of eleven years after his ejection. Judging from the actions against him for debts, recorded in the Court Books of Newburgh, he appears to have been reduced to great straits. The latest of these actions is dated the 26th March 1701. Mr Grant subsequently removed to Edinburgh, and died there on the 21st January 1715, in the fifty-sixth year of his age.[1]

The number of clergy who were ejected from their pulpits at this period was very great. Out of the twenty members of the Presbytery of Cupar,—of which one charge was vacant,—all but one suffered ejection rather than take the oaths imposed. In St Andrews Presbytery, seventeen out of twenty-one were deprived, and in the whole of Fife and Kinross-shire only sixteen ministers adhered, fifty-five were deprived. In the Presbytery of Perth, seventeen out of twenty ministers were ejected; in that of Auchterarder, fourteen out of fifteen; in Dunblane, ten out of twelve; six ministers only adhering in these three Presbyteries. A self-sacrifice so great and so general, shows a deeper and more wide-spread attachment to the House of Stuart and to the existing ecclesiastical polity, than is commonly supposed. A like proportion of ejections prevailed in many other Presbyteries. The ministers of Cupar, Auchtermuchty, Kettle, Logie, and Strathmiglo, were ejected on Wednesday, the 29th August 1689; those of Dairsie, Creich, Flisk, Dunbog, Abdie, and Newburgh, on the Tuesday following.[2]

These deprived ministers were not allowed to exercise their ministerial functions without hindrance, as in modern times. On the 22d July 1690, an Act was passed by Parliament, 'discharging and prohibiting them from preaching or exercising any part of their ministerial functions, either in churches or elsewhere, until they present themselves before the Privy Council, and in their presence take and subscribe the oath of allegiance, and also engaged, under their hands, to pray for King William and Queen Mary, as King and Queen of the Realm. . . . Certifying such

---

[1] H. Scott's *Fasti Scoticana*, Fife.　　[2] *Ib.*, *Fife.*

ministers as shall do in the contrary that they shall be prosecuted as persons disaffected and enemies to their Majesties
Government with all rigor.'[1] Three years later, they, in common
with all official personages, were called upon to make the prescribed
Declaration of Assurance, that William and Mary were *de jure*,
as well as *de facto* King and Queen. Preachers not provided with
Kirks who refused to take the oath and make the Declaration,
to be punished by banishment or otherwise, as the Council shall
think fit.'[2] The deprived ministers refused to forswear themselves by taking the oath, and they were in consequence called
non-jurors. The punishment imposed by the Acts mentioned was
left to the discretion of the Privy Council; but in July 1695 an
Act was passed, which left no option to the presiding magistrate.
This Act strictly prohibited and discharged any *outed* minister
from baptizing any children, or solemnizing any marriage under
pain of imprisonment, 'ay and while he finds caution to go out of
the kingdom, and never to return thereto.[3]

The closing of the pulpits against so many of the clergy
necessarily deprived many parishes of public worship. For nearly
eight years (1689–1697) there is no record of public worship
having been observed in Newburgh Church, and similar neglect
occurred in numerous other parishes. In May 1697, Mr James
Haddo, minister of Cupar, met the magistrates and elders, and
'declaired that the Presbytery were willing to give their concurrence to the planting of this place with a minister as mutch as
possible to the satisfaction of all.'

One of the first entries in the Session Books under the new
order of things, is a record of the purchase of meal for distribution
among the poor (January and May 1697) and thereafter immediately follows entries of payments 'for mort-chists for the poor,'
proving that Newburgh did not escape the terrible famine which
prevailed for several successive years towards the end of the
sevententh century. A cotemporary writer, speaking of the dearth,

---

[1] 1st. Parl. William and Mary, 2d Sess. Chap. 35. [2] *Ib*. 4th Sess. Chap. 6.
[3] *Ib*. 5th Sess. Chap. 12.

says, 'these unheard-of manifold judgements continued seven years, not always alike, but the seasons, summer and winter, so cold and barren, and the wonted heat of the sun so much withholden that it was discernible upon the cattle, flying birds and insects decaying, that seldom a fly or cleg was to be seen. Our harvests not in ordinary months, many shearing in November and December, yea some in January and February, many contracting their deaths, and losing the use of their feet and hands, shearing and working in frost and snow, and after all some of it standing still, and rotting upon the ground, much of it for little use either to man or beast, and which had no taste or colour of meal.' The same writer continues: 'Through the long continuance of these manifold judgements, deaths and burials were so many and common that the living were wearied with burying the dead. I have seen corpses drawn in sleds. Many got neither coffins nor winding-sheet. I was one of four who carried the corpse of a young woman a mile of way, and when we came to the grave, an honest poor man come and said, "you must go and help me to bury my son, he has lain dead these two days, otherwise I shall be obliged to bury him in my yard."[1] The sufferings of these years must have been terrible, and the entry 'for mort-chists' tell with unequivocal certainty that the famine did its fearful work.

The subsequent entries in the Kirk Session Records are of a more common-place character; still there are notices connected with events of historical importance, which possess more than local interest. Under the year 1715, but unfortunately without any more special date, the following entry occurs: —

'Altho sermon, yet no collection because of disturbance.'

The following account, presented by the magistrates of Newburgh to the commissioners of supply for the county of Fife, throws some light on this 'disturbance,' and affords a glimpse of

---

[1] Chambers's *Domestic Annals*, Vol. III., pp. 196-7.

the movements of the Highland troops, and of the frequency of
their visits to the neighbourhood :—

Accompt of the loss sustained by the toune and inhabitants
of Newburgh by the rebells dureing the tyme of the late
Rebellion, as Follows :[1]

	lib	sh.	d.
'Imp^r Payed of Cess to John Smith, Collector to the rebells conforme to his discharge yrof dated 20 Oct. 1715'	85	12	2
'It. There was quartered of Strathmores men Sevintein, John Strachan being commander, and that for the space of twenty ffour hours, who took frie quarters. Referred to ye Judges modification	5	6	0
It. There was quartered fifty seven men twenty four hours, also commanded by Captaine Farquarsone'	17	4	0
It. there was twenty men took frie quarters also, for two days, commanded by Ensign Ogilvie'	12	8	0
It. there was twenty seven took frie quarters also sixtein days, commanded by Alexander McKenzie'	69	12	0
It. there was seven men for three days commanded by Lieutenant McKenzie'	7	16	0
'It. Captain McKenzie and seventein men for five days got frie quarters also'	27	0	0
'It. A large Drum and Drumsticks, taken of by the party of gentlemen, when they came first to Fife about Michaelmas last, referred to the judges modificatione'[2]	6	0	0
	£230	10	2

---

[1] The original was in the possession of the late Thos. Shaw, Cupar.
[2] Leighton's *History of Fife*, Vol. II., p. 164.

'This is the generall accompt relating to the toune, but each
particular person's loss sustained by them is to be given
in by their Accompts signed with their hands. As witness
qrof this signed by the baillie's att Newburgh the ffour-
teen of March, jajvijc and sixtein years.'

R. SMITH.   JOHN LYELL.

Several of the proprietors in the neighbourhood of Newburgh
were friendly to the Stuarts in the rising of 1715.   The most
prominent was Major Henry Balfour of Dunboig, son of Lord
Balfour of Burleigh.   He was severely satirised at the time for
having deserted the cause ; but, notwithstanding his defection, he
was seized and imprisoned in Edinburgh Castle, and his estates
confiscated.[1]   He was one of the members for Fife in the last
Scottish Parliament, and strenuously opposed the union.'

The following entry in Newburgh Session Books records the
suppression of the rebellion :—

1716 June 7 being thanksgiving for the defeat of the Rebels
            [Collected]   .   .   02 17 00

' 1739 January 22.   Given for mending of the Kirk after the
excessive wind.'

'This was a hurricane from the southwest, commencing at one
in the morning of the 14th January, and accompanied by light-
ning ; it swept across the south of Scotland, and seems to have
been beyond parallel for destructiveness in the same district before
or since.   It tore sheet lead from churches and houses, and made
it fly through the air like paper.   Houses were thrown down,
trees uprooted by hundreds, and corn stacks scattered.   At Loch
Leven great shoals of perches and pikes were driven a great way

---

[1] Spottiswood's *Miscellany*, Vol. II., p. 435.

into the fields, so that the country people got horse-loads of them, at one penny per hundred.' [1]

> ' 1740, January 31. For meal and coals to the poor under
>   the storm   9   04   00
> ' June 21. To Peter Miller for two Bolls of
>   Oatmeal at 7 lib per boll, and two Bolls
>   of Peasmeal at 4 lib 8 sh per boll dis-
>   tribute among the poor under the storm   22   16   00

The storm here referred to was a severe frost, 'which began on the 26th December 1739; it lasted till the end of January, and was long remembered for its severity.   The principal rivers of Scotland were frozen over [the Tay at Perth was frozen nearly to the bottom], and there was such a general stoppage of water-mills, that the knocking stones usually employed in those simple days for crushing grain in small quantities, and of which there was one at nearly every cottage door, were used on this occasion, as a means of grinding it.   Such mills as had a flow of water were worked on Sundays as well as ordinary days.   Food rose to famine prices, and large contributions were required from the rich to keep the poor alive.   People perished of cold in the fields, and even in the streets.' [2]

This trying calamity was followed by a failure of the crop of the ensuing season (1740), which was productive of great distress. Many were reduced to absolute want, and starving men ravenously seized on any food within their reach for themselves and their children.   The magistracy, both in the towns and the country, made the most strenuous efforts to meet the fearful emergency; and the rich came liberally forward with their means to procure meal to retail to the poor at comparatively low prices, but still the fearful distress prevailed.   The Kirk Sessions, as guardians of the poor, were most indefatigable in their exertions.[3]   The Kirk

---

[1] Chambers's *Domestic Annals*, Vol. III., p. 603.   [2] *Ib.*, p. 605.   [3] *Ib.*, p. 606.

Session of Abdie, with the commendable object of affording work to the poor in their distress, and at the sametime maintaining a proper spirit of independence and self-respect, bought flax to be given out to spin. On the 19th January 1741, the following entry occurs in their records :—

> ' ffor one hundred weight of lint to be given out to the poor
>   people of the paroche to spine .   27   00   00'
> ' ffor the carriage from Dundie of two hun-
>   dred weight   00   18   00'

Both in the records of the Session of Newburgh and of Abdie, entry after entry occurs during the year 1741, 'for meal bought to the poor.' On the 1st of June the Kirk Session of Abdie paid the unusually high price of thirty six pounds for three bolls of bear, the average price at that time being about four pounds fifteen shillings the boll. So late as the 3d October, when the harvest ought to have been gathered in, the following touching entry occurs in Newburgh Session Book ·—'To several of the Poor when there was not meal for them 1   07.   00.' Notwithstanding the bounty of the rich, and the active exertions of the magistracy and of the Kirk Sessions, the famine did its fearful work, and disease and death followed in its wake. In the Records of the Kirk Session of Abdie the following significant entry occurs :—

> ' 1741 August 10.   to John Wilkie in full pay[t] of all the poors
>   coffins to this date   08   13   0

> ' 1742 Dec 20. To candle and other charges
>   when Margaret Peatt was a corpse   .   0   12   00
> ' 1750, Oct. 5.   To John Laing for Isabel
>   Clow's coffin   4   10   0
> ' To sake [sack] and sugar before her death,
>   and ale, bread, and candle after funeral   2   18   6

These records of the countenance of lychwakes (so called from the old English word *lych*, a corpse, and *wake* to watch) by the Kirk Session, is a relic of a custom now quite obsolete in this neighbourhood, but which, at the dates mentioned, must have universally prevailed, as the providing funds for the *wakes* of those on the roll of paupers proves. It would naturally be supposed that the custom of burning lights, and watching by a corpse, sprang from the desire of mourners to be near the object of their affection, and from the assembling of neighbours to sympathise with them in their affliction. Feelings so natural and so commendable, tended to keep alive the custom; but there is reason to believe that it had its origin in primeval times, and out of a very different set of feelings, affording one more evidence of the vitality of customs having their origin in the childhood of the human race. 'It is a prevailing belief in countries widely separated, that especially in the dark, harmful spirits swarm. In broad daylight the Hindu lights lamps to keep off demons. In Europe the details of the use of fire to keep off demons and witches are most explicit. The people of the Hebrides continued till recent times to protect mother and child from evil spirits by carrying fire round them before baptism, and in Bulgaria candles are still lighted on the feast of St Demetrius in stables and sheds, to prevent evil spirits from entering into the domestic animals.'[1] The Roman Catholic Church, finding this belief so deeply rooted, endeavoured to give it a Christian direction, and it instituted a special office for blessing candles so used, which were held as symbolical of the True Light. Great importance was, in consequence, attached to the burning of lights beside an unburied corpse in medieval times; and as in the case of providing lights at the tomb after burial, craftsmen united to secure candles for burning at the Lychwake of one another. The Gild of the Holy Cross, established at Stratford-on-Avon A.D. 1389, ordained, 'that when any of the bretheren or sisteren of the Gild dies, one large and eight small wax lights

---

[1] E. B. Tylor's *Primitive Culture*, Vol. II., p. 178.

S

shall be carried from the church to the house of the dead, and
there they shall be kept alight before the body until it is carried
to the church, and the waxes shall be carried and kept alight
until the body is buried.'[1] Though funerals at that period, and
for long afterwards, almost invariably took place after sunset,
rendering torches necessary, yet superstition largely mingled with
the practice. It was firmly believed that the lights had a potent
effect in shielding the dead from the malevolence of evil spirits.
A medieval writer says :—

> 'A wondrous force and might
> Doth in these candels lie, which at any time they light,
> They sure beleve that neyther storme or tempest dare abide,
> Nor thunder in the skies be heard nor any devil's spide,
> Nor fearfull spirites that walk by night.'[2]

Notwithstanding the religious direction given to lychwakes by
the Roman Catholic Church, which among other things enjoined
the offering up of prayers and singing of psalms at these meetings,
they became occasions of intemperance and debauchery, from
which every sacred feeling was banished. So early as the middle
of the 13th century, the church protested against these excesses,
and threatened excommunication against all who joined in them.
These threats were unavailing ; and both in Roman Catholic and
Protestant countries, lychwakes became mere gatherings for unbridled license, from which, in Scotland, even superstitious feelings
were latterly thoroughly eliminated.[3]

From the Records of the Presbytery of St Andrews, under date
20th March 1644, we learn that it was the custom when a death
took place in a family, for 'confused multitudes' to frequent the
house of the deceased uninvited, for the purpose of obtaining a
share of the meat and drink that was provided on the occasion.
And that it was usual to distribute money among the poor at the

---

[1] *Old English Gilds*, p. 215.
[2] Brand's *Popular Antiquities*, Vol. I., p. 46.   [3] *Ib.*, Vol. II., pp. 225, 230.

time of the funeral. The Presbytery issued an ordinance forbidding these excesses, and recommended that the money to be distributed, should be given to the Kirk Session of the parish for distribution, and not 'in so great a tumult of beggars as vse to be at the buriall place, when they that cryes most and have least neid, come often best speed.'[1]

The following extract from the Records of the Town Council of Newburgh, shows the extent to which the drinking customs at lychwakes and funerals were carried in Scotland in the last century :—

> 18th Aprile 1759. This day the Counsel mett after calling of the Pasch Head Court, and there was laid before them a Long Petition, signed by the Plurality of the Inhabitants of the Burgh representing and holding forth the many Disabuses that are committed at Burials both before and after the corps is interred, whereby many become mortally drunk, to the scandal of the Burgh, and Therefore the said Petitioners earnestly require that the Bailies and Counsel, shall make an Act for regulating such Disabuses, and against drinking before the Interment or at Dargies.'

The following resolutions were unanimously passed :—

> ' 1[mo.] That no Inhabitant within the Town of Newburgh shall invite either one or other of the Inhabitants to drink before the Corpe be interred, nor shall any of them go in under the penalty following.
> ' 2[do.] They also discharge all publick Dargies, excepting Relations and near neighbours, or those that may be serviceable to the concerns of the Defunct,—But that the country people may be taken in before the lifting of the corpse if they please.'

Selections from the Records of the Presbyteries of St Andrews and Cupar, p. 20.

'3^{tio.} That any of the Inhabitants transgressing the foresaid
Regulation whether the Inviter or the Invited of them
shall pay twenty pounds scots *Toties Quoties*, and ordains
this to be intimate to the Inhabitants by the tuck of
drum that none pretend ignorance.'

This public movement was the dawn of a better day, and for
more than one generation back, absolute sobriety at funerals has
prevailed.

Before the country had time to recover from the calamitous
effects of the storm of 1740, came the troublous era of the 'Forty-
five.' The following entry in Newburgh Kirk Session Records,
shows the anxiety with which the anticipated approach of the
Highlanders was contemplated :—

'1746 Januar 24. To Robert Ferrier to bring news from
Stirling . . . . . . 3 00 00'

A party of Highlanders came to Newburgh on a Sunday while
the people were in church ; the congregation dispersed immediately, and instead of going home by the middle of the street, as
was their wont, they kept along by the sides of the houses. One
man named Thomas Kinloch, said he would not be turned out of
his way by rebels, and he kept his accustomed path on the crown
of the causeway ; but he had to learn the Falstaffian maxim, that
'discretion is the better part of valour;' for the Highlanders,
seeing his temper, pricked him on before them to Lindores, a distance of two miles, and would not allow him to return until he
cried aloud, 'Prince Charlie for ever.' This episode seems to have
been a subject of merriment in aftertimes, when all danger was
past. An eye-witness of the entry of the Highlanders into Newburgh in 1745, in narrating the incident, laughed heartily, nearly
eighty years after the event, as he recounted the stern old whig's
discomfiture. Prince Charles Edward did not come to Newburgh,

but there is a tradition that he slept one night in the old mansion-house of Carpow, two miles to the westward, then the residence of John Oliphant, whose kindred were all staunch adherents of the Stuarts. The room which the Prince is said to have occupied is still pointed out.

THE OLD MANSION HOUSE OF CARPOW. *(From a Photograph.)*

There is a tradition that the Highlanders made search for the magistrates of Newburgh, to compel them to swear allegiance to the 'rightful King,' and not finding them, they threatened to burn their houses when they came back; but Culloden intervened, and the threat remained what it was intended to be, unfulfilled.

Lord George Murray, Princes Charles's ablest adviser, lived at Mugdrum (A.D. 1730), of which he was proprietor, and to him the inhabitants of Newburgh are indebted for the right of property, which still affords them the only access to the river that they can claim as their own. He was the fifth son of the first Duke of Athol, and ancestor of the present duke. He had served abroad, and had acquired that knowledge of his profession which fitted

him for the command of an army. Like almost all his family and
clan he was devotedly attached to the exiled Royal family. He
joined the Chevalier at Perth, who immediately appointed him
Lieutenant-General of his forces. Lord George acted in that
capacity all through the expedition, and occupied the post of
danger in bringing up the rear in the retreat from England. ' He
was tall, robust, and brave,' and humane as he was brave. After
the battle of Prestonpans there was difficulty in finding accommodation for the wounded on both sides. Lord George busied
himself in finding and providing food and lodgings for the wounded
officers of Cope's army, and when no better could be had purchased
dry straw for them to sleep on, and at their earnest entreaty slept
beside them on the floor for their protection.[1] It was said by one
who took part in the expedition, that ' had the Prince slept during
his entire Scottish residence, at least for a proper time after the
battle of Preston, and left the entire guidance of his affairs to
Lord George Murray, when waking, he would have found the
diadem on his father's brows.'[2] After the defeat of Culloden, Lord
George escaped to the continent never to return to his native land.
He was attainted for high treason, and died at Medenblinck in
Holland, on the 11th October 1760. There is preserved among
the public documents of Newburgh, a letter written by him to the
magistrates; a fac-simile of which is annexed as a memorial of
one who bore so prominent a part in the chivalrous enterprise of
the ' Forty-five,' and of his peaceful avocations at Mugdrum. One
who had conversed with those who were present at the scene, used
to tell that during Lord George Murray's residence at Mugdrum, in negotiating some matters with the magistrates and councillors of Newburgh, about their respective marches, a rude remark
was made to his lordship by a burgess named David Blyth, better
known as ' Earl Davie.' Lord George resented, by asking if he
knew to whom he spoke ? ' I'm speaking to a Lord, but ye ought

---

[1] Browne's *Highlands*, Vol. III., pp. 87–8.
[2] Spottiswoode, *Miscellany*, Vol. II., pp. 484–5.

Having occasion for some quarrie stones for my biggings and Dykes I am obseruing that there is good quarrie in the hill at the head of one of my riggs that leads down to my ferme. I shall therefore take it as a favour that you'll allow me to won stones as I may have use for them out of that place) Which is all at present from—

Your very humble Ser

George Murray

Mugdrum 15th Sepr 1730

For the Baillies and Towns Councill of Newburgh

to ken ye're speaking to an Earl,' was the reply; a hearty laugh ensued, and good humour was restored.[1]

The exactions of the Highlanders in Newburgh seem to have been more of a trivial than an oppressive character. Tradition tells that a pair of good shoes, whether off the feet or on the feet of a burgess were immediately appropriated. It is said that a party of Highlanders went into Arngask church on a Sunday, sat down beside the worshippers, and quietly relieved them of their shoes, leaving them to find their way home barefooted as they best could.

The troubles, however, paralyzed business, and the markets were unfrequented. The following entry, which occurs in the Records of the Town Council of Newburgh, gives abundant evidence of this, and testifies to the sense of insecurity which prevailed:—

'1746 Decr 31. John Dall, Customer, [Tacksman of Customs] to be discharged to six pounds scots, instead of twelve pounds, on account of the troublesome times during ye late Rebellion.'

The events connected with the last attempt of the Stuarts to regain the throne of their ancestors, are separated from the present time by such a wide gulf in modern thought, that it seems like stepping back centuries to recall them; and yet there was one alive in the beginning of the present year (1874), who had conversed with the last representative of the family. John Christian Schetky,[2] well known in the brilliant literary society of Edinburgh

---

[1] The family to which David Blyth belonged is invariably designed in the public records, for nearly two centuries, as Blyth Earle. The last of the family died in 1814; he was known to all as ' Earl Davie.'

[2] Mr Schetky, descended from an ancient Transylvanian family, was born in Edinburgh (where his father had come to reside) on the 11th August 1778, and died at his residence, 11 Kent Terrace, Regent's Park, London, in the 96th year of his age, on the 29th January 1874. He was the contemporary, at the High School of Edinburgh, of Walter Scott, Lord Brougham, and many others, after-

of sixty years ago, accompanied by his friend Francis Horne (afterwards Colonel Horne, the brave defender of Hougoumont) went in 1801, during the short peace of Amiens, on an excursion to Italy, to see the art treasures so long shut to the British world. They walked from Paris to Rome ; when near the latter city, in the Campagna, the pedestrians had to get out of the way, at a narrow part of the road, to allow one of the heavy coaches of those days to pass; when it approached where they stood, the oc-cupant ordered the driver to halt, and immediately saluted the young travellers, by asking if they were Englishmen. On their answering in the affirmative, he immediately said, 'I love to see Englishmen.' Inquiring the object of their journey, he expressed the hope that their anticipations would be realised, and that they

---

wards the great men of their day. In after life he and Sir Walter were bosom friends, and at the request of the latter he published a volume of illustrations of the scenery described in the 'Lay of the Last Minstrel.' Besides meeting with 'the last of the Stuarts,' Mr Schetky used to tell with pride that he had been in the company of Robert Burns; the poet, by his intercession, saved him from a flogging from his father (with whom Burns was intimate) for playing truant to sail a boy-made ship at Leith. This incident in his life shows the bent of his genius, for in his later years Mr Schetky's most admired paintings were naval scenes ; many of which are of great excellence ; and at the time of his death, and for many years previous, he was Marine Painter to the Queen. Mr Schetky, in 1848, accompanied the late Duke of Rutland in a cruise in the duke's yacht round the coast of Scotland, and in conjunction with Lord John Manners, the duke's son (who furnished the letter-press), published, in a large folio volume, a series of chromolithographic views of the scenes they visited. Mr Schetky cruised on more than one occasion with her present Most Gracious Majesty, for whom and the late Prince Consort, he executed at various times many commissions. Besides being an accomplished artist, Mr Schetky was an excellent musician, and both sung and played old Scotch ballads and songs with exquisite taste and pathos. He was an early and esteemed friend of Professor Wilson's. In the *Noctes Ambrosianæ*, Wilson, in the character of *Christopher North*, speaking of him, says, 'In his company care loses her name and forgets her nature;' and the *Shepherd* adds, 'I howp I'll no gang to my grave without forgathering wi' John Schetky.' It was indeed a pleasure to 'forgather' with him. Mr Schetky retained his elas-ticity of spirits in his advanced years.

would enjoy their visit to Rome. He then asked them of the state of affairs in Britain, and said, 'How are my fleets and armies getting on?' Noticing their surprise at the question, he immediately added, 'I mean of Great Britain.' He parted from them with a kindly farewell, and almost immediately after he left, they learned that the person they had conversed with, was Cardinal York, the last of the Stuarts.

The study of the Ecclesiastical Records from which most of the foregoing selections have been made, is suggestive of varied reflections. The indulgence in violent and abusive language, instances of which occur in almost every page, and the open disregard of the Lord's-day, of which there are such frequent notices, come upon the reader with surprise, and rudely dispel the idea of greater sanctity in those times. Toleration was utterly unknown; not the slightest indulgence being shown towards any opinion that differed from the principles of those who were in power at the time; but through all the intolerance it is most pleasing to find that the church, through its local courts, whether under Episcopacy or Presbytery, ever appears as the friend of the poor; caring both for their temporal and spiritual interests. Every page of the Records bears evidence of solicitude for the comfort of the distressed.

The following extracts are taken, at distant intervals, from Newburgh Session Records:—

> 'Jan. the 3, 1686. Given to James Cŭick on of our paroch
>   being tristed with sicknes   .   .   .   01   04   00.'
> '1729, March 10, To Matthew Davidson, Glas-
>   cow, a poor man   00   12   00.'
> '1747, To a poor man with a Dropsie   00   12   00.'

As instances of the church's concern for the education and spiritual welfare of the destitute, such entries as the following constantly occur:—

'1739 June 28, Payed to the schoolmaster for teaching poor
scholars, preceding 27 Augt 1738 . . 3 18 00.'
'Decr 30. Payed to Mr Taylor, Schoolmaster, for
poor scholars from 3 Octr 1738 to 3 Septr 1739 4 03 00.'
'1742 Nov. 24 ffor a bible to a poor lass 01 04 00.'

Page after page tells of similar payments to the schoolmaster
for the instruction of poor children, evincing laudable anxiety lest
any should grow up uneducated.

With a still wider philanthropy, the church was instrumental
in promoting the material improvement of the country, by raising
contributions for the making of harbours and building of bridges,
those sinews of commerce and trade. And there is scarcely a
town or district in the kingdom, however great and opulent it
may now be, that has not at one time or other, partaken of the
substantial benefits conferred on it by the enlightened patriotism
of the church.

CHAPTER XXII.

ECCLESIASTICAL AND MAGISTERIAL RULE.

'A land of settled government,
  A land of just and old renown,
  Where freedom broadens slowly down
From precedent to precedent.

'And let the change which comes be free
  To ingroove itself with that, which flies,
  And work, a joint of state, that plies
Its office moved with sympathy.'

Tennyson.

On the abolition of hereditary jurisdictions in 1747, personal authority gradually disappeared from the exercise of magisterial functions, and the majesty of the law became the great regulating power between man and man in public life. In the transition, lingering traces of the older system continued, and in the public records of the period there are many notices of customs and regulations which are now entirely obsolete. The following extracts from the Court Books of Newburgh, beginning with some anterior to the date mentioned, throw light on the social life of our forefathers, and are sufficiently curious to merit attention :—

'27 Feby 1706. *In causa* Kirk Session contra John Bet for crossing the water [the Tay] on the Sabbath day, compeared John Bet and confest the samen, the baillies fines him in four pounds scots as the penaltie, as he enacted himself not to row on the Saboth day.'

'9ᵗʰ Septʳ 1707. James Sword enacts himself that he shall
not admitt of any Table reckoning late on Sabbath night
or early in the morning above ane chappin of eall the
piece, under the pain of four pounds Scotts *toties quoties.*
James Sword.'

'August 18, 1708. *In causa* proketor fiscal against David
Blyth eldʳ Earle, for being drunk upon the twelfth and
thretteenth instant, and did curse and swear and abuse his
neighbours and his own familie contrair to the Acts of
Parliament, and being frequentlie convict of the said
faults formerly and therefore craves that he may be punished conform to law.'

The Act of Parliament referred to is that of Charles II., A.D.
1661, chap. XIX., which imposed a fine of twenty pounds on a
nobleman for cursing or swearing; on a baron twenty merks,
gentleman, heritor, or burgess ten merks, a yeoman forty shillings, a servant twenty shillings, and a minister the fifth part of
his stipend. Any judge or magistrate refusing to put the law
in force, 'shall be liable and subject to a fine of one hundred
pounds Scots for the poor of the parish where the scandal happened.'

John Bet appears to have been a confirmed offender, for on the
31st May 1710, he is brought before the magistrates, 'confessing
that he had crossed the water with Mr David Nairn, who obtained
leave from the Minister. Therefore the Baillyies considering the
same *assoilzie the said John Bate and his servant*' [the words in
italics are deleted],—then follows, 'And the minister also compearing and denying that he gave any liberty to the said Mr
David, and declares that the said John never sought leave from
him to that effect.' 'Therefore considering the minister's declaration, fines the said John Bate conform to the Act made yʳ-anent,
which is dated 21st March 1705.'

The following cases of breaches of the Sabbath occur in
Abdie Session Records about the same period :—

'1704 Nov. 12. George Paterson, Milner of Denmyln, John Lilburn and Michael Hog delated for grinding corns on the Sabbath, and being cited, compearing and examined Denyed the charge.'

1705 April 22. John Lilburn compeared not, being sick, but George Paterson did confest his fault, and was appointed to public rebuke next Sabbath. And this day Michael Hog appeared publicly and was rebuked.'

'1710 May 18. Mungo Neish and Michael Wilkie delated for scandalous drinking and vaging to ale-houses on the Sabbath day, they compeired and were rebuked for Sabbath breaking.'

'1711 April 29th. Margaret Murray in the Grange being delated for bringing in water on the Sabbath, is ordained to be rebuked by an Elder, and if obstinate to be cited before the Session.'

1713, Feb. 29. Complaint being this day entered against the people of Grange, their profanation of the Sabbath, by a scandalous crowding together in heaps after sermons, about worldly discourses and diversions, and suffering their children to play that day openly before their faces without rebuke. . . . .
. . . The Beadle to summon them to the Session to be rebuked for such a scandalous practice.'

A few years previous to the breach of the Sabbath by the Grange folks, the following threatened exercise of a law apparently in force at the time, occurs —

'1708 October 31. James Scot entered the pillar and was rebuked.'

'1709 Feb. 20. The Beadle ordered to tell James Scot that if he pay not his penalty instantly, and subject to discipline, They will give him up to be a Sojor, according to the Proclamation.'

James, however, was not ambitious of military honours, for on the 13th March following, he 'granted bond for his penalty and satisfaction, and was appointed to the stool on Sabbath next.'

Reverting to Burgh Records of Newburgh, the following occurs ·—

> '1709 May 19. The Qlk day Gavin Spens lait Bailie ther gave in ane complaint upon Katharin Baxter that where-as ther was depositat in his hands with consent, ane con-tract of marriage betwixt her and James Imbrie, and the said Katharin desyring to hear the said contract read, she violently took the said contract out of the hands of John Houg tennant in Mugdrum, whom she. brought along to read it, and she brunt the samen   The Baillies taking this business to their serious consideration appoints the said Katharin to be confynd to the Tolbooth till sutch tyme as she shall make up the sd contract in all its heads and contents, and till she return to ·her husband, James Imbrie, and cohabit with him.'

As there was no escape from such a sentence, 'Katharin' com-plied, 'made up the contract anew,' and offered to return to her husband.' The magistrates, therefore, went to the domicile of the refractory couple, and in their presence, the town officer formally announced to the husband the magistrates' decision, and the of-fending wife's willingness to return to his house.

> '15 day of June 1709. 'In causa ag^t Katharin Smart the Baillies appoints her to be putt in the stocks for ane certain short space, as a punishment for her misdy-manners.'

On the 5th Oct. 1709, David, Lord Lundores appears as a wit-ness in a case before the magistrates, and signed his deposition. On the same day the following entry occurs:—

'David, Lord Lundores protested that there should be no Magistrates elected for this burgh without his warrand and Commission, To which the Councillors Electors replied that they were not oblidged to have his warrand and Commissione. In respect they have their surbys under ye Abbott of Lundores hands, and after him by Confirmation of his Majestie the year of God 1632 and yrfor they would proceed conform to their Chartours use and wont.'

'1711 May 30th. The said day anent ane complaint given in by ye Fiscall and John Lyell younger informer ag^{t} Margt Ballingall for scolding abusing and using most hellish expressions ag^{t} the said John Lyell and his wife, and ag^{t} oyr^{s} in ye Burgh. And ye Baillyies considering the samen, and she confessing she made use of some base expressions. And furder considering ane act made off before for banishing her fourth of ye toune for thift, yet ye said toune is furder molested with her by retourning again to ye Burgh. Therefore the Baillyies ordain her to find caution and allows her tyme to write to her husband, with this express provision that if the saids Baillyies shall be instrumented, by any person leased or who shall suspect, for ane act of banishment, or ye former to be yet put in execution ag^{t} her, then and at the same tyme the said Baillyies enacts and ordains that she be presently thereafter banished furth ye toune. And if she shall return they ordain her yrafter to be burnt [branded with a hot iron] and scourged out att ye ports. And furder enacts that after ye said act shall be put in execution, any person who shall resett her shall be held and repute as airt and pairt with her, and shall be lyable to make up all damnadge and losse any person may sustain by her. And furder ordains all her moveable goods and gear to be confiscatt either in her custody, or where it can be found, and to be Escheit and inbrought to her Majesties use.—

DAVID BICKERTON.'

' 1726, Decr 7. In the action Wmson Pro^r ffiscal ag^t William Watsone, shoemaker in Newburgh and James Fotheringham, weaver there, for haveing within these few days bygone a numerous company att their marriadge contrair to the Law. Def^{rs} called and both of them compeared and judicially acknowledged they had upwards of thirty persons att each of their weddings. The Baillies considering the same finds both to have contravened ye act of parliament, and that that number is more than the Law allows. Therefore the baillies fines each of them for these facts conform to act of parliament, and ordains them to make payment wtin form of Law. '

'The said day compeared William Watsone, Shoemaker . . . desyring to be admitted burges of Newburgh, which being considered, the baillies, with consent of the Councill, Doe hereby admitt him to be Burges of the said burgh ' and after taking the oath of fidelity in common form. He requyred act of Court and took instruments. '

In the Burgh Records there are many entries similar to the foregoing, recording decisions against offenders for having more than the legal number at their marriage, and almost invariably, as in this instance, there follows an application by the prosecuted person craving to be admitted a burgess. It would seem as if becoming a burgess mitigated the fine, but it is nowhere so expressed. The Act of Parliament referred to is that of Charles II., 13 Sep. 1681, intituled—' Act restraining the exorbitant expenses of Marriages, Baptisms and Burials.' The enactment regarding marriages is, ' that besides the married persons, their parents, children, brothers and sisters, and the family wherein they live, There shall not be present at any contract of marriage, marriage or In-fare or meet upon occasion thereof above four friends on either side with their ordinary domestic servants, and that neither Bridegroom, nor Bride, nor their parents or Relations, Tutors, or Curators for them, and to their use, shall make above two changes of raiment at that time, or upon that occasion, certifying such persons as shall contraveen, if they be landed persons. They shall be liable in the fourth part of their yearly valued rent, and those who are not landed persons in the fourth part of their moveables. Burgesses according to their condition and means not exceeding five hundred merks scots. And if there shall be any greater number of persons than aforesaid in any House or Inn within Burgh, or suburbs, or within two miles of the same, where Penny Weddings are made. That the master of the House shall be fined in the sum of Five hundred merks scots.'

Besides the question of expense, which was excessive, and entailed in many cases a heavy burden of debt, and much subsequent privation, both among rich and poor, there were evils attending Penny Weddings, which the ministers of religion set their faces against, and strove to correct. The ministers alleged, and there is reason to believe justly, that these meetings were often the occasion of immorality, and that 'the piping and dancing and profane ministrelling tended to desboshry.' To make sure that their edicts for the repression of irregularities were enforced, some kirk sessions and presbyteries enacted, 'that nane be married till ten pounds be consigned for the better security that thar be nae mair taen for an bridal lawing than five shillings according to order, with certification, gif the order of the bridal lawing be broken the said ten pounds sall be confiscat.'[1] The efforts of the church to restrain 'deboshry' were praiseworthy, and it is reasonable to suppose that they had some effect in restraining the grosser irregularities complained of; but, besides the suppression of immorality, they attempted to restrain the rejoicings which are so natural and so universal on marriage occasions, and there they failed. Though edict after edict was issued, 'the piping and the dancing and the minstrelling' continued, and still continues, at marriage festivities.

'27 Nov. 1728. In causa David Jack agᵗ Ann Robertson

---

[1] Chambers's *Domestic Annals*, Vol. I., p. 333.

servitrix to Margaret Robertson, who fied herself with the said complainer from Mart[s] 1728 to Mart[s] 1729 at ten pounds, ane pare of shoes and ane eln of lining'

The Baillies decerns Margaret Robertson with whom she continues servant to pay the half of the above years fie being ffyve pound, nyne pence for on shoe and a groat for ye half eln linning,'

'1st January 1729. The Baillies haveing considered the complaint exhibited by James Wilkie as to his haveing sheep stollen from him, and thereupon craveing warrand for a search, which search was accordingly made, and also considering ye mutton, sheep skins, and oyrs mentioned in ye minute were found in ye house of Richard —— in Newburgh, and the saids Baillies have also considered that R. —— had deserted and fled, and haveing also considered ye judiciall confession of Margaret Bett his spouse the pannell and ye haill oyr minuts of proces, and being with the whole affair Deliberately and weill advised. They find that R. —— has been guilty of stealling sheep and other things, and that he has had a practise in so doeing for sometyme bygone, and that his spouse Margaret Bett ye pannell has been airt and pairt with him in the stealth for this while bygone and has connived wt him yrin, Resett, and made use of ye stollen goods equally with himself. And therefore they decern and ordain out of the first end of his moveable effects, household plenishing and debts dew to him, that the haill debts dew by him and contained in ye minuts be payed, and ye remander therof to belong to the pror[r] ffiscal and to be intromitted with and disposed upon by him for ye use of ye members of Court; And decerns and ordains Margaret Bett ye pannell to be punished by being immediately putt in ye stocks there to remain with a sheep's skin about her att ye cross for ye speace of two hours and yrafter to be putt in ye jougs there to remain with a sheep's skin about her for ye speace of on hour, and thereafter to be banished ye toune by touck of drum to ye westport yrof never to return to ye same in any tyme comeing, and att ye said west port to be burnt on ye hand and dismissed. The Baillies not haveing thought fitt to cause scourge her in reguard it is informed she is with child and hereby discharge any persons within ye burgh to give any harbry or residence to ye said Richard —— and his said spouse in any tyme comeing under ye penalty of twenty pound scots toties quoties, seeing that both he and she are both banished ye toune in all tyme comeing, and ordains this to be advertysed by touck of drum, and if any person can hereafter apprehend Richard —— upon their delyvering him to the ffiscall they shall have a crown of reward.— WILLIAM ANDERSON, WILLIAM BALLINGALL.'

'Februar. the 27th 1729. Court off the brough Newbrugh holdn be Wm Anderson and William Ballingall present bailies.' 'Anent ane complaint given in to ye Bailies be David Anderson portioner of Newburgh shewing that David Blyth alias Earl hath his midden stead before his entrie to his house which is greatly to his prejudice. The said Baillies called men to boun the ground off the two midden steads, and then tooke in their report how they should be marched for both ther conveniency. The men are as follows David bickertoun,—Mathew Lyal,—John Halibourtoun,—William Ballingall,—David Spence,—who judged it ffitt that David Anderson have the miden stead westmost before his own door, that belonged formerly to David Blyth, and David Blyth the eastmost midden stead, and both are equally to be divided. And David Anderson is oblidged to feace up the brae above the eastmost midden-stead on the westmost. And that the stones of the westmost midden are to be still as they ar till the Bailies find convenience, because David Blyth owned he toock them off the Cassa. The Bailies haveing taken the men's

verdict to their consideration, do decern and ordain the
westmost midden stead to belong to David Anderson
without any trouble or molestation to any of the parties,
under the paine of ten pound scots to be payed in to the
treasurer, and the said midden-steads to be marched at
the sight of honest men of the bailies apoynting.'

This grave judicial decision, there is too much reason to
believe, presents a faithful photograph of the condition of the
streets of Newburgh and other Scottish towns one hundred and
fifty years ago. It corroborates to the letter the representation
which James VI. made to the Convention of Royal Burghs in 1608.
Among other matters he says: 'In regard that the lying of the
muk and fewell in grit heapis and myddingis upoun the hie
streitis, or within ony uther place of our saidis burghis and cityis,
is nocht only noysum to all strangeris and passengeris bothe in
smell and sicht, bott is dangerous also in tyme of plague, being a
speciall neurescher thair-of, that thairfor thai sould appoint the
streitis of thair tounis to be keipit cleyne; as also that within
thair gret cityis and tounis skaviengeris may be appointit, efter
the form usit heir [England] for carying furth of these tounis all
sort of filth that so the cuntrey people attending us in our
intendit journay thither the next yeir may nocht reproche the
uncleynes of the touns and cityis of that our kingdome; and als
that all filthie beastis, such as swyne, be nocht sufferit to hant in
the oppin streetis.' [1]
The records of the negotiation in 1697-8 for the removal of the
University of Andrews to Perth, bring before us the filthy state of
the streets of St Andrews at that period,—the eighth reason given
for the change is as follows:—'This place [St Andrews] being
now only a village, where most part farmers dwell, the whole
streets are filled with Dunghills, which are exceedingly noisome
and ready to infect the air, especially at this season when the

---

[1] *Record of Convention of Royal Burghs*, 1597; 1614, p. 253.

herring gutts are exposed in them, or rather in all corners of the Toune by themselves, and the season of the year apt to breed infection, which partly may be said to have been the occasion of last year's dysenterie, which from the beginning here raged through most part of the Kingdom.' [1]

It is worthy of mention, that the Commissioners appointed for the removal of the University to Perth, held a number of meetings for the purpose. One of these meetings was held at the village of Glenduckie, and another was held at Newburgh on the 21st March 1698; but as the continuance of the University at St Andrews attests, their deliberations came to nought, which is the more surprising, as the preliminaries were all but arranged, and both sides were desirous for the change.[2]

It was long ere the streets of country towns were brought into a condition even approaching to cleanness. In 1793 the Magistrates of Newburgh issued an order that dung was not to be allowed to lie on the street longer than forty-eight hours;—and even thirty years later, the inhabitants were duly warned by tuck of drum, to remove all accumulations of manure from the street in front of their houses previous to the half-yearly fairs. The street of Newburgh is wide and spacious, but the following decision of the Town Council, on a petition from a number of the inhabitants, presents us with a picture more like a scene in pastoral life, on

'Some flowrie holm between twa verdant braes
Where lasses used to wash and spread their claes,' [3]

than the High Street of a Royal Burgh.

'June 29th 1771. The Councill being mett, the within Petition was read and being considered, the voats called, they were unanimous that none shall be allowed to bleach

---

[1] *Perth,—its Annals and Archives*, p. 341.   [2] *Ib.*, pp. 345–351.
[3] *'Gentle Shepherd.*—Scene II.

weabs on the high street or tramp cloath of any kind within six yards and even that at the under side of the wells, and . . . the Councell orders their act to be published by tuck of drum that none may pretend ignorance, and that transgressors shall be punished according to Justice, in terror to others, signed by the Baillie in name of the Councell.—David Ballingall.'

1729, Sepr 22. George Sim in Newburgh is accused of stealing wheat and bringing it from the Cars of Gowry . .
the Bailies finds him guilty of theft and therefore decerns and ordains him to be taken immediately from ye tolbooth and to be put in ye jougs there to remain for ye speace of ane hour, and immediately thereafter to be banished and putt from ye cross out at ye east end of the toune by ye touck of drum, and there to be burnt on ye hand with ane burn-iron and ordains his wife and family immediately to remove furth off ye toune also, and never any of them to return y^runto, and if any person in tyme coming shall harbry or reset the said George Sim his wife or family within ye burgh, or entertain them with meat, drink or house-roome, they shall for each such transgression incur the penalty of twenty pounds Scotts *toties quoties*, and ordains the same to be published and intimate to ye inhabitants by ye bell or oyr ways. And decerns and ordains the haill moveable goods and gear of the said George Sim to be escheat at the instance of the pro^r Fiscall, and ordains ye inhabitants to see and witness his above punishment and banishment forsaid put to dew Execution.'

The following is one of the latest prosecutions for breach of the Sabbath:

'9 Feb: 1743. A complaint being exhibit ag^t Andrew Currie, William Winton, Alex^r Currie, Alex^r Clow, John Tod,

Alex^r Hoy, David Lyell and Robert Dowie for committing abuse on ye Sabbath day in ye church and oy^r young boys in this Burgh. The Baillies enacts statutes and ordains that not only they but all other young people within the Burgh, shall not in time comeing goe to church either fore-noon or afternoon till ye ringing of ye last bell, and that they goe along to church with their parents or master, and behave civilly therein during the whole time of wor-ship, and that if they doe otherways, they shall be fined in ten pounds scots for each transgression. And ye masters to be lyable for their servants, and parents for their children for ye said fines and penaltys and ordains this Act to be published through the brough by the Bell or Drum. And that besides if any abuse be committed in tyme of worship the Committer shall be corporally pun-ished besides paying such fines.'

The formula of 'parents being liable for their children, and masters for their servants,' continued to be proclaimed by the town officers when publishing a magisterial edict, down to about the year 1830. This was a far-off echo of a principle which lay at the foundation of society among all the Teutonic races. 'Teutonic Law based itself on the family bond. The community in which a man was born and lived, the gild to which he had bound himself, the master he had served were responsible for citizen, craftsman, or servant.' So thoroughly did this principle of responsibility pervade the law, that 'if a man entertained a merchant or stranger for the night, and supplied him with food, and the guest commit a crime, the host was bound to bring him to justice, or answer for it himself.' [1]

The following extract from the Burgh Court Book of New-burgh, shows the mode of procedure in cases of defamation in the middle of the last century. James Beatt having been accused of

---

[1] J. M. Kemble, quoted, Hughes's *Alfred the Great*, pp. 28, 29.

defaming the character of Mr Taylor, the schoolmaster, was brought before the magistrates; who, after hearing the evidence adduced, pronounced the following sentence:—

> '1748 April 14. James Beatt found guilty of taking away the reputation of Mr Taylor, and therefore not only fines him in the sum of foure pounds sterling, but Ordains him betwixt and Sabbath next, in fair sunshine and before a good many famous honest men in the place, to goe to the public Cross of Newburgh, When Mr Taylor is called to be present, and there beg Mr Taylor's pardon, and acknowledge he had injured him in his reputation and say, "False tongue he lyed," and that under the penalty of foure pounds sterling. And hereby grants warrant to the officers, who are to call the assistance of Burgesses to apprehend the person of the said James Beatt and to put him in closs prison, there to remain while the whole sentence is fulfilled, and with certification if any burgess refuse to assist, each of them so doing shall be lyable to a fine of ten pounds Scots. — John Small, David Lyell, Bailies.'

The latest case that occurs in the Burgh Court Books of the use of the 'Jougs' as an instrument of punishment, is that of Peter Gibb. It is as follows:—

> '1757 20 July. The Baillies considering the complaint and the judicial acknowledgement of Peter Gibb y^r son of Peter Gibb, Taylor,—and also of Peter McClachlan, son to Sonsan Dewar finds that they are both guilty in being airt and pairt in breaking in on John Smiton's house and carrying off his kypper, and therefore decerns and ordains that each of them stand two hours in the *jugs* with the kypper tyed about their necks. And their parents as they are under non age bind and oblidge themselves for their

honest and good behaviour in tyme coming under penalty of being banished the toune; And further Decerne that the said Peter Gibb and Sousan Dewar shall be fined for their interests of a ⁻crown each and remain in prison while payment shall be made.'

The practice of compelling those guilty of theft to appear in public with the article stolen tied about them, was an ancient one. 'In 1327, several bakers in London were accused of stealing dough, by making holes in the baker's moulding boards. They were sentenced to stand in the pillory with the dough hung about their necks, until vespers at St Paul's should be ended.' [1]

The somewhat arbitrary sentence pronounced by the Magistrates of Newburgh on Peter Gibb and his companion, fitly closes our extracts from the Judicial Records of the Burgh. Since then their decisions are more in accordance with modern ideas of justice, than a sentence of indefinite imprisonment until the fine is paid.

Arbitrary though this sentence was, it was merciful when contrasted with the judicial decisions of an earlier age. In the Records of the Burgh of Edinburgh, the following enactment occurs:—'22 December 1515. Ane Minor of less aige airt and part with ane common theif adjugeit to be scurgeit to the gallows and thair his lug takkit to the beame, and banist this toune and four myle about for all the dayes of his lyfe, and neuir to cum thairin under the payne of deid [death].' [2]

The following quaint obligation, preserved in the Town's Charter Chest, shows that Peter Gibb, junior, nearly thirty years after his early offence, continued to require magisterial attention:—

'I Patrick Gib, Carter in Newburgh hereby bind and oblige myself, and my heirs acted in the burrow Court Books of

---

[1] *Long Ago*, Vol. I., p. 264.
[2] *Extracts from the Records of the Burgh of Edinburgh*, 1403–1528, p. 159.

Newburgh that I shall keep his Majesty's peace in all time coming, and that I shall behave and carry myself decently and soberly as becomes, and that I shall abstain from insulting, maltreating, injuring any person within the Burgh of Newburgh, and from cursing and swearing within the said Burgh in all time coming, under the penalty of Five pounds Sterling.—P K. GIBB.'

Notwithstanding this obligation, there is reason to believe, from what is known of the culprit's history, that if he forbore to swear within 'the Burgh,' he did not seem to think the obligation was binding beyond it.

INDUSTRIAL PURSUITS.[1]

' Blest is this Isle,—our native land
  Where battlement and moated gate
  Are objects only for the hand
  Of hoary Time to decorate;
  Where shady hamlet, town that breathes
  Its busy smoke in social wreaths,
  No ramparts' stern defence require,
  Nought but the heaven-directed spire
  And steeple tower (with pealing bells
  Far heard) our only citadels.'

Wordsworth.

AFTER the suppression of the rising in favour of the Stuarts in 1745, the country made rapid strides in material progress; manufactures were developed and agriculture improved. The improvement was sometimes faster and sometimes slower, but ever since then, the blessings of immunity from invasion and freedom from civil war have manifested themselves in increased prosperity and comfort. The manufacture of linen was considered of prime importance at that period, and the government held out great encouragement for its extension and improvement. Bounties were offered for every yard of Scottish linen exported; penalties were imposed on the importers of damaged seed, and a bounty of

---

[1] The substance of what is said in this chapter regarding manufactures, was delivered as a lecture in the Town Hall, Newburgh, and was afterwards published, under the title of ' The History of Linen, and of Linen Weaving in Newburgh.

fifteen shillings, which was afterwards increased to twenty shillings, was paid for every acre of ground sown with lint or hemp. The Convention of Royal Burghs, and the Board of Trustees for Manufactures, brought weavers from abroad to exhibit and teach others the most improved methods of weaving.[1] Large rewards were offered for the improvement of looms, and other manufacturing utensils; prizes were given to housewives for the best made pieces of linen, and aid was given towards the establishment of spinning-schools for the instruction of the young in the art of spinning. The following entry on this subject occurs in the Records of the Burgh of Peebles :—

> '27 May 1633. Appointis Weddinsday nixt to convene the haill persones and parentis of these bairnes gevin up in roll to be bound for ane yeir to the small quheill in the hous to be erectit to lerne the young anes to spyn.'[2]

The efforts made to establish manufactures in Scotland at this earlier period failed, through the breaking out of the civil wars shortly afterwards; those of the eighteenth century fell on happier times, and were more successful. The encouragement given by the Board of Trustees for Manufactures, induced an extension of the cultivation of *lint;* there was not a farm in this neighbourhood, or in the country generally, on which there was not more or less of it sown. It was cultivated largely on the Burgh Acres; the cottar had his little plot; and so much did it enter into social arrangements, that domestic servants had a small ·patch (two *lippies-bounds*, equal to about five and a half poles) allotted to them, and even herd-boys had their wages paid in *lint*. A corresponding activity was manifested in its manufacture; one or more spinning-wheels were in active operation in every house,—female servants were bound to spin two spindles and a half, or thirty-six thousand

---

[1] *Records of the Convention of Royal Burghs*, 1597–1614, pp. 116, 117.
[2] *Charters and Documents of the Burgh of Peebles*, Burgh Record Society, p. 372.

yards of yarn weekly, besides performing their usual work. Cottar wives assembled under the eye of the mistress of the homestead, and had a 'rockin,' striving who could spin the greatest quantity in a given time. Such scenes of household industry have utterly past away,—few of the present generation have seen a spinning-wheel, and even the terms used in speaking of the art, which, up to the third decade of the present century, were familiar as household words, are now utterly unknown. But it was by this domestic industry that all the linen manufactured was produced, and it brought comfort and independence to many a humble home. The drying up of this industry had this injurious effect, that it tended to depopulate the rural districts, by driving the people to seek for work and livelihood in the towns, which they could no longer find in the country.

Towards the end of the last, and even in the beginning of the present century, most of the ordinary clothing of both young and old in this neighbourhood was of home-made woollen. The cottar-folk, who were unable to have a whole web of their own, joined together for a warp, and each had their own weft woven on it. This was called a *mein*, or common web. If it was of woollen, it was sent to the litster, or dyer, of whom there was one or more in every district, to be waulked (fulled), and then dyed; but hodden-grey (which was simply the natural colour of the wool) for common use prevailed. The getting of a new gown at that era was a matter involving much time and preparation; the lint had often first to be sown in the field, then spun, woven, bleached, and latterly sent to the printfield, to be printed of a selected pattern. As may readily be conjectured, a gown so prepared was not often replaced by a newer fashion.

In the year 1749 linen manufacture, which has ever since been the staple trade of the town, received a great impetus in Newburgh. At that period an enactment required that every master-weaver should become bound to manufacture faithful and honest goods, the object being the production of cloth that would secure a good name for the linen manufactures of Britain in the markets of the world. The regulations for securing this have so utterly passed out of memory as to make them curious. The Act required ' that no weaver shall set up for himself as Master-Weaver until he give security before a Justice of the Peace or Magistrate within any Burgh, under such penalties as the Justice or Magistrate shall think fit, that neither he nor any person to be employed by him shall weave any linen cloth for sale or otherwise than according to the Rules and Directions prescribed by this Act. And if any person shall set up for himself as Master-Weaver without giving such security, he shall forfeit for every web of linen cloth so wrought or wove by him, or them, or any employed by them, the said web or piece of cloth, or the value thereof for the benefit of the Informer, and shall further forfeit the sum of Five pounds.'[1]

The first entry that occurs in the Court Books of Newburgh, in terms of this Act, is on the 31st January 1749, and is as follows:—

> 'Compeared before John Small and John Lyell, younger, baillies of the Burgh of Newburgh, Alexander Lyell, weaver and present stamp-master there, Thomas Spence, Weaver there, who in terms of ye Act Enter themselves as Master-Weavers and became bound each of them Cautioners for the other in terms of the Act of Parliament.'

This is followed by twenty-eight other weavers coming forward on the same day, and becoming bound in like manner.

The duty of the stampmaster, whose name is incidentally mentioned in the foregoing extract, was to examine all the linen cloth woven in the town and neighbourhood, and to impress it with a stamp specially entrusted to him, if he deemed the web honestly and properly manufactured. The following process,

---

[1] Act Geo. I., 1727.

preserved in the archives of Newburgh, exhibits the form of procedure when the stampmaster refused to stamp the cloth presented:—

'Complains Alexander Lyell, Stampmaster in Newburgh upon James Thomson, younger weaver in Newburgh, That upon ye day and date of thir presents, the said defender presented a Brown web of Linnen Cloath containing fyftie-thrie yeards of lenth to be stamped, and after inspecting ye same the said complainer found it altogether insufficient. Therefore may it please your Lordships the Magistrates of Newburgh to appoint tradesmen to inspect the same, and if found insufficient the said web ought to be con-demned in terms of ye act of parliament, and the defender ought to be fined according the said act. "Court held 5th March 1753. The Bailies appoint John Lyell y^{r}., weaver at the west port of Newburgh, James Nairn in the said Brugh, James Anderson, Weaver y^{r}., and Joseph Lyell to goe and inspect the said web and to Retourn their verdict to them. Having inspected and considered the said web unanimously declare upon oath that the same is insufficient, and spoilt in the working and not merchant-able goods." The Bailies have received this verdict "condemns the said web and decerns ye same to be cutt in six elns according to the act of parliament and fines the defender in terms of the act of parliament.

'W^{M}. BALLINGALL, JOHN LYELL.'

Long before these provisions, however, for the manufacture of 'honest and merchantable goods,' it was enacted in the reign of James VII. (1686), 'for the encouragement of the Linen Manu factures of this Kingdom, and prevention of the exportation of monies thereof by importing of linen, that no corps of any persons whatever shall be buried in any shirt, sheet, or any thing else except in plain linen or cloth of hards made and spun within the kingdom under a penalty of £300 Scots for a nobleman, and £200 for each other person.' This Act was ratified by the first Parliament of William and Mary, with, among other additions, 'that the nearest Elder or Deacon of the parish with one neighbour or two be called by the persons concerned and present, to the putting of the dead corps in the coffin that they may see the same done;' and they were required to subscribe a certificate to that effect.

This Act was repealed in the last Scottish Parliament,[1] 'and for the encouragement of the manufacture of woollen' (which was depressed at the time), it was enacted, 'that hereafter no corps of any person, of what condition or quality soever shall be buried in linen of whatever kind, but plain woollen cloth or stuff shall be. made use of, and that under the same penalties as were imposed by the Act anent Linens.' This law did not remain a dead letter. In the Court Books of Newburgh the following entry occurs :—

> 'At a Court holden by Richard Smith baillyie upon ye 14 May 1712, Court lawfully fencit. The qlk day ye ffiscall of Court ag^t ye persons afternamed, for winding of their dead in Lining since ye Act of Parliament made ag^t winding of dead in Lining; And that contrair to the said Act of Parliament, vizt., John Small for winding his wife, Janet Stinnes for winding John Smith her husband in Linning; John Brown for winding two of his children, Robert Allan for winding his wife, Jean Daniel for her daughter, Rebecca Stinnes for Thomas Matheson her husband, John Blyth, talyeour, for his father,—All for winding in Linning contrair to the said Act of Parliament. And they being all summoned to this day personally apprehended, John Small, John Brown, Janet Stinnes, Jean Daniel all confessed, and John Blyth absent, held as confessed, and Rebecca Stinnes absent, held as confest. And Robert Allan not being able to come, and it

---

[1] Anne, Cap. XIV., 1707.

SPINDLE AND D STAFF, AND SP NN NG-WHEEL.

being attested and verified by sundrie honest men that he was not guilty, Therefore the baillyie fines those guilty conform to Act of Parliament, and assoilzies Robert Allan.'

The prejudice in favour of burying in linen must have been strong, to have induced so many to run the risk of the heavy penalty which the act imposed; and yet, in all likelihood in consequence of this very act, a white woollen stuff (called burial crape) continued to be used, especially by the rich for winding their dead, so late as the year 1820. John Wesley, on his death-bed, gave instructions that his body should be buried in woollen.[1]

It is an interesting instance of the tenacity with which old habits and customs keep their hold, that primitive modes of spinning and weaving should have continued in use so long after improved methods were discovered. We have evidence, in a manuscript in the British Museum, written early in the 14th century, of the use of a spinning wheel at that date.[2]

Two centuries later, in 1533, a wheel at which the spinner sat and turned with her foot by a crank was invented.[3] In or about 1764 the two-handed wheel, which enabled the spinner to spin two threads at once, was discovered, and yet most of the old people in the neighbourhood of Newburgh and in the country generally continued to spin by the spindle and distaff up to the beginning of the present century. A weaver of Newburgh, still alive (1874), wove in his youth a web of linen spun entirely by the Balk and Rock, as the spindle and distaff were named in Scotland.[4] The spinning-wheel

---

[1] Southey's *Life of Wesley*, Vol., II., p. 566.

[2] Wright's *History of Domestic Manners*, p. 238.

[3] Chambers's *Book of Days*, Vol. I., p. 68.

[4] This primitive mode of spinning continued much longer in more secluded districts. Dr Arthur Mitchell, whose knowledge of archaic usages is so extensive, has seen the spindle (but not the distaff) in practical use 'in Fetlar in Shetland; on the west coast of Sutherlandshire; in the parish of Daviot, near Inverness, and in the parish of Balmaclellan, in Galloway, besides other places in

lingered in this neighbourhood until somewhere between 1820 and 1830, but it has now as entirely disappeared as the Balk and Rock which preceded it. The fly-shuttle, which greatly increased speed in weaving, was invented in 1738, and yet so late as the beginning of this century, all the old weavers in this neighbourhood continued to use the hand-shuttle, driving it first with the right hand and then with the left, as in ancient times. One old man continued to use it to about the year 1820.

Though so many of the inhabitants of Newburgh enrolled themselves as master-weavers in 1749, yet for a long time the manufactures of the town were of limited extent. Dr Stuart, minister of Newburgh, in his admirable Statistical Account of the Parish, written in 1792, says, 'no trader has yet appeared whose extensive transactions in commerce would entitle him to the name and character of a merchant, though perhaps the time is not far distant when many will be found of that respectable description.'[1] That time has since arrived,—but up to the end of the last century the main occupation and dependence of the burgesses was in the grazing of their cattle on the common hill, and on the cultivation of their share of the burgh lands.

These lands, in common with a great portion of the arable land of the country generally, were cultivated under the system of run-rig. This system sprang from a principle of fair-play ; each burgess having alloted to him a portion of the good land, then a portion of middling, next of inferior, and last of all a portion of the worst, each lot running side by side with that of a neighbour, hence the term run-rig. One lot, perhaps at one extremity, another it

---

Scotland, within the last ten years.' And, he adds, ' in Fetlar and other parts of Shetland it is common.' The term *Balk-and-Rock* does not occur in Jamieson's Scottish Dictionary. *Balk* signifies a beam ; we still say *weigh-balk*, Anglice, weighing-beam. *Rock* originally meant a bundle of anything loosely thrown together ; hence we speak in Scotland of a *ruck* of hay. Latterly *Rock* came to signify the piece of wood round which the flax or tow to be spun was loosely twisted ; hence the name tow staff or distaff.

[1] Sinclair's *Statistical Account*, Vol. VIII., p. 182.

may be in the centre, or at some corner, and another at the other extremity of the lands. Though springing from such a commendable principle, the run-rig system was a source of endless disputes. It has been thus described as seen in operation in the west of Ireland a few years ago, where it seems to have prevailed (if it does not still) in a very aggravated form. 'In some instances a tenant having any portion of a town-land, had his property in thirty or forty different places, and without fences between them, it being utterly impossible to have any, as the portions were so numerous, and frequently so very small, that not more than half a stone of oats were required to sow one of these divisions. Trespasses, confusions, disputes, and assaults, were the unavoidable consequences of this sytem.'[1] The *Wodrife* or burgh acres of Newburgh were divided into portions called *half-parts*, containing usually about two acres each; these were made up of five or six rigs, scattered in as many different places, intermixed with those of others in the manner described, the whole sixty-four half parts containing in all 156 acres, were subdivided into upwards of 350 patches.

In addition to the evils attending this minute subdivision—the burgesses had a right to send their cattle from a certain day in autumn to a certain day in spring to pasture over the whole arable lands of the burgh. Such a system was a bar to all improvement; and had it continued, the sowing of clover or the cultivation of turnips, or of any winter crop, would have been impossible.

To remedy such a state of matters, an Act was passed in the reign of William I. (1695), but burgh acres were expressly excluded. The burgh lands of Newburgh therefore remained under the system of run-rig, till the increasing importance of the linen manufactures, towards the end of the last century, made it more profitable to devote attention to them, and gradually the much-divided *half-parts* of the Wodrife, with four or five exceptions, have fallen into the hands of a neighbouring proprietor.

---

[1] Coulter's *West of Ireland*, p. 182.

So long as the main dependence of the burgesses was on the cultivation and pasturage of their lands, the records of the burgh teem with enactments for preventing trespasses and encroachments. An instance occurs in the very first page of the oldest Court Book of the Burgh.

> ' 1471, May 8. It was ordand be ye ballyeis i-ye Cossell of ye ton y^t John Layll suld keip ye corn of ye wydd^r-off, and ye hyll, and all ye grysse of ye com^n fra Whytsonde to ye tym y^t ye corn ye leyde i.'

The corn and grass were 'pryssed' at the entry of the person entrusted with charge of them, and if found damaged ' be ye pryssere,' the keeper was bound to make it good out of his ' pay^t to hym at Sanct Katryn-day.' For upwards of three hundred years similar appointments continued to be made, and very frequently the town-herd was the person appointed, but it also frequently occurred that the heritors did the duty in person. Whoever was appointed to the office was empowered to poind cattle found among the growing corn, hence he was named the *Punler*. The following is one of many records of an appointment under this primitive institution :—

> ' 1717 May 29. This day being appointed for choising of a Punler, and ye heritors being advertyssed for that effect, and they not compearing only David Lyell acknowledged that he had ye *punler* staff, and yrfor in respect of ye heritors not compearing to give their vote for a punler, Therefore the Baillzies statutes enacts and appoints that David Lyell begin to punle, and so that he delyver the staff to his nixt neighbour concerned that he may punle nixt, and that accordingly it goe round thorrow the whole heritors concerned, and that they punle each of them *per vices* day about for the present year, and who shall refuse or neglect their duty as it comes to their door, that they

be liable to a fine at ye Baillzies modification and discretion.'

The latest appointment of such an officer occurs in 1777.

The silent on-goings of peace pass un-noted by tradition, and it is only by comparing results at distant periods that the great advances and improvements in agriculture is perceived. For years after the last rising in favour of the Stuarts, the mode of conveying manure to the fields of the Wodrife was in *creels* or panniers, strung across a horse's back. Potatoes, which now form such an important crop, and have become such an indispensable necessity in modern life, were not introduced to this neighbourhood till some years after the 'Forty-five.' One who was born in 1743 remembered the introduction of potatoes to this neighbourhood. He used to tell, in the third decade of the present century, that when a boy he went and searched the ground after the crop was lifted. He found two or three not bigger than small plums, which he took home, and after they were boiled, they were divided, that all the household might taste them. Balks (waste stripes betwixt ridges) continued till after that period, and it was only by slow degrees, and within comparatively recent times, that the country became so highly cultivated, and assumed that garden-like appearance which it now presents.[1]

When enlarged spheres of industry had opened up and brought the inhabitants within the range of commercial activity, old modes of life and primitive institutions disappeared. This is notably the case with the town-herd ; this functionary and his duties are as utterly unknown to the present generation, as if he had never existed. And yet so late as the year 1830, he continued to drive out, twice a day, the *town-kye* to the pasturage of the Common Hill. The blowing of his horn, and the lowing of his charge, as he collected them one by one, was a sight and sound as familiar as the returning summer morn, and yet it is as completely buried

---

[1] Appendix No. X.

in the past as the fossil formations of a past era. Generally it
was an old man who was appointed to the office of town-herd;
and so important was the trust considered, that there was frequently a contest for the situation; the appointment depending
on the votes of the Wodrife Heritors. The last who held the
office (George Birrell) wore a broad blue bonnet of the old Cove-
nanter type, and his picturesque appearance, as he followed his
charge along the street, would now be eagerly seized by artists
as a subject for their pencil.

The following extract from the Town Council Records of Newburgh brings the duties and emoluments of this extinct official
vividly before us :—

' Court of the brough off Newburgh holdn be the baillies the
eighth day off December 1725 lawfully ffenced. . . .
' The whilk day being apoynted for choysing ane nolt-
heard ffor the inshewing yeir 1726   . The wholl
heretors and others conserned being ŭarnd to this dyet, to
give ther vots who shall keep the kyn the fforesaid yeir
publickly by the bell as ūse is.'
' And who shall succeed to the said kyn keeping ar to enter
with said service att the 25t off march nixt and to continoŭ
till mertimis therafter and cairfully to keep them and not
to preffer on by ane other in baiting, or his oŭn Coŭ and to
tak them out in the morning tymously and bring them in
betwixt elevn and tŭell and tak them oūt betwixt tŭo and
three afternoon, and give ŭarning by ane horn morning
and att noon, and that he shall not cast any toŭffs bot
only whair the rest of the heritors casts ther oŭn, and also
to ñait on the saids goods—alsūeel in the harvest as any
other tym in his oŭn person (he having his health) and
keep the grasse from others.'
' The bailies and all conserned ar to pay the said herd ffor
ilk beast off Coŭ six lippies off good and sufficient bear the
on halfe at bear-seed closing, the other halfe betwixt

mertimis and yooll and any other deŭs conform to use and
ŭont. D. BICKERTON. Ri : SMITH.'

' The ŭhilk day after a ffull and ffree vot of all conserned in
choysing ane nolt heard ffor the insheŭing yeir jajvij and
tuentie and sixe yeirs and Gorge fotherengham leat
sheepheard in parkhill caried the vot by nynteen vots and
Ingadges to the said service on The terms above ŭrytn
and ŭith him John Tod as Cautioner ffor the said Gorge
ffotherengham and that he shall perfform his pairt and
that the said gorge shall keep the gress from other fflocks
in goesomer. And on the other pairt, the bailies and ther
sucessors oblidges Them in name of the rest ffor payment
of the fforsd bole at the terms above ŭrytn, and That he
shall have his oŭn Coŭs grasse ŭithe therest alenerly, and
iff any beis deficiant The bailies is to give sentance in
his ffavors against them gratis, and bothe pairties have
subscrivit thir presents as ffollows. D. BICKERTON, Rᶦ SMITH,
GEORG FOTHERENGAHM, JOHN TOD.'

On the 10th December 1740, Patrick Glass, pyper in Newburgh, after competition between him and another, was elected
to the office of Cow-herd, on the condition, however, ' that he
shall goe to no wedding to play thereatt with his pypes, unless
he put a sufficient man in his Roume to hird for him, who shall
satisfy the Baillies.' Besides the emoluments mentioned, there
was a ' rig' of land in the burgh acres allotted to the herd. It is
still known as the Cow-herd's rig.

From the very earliest record of the burgh life up to the year
1830, the bestial of the burgesses (those, however, who were owners
of lands in the burgh acres having a special claim to it) pastured
daily on the Common Hill; but for reasons which seemed good to
many at the time, the hill was alloted, and turned to arable purposes, and the burgesses generally were denuded of a privilege
which, though those who kept cattle were gradually becoming
fewer and fewer, eked out the means of living, and diffused an

amount of comfort among the inhabitants, which has no equivalent in modern life.

The increasing activities of manufactures required more communication with the outside world, but the *unmade* state of the roads up to the end of the last century, rendered travelling difficult, and excepting on foot or horseback, next to impossible. Wheel-carriages were consequently all but unknown. The visits of strangers were few and seldom. The little world lived within itself, and news from the outside came only by some chance visitant, or the arrival of a vessel at the port. But in the year 1782, at a meeting of the Town Council,—

> 'Oct. 24th It was moved by Mr Brown, Clerk of Court, that he had some hopes of procuring a bye-post bag for conveying letters and other dispatches betwixt Perth and this Town three times a week, and it being put to the vote it was carried unanimously that the town pay sixpence per week towards defraying the expense of that bye-bag for one year's duration after its commencement, and appoint the Treasurer to pay the same.—JOSEPH LYELL, HENRY HARDIE.'

A brass plate, which the postman used to wear, engraved with the words 'Newburgh Post,' and the date 1792, is preserved among the Town's Records.

Little by little the old life gave way. The ports or gates of the town, were the boundaries within which none, however powerful, dare pass without becoming amenable to the authority within —they were raised perhaps more to mark the limits of the burghal jurisdiction than for protection against any hostile force. But what in a former age was looked upon with special pride as the *insignia* of authority and privileges, in the widening spheres of industry, were condemned as incumbrances.

On the '4 January 1785 It was moved in the Council that the West port cheeks and the north cheek of the East port were incumbrances and a nausiance to the Town, and it would tend to the ease and conveniency at the going out and the coming in to the Town if they were removed. It is therefore agreed that the said three cheeks shall be removed, and that the same be sold by public Roup for the use of the Common Good, only it is agreed that the north cheek of the West Port shall not be removed till the passage on the west port burn be widened more towards the north, for fear of danger to passengers there.—ANDREW FERNEY, JOHN ANDERSON, Bailies.'

Besides marking the limits of burghal jurisdiction and privileges, the burgesses perhaps felt a fancied security within the frail defences of their Posts, but the time had come when all civil commotions had ceased, when equal freedom prevailed within and without the Burgh Gates; when the feudal castle was deserted, and allowed to crumble into decay, and greater security was felt in the supremacy of law, than in walls and battlements. Henceforth there is nothing peculiar in the Records of the Burgh, and therefore its ancient history happily closes in the triumph of industry and peace.

CHAPTER XXIV

SCULPTURED STONE AT LINDORES; MUGDRUM CROSS, AND CROSS MACDUFF.

> ' Homeward let us take our path,
> Through the glowing purple heath,
> O'er the height that looketh down,
> On loch and river, strath and town,
> Past the cairn where legends tell,
> Of passions fierce and violence fell;
> By the *Cross* whose storied name
> Is blazon'd on the roll of Fame.'
>
> *Anon.*

THERE are three remarkable ancient monuments in the neighbourhood of Newburgh. A 'Sculptured Stone,' Mugdrum Cross, and Cross Macduff. The sculptured stone is one of the class peculiar to the east coast of Britain, and with one or two exceptions, found solely north of the Forth. It is situated on the north side of the public road near the village of Lindores, formerly it stood on the crest of the adjoining ridge called the Kaim Hill, until it was removed to its present situation, when the ridge was brought under the plough about thirty years ago.

The interest that attaches to the class of monuments to which the stone at Lindores belongs, arises from the peculiarity of the symbols sculptured upon them, and the mystery which surrounds them; nothing exactly similar having been found in any other part of the world.

The fact that these peculiar symbols are only found in the eastern parts of Scotland, tends to show that they are the work of the people who inhabited that district, which 'we learn from the venerable historian of the Angles in the beginning of the eighth century, was known as Pictavia and Alba, the country of the Picts, whose southern boundary was the Firth of Forth.'[1] It seems also reasonable to conclude from the absence of any Christian symbol on very many of these stones, that the earliest and rudest of them were raised in heathen times. This conjecture is strengthened by the fact of a fragment of one of these peculiarly sculptured stones having been found, forming part of a cist in a burial mound (at Cairn Greg, in the parish of Monifieth) of acknowledged heathen character. In the cist, a bronze dagger was found lying beside an urn very rudely made, containing the ashes of the individual over whom the mound was raised. The dagger laid beside the deceased clearly points to heathen usages and beliefs, and the appropriation of the 'Sculptured Stone' towards the formation of the cist, is a convincing proof that it was carved when these usages and beliefs prevailed.[2] Putting all these circumstances together, it may reasonably be assumed that the oldest of these 'Sculptured Stones' dates back to a period preceding the introduction of Christianity to the eastern coast of Scotland, and as far back, if not even earlier, than the third century of our era.

What is called the crescent and sceptre, which appears on the stone at Lindores, is found with various modifications on a very large proportion of this class of monuments, and the constant repetition of these figures has led many to entertain the opinion that these and the other figures, which so frequently occur, are symbols having a religious meaning. Mr Ferguson, in his 'Tree and Serpent Worship,' speaking of the symbols on the sculptured stones, says, 'among them the serpent appears frequently, and so prominently that it is impossible to doubt that it was considered

---

[1] *Sculptured Stones of Scotland*, Vol. II., Pref. p. iii.
[2] *Proceedings of the Society of Antiquaries*, Vol. VI., pp. 98-103.

an object of veneration by those who erected those monuments.'
He conjectures that the broken sceptre, which occurs so frequently
and appears on the stone at Lindores, 'may be a hieroglyph for
God or King　　　We shall,' he says, 'probably not err far, if
we regard these traces of serpent worship, as indicating the presence in the north-east of Scotland of the head of that column of

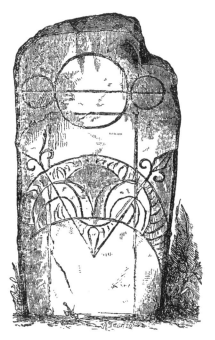

SCULPTURED STONE AT LINDORES.

migration, or of propagandism, which, under the myth of Wodenism,
we endeavoured, in a previous chapter, to trace from the Caucasus
to Scandinavia. The Edda seems sufficient to prove that a form
of serpent worship did certainly prevail in the latter country in
the early centuries of the Christian era; and nothing seems
more possible, or more in accordance with Pictish traditions,

than it should have passed thence into Scotland, and should have left its traces everywhere between the Orkneys and the Friths.'[1]

These are some of the most recent speculations of those who entertain this view, but the generally received opinion now is that of the author of the 'Sculptured Stones of Scotland,' who has made the subject his special study. He says in his second volume, published many years after the first, ' the result of wider investigation and further thought has led me to believe that the peculiar symbols of the Scotch pillar-stones are to be ascribed to the Pictish people of Alba, and were used by them mainly on their tombs, as marks of personal distinction, such as family descent, tribal rank or official dignity.'[2] In support of the opinion that the figures on the sculptured stones are symbols assumed by families, Dr Stuart cites ' the ancient Ditmarshers as having a symbol or sign by which they distinguished their lands, their houses, their stalls in the Church and their graves.'[3] This opinion receives confirmation from an unexpected quarter. In the course of the recent systematic exploration of the desert of Sinai, remains of primeval dwellings and ancient tombs almost identical with those of Great Britain, and also large stones set up of old by the inhabitants to mark the boundaries of their land, have been discovered; each stone having cut upon it the symbol of the tribe to which the district belonged.[4] The conclusion arrived at by Dr Stuart does not, however, preclude the supposition that some of the mysterious figures on the sculptured stones were originally hieroglyphs or

---

[1] Ferguson's *Tree and Serpent Worship*, pp. 31, 32.

[2] *Sculptured Stones of Scotland*, Vol. II., Pref. p. iii.

[3] *Ib.*, p. 29.

[4] E. H. Palmer's *Report to the University of Cambridge*, 1869. A recent writer says, ' I noticed mystic signs on an ancient bridge on the borders of the Dead Sea ;' and, he adds, ' I have seen similar signs on the flanks of Jellahin camels, and believe it to be a Bedouin mark for the district or tribe.'—*Quarterly Statement.* Palestine Exploration Fund, 1869, p. 148.

symbols of religious import; just as the cross in various forms appears as a cognizance in modern heraldic distinctions. The fact of their being so, would make them all the more prized by families who claimed descent from deified ancestors.

Mugdrum Cross, situated on a ridge about a quarter of a mile from Newburgh, within the grounds of Mugdrum, is of more recent date than the Lindores stone, though undoubtedly of great antiquity. It is of yellow sandstone, about eleven feet high, firmly fixed in a socket or pedestal of the same material.[1] The sculptures for which it is distinguished are on the eastern side of the shaft. On the lower and larger compartment there is a representation of a boar hunt. In the compartment immediately above, are the figures of two men on horseback, armed with hunting spears. In each of the two upper compartments, the head and fore-quarters of a horse bridled and represented as if in the act of moving, are very artistically cut, but the figures of the riders, and of the hind quarters of the horses are entirely eroded by the wasting of the stone.

The sides of the shaft are sculptured with the interlaced work characteristic of the class of monuments to which Mugdrum Cross belongs. It is very distinct on the north side, of which an illustration is given in the frontispiece, but the south side is so weather-worn that the interlacing has almost entirely disappeared. The figures on the Lindores stone are incised, but the whole of the sculpturing on Mugdrum Cross is highly relieved. Near the top of the shaft of the latter on the north side, there is a niche, as if it was the remains of the arm of a cross; but whether it ever had arms, which is probable, or had a cross cut within a circle on the back, similar to the sculptured stone formerly at Largo, cannot

---

[1] The shaft of Mugdrum Cross is 10 feet 10 inches in height, the pedestal is 1 foot 9 inches in depth, making the total height of the Cross from the surface of the ground 12 feet 7 inches. The shaft is 2 feet $3\frac{1}{2}$ inches in width and 15 inches in thickness where not wasted. The pedestal or socket is 5 feet 8 inches in length by 3 feet 9 inches in breadth.

MUGDRUM CROSS.

FRONT VIEW, EAST SIDE

now be positively determined, the upper portion of the shaft being much wasted all round.

The representation of a boar hunt is significant when taken in connection with the name of the Cross; the most ancient spelling, 'Mukedrum,' signifying in the original Gaelic 'The Sow's Ridge,' (*muc*, sow; *druim*, ridge). The prefix *muc* enters largely into the topography of Scotland, and is indicative of the prevalence of the boar tribe at the time that Gaelic was the spoken language of the Lowlands. Muc-ros, the boar's head-land, is the ancient name of St Andrews, and we know that 'the chase of the boar was a favourite employment among the ancient Celts. It is celebrated in many of their tales, and the sow enters largely into their ancient mythology.'[1] The sculpture on Mugdrum Cross does not show any veneration in this direction, but rather the reverse, the herd of swine being represented in the attitude of flight, with the hounds in full chase after them. The erection of so stately a cross, so elaborately and beautifully sculptured, was undoubtedly to mark a sacred spot, or to commemorate some remarkable event, the memory of which has perished.

The beautiful interlaced sculpture which is seen on the sides of Mugdrum Cross, is characteristic of the crosses found within the north-western parts of Scotland and the Islands where St Columba and his Irish followers, and their successors chiefly penetrated and settled. The similarity of the designs on these crosses to those still seen on the ancient Irish manuscripts, has led to the conclusion that they are the work of the same hands. 'We know,' says the author of the Sculptured Stones of Scotland, 'that in Ireland the monks were the artificers of the shrines, croziers, book-covers, and bells which yet exist to excite our wonder by the grace, and at the sametime the minute intricacy of their style, while they were also the writers of those manuscripts of matchless caligraphy,' which are still extant.

The inference from all this is, that the class of sculptured pillars

---

[1] *The Dean of Lismore's Book*, Note, p. 31.

to which **Mugdrum** Cross belongs, were erected after the arrival of St Columba and his followers (A.D. 563). The cross is conspicuously prominent on most of these pillars, occupying in many of them the whole length of the shaft. It is worthy of note, that the **mysterious** symbols of the more ancient stones appear on some of these undoubtedly Christian monuments; almost invariably, however, in a most inconspicuous position. On the sculptured stone at St Madocs, in the Carse of Gowrie, the cross occupies the whole face of one of the sides; on the other, the crescent and sceptre symbols appear, but of a diminutive size. The same remark applies to ' the Bore Stone of Gask,' on which the cross appears and occupies the whole length of the stone on both sides, while the peculiar symbols are small and are relegated to obscure positions. The appearance of these mysterious symbols on Christian monuments strengthens the conclusion arrived at by Dr Stuart, that they are family or tribal marks; as otherwise it is scarcely conceivable that the early founders of Christianity in Scotland, would have carved on Christian monuments emblems of direct heathen import unless on the supposition that at the time of the carving of these pillars their heathen significance had been forgotten. Whatever doubts may exist as to the origin and meaning of these peculiar symbols, there can be none regarding the most ancient pillar-stones on which the cross appears. These crosses are memorials of the triumph of Christianity over Heathenism, and it invests them with special interest when they are looked upon as having been reared in different parts of the country, as the influence of the early missionaries extended and Christianity prevailed.

Cross Macduff, which has a wider celebrity than that of Mugdrum, is situated about a mile southwest of Newburgh, on the water-shed of a wide pass through the Ochils from Fife to Strathearn. Sir James Balfour calls it ' Our ancient **Limitt** or march stone which devydit this Countrey [of Fife] from the Countrey palatine of Stratherne.'[1] The cross is the property of

---

[1] Balfour's M.S., Advocates' Library.

the burgesses of Newburgh (if a historical monument can be called the property of any one in particular), and it stands on the land bestowed on them by the monks of Lindores. It is no slight honour for the burgesses to have in their keeping a monument which has engaged the pen of the great Minstrel of the Border, and has also the lustre of Shakespeare's genius shed upon it; he

> 'Tuned but his harp to this wild northern theme
> And lo! the scene is hallowed.'

When the ground was first let for cultivation the Town Council took the tenant bound not to plough within twelve feet of the Cross, and not to injure it in any way, but the love of gain gradually got the better of reverence for antiquity, and little

CROSS MACDUFF.

by little the Cross was encroached upon until it was all but toppling from its foundation. On its insecure condition being represented to the Town Council, they again interposed, and in the spring of 1851, it was enclosed with the circle of boulders which now surround it. The Cross (for only the pedestal remains) 'was all torn in pieces by the furie of the Congregatione, as they named them in the tyme of the reformatione of

religion.'[1] Very probably this destruction took place on the
13th June 1559, when the troops under Lord Ruthven went from
Perth to join the forces of the Congregation in the neighbourhood of Cupar, Cross Macduff lying directly in their route. The
pedestal is an uneven four-sided block of yellow sandstone, three
and a half feet in height, and measuring from four and a half
feet in length, and three feet eight inches in breadth at the base.[2]
The nearest locality from which such a stone could have been
obtained is the Lomonds, near Falkland, eight miles distant.

Utterly featureless though the Cross now is, the poet has truly
said—

> ' None shall pass,
> Now, or in after days, beside that stone,
> But he shall have strange visions ; thoughts and words
> That shake or rouse the human heart
> Shall rush upon his memory, when he hears
> The spirit-stirring name of that rude symbol.'[3]

All that is authentically known of Cross Macduff has been told
by Dr Stuart in the second volume of the 'Sculptured Stones of
Scotland,' and therefore it is only needful to endeavour to con-
dense what he has collected with so much research.

Before doing this, however, it is proper in any history of the
Cross to give the traditionary account of the events that led to
Macduff's obtaining the privileges which are said to have been
connected with the Cross, only premising this, that the first *Earl*

---

[1] Balfour's M.S., Advocates' Library.

[2] The pedestal tapers very slightly from the base upwards. The exact measurement at the top on the west side is three feet six inches, on the north side it is two
feet ten inches, which all but corresponds with the measurement given by Camden (*Britannia*, Vol. III., p. 376) nearly two hundred years ago. There is, however, some manifest error in what he says of the ' length and breadth of the socket
where the cross was fixed.' These he gives as four and a half feet and four feet
respectively, a socket which it was impossible to make in a stone of three feet by
two feet ten inches.

[3] Scott's *Poetical Works*, Vol. XII., p. 96. (Ed. 1857).

of Fife known in record is Ethelred the son of Malcolm Ceanmore and St Margaret, who was at once Earl of Fife and Abbot of Dunkeld. [1]

Wyntoun, our earliest historian, in his 'Cronykil,' thus sets the circumstances forth—

> ' And in Scotland than as Kyng
> This Makbeth mad gret sterying;
> And set hym than in hys powere
> A gret hows for to mak of were
> Apon the hycht of Dwnsynane; [2]
> Tymbyr thare-til to drawe and stane,
> Of Fyfe and of Angws, he
> Gert mony oxin gadryd be.
> Sa on a day in thare trawaile
> A yhok of oxyn Makbeth saw fayle;
> Than speryt Makbeth, quha that awcht
> The yhoke, that faylyd in that drawcht.
> Thai answeryd till Mackbeth agayne,
> And said ' Macduff of Fyfe the Thayne
> That ilk yhoke of oxyn awcht
> That he saw fayle in-to the drawcht.'
> Than spak Makbeth dyspytusly,
> And to the Thayne sayd angryly,
> Lyk all wrythyn in hys skyn,
> Hys awyn nek he suld put in
> The yhoke, and ger hym drawchtis drawe.'

---

[1] Robertson's *Scotland under her Early Kings*, Vol. I., pp. 124–255.

[2] Dunsinnan is one of the interesting class of forts which are vitrified. A very fine specimen of the vitrification (binding together several stones) dug from its walls in 1867, may be seen in the National Museum of Antiquities, Edinburgh. In making some excavations within the walls of the fort in the summer of 1857, a bronze spiral finger ring was discovered. The Rev. Mr Brown, minister of the parish of Collace, who was present when it was found, says, that it was most artistically made in the form of a serpent; the head, eyes and scales being distinctly and minutely carved; so minutely, that a microscope only fully revealed the exquisite beauty of the workmanship. The vitrification of Dunsinnan, and the character of the ring, throws back the erection of the fort to a period of great antiquity. The ring unfortunately has been lost.

As may readily be imagined, Macduff did not wait to give the king an opportunity of putting his threat into execution.

> 'Bot prewally owt off the thrang
> Wyth slycht he gat, and the spensere
> A laffe hym gawe till hys supere;
> And als swyne as he mycht se
> Hys tyme and oportunyte
> Owt off the curt he past and ran,
> And that layff bare wyth hym than
> To the wattyre off Eryne.   That brede
> He gawe the batwartis hym to lede,
> And on the south half him to sete,
> But delay or ony lete,
> That passage cald wes efftyre than
> Lang tyme Portnebaryan;
> The Hawyn of Brede, that suld be
> Callyd in tyll propyrte.' [1]

Port, in Gaelic, signifying a haven or ferry, and *arain* is the genitive of *aran* a loaf.   The direct road to Macduff's stronghold in the south of Fife, was by the 'Ferry of the Loaf,' and through the pass in which the Cross is situated.   Macbeth, the story says, pursued the Thane 'till Kennawchy,' and demanded his surrender at the gate of his castle; but Macduff had fled at his approach, and set sail across the Forth.   Lady Macduff made many excuses till she saw her husband safely out at sea; then looking over the castle wall said, 'Do you see yon white sail upon the sea? yonder goes Macduff;' or, as the old chronicler has it,

> 'Makbeth, luke up, and se,
> Wnder yhon sayle forsuth is he,
> The Thayne of Fyfe that thou has sowcht;
> Trowe thowe welle, and dowt rycht nowcht
> Gyve evyr thow sall hym se agayne,
> He sall the set in tyll gret payne;

---

[1] Wyntoun's *Cronykil*, Book VI., Chap., XVIII.

Syne thou would hawe put hys neke
In till thi yhoke. Now will I speke
With the na mare, fare on thi waye.'

'That passage syne was comownly
In Scotland called the Erlys-Ferry.'[1]

Fordun's account of the flight and escape of Macduff is similar
to that of Wyntoun, but he does not associate it with Dunsinnan
or any locality. He says, 'The greatest and chief of those who
laboured to advance Malcolm to the throne was a distinguished
noble, and trusty man, named Macduff, thane of Fife. Macduff kept
the unknown purpose of his heart hidden longer and more carefully
than the rest, but he was, nevertheless, again and again denounced
to the king, until, at length, he was viewed with suspicion. Mean-
while the king, one day, took occasion, I know not on what
pretext, first to upbraid him, more cruelly than usual, perhaps on
account of his disloyalty, with his shortcomings towards him, and
then added plainly that he would put his neck under his yoke, as
that of the ox in a wain; and he swore he would do it before long.'
The narrative proceeds to tell that Macduff fled privily, and 'when
his secret departure became known to the king, the latter was
furious, and calling his horses and horsemen every one he has,
hastily followed the fugitive, until he saw out at sea the little
vessel in which Macduff had sailed. Macbeth 'besieged all Macduff's castles and confiscated and took away all his substance.
Moreover, he caused him to be proclaimed by the voice of a
herald, an exile for ever, and stripped of all his estates and
other property whatsoever. Thereupon there rose great mur-
murings throughout the whole kingdom, and especially among
the nobles (for the thane was beloved by them with kindly
affection), for that the king, led rather by wrath than by reason,
had been too hasty in rendering so doughty and powerful a man

---

[1] Wyntoun's *Cronykil*, Book VI., Chap. XVIiI.

exile or disinherited without a decree of a general council and of
the nobles. They said that it was quite wrong that any noble or
private person should be condemned by a sudden sentence of
exile or disinheritance until he had been summoned to court on
the lawful day of the appointed time, and if then, when he came,
he justified himself by the laws, he should thus go forth free, but
if he were worsted in Court, he should atone to the King, at the
cost of his body, or otherwise; or if he should neglect to come
when summoned, then first ought he to be outlawed as an exile,
or if he should plead guilty, disinherited.'[1]

The sequel of the story is well known. Macduff bore a conspicuous part in the overthrow of Macbeth, and on Malcolm obtaining the victory, he rewarded the valiant thane by conferring
on him and his descendants the honour of placing the Scottish
monarchs on the Coronation Stone on their accession to the
throne; of leading the vanguard of the Royal Army in battle, if
the Thane or his successor and descendant be on the field; and
in addition to these honours, that the Thane and his kindred
should be entitled to the benefit of the privilege of the 'Law of
Clan Macduff,' of which it has generally been assumed, that a
Girth or Sanctuary at Cross Macduff was the most distinguishing
feature. All this is succinctly set forth by Scott.

> 'Know then, when fell Macbeth beneath the arm
> Of the predestined Knight, unborn of woman,
> Three boons the victor ask'd, and thrice did Malcolm,
> Stooping the septre by the Thane restored,
> Assent to his request. And hence the rule,
> That first when Scotland's King assumes the crown,
> Macduff's descendant rings his brow with it,
> And hence when Scotland's King calls forth his host,
> Macduff's descendant leads the van in battle;
> And last, in guerdon of the crown restored,
> Red with the blood of the usurping tyrant,
> The right was granted in succeeding time,

---

[1] Fordun's *Chronicle*, Book IV., Chap. XLVI.

That if a kinsman of the Thane of Fife
Commit a slaughter on a sudden impulse,
And fly for refuge to this Cross MacDuff
For the Thane's sake he shall find sanctuary :
For here must the avenger's step be staid,
And here the panting homicide find safety.'[1]

Mr W. F. Skene, in his valuable notes to 'Fordun's Chronicle,' adduces evidence to show that anciently before the introduction of the feudal principle, there was a 'constitutional body termed the Seven Earls of Scotland,' which formed the 'curia regis,' and the Great Council of the Kingdom; and that they claimed to exercise certain privileges, and occasionally did exercise them, long after they were superseded by the feudal 'communitas,' or system. 'The number seven,' Mr Skene adds, 'seems to point to the old division of Albania into seven provinces, as the source of their constitutional privileges. The Earl of Fife seems always to have held the foremost position among the old traditionary Earls of Scotland, and to have belonged to this body, and it was probably from his position at the head of the Seven Earls that he possessed the privilege of placing the King in the Royal Chair.'[2] Fordun, in his account of the coronation of Alexander II., relates that 'the Earls of Fife, Stratherne, Atholl, Angus, Menteith, Buchan, and Lothian, took the young king, a lad of sixteen years and a half, to Scone, and raised him to the throne, in honour and peace, with the approval of God and man, and all wished him joy, and none gainsaid him.'[3] The Seven Earls, and in conjunction with them Seven Bishops, were present with Alexander III. in Dunfermline Abbey, on the great state occasion of the translation of 'the bones of Saint Margaret, the Queen, from the Stone Monument where they had lain, to a shrine set with gold and precious stones.'[4] The express mention of the presence of a body of Seven Earls

---

[1] Scott's *Poetical Works*, Macduff Cross, Vol. XII., p. 100.
[2] The Historians of Scotland, Fordun's *Chronicle*, Vol. II., pp. 436, 437.
[3] *Ib.*, pp. 275, 276–433.   [4] *Ib.*, pp. 290, 291.

on these state and ceremonial occasions, and the position which the Earl of Fife held in the 'Magnum concilium regni,' adds force to Mr Skene's conjecture, and renders it extremely probable that the honours and privileges recorded by Wyntoun, as having been conferred by King Malcolm on Macduff, were a reinstalment of the Thane (after his exile) in his ancient constitutional privileges.

The earliest writers who mention the privilege of the 'Law of Clan Macduff' are Fordun and Wyntoun, neither of whom allude to the Cross. 'According to Fordun, the 'Law, conferred on the Thane, and all his posterity for ever, the right that if a noble person of their number shall commit a sudden and unpremeditated slaughter, he shall be free, on payment of twenty four merks of kinbot (Anglo Saxon *Cynn*, kindred *bot*, compensation) and if a common man of twelve merks.' [1]

Wyntoun's account of it is as follows :—

> ' Gyve ony be suddane chawdmellè
> Hapnyd swa slayne to be
> Be ony of the Thaynys Kyne,
> Off Fyff the Kynryk all wyth-in,
> Gyve he swa slayne wer gentill-man,
> Foure and twenty markys than
> For a yhwman twelf markys ay
> The slaare suld for Kynbwt pay,
> And hawe full remyssyowne
> Fra thine for all that actyowne,
> Gyve ony hapnyd hym to sla,
> That to that lawch ware bwndyn swa ;
> Off that priwylage evyrmare
> Partles suld be the slaare.
> Off this lawch are thre capytale ;
> That is the Blak Prest of Weddale,
> The Thayne of Fyffe, and the thryd syne,
> Quha ewyre be Lord off Abbyrnethyne.' [2]

---

[1] *Sculptured Stones of Scotland*, Vol. II., Cross Macduff.
[2] Wyntoun's *Cronykil*, Bk. VI., Chap. XIX.

'The account given by Boece differs entirely from either Fordoun or Wyntoun, and defines the privilege as a right of regality conferred on the Clan Macduff, by which its head could repledge from other courts in any part of the kingdom to his own court, any of his own clan or tenantry.'[1]

Sir John Skene says, 'The croce of Clan Makduffe had priviledge and libertie of Girth in sik sorte, that quher ony man-slayer being within the ninth degree of kin and bluid to Makduffe sometime Earl of Fife, cam to that croce, and gave nine kye, and ane colpindach, he was free of the slauchter committed be him.' A colpindach, he elsewhere explains, 'is ane young beast or kow of the age of ane or twa yeiris quhilk now is called an cowdach or *quoyach*.'[2] The same author states in the '*Regiam Majestatem*,' that by a statute of William the Lion, those who had a right to the privilege of the 'Law of Clan Macduff,' could, in virtue of that law, refuse to decide their case by single combat; another indication of the comprehensive nature of the privilege.[3]

The preceding notice by Sir John Skene is the first in which the Cross is mentioned, and that assigns a right of Girth to it; it is also the first which limits the privilege of the 'Law' to those within the ninth degree of kindred of Macduff. It differs from the earlier narratives in fixing the penalty at the apparently mystical number of nine.

There are two copies of the Inscription said to have been on the Cross. Sir James Balfour, in his 'Notes on Fife' says, 'the inscription even at that time [shortly before its destruction] was so out-worn that he who copied samen (given to Sir James by his son) had much ado to mak words of some dispersed and out-worne bare characters.'[4]

---

[1] *Sculptured Stones of Scotland*, Vol. II., Cross Macduff.
[2] Skene *De verb., Sig.* voce—*Clan Macduff, and Colpach.*
[3] *Regiam Majestatem Stat.* William 'The Lion,' Chap. XXVII.
[4] Balfour's M.S., Advocates' Library.

The reading of the inscription given by Sir James is as follows :—

> ' MALDRARADUM DRAGOS, MARIA LAGHSLITA, LARGOS,
> SPALANDA SPADOS, SIVE NIG FIG KNIGHTHITE GNAROS
> LOTHEA LEUDISCOS LARICINGEN LAIRIA LISCOS
> ET COLORVURTOS SIC FIT TIBI BURSIA BURTUS
> EXITUS ET BLADADRUM SIVE LIM SIVE LAM SIVE LABRUM.
> PROPTER MAGRIDIN ET HOC OBLATUM
> ACCIPE SMELERIDEM SUPER LIMTHIDE LAMTHIDA LABRUM.'

Cunningham in his essay on this version of the Inscription published in 1678 says, ' Though I had this of an ingenious Gentleman telling me he came by it from the Clerk of Crail, who informed, that several succeeding clerks there have for a considerable time, engrost this as a true copy in their Books to preserve it from utter perishing; for it is now quite worn off the stone, at least altogether illegible.   But be it so recorded in Crail, Newburgh, or elsewhere, yet with their good favour scarcely can I judge this a true and exact copy, whether the fault has been with the first copiator from the stone, or from the engraver, or partly both.' He endeavours to find the meaning by assuming ' the Inscription to be Saxon (as to the main) aped in a Latin dress, as to the main I say, for I suppose some words might savour of a Danish, or old French extract.' [1] Notwithstanding this latitude of interpretation, he leaves the subject after a lengthened disquisition as dark as he found it.

In a postscript to his essay he says—' That Gentle reader I may conceale you nothing, just now, as it was doing under the Irons, am I told there is an exact coppie, with a true exposition of this Inscription at the Newburgh, in the hands, or books of the Clerk there.   And yet my Informer though with us a good Antiquarie and Historian could neither tell me the lines nor the exposition, and pitie it were that so old and famous a monument in this our

---

[1] *Essay upon the Inscription of Macduff's Crosse*, pp. 3, 4.

Kingdom, should be closelie dormant in a poor countrey village without being communicate (for ought I know) to any. For it should seem our Clerk-register Skeen had neither seen nor heard of it otherways (methinks) he would hardly have called the lines so barbarous. But this however I hope may invite those of the *Newburgh* to divulge it (if any such thing they have) for it is onely truth that here I am in quest of.' [1]

The Court Books of Newburgh, between the years 1480 and 1697, have disappeared, but in none of those remaining, or in any of the documents belonging to the town does the name of Cross Macduff once occur; until the year 1814, when the field in which the Cross is situated was first let for cultivation.

Sir James Dalrymple, in his second edition of Camden's Description of Scotland, publishes a version of the Inscription, which, he says, 'one Douglas of Newburgh had by him.' It is possible that it may be the version of which Cunningham heard. It reads thus :—

> ' Ara urget lex quos, lare egentes atria lis, quos,
> Hoc qui laboras hæc fit tibi pactio portus,
> Mille reum drachmas mulctam de largior agris
> Spes tantum pacis cum nex fit a nepote natis
> Propter Macgidrum, et hoc oblatum accipe semel
> Hæredum, super lymphato lapide labem.'

The reader, after perusing both of the alleged inscriptions, will be inclined to agree with the poet, that the cross was 'carved o'er with words which foiled philologists.' Certainly the copies of the inscription have done so ; both of them, it is evident, cannot be correct, and perhaps neither of them are so. A very ingenious solution of the discrepancies of the two versions has been suggested by the author of the history of the ' East Neuk of Fife,' which carries much probability with it. He says, the singular thing is that none of the writers on the subject seemed to have

---

[1] *Essay upon the Inscription of Macduff's Crosse,* p. 20.

discovered that the two inscriptions are the same, the one being a corrupted form of the other. To prove this we shall write the one under the other, premising that the lines have been disarranged in the first inscription, and should be taken in the order 3^d, 4th, 1st, 2^d, 6th, and 7th; the 5th line being an interpolation, and merely a variation of the last :

> Ara urget lex quos lare egentes atria lis quos
> *Lothea ludiscos laricingen lairia liscos*
> Hoc qui laboras hæc fit tibi pactio portus
> *Et colovurtos sic fit tibi bursia burtus*
> Mille reum drachmas mulctam de largior agris
> *Maldraradum dragos mairia lagslita largos*
> Spes tantum pacis cum nex fit a nepote natis
> *Spalando spados sive nig fig knighthite gnaros*
> Propter Macgidrum et hoc oblatum accipe semel
> *Propter Magridin et hoc oblatum accipe smel*
> Hæredum super lymphato lapide labem
> *eridum super limthide lamthida labum.*

'The coincidences are evidently such as can easily be accounted for on the supposition that Douglas's reading of the inscription was the true one, and that Balfour's one was taken down from oral recitation of some one who had committed it to memory without understanding it, so that he possessed little more than the jingle of the Latin verses.' [1]

Of the authenticity of these inscriptions there is no positive evidence, but there is nothing improbable in an elaborate inscription being on a cross at an age even preceding the date of its alleged erection into a sanctuary. Ruthwell Cross had a much

---

[1] Wood's *East Neuk of Fife*, p. 13. Mr Wood gives the following literal translation of Sir James Dalrymple's version :—'An altar for those whom law pursues, a hall for those whom strife pursues to thee this paction becomes a harbour. But there is hope of peace only when the murder has been committed by those born of my grandson. I set free the accused, a fine of a thousand drachmas from his lands. On account of Magridin and his offering take once for all the cleansing of my heirs beneath this stone filled with water.'—P. 14.

longer inscription carved upon it, part of which is still legible, and upon good grounds it is believed to have been erected about the year 680.[1]

In Sibbald's *History of Fife*, the following paraphrase of the version first printed by Sir James Dalrymple appears. It is manifestly incorrect, as it introduces names and things which do not occur in either of the two copies transmitted to us.

> ' All such as are within the ninth degree
> Of kindred to that antient Thane Macduff,
> And yet for slaughter are compelled to flie
> And leave their houses, and their household stuff;
> Here shall they find for their refuge a place,
> To save them from the cruel blood avenger,
> A privilege peculiar to that race,
> Which never was allowed to any stranger.
> But they must enter heir, on this condition,
> (Which they observe must with faith unfeignyied)
> To pay a thousand groats for their remission,
> Or else their lands and goods shall be distrenyied.
> For saint Mackgidder's sake, and this oblation
> And by their only washing at this stone,
> Purged is the blood shed by that generation;
> This privilege pertains to them alone.'[2]

The only direct evidence for the inscription on Cross Macduff is that given by Sir John Skene, who examined it personally. He says, 'In the stanes of this Croce I saw barbarous words and verses written quhilk here I willingly pretermit, and yet sum of them appears to be conform to this purpose:—'PROPTER MAKGIDRIM ET HOC OBLATUM—ACCIPE SMELERIDUM SUPER LAMPADE, LIMPADA LABRUM.'[3] 'In the first edition of Sibbald's History of the County [published in 1710], a drawing is given of a cross, with the socket in which it is inserted. The inscription is made to extend across the transverse arms of the monument and down the face of

---

[1] Professor Stephen's *Ruthwell Cross.* [2] *Ib.*, p. 21.
[3] *De verb. signif.* voce *Clan Macduff.*

the shaft. . . . The rest of the inscription is on the pedestal
in eleven lines, many of which are incomplete.' Judging from a
representation of another cross (still extant at Docton in Fife) in
the same work, not much confidence can be placed on the accuracy
of Sibbald's engraving of Cross Macduff.[1]

The inscription seen by Sir John Skene (1597) had disappeared
before Sir Robert Gordon visited the Cross previous to 1648. In
1710 Sir Robert Sibbald says, ' Time had so defaced them, I could
discover none upon the pedestal of the Cross, the rest of it is
not to be seen.'[2] When Sir Alexander Gordon visited it in the
early part of last century (A.D. 1727), he found a large cavity (in
the pedestal) where the Cross anciently stood. ' So completely
have the marks been obliterated, that in all recent notices of the
pedestal it has been taken for granted that there never was a
socket. There is now only a very slight depression, which it
would be unsafe to take as the mark of a socket. Nodules of
iron pyrites occur in the stone, some of which have fallen out,
leaving small holes in the sides. In the progress of tradition
these were represented as nine in number, and as having each
contained an iron staple and ring to which the nine cows supposed
to be payable to St Magridden by the culprits were fastened. It
was also alleged that they had to wash nine times at the nine
wells which still bubble up a short way northward of the Cross.'[3]

Almost the only thing certain about the inscription on Cross
Macduff is that the name of *Magidrin* formed part of it. It is
therefore an interesting inquiry to ascertain who Magidrin was, and
his connection with the Cross. In a very able disquisition by Mr
W. F. Skene on the Early Ecclesiastical Settlements of St Andrew's,
Magidrin is identified with Adrian, who was martyred by the
Danes on the Isle of May.[4] The legendary account of this saint

---

[1] *Sculptured Stones of Scotland*, Vol. II., Cross Macduff.
[2] *History of Fife*, p. 219.
[3] *Sculptured Stones of Scotland*, Vol. II., Cross Macduff.
[4] *Pro. of Soc. of Antiquaries*, Vol. IV., pp. 300–321.

is, that he and a 'company' came from Hungary to the eastern
parts of Scotland, inhabited by the Picts, to preach the gospel.
The first scene of their labours was the coast of Fife, but they
subsequently fixed their abode in the Isle of May, near enough
the coast to allow them to continue their work of converting the
heathen of the mainland, and yet sufficiently removed to afford
retirement and security.

'Wyntoun who towards the end of the fourteenth century,
was Prior of the Monastery of St Serfs Inch, Lochleven, and there
composed his Chronicle from many authentic sources now lost to
us, says—

> 'Adriane wyth hys cumpany
> To-gydder cam to Caplawchy;
> Thare sum in-to the Ile of May
> Chesyd to byde to thare Enday.
> And sum of them chesyed be-northe
> In stedde's sere be Watter of Forth.'

'And there may yet be seen, in a grey weather-beaten cliff at
Caplachie or Caiplie, in the shire of Fife (in the parish of Kilrenny)
opposite the Isle of May, a group of caves hollowed out of the
rock. Of these the middle and largest has many small crosses
rudely incised in its walls, while over the cave, and entering from
it by steps cut in the rock, there was till lately a little chamber
with a bench on its inner side cut in the rock, both of which have
been traditionally associated with St Adrian as his oratory or
abode.'[1]

The retirement of the saint to the Isle of May did not afford
protection from the fierce inroads of the Northmen, who, previous
to their conversion to Christianity, made frequent descents on the
coasts of Britain, carrying fire and sword wherever they went,
and laying waste all within their reach. In one of these terrible

---

[1] *Records of the Priory of the Isle of May*, pp. iv., v.

incursions (A.D. 875) they landed on the Isle of May, and barbar
ously massacred Adrian and his companions.

> 'Hwb, Haldane, and Hyngare
> Off Denmark this time cummin ware
> In Scotland wyth gret multitude,
> And wyth thare powere it oure-yhude
> In Hethynnes all lyvyd thai,
> And in despyte of Crystyn Fay
> In-to the Land thai slwe mony,
> And put to Dede by Martyry
> And a-pon haly Thursday
> Saynt Adriane thai slwe in May
> Wyth mony of hys Cumpany.
> In-to that haly Ile thai ly.'[1]

According to Mr Skene, the true history seems to be (and
tradition and circumstances support it) that Adrian was at the
head of a 'company' of Scottish (Irish) clergy, who arrived about
the time of Kenneth Macalpin's 'accession' to the Scottish throne.
'The saint's true name, if a Scot, was probably Odran, as the
name of the patron saint always enters largely into those of the
clergy of the place, and we find a subsequent Bishop of St
Andrew's, Macgilla Odran, son of the servant of Odran,' the
change from Odran to Adrian arising from the practice of the
monks of almost invariably putting names in a Latin form. 'The
corrupt form of the name was Magridan, which is simply the Irish
Mo (my) with a g inserted for euphony.[2] The parishes of Flisk
and Lindores, both within the *parochia*, are dedicated to Macgidrin.'[3]
Cross Macduff is within what originally constituted the latter
parish.

---

[1] Wyntoun's *Cronykil*, Bk. VI., Cap. VIII.

[2] 'The syllable *mo* (my) was often prefixed to the name of Irish saints as a
term of endearment or reverence, thus Conna, becomes Mochonna.'—*Joyce's Irish
Names of Places*, p. 141.

[3] W. F. Skene, *Pro. Socy. of Antiq. Scot.*, Vol. IV., p. 318.

In the absence of authentic records there is nothing to show how Magidrin came to be connected with Cross Macduff, and therefore anything that can be said on the subject is only founded on conjecture. He is named by some authorities as Bishop of St Andrews, and there is nothing very improbable in a cross being erected to his memory on the boundary of his diocese. The reverence which the saint's martyrdom must necessarily have inspired, would throw a fence of great sanctity around a cross dedicated to his memory: and as the clergy strove by all means in their power, and embraced every opening for allaying the fierce passions of their turbulent flocks, there is a strong presumption that they may have declared the Cross a sanctuary for the man-slayer, a crime so rife in those days.

On this point the late Joseph Robertson says, 'It was to its ecclesiastical descent (the family of Abernethy sprung from the Lay Abbots of Abernethy) that its chief owed the distinction which he shared with the Earl of Fife and the priest of Wedale (now Gala Water), of being one of the three judges of the law of Clan Macduff, itself perhaps a privilege of mixed ecclesiastical and judicial origin, a right it would seem partly of a 'Sanctuary,' partly of a regality distinguished from the common mass of such jurisdiction by being personal not territorial, inherent in a tribe, and not attached to a church or barony.'[1]

Mr E. W. Robertson, in his history of 'Scotland under her Early Kings,' says, 'the "Law" was probably a relic of the old right once belonging to every *Mormaor* or *Oirrigh* of retaining all his kindred in his *mund*.'[2] A supposition which does not militate against what has been said, as the clergy of that age invariably engrafted religion on ancient institutions. Sanctuaries or Girths, were not confined to the Jewish polity, they were recognised institutions of Pagan Greece and Rome, and seem, under one form or another, to have been as universal as the human race. The

---

[1] *Mis. Spald. Club*, Vol. V., App. to Pref. p. 75.
[2] *Scotland under Her Early Kings*, Vol. I., p. 215, Note.

fact that the conservators of the 'Law of Clan Macduff' were of spiritual descent, tends to show that whatever may have been the origin of its privileges, the clergy had at an early period thrown around the 'Girth' the sanctities of religion, as to them undoubtedly must be ascribed the erection of Cross Macduff. This supposition is strengthened by the only authenticated words of the inscription, which bear that the fine was more in the light of an offering to Saint Magidrin, then a compensation to the injured person. 'By the ancient statutes of the Scottish Church, every church which was consecrated, and had the right of baptism and burial, had the privilege of sanctuary, which extended for thirty paces around the burial ground,'[1] and the clergy were the guardians of this privilege. This privilege may account for hostelries in old times being so near the Kirk Style. Some churches had a wider range of sanctuary attached to them, and the limits were marked by crosses. In A.D. 1144, David I. granted the Church of Lesmahagow as a cell to the Abbey of Kelso, with, among other privileges, 'that it shall be a place of refuge, or sanctuary, for those who in peril of life and limb should flee to the said cell, or come within the four crosses standing around it.' These crosses have been destroyed, but a fragment of what is supposed to be a portion of one of them was discovered in 1866.[2] Crosses marking the limits of the sanctuaries of Dull and Torphichen are still extant.[3] In Ireland, where these relics have been better preserved, there are four splendid crosses at the four roads entering the town of Kilfenora; and though their original use is gone, there is a saying still current, that 'who should spill blood within the four crosses of Kilfenora will be accursed, and will meet his death within the year.'[4]

We have, in the county of Fife, in the parish of Markinch, a cross of a most ancient type, which there is reason to think marks the boundary of an early sanctuary. This relic, known as

---

[1] *Sculptured Stones of Scotland*, Vol. II., Cross Macduff.
[2] *Proceedings of the Soc. of Antiq. of Scotland*, Vol. VII., pp. 256–265.
[3] *Sculptured Stones of Scotland*, Vol. II.   [4] *Dr Petrie's Life*, p. 342.

Stob Cross, of which an engraving is here given, is similar in many respects to the Cross in the village of Dull, which bears all the marks of great antiquity.   There are circumstances in the history of Markinch, which show that it was an ecclesiastical site at a very early period, and which tend to confirm the conjecture that Stob Cross is an ancient Girth Cross.   Somewhere between A.D. 1034 and 1055, Malduin, Bishop of St Andrews, gave the Church

STOB CROSS, MARKINCH.

of 'Marchinke,' and the land belonging to it, to God and Saint Servanns, and to the 'Keledeis' of the Isle of Lochleven.[1]   After the Culdees were superseded by David I.,[2] Duncan, Earl of Fife, not later than A.D. 1203, gave the Church of Markinch to the Priory of St Andrews; and his son, Earl Malcolm, added to the gift, by

---

[1] Reeves' *Culdees of the British Islands*, p. 246.
[2] *Scotland in the Middle Ages*, p. 111.

giving 'to God and the Church of Modhrust of Markinge,' an acre of land on the north-east of the *cimiterium*, or old burying ground of Markinch.[1] Modhrust (to whom the Church of Markinch was dedicated), shorn of the customary prefix Mo, is Drostan, the disciple of St Columba, and whom that saint left in charge of the first Christian mission to the Pictish tribes in the north-east of Scotland.[2] At a later date, and in all probability when a new church was erected on the old site (of which the noble old tower only remains), Markinch Church was consecrated on the 19th August (A.D. 1243), by David de Bernhame, Bishop of St Andrews, and in addition to the native saint, it was dedicated to John the Baptist.[3] The festival of St Drostan was celebrated on the 15th December, and that of John the Baptist on the 24th June, and on these ancient festivals, allowing for the difference of the old and new styles, and a fixed day of the week, fairs are still held in Markinch; one on the third Tuesday of December and the other on the second Tuesday of July. Mr Cosmo Innes says, 'It is curious how often a chapter of old history is preserved in such memorials. The dedications of many of our churches to the first preachers of the faith, despised and forgotten in Scotland, are often preserved by the name of a well beside the church, at first hallowed as the baptismal source, or by the name and day of the village fair, which was of old held on the day of the patron saint.'[4] Drostan, the patron saint of Markinch, was of royal descent, and the following verses continued to be sung in his praise :—

' Vir Drostanus	Veneremur
Christianus	Et precemur
Fidei constancia,	Ipsum cum instancia,
Vita clarus	Vt spe precum
Deo carus	Ducat secum
Fuit ab infancia.	Nos ad celi gaudia.'[5]

---

[1] *Reg. Priory of St Andrews*, pp. 242-245.
[2] *Book of Deer*, pp. 47-57.   [3] *Conciliæ Scotiæ*, pp. 185-301.
[4] Innes' *Scotland in the Middle Ages*, p. 323, Note.
[5] *Collections in the Shires of Aberdeen and Banff*, p. 443.

These facts in the early ecclesiastical history of Markinch have been adduced to show that there is nothing improbable in its having had around its church an extended Girth or Sanctuary, and that the Stob Cross is one of the very few remaining Girth Crosses in Scotland. The name of the Cross confirms this : *Stob* in Gaelic signifies to mark off with stakes, and in the Cleveland dialect, in which so many old words are preserved, Stob still signifies, ' a stake defining the limits of an enclosure.'[1] It is a further corroboration of this signification and use, that the places known as Stob Cross in Scotland are invariably at the outskirts of towns or villages ; that of Markinch stands beyond the town on the roadside about an eighth of a mile from the churchyard. The name 'Holy Ground,' which still attaches to a spot within the precincts of Markinch Stob Cross, is confirmatory evidence that the picturesque old relic is what its name implies, an ancient Girth Cross.

The earliest authorities who write on the subject, make no mention of a right of Girth at Cross Macduff, but the considerations that have been adduced, and the concurrent testimony of writers of considerable antiquity make it more than probable that it was a sanctuary. The fact recorded by Wyntoun, that those claiming the privilege of the Law of Clan Macduff, were required to appear before the judges assembled ' at Cowper in Fyfe,' does not contradict this supposition, as the accused may have previously sought and found refuge at the Cross, though not mentioned, in consequence of sanctuaries being a common and understood institution at that period.

Wyntoun's words are as follows :—

' Gywe thar be ony that lykis
The Lawch for to se led of this,
Quhen be crye the day is set,
As fallys to be done of dete,
To Cowper in Fyfe than cum he
Welle led that Lawch thare sall he se.'[2]

Atkinson's *Glossary of the Cleveland Dialect*, voce *Stob*.   [2] Bk. VI., Cap. XIX.

The first person who mentions the right of sanctuary at Cross Macduff is Sir John Skene (1597), but his statement receives no direct support from recorded events connected with 'the Law of Clan Macduff.' The events show that it was a privilege of re-pledging from other courts the kindred of the 'Earl' of Fife, accused of unpremeditated slaughter. So great was the privilege that 'it would seem that the Earl of Fife could repledge even from the Court of the King. He was equal in some respects to the king and his territory like a little kingdom.'[1] Sir John Skene states that this privilege only extended to those within the ninth degree of kindred to the Earl of Fife; those within that degree were reckoned of pure blood.[2]

The fine of nine kye and a colpindach payable by the man-slayer, is the same as that which was payable to the king when the rights of the crown were infringed.[3] This similarity shows that the privilege was guarded by the highest sanction which law afforded. The fine of *nine* kye, and the traditionary necessity of washing *nine* times in the Nine Wells (which rise on the lands of the town of Newburgh, in a field adjoining that on which Cross Macduff is situated), tends to show that there was a mystical pro-perty connected with the number *nine*, and that the tradition had its origin in some principle, which is lost in the mist of antiquity.

In Scottish superstition the number *nine* held a prominent place, and arising out of this source there are various places in Scotland named Nine-wells; as the Nine Maiden Well of Glamis; Nine-wells in Berwickshire and elsewhere.[4] 'Nine enchanted

---

[1] *Sculp. Stones of Scot.*, Vol. II., Cross Macduff.

[2] Great stress was laid on purity of blood in ancient times. The author of 'Scotland under her Early Kings,' says, 'the purity of the Hebrew and Teutonic mægs (clan related by blood) appears to have been identical, but not even in his *tenth* generation could the descendant of the Moabite or the Ammonite be reckoned as a child of Abraham.'—See Vol. II., pp. 314, 5, where the whole subject is ably discussed.

[3] *Act of Par. Scot.*, Vol. I., p. 72.

[4] Jervise's *Memorials of Angus and Mearns*, p. 334, 5.

stones were cast or laid in a field for destruction of the crop. A skein of yarn through which a patient has been transmitted *nine* times was cut into *nine* parts and buried in three Lairds lands for a cure.'[1] On the 11th August 1623, a mother hired a woman to go silent to bring water from the well of Ruthven, ' to wash her bairn for the restoration of its health, the woman, the mother averred before the Kirk Session of Perth, put her bairn through ane cake made of *nine* curnes of meal gotten from women married maidens, and that it is ane common practice used for curing bairns.'[2] 'A draught repeated *nine* times from the horn of a living ox was prescribed for hooping cough, together with putting the patient *nine* several times in the happer of a grinding mill.'[3] Numerous other instances might be adduced of superstitions reverence for the number nine. One of the very latest that has come under our notice, shows that the superstition is widespread, and still bears sway over the minds of men. In 1869 the Emir of Bokhara to propitiate the favour of the Emperor of Russia when suing for peace, sent a costly present by an embassy to that monarch, consisting of nine valuable gifts, the number *nine*, it was stated, being strictly adhered to, in accordance with the custom of the Turko-Tartaric races.[4]

In the Norse mythology, from which so many of our superstitions and customs have descended, the same mystical quality is attached to the number *nine*. 'In front of the great Temple of Upsala, in Sweden, there was a grove sacred to Odin, in it the most solemn sacrifices were performed, especially every ninth year, when *nine* human victims were sacrificed from among the captives, if in time of war, or nine slaves in time of peace.'[5]

In Scotland relics of this custom prevailed to the end of the last century. 'Highland Shepherds prepared an oaten cake with *nine* knobs on the surface. 'Each of these dedicated to a con-

---

[1] Dalyell's *Darker Superstitions of Scotland*, p. 392.   [2] *Book of Perth*, p. 304.
[3] Dalyell's *Darker Superstitions of Scotland*, p. 117.
[4] Vambery's *History of Bokhara*, pp. 416, 417.
Ferguson's *Tree and Serpent Worship*, p. 25.

servative or destructive being, was broke off and thrown over the shoulder with an invocation for protection of the herds.'[1]   In England there is still a game in which one party plays against another with *nine* stones each. · The point of the game consists in who shall first strike off the stones of his neighbour; each stone removed is placed in an inner square cut on the turf, and the men, as the stones are called, are therein impounded.[2]   That there is here a direct relic of human sacrifice there can be no doubt. Religious rites and superstitions survive in the games of men and children long after their original significance is utterly forgotten. Customs too, which had their origin in remote antiquity, long hold their place in the judicial proceedings of the country, and thus the *nine* kye of Cross Macduff are the far-off representatives of the human sacrifices of darker ages.

The tradition regarding the necessity of those who sought the asylum of Cross Macduff, washing at the Nine Wells; only occurs in comparatively recent times, and it is not mentioned in any ancient record.   The same remark applies, with still greater force, 'to the holes in the pedestal, caused by the wearing out of nodules of iron pyrites, which oral tradition tells us were holes in which staples and rings were fixed, for fastening the nine kye payable by the culprit.'.

Though there is no mention in any ancient record of the manslayer washing at the Nine Wells, there is much in support of the tradition, in the universality of the practice of cermonial washing before sacrifice.   Egyptians, Jews,[3] Greeks, Romans,[4] and other nations practised it. 'Go and wash, that you may sacrifice,'[5] was an injunction among the Romans; and among the Greeks, solemn ablutions were essential to the removal of the guilt of the homicide whether accidental or intentional.[6]   That the Celtic and

---

[1] Dalyell's *Darker Superstitions of Scotland*, p. 167.

[2] Brand's *Popular Antiquities*, Vol. II., p. 430.

[3] Exodus, chap. xl. vers. 30–32.

[4] Smith's *Dictionary of Antiquities*, voce *Sacrificium*.

[5] *Plautus Aulular*, III. 6, 43.   [6] *Sophocles Ajax*, 654, 6.

Teutonic races practised rites similar to their Aryan kindred the Greeks and Romans, is testified by their going to wells from superstitious motives, and leaving donations there, down to comparatively recent times. A practice which must have had its origin in pre-Christian times, and which the church invoked the strong arm of the law to put down. In 1573 the General Assembly resolved, 'For punishment of persons that pass in pilgrimages to *wells*, lett the discipline of the kirk be used against the users of such Superstition, and the civill Magistrat shall also hold hand to the punishment.'[1] And on 17th October 1581, the Assembly besought that an Act of Parliament be made for suppressing the custom.[2] On the 24th of the same month it was accordingly enacted by Parliament, that 'Forsameikle pairtlie through the perverse inclination of Mans ingine to Superstition, the dregges of idolatrie yit remaines in divers pairtes of the Realme be using of pilgrimages to some Chapelles, Welles, Croces, and sik uther monuments of Idolatrie. As also be observing of the festival dayes of the Sanctes, sumtime named their Patrons; in setting furth of bane-fyers, singing Carrales within and about Kirkes. That the punishment for the first offence for ilk Gentilman or Woman landed, or Wife of Gentilman landed ane fine of ane 100 punds. The unlanded ane hundred markes and the Yeaman fourtie poundis for the first fault, And for the second fault the offenders to suffer death as Idolaters.'[3] A punishment so severe shows that these superstitions were deeply rooted in the minds of the people, and warrants belief in the truth of the tradition, that the manslayer who sought protection at Cross Macduff had to wash at the Nine Wells.

Whatever may have been the origin of the 'Law of Clan Macduff,' a privilege so valuable was not likely to remain a dead letter. Sir John Skene says that 'King David II. (1348–1370) gave and disponed the Earledome of Fife, with all its priviledges,

---

[1] *Book of the Universal Kirk of Scotland*, p. 280. [2] *Ib.*, p. 535.
[3] James VI., Parl. VII., Cap. 104.

and with the law which is called Clan Makduff to William Ramsay (who married Isabel, Countess of Fife) and his aires, quhilk charter is yet extant in the Register.'

He further says, 'I saw ane auld evident bearand that Spens of Wormeston, beand of Makduffis Kinne, injoyed the benefite and immunitie of the Law for the slauchter of ane called Kynnyn-month.'[1]

'Sir Alexande de Moravia of the Morays of Abercairney was accused of the slaughter of William de Spaldyne and indicted for the crime in the Court of the High Justiciar held by his deputies Sir John and Maurice de Drummond at Foulis. On the 7 December 1391 he appeared with his fore-speakers, protested that inasmuch as he had been once before called in judgement of that slaughter, and repledged to the Law of Clan Macduff by Robert Earl of Fife he was not obliged to plead before any other judge to that charge, until the said law of Clan Macduff should have had its privileges in regard to him thus repledged to its jurisdiction, and he demanded to be lawfully discharged. The judges made answer that they could not discharge him, but would respite him until the Lord of Brechin, the principal Justiciar, should take order in the matter.'[2]

The next case on record is that connected with the inhuman murder of Sir John Melville of Glenbervie, Sheriff of Mearns. We are told by Sir Walter Scott, that 'the sheriff bore his faculties so harshly, that he became detested by the barons of the county. Reiterated complaints of his conduct having been made to James I. (or, as some say, to the Duke of Albany), the monarch answered in a moment of unguarded impatience, 'Sorrow gin the sheriff were sodden and supped in broo'l' The complainers retired perfectly satisfied. Shortly after the lairds of Arbuthnot, Mathers, Lauriston, and Pitarow decoyed Melville to the top of the hill of Garvoch, under pretence of a grand hunting party. Upon the place still

---

De Verborum Sig.—voce *Clan Makduff.*
Innes' *Sketches of Early Scottish History*, p. 214.

called the Sheriff's Pot, the barons had prepared a fire and a boiling caldron, into which they plunged the unsuspecting sheriff. After he was *soddin*, as the king termed it, for a sufficient time, the savages, that they might literally observe the royal mandate, concluded the scene of abomination by actually partaking of the hell-broth.[1] The three lairds were outlawed for the crime, and Barclay, one of their number, to screen himself from justice, erected the Kaim (*i.e.*, the fortress) of Mathers, which stands on a rocky and almost inaccessible peninsula overhanging the German Ocean. The Laird of Arbuthnot is said to have eluded the royal vengeance, by claiming the benefit of the Law of Clan Macduff. A pardon, or perhaps a deed of replegiation, is said to be still extant among the records of the Viscount Arbuthnot.'[2]

The following is a copy of the letter of remission :—' Tyll all men thir present letters to comes, I, Johnston, Stuart of Fyfe, sends greiting in God, witt ye, wee have resavit Hugh Arbuthnot, George Barclay, Alexander Falconer, William the Græm or Graham, Gilbert Middleton, Patrick Barclay, Alexander of Graham to the lawes of Clane Mackduff for the deid [death] of quhillome John the Malaville, Laird of Glenbervy, and certain and sicker burrowise [borch's, sureties], that is to say David Barclay of Collarnis [Collairnie] the first broych that they ought of the lawes, David the Barclay of Leuchry [Luthrie?] the second broych that they ought to have the lawes, Robert of Barclay of Towch or Towy the 3^d burghe that they shale fulfill the lawes as the law will. Quhairfore to all and sundrie that it efferis, firmly wee forbidd on the King's halfe [behalf] of Scotland, and our Lord Mackduff, Duke of Albany,

---

1 We stand astounded at this wild act of revenge; but, in the comparatively late reign of Henry VIII., in an outburst of popular fury against an aggravated case of poisoning, an Act was passed in England, sentencing poisoners to death by boiling them alive. This enactment was so revolting to public feeling, that it was rescinded in the succeeding reign.[1]

2 *Minstrelsy of the Scottish Borders*, Vol. IV., p. 265—Edition 1859.

---

1 Edward VI., cap. 12.

Earle of Fyfe and Menteith and Governor of Scotland, that the said lawes hes in keeping, that no man take in hand to doe, molest, greive, or wrange the foirsaid persons in their bodies, or in thir geire, because of the deid of the said Johne of Malavill and the payne that after lyes, and forfalting of the Lawes forsaid and this present Letter.—In Witness of the whilk this our Seale to this present hes putt. At Falkland the first of September, the year of God 1421 yeirs.'[1]

Such is all the authentic information that is known regarding the Law of Clan Macduff; and in none of the earliest notices of it is there positive evidence that the Cross was a Girth or Sanctuary. From the paucity of records concerning this ' Law,' and perhaps from the extreme antiquity of the privilege, the subject is surrounded with obscurity. Still it is not improbable that with the right of regality and replegiation there was also a right of Girth. Sir John Skene was not likely to have made such a positive statement, unless he had some evidence to that effect, which is now lost. Such a privilege was in keeping with the state of society, and necessities of the times. Every consecrated churchyard we have seen, was a sanctuary; but some of our early Christian settlements, as Dull, had a much wider space around the monastery marked by crosses as a Girth. ' When we remember Ethelred (son of St Margaret), the first known Earl of Fife, was also Abbot of Dunkeld, and that tradition represents Macduff to have been the progenitor, as well of the Mackintoshs as of the Abernethys, both of them of spiritual descent, we need not be surprised at such a combination (of ecclesiastical and civil privileges), or refuse to believe that the first Macduff may have represented a line of ancient Abbots on whom a privilege of girth had been conferred.'[2]

Later tradition is uniform on the subject; and about a quarter of a mile south-east of the Cross there is a small hillock, now part of a ploughed field, commanding a view of all the roads leading

---

[1] *Analecta Soctica*, Vol. IL, pp. 30, 31.
[2] *Sculptured Stones of Scotland*, Vol. II., Cross Macduff.

to it, called 'The Coucher's Knowe,' so named, it is conjectured, from the circumstance of watchers *couching*, or lurking there to waylay the manslayer ere he reached the sanctuary. When the field in which Cross Macduff is situated was first brought under the plough, there was a rude sort of pavement discovered on the small mound-like hillock, thirty paces south of the Cross. It has been conjectured, and it is not improbable, that this pavement was the floor of a small rude cell or oratory in connection with the Cross, such as are still to be seen on the early Christian sites in Ireland and in the Hebrides.[1]

In that turbulent age, when might was too often the measure of right, a sanctuary was of great value in restraining the hand of violence; and it was a noble aim on the part of the clergy in the prosecution of their work of mercy, to secure one spot where the defenceless could find safety. The undefined dread with which our ancestors regarded any attempt to violate such places of anctuary, bore upon them with a weight of awe that curbed their revenge, when mere law or authority would have been despised.

So long as the orginal purposes of their institution were strictly adhered to, sanctuaries had this good effect; they kept alive the distinction betwixt murder and manslaughter. But it is much to be feared that they were sometimes perverted from their original aim, and gave shelter to criminals to whom it was never intended they should afford protection. Laws had to be passed to remedy

---

[1] Besides the rude pavement, there was in Cross Macduff field when it was broken up in 1814, one very large and several small cairns, which were, without doubt, ancient burial places. The cells mentioned in the text as being still extant in Ireland and in the Hebrides are most primitive in their construction; they are built and covered by a gradually converging roof of unhewn stones, without lime or cement. Illustrations of some of the most ancient of these are given in Dr Petrie's work on the *Round Towers of Ireland* (pp. 129, 130); and in *Characteristics of Old Church Architecture in Scotland* (pp. 180, 181, 205). There is one of these rude cells on Inchcolm; an engraving of it from a drawing by Mr Drummond, R.S.A., appears in Sir James Simpson's paper on Inchcolm.—*Proceedings of the Society of Antiquaries of Scotland*, Vol. II., p. 501.

this evil, the latest of which, passed in 1535, enacted that Masters of Girths must be appointed, who were to be held personally responsible for the proper management of the sanctuaries under their charge.[1] Numerous instances of their perversion might be adduced; still—

> ' If full oft the sanctuary saves
> Lives black with guilt, ferocity it calms.'[2]

The fierce warrior, who would not have shrunk from the face of man, quailed and sheathed his sword before the spiritual and unseen power.

If obscurity attaches to the right of the Girth at Cross Macduff, and history is silent regarding the fitness of the descendants of the Thane of Fife for leading the van of the royal army in battle, we are left in no doubt as to the exercise of the right of placing the Scottish monarch on the throne. On the occasion of the coronation of Robert Bruce, Isabel, Countess of Buchan, sister of the Earl of Fife, knowing that her brother was in the power of Edward (and therefore could not exercise his hereditary right), hastened to Scone, and insisted on the ceremony being performed a second time, as she alone, as the representative of the Thanes of Fife, had the right to place the king on the 'Royal Seat.' That no informality might attach to his title to the Crown, Bruce consented, and regardless of the risk (for only a small band of patriots adhered to Bruce), the Countess placed the crown on Bruce's head.

> ' There steps a noble lady forth, and cries the right is mine,
> My fathers for long ages past, crown'd Scotland's royal line:
> She placed the circlet on his brow,—her hand ne'er shook nor quail'd;
> Go forth, she said, and fight for us, and God defend the right.'

This patriotic act brought down on the brave Countess the wrath of Edward I., and unfortunately she did not escape it. She

---

[1] James V., Parl. IV., Cap. 23.   [2] Wordsworth, *Ecc. Sonnets*, Pt. I., xxiv.

was taken prisoner shortly after Bruce's defeat at Methven, and for four years confined in a cage made of sparred wood, bound with iron, placed on one of the turrets of Berwick Castle, exposed to the severity of the weather and the gaze of every passer-by. This barbarous treatment was afterwards so far mitigated, that she was allowed to reside in strict retirement in a convent in Berwick.'[1] Had ambition not quenched Edward's better feelings, he would have admired the patriotism of the woman who had so daringly defied his power—for the beautiful crosses erected by him to the memory of his wife, on the spots where her body rested on the way to the tomb, testify to the depth of his affections. The conquest of Scotland had become with him an absorbing passion; he thought it within his grasp, and he wreaked his vengeance on all who had in any way helped to balk him of his coveted prize.

Such is the story of Cross Macduff. Sir Walter Scott, who visited it in 1822, thus speaks of it in the Prelude to his poem of Macduff Cross—

> ' Mark that fragment,
> I mean that rough-hewn block of massive stone,
> Placed on the summit of this mountain pass,
> Commanding prospect wide o'er field and fell,
> And peopled village and extended moorland,
> And the wide ocean and the majestic Tay
> To the far distant Grampians—Do not deem it
> A loosen'd portion of the neighbouring rock
> Detach'd by storm and thunder,—'twas the pedestal
> On which, in ancient times, a Cross was rear'd,
> Carved o'er with words which foil'd philologists;
> And the events it did commemorate
> Were dark, remote and undistinguishable,
> As were the mystic characters it bore.
> But, mark—a wizard born on Avon's bank
> Tun'd but his harp to this wild northern theme,
> And, lo! the scene is hallow'd—none shall pass
> Now or in after days, beside that stone,
> But he shall have strange visions; thoughts and words

---

[1] Note to *The Bruce*, Barbour, p. 438, Ed. 1869.

That shake, or rouse, or thrill the human heart
Shall rush upon his memory when he hears
The spirit-stirring name of this rude symbol ;—
Oblivious ages, at that simple spell,
Shall render back their terrors with their woes,
Alas! and with their crimes.'

Pilgrims attracted to the spot by the associations connected with the Cross may be disappointed in the little that remains of the ancient relic ; but they will be amply gratified by the magnificence of the prospect which stretches out before them.   For even the great Minstrel has failed to do justice to the surpassing beauty of the scene.

CROSS MACDUFF (FROM THE SOUTH-EAST.)

DENMILN CASTLE.

CHAPTER XXV

DENMILN CASTLE.

Denmiln ! upon thy battlements
The bearded thistle waves ;
Thy Halls with moss are carpeted,
Thy sons are in their graves.

  .   .   .   .

The mind, that loveth olden days,
Will long delight to dwell,
Sir James ! upon the storied page
Of thy quaint Chronicle,—
Where like a place of burial
Amid the Past we tread,
And gather sober wisdom
From the legends of the dead.'

                        John Anderson, D.D.

THE Castle of Denmiln, situated about a mile south-east from New-burgh, is deserving of more than a passing notice, from its having been the residence of Sir James Balfour the well-known antiquary, and for the tragic fate of more than one of his successors in the family honours and estate. The castle, which stands in a narrow sheltered valley or *den*, is now roofless, and only the bare walls remain. Judging from the style of its architecture, the probability is, that it was erected in the end of the 15th or the beginning of the 16th century. Sir James, in his Topographical Notes, preserved in manuscript in the Advocates' Library, says, ' A lytle southe of Lyndores [Abbey] standis Denmill, of old perteining to the Earllis of Fyff, till King James II. in the 14th year of his reign (1452) gave it to his beloved and familiar servitor James Balfour sone to

Sir John Balfour of Balgarvy, Knight.' Denmiln came into the possession of the Crown by the forfeiture of Murdoch, Duke of Albany, A.D. 1424.[1]

The family of Balfour, from whom the Balfours of Denmiln sprang, have long held a prominent place in Fife. Like most of the old territorial families, they acquired their surname from the name of the lands they occupied. Their original seat in Fife was named Balfour, from the Gaelic *Bal foidh or*, the town at the foot of the Or (the *dh* in *foidh* is silent). The family reckon their descent from the time of King Duncan, but it is certain that Sir Michael Balfour obtained a charter from William the Lion, A.D. 1214. In the struggle for the independence of Scotland, the Balfours were found on the side of their country ; Sir John Balfour fell in the defence of Berwick, when that town was besieged by Edward I. (A.D. 1296). Sir Duncan, Sheriff of Fife, fell at the battle of Black Earnside, in the gallant fight under Wallace. Half a century later Adam Balfour, a younger brother, died of a wound received at the disastrous defeat of Durham, and was buried in Melrose Abbey.

The ancestral property of Balfour passed into the family of Bethune by the marriage of Sir Robert Bethune to the only daughter and heiress of Sir John Balfour, who died A.D. 1375. Sir John Balfour of Balgarvy, whose son James acquired Denmiln, was a cadet of the Balfours of Montquhany, who were descendants of Adam Balfour, who received his death-wound at Durham.

James Balfour, the first of Denmiln, fell at the siege of Roxburgh, where his benefactor James II. accidentally met his death. He was succeeded by his son John, who was killed fighting on the fatal field of Flodden. Sir Michael, the great grandson of John who fell at Flodden, ranked high in public estimation both as a soldier and as a statesman, he being equally celebrated for his courage in the field and for his prudence in council. Charles I. selected him as Comptroller of his Household, and conferred the honour of knighthood upon him.

---

[1] Tytler's *History of Scotland*, Vol. II., p. 50.

Sir Michael married Joanna Durham, daughter of James Durham of Pitkerrow, by whom he had five sons and nine daughters, all of whom except two (who died unmarried) formed honourable alliances. He bestowed on his sons the best education the times could afford, and they all rose to distinction in their several paths. It is said that Sir Michael lived to see three hundred of his descendants, which, if correct, is the more remarkable, as within one hundred years of his death the male line of his family became extinct. He died at Denmiln, on the 4th February 1652, at the age of 72, and was buried in Abdie Church on the 20th of the same month.

The great length of time which was allowed to elapse betwixt Sir Michael's death and burial cannot fail to strike modern readers with surprise. It arose from the custom of entertaining all relatives and neighbours so long as the body lay unburied, with a profuse hospitality, which was not bounded by temperance.[1] Day after day scenes of conviviality went on, most unbecoming the solemn occasion, and expenses were incurred which often embarrassed the family of the deceased for generations. Instances are on record of two years rental of large estates having been spent in this wasteful manner at the funeral of the proprietors; and yet, had the family of the deceased set themselves against the custom of the time, they would have been branded as disregardful of their father's memory.

An Act was passed in the reign of Charles II. to curb these excesses and to restrain the ' exorbitant expense of burials because of the hurt and prejudice of the kingdom.'[2] It was ordained by this Act that 'there shall not be invited to the burial of noblemen and Bishops, and their wives, not above one hundred noblemen and

---

[1] One instance will suffice. At the Laird of Calder's funeral in 1716, sixteen bolls and a half of malt were brewed to provide ale (besides other liquors in proportion) for those who came during the eighteen days his corpse lay unburied. —Chambers's *Domestic Annals*, Vol. III., p. 309.

[2] Charles II., Par. III., Cap. 14.

gentlemen. To the burial of a Baron of quality, not above sixty, and other landed gentlemen, not above thirty.' Besides the ordinary attendants, special mourners were engaged, and it was specially ordained by the same Act, 'that the Mourners at the burials of Noblemen, and Bishops and their Ladies, do not exceed thirty, and at the burials of Privy Counsellors, Lords of Session, Barons, Provests of Burghs, and their wives, the number of Mourners doe not exceed twenty four, and at the burial of all other Landed Gentlemen and Citizens within Burgh they do not exceed the number of twelve.' The Act further prohibits and 'discharges the using or carrying of any Pencils, Banners and other Honours at Burial, except only the eight Branches to be upon the Pale [Pall], or upon the coffin where there is no Pale. Under the pain if a landed person of a fourth part of their yearly valued rent, and others, a fourth part of their moveables; Burgesses, five hundred merks, Craftesmen and Servants not exceeding one hundred merks.' Mourning cloaks were also strictly prohibited at burials 'under pain of a fine of one hundred merks.'

Notwithstanding this enactment, such is the tyranny of fashion, it was disregarded, and funerals continued to take place at which the attendants mustered in such numbers, marching in regular order, according to rank, that a procession has been known to extend upwards of four miles; the family honour depending on the rank and number of the attendants.[1]

In a very curious collection of Tracts by Sir James Balfour, there are several containing regulations for the order of funerals of persons of distinction, in which the most minute directions are laid down for marshalling the procession according to rank and precedence.[2] We have gone to the other extreme in Scotland, order and regular procession is disregarded, and apart from the solemnity of the occasion, a Scottish funeral cannot be said to be impressive.

---

[1] Chambers's *Domestic Annals*, Vol. III., p. 308.
[2] Sir James Balfour, *Ancient Heraldic and Antiquarian Tracts.*

The following is a copy of the inscription on the monument in Abdie Church, raised to the memory of Sir Michael Balfour, by his grandson Sir Robert Balfour.

D. O. M. S.

D. MICHAELIO BALFURIO A DENMIL EQUITI AURATO AUO PRÆSTANTIS PIETATE INSIGNI IN PATRIAM FIDE SPECTATO AULAM IMPERIALEM EXCELLENTISS. CAROLI II. IN SCOTIÆ, ANGLIÆ, FRANCIÆ ET HIBERNIÆ MONARCHEI CELCIS, TRIUM REGNI ORDINUM STATUO OB SUMMAM PRUDENTIAM CO-OPTATORET EIUS CONTRA ROTULIATOR PRONUNCIATO SENIOMORBOQUE CONFECTO IIII FEB: AN. CIɔ. IDCLII. AETAT. LXXII.

D. JOANNÆ DURHAMIÆ AVIÆ PAT: DIGNISS: RELIGIONE IN DEUM, CHARITATE IN EGENOS CLARISS. UT AMARANTINA FRUERETUR GLORIÆ CORONA IMMATURE EXTINCTÆ, 1ο. NOVEM. AN. CIɔ. IDCXL. AETAT LIX.

Sir James Balfour of Kinnaird, the eldest son of Sir Michael, and the heir to his title and estates, is the most widely known of the family, from the writings he has left behind him on antiquarian subjects. He was born in the year 1603 or 4. In the early part of his career he displayed a taste for poetry. Contemporary writers complimented him in verse, on his poetical compositions, several of which were in Latin and others in Scotch, but none of them have descended to posterity. Sir James was in terms of the closest intimacy with Drummond of Hawthornden, the well-known Scottish poet. In some of Sir James' correspondence, preserved in the Advocates' Library, he says, in a letter to Drummond, 'your starrie "Urania," on the wings of a strong wind, flees by us, in every ones handes; quherfor I intreid you wold you have me deprived of it? Have you thought me dead to the Muses that either I could not judge of it, or so dull that I could not praise it.' The starrie 'Urania' to which Sir James alludes, is a collection of spiritual poems published by Drummond under that title. Many of Drummond's poems have a grandeur of conception, and are pervaded by a penetrating sense of beauty, which makes them worthy of being more read and better known.

The following sonnet from the 'Urania' which Sir James was so impatient to see, is admirably conceived, and has a sustained thought running through it, which gains on reperusal :—

> ' To spread the azure canopy of heaven,
>   And make it twinkle with those spangs of gold,
>   To stay this mighty mass of earth so even
>   That it should all, and nought should it uphold ;
>   To give strange motions to the planets seven,
>   Of Jove to make so meek, and Mars so bold ;
>   To temper what is moist, dry, hot, and cold
>   Of all that jars that sweet accords are given ;
>   Lord, to thy wisdom nought is, nor thy might ·
>   But that thou shouldst, thy glory laid aside,
>   Come meanly in mortality to bide,
>   And die for those deserv'd eternal plight,
>   A wonder is so far above our wit,
>   That angels stand amazed to think on it.'

The reading of a sonnet like this, or the following (also by Drummond), which were often read within the walls of Denmiln when they were warm with life and happiness, brings before us the thoughts and feelings of the inmates, far more vividly than the most laboured description could convey.

> ' Sweet bird, that sing'st away the early hours,
>   Of winter's past or coming void of care,
>   Well pleasèd with delights which present are,
>   Fair seasons, budding sprays, sweet-smelling flowers ;
>   To rocks, to springs, to rills, from leafy bowers
>   Thou thy Creator's goodness dost declare,
>   And what dear gifts on thee he did not spare,
>   A stain to human sense in sin that lowers.
>   What soul can be so sick which by thy songs,
>   Attir'd in sweetness, sweetly is not driven
>   Quite to forget earth's turmoils, spites, and wrongs,
>   And lift a reverend eye and thought to heaven ?
>   Sweet artless songster, thou my mind dost raise
>   To airs of spheres, yes, and to angels' lays.'

After the completion of his academical course Sir James seems to have spent some years subsequent to 1626 abroad, availing himself of every opportunity of adding to his stores of knowledge and of improving himself by intercourse with eminent literary men. 'At the close of his continental travels he spent sometime in London, and obtained the friendship of the distinguished antiquary Sir Robert Cotton, of Sir William Dugdale, the author of the '*Monasticon Anglicanum*,' and others eminent in literature at the time.' His intercourse with Sir Robert, and other men of similar tastes seems to have given a bent to his future studies. He turned his attention to the study of heraldry and of historical antiquities, and on his achievements on these subjects his fame chiefly rests. These studies marked him out as a fitting person for holding the important position of Lyon King of Arms, an office to which he was appointed by Charles I. (15th June 1630) having previously received the honour of knighthood and the dignity of a Baronet from that monarch. Sir James held the office of Lyon King of Arms for many years, till, on account of his attachment to the royal family, he was deprived of it by Cromwell.

Sir James was animated by the praiseworthy ambition of rescuing from neglect the history of his native land, by recovering the charters of the various abbeys of the kingdom, and the chronicles which were so frequently compiled in these establishments; documents which, after the alienation of the abbeys, were fast passing into careless hands. For this purpose he visited all the cathedrals and principal parish churches in the kingdom, and examined the sepulchres and other monuments, from which he copied the most remarkable epitaphs and inscriptions, carefully preserving them in a volume. His largest work, entitled 'The Annales of Scotland MLVII–MDCIII.,' which lay in manuscript until it was published in 1824, is the result of these investigations. It contains many facts not now otherwise to be found on record. Considering the early age at which he died, and how much he did, it is not surprising that inaccuracies have crept into his writings.

Sir James's appointment as Lord Lyon King of Arms necessarily drew his attention to the science of heraldry, and on this subject he wrote numerous treatises, a list of the most important of which is given in the Memoir of his Life prefixed to the published edition of '*The Annales of Scotland.*' He also wrote a Topographical Account of Fife, which is preserved in manuscript in the Advocates' Library. It contains interesting facts regarding the county generally, and is well worthy the examination of students of local history. There was no subject, whether of literature or of natural history, in which Sir James did not take an interest. He entered most zealously into the Geographical Survey of Scotland, and helped forward the construction of the first series of maps of the country that were ever projected. They were published under the title of *Theatrum Scotiæ* by the Dutch Geographer Bleau. The map of Lorn is dedicated to Sir James, and is embellished with an engraving of his coat of arms.

Sir James collected with unwearied industry, and at great expense, a voluminous library stored with the most choice works in every department of literature, but more especially illustrative of the history, antiquities and heraldry of Scotland. Many of the original documents which he collected with so much zeal, and at so great expense, during the greater part of his life, were unfortunately lost or dispersed in the sack of Perth by the English under Cromwell, whither they had been sent for security. Those which were preserved were advertised for sale in 1698, and were purchased by the Faculty of Advocates. A copy of the printed catalogue, issued at the time, is preserved in the Signet Library. The title page sets forth that it is 'a Catalogue of Curious Manuscripts, collected by Sir James Balfour of Kinnaird, Knight-Baronet, and Lyon King at Arms, kept by him in his Famous Study of Denmilne.' The advertisement prefixed states 'that many of the manuscripts are in parchment, and more ancient than printing,—severals of them are curiously guilded and painted. Diverse of them are autographs, and original Papers of Latter times, affording thereby great light to History and the transactions of these times.'

Among the manuscripts, the most important are the Liber Carthusianorum de Perth, seu Scotichronicon abbreviatum; Winton, his Chronicle in Scottish verse; The Chartulary of the Monastery of the Holy Trinity at Scone; Liber Sanctæ Mariæ de Balmerinoch; Liber Sanctæ Mariæ de Dryburgh; Liber Arbrothiensis, and the Great Chartulary of the Monastery of Aberbrothock. Also, though not mentioned in the catalogue, Liber Sanctæ Mariæ de Lundors.

So late as the third decade of the present century, a farmer in the neighbourhood of Perth had a pair of shoes sent to him by his shoemaker wrapt in paper, which proved to be a manuscript from the collection of Sir James Balfour. In the middle of last century, one who saw them stated that chests filled with manuscripts stood in Denmiln Castle, and they were so little cared for that the doors of the castle stood open, and any one helped himself to what papers he chose without hindrance.

Many valuable manuscripts were preserved from destruction by Sir James, and 'posterity' (says the author of Memoria Balfouriana) 'ought to be deeply grateful to him for the labour and expense which he lavished in the collection and preservation of these manuscripts, which during his whole life he continued to accumulate, not so much for his individual utility as for the common benefit of literary men,' and, it may be added, for the elucidation of the history of the country.

Sir James, who previous to the death of his father is always styled of Kinnaird, as owner of that estate, married Anne Aiton, sister of Sir John Aiton of that Ilk (21st October 1630). She bore him three sons, who all died young, and six daughters, who all died unmarried.

After the death of his first wife Sir James married his cousin Jean Durham, who died within a year of her marriage. His third wife, Margaret Arnot, only daughter of Sir James Arnot of Ferney, bore to him three sons and three daughters, all of whom died young except Robert, who succeeded to the title and estates. On the death of Margaret Arnot, Sir James married Janet Auchinleck, daughter of Sir William Auchinleck of Balmanno, by whom he had two daughters. Sir James died on the 14th February 1657, at the early age of fifty-two. A tablet, erected by his son Sir Robert, in the aisle of Abdie Old Church, contains the following inscriptions :—

D. O. M. S.

D. JACOBO BALFURIO A DENMIL MILITI BARONET LEONI ARMORUM REGI PATRI DESIDERATISS, VERO HONORIS ET PROBITATIS EXEMPLO, LITERARUM OMNIUM CUM GRAVIORUM TUM POLITIORUM PERITISS, PENITORIS ANTIQUITATIS NON MINUS CERTUS QUAM INDAGATORI CURIOSI MUSARUM ET GRATIARUM CORCULO ET OCELLO ORBI ADEMPTO XIIII. FEB : AN. CIƆIDCLVII ÆTAT. LII.

D. MARGARITÆ ARNOTÆ MATRI CHARISS ; VIRTUTE ET FORMA ULTRA SEXUM EXIMIÆ, IN IPSO JUVENTUTIS FLORE UT SUPERIS ASSOCIARETUR TERRIS EREPTAE XV. DECEMB. AN. CIƆIDC. LIII ÆTAT XXV.

D. ROBERTUS BALFURIUS A DENMIL MILES BARONET FILIUS ÆTAT IO CURA ET AUTHORITATE MICHAELIS BALFOURII A PITMEDIN TESTAMENTO PATRIS TUTORE DATI EX PRESENTIBUS FUTURA PROSPICIENS MAUSOLEUM HOC M. S. ET P.F.J. AN. CIƆIDC LXI.

Prefixed to the edition of his 'Annales' published in 1824, is an engraved portrait of Sir James, from an original which was in the possession of the late Lord Belhaven. The expression of his countenance indicates a thoughtful and cultivated mind. He is represented leaning on a table covered with books and parchments, and in the dress and long hair of the cavaliers of the time of Charles I. The only relic at Denmiln which is likely to be connected with him, is a lintel over the orchard gate, bearing the inscription

'Hic Argus non Briareus esto.'[1]

Alexander, the immediate younger brother of Sir James,

---

[1] In the front of the steading of Denmiln there is an elaborately carved stone, bearing the arms of Balfour and Durham. with the initials, M. B. & J. D.

designed 'of Lumbanie,' from his having possessed some portion of that farm, became 'minister of the Word of God' in his native parish of Abdie. He held that charge, first as *helper* to Mr Andrew Murray, Lord Balvaird, and afterwards as incumbent of the parish from at least A.D. 1634 until 1673. During his incumbency his nephew, Sir Robert Balfour, built the addition to Abdie Old Church, known as Denmiln aisle, as appears from his initials and date 1661, and his coat of arms over the entrance. This aisle is devoid of all architectural elegance; had it been built in the same chaste style as the ancient structure, it would still have met the requirements of the parish, and the parishioners of Abdie might have boasted of a parish church second almost to none in antiquity in Scotland. · 'Mr Alexander Balfour who was venerated for the dignity of his deportment, and for the wisdom and piety of his life, had a promise from James, Archbishop of St Andrews (better known as Archbishop Sharpe) of the first vacant Bishopric in Scotland.'[1] He married Janet Hay, and on the death of his nephew Sir Robert, he succeeded to the baronetcy and estate. Abdie Church bell, which was recast in Alexander Balfour's time, bears the following inscription, 'Joannes Burgerhuys me fecit 1671. *Soli Deo Gloria!* Mr Alexander Balfour, minister there, of the parish of Ebde.'[2]

Michael, third son of Sir Michael Balfour, was born at Denmiln, and baptised on the 25th October 1623. He devoted his attention to agriculture, and stood high in the estimation of his contemporaries for his skill in rural matters.[3] He was proprietor of 'Pitmedin,' and is so designed on a monument erected by him in Abdie Old Church to the memory of his wife Katharine Napier who died in 1652, at the early age of twenty five. He appears to have sold Pitmedin in 1663, when he purchased the estate of Randerston (anciently Randalston) as he is thereafter designated by the name of that estate. The purchase is thus recorded in *Lamont's*

---

[1] Scott's *Fasti.*   [2] *New Statistical Account, Fife,* p. 54.   [3] *Memoria Balfouriana,* p. 3.

Diary—' 1663. This summer.   Balfour of   second
ˉthird] son of the deceased old Laird of Dinmille, in Fyffe bowght
the lands of Randerston at Craill, from Mr James Sharpe, Archbishop of St Andrews, and Alexr Inglis of Kingask the two sons
in law of the deceased Laird of Randerston : it stood him about
sextie thousande merkes or thereby.'[1]   His nephew James, son of
Lord Forret, succeeded to the estate.   James' daughter married
George Hay of Leys, whose descendant, Edmund Paterson Balfour
Hay, is now proprietor of Randerston.

In Abdie Old Church there is a tablet raised by Michael Balfour
to the memory of his wife; the arms of the Balfours, and the
engrailed cross of the Napiers, are very beautifully cut upon it.
The tablet bears the following inscription :—

P. M. E.

CATHARINE NÆPARÆ QUÆ RARIORUS VIRTUTIS QUÆ IN CLARISS. E-MINIS
SPLENDESCERE SOLET DITISS. EXHIBUIT APPARATUM NATURÆ PARTUM DUM
EDERET PUELLÆ VITAM SIBI MORTEM, PROH FLENDUM ADSCIVIT VIII. FEB.
AN.   CIƆ. IDC. LII. AETAT. XXV.

MICHAEL BALFOURIUS, A PITMEDIN AMATISS. CONJUGI CUJUS CINERES DONEC
LUX POSTREMA REFULGEAT IN HIS REQUIESCENT TENEBRIS CIPPUM HUNC.
P.S.D.D. AN. C.I.Ɔ.I.D.C. LXI.

Sir David Balfour of Forret, fourth son of Sir Michael, was
born in 1623. 'David, Viscount of Stormonth, and Sir David
Barclay of Cullernie, Knycht,' were witnesses to his baptism in
Abdie Church, on the 12th September of that year.   David
Balfour adopted the law as his profession.   He was admitted Advocate on the 29th January 1650.   Previous to his elevation to
the bench, as one of the Lords of Session in 1674, under the title
of Lord Forret, he had the honour of knighthood conferred upon
him, and in the following year was appointed one of the Justiciary
Judges.   In 1685 he was elected a Commissioner for the County
of Fife, to the Parliament which met in that year.   In the same

---

[1] *Lamont's Diary*, p. 210.

year he was chosen one of the Lords of the Articles, a body invested in some degree with the power of deciding what measures should or should not be brought before Parliament. Sir David died shortly after the Revolution.[1]

An interesting relic of Sir David Balfour is still extant. In the year 1683 he presented a Pulpit Bible to the parish of Logie, Fifeshire, in which the estate of Forret is situated. It bears the following inscription, both at the beginning of the Old, and also at the beginning of the New Testament:—'For the Glorie of God and edification of his People within the Paroshin of Logie—Sir David Balfour of Fforret, Knight, one of the Senators of the Colledge of Justice, gave this Bible, upon the 28th of April 1683.' Sir David's pious gift continued to be used by the minister in his pulpit ministrations up to the year 1855. Though now disused it is carefully preserved.[2]

Sir Andrew Balfour, the fifth, and youngest son of Sir Michael, was born in the Castle of Denmiln on the 10th January 1630, and was baptised on the same day in the parish church by the minister, Sir Andrew Murray of Balvaird. Sir Andrew appears to have received his early education at the parish school; he afterwards entered the University of St Andrews, where he continued until he took his degree of Master of Arts.[3]

---

[1] *Memoria Balfouriana*, p. 3, Haig's *Senators of the College of Justice*, p. 402.

[2] The Bible is in folio, and bears to have been printed at 'The Theater, Oxford, 1680.' It contains two illustrations of passages in the Revelation.

[3] The following graceful notice in the Records of the Kirk Session of Abdie, penned by the schoolmaster, shows the scholarly tastes of the parish schoolmasters of that day:—'1711 June 3. This day was buried here a stranger, called David Shearer, Merchant in Crief, who as he was swimming his horse and washing him yesterday forenoon, in the Loch of Lindores, by north of the Dove-Cote perished in the waters. Ah!

Quid quisque vitet, nunquam homini satis
Cautum est, in horas.

Horace, Bk. IL, Ode XIII.'

Sir James, his eldest brother, directed his studies and inspired him with that love of learning, especially of natural history in all its branches, which distinguished him through life.

The young student of Denmiln chose the science of medicine for his profession. After leaving St Andrews he went to London (1650), where he enjoyed the friendship of Harvey, the celebrated discoverer of the circulation of blood, and of other physicians eminent in medical science. After a residence of several years in London, and an attendance at the University of Oxford, he went to Blois in France, to be near the Botanic Garden there, then the best in Europe. He afterwards proceeded to Paris, where he prosecuted his studies as a physician with great ardour, embracing every opportunity of anatomical dissection, and attending constantly on the practice of the public hospitals. Subsequently he travelled through the whole of France with Sir Watkinson-Pelior (at whose seat in Yorkshire he afterwards resided for sometime). At the University of Caen in Normandy, he entered on a public disputation, according to the fashion of the time, and obtained the degree of Doctor in Medicine from that university.

On his return to London, Dr Balfour was introduced to King Charles II., who selected him as a fit person to travel abroad as governor to the Earl of Rochester, a young nobleman (who ranks among British poets) of whom great hopes were entertained, but who had fallen into dissolute habits. Dr Balfour travelled with the Earl four years, returning in 1667. He endeavoured to recall the young nobleman to a true and noble life, and his counsels and example were so far successful, that the Earl totally subdued his inclination to intemperance during the whole course of his travels. Johnson, in his *Lives of the Poets*, says of Rochester's works, 'there is in all of them sprightliness and vigour, and everywhere may be found in them tokens of a mind which study might have carried to excellence.'[1] Unhappily on his return to Britain the Earl again gave way to vicious indulgence, and

---

[1] Johnson's *Lives of the Poets*—Rochester.

'blazed out his life in lavish voluptuousness' and daring impiety at the early age of thirty-one.

'Rochester often acknowledged, and to Bishop Burnet in particular only three days before his death, how much he was bound to love and honour Dr Balfour, to whom, next to his parents, he felt he owed more than to all the world.'[1]

In the course of his travels, which at intervals extended over a period of fifteen years, Dr Balfour was indefatigable in his researches on every subject of interest, whether of science or of art, and lost no opportunity of collecting specimens illustrative of the natural history of the counties through which he past. On his return to his native country 'he brought with him the most extensive and valuable library, especially in works of medicine and natural history, that till then had appeared in Scotland.' A list of several of these books is given in the *Memoria Balfouriania.* They embrace almost every variety of subject,—among them were 'books even from China, India, and other parts of the East.' He brought also maps, plans of ancient buildings, statues and busts of famous men, and a collection of surgical, mathematical, and what is remarkable at that early age, microscopic instruments. His museum contained, besides anatomical preparations of the human frame, quadrupeds, birds, reptiles, fishes, specimens of minerals, of metals and various kinds of stones and fossils, anticipating in this respect the geological inquiries of the present age. The marine productions consisted of corals, white and red (*stellata, articulata* et *verruscosa*), and the vegetables embraced various kinds of wood, fruit, and gums. The plants which he collected were bound in several large volumes, and as well as some of his other specimens were deposited in the College of Edinburgh. No such collection having previously been seen in Scotland, it attracted great attention, and must have given an impetus to the study of natural history, and to the cultivation of the fine arts. Had Dr Balfour's collections been carefully preserved, they would have proved an interesting

[1] Walker's *Mem. of Sir Andrew Balfour,* p. 351.

feature in the Museum of the University of Edinburgh; but, unfortunately, towards the end of the last century only a small portion of them remained.

On his return to Scotland, Dr Balfour commenced practice as
a physician in St Andrews. He employed his leisure hours there
in the study of anatomy and natural history, and in the dissection
of the human body, which was then for the first time practised in
Scotland. The ancient city has therefore the honour of leading
the way to that eminence in medical science which Scotland has
since attained. Ever active in his scientific pursuits, Dr Balfour
collected during his residence in St Andrews the indigenous plants
of the country; and discovered several which were previously
unknown to botanists.[1] Of a truly scientific mind, he seems to
have taken no fact in natural history on trust which he could
examine for himself. He sent to the Hebrides for specimens of the
barnacle, and by accurate dissections exposed the errors, which
till then, even the learned believed, of its marvellous transformation into a bird. With the true characteristic of a great mind,
widened by travel, he rose superior to the vulgar errors of his
age, and in a letter which was published, but unfortunately has
been lost, he endeavoured to free his countrymen from the belief
in witchcraft, which then held them in such painful bondage.

In 1670 Dr Balfour removed from St Andrews to Edinburgh,
where he immediately came into an extensive practice, more
remunerative than any physician had ever before obtained in
Scotland. His health broke down in a few years after his removal,

---

[1] It sounds strange to botanists now to be told that Dr Balfour first made
known the Rubus Chamœmorus, or Cloudberry (found in so many mossy mountain ridges in Scotland) as indigenous. He first discovered the *Pulmonaria
Maritima Linn*, now *Mertensia Maritima*, known, from the flavour of its leaves, as
the Oyster plant, to be a native of Scotland. This plant, which grows on the
shores of the Forth near Earlsferry, is rare on the east coast of Scotland, and it
was probably there that Sir Andrew discovered it. The extreme beauty of its
purplish blue flowers attracts the notice of casual visitors, and the plant is in
danger of being extirpated, to the regret of all students and lovers of nature.

notwithstanding he continued to interest himself in his favourite studies. He was an excellent linguist, and kept up a correspondence with commercial, as well as literary friends in various countries on these subjects. Year by year he received specimens from the *Indies* and from Europe, and, what scientific journals now convey—information of the latest discoveries in science. His intimate acquaintance with the manners, customs, and institutions of foreign countries, made him a valuable adviser in the establishment of similar institutions at home. He suggested and assisted in carrying out the establishment of the Royal College of Physicians in Edinburgh, and was elected one of the first Presidents of that Institution. He projected and established an Infirmary in Edinburgh—the first in Scotland—for the cure of the diseased poor and friendless; it was originally of humble dimensions, but from it has sprung the noble Institution which now fills its place.[1]

The love of botany, which he imbibed from his elder brother Sir James, seems to have been the solace of his life. In a small garden adjoining to his house, he raised many plants from seeds which he received from his foreign correspondents, and which were then first introduced into Scotland.

The death of Murray, Baron of Livingstone, a young and ardent botanist who travelled abroad at Dr Balfour's suggestion, placed a thousand species of plants at his disposal. To prevent this valuable collection from being scattered and lost, Sir Robert Sibbald and the Faculty of Advocates assisted Dr Balfour in defraying the necessary expenses incurred in preserving and cultivating them. The rare plants collected by the indefatigable perseverance of Dr Balfour attracted the notice of eminent botanists abroad, and at length the Magistrates of Edinburgh awakening to the importance of the institution, allotted a piece of ground near Trinity College Church, for what they called a 'Physic' garden,[2] and a

---

[1] Walker's *Essays on Natural History*, pp. 361, 2.

[2] The ground is now occupied by the North British Railway; the garden was removed to Leith Walk in 1763, and to its present site, in Inverleith Row, in 1819.

A A

salary to a curator. To Dr Balfour therefore belongs the honour of founding the first public botanic garden in Scotland.

Dr Balfour received the honour of knighthood in the reign of Charles II. Sir Robert Sibbald, in a memoir of his own life, gives the following account of the bestowal of this honour :—'In the beginning of the year 1682, I was advertised upon a Saturday night to bring with me Dr Steinson and Dr Balfour to wait upon the Duke of York, after the forenoon sermon. The Earl of Perth and Sir Charles Scarborough had concerted the matter, wee indeed knew nothing of the designe, but thought that we had been sent for to receive his Royal Highness's commands anent the Colledge, for that he was to goe away shortly. Bot to our surprisall ther was ane carpet layed, and we were ordered to kneel, and were each of us Knighted by his Royall Highness, then Commissioner.'[1] Dr Balfour was eminently deserving of this honour ; he was the representative man of science in Scotland at the time, and there was no subject in any department of learning, or indeed anything which tended to promote the prosperity of the country in which he did not take an interest.

Having made himself acquainted, as opportunity offered, with the processes of manufactures abroad, and having seen the advantages arising from manufacturing activity, Sir Andrew was naturally desirous of imparting the advantages to his own country, and of raising Scotland to the level of other nations. Though for one hundred and twenty years previous, paper had been manufactured in England, the attempts that had been made to introduce its manufacture into Scotland had hitherto failed. Sir Andrew projected, and with that successful energy which seems to have attended all his efforts, succeeded in introducing, the manufacture of this useful material,—and it has ever since been carried on extensively in the neighbourhood of Edinburgh.[2]

---

[1] *Analecta Scotica*, Vol. I., p. 147.

[2] The first time that the manufacture of paper is heard of in Scotland is in the year 1590. A German in that year petitioned government for certain ɪ ri-

Raised to the pinnacle of professional eminence in Scotland, the suavity of his manners and his extensive stores of knowledge, secured for Sir Andrew the friendship of the learned and the great. He was the friend and medical attendant of the Duke of Rothes, and was on terms of intimate intercourse with the Earls of Moray, Morton, and Strathmore, Viscount Tarbat, Sir James Murray of Drumcairn, and the other leading men of the time; but his consideration for the poor, and the kindliness of his disposition made him beloved by them and universally esteemed.

After many years of impaired health, Sir Andrew Balfour died in 1694, in the sixty-third year of his age. He was prepossessing in his appearance, 'of a handsome figure, and with a pleasing and expressive countenance. There was a print of him executed in Paris, but no copy of it is known to exist.' After Sir Andrew's death his son published a volume of letters addressed by his father to his friend Murray, Baron of Livingstone, while on his travels. These letters contain directions and advice to the young naturalist to guide him to the places where the most note-worthy objects of scientific interest and art were to be found. The volume, only that it is more exclusively scientific, is exactly what a guide-book is to the modern tourist. The author's remarks on the natural phenomena and objects of taste which he visited and examined, display a thorough appreciation of art, and an independent judgment in matters of science. 'After experiments on the vapour of the famous *Grotto del Cane*, he came to the conclusion that it was the same as the choke-damp of the coal mines of Britain,'—a conclusion which modern chemistry has completely verified. His learning

---

vileges in connection with its manufacture, which were granted, but the attempt seems to have been unsuccessful. In 1675 a paper-work was established on the Water of Leith in which was made (in 1679) 'gray and blue paper much finer than ever this country offered to the Council.' In 1697 'a paper manufactory was going on prosperously under a joint-stock company, producing 'good white paper; and it is spoken of as the only one in the kingdom 'that has either work or design for white paper.'—Chambers's *Domestic Annals.*—These two latter works were undoubtedly the offspring of Sir Andrew Balfour's enterprize.

and his scientific knowledge only made him more stedfast in his faith, and more humble and more ardent in his love to God. 'He was' (says Sir Robert Sibbald) 'beyond most of his time in wisdom, in moderation of mind, and in learning, he excelled all his contemporaries in his knowledge of natural history and antiquities; in these studies he was the foremost of Scotsmen, and was justly awarded the palm.'

The following eulogium, published at the time of his death, expresses the opinions entertained by his contemporaries of his worth—

> 'The great Balfour is dead, too soon alace!
> Who was his countries' ornament and grace,
> But his great name still lives, and shall allwayes,
> A garland wear of never-fading bayes,
> His heaven-born soul to great things did aspire,
> Nor sea, nor land could bound his vast desire ;
> And when the wonders these contain'd he knew,
> He passed hence, Heaven's wonders next to view.' [1]

Denmiln Castle for a generation was a centre of learning and refinement, the resort of the most eminent in literature at the time, and the meeting-place of all who had the promotion of learning and the intellectual advancement of Scotland at heart. In the immediately succeeding generation this fair picture was dashed with bloodshed and violent death. Sir Robert Balfour, the only surviving son of Sir James, was killed in a duel with his neighbour Sir James M'Gill of Lindores, when little more than twenty-one years of age. A small Cairn on the roadside, about a quarter of a mile west from Cross Macduff, known by the name of Sir Robert's Prap, marks the spot where the unhappy young man fell, A.D. 1673. Though judicial action was taken in the matter, the record does not mention the cause of the conflict. Tradition has uniformly narrated that the two

---

[1] *Memoria Balfouriana*, p. 98. Walker's *Essays on Natural History, passim.*

neighbours had been at Perth together attending a fair, and that they quarrelled on their way homewards. M'Gill is reported to have said to Sir Robert, 'Yon Hielandman would have been ow'r able for you, if I had not interfered.' Nettled at the remark, Sir Robert retorted angrily, and a violent altercation ensued; when, riding at full gallop through the standing corn towards the foot of the hill, they came to a stand, and the flashing of their swords told that they were engaged in mortal combat. A neighbouring miller who was a spectator of the scene hastened after them, but before he reached the spot Sir Robert was lying lifeless on the place now covered by the Cairn known by his name.

> ' Saddled and bridled
> And gallant rode he ;
> Hame came his gude horse
> But never cam he.'

Tradition relates that a shepherd who was near the scene of the fight heard M'Gill entreating Sir Robert to stand off, lest in self-defence he should kill him ; but Sir Robert was furious, and compelled him to fight.

This tradition places M'Gill in a more favourable light than the sentence pronounced against him would seem to warrant. He had to lie concealed, and the king only granted him remission on condition 'that he should never again be seen in Fife,' a condition which implies that the duel was accompanied by aggravations which are not recorded. Eight years after the fatal event, Fountainhall records, that on '4th and 5th May 1681, Rankiclour gave in a Bill to the (Privy) Councell, bearing that Sir James M'Gill his sone having been so unfortunate as to kil Balfour of Denmiln, and his Majesty having granted him a remission, to which the Councell added this quality, that he should never be seen in Fife to prevent bloodshed; and that the petitioner being now a-dying, and earnestly wishing to speak with and see his sone, therefor begged they would relax so much of the punishment as to allow his sone to come and see him. The Councell doubted if they might doe this; but the Duke of Albany affirming that he believed the king would not refuse this desire of any old dying gentleman, they grantit it in thir termes, that he should go with a guard like a prisoner, and stay but twenty-four houres, and then depart out of Fyfe where the friends of him that was killed live.'[1]

'Encouraged by the liberality of the Council, Sir James M'Gill petitioned them anew in December for a removal of all restriction upon his remission, alleging that it was required on account of the decayed and infirm condition of his parents (he being their only son), and the ruin into which his affairs had fallen in consequence of his long exile. Against this petition, however, the friends of Sir Robert Balfour gave in answers, showing how green such a wound could then be kept for eight years. They urged that the slaughter of their kinsman, so far from being done, as alleged by Sir James in self-defence, was in forethought felony, and it was only owing to an undeserved clemency on his Majesty's part that he had not been brought to condign punishment. The pretexts regarding his parents and estate were frivolous when the nature of the offence was considered.' 'Though it is insinuate that the said Sir James desires only to live in the parish of Monimail, and not in the parish of Ebdie, where Sir Robert's nearest relatives are, this is a very silly pretence, for this is the very next parish, and Sir Robert's nearest relatives have their interests in this parish itself, and it may easily be considered, that, if this is allowed, Sir Robert's friends will be punished for Sir James' crime, since they must, to shun his company, neither go to the meetings of the shire, baptisms, nor marriages, burials or churches; nay, nor to see their friends nor neighbours lest they should *fall in inconveniences with him*, which was the ground upon which the restriction was granted at first.' To prove how unworthy Sir James was of the favour extended to him in May last, it was set furth that, on that occasion, 'he must ride insolently by the very gate of the gentleman he had murdered, with a great train of friends,

---

[1] Fountainhall's *Historical Notes*, p. 292.

and in passing the road they did also very insolently boast and upbraid the poor people with whom they met.' 'If this,' it was added, 'was done in the very first time, what may be expected when his confidence is increased by renewed favours, and when Denmiln's friends see that the only satisfaction they got (which was not to see him at all) is taken from them.'[1] This representation on the part of Sir Robert's friends is no doubt highly coloured; but even making deductions for exaggeration, the conduct of Sir James ill-accorded with his being the unwilling cause of the young baronet's death. The petition was refused.

Sir Robert Balfour was succeeded by his uncle Alexander, the minister of Abdie, who lived little more than a year after he came into possession of the family honours and estate. Sir Alexander was succeeded by his son Michael (22d July 1675).[2] Sir Michael married Marjory, daughter of Moncrieff of Reidie, and was one of the members for Fife in the Scottish Parliament in 1685. In the spring of 1709 Sir Michael rode away from Denmiln Castle with the expressed intention of visiting some friends, and never returned. Search was made in all directions, and advertisements were inserted in newspapers both at home and on the continent, but no tidings of him were ever received. On the 17th January 1710, 'Lady Denmiln, gave in a bill to the Lords bearing that Michael Balfour her husband went from home in March last to visit some friends and for other business, and in his return home, he sent his servant an errand into the town of Cupar, and told him he would be at home before him, and yet he never yet returned to his house, notwithstanding all the search and enquiry made for him, and the horse he rode on; and no account can hitherto be got what is become of him; by which misfortune his creditors are falling upon his estate, and proceeding to diligence which may encumber and embarass his fortune, though it far exceeds his debts, unless prevented. Therefore craves, in this extraordinary case, the Lords may name a factor to uplift the rents

---

[1] Chambers's *Domestic Annals*, Vol. II., pp. 424-6.   [2] *Fife Retours*, 1143.

and out of it [them] to pay the current annual rents, and give an aliment to her and her seven children.'

Fountainhall, who records the foregoing petition, says, ' There were many conjectures about him, for some have been known to retire and go abroad upon melancholy and discontent; others have been said to be transported and carried away by spirits, and a third sort have given out that they were lost, to cause their creditors compound; as the old Lord Belhaven was said to be drowned on Solway Sands; so of Kirkton, yet both of them afterwards appeared. The most probable opinion was that Denmiln and his horse had fallen under night into some deep coal pit, though these were also searched, which lay on his way home. The Lords thought the case craved some pity and compassion, and that their interposing would come better if the creditors had applied; yet they appointed a factor to last only for the year 1710, to uplift and manage the rents for the creditors and relict, before which were [was] expired they would be at more certainty whether he was dead or alive.'[1]

Sir Michael's mysterious disappearance excited much interest in the neighbourhood of his residence, and the elders of a preceding generation used to tell that there were those living in their youth, who saw the baronet ride away from the castle on a black horse accompanied by a servant on horseback, and that he never came back. The interest excited by the mystery which shrouded the baronet's disappearance extended far beyond his own neighbourhood. Fifteen years after he rode away, a broad-sheet entitled ' Murder will out,' was hawked about the country. This document, of which a copy is preserved in the file of the ' Courant' newspaper, purports to be the confession of a woman on her deathbed, to the effect that her father, who was a tenant of Sir Michael Balfour at the time, had secretly stabbed and buried him to get quit of arrears of rent.

Sir Michael, the son of the missing baronet, contradicted the

---

[1] Fountainhall's *Decisions*, Vol. II., p. 554.

statement of the broad-sheet, which is of a most sensational character; and in a letter which he sent to the publisher of the newspaper he said, that the 'story was false in all the circumstances,' and the printer apologized for having been instrumental in giving circulation to a false report. There is reason to believe that Sir Michael was involved in pecuniary embarrassments. On the 25th May 1684, the following entry occurs in Newburgh Kirk Session Records, 'ye minister and Elders unanimously agreed that diligence should be used against Sir Michael Balfour;' a prosecution which he got rid of by granting an assignation to the rent of Wester Lumbennie, then part of his property. It is on record also that he granted a bond (25th May 1705) for 1100 merks in favour of his brother, Mr David Balfour, Doctor of Medicine, which was not paid at the time of his disappearance, as the amount was arrested subsequently in the hands of James Balfour of Randerstone. These and other pecuniary difficulties may have had something to do with Sir Michael's disappearance, but whatever was the cause, no clue to his fate was ever obtained, and

'The secret sleeps in death.'

CHAPTER XXVI.

OLD CUSTOMS AND FOLKLORE.

' Hail ancient manners! sure defence
Of wholesome laws.'

Wordsworth.

LESS than two generations back any grave notice of the games of children would have been reckoned a waste of time, and the very essence of childishness; but the researches of scholars both on the continent of Europe and in Britain have shown, that these boyish sports are often far-descended imitations of the doings of grown men in the early stages of society. Even apparently meaningless expressions reflect phases of belief which have long since past away. The expression, ' Gae to Hackelbirnie!' which is still current in this neighbourhood, and used as a mere playful expletive (commonly in answer to a request not to be complied with), has come down from the days when our fathers believed in heathen gods. Hackel-bærend was the Norse Spirit of the storm. To threaten to send a fretful child to Hackel-bærend, therefore, in the days of heathendom, was to send him to the spirit whose angry voice was heard in the wild tumult of the wintry wind.

The tales too which have come floating down in the traditions of the people, are far off echoes of the hopes and fears of the human race, ere the light of the gospel had dawned upon them; many of them containing distinct traces of heathen beliefs. These tales are common to many lands; one known as ' Johnny Trotter,' still current among the peasantry of Fife, is identical with a tale popular among the peasantry of Norway, under the title of ' Not a

pin to choose between them,'[1] and it is known as ' Jack Hannaford '
in Devon.

The latest writer who has treated of the games of children and
kindred subjects philosophically, says, ' If they be examined with
an eye to ethnological lessons, one of the first things that strikes
us is, how many of them are only sportive imitations of the serious
business of life.'[2]   He cites the act of a Scottish mother playfully
reducing her obstreperous youngling of a son to submission, by
taking him by the forelock and saying, ' Tappitousie ! will ye be
my man ?' as a relic of the time when serfdom prevailed, and
when the owner led the serf by the forelock in presence of witnesses, in token and admission of servitude.   The following are
some of the lines of this far-descended rhyme, which are still
repeated in Newburgh :—

> ' Tappitousie ! will ye be my man ?
> O, yes ! I'll do the best I can.
> Come to me, come to me, come to me !
> Tappitousie ! will ye be my wife ?
> Eh, na ! I canna, for ye'll tak my life.
> Gae fae me, gae fae me, gae fae me !

In the collection known as ' *Quoniam Attachiamenta,* or *the Baron
Lawes,*' we have the mode in which serfdom was acknowledged
and carried out in reality.   In these ' Lawes ' it is stated that ' the
thrid kinde of nativitie or bondage is, quhen ane frie man, to the
end he may have the menteinance of ane great and potent man,
randers himself to be his bondman, in his court, be the haire of
his forehead, and gif he thereafter withdrawes himselfe, and flees
away from his maister, or denyes to him his nativitie, his maister
may proue him to be his bondman, be ane assise before the justice,
challengand him, that he sic ane day, sic ane yeare compeared in
his court, and there yielded himselfe to him to be his slave and

---

[1] Dasent's *Popular Tales from the Norse,* p. 178.
[2] Tylor's *Primitive Culture,* Vol. I., p. 65.

bondman. And quhen any man is adjudged and decerned to be native or bondman to any maister, the maister may take him be the nose, and reduce him to his former slavery.'[1]

The game which less than fifty years ago was known in this neighbourhood as 'Burnt Witches' (and may be still so known), is an undoubted survival in sport of the terrible hallucination which subjected helpless women to an agonizing death for the imaginary crime of witchcraft. In a game still practised by the boys of Newburgh, we appear to have represented in sport the exaction of the fine known as the *Cro* among the ancient Celtic population of Scotland. The *Regiam Majestatem* defines *Cro* to be compensation for slaughter.[2] The *Cro* for the slaughter of the king was a thousand *kye;* for the son of an Earl or a Thane a hundred, and lower grades less; that of a husbandman or yeoman being saxtene kye.'[3] From the circumstance that there are stones in Scotland known as the Cro or Crawstanes, it is conjectured that the judicial proceedings connected with the exaction of the *Cro* may have taken place at them. 'At the perambulation of the lands of Melgow or Melgum in Nithbrenshire (Newburnshire), held at Largo Law by the Justiciar of Fife in 1306, one part of the boundary ran *ad lapidem que vocatur le Crawstane;* and one of the Sculptured Stones at Rhynie, in Aberdeenshire, is known as the Cro or Crawstane.'[4] In the game, a boy named the *Cra*, sits on a stone in the centre of a circle of companions, who stand ready to strike him with plaited handkerchiefs as soon as the judge of the game permits; but the moment that the judge (whose duty it is to decide when due punishment is exacted), proclaims that his '*Cra's* no free,' that moment every one is obliged to desist. In this game there seems to be an undoubted representation of a grave proceeding in the criminal judicature of remote antiquity; a supposition which the identity of the name strongly corroborates.

---

[1] *Quoniam Attachiamenta*, chap. lvi.   [2] *Reg. Majest.* Book iv. 36.
[3] W. F. Skene, *Tribe Communities of Scotland.* Fordun, Vol. II., Appendix, p. 448.
[4] *Sculptured Stones of Scotland*, p. xlv. *Regis. de Dunfermelyn*, p. 410.

St Chrysostom truly said fourteen centuries ago, that super-stition enslaves men. It subjects them to a thraldom stronger tenfold then human laws; the spiritual and unseen having far greater power over the human mind than any threatened infliction of mere bodily punishment. Innumerable instances of this truth might be adduced from the annals of superstition.

Towards the end of the last century the corpse of a suicide had to be lifted over the walls of the churchyard in Newburgh; the superstitious belief being that if it was permitted to enter by the gate, the next child that was carried to the church for baptism would end its days by self-destruction. This superstition died out by slow degrees. Scarcely fifty years ago, two old women remembering what they had seen in their youth, watched with eager curiosity the funeral procession of a suicide in Newburgh, as it approached the churchyard porch, where a very slight accidental stoppage took place. Imagining that the old super-stitious practice was to be put in force, they immediately set off to see the end, exclaiming, 'They're no gaun to let her in yet!' but they had not run many paces when the whole procession disappeared within the churchyard gate, and this form of super-stition was for ever extinguished amongst us.

In the beginning of the present century a reputed witch named Jean Ford was living in Newburgh. The belief in her occult powers was so strong, that sailors before setting out on a voyage were accustomed to propitiate her with a present to ensure a safe return. Jean, in her latter years, was warned to remove from her house by her landlord, who had no dread of her hidden powers; not so, however, his wife. After receiving the notice of removal, Jean went to the landlord's residence (and taking care to stand where she could be seen by the inmates), she began to make mystical signs on the ground with her staff, muttering all the while some words to herself. The servants who had a wholesome dread of her powers, attracted the attention of their mistress towards her. The spell was successful; the warning was removed, and Jean was allowed to remain in her house all

her life. Still later, the wife of an elder in Newburgh had a
valuable plaid stolen, and the threatenings of the law proved
powerless to recover it. The worthy elder, however, caused it to
be widely known that he was going to consult a spaewife in the
neighbourhood, when the plaid was secretly returned and laid
where it could be seen. Superstitious fears had more power than
the law, but the spaewife might now spae in vain. Barely two
generations back the belief in ghosts was firmly fixed in the
popular mind. It was implicitly believed that the ghost of 'the
Leddy of Denmiln' wandered; or, to use the expression invariably
applied to ghosts, 'gaed' at nights around her old residence,
restless because of her cheatrie in selling the meal ground at her
mill, and muttering to herself,

> 'The little lippie and the licht stane
> Gars me wander here my lane.'

Mild forms of superstition still unconsciously linger. If a boy
and girl are brought to the church for baptism at the same time,
the boy must be baptised first, the belief being, that the girl would
otherwise have the unfeminine appendage of a beard. The custom of taking a bit of *shortbread*, or other kind of cake, along
with, and sometimes pinned up in the dress of a child conveyed
to church for baptism, still prevails in Newburgh. This cake is
known as 'The Bairn's Piece,' and it is presented to the first person
that is met on the way to the church. This old custom seems to
have had its origin in the times when bread was distributed to
obtain the prayers of the recipients. The survival of the custom
is calculated to inspire kindly feelings; which, though the origin of
'The Bairn's Piece' is forgotten, may be productive of unspoken
prayers for the well-being of the unconscious infant. This custom
still survives in many other places. In 1871 a gentlemen was
accosted on a Sunday forenoon by a lady accompanied by an
attendant carrying an infant, in one of the principal streets of
Edinburgh. On his stopping, the lady offered him what she said

was ' the Christening bit,' which, on explanation of the custom, to her apparent delight, he accepted.[1]

There is a remarkable superstition still prevalent in this neighbourhood. It is firmly believed that if a child or other relative is withheld from dying by being 'Cried back' (as the prayers for its continuance in life are called), it will be deprived of one or more of its faculties, as a punishment to the parent or other relative who would not acquiesce in the Divine Will. Mrs Barrett Browning has made use of this superstition in her exquisite poem of ' Isobel's Child.' She thus writes—

> Dear Lord who spreadest out above
> Thy loving, transpierced hands to meet
> All lifted hearts with blessings sweet,—
> Pierce not my tender heart, my tender heart
> Thou madest tender! Thou who art
> So happy in Thy heaven alway,
> Take not mine only bliss away!'
>
> 'Mother, mother,
> Suffer me to go to Him.'
>
> 'Loose thy prayer and let me go
> To the place which loving is.'
>
> 'Wake nurse!' the lady said.
>
> 'I changed the cruel prayer I made,
> And bowed my meekened head and prayed
> That God would do His will.'
> 'He parted us;
> And His sun shows victorious
> The dead calm face, and I am calm,
> And Heaven is harkening a new psalm.'[2]

Many things continue to be done in daily life in a certain fixed

---

[1] *Notes and Queries*, Vol. IV., S. VIII., p. 506.

[2] E. Barrett Browning, *Poems*, Vol. I., p. 293, Ed. 1866.

way, solely because it has been the custom to do so, which could
be as well done in another; such as the glass in social intercourse
following the path of the sun instead of *withershins*, or the contrary
direction, which is deemed unlucky. The influence of custom is
specially dominant at births, marriages, and deaths, and other
important occurrences in life. The more important these occurrences are, the more do men continue to throw the requirements
of custom around them, lest the welfare of the person concerned
should be imperilled. It is still considered unlucky by many to
use a new cradle for a new-born infant; old cradles are therefore
in special request, and are constantly borrowed to avoid the
mysterious peril of using a new one. The family clock used to
be stopped when a death occurred in the house, and the looking-
glass was invariably (and perhaps still is) covered up in the
chamber where the dead lay. There were those in this neighbourhood, long after the beginning of the present century, who believed that a slip of rowan tree carried on their person dispelled
glamour, and rendered nugatory all the powers of sorcery and
witchcraft. This superstition is of very remote antiquity. In
Norse mythology the rowan is associated with the stealing of fire
from heaven; the traditions of which our Celtic and Teutonic
forefathers brought with them from the far east. The rowan,
in their belief, having sprung from a feather of the bird that stole
the fire. Its connection with an event of such supreme importance
to man as the acquisition of the use of fire, invested the rowan
with those mystic powers which superstition gathered round it.
This superstition continued to exert its power on men otherwise intelligent. Impelled by ancient custom, they bore on their
person on the eve of Mayday, a slip of rowan tied with red
thread (the red thread and the scarlet berries of the rowan
being typical of fire), as a charm against ill luck, and with an
undefined hope that it would avert evil from their flocks and
herds.[1] It is still an article of belief with some, that eggs must

---

[1] Kelly's *Indo-European Folklore*, pp. 161-168.

be set below a hen, or other fowl for a brood, when the tide is rising, and when the moon is on the increase, to make sure of the full tale of chickens. In the early years of the present century a horse-shoe was affixed to the mast of ships, to ensure safe and prosperous voyages, the belief being that it was a spell against which the machinations of witchcraft were powerless The horse-shoe is still to be seen nailed to doors in this neighbourhood; more, however, from old custom than from any fancied benefit.

A thousand years, or nearly so, have passed away since Odin was worshipped by the inhabitants of this island; and yet the magpie, which was sacred to him, is still invested with superstitious fears due to this cause. Notwithstanding better knowledge, uncomfortable misgivings, of which they cannot altogether divest themselves, still come over the minds of many, if, while on a journey they observe one of these birds crossing the road on which they are travelling. In the last generation, if two magpies were seen flying over a house in which a person lay ill, it was held to be a sure omen that the sufferer would not recover. 'She'll no get better,' was the saying (which living ears have heard), 'I saw twa piets flee ower the hoos this mornin.'

The vitality of old customs is specially observable on the occasion of a marriage. The author of 'Primitive Marriage,' in his able inquiry into the origin of marriage ceremonies, adduces the hurling of old shoes after the bridegroom when he takes away the bride from her maiden home, as a relic of the practice of obtaining a wife by capture;[1] the throwing of the shoes being a surviving symbol of the efforts that were made to detain the bride when seizure of one by violence was a reality. Whatever may have been the causes which rendered the obtaining of a bride by capture necessary, the practice seems to have been almost universal. The universality of the practice indicating a common cause. Relics of this custom prevailed in the celebration of marriages of ancient Greece and Rome. Symbols of it of more

---

[1] Maclennan, *Primitive Marriage*, p. 29. *Note.*

or less significancè are still found in the steppes of Tartary;
among the native races of America; in the interior of Africa;
among the hill tribe of the Khonds in Hindostan, and all over the
continent of Europe.   The ceremonies which still prevail in
Khondistan, and which until lately prevailed in Wales, are adduced by the same author as significant relics of marriage by
capture.   In Khondistan the young female companions of the
bride chase the bridal party, throwing stones at the head of the
bridegroom until he reaches the confines of his own village.   Lord
Kames says, that the following marriage ceremony was in his
day (1774), or at least had, till shortly before, been common among
the Welsh.   'On the morning of the wedding-day the bridegroom,
accompanied by his friends on horseback, demands the bride.   Her
friends who are likewise on horseback, give a positive refusal,
upon which a mock scuffle ensues.   The bride, mounted behind
her nearest kinsman, is carried off, and is pursued by the bridegroom and his friends with loud shouts.'   He is, however, suffered
to overtake her, and to carry her to his home in triumph.   'Two or
three hundred horsemen might have been seen in Wales on some
occasions engaged in this mock flight and pursuit.'[1]

In Scotland the mock capture of a bride, known as 'Riding the
Broose,' continued in this neighbourhood down to about 1820.   The
moment the bride left her home, mounted horsemen set off at full
speed, striving who would soonest reach the bridegroom's house,
and the first person to arrive there was said to have *won the Broose;*
a term of which no satisfactory etymology has been given.   Those
who can remember the 'Riding the Broose,' can testify that the head-
long gallop, to which Burns bears testimony in his 'Address to his
Auld Mare '—

> ' At Brooses thou had ne'er a fellow
> For pith and speed,'

was too noisy an episode to be forgotten, and it gave some indication of what a real capture must have been.

---

[1] Maclennan, *Primitive Marriage*, pp. 28, 29, 36, 37.

Marriages are now celebrated in this neighbourhood without this noisy relic of capture, but they are attended with customs of which no positive explanation can be given. The best-man (groomsman) and the bridesmaid go arm in arm to fetch the bridegroom, and conduct him (and afterwards the other guests) to the dwelling of the bride, where the marriage ceremony is performed, though less than a hundred years ago it was usually performed in the church. After the ceremony, and just as the newly married couple are leaving the house, a plate containing salt is at some marriages stealthily broken over the head of the bridegroom, and as they leave the door the customary shower of old shoes is thrown at them. The bride and bridegroom head the procession, they are followed by the bridesmaid and best-man, and the rest of the bridal party, all walking two and two, arm and arm, to the bridegroom's house, where a supper is prepared for the wedding guests. On the arrival of the bridal party at the bridegroom's house, his mother, or nearest female relative, breaks a cake of *shortbread* over the head of the bride as she sets her foot on the threshold, and throws the fragments to the door to be scrambled for by those who assemble outside on marriage occasions. A fragment of the cake is coveted by young maidens, to lay under their pillows at night, as a spell for ensuring dreams of those they love. It is deemed specially unlucky for a marriage party to take any by-path, or to turn back after they have once set out for their new home.

Keeping the highway holds equally true of funeral processions; by tacit consent they keep the old accustomed path. Kirk-roads, disused for most other purposes, continue to be used for funerals. To take any by-path would be held to be derogatory to the deceased. The good old custom of 'bidding' the friends and neighbours to a funeral, by the beadle going from door to door, is still practised in Newburgh. Formerly it was the custom for the beadle to walk before the coffin ringing a hand-bell, all the way to the churchyard. This practice was discontinued in Newburgh sometime between the years 1780-1790, but it continued in the neighbouring parish of Abdie down to a more recent period. The ringing of the church bell at a funeral was to give notice of the hour of 'lifting' to the neighbours, but in medieval times, super- stitions arose out of the practice, and the belief prevailed that evil spirits were driven away, and could not come within the sound of the bell.[1] The belief in the exorcising power of bells has totally disappeared; but the tolling of the great bell has continued un- interruptedly in Newburgh, and it is now the one solemnising public accompaniment of a Scottish funeral. One other outward token of respect still continues. If a wayfarer meets a funeral procession he reverently uncovers his head; and the same mark of respect is shown by the attendants the moment that the coffin is lowered into the grave, no other outward demonstration being exhibited. Women have long ceased to attend funerals in Scot- land. This is the more remarkable, as so late as the year 1715 they formed part of every funeral procession, walking in regular rank, as they still do in the north of England. The men, how- ever, in Scotland, walked in front and the women behind.[2] The disappearance of women from funerals in Scotland seems to have been so gradual, that no contemporary notice of it appears; and so utterly has their attendance on these occasions passed out of remembrance, that were they now to appear, their presence would excite comment and astonishment.

The enduring nature of old customs is nowhere so apparent as when they are linked with some day in the calendar. This is specially the case with Halloween, Hogmanay, and Handsel-Monday, the popular festivals in Newburgh and in other places in Scotland.

There are some features in the mode of keeping Halloween in Newburgh which are not touched upon by Burns in his celebrated poem; though several of the customs so inimitably described by him are still kept up amongst us. Nuts are burned; *kail-stocks* are pulled; young maidens carrying them home backwards, to

---

[1] Brand's *Popular Antiquities*, Vol. III., p. 217.
[2] *Selections from Ecclesiastial Records of Aberdeen*, p. lxix.

lodge them behind the door ; and the ordeal of the *luggies* is tried, in order to obtain, in vision, a glimpse of their future husbands. But besides these playful divinations, fire has always been an indispensable element on Halloweèn. Whin bushes were kindled on the hills and set a blazing ; and the most mischievous among the boys sometimes barricaded the door of a dwelling-house from the outside, and then through the keyhole filled the house with smoke, by blowing a hollowed *kail-runt*, filled with burning tow. Similar customs, in which fire predominated, were practised on Halloweèn in other localities. In the Highlands of Perthshire (A.D. 1835) the boys for weeks beforehand gathered *pob*, heather, and other inflammable materials in a great heap, to which they set fire on Halloweèn, with great rejoicing. The older folks came and looked on for a while, and before retiring, each of them took up a stone, and cast it into the blazing pile, leaving the boys to finish the revel. The constant use of fire on Halloweèn has led to the supposition that the customs in which it forms a part are relics of ordeal by fire. The practice (which is still continued here) of trying to catch with the teeth an apple fixed to one end of a rod with a lighted candle at the other, suspended from the ceiling and quickly twirled round, is believed by some to be a survival in sport of the ordeal by fire. The endeavour to catch with the mouth an apple floating in a tub in water, having the hands clasped behind the back, which is still a never failing accompaniment of Halloweèn, is believed on the same ground to be a survival of the ordeal by water.[1] But the special amusement of the boys in Newburgh was to arm themselves with *kail-runts*, and to run knocking with them at the doors of the houses as they passed ; a practice which was tolerated by the inmates on that special evening all the more readily, as the doors fifty years ago were for the most part of plain deal without paint. Observances of a similar kind prevailed all over Western Europe ; but what had degenerated in this neighbourhood into mere boyish licence,

---

[1] Henderson's *Folk Lore of the Northern Counties*, p. 75.

is still kept up in other countries in a form nearer to the original
practice. This is specially the case in Brittany; and the customs
now observed there, put side by side with those practised here,
like the piecing together of the fragments of an ancient manuscript, throw light on the apparently meaningless knocking at the
doors of the houses of Newburgh by the boys on Halloweèn. The
desire to pry into futurity, which is such a prominent feature of
the customs so felicitously described by Burns, indicates very
strongly that Halloweèn is of heathen origin. This appears
certain; but the observances kept up in Brittany clearly show,
that the clergy had at an early period endeavoured to divest it
of heathen practices, and had made the festival a means of im-
pressing on their flocks the reality of purgatory. On 'All Saints
Eve' [Halloweèn] 'in Brittany, crowds flock to the graveyards to
pray by the family graves, to fill with holy water the little hollows
left for this pious purpose in the Breton gravestones, and in some
places to offer libations of milk. All night masses for the dead
are said, and bells toll. . . . When supper has been eaten by
the living, in every house the cloth and the remains of supper are
left, that the souls of the dead may take their seat at the board,
and the fire is left burning on the hearth, that the dead may warm
their hands at the embers as they did when in life. . . . And
when the household are abed, weird wailings are heard outside the
door. 'These wailings are the songs of the parish poor, who on
this night represent the souls in purgatory.' The following are
some of the verses of their song :—

> 'When death knocks with his hands so thin,
> At midnight asking to come in,
> No heart but with a quake doth say
> Who is it death would take away?

> 'To wake you in this house that bide,
> To wake you old and young beside,
> If ruth, alack live under sky,
> For succour in God's name we cry!

'They that we fed upon the breast,
Long since to think of us have ceast ;
They that we held in our hearts' core
Hold us in loving thought no more!

' Up from your beds, and speedilie,
And throw yourselves on bended knee,
Save those whom ailments sore make lame,
Or death, already, calls by name!'

'Hearing this lamentable cry, the inmates rise from their beds, fall on their knees, and pray God for the departed, not forgetting their representatives—the poor at the door.'[1]

We have in these observances a full development of what the knocking on the doors in Newburgh on Halloweèn is a mere sportive relic.

Hogmanay, or Singin' E'en is, however, the festival which is most popular in Newburgh among the young. On this, the last evening of the year, the youth of both sexes, as in other parts of Scotland, go about disguised from house to house in bands, singing songs in every house they visit. The custom of going about disguised on the last night of the year, had its origin in pre-christian times, and is of great antiquity. The practice was vehemently denounced from the pulpit in the early ages of Christianity as a remnant of paganism. In the fifth century, Salvianus, a pious writer, inveighed against the custom in these terms:—'Men dress themselves up like women ; they put on their robes and assume their manners. They transform themselves into monsters, as if they were sorry they are men.' What was justly censurable at that time, as paying a lingering religious homage to heathenism (the intention constituting the guilt), has been softened down by the intervening centuries into harmless amusement and unobnoxious mirth. Many grave consultations are held by the young beforehand as to the special disguises to be worn

---

[1] *Ballads and Songs of Brittany*, Taylor, pp. 213–216.

on Singin' E'en, and it is looked forward to with impatience, and entered upon with a heartiness, which bespeaks thorough enjoyment. The young Guisers, a generation back, were rewarded with a ferl, (*feorth-dael*—Anglo Saxon fourth part) of oaten cake, many families specially baking them for the purpose. The dole is now mostly bestowed in money, which is paid to the purser of the band, and is divided equally at the conclusion of the evening's peregrinations. The songs sung are sometimes of a kind that are popular at the time, but old and enduring favourites, and old rude rhymes, which have been handed down orally for many generations, never fail to be also sung on that night. Among these latter, the following is the most common, and holds its place most tenaciously :—

> ' Rise up gudewife ! an' dinna be sweir,
> An' deal your gear as lang's you're here ;
> The day'll come whan ye'll be dead,
> An' ye'll hae naither meal nor bread.

> ' Lay by your stocks ! lay by your stools !
> Ye maunna think that we're fules ;
> We're bairns come to play,
> Gie's oor cakes an' lat's away.'

From those whose musical powers are not of a high order, the following rhyme, which sets both music and grammar at defiance is occasionally heard :—

> ' Round the midden I whuppit a geese ;
> I'll sing nae mair till I get a bit piece.'

These ditties are so rude that they may well provoke a smile, but they are part of the life of the people ; and though the festival is now mainly the province of the young, yet even to the old

> ' Pleasure hath not ceased to wait
> On these expected annual rounds.' [1]

---

[1] Wordsworth, Vol. III., p. 240.

Handsel-Monday (the first Monday of the new year) is, however, the great festival of the year in this neighbourhood. The name arose out of the custom of presenting gifts at the new year, the first gift being the receiver's *handsel*. This signification is most clearly expressed in the words *hand* and *syllan* (Old English), to give or clasp hands, in token of a concluded bargain. Handsel-Monday (where it is kept) holds socially the same place in Scotland that Christmas-day does in England; there is a cessation of all labour, but the day is not observed by all classes; religious observances form no part of it, and it has not that thorough hold on the whole nation that Christmas rejoicings have in England.

The most remarkable feature in the observance of Handsel-Monday in Newburgh, and which seems peculiar to the town, is the blowing of horns in the street by the boys the moment that the clock strikes the twelfth hour on Sunday night. They continue this unmelodious music until daylight, kindle bonfires, and a generation back removed tradesmen's signs to private dwellings, and perpetrated other mad pranks. The adherence of the boys to these old usages is a striking instance of the toughness of long-descended customs. Those who would not lose an hour's sleep on any other occasion, conceal themselves from their friends, that they may go out on an inclement winter night, to be ready to begin the old demonstration at the exact hour.

These peculiar customs have their root in beliefs and usages prevalent in remote antiquity. That they are of heathen origin is placed beyond a doubt, by the denunciations uttered against their observance by zealous bishops, more than a thousand years ago. In the fifth century, St Maximus of Turin, raised his voice against the superstitious follies of the 1st of January, 'when Christians put on habits of intemperance, and seek to forestal their friends with early visits in the morning, bringing them petty presents as New-Year's gifts.[1] St Eligius, Bishop of Noyon, preached against them in the ninth century: 'Above all,' he says,

---

[1] Quoted *Notes and Queries*, 4th *Series*, Vol. VI., p. 493.

'I implore you not to observe the sacrilegious customs of the pagans. . Let no one do on the kalends of January those forbidden, ridiculous, ancient, and disreputable things, such as dancing or keeping open house at night, or getting drunk.'[1]

The chief redeeming feature of Hansel-Monday is the reunion of families; but there is no bond uniting all classes in a common brotherhood, such as the celebration of the birth of the Saviour of men gives in countries where Christmas is observed. It required the long continued exercise of ecclesiastical discipline to extirpate the observance of Christmas in Scotland. The folks of Perth and Aberdeen required stringent measures to compel them to desist from their wonted celebrations.[2] The following extracts from Aberdeen Kirk Session Records are instances of this:—'10th January 1575-6. The said day, the haill deacones of craftes within this burt, ar ordanit to tak trial of thair craftes *respective* for sitting ydill on Yoill day last wes, and to gif answer thairin on Thuirsday nixt.'[3] Nearly eighty years later the following occurs in the same Records:—'12th January 1657. Compearit John Cowtes, and also compearit Patrick Murray, baxter, and declaired that the said John Cowtes said to William Smart, his servitor, quhen he was biddenne work with his mill one Yule day, he wished that the baxtar boyes brake ther legges that bade him worke one Yuillday, and that he wold worke none till Twyseday thaireftir, notwithstanding the mill was not broken, as wes alledgit be him, but able for grindeing.' Other witnesses appearing and testifying to the same effect, the session 'apoints the said Johne Cowtes to appear before the pulpit and to be rebuked therfor.' He did not appear on the two succeeding Sundays, but there was no escape from the sentence, as continued refusal would have led to excommunication, and excommunication would have deprived

---

[1] Quoted Ferguson's *Folk Lore of the Northern Counties*, p. 23.

[2] *Book of the Universal Kirk*, pp. 334, 374. Chambers's *Domestic Annals*, Vol. I., pp. 326, 327.

[3] Spalding Club, *Seclections from Aberdeen Kirk Session Records*, p. 21.

him of all employment. We therefore read in the same Records:—
'2d February 1657. John Cowtes yesterday publictlie rebuked for
refuseing to grinde flower on Yuleday, conforme to former Acts.'[1]
The suppression of Christmas in Scotland has been attended with
this effect, that it has left to the people festivals which have
degenerated into occasions for mere indulgence, unredeemed by
any opportunity for the expression of these higher impulses which
religion fosters and affords. There has grown up around Christmas
in those countries where it is religiously observed, kindly feelings
which foster the best traits of which our nature is capable. In
Sweden, on Christmas eve, just before the sun goes down, even
the very poorest peasant puts a small sheaf of corn on a high pole
near his house, or on the house itself, that the little birds may
feast and rejoice on the anniversary of Christ's coming into the
world.[2] Such kindly offshoots of the Christmas festival humanize
and bless; for truly

'He prayeth well, who loveth well
Both man and bird and beast.

He prayeth best, who loveth best
All things both great and small;
For the dear God who loveth us,
He made and loveth all.'[3]

The improvements in manufactures effected by machinery have
produced great changes in the clothing of the people. Fifty years
ago tailors went from house to house to make up home-made cloth
into garments, which were not always of the most artistic shape,
new fashions penetrating slowly. Up to the year 1820 some old
men continued to wear and go to church with the broad blue
bonnet, which was universal (excepting among the wealthy), in
the second half of the preceding century. Later still, onwards

---

[1] Spalding Club, *Selections from Aberdeen Kirk Session Records*, pp. 138, 139.
[2] Loyd's *Peasant Life in Sweden*, p. 168.
[3] Coleridge's Poems, *Ancient Mariner*.

to 1830 (what would now be considered a strange apparition), old women went to church wearing white linen caps or mutches, with a scarlet or bright tartan plaid thrown over the head and falling over the shoulders. Others wore a white woollen mantle of the Spanish type, and a white muslin cap tied with a silken snood. The disappearance, one by one, of these old women from their accustomed stools in the Church, from which they were rarely absent, broke a link which has severed us from preceding generations.

Down to about the year 1830 the spinning-wheel enabled old women to maintain themselves in honest independence. But they required to exercise many thrifty expedients, of which the present generation have no knowledge. It was common then, in the dearth of coals, or *eldin*, as they named fuel, to make peats of coal-dross and cow-dung, and to dry them in the sun to help their scanty fires. *Sowens*, which Burns tells us was the dainty provided for supper on Halloweèn (prepared, however, on that special evening with butter instead of milk), and which, he says, 'Set a' their gabs a-steerin,' are now almost as mythical as the heather-ale of the Picts. The art of making sowens is now all but forgotten; and yet out of what is now thrown away they were prepared in almost every family two generations ago. A lady, who died in Newburgh in the year 1860, at the advanced age of 92, used to tell that when the winter *mart* was killed, her mother strung the marrow-bones together and hung them up, ready to be lent to the cottars to make kail-broth for their families. 'Sabine fare, which could not long ward off vigorous hunger.' She also used to say that her mother attended to the ailments of the poor, and that one of her prescriptions for diseases of the throat was to sew a living caterpillar between two plies of flannel, leaving the animal sufficient room to crawl, and then to tie the flannel around the neck of the person affected. This cure was prescribed in other parts of the country for hooping-cough; the belief being that as the worm died the cough disappeared.[1]

---

[1] Henderson, *Folk Lore of the Northern Counties*, p. 110.

Long after the middle of the last century, the dainty provided for friends and neighbours on the occasion of the birth of a child, was oatmeal cakes crumbled and fried in butter, which were named butter-saps. To say that you had partaken of these saps in a house, was equivalent to saying that a birth had occurred in the family. At that time, and long afterwards, ale was the universal beverage in Scotland. The brewsteads, of which the names or foundations remains in almost every hamlet throughout the country, testify to this. It would then have been as uncommon to have asked for a glass of whisky in a public-house in Newburgh, as it would now be to ask for a glass of wine. The early literature of Scotland incidentally testifies to ale being the national drink, and ancient records corroborate it. In the Royal Household Books of James IV., the following occurs, A.D. 1512. 'Friday, the Seller [cellarer] spendit IX. gallonis aill. Item, for wyne X^d. Setterday spendit V. gallonis, ij quartis aill. Item, coft iiij gallonis aill, pryce VT. iiijd. Sonday XXIX August the seller coft lviij gallonis aill, pryce iij lib xvis iijd and spendit viii gallonis iij quarts. Item, for wyne Xd.'[1] The small quantity of wine provided shows the preponderance of ale even in the royal household. From the close connection of Scotland with France, claret and other French wines was largely used in Scotland,[2] and they continued in use for a considerable period after the union with England; but even when that connection was closest, ale was the staple beverage. In the time of James V., Sir David Lyndsay in his 'Satyre of the Thrie Estaitis,' makes an Abbot say of his Abbey :—

> 'There is na monks from Carrick to Carraill
> That fairs better, and drinks mair helsum aill.'[3]

In the reign of Mary, the allowance for the Queen's table 'at

---

[1] *National Manuscripts of Scotland*, Part III., No. X.
[2] Joseph Robertson, *Proceedings of Society of Antiquaries*, Vol. III., p. 424.
[3] Lyndsay's *Poetical Works*, Ed. 1871., Vol. II., p. 264.

dinner and supper was vi. quartis white wine and ale.' At the
table of the Master of the Household, the allowance was a pint of
ale and wine; at the next table the sole beverage allowed was
ale.[1] Four hundred years ago town councillors in Newburgh
were fined a gallon of ale for non-attendance. Two hundred and
fifty years later, kirk sessions supplied ale for the Lychwakes of
paupers. Even the burial of a pauper child could not take place
without an allowance of this beverage. The following extract
from Abdie Kirk Session Records is an instance of this:—' 1721,
December 3. To Robert Stuart for ale at the burial of a poor
child, 01 .. 02 .. 00.' Numerous other entries of a similar kind
occurs. Allan Ramsay, in an epitaph on a noted 'Browster wife,'
in his time, says—

> ' Hast thou left to bairns o thine,
>   The pauky knack
> O brewing ale amaist like wine,
>   That gar'd us crack.' [2]

Later still (1787) Burns declares ale to be

> ' The life o' public haunts.'

And from numerous passages in his poems we learn that it was
the customary drink of the people on all social occasions, of which
that memorable night that ' Tam got planted unco richt,' when

> ' The night drave on wi sangs and clatter,
>   An' aye the ale was growing better,' [4]

is enduring evidence.

Ale was displaced by the taxes imposed on malt in the end of
the last century, which increased the cost and interfered with its
production. This interference with the accustomed beverage of

---

[1] *National Manuscripts of Scotland*, Part III., No. XLII.
[2] Ramsay's Poems, *Maggie Johnston's Epitaph.*
[3] Burns' Poems, *Scotch Drink.*   [4] Burns' Poems, *Tam O' Shanter.*

the people was the cause of much irritation; and the lines in Burns' song—

'We'll mak our maut, we'll brew our drink,'
We'll laugh, sing, and rejoice man,'[1]

were only the embodiment of the public feeling at the time. Most families in the country of any consequence, brewing ale for household use.[2] To obviate the increased cost of malt, ale was made weaker and less exhilarating, and whisky, which was allowed to be sold in public-houses with a lower licence, gradually came into general use.

Modern inventions have within the last generation silently displaced articles of household use, which are now as obsolete as the stone implements of former ages. The flint-and-steel, which five and twenty years ago, was in every house, and which has been the fire-producer for immemorable ages, now stands in need of explanation to the rising generation; and the primitive cruisie, with its wick of *rashie-rind* (pith of rushes), the sole light of every weaver, and of most of the householders in Newburgh thirty-five years ago, is now utterly unknown.[3]

The facilities for travelling which are now available, have also made, and are making, many inroads on old habits and modes of living. Those who cannot look back to the time anterior to the introduction of these facilities, can form no adequate conception of the quiet flow and unruffled current of life in small communities fifty years ago. There were at that period itinerant preachers, who went from place to place exercising their calling for a livelihood. When one of these worthies appeared, dressed in his rusty

---

[1] Burns' Poems, *The Deil's awa wi' the Exciseman.*

[2] Chambers's *Book of Days*, Vol. I., p. 372.

[3] The discovery of the art of producing fire at will, was of momentous import. It relieved man from the dread of losing the use of fire, and an expeditious mode of producing it was justly deemed a conquest for the whole human race; the mythology of most nations exhibit traces of it.—*Kelly's Folk Lore*, p. 40.

suit of black, a little knot of working men would gather around him, and after having settled with the preacher whether it was to be a sermon of Logan or of Blair, he would lay down his hat to receive their contributions, mount the pedestal of the Cross, or some convenient *Loupin-on-stane*, and then proceed with the delivery of his discourse, which was gravely listened to, to the end.

There was at that time no public conveyance from Newburgh for travellers by land. Husband and wife rode to church and market on one horse, the wife sitting behind on a pad, and there was a Loupin-on-stane at almost every door, to enable her to mount to her seat. Loupin-on-stanes were frequently of a single block or boulder, but many of them were built. The following extract from the Council Books of Newburgh shows the importance that was attached to the possession of one of these conveniences :—

'20ᵗʰ March 1728. The said day upon a petition given in by George Grant, Vintner in Newburgh, To ye baillies and Councill, met in Councill, for ye liberty of building a loŭping on ston at the south side of the house in Newburgh he possesses. By plurality of vots of Councill it was condescended and agreed upon that the said liberty be granted to him, provided he goe not farder than six foot from the root of ye wall of his house in building ye said loŭping on ston, and that he build nothing else there than a louping on ston, and also that provided for the said Liberty, and before ye said loŭping on ston [is built] he pay in for behove of ye Common good of ye burgh thrie pound scots, or lay a sufficient Cassy without ye said louping on Ston as far as his house goes that shall satisfy them as to ye sufficiency yrof, and that before ye building of ye said loŭping on ston, and that it shall be in ye option of ye baillies and Councill, either to take ye Crown from ye said George Grant, so obleidge him to lay ye said Cassy as said is, for ye said liberty so granted him. William Anderson, Matthew Lyell.'

Newspapers, fifty years ago, were the luxury of the rich. The minister of the parish, and one or two others got a paper twice or thrice, but mostly once, a week. These newspapers were afterwards read by other families. Working-men clubbed together for the purchase of a paper, which was handed from one to another, until it had been perused by a dozen or more readers. The ballads sold by wandering singers, and the broad-sheets which were sold by itinerant venders, proclaiming them through the town, especially the dying speeches of those who suffered death at the hands of the public executioner, were the periodic literature of the people, and were eagerly bought by them. From a statement drawn up at the time, we learn that the revenue derived from letters received by post in Newburgh in 1801, was £137, 6s. 6d. Calculating the postage of each letter at sixpence (a low rate, as letters from Edinburgh before the reduction of postage were $7\frac{1}{2}$d., from Glasgow $8\frac{1}{2}$d., and from London 1s. $2\frac{1}{2}$d.), we find that only fifteen letters on an average were then received daily by the whole town and neighbourhood. Even assuming an average rate of 4d., the daily number of letters received did not exceed twenty.

The contrast is now great. What was the privilege of the few little more than half-a-century ago, is now the heritage of the many. Showers of periodic publications now find their way into the most secluded hamlets. Science has extended her domain, curtailing the region of superstition, and ameliorating the condition of man. The present generation enjoys advantages which their grandfathers knew not of. The unexampled freedom and the blessings which we now enjoy, are the long, slow growth of ages; and the foregoing pages will have failed in their purpose, if they do not beget a more intelligent reverence of the past; a juster sense of what we owe to our forefathers, and a stronger attachment to the beneficent laws and institutions which they have handed down to us. These blessings, and the exceeding

C C

grandeur of the scene amid which Lindores Abbey and its Burgh of Newburgh are placed, are sufficient, and ought to inspire every native and denizen of the Burgh with a deeper and more active interest in its welfare and prosperity; and they amply justify us in applying to them the valedictory lines of the poet, with which we conclude.

'Fair Land! by Time's parental love made free,
  By social order's watchful arms embraced;
  With unexampled union meet in thee,
  For eye and mind, the present and the past;
  With golden prospect for futurity,
  If that be *reverenced* which ought to last.'[1]

---

[1] Wordsworth's *Poems*, Ed. 1857, Vol. IV., p. 145.

WINDOW IN GABLE OF DUNDEMORE CHAPEL.

APPENDIX.

No. I., p. 130.

THE FAMILY OF LESLIE, LORDS LINDORES.

THE family of Leslie of Ballinbriech, seems to have acquired an interest in the temporalities of Lindores Abbey immediately after the Reformation, for, ' in 1561, Andrew, Earl of Rothes, oblessis hymself, as fermorar of the fruits of the Abbay of Lindores, to pay William Symson, minister in Ebdie, iiij^{xx} li. yeirly.'[1] Sir Patrick Leslie of Pitcairlie, commendator of, and afterwards first Lord Lindores, was the second son of Earl Andrew, who was fourth Earl of Rothes. Sir Robert Sibbald, in his History of Fife says, ' north of Lumwhat and in a glen is Pitcairlie, an old Tower, of old the seat of Patrick Leslie, first Lord Lindores.' The ' old Tower' still forms part of the present mansion-house, and bears marks of having been erected about the end of the 14th century. The estate of Pitcairlie formed part of the great Lordship of Abernethy. Sir Alexander of Abernethy, somewhere between 1296 and 1314 A.D., gave the lands of Petcarlingis in the barony of Ballynbriech, to Sir John de Moravia of Tullybardine. This grant was confirmed by David II. at Elgyne on the 7th December, in the thirty-third year of his reign [1362].[2] Sir Alexander of Abernethy joined the band of patriots who opposed the ambitious attempts of Edward I. on Scotland, and took up arms in concert with the brave Sir Simon Frazer, but latterly he espoused the cause of Edward.[3] On the success of Bruce's arms, the immense estates of Sir Alexander were confiscated, and in the fifteenth year of his reign Bruce gave ' to his beloved son Robert, the lands of Alexander Abernethy, and of Margaret

---

[1] Scott's *Fasti Scoticanæ*, Vol. II., Part 2.

[2] Robertson's *Index of Charters*, 72, 29.

[3] *Historical Documents, Illustrative of the History of Scotland*, Vol. II., pp. 431, 490.

his daughter and ane of his three aires, by reason of his forefaltrie.'[1] The lands of Pitcairlie reverted to the descendants of Sir Alexander of Abernethy, for the barony of Ballinbriech, of which Pitcairlie forms a part, and that of Cairnie in Perthshire, and of Rothes in the county of Elgin, came into the possession of the family of Leslie by the marriage of their ancestor Sir Andrew Leslie, *circa* 1312, with Mary, one of the daughters and coheiresses of Sir Alexander of Abernethy. Andrew, fourth Earl of Rothes bestowed the lands of Pitcairlie and other estates on his second son Patrick, who is thenceforth styled of Pitcairlie.

I. Sir Patrick Leslie, first Lord Lindores, married Lady Jane Stewart, daughter of Robert, Earl of Orkney, and had issue ·—

1. Patrick, his successor.

2. James, who succeeded his brother Patrick as third Lord Lindores.

3. Robert, who had a nineteen years' lease of the revenues of the Bishopric of Orkney, 1641. He married and had issue, but his male line is extinct.

4. Ludovic. He entered the service of Gustavus Adolphus, and attained the rank of Colonel in his army. On his return to Scotland he was appointed to the important post of Governor of Berwick Castle. He bought ' the Reid Insche,' now Mugdrum Island, from William Oliphant of Balgonie in 1647, and the lands and fortalice of Mugdrum in 1648 from George Orme. He sold them both to William Arnot in 1663. He died unmarried.

5. David, the most distinguished of the family, also entered the service of Gustavus Adolphus, and speedily rose to distinction. On the breaking out of the unhappy civil and religious wars in Britain, he returned to Scotland, and was immediately appointed Major-General of the army sent into England under the Earl of Leven in 1644, to the assistance of the English Parliamentary forces. He effectually stopped the brilliant career of the Marquis of Montrose by the decisive victory he gained over him at Philiphaugh. He was present at Newark on Trent when Charles I. came into the Scottish camp a disguised fugitive. At a subsequent period of his career he accepted the command of the army raised to oppose Cromwell, where, with inferior numbers, he shut him up in Dunbar, and but for interference with his plans would have compelled Cromwell to submit. Leslie's better judgment was overborne, and he was defeated and retired to Stirling with the

---

[1] Robertson's *Index of Charters*, 15, 3.

fragment of his forces. He took command under Charles II., only to sustain defeat at the battle of Worcester in 1651. Leslie was captured in Yorkshire, on his way to Scotland, and was sent to the Tower, where he lay a prisoner for nine years. At the Restoration he was created Lord Newark with a pension of five hundred pounds a-year. Those who had been unflinchingly loyal during the whole period of the Civil war, spoke and felt bitterly at the bestowal of these honours on General Leslie, who only latterly joined the cause of the King. In 1649 he purchased the lands of Abercrombie and St Monans. The purchase is thus quaintly recorded in Lamont's Diary: 'This yeare David Lesly L. Generall of the forces standing for the tyme in this kingdome bought the lands of Abercrombie and St Monan's in Fyfe from James Sandielands L. [Lord] Abercrombie, a ryotous youth, who spent ane old estate in the space of 4 or 5 yeares.' The ruins of the Castle of Newark, from which General Leslie took his title, still stand on a rock overhanging the Firth of Forth. He died in 1682, and was succeeded by his only son David, second Lord Newark, who left no male issue. Jean, the eldest daughter of the second Lord Newark, who married Sir Alexander Anstruther, fifth son of Sir Philip Anstruther of Anstruther assumed the title of Baroness Newark; and after her death her sons William and Alexander successively took the title of Lord Newark; but in the elections of Peers their votes were objected to on the ground that the original patent restricted the title to heirs male. The House of Lords sustained the objection A.D. 1793, and the title is in consequence now extinct.

Patrick, first Lord Lindores, left five daughters:—

1. Elizabeth, married to Sir William Sinclair of Moy.
2. Jane, married to John Forbes of Leslie.
3. Margaret, married to John, second Lord Maderty.

The following love sonnet addressed to this lady by the courtly poet Sir Robert Ayton, appears among his published works. It incidentally shows that Lord Lindores and his family resided at Lindores Abbey; though, as will afterwards be seen, Patrick, second Lord Lindores, died at Pitcairlie.

> 'Religious relics of that ruinous place,
> Which sometime gloried in the glore of saints,
> Now hath no glore but one, whereof it vaunts,
> That one saint's beauty makes it heav'n of grace.

> In balmy fields which fards her flow'ry face
> With sweet perfumes of corns, of trees, of plants,
> And laughs for joy such beauty to embrace ;
> Bear me record, that while I passed by,
> I did my duteous homage to your dame ;
> How thrice I sighed, thrice on her name did cry,
> Thrice kissed the ground for honour of the same,
>   There left those lines to tell her, on a tree,
>   That she made them to live, and me to die.'

4. Janet, married to Sir John Cunningham of Broomhill.
5. Mary, married to Sir David Barclay of Cullairny.

II. Patrick Leslie, second Lord Lindores was served heir to his uncle the Hon. Andrew Leslie of Lumbenny, in five seventh-parts of the town and lands of Eister Lumbennene on the 19th April 1609.[1] He was a dissolute man, and squandered the revenues and estates of Lindores Abbey in riotous and profligate living. He sold most of the abbey estates in the north to his brother-in-law, John Forbes of Leslie.[2] Among the archives of Mugdrum there are documents which show that within fifteen years after his accession to the title and estates, he granted innumerable obligations and bonds over his lands to raise money, which ultimately comprised his whole estate. Sir James Balfour records that Patrick Lesley, Lord of Londors, died at Pitcairlie on ' Sunday 12 August 1649, about 3 in the afternoone.' He was never married, but he had a numerous issue of illegitimate sons and daughters. Contrary to the prevailing custom of keeping the corpse many days unburied, Sir James records that ' Lord Lindores' was interrid priuately at the east end of Neuburghe Church, one Tuesday in the night the 14 of the same monthe.'[3]

Mr John Bayne, writer to the signet, raised a process of apprising for money advanced to Lord Lindores, and by a decision of the Court of · Session he obtained on the 20th February 1667, an order for infeftment in the estate, which belonged ' to the deceased Patrick, Lord Lindores.' Pitcairlie subsequently came into the possession of the family of Cathcart of Carbiston in Ayrshire, and it is now the residence and property of Robert Carthcart, Esq., the representative of that family.

---

[1] *Fife Retours*, No. 200.
[2] *Historical Records of the Family of Leslie*, Vol. II., p. 191.
[3] Balfour's *Annals*, Vol. III., p. 425.

III. James, second son of Patrick, Commendator of Lindores, first Lord Lindores, succeeded his brother Patrick as third Lord Lindores in 1649. He was a man of estimable character, but he inherited little more than the title. He married, first, a daughter of Ormestone of Ormestone, but had no issue by her. He married, secondly, Mary, third daughter of Lord Gray, by whom he had a son :—

1. John.

He married, thirdly, Miss Clepburn, by whom he had a daughter.

2. Hon. Jane married first, to John Stewart of Innernytie, and secondly to John Bruce of Blairhall.

James, third Lord Lindores died abroad before 20th July 1667, and was succeeded by his son :—

IV. John, fourth Lord Lindores. By the interest of John, Duke of Rothes, John, Lord Lindores, obtained a grant of the house and grounds of Lindores, and some portions of the property around the Abbey, and he got a charter to the same 1st August 1694, to himself in liferent, and to his son David, Master of Lindores, in fee. He married, first, Lady Marion Ogilvie, daughter of James, second Earl of Airlie, and relict of James Elphinston, Lord Cowper. By her he had a son :—

1. David, who became fifth Lord Lindores.

He married, secondly, Jane Gibson, relict of Sir Hugh Macculloch of Pilton, in the county of Edinburgh, but had no children by her. He died in 1706, and was succeeded by his only son —;

V. David, fifth Lord Lindores. He married Margaret, daughter of Archibald Stewart of Dunearn, relict of Archibald Stewart of Burray. Having no issue, he executed, on the 18th December 1718, a disposition bearing that being desirous to settle what remained of his estate of Lindores in the best manner for the preservation of the memory of the family, he settled the estate on Dame Jane Leslie, grand-daughter of David, first Lord Newark, and great grand-daughter of the Commendator.

David, fifth Lord Lindores, and the last in the direct line, died in July 1719. Dame Jane Leslie, with consent of her husband, Sir Alexander Anstruther, conveyed the estate of Lindores to Alexander Leslie of Quarter, in the parish of Burntisland, great-grandson of Sir John Leslie of Newton, brother of Patrick Leslie, the Commendator, who assumed the title.

VI. Alexander, sixth Lord Lindores, was Lieutenant in the 3d Regiment of Foot Guards in 1734, Captain in 1745. Had the rank of Major-General in the army in 1761, and was appointed Colonel of the 41st Regiment of Foot in 1764. He died at London in August 1765, and was buried at Chel sea on the 3d September following. He married Jane, niece of Sir James Campbell of Aberuchill, by whom he had a son :—

VII. Francis John, seventh Lord Lindores, had a company in the Marine forces in 1757. He died on 30th June 1775, and was buried at Hackney on the 4th July following.

On the death of Francis John, seventh Lord Lindores, the title was claimed by the Leslies of Lumquhat, who were descended from James Leslie third son of Sir John Leslie of Newton, brother of the Commendator. James Leslie acquired Lumquhat in 1669, and had a son, Captain John Leslie, who was served heir to his father in 1706. From an entry in Abdie Session Records, we learn that John Leslie of Lumquhat, married Mrs Mary Gibb, Lady Ormeston, on the 14th January 1703. Captain John Leslie was succeeded by his son John, who married Janet, daughter of Arnot of Woodmilne, by whom he had a son, born 1723. He was an officer in Gardiner's Dragoons, and took an active part in the army of the royalists, under William, Duke of Cumberland, and long survived that period. He married Antonia, daughter of Barclay of Cullairnie, by whom he had nine children, of whom John Leslie of Lumquhat, the eldest son, who was served heir to his father 2d February 1774, assumed the title of Lord Lindores. He was present, and voted at the elections of Peers on the 17th October 1780, and on 8th May 1784, and on 28th March 1787. But at the General Election 24th July 1790, his votes were objected to, and the House of Lords, 6th June 1793, resolved that ' the votes given by the Lord Lindores at the said election were not good.' The Title is therefore disallowed, because the Lords held that the patent limited the honours to heirs-male of the body and not to heirs-male whomsoever, as was contended. According to this decision David, fifth Lord, was the last who had a legal right to the title. John Leslie, the last heir male of the family of Lumquhat, married 22d March 1789, Janet, youngest daughter and co-heiress of Sir Thomas Reeve of Hendens, in Berkshire, and died 4th May 1814, without issue.

The following are the names of the other children of John Leslie and Antonia Barclay :—

1. Elizabeth, born 5 March 1745, and died in 1802.

2. Hugina was born 15 March 1746. She attained the great age of one hundred years and one month, and was the last survivor of the house of Lumquhat. Miss Leslie was of a cheerful and most benevolent disposition ; no needy or helpless sufferer was ever allowed to leave her door

without receiving more or less relief. She died at Cupar in Fife on the 22d April 1846.

3. Jane, killed by a fall in infancy.

4. John, who assumed the title of Lord Lindores.

5. David, drowned at sea.

6.-9. Norman and three others, who all died in infancy.

Elizabeth Leslie, the eldest daughter, was the only member of the Lumquhat family who left issue. She married Captain Hewan of the 4th Dragoon Guards, a gentleman belonging to Yorkshire, and had by that marriage six sons and seven daughters :—

1. Thomas Barstow Hewan, Captain 25th Regiment of Foot, killed in action with the French troops at Granada 3d April 1795.

2. John, died in the West Indies. Had a son John, whose son Archibald Hewan is now a physician in London.

3. Joseph, Captain in the army, died in Ireland.

4. David, Captain 21st Regiment of Foot, died in Edinburgh 1818. His daughter, Helen Hewan resides in Liverpool.

5. Michael, Captain 95th Rifle Regiment, severely wounded at Tolouse, 1814, died 1818.

6. George died in infancy. The daughters were ·—

1. Antonia.

2. Helen, married —— Thomson, a physician.

3. Elizabeth died unmarried.

4. Anne, married —— Duff.

5. Louisa, married Rev. William Archdall. Her son is Rev. John Archdall of Newton-Barry, Ireland.

6. Catharine died in infancy.

7. Mary, married —— Findlater, she died at Portobello in 1870. Had a daughter, Elizabeth Leslie, who died in Edinburgh in 1863, leaving an account of her ancestors in manuscript, and besides other poems set to music, one of thirty stanzas, written in old Scotch, founded on the bestowal of the title of Lord Lindores.

No. II., p. 132.

THE reference at page 132 is made to the Rental marked Appendix No. III. (which immediately follows this); but as the following Rental is of an earlier date, it is inserted here. It, as well as No. III., is preserved in Mugdrum Charter Chest. Judging from the style of the handwriting, the old 'Rentaill' was to all appearance drawn up about the end of the 15th century. The paper on which it is written bears a maker's mark (an open hand) that prevailed about the year 1480. The 'Rentaill' is in the form of a book, and is covered with a leaf of an old service book (of parchment) of an early date, the penmanship of which is most beautiful, and the initial letters are illuminated. At the end of the volume the scribe has written

> ' In my defence, god me defend,
> and bring my sawel to ane good end,
> In quhen I am sike and lyk to dei,
> the son of god haive mynd of me. '

The Rentaill of the Abbey of Lundoris into the northe as followis of the barrones of Fyntres and Wranghame.

In premis Cregtone,	viij$^{\text{lib.}}$	vj$^{\text{s.}}$	viij$^{\text{d.}}$
Kyrkhill, Flenderis,	xxiij$^{\text{lib.}}$		
Crystis kirk, Hedderlek, Inche,	xxix$^{\text{lib.}}$	xiiij$^{\text{s.}}$	viij$^{\text{d.}}$
Lergies,	iij$^{\text{lib.}}$	vj$^{\text{s.}}$	viij$^{\text{d.}}$
Tylliemorgane,	xvj$^{\text{lib.}}$		
Wranghame, Newtone,	iij^{xx}vj$^{\text{lib.}}$	vj$^{\text{s.}}$	viij$^{\text{d.}}$
Wilyemsone, Heddenhame,	xlviij$^{\text{lib.}}$	xiij$^{\text{s.}}$	iiij$^{\text{d.}}$
Mylne of Willemsone, withe the pertinentis,	vj$^{\text{lib.}}$	xiij$^{\text{s.}}$	iiij$^{\text{d.}}$
Pow quhit,	xxiiij$^{\text{lib.}}$	v$^{\text{s.}}$	viij$^{\text{d.}}$
Mellensyde,	xxviij$^{\text{lib.}}$	ix$^{\text{s.}}$	viij$^{\text{d.}}$
Kirktowne of Colsamond,	viij$^{\text{lib.}}$	iiij$^{\text{s.}}$	vj$^{\text{d.}}$
Premmey vne fewit,	vj$^{\text{lib.}}$		
Logie dornocht one fewit payit,	xl$^{\text{lib.}}$	xiij$^{\text{s.}}$	iiij$^{\text{d.}}$

Ane costome mart; iiij. vodderis: iiij. bollis malt; iiij. bollis aittis; iiij. dusone powtrey.

The Rentaill of the barony of Fynteis. [*Fyntry.*]

In premis Logiefyntry,	viij$^{\text{lib.}}$		
Eister Disblair,	xvj$^{\text{lib.}}$	xj$^{\text{s.}}$	
Myddil Disblair,	xxiiij$^{\text{lib.}}$	v$^{\text{s.}}$	iiij$^{\text{d.}}$

Wester Disblair,	xxiiij$^{lib.}$		
Monkegie.			
West Bynd,	xix$^{lib.}$	xiij$^{s.}$	iiij$^{d.}$
Kilmvkis,	xxj$^{lib.}$	ix$^{s.}$	ij$^{d.}$
Heddervek Bawethene,	xvi$^{lib.}$	xiij$^{s.}$	iiij$^{d.}$
Mylne of Fyntry, .	vij$^{lib.}$	v$^{s.}$	viij

Vne fewit the Haltone of Fyntry.

viij plewis everilk pluche, pays of maill iiij merkis.

ane quarter cvstome mart.

ane cwstome wodder.

iiij caponeis. viij powtrey.

ij ferlotis cvstome malt.

vj ferlettis costome meill.

ij bollis costome aittis withe fodder, withe hareage and carrage.

Westar Fyntrey viij plewis vnefewit.

everilk pluche payit iiij merkis.

Ane quartar cvstome mert.

ane cvstome mert.

iiij caponeis ; viij powtrey.

ij ferlottis cvstome malt.

vj ferlottis cvstome meill.

ij bollis cvstome aittis withe fodder, with harrage and carrage.

The medowis withe the thre aikrs of the Wod, vij$^{lib.}$ xiij$^{s.}$ iiij$^{d.}$

Lang Crvk.

Baddeforra vne-fewit payit in maill and teynd silver, viij$^{lib.}$

iiij caponeis, viij powtrey with harrage and carrage

The annewellis of Kyllar, Balhagertei and Indorrowry, xiij$^{lib.}$ vj$^{s.}$ viij$^{d.}$

The mylne of Leslei, xxvj$^{s.}$ viij$^{d.}$

The rentaill of the Mernes and Angus.

Item the hall of Witstones. fysche hill. Hilend,	xxvj$^{lib.}$	xvj$^{s.}$	viij$^{d.}$
Litil Vitstone, .	vij$^{lib.}$	xviij$^{s.}$	x$^{d.}$
Nedder Vitstones and Pettenhous,	xxix$^{lib.}$	ij$^{s.}$	viij$^{d.}$
Scotstone and Marcarey. Offeciaris landis. meill	xxij$^{lib.}$	xvij$^{s.}$	viij$^{d.}$
Ardoche, .	viij$^{lib.}$	xiij$^{s.}$	viij$^{d.}$
The annewellis of Bervay,		viij$^{s.}$	
The annewellis of Mvnrois, .		iij$^{s.}$	
The cley pottis, and ferretone, .	xi$^{lib.}$	xix$^{s.}$	iiij$^{d.}$
Westar Cregy set to David Wodderburnis, .		xiiij merkis.	
Hiltone and Myltoune of cregy set in few,		xvj$^{lib.}$	
Balmaw fewit for		xv$^{lib.}$	

xij geis, xxxvj powtre.
withe harrag and carrage.
tempill hilend,   xj$^{s.}$ xij capones.
Inderrarettie, .   iij$^{lib.}$ vj$^{s.}$ viij$^{d.}$
The annewellis of Dundy,   vj$^{lib.}$ vj$^{s.}$

The Feddellis.

Item wester feddellis,   .   .   xvj$^{lib.}$ xiij$^{s.}$ iiij$^{d.}$
Beney,   x$^{lib.}$ xiij$^{s.}$ iiij$^{d.}$
Eister fedellis,   xxiiij$^{lib.}$ xiij$^{s.}$ iiij$^{d.}$
Mylne of Feddellis,   viij$^{lib.}$
The annewellis of Petcarne,   .   .   .   iiij$^{s.}$
Annewellis of Forgowne,   ij$^{s.}$
Annewellis of Perthe,   .   iiij$^{lib.}$ iiij$^{s.}$ iiij$^{d.}$
Exmakgyrdill iiij plewis, set for ferme vij chalder xj bolls.
vizt. j chalder frumenti.
    iii Chalder iij ordei.
    iij chalder viij bollis farine.
    teynd of Eglesmagyrdill,   xx$^{lib.}$
    The mylne of the saim,   viij$^{lib.}$ xiij$^{s.}$ iiij$^{d.}$
    The Brewhous, .   xxvj$^{s.}$ viij$^{d.}$

The rentaill of the landis within Fyfe.

Item cluney in feu, ...   xvj$^{lib.}$ vj$^{s.}$ viij$^{d.}$
the borrow maillis of Newburghe,   iiij$^{lib.}$ xv$^{s.}$ iiij$^{d.}$
Johne Lowtfutis hous,   xi$^{s.}$
the annewellis of Newburghe,   xxx$^{s.}$
Denemylne,   .   .   .   liij$^{s.}$ iiij$^{d.}$
Kyggis hoill,   xx$^{s.}$
the segis,   .   ,.   .   xi$^{s.}$
Marie croft   xl$^{s.}$
Cregmylne iiij chader wictuall viz.
    viij. bollis quheit xxviij bollis beir
    xxviij bollis meill xlviij caponeis.

The Grange of Lundoris.

xvj plewis everilk pleuche in maill zeirly   .   .   iiij$^{bs.}$ iij$^{s.}$ iiij
    xxvj$^{s.}$ viij$^{d.}$ in gersum zerly
      ij$^{s.}$ fyne siluer i boll ber
        i boll meill xij caponeis
      viij powtre with harrage and carrage.

The Luging of Sainct Andros set in feu to Johne
  Brownehill, ... xxvj^{s.} viij^{d.}

Lumquhat on fewit of maill ȝeirly viij merkis ij
  bollis beir ij bollis meill of dry mowters.

The Wodheid of mail on fewit iiij^{lib.} 1 Wedder.
  1 Lame, xij powtry.

The Southe wodis of maill and teynd yerly xvi
  merkis, ... x^{lib.} xiij^{s.} iij^{d.}

The Brewhous of the Grange . . . xiij^{s.}

The teyndis of Forrat, . xiij^{lib.} vj^{s.} viij^{d.}

The toftis of Auld Lundoris, vj^{s.} viij^{d.}

The toft of Littlekylloche, x^{s.}

The Brewhous of Collessy, . xlvj^{s.} viij^{d.}

The Abbottis Luging in falkland, xl^{s.}

The brewhous of Awchtermowchtie, xl^{s.}

The teyndis of Clevege, xviij^{lb.}

The annewellis Sanctandros, vj^{s.}

The annewellis of Cowper, . . . viij^{s.}

The Durrieland of Creiche, . . . xl^{s.}

The wiccarag Dundy, . . . vi^{lb.} xiij^{s.} iiij^{d.}

The annewellis of Creill, v^{s.} x^{d.}

The annewellis of Petfour, xxvj^{s.} viij^{d.}

The annewellis of Ruthuene, viij^{s.}

Ebdey.

The hallow brokis, . . . iij^{lib.} vj^{s.} viij^{d.}

The teynd wollis, xiij^{lib.} vj^{s.} viij^{d.}

The teynd Lames, xiij^{lib.} vj^{s.} viij^{d.}

The teynd cleiche, . . . xiij^{lib.} vj^{s.} viij^{d.}

The mekle orchart, x^{lib.}

The kyching fe, . . . iiij^{lib.}

The teynd silver of the fyve kyrkis be yound
  the monthe yerly vj^ciij^{xx.} iij^{lib.} xiij^{s.} iiij^{d.}

The kirk of Kynnawhmont, xxviij^{lib.}

Crystis kirk, . xij^{lib.}

The tempilland, vj^{s.} viij^{d.}

The Flenderis, xx^{lib.}

Kirk of the inche.

The towne of the same, iij^{lib.} vj^{s.} viij^{d.}

Mekle wardes, xviij^{lib.} vj^{s.} viij^{d.}

Nedder and Vuer boddame,	iiij^lib.		
Knoknaberde,	xiij^lib.	vj^s.	viij^d.
Donedure,	xv^lib.	vi^s.	viij^d.
Litill wardes, . . .	iiij^lib.		
Jôhneis leis,	iiij^lib.		
Wraithis	iii^lib.		

The Kirk of Leslie.

The maneis of auld lesly, . .	xiijj^lib.	xiij^s.	iiij^d.
Cweterstowne,	xiij^lib.	vj^s.	viij^d.
The Chepeltowne,	iiij^lib.		
New leslie,	vj^lib.	vj^s.	viij^d.
Duncastone,	vj^lib.	xiij^s.	iiij^d
Johnestone,		xl^s.	

The Kirk of Premmey.

payis,	xlvij^lib.	vj^s.	viij^d.

The Kirk of colsamond.

Telle morgane ij plewis	iiij^lib.		
The Kirktowne 1 plewche,	iij^lib.	vj^s.	viij^d.
Powquhit iiij plewis, .	x^lib.	xiij^s.	iiij^d
Williamstone iiij plewis,	x^lib.	xiij^s.	iiij^d.
The mylne of Willistone, brewhous and Walkeris croft, ...		xl^s.	
Melenesyde iiij plewis.			
The newtone iiij plewis, . .	xvi^lib.		
Wranghame v plewis uithe the walk mylne, .	xviij^lib.	xiij^s.	iiij^d.

The Kirk of Loge dornocht.

The Kirktone of the same, .	xiiij^lib.		
Lethentie, .	xj^lib.		
Myltowne of Dorno, ...	xxxiiij^lib.	xiij^s.	iiij^d.
Balhagertie, .	xvj^lib.		
Pctbie,	vj^lib.		
Harlaw,	viij^lib.	xiij^s.	iiij^d.
Cregtowie,	iij^lib.	vj^s.	viij^d.
Ester ramsay,	vj^lib.	xiij^s.	iiij^d.
Broko, . . .	iij^lib.	vj^s.	viij^d.
Drumdorne, .	ix^lib.		
Drumlethene, .		xxxiij^s.	iiij^d.

Knokhallothie	.	.	.	.	viij$^{lb.}$	xiij$^{s.}$	iiij$^{d.}$
Buchquhene,	.	.	.	.	viij$^{lb.}$		
Petscurrey,	.	.	.	.	viij$^{lb.}$	x$^{s.}$	
Pettepill,	.	.	.	.	xiiij$^{lb.}$		
quhitcros,	.	.	.	.		liij$^{s.}$	iiij$^{d.}$
Pettoddertie,	.	.	.	.	vj$^{lb.}$	xiij$^{s.}$	iiij$^{d.}$

The Kirk of inderrowrie.

The Kirktowne,	.	.	.	.	xxiiij$^{lb.}$		
Awchforthy,	.	.	.	.	vj$^{lb.}$	xiij$^{s.}$	iiij$^{d.}$
Blakhall,	.	.	.	.	iiij$^{lb.}$		
Drymmeis,	.	.	.	.	vij$^{lb.}$	vj$^{s.}$	viij$^{s.}$
Haltone of knoknablew,		.	.	.	vj$^{lb.}$		
Newtone,	.	.	.	.	iiij$^{lb.}$		
Meddiltowne of Knoknablewis,					x$^{lb.}$	xiiij$^{s.}$	iiij^{s}

The Kirk of Monkege.

The Kirktone of the samen,		.	.	.	iiij$^{lb.}$	xiij$^{s.}$	iiij$^{d.}$
Caskebene,	.	.	.	.	xx$^{lb.}$		
Cremownche.							
Boyndis,	.	.	.	.	viij$^{lib.}$		
Lochtullo,	.	.	.	.	iij$^{lb.}$	vj$^{s.}$	viij$^{d.}$
Selbie,	.	.	.	.	v$^{lb.}$	vj$^{s.}$	viij$^{d.}$
Porterstone,	.	.	.	.	iij$^{lb.}$	vj$^{s.}$	viij$^{d.}$

The Kirk of Fyntres.

The haltowne of Fyntrey,		.	.	.	xxj$^{lb.}$	vj$^{s.}$	viij$^{d.}$
Westar fyntrey,	.	.	.	.	xxj$^{lb.}$	vj$^{s.}$	viij$^{d.}$
Westar Disblair,	.	.	.	.	viij$^{lb.}$		
Meddil Disblair,	.	.	.	.	iij$^{lib.}$		
Eister Disblair with Cavellis mylne,					v$^{lb.}$	vj$^{s.}$	viij$^{d.}$
Logie fyntrey.							

The Kirk of Dundy teynd siluer.
ij$^{clib.}$

The teyndis of the Kirk of Ebdey.

Vuer Denemvre ij chalders xj bollis i firlot viz. viij bollis frumenti xv
bollis i firlot ordei i chalder iiij bollis farine.

Nedder Dene mvre iij chalder viij bollis viz. viij bollis quheit; xvi bollis
ordei ij chalder meill.

Carpowie vj bollis vizt.
   iij bollis quheit, iii bollis farine
Kynenerdi iij Chalder xiiij bollis viz. :
     x bollis quheit, xx bollis ber, xxxij bollis meill.
Wodmylne j Chalder xiijj bollis ij firlots, viz. :
       v bollis ij firlotis quheit
       x bollis ij firlotis ordei
       xiijj bollis ij firlotis farine.
Freland vij bollis ij firlotis viz. : iij bollis
   ij firlotis ordei iij bollis ii firlottis farine.
Inchery
   Ane Chalder viz. : i boll quheit, v bollis beir
           x bollis farine.

Lundoris.

iiij chalder viij bollis viz. ii chalder quheit xxiij bollis ber xxxii bollis meill.

Denemylne.

vij bollis j boll ij firlotis quheit iij bollis ordei ij bollis ii firlotis farine.

Parkhill.

xv bollis viz. ij bollis quheit iiij bollis ber ix bollis meill.

Wodheid xvj bollis.

Ane chalder viz. ij bollis quheit iiij bollis ordei iix bollis farine.

Toftis of William Chepman iij ferlotis.

Ane ferlet beir ij ferletis meill.

Toftis of Johne Blyth iij ferletis, ij pekis viz.

sax pekis ber ij ferlettis farine.
Toftis of the Mylne—Tua ferlettis meill.
Cregend vj ferlettis viz. ane boll beir tua ferlettis meill.
Marie croft ij bollis viz. ane boll beir, ane boll meill.
Segis ij bollis viz. ane boll beir—ane boll meill.
Almerey cruk ix bollis ordei.
Akeris vnder the wod x bollis ordei.
Wodrufehill; threpland ij chalder x bollis ordei.
Hauche, iij chalder ordei.
Brodland, ij chalder viij bollis ordei.
The teyndis of Newburgh vj chalder viz. iij chalder ordei iij chalder farine.

Clayis iiij chalder ordei a. a.
Litill medowis viii bollis ordei a. a.
West medow iiij chalder.
Teyndis of the Grange xij chalder viz. :
Drymowteris i chalder xij bollis ordei i chalder xij bollis farine.

Kyrk of Collessy.

Hahill ij chalders x bollis viz. vj bollis frumenti xij bollis ordei i chalder
    viij bollis farine.
Scheillis and Bowhous xxiiij bollis viz. xij bollis ordei xij bollis farine.
Prestis croft iij ferlettis ij pekis frumenti.
Neutowne i chalder xij bollis viz. iij bollis frumenti xi bollis ordei xiiij
    farine.
Petlair i chalder x bollis viz. x bollis ordei i chalder farine.
Dafmylne vj bollis ij ferletis viz. ij bollis ij ferlettis ordei iiij bollis farine.
Ballowmylne xi bollis viz. iiij bollis ordei vij bollis farine.
Petcunertey viij bollis.
Mairstone xij bollis ane boll corne.
Lawfeill and menisgrene viij boll ane corne.
Drumtenend i chalder viij bollis vj bollis ordei xviij bollis farine.
Ester Kylquhys xi bollis viz. i boll ordei x bollis corne.
Est pairt of Kylloche ij chalder, ane boll iij pekis viz. ij bollis i ferlett
    frumenti xi boll i ferlet ordei and xix bollis ij ferlettis iii pekis.
The west pairt of Kylloche withe the half pairt of the mylne land and haill
    ij chalder xiiij bollis viz. iiij bollis frumenti xiij bollis ordei xxviii bollis
    farine.
Mychell Kuikis toft ij bollis ane corne.
David Jop croft with the half rud of the brewland ij bollis ordei.
Ester Rossie ij chalder xiiij bollis viz. vj bollis frumenti xx bollis ordei xx
    bollis farine.
Westar Rossie xi bollis viz. vj bollis frumenti xiiij bollis ordei xx bollis
    farine.
Wedderisbie vj chalder vj bollis viz. x bollis frumenti xxxvj bollis ordei
    iij chalder vj bollis farine.

Kirk Awchtermowchtie.

Auchtermowchtie iii chalder viij bollis ij ferlettis ij pekis cum bina pairt
    peci viz. vij bollis iij ferlettis ij pekis peces cum bena.

The southe quarter.

quarter iij chalder x bollis ij ferlettis cum bina parte viz. viij bollis ix
ferlettis i pec cum bina parte frumenti.

At the end of the book the following entry occurs ' Item for colls xliiij lib.
iiijs.'

No. III., p. 132.[1]

*The Rentall of the kirkes and teindis pertenying to the place of Lundoris sett for
money.*

1. The kyrk of Kynnathmonthe be yound the monthe payis yeirlie	xxviij ƚi thairfor
Lord Forbes for his bailyie fie yeirlie	xiij ƚi vj viijᵈ·
and so we get bott	xiiij ƚi of the said kirk
2. Christis kirk payis yeirlie	xxxij ƚi quhilk
is bott ane pendicle of Kynnathmonthe.	
3. The kirk of Inche payis yeirlie	lxxvij ƚi vi s̃ viijᵈ·
4. The kirk of Leslie payis yeirlie	xlv ƚi vi s̃ viijᵈ·
5. The kirk of Primethe payis yeirlie	L ƚi.
6. The kirk of Colsalmonthe payis yeirlie	lxxx j ƚi vj s̃ viijᵈ·
7. The kirk of Logydornothe payis yeirlie	iᶜ lxj ƚi xiij s̃ viijᵈ·
8. Innerrowrie payis yeirlie	lxij ƚi xiij s̃ iiijᵈ·
9. The kirk of Monkegy payis yeirlie	lvij ƚi
Quhilk is but ane pendicle of Innerrowrie.	
10. The kirk of Fyntrie payis yeirlie	lx ƚi
11. For the teindis of Baddyforrow yeirlie	liij s̃ iiijᵈ·
12. For the schewis of Wester Disblair	xijᵇ bƚ malt iiij bƚ meill
13. The kirk of Dundie	iijᶜ merkis in all
tymes by past and this last crope and all tymes to cum I traist it sall be ane hundrethe merkis mair heirof the Minister gattis yeirlie	iᶜ ƚi

---

[1] The numbers inserted before the names of the various places in the following Rental are not in the original; they are prefixed for reference to the Notes
on the Rentall, Appendix No. IV.

14. The kirk of Eglismagill, viz. the toun of the samyn payis
    yeirlie   xiij li vj s̃ viij^d.
15. The teind schewis and vicarage of the toun of Clawage yeirlie xviij li
16. The teind schewis of the Eister Feddellis and Bene yeirlie   xviij li
17. The teind schewis of Forrett yeirlie   xiij li vj s̃ viij^d

The kirkis of Fyfe sett for Victuallis.

18. *The paroche of Ebdy.*
19. The Wodruife with the hill and Thraiplandis payis of ferme
    yeirlie   ij ch viij bl beir
20. The Brodlands payis of ferme yeirlie   i ch vij bl beir
21. The hauche payis of ferme yeirlie   ij ch xv bls beir
22. The eist pairt of Dunmure ⎱ viij bls quheit, i ch beir, xxiiij bl meill
    pays yeirlie of teind ⎰
23. Carpowy payis yeirlie   iij bl quheit iij bl beir
24. Kynnard payis yeirlie   x bl quheit
    and   i ch iiij bl beir ij ch meill
    And the said toun of Kinnard ⎱ viij bls beir viij bls meill
    payis yeirlie of dry multer ⎰
25. The Wodmyln payis yeirlie   ⎰ iij bl ij fr quheit.
                                ⎱ xiij bl beir and xxiiij bl meil
26. The frieland payis yeirlie   ⎰ ij fr quheit iij bl beir
                                ⎱ and iiij bl meill
27. Inchery payis yeirlie   ⎰ i bl quheit v bl beir
                                ⎱ and x bl meill
28. Loundoris payis yeirlie   ⎰ i ch quheit xxiiij bl beir
                                ⎱ and ij ch meill
29. The Denmill payis yeirlie   ⎰ i bl quheit ij bl beir
                                ⎱ and ij bl meill
30. The Parkhill payis yeirlie   ⎰ iij bl quheit v bl beir
                                ⎱ and viij bl meill
31. The toft of Andrew Downy withe ⎰ viij bl meill iij bl
    the southwod payis yeirlie ⎱ quheit and iij bl beir
32. The toftis of Henrie Philip and ⎱ ij^{fr}l ij^{pks} beir and i bl meill
    Niniane Blythe payis yeirlie ⎰
33. The toft of the Craig myln withe ⎱ i bl beir i bl ij^{fr} meill
    the Seggis payis yeirlie ⎰
34. The Marie croft payis yeirlie   i bl beir i bl meill
35. The cartward payis yeirlie   iiij bl beir
36. The Craigend payis yeirlie   i bl beir ij^{fr} meill

37. The teind of the Newbruiche   ij ch viij bł beir and ij ch viij bł meill
38. The teind of the barony of the Grange,   ⌈ viij ch thairof
      viz. vnj plewis of the Grange four | i ch quheit
      of the Berreholl tua of Ormestoun   ⌡ ij ch xij bł beir
      and tua of the Hiltoun hill payis | and iiij ch
      of teind   ⌞ iiij bł meill

Beir   xviij ch xv bł ijp^{ks} quheit iiij ch ix bł
Meill   xviij ch xij bł ij^{fr}ł

The paroche of Cullessie.

39. Halhill payis yeirlie   i bł quheit vij bł beir and x bs meill
40. The Mylhill Scheillis and Bowes payis
      yeirlie   xxij bł beir and xxij bł meill
    The croft of Sir Johnne Youngis payis yeirlie   i bł meill
41. The Newtoun of Cullessie payis yeirlie   vj bł beir viij bł meill
42. Pitlair payis yeirlie   i bł quheit vij bł beir and xiiij bł meill
43. Daftmyłn payis yeirlie   ij bł ij^{fr} beir iiij bł meill
44. Maristoun payis yeirlie   i bł beir xj bł meill
45. Lawfield and Menysgrene payis yeirlie   viij bł aittis
46. Bellowmyll payis yeirlie   iiij bł beir vij bł meill
47. Drumtennent payis yeirlie   vj bł beir xviij bł meill
48. The eist pairt of Kinloyche   �{ iiij bł quheit xijj bł iij^{fr}
      ij p^{cts} beir and i ch vij bł i^{fr} ł meill
48. The wast pairt of the same   ⌉
      payis yeirlie   ⌋ iij bł quheit, xiij bł beir and i ch x bł meill
48. The toft of Kinloiche payis   ij bł beir ij bł aittis
49. Rosse Eister payis yeirlie   iiij bł quheit xiij bł beir and xiiij bł meill
49. Rosse Waster payis yeirlie vj bł quheit xiiij bł beir and i ch iiij bł meill
50. Weddersbie payis yeirlie viij bł quheit i ch xij bł beir and ij ch iiij bł meill
    The pendiclis of the same payis yeirlie   ij bł i^{fr} beir ij bł meill
51. Lumquhat payis yeirlie   vij bł beir xiiij bł meill
52. Kilquhyss Eister payis yeirlie   i bł beir x bł aittis
    Summa i ch xi bł ij^{fr} quheit
    Summa of the beir ix ch vij bł ij^{fr} ijp^{ks} beir
    Summa of the meill xiiij ch xj bł ij^{fr} ijp^{k} meill
    Summa of the aittis i ch xv błs
53. *The paroche of Auchtirmochtie*
    The northe pairt of Auchtermuchtie ⌠ x bł quheit xxij bł i^{fr} ijp^{et} beir
      ⌡ and xxviij bł meill
    The southe pairt of the same payis ⌠ x bł quheit xxj bł ij p^{et} beir
      yeirlie   ⌡ xxxj bł ij bł meill

The bound half payis yeirlie { x b^t iij^{fr} ij p^{ct} quheit and i ch viij b^t / ij^{fr} beir ij ch iiij b^t ij^{fr} meill

54. Cotlandis withe Marislandis payis yeirlie   ix b^t beir viij b^t ij^{fr} meill
55. Gerusland payis yeirlie   iij b^t quheit vj b^t ij^{fr} beir and vij b^t iJ^{fr} meill
56. The Myris Over and Nethir payis yeirlie { vi b^t quheit x b^t beir and / xviij b^t meill
57. Burnegrenis payis yeirlie   viij b^t aittis
58. Demperstoun payis yeirlie vnj b^t quheit i ch beir and ij ch viij b^t meill
59. Redy and Longiswaird   iij b^t quheit v b^t beir and i ch meill
(52.) Kilquhyis Westir payis yeirlie   iiij b^t beir viij b^t meill
    Summa of the quheit iij ch ij b^t iiij^{fr}t ij p^k
    Summa of the beir vi ch ij b^t ij^{fr}t
    Summa of the meill xij ch i b^t ij^{fr} ij p^k
    Summa of the aittis viij b^t

60. *The paroche kirk of Creiche.*
61. The toun of Creiche payis yeirlie ij b^t quheit iiij b^t beir and xij b^t meill
62. Perbroithe payis yeirlie   iij b^t quheit xij b^t beir and i ch meill
63. Luthre payis yeirlie x b^t quheit ij ch iiij b^t beir and iij ch iiij b^t meill
64. Kynsleif ester payis yeirlie   iij b^t quheit vj b^t beir and x b^t meill
64. Kynsleif westir payis yeirlie   iij b^t quheit vj b^t beir and x b^t meill
65. Balmadysyde payis yeirlie { xij b^t quheit xviij b^t beir / and i ch iiij b^t meill
    Summa of the quheit ij ch ij b^t
    Summa of the beir v ch ij b^t
    Summa of the meill v ch viij b^t
    Summa totie of quheit xj ch xij b^t iiij^{fr}t iiijp^{ct}
    Summa of Beir and malt, xl ch vij b^t i^{fr}
    Summa of Meil xlix ch v b^t iiij^{fr}t
    Summa of aittis ij ch vij b^t

The Assumption of the thrid of the Abbay of Lundoris.

Thrid of the money   vij^c xlvj li xviij s i^d
66. The barone of Wranghame   iij^c i li vj s ij^d
67. The barone of Fyntray   ij^c xlv li vnj s iiij^d
68. The landis of Balmaw and Newtyld for   xvij li viij s
69. Hiltoun and Mylntoun of Cragy for   xxv li vj s viij^d·
70. Claypottis and Friertoun for   xj li xnj s iiij^d.
71. The barone of Mernis by the annuellis of
    Bervy for   lxxxxij li xv s viij^d·
(14). Egleismagreltoun myln with the brew-
    houss's for   i^c· merkis vj s vnj^d·

Gif in xiiij ƚi iš xj^d

Thrid of the quheit	iij ch xij bƚ ifr i p^{k.}
(28). Lundoris for	i ch
(22). The eist pairt of Dunmure	viij bƚ
The west pairt thairof	viij bƚ
(24). Kinnarde	x bƚ
(31). The toft of Andrew Downy withe the southwod	iij bƚ
(38). The teindis of the Grange	i ch

Gif in ij frl iiij p^{ct.} eq.

Beir thrid thairof	xiij ch vij bƚ ij^{frs.}
(19). Tak the Wodruf Hill and Treiplandis for	ij ch viij bƚ
(20). The Brodland	i ch vij bƚ
72. The Hauche	i ch xv bƚ
(22). The west pairt of Dunmuire	i ch
(24). Kynnaird	i ch iiij bƚ
(37). Newbruiche	ij ch viij bƚ
(38). The teind of the Grange	ij ch xij bƚ
(22). The eist pairt of Dunmuire	xv bƚ

Gif in xiij bƚ i^{frc.} eq.

The beir that is tane mair is in respect of the malt.

Thrid of the meill	xvij ch vij bl. ƚi fr

Tak the haill meill of the paroche of Ebdy gevand be yeir

Gif in i ch v bƚ i^{fr}

Thrid of the aittis	xiij bƚ
Tak it out of Cullessy paroche gevand	i ch xv bƚ

Omittit grassumes entre siluer, yairdis fyschingis caponis pultrie canis custumes mertis cariagis and all vtheris dewteis.

The Rentall of Lundoris in money teindis and fermis—

The baronie of Grange lyand within the Schirrefdome of Fyfe.

(38). Imprimis the tovne of the Grange, aucht pleuichis sett in few tua thairof for yeirlie maill ilk plewche aucht pound x schillingis summa sevintyne poundis and sax pleuichis payis bot ilk pleuche fyve poundis fourtyne schillingis summa thrittie four poundis iiij š during the Tennentis lyftymes—The Berryhoill four pleuchis sett in few thrie thairof for yeirlie maill ilk pleuiche aucht pound x š summa xxv ƚi x š and ane pleuiche payis bot fyve poundis xiijj š during the tennentis lyftymes, ormestoun twa pleuchis sett in lyfrent for yeirlie maill allyvin pound viij š.

(51). Lumquhat tua pleuichis sett in few for yeirlie maill fyve pound vij s̄ viij^d· The remanent of the tua plcuichis sett in few for yeirlie maill is payit to the Quenis grace chepill in Falkland and to my Lord Angus College in Abirnethie.

73. The toft of the Wodheid in few withe the souithe wode for yeirlie maillis   merkis

74. The Eist wod withe the teindes thairof sett in few for yeirlie maill   x li xiij s̄ iiij^d·

75. The Brewhouss of the Grange sett in few for yeirlie maill   xvij s̄

76. The barrow (burrow) maillis of Newbruiche yeirlie four poundis tuelf schillingis.

76. The tennentis of Newbruiche yeirlie thrie poundis fyve schillingis.

77. The annuellis in sanctandrois yeirlie   xxvij s̄ viij^d·

78. The Derachland of Creich payit na thing thir xxij yeiris.

(42). The toft of Cullessie yeirlie fourtie sax schillingis.

(48). The toft in Kinloche yeirlie vij schillingis.

(53). The Brewhouss's of Auchtermuchtie yeirlie   xxiiij s̄

(28). The toft of Auld Loundoris yeirlie   viij s̄

79. The luidging in Falkland payit nathing thir tuentie tua yeiris.

80. Cluny Eister yeirlie saxtyne pound xvj s̄ viij^d·

(36). Cragend and Keggishoill yeirlie fourtie tua schillingis.

(34). Marie croft and seggis yeirlie four poundis.

81. Craigmylne yeirlie thrittie tua pound

82. The Clayis withe nyne aikaris of the West medew yeirlie sevintyne poundis vj s̄ viij^d

The teind thairof yeirlie sax pound xiij s iiij^d·

Thrittie ane aikeris and ane half in the

(20-21). Hauch medows. Brodland respective ilk aiker tua merkis. Summa fourtie tua poundis.

83. The Almerie Cruike yeirlie sax pound xiij s iiij^d·

The aikeris under the wod yeirlie sax pound.

84. The Reid Insches saltgress Kow Insches.

85. Park est yaird fruit yairdis and fyschingis in Tay yeirlie ane houndrethe poundis.

The teind of Auld Lundoris yeirlie thrittie pound.

The teindis of Forret yeirlie tuentie merkis.

The teind of Den mylne yeirlie four pound.

The Maillis of the landis in Anguss.

(68). Balmaw and Newtyld yeirlie sevintyne poundis viij s̄.

(69). Ouretoun of the Hiltoun and Mylntoun of Cragy yeirlie tuentie fyve poundis vi s̄ viij^d·

(70). Claypottis and Ferrietoun allyvin poundis xiij $\bar{s}$ iiij$^{d.}$

86. Innerraritie iij $\bar{\text{li}}$ vj $\bar{s}$ viij$^{d.}$ payit nathing thir tventie tua yeiris. The vicarage of Dundie payit na thing sen ye beginnying of the toun. The annuellis of Dundie payit x merkis na thing sen the begynnyng of ye toun.

The Maillis of the landis in the Mernis.

87. The haill of Vistownis hillend and Fyscher hill yeirlie tuentie sax poundis saxtyne schillingis aucht penneis.
88. Lytill Wistonis yeirlie sevin pound viij $\bar{s}$ x$^{d.}$
89. Nedir Wistonis pittargus and pittemuis yeirlie tuentie pound xiij $\bar{s}$ iij$^{d.}$
90. Scottistone and mercorie yeirlie tuentie tua pound sevintyne schillingis vj$^{d.}$
91. Myltoun of Wistonis yeirlie fyve pound aucht schillingis four penneis. Brewhouse of Westonnis yeirlie fyve poundis ij$^{s.}$
    Ardoche yeirlie sax pound.
    Annuellis of Bervie yeirlie aucht schillingis.

The Maillis and Annuellis of the landis within the Schirrefdome of Stratherne.

(16). Westir Feddellis yeirlie tuentie sex poundis sax schilling aucht pennies.
(16). Estir Feddellis yeirlie aucht poundis.
(16). Bene yeirly tuelf pound.
    Eclismagirdill the toun thairof withe the mylne and Brewhous thrie scoir sevin poundis tua schillingis.
92. The greit luidging in Perthe yeirlie ten pound.
    The luidging in the watir gaitt yeirlie fyve pound.
    The fore luidging yeirlie iij $\bar{\text{li}}$ vi $\bar{s}$ viij$^{d.}$
    Thairof to Dunkeld be the tennentis fourte schillingis.
    The annuellis of Perthe fyve merkis fyve schillingis.

The Barone of Wranghame lyand within the Schireffdome of Abirdyne.[1]

The Craigtoun yeirlie thrittyne pound vj $\bar{s}$ viij$^{d.}$
Kirkhill   vj $\bar{\text{li}}$ xuj $\bar{s}$ iiij$^{d.}$

---

[1] A Barony of Newton of Wranghame in the parish of Culsamond, George Gordon of Newtoun, succeeded to it 1644, and the corn and pulling, or 'winde mills,' and also ta the Kirkton of Culsamond.

The Towne of Christis kirk withe Hedwlyke[1]   xvj ℔ iiij ₴ viij$^{d.}$
The mylne of Leslie tuentie sax schillingis viij$^{d.}$
Na payment Largie yeirlie thrie poundis vj ₴ viij$^{d.}$
Newtoun of Wranghame yeirlie withe the waike mylne and waird Thrie
     scoir sax poundis xiij ₴ iiij$^{d.}$
Kirktoun of Colsalmound   viij ℔ iiij ₴ vj$^{d.}$
Powquhite yeirlie   xxiij ℔
Lyddinghame and Williamsoun yeirlie   xlviij ℔ xiij ₴ iiij$^{d.}$

To my Lord Rothes's fie.

The mylne and Brewhouse of Williamstoun yeirlie sax pound xiij ₴ iiij$^{d.}$
Malingsyde yeirlie twenty-aucht pound ix ₴ viij$^{d.}$
Flendaris yeirlie tuenty-four pound ix ₴ viij$^{d.}$
Logydornoch with the Brewhouse of the samyne twenty pound xviij ₴.
The kirktoun of Inche with the mylne and brewhouse of the samyn
     thirttyne pound vij schillingis.
The kirktoune of Premethe   iiij ℔ xiij ₴ iiij$^{d.}$
yeirlie   xij ℔

The barony of Fyntray.

Logyfintry with the Froster' sait yeirlie   viij ℔
Haltoun of Fyntray and Westir Fyntray withe the place and wod thairof
     yeirlie   lxxxvij ℔ ij ₴ viij$^{d.}$
Myltoun of Fyntray yeirlie sevin pound vj ₴ viij$^{d.}$
Balbuthnie Haddirweik and Craigforthie   xviij ℔
Baddifforrow yeirlie fyve poundis vij ₴ ix$^{d.}$
Moukegy and West bowndis   xix ℔ xiij ₴ iiij$^{d.}$
Kynmok yeirlie tuentie pouudis ix ₴ ij$^{d.}$
Tillykerne fyve pound vj ₴ viij$^{d.}$
Westir Disblaire yeirlie xxiiij ℔
Middill Disblair yeirlie tuentie-four poundis v ₴ viij$^{d.}$
Eister Disblair withe the Cavillis mylne xvj ℔ xij ₴
The tua brewhoussis of Fyntrais withe medow and croftis respec-
     tive   viij ℔ xiij ₴ iiij$^{d.}$

Assignit to the Chalmerlane.

The Annuellis of Balhalgarthy Kelly and Innerrowry   xiij ℔ vj ₴ viij$^{d.}$

---

[1] 'Hedwlyk,' Hedderlick in the parish of Premnay. In 1680 Mr John Ross
was served heir to his father in the lands of Insch, the burgh of barony of Insch,
the mill of Insch, and the restricted multures of the lands of Flinders, chartulary,
Insch of Hedderlick, and the Temple croft 'in per registilulum de Lundoris.'—
Retours of Aberdeen.

The Rentall of the kirkis lyand within the Schirrefdome of Abirdyne and teind schewis thairof sett for money.

The Kirk of Kinathmonthe	xiiij ƚi

The rest thairof to my Lord Forbes bailie fie extending in the first rentall
to   xiij ƚi vj s vuj[d.]

Christis kirk yeirlie thrittie tua pound.

The kirk of Inche	lxvj ƚi xiij s̃ iij[d]

The kirk of Leslie fourtie-five pound vi s̃ viij[d.]

The kirk of Premeth yeirlie fyftie pound.

The kirk of Culsalmound	lxxxxj ƚi vj s̃ iiij[d.]

The kirk of Logydornoch ane houndrethe thrie scoir ane pound xiij s̃ iiij[d.]

The kirk of Innerrowrie thrie scoir tua pound xiij s̃ iiij[d.]

The kirk of Monkegy yeirlie	lvij ƚi
The kirk of Fyntray yeirlie	lx ƚi
The teindis of Baddyforrow	lij s̃ iiij[d.]
The teindis of Wester Disblair yeirlie	viij ƚi

The kirkis within the Schirrefdome of Forfar.

The kirk of Dundie yeirlie	ij[c] ƚi

The kirkis within the Schirrefdome of Perthe.

The kirk of Eglismagreill	xiij ƚi vj s̃ viij[d.]
The teindis and vicarage of Clavege	xviij ƚi
The teindis of Eister Feddellis and Bene	xviij ƚi

The kirkis within the Schirrefdome of Fife sett for victuallis.
the kirkis the teind schewis thairof.

The Wodrwf hill and Thraiplandis	ij cħ iiij bƚ beir
The Brodland	i cħ vij bƚ beir
The Hauch	i cħ xij bƚ beir
The eist pairt of Dunmuire viij bƚ quheit xv bƚ i frl beir and	i cħ iiij bƚ meill
The West pairt of Dunmuire viij bƚ quheit i cħ beir xxiiij bƚ meill	
Carpowe	iij bƚ quheit iij bƚ beir
Kinnard ten bollis quheit xx bƚ beir and ij cħ meill	
The dry muttar of Kinnard	viij bƚ beir viij bƚ meill
Inchyray i bƚ quheit v bƚ beir and	x bƚ meill
Parkhill ij bƚ quheit v bƚ beir and	vj bƚ meill
The toft of Andrew Downie with the Southe wod iij bƚ quheit iij bƚ beir and	viij bƚ meill
The Croft of James Philpe ij frl ij p[ct.] beir and	ij bƚ meill

The toft of Craigmylne and seggis	i bŧ beir and i bŧ ij frŧ meill
Mary Croft	i bŧ beir and i bŧ meill
Cartward	iiij bŧ beir
Craigend	i bŧ beir
Newburgh	ij ch viij bŧ beir ij ch viij bŧ meill
Berrihoill and the Grange	i ch quheit ij ch x bŧ beir and iiij ch meill

Cullessie kirk teynd schewis thairof.

Halhill	ij bŧ quheit iiij bŧ beir and vj bŧ meill
Mylhill scheillis and Brewhouse	ij ch vj bŧ beir and i ch vj bŧ meill
Myln croft of Cullessie	i bŧ meill
Newtoun of Cullessie	vj bŧ beir and viij bŧ meill
Pitlair	i bŧ quheit vij bŧ beir and xij bŧ meill
Daftmyln	ij bŧ ij frl beir and iiij bŧ meill
Maristoun	i bŧ beir and xj bŧ aittis for horse
Lawfield and Menisgrene	viij bŧ aittis for horse corne
Ballowmylne	iiij bŧ beir and vij bŧ meill
Drumtennent	vj bŧ beir and ch ij bŧ . . .
Eist pairt of Kinloyche [1]	quheit x . . beir and i ch vj bŧ meill
Wastir pairt of Kinloyche	iiij bŧ quheit xij bŧ beir i ch vj bŧ meill
Toft of Kynlocht	ij bŧ beir ij bŧ aittis for horse corne
Rosse Eister	four bollis quheit xiiij bŧ beir and xiiij bŧ meill

Assignit to James Calwie and sua payis na thing to the place.

Rosse Westir	vj bŧ quheit xiiij bŧ beir xx bŧ meill

Weddersbie James Sandelandis pairt thairof tua bŧ quheit viij bŧ beir and xij bŧ meill

The vthir half thairof four bollis quheit tuelf bollis tua furlottis beir and i ch iiij bŧ meill

. . . . . . samyn. . . bŧ. frŧ. . . . . . .

Extract furthe of the Registir of the Rentallis Demissionis and Assumptionis thairof be me Mr Johnne Nicolsoun, collectour clark, keipar and extracter of the same.

JO. NICOLSON.

---

[1] Manuscript imperfect.

No. IV., p. 132.

Notes on the preceding ' Rentall of Lundoris.'

No. 1. *Kynnathmonthe be-yound the monthe,*—now Kennethmont, beyond the Grampians, was one of the churches bestowed on the Monastery of Lindores by the Founder. In the Foundation Charter it is named Kelalcmund, and Chelalmund in the Confirmation of the same Charter, A.D. 1198, by Pope Innocent III. The Charter erecting the possessions of Lindores Abbey into a temporal Lordship in favour of Patrick Leslie, binds him to pay the minister of Kynnathmount and Christiskirk one hundred and twenty merks, besides the small tithes.

2. *Christis Kirk*, formerly a hamlet in the parish of Kennethmont, now represented by two or three small farm steadings. The church stood on a hillock, and a Fair used to be held on the green around the church yearly in the month of May. The Fair began 'at night about sunset and ended next morning an hour after sunrising; the people buying and selling mercat goods during the night, which is not then dark, a very singular kind of mercat as any ever was. About the year 1760 the proprietor changed the Fair from night to day; but so strong was the prepossession of the people in favour of the old custom, that rather than comply with the alteration they chose to neglect it altogether.'—*Collections on the Shires of Aberdeen and Banff, Spalding Club*, p. 623. The name Christis Kirk, its position on the Green, and the singular circumstance of a Fair at night, where 'dancing and deray' were indulged the whole night through, have inclined many to think that it is the scene of James I.'s Poem of ' Christis Kirk of the Grene.' This honour is claimed also for the parish kirk of Leslie in Fifeshire, which stands on a green, and its proximity to the royal palace of Falkland is urged in support of it. The author of the ' Statistical Account of the Parish of Kennethmount,' in speaking of Christs Kirk and the Fair held at night, says, ' What more likely to strike the fancy of the monarch, in his progress through his kingdom than the market at mid-night; the circumstance may be supposed to fall in with his humour, and give birth to such scenes as he describes.'—*Old Stat. Account* Vol. XIII., pp. 77, 78, *Note.* It is remarkable, however, that the poet does not once allude to the singular circumstance of the Fair being held at night, but, on the contrary, every verse has the refrain ' At Christis Kirk of the Grene *that day.*'

Chalmers, in his edition of ' The Poetic Remains of Some of the Scottish Kings,' p. 135, says, ' Ramsay learned that Christs Kirk was not far from

Leslie ; he mistook Leslie in Fife for Leslie in the Garioch, and he laid the scene of his two additional cantos at Leslie in Fifeshire. The error was corrected in the last edition of Ramsay's Poems. Mr Sibbald, substituting conjecture for facts, laid the scene at St Andrews, and supposes that the author may have given the name of Christis Kirk to the College Kirk of St Salvador. Pinkerton, in his edition of ' Scots Ballads,' Vol. II., p. 176, says, ' Christs Kirk on the Green means the kirk town of Leslie, near Falkland in Fife.' He did not recollect that there was an elder Leslie in Aberdeenshire, where there was a Christ's Kirk on the Green. But this conjecture he afterwards gave up as unfounded.'—*Chalmers, Ib.*, p. 449. The fact that Christis Kirk in Kennethmount is the only place in Scotland which bears that name, is a strong corroborative plea of its being the scene of the Royal author's graphic poem, and the weight of evidence is in its favour.

3. *The Kirke of Inche*, in the Presbytery of Garioch, Aberdeenshire, is named Inchmabanin in the Foundation Charter, Lord Lindores was bound to allow the minister eighty pounds yearly together with the small tithes of the vicarage.

4. *Lesly, in the Presbytery of Garioch.*—We learn from a Charter by John, Earl of Huntingdon, A.D. 1219–1237, that this Church was bestowed on Lindores Abbey by Norman, the son of Malcom, an ancestor of the family of Leslie. In confirming the grant of the lands, the Earl of Huntingdon expressly excepts ' the church of Lessellyn which the said Norman gave to that Abbacy.' This parish, an old writer informs us, ' is the original Seat of the family of Leslie (now represented by the Countess of Rothes), whose ancestor, in memory of this, named his house in Fife, Leslie.'—*Collections on the Shires of Aberdeen and Banff*, p. 455. From three Charters quoted in the ' Collections on the shires of Aberdeen and Banff, pp. 546–8,' we learn the names of four of the ancestors, in lineal descent, of the Countess of Rothes before they had assumed the surname of Leslie. By one of these Charters, David, Earl of Huntingdon, A.D. 1171–1169, confirms the lands of Lesslyn to Malcolm the son of Bartholf ; and in the Charter by John, Earl of Huntingdon, A.D. 1219–1237, the same lands are confirmed to Norman the son of Malcom. In the third Charter by Alexander II., A.D. 1247, 1248 they are again confirmed to Alfornus, the son of Norman. The surname Leslie was derived, as was then usual, from the lands the family possessed ; and if a conjecture may be hazarded, perhaps the origin of the name may be found in the word *Less*, which in Gaelic signifies a circular earthen fort, and *linn*, a pool. The burn of Leslie, and the river Gawdie renowned in song, flow through the parish, the latter passes close by the old castle of Leslie. If this etymology of Leslie is correct, it is not a little remarkable that the title Rothes should have the same signification. *Rath*, in Gaelic

means a fort, and *es* water; Rath-es, a compound which Mr Jervise of
Brechin, who is familiar with the locality, says is admirably descriptive of
a circular fort still extant at the confluence of two streams in the parish of
Rothes. Lord Lindores was bound to pay the minister of Leslie one
hundred merks yearly. On the 10th October 1546, the Abbot of Lindores
granted a tack of the titles of Mains of Lesly to John Leslie of that ylk:
it is dated at the Monastery of Lundoris, and is interesting as being signed
by the abbot and monks; their names are as follows:—

Johannes Abbot of Lundoris.	Alex^r. Patonson.
Johannes Brownhill, supprior eiusdem.	Robertus Jameson.
Johannes Blair.	Robertus Wilyemson.
Ricardus Barcar.	Robertus Westuatter.
Patricius Steill.	Jacobus Carstairs.
Willilmus Messon.	Johannes Skynnir.
Alexr. Wrycht.	Willelmus Walhand.
Alex^r Richardsoun.	Gilbertus Marischell.
David Orem.	Andreas Vod.
Andreas Lesly.	Johannes Smyth.

John Philp, vicar of Logiedorno, is one of the witnesses.—*Antiq of
the Shires of Aberdeen and Banff, Spalding Club*, Vol. III., p. 393–4.

5. *Primethe*, now Premnay, in the same presbytery as the foregoing.
The church was bestowed by David, Earl of Huntingdon, on Lindores
Abbey, and is named in the Foundation Charter 'Prame.' The stipend
payable by Lord Lindores to the minister was forty pounds yearly.

6. *Culsalmonthe*, now Culsalmond, also in the Presbytery of Garrioch,
and bestowed by the Founder on Lindores Abbey; it is named in Original
Charter 'Culsamuel.' The stipend payable to the minister by Lord Lindores
was one hundred merks yearly. John, Abbot of Lindores, conveyed the
lands of Largye, in this parish, to Henry Leslye and his spouse in feu ferme;
the charter is dated 10th December 1545, at the Monastery of Lundoris, and
is signed by the abbot and monks. Mr John Rolland and Mr John Philp,
chaplains, are witnesses.—*Antq. of Aberdeen and Banff-shires*, Vol. III., pp.
409–10.

7. *Logydornoche*, named the church of 'Durnach,' in the Foundation
Charter. 'Before the Reformation it would appear that there were three
places of worship in this parish, namely, Logie Durno, Fetternear, and a
chapel, formerly called 'Capella Beatae Virginis de Garvyach.' Early in
the 17th century the parish church was built on the site of this chapel, and
was then appointed to be called the Chapel of the Garioch.' Lord Lindores
was bound to pay the minister one hundred merks of stipend. Sir John
Leslie of Balquhain in this parish, who died in A.D. 1561, 'purchased many

lands belonding to the Abbey of Lindores.'—*Collections on the Shires of Aberdeen and Banff*, p. 530. Had abstracts of the Charters of these purchases been given in the elaborate ' Historical Records of the Family of Leslie,' published 1869, additional light might have been thrown on the transference of the lands of the Abbey.

8. *Innerowrie*, named ' Inverurin ' in the Foundation Charter, one of the original churches bestowed on Lindores Abbey by David, Earl of Huntingdon ; in addition to the church the Pope's Confirmation of the same Charter (1198) specifies 'one full toft in the burgh of Inverurie.' The stipend payable by Lord Lindores to the minister of Inverurie and Monkegie ' because it was a pendicle of the same,' was one hundred merks yearly. The Burgh of Inverurie still pays 2s. 2½d. yearly of feu-duty to Sir William Forbes, Bart., of Craigievar, ' Hereditary Collector of the Feu-duties of the North Abbacy of Lindores.'

9. *Monkegy*, named ' Munkegin ' in the Foundation Charter; another of the churches bestowed on Lindores Abbey by the Founder. The church and parish is now known by the name of Keithhall, the name of a property in the parish.

10. *Fyntrie*, now Fintray, in the Presbytery of Aberdeen ; the church is named ' Fintreth ' in the Foundation Charter, having been bestowed on Lindores Abbey by the Founder. The Abbot ' had a summer seat at Saint Giles in Hatton ' in this parish.—*Collect. Aberdeen, etc.*, p. 245. In A.D. 1216, Alexander II. erected the wood of Fyntreth into a forest for the preservation of game in favour of the abbot and convent (Charter No. 8). The stipend payable by Lord Lindores to the minister was one hundred merks yearly. In the reign of James VI. an Act was passed (A.D. 1621) separating the barony of Logyfintray from the Regality of Lundoris. It is therein enacted, as more fully stated in a preceding page, ' that Courts be held at the Haltoun of Fyntrey instead of the Tolbuith of Newburgh.'

11. *Baddy-Forrow*, a property in the parish of Inverurie, now called Manar.

12. *Wester Disblair*, a property in the parish of Fintray.

13. *Dundee*, see *antea*.

14. *Eglismagill*, named Eglismagwll in the tack in favour of George Muncrefe (see *antea*) ; latterly it was known as Exmagirdle, but recently the name has been changed to Glenearn. It is situated in the westmost corner of the parish of Dron, in a small secluded valley lying between the Bridge of Earn and the Ochils. ' There is a roofless chapel, with a burying ground surrounding it, close by the old mansion house of Exmagirdle.' The author of ' Characteristics of Old Church Architecture,' says, ' there are features in the chapel indicative of the First-pointed Period,' which ranged

in Scotland from A.D. 1170 to 1250 (p. 47). In the churchyard there is a stone which commemorates the death of one of the martyrs of the Covenant, in these words : ' Heir lyis ane vertous Husbandman, Thomas Smal, who Died for Religion, Covenant, King and Countrie the 1st of September 1645, his age 58. Mementi mori.' The burying-ground is still used as such by the old families in the neighbourhood. There is no record as to how Exmagirdle came into the possession of Lindores Abbey, but that it was a dependent chapel of that monastery, where one or more of the monks celebrated divine worship, is evident from the record of the provision that was made for their comfort by the Steward of the Abbey. At page 31 of the ' Liber Sancti Marie de Lundoris,' the following occurs :— ' Memoradum of the bedds in Exmag. by this compt due of this compt and fyue diueriss claths bath for bed and burd.' ' The yeyr of God Ane mi° v°. & xxx yers.' But besides this memorandum, the Charter by James VI., erecting the lands which belonged to Lindores Abbey into a temporal Lordship in favour of Patrick Leslie, expressly sets forth 'that because from old times there was a chaplain who celebrated divine worship in the chapel of Eglismagirgill . . . therefore, we for the zeal, affection and love which we bear to the true religion, . . . give commission to Patrick Leslie to nominate a Reader to the said chapel, who shall have a stipend of forty merks yearly.'

In the preface to the ' Liber Sancti Marie de Lundoris,' the editor contraverts a statement of the Rev. Dr Anderson of Newburgh, and asserts that ' in the calendar of no church is such a saint enrolled' as St Magidrin. W. F. Skene, Esq., F.S.A., has conclusively shown in an able paper (*Proceedings Society of Antiquaries*, Vol. IV., p. 318) on the ' Early Ecclesiastical Settlements of St Andrews,' that this saint can be identified with St Adrian, who was martyred in the Isle of May. The parish of Lindores, of which Newburgh forms a part, was dedicated to St Magidrin, and, as already stated, his name appeared on Cross Macduff.

The editor is also in error in allowing the statement, which he has quoted in the same preface, from the Statistical Account of the Parish of Dron, that the chapel of Potie, at the mouth of Glenfarg, was a dependency of Lindores Abbey. In an Act passed in the reign of James VI. (cap. 162, A.D. 1592), the Kirks of Potie and Moncrief are designated ' pendicles of the College and Hospital of Dunbarney.' The chapel of Potie has been entirely swept away by the impetuous torrents of the Farg, and not a vestige remains above ground. A lead seal of a Papal Bull was found, in what constituted the burying-ground of the chapel, about twenty years ago. On one side is 'Nicolaus P.P. IIII., and on the other, ' SPA, SPE,' under which are heads of St Peter and St Paul. Nicolas IV. held the

Papacy from A.D. 1288 to 1292. The seal is deposited in the Museum of the Society of Antiquaries, Edinburgh.—*Proceedings of Society of Antiquaries*, Vol. IV., p. 296.

15. *Clavage*, a property in the parish of Dunning.

16. *Eister Feddellis* and *Bene*, now *Bennie;* both these properties are in the parish of Ardoch. The owner of one of the halves of Wester Feddellis was bound to carry two horse loads of herring yearly from Glasgow to the monastery of Lundoris for the use of the monks. John Chisholm was served heir to his father, Sir James Chisholm, in the lands of Wester Feddellis, in the Regality of Lundoris, 30th April 1642, under this burden. —*Perth Retours*, No. 503.

17. *Forrett.* There is no indication of the situation of this property, but in all likelihood it was Forrett in the parish of Logie, Fifeshire.

18. *Ebdy*, designated ' Ecc^a Lundors *vel* Ebedy,' *Reg de Dunfermelyn*, p. 208, now *Abdie*, see *antea*. By his charter, Lord Lindores was bound to pay the minister of ' Ebdie' 16 bolls of oatmeal, commonly called ' teind ait meall,' 4 bolls of barley and one hundred pounds Scots of stipend.

19. *The Wodriffe*, the arable portion of the lands bestowed by the Abbot of Lindores on the Burgesses of Newburgh, under payment of ' 40 bolls of beir,' which is still paid by the proprietors of the Wodriffe Lands (see *antea*).

Thraiplands, in Newburgh parish ; name obsolete.

20. *Brodlands*, part of the burgh lands lying between the Woodriffe and Mugdrum ; the name is now obsolete.

21. *The Haugh ;* the rich alluvial soil lying between Newburgh and the Tay ; the name is now disused, but it was familiarly known forty years ago.

22 *Dunmuir*, more correctly *Dunmore*, in the parish of Abdie. In the confirmation of the Foundation Charter of Lindores Abbey by Pope Innocent III., A.D. 1198, ' the chapel of Dundemore' is described ' as belonging to the church of Londors.' The name is undoubtedly derived from the Gaelic *Dun more*, the great *dun* or *fort* on Norman's Law, the Northman's or Norwegian's Law.—*Glossary of Cleveland Dialect*, p. xx. There is a small chapel on the property, the walls of which are nearly entire, but roofless. It is of comparatively modern erection, but the stones of a much older chapel have been used in its construction and it is a legitimate inference to presume that they formed part of the chapel existing A.D. 1198. Besides hewn work built among the rubble, the lintels of the gable windows are specially noticeable. They consist each of a single stone hewn into a semicircular or arched form, almost identical with some described by Dr Petrie, as seen in very ancient Irish churches.—*Round*

E E

Towers of Ireland, p. 181. The engraving of the window in the east gable of the chapel, at page 402, is from a drawing by Mr Jervise of Brechin. It gives a most accurate representation of the original.

The lands of Dunmore belonged to a family of great antiquity, who took their surname from the name of their property. Henry of Dundemore was a witness to the conveyance of the lands of Rathmuryel to the Monastery of Lundoris, at Lundoris Abbey, in the year 1245.—*Collections on Aberdeen and Banffshires*, p. 626. John of Dundemore was one of the Regents of Alexander III. in his minority, 1249-1262.—In the year 1260, '.a controversy arose between the monks of the Isle of May and Sir John of Dundemore, relative to the lands of Turbrech, in Fife, which, after many altercations, was settled by Sir John relinquishing all claim to the lands; in consideration of which the prior and monks granted him a monk to perform divine service in the chapel of the Blessed Virgin Mary in the Isle of May, for his soul, and the souls of his forefathers and successors. They were also to pay him half a merk of silver yearly, or sixty 'mulivelli' (a kind of fish abounding in the northern seas—the word has been translated mullet and haddock), at their option; and they also granted to him and his heirs a lamp of glass (to burn continually) in the church of Syreis, or Ceres, and for feeding it two gallons of oil, or twelve pence yearly. If they should fail to observe these conditions, Sir John was to have right of regress to the lands.'—*Preface to the Records of Priory of the Isle of May*, pp. xvi. xvii.

Henry of Dundemore, the successor of John, apparently not afraid for the loss of the prayers of the monks, seized a horse belonging to them, because they would not swear fealty to him for the lands of Turbrech; but in 1285 the Bishop of St Andrews, as arbiter, decided 'that the monks were not bound to make the fealty claimed, and gave sentence that the horse be restored.'—*Ib.*, p. xvii.

The Dundemores' seem to have been a family of great ability, and their talents raised them to high positions both in Church and State. In the struggle for Independence, they adhered to the patriotic side, and suffered in consequence. Among the petitions presented to Edward I. for maintenance by the wives of those whose estates had been seized because of their opposition to his claims, appears that of Isabella, the widow of Simon of Dundemore, 3d September 1296. Her petition was indorsed with these words, *Habeat quiete totum*—Let her quietly have the whole. Sir Richard of Dundemore was taken captive at the battle of Dunbar in 1296, and imprisoned in Winchester Castle, where he was confined for at least two years. On the 30th September 1298, an order allowing him fourpence a day for his maintenance while in prison, is preserved among the English Public Records.—*Historical Documents*, Vol. II., pp. 93, 94-307. Thomas of Dundemore, Bishop of Ross recognised the title of King Robert Bruce to the Crown of Scotland, A.D. 1309. In the same year John of Dundemore affixed his seal as a witness to the settlement of the dispute between the Abbot and Convent of Lundoris and the Burgesses of Newburgh. Stephen of Dundemore, who is expressly mentioned as being descended from the Dundemores of that ilk in Fife, was elected Bishop of Glasgow A.D. 1317. The Bishop-elect being a keen supporter of Bruce, Edward II. wrote to the Pope not to admit him to the Bishopric ; and it would appear that he never was consecrated, having died, it is said, on his way to Rome.—Keith's *Scottish Bishops*, pp. 187-242. On the 27th June 1331, Sir John Dundemore conveyed by charter in free gift to the monks of Balmerino, the right to the water running through his land of Dunberauch for the use of their mill at Pitgornoch. The bestowal of this gift was apparently made the occasion of a festive gathering at Dunmore; the Bishop of St Andrews, the Abbot of Lundoris, Sir David de Berkeley (of Cullairnie ?) Sir Alexander of Seton, the Governor of Berwick, Alex of Claphain, and others, were present as witnesses ; most of whom had borne their part in the great struggle for Independence.—*The Chartulary of Balmerino*, pp. 40, 41. In the reign of David II., 1346-70, Marion Dunmore gave a Charter to Robert, Stewart of Scotland, of the lands of Dunmore in Fyfe in favour of Roger Mortimer.—Robertson's *Index of Missing Charters*, 45-35. Another Stephen of Dunmore appears as a witness to an agreement by Fergus, Perpetual Vicar of the Church of Dunbulg, A.D. 1395.—*Register of the Priory of St Andrews*, p. 49.

In the year 1483, Isobel, spouse of umquhile Richardsoun, is named as proprietor of Dunmore, but whether in her own right as a descendant of the Dundemores, does not appear. On the 11th October of that year, she was summoned before the Lords of Council by Andrew, Abbot of Lundores, for the payment of ' viii chalders of vittale of the teynds of Dunmure,' which she was decerned to pay. *Acta Dominorum* p. 119.*—On the 19th February 1483-4 George, Lord Setoun, raised an action against John Bercla, brother to David Bercla of Cullerney and others, for the wrongous occupation of Dunmore, on the ground that he had received a tack of the lands from the Crown ; Bercla and his friends alleging, on the other hand, that they had a warrand from Andrew Richardson for the occupation of the lands.—*Ib.*, p. 130.* Dunmore seems subsequently to have come into the hands of the Crown.

James III. bestowed 'the lands of Dunmuir on his servitor, James Paterson, 1460-1488.—*Sibbald* p. 408. James V., about two months before his death, conferred on Sir David Lyndsay of the Mount, as Lyon King of Arms 'two chalders aittis yearly for hors corn all the days of his life, out of the Kings lands of Over-Dynmure now being in the hands of Walter Paterson, fewar of the samyn.' This was in augmentation of Lyndsay's ordinary fee assigned by the same monarch out of the lands of Luthrie. *Sir David Lyndsay's Works, Chalmers' Edition*, Vol. I., p. 26.

This addition to his salary must have been doubly gratifying to Lyndsay, coming from the Prince whom he had nurtured in his youth, and at the time that the out-spokenness of his writings must necessarily have begat him many enemies. In his first poem Lyndsay, addressing the King, says—

> ' Quhen thow wes·young I bure thee in myne arme
> Full tenderlie, tyll thou begouth to gang ;
> And in thy bed oft happit thee full warme,
> With lute in hand, syne sweitlie to thee sang,'

and in his latter years he counselled James to ' Lerne to be ane King.'

Lyndsay's denunciations of the vices of the clergy are unsparing, and David Laing, in his Memoir of him says, 'It is a remarkable fact, that in such troublous times, Lyndsay should have been allowed to escape persecution in some of its various forms, whether deprivation of property, imprisonment, torture or death,' p. xlix. Lyndsay's Poems, written in the vernacular, came home with power to the people, and his unsparing exposure of the vices and errors of the clergy powerfully helped on the cause of Reformation, so much so, that one writer does not hesitate to affirm that ' Sir David Lyndsay was more the Reformer of Scotland than John Knox.' —*Pinkerton, quoted by Joseph Robertson. Preface to Statuta Ecc. Scoticanae*, p. cccix. It has been said that Lyndsay never joined the Reformers, but Mr David Laing has shown that he ' died some time previous to the 18th April 1555,' upwards of four years before the consummation of the Reformation. Had he lived, the whole tendency of his writings shows that he would have thrown himself in the cause which he had advocated into his writings.

In Lamont's Diary, under date 1669, the following occurs :—' About Whitsunday, Andrew Patersone, one of the baylies of Cupar in Fyffe bought the lands of Dunmwre, nire Aytown in Fyffe from the Laird of Dunmwre, and ane Hew Patersone, writer in Edb. It was estimat about 16 chalders of victual and money rent, it stood him about 32 thousand merkis.' P. 263. It would appear, however, that the laird had only sold one of the portions into which estates were at that period subdivided, for, on the 6th January 1686, Andrew Paterson of Dinmwr was served heir to his father George Patersone in the east half of the lands of Dinmwr, known as Over-Dunmoore and in the Mill of Dunmoore. On the 19 Jany[r] 1699 George Paterson was served heir to his brother Andrew in the same lands. —*Fife Retours, No.* 1280-1424. Sibbald, in his History of Fife, 1710, says,

'South east of Dinbug is Dinmuir, a new house the seat of Mr George Paterson whose ancestors have been heritors of this estate since the reign of James III.'—P. 408. A portion of this house still remains, forming part of the steading. A coat of arms, carved in oak, is built into the wall, but the carving is so much wasted that it is not decipherable. George Paterson married, in 1710, Elizabeth, eldest daughter of Major Henry Balfour of Dunbog. The building of the new house, or other causes, seems to have brought him into difficulties, for, in 1729, he conveyed Over or Easter Dunmure to his creditors. The property was bought at a public *roup* by Major Balfour, who sold it in 1742 to William Imrie. Over Dunmure remained in possession of the Imries until 1805; in which year Lieut.-Col. Ninian Imrie sold it to the late Alexander Murray and his son Joseph Murray of Ayton, the present proprietor.

In 1507, by a Charter under the Great Seal, 'James IV. bestowed the west half of Dinmuir or Nether Dinmuir, now called Ayton, on Andrew Aiton, Captain of the Castle of Stirling, of the family of Aiton in the Merse, for good and faithful services.'—*Sibbald*, p. 409. Andrew Aiton had also a charter to Glenduckie, 1506. The following notice of the descendants of Andrew Ayton is from Sir James Balfour's M.S. Collections on the Shires,' preserved in the Advocates' Library :—

> 1. 'Andrew Aytone 2^d sone to the Laird of Aytone in the Merss and Capitane of the Castell of Streweling wes the first that had the Landes of Nether Dunmore in few farm from K. Ja. He married Isobel, daughter to Kincragey of that ilk and had issew 3 sonns and 7 daughters. The sonns, Johne the eldest succidit him.

Robert the 2^d wes the first goodman of Inchdarney.

Mr Johne [Andrew?] hes 3^d sone wes first goodman of Kinaldey.[1]

His daughters ver :—

the eldest wes Lade (Lady) of Balthayock in Perthshyre.

Hes 2^d daughter wes maried to Straquhaine, Laird of Brigtoune in Forfarshyre.

Hes 3^d daughter wes maried to Cunninghame, Laird of Polmais in Streueling.

Hes 4^t daughter ves maried to Shaw of Knockhill in Strevelingshyre.

Hes 5^t daughter was married to Lindesay of Dowhill.

Hes 6^t daughter wes married to Hackett of Pitfirrane.

---

[1] There is evidently an error here. There was a John Aytoun of Kinaldie about 1539, 'who, there is reason to believe, was a younger brother of the Captain of Stirling Castle. His son left that estate to Andrew, his uncle's youngest [3d] son.—*Memoir of Sir Robert Aytoun, by Rev. Dr Rogers*, p. 153.

Hes 7 daughter wes maried to Dudingstone of Sanford for his 2^d vyffe.

2. Johne Aytone succidit hes father [19th April 1558] and ves 2^d goodman of Dunmore, maried Barclay daughter to Dauid Barclay of Cullerney and had issew one sone Androw.

3. Androw Aytone only sone to John Ayton of Dunmore succidit hes father [1581] and maried Elizabeth Weymes daughter to the Laird of Pittincreiffe had issew 3 sonns.

John his eldest sone succidit him.

Robert his 2^d sone of Craidfudey, married Ingliss, daughter of Inglis of Ingilishtaruett, and had issew, Mr Robert Aytone of Cluny now living &c.

Andrew his 3^d wes neuer maried, bot he had a Basse son Mr Androw Aytone, Adwocat now Laird of Logie 1637; and 4 daughters, the eldest wes maried to John Pitcairne of forther and had issew.

Hes 2^d daughter was maried to Alexander Lindesay of the Mounth and had issew.

Hes 3^d daughter wes maried to David Balfour of Pouis in Streveling-shyre and had issew.

Hes 4^t daughter wes maried to John Arnott of Voodmyle and had issew.

4. John Aytoune 4^t of Dunmore did succeed hes father Androw and maried Anna Weeymes daughter to Sir John Veeymes of Wymes, and had issew one sone Androw and 2 daughters.

Margarett his eldest daughter wes maried to George Settone of Carrilstoune and had issew.

Catherine hes 2^d daugher wes maried to George Patersone of Luthrey for his first Wyffe and had issew Robert Patersone now of Dunmore, &c.

5 Androw Aytone first Laird of Aytone had hes Lands of Dunmore vith vthers by K. Ja: 6 in free Barroney: to be callid in all tyme coming the Lairschipe and Barroney of Aytone, succidit his father Johne, and maried Anna Loudone 3^d daughter of Mr William Loudone of the same, by Elizabeth Loudone hes 2^d Wyffe daughter to the Laird of Balgoney, and had issew one sone Johne that succidit him, and 4 daughters, Margaret his eldest daughter wes maried to Sir Thomas Blair of Balthayock and hes issew.

Anna hes 2^d daughter wes maried to Sir James Balfour of Kynaird Knight and Barronett and hes issew.

Elizabeth hes 3^d daughter was maried to Sir Johne Weeymes of Bogey knight and hes no issew.

Helena hes 4^t daughter wes maried to Sir Dauid Barclay of Culerney Knight and left no issew.

6. Johne Aytone 6^t of that family did succeid hes father Androw quho deyed——at Aytone in February in A° and wes interid at Ebdey Church that same month. He maried Elizabeth Weeymes 4 daughter to Johne, Earle of Weeymes one the 18 day of Appryll 1636 and hes isseu liuing in this yeir of God 1654.

' 2. Sonnes John and Dauïd and six daughters.'

John, the eldest son, received the honour of knighthood. This is recorded in Lamont's Diary as follows :—' 1665 This summer, yo Ayton in Fyffe, was knighted, as also Balbeadie's eldest son, surnamed Malcome was made a knight baronet, att Edb. Sir John married a daughter of Sir William Stewart of Enderneath; this event is also recorded by Lamont— ' Sept. 1. 1670, Ayton married Sir William Stewart of Enderneath, att Perth, his daughter, the marriage feast stood att hir father's house in Pearth.'—*Lamont's Diary*, p. 231. Sir John married as his second wife Margaret Colville, daughter of Lord Colville of Ochiltree, in 1701. He died in 1703, and was succeeded by his eldest son William. Sir John, shortly before his death, settled on his second wife and her children (besides a jointure), 40,000 merks and half the lands of Kincraigie. His eldest son raised an action to reduce this settlement, on the ground that it left him less than he was entitled to as heir. The question was litigated in the Court of Session for eleven years, and in 1716 it was decided, mainly on technical grounds, that he 'could quarrel none of his father's deeds.'—*Morrison's Dictionary of Decisions*, Nos. 6710, 14009, 14012. This long litigation empoverished the heir, and he sold Ayton on the 7th December 1723, to Patrick Murray, second son of Sir Patrick Murray of Ochtertyre, whose great-grandson, Joseph Murray, is now proprietor of Ayton and Dunmore.

The family of Ayton buried in the old chapel of Dundemore. On the inside of the east gable there is a sandstone panel bearing four shields with the date 1683, and the initials J. A. carved on it. Mr Jervise of Brechin, who has examined the monument, is of opinion that ' the third as well as the first shield has been charged with the Ayton arms (a cross engrailed between four roses). The arms on the second shield are very much defaced, but enough remains to show that it had borne four lions rampant (for Wemyss), which is confirmed by the faint traces of the letter W. below the shield. The arms on the fourth shield, although only two stars in chief are now visible, are probably those of Lindsay of Kirkforthar, which are described as a fesse-chequee between three stars in chief, and a hunting horn in base.' The initials and date prove that the panel was erected by Sir John Ayton, and the preceding pedigree shows the connection of the Ayton's with the Wemyss family, but no record has appeared to show their connection with the Lindsays of Kirkforthar. The son of

Patrick Murray who acquired Ayton, is said to have been buried in the chapel. In 1710, when Sir Robert Sibbald wrote his History of Fife, there was, he says, 'a good house with all conveniences of gardens and inclosures belonging to Mr William Ayton, the lineal successor of Andrew Ayton, Captain of the Castle of Stirling.'—P. 406. Not a vestige of the house now remains. William Edmonstone Aytoun, the author of the 'Lays of the Scottish Cavaliers,' was a descendant of the Aytons of Ayton.

23. *Carpow*, the name of a small farm absorbed into the adjoining farm of Glenduckie. A portion of the lands are still known as Carpow Rigs.

24. *Kinnaird.* Sir James Balfour, in his manuscript preserved in the Advocates' Library, says, 'With Lochindoir bordires Kynaird the heritage of Sir James Balfour, Lyone King of Armes ; these lands formerlie belonged to David Earll of Huntingdone who dysponed the tyndis anno 9 regis Willielmi under the tenour Omnes decimas villae *nostre de Kynnaird Beata Mariae et monochis de Londores in Sylvis.* (All the teinds of our town of Kynnaird to the Blessed Mary and the Monks of Londoris in the Woods) wch he himself foundit not a yeir befoir, and the lands within 3 yeiris following to Gilbert, Earll of Stratherne his cousigne quhos sone Madoc, Earl of Stratherne with consent of his son Malise dated [doted] the property of the said land to the Prioress and Holy Virgins of Elchok in the reign of Alexander II. A.D. 1214-1247. Magdalen, prioress of Elchok sett thir lands, Reg. Ja. 5 (1528–1542) in heritabill feu, but any reversioune to Robert leslie Advocatt to the Kingis Majestie quhose ischew failling in the air maill by his grand chyld Elizabeth married to James Barron ane Merchant in Edinburgh quhos sone George barone [who had a charter to Kynnard in favour of himself and Elizabeth Linmouth from James VI., dated 21st July 1587] disponed them to Sir Michael Balfour of Denmylne knight.' According to the Retours of Fife, Alexander Leslie succeeded to the lands of Kinnaird as heir to his father Mr Andrew Leslie of Innerpeffer in 1544. (No. 4) Thomas, his brother, succeeded to him in 1556, (No. 28) and Helen their sister, in 1561 (No. 47). Assuming Mr Andrew to be the son of Robert Leslie, the 'Advocatt,' Elizabeth must have been his great-grandchild. On the 29th January 1630 Charles I. granted a Charter of Confirmation under the Great Seal to the lands of Kynnaird in favour of Sir James Balfour, Lyon-King-of-Arms, and his spouse, Nos. 53, 113, 6, 1, 6.

Lord Balvaird must have acquired the right to the feu-duties payable out of Kinnaird to the nunnery of Elcho, for, on the 12th May 1643, Andrew, Lord Balvaird, conveyed them by Disposition to Sir Michael Balfour of Denmiln, and to his son Sir James Balfour of Kinnard. On the 5th September 1675, Sir Michael Balfour of Denmiln, with consent of Dame Katherine Pitcarne his mother, conveyed to Sir James Sinclair and Dame Elizabeth

Balfour his spouse, ' the lands and barony of Kinnaird and thretty four pounds Scottis money formerlie payable to the Priory of Elcho, acquired by umquhile Sir Michael Balfour my grandfather and Sir James Balfour his sone.' On the 25th September 1702, Sir George Sinclair, son of Sir James Sinclair, had a precept of Iufeftment to the lands of Kinnaird. On the 24th January 1726, Sir George, with consent of Dame Margaret Crawford his spouse, sold the Barony of Kinnaird to Sir Edward Gibson of Keirhill, Baronet. After Sir Edward's death the property passed successively through the hands of Alexander Cameron, writer in Edinburgh, 1739. Walter Ferguson, also writer in Edinburgh, 1758. Dr James Walker, physician in Edinburgh, 1764. John Lyon, merchant in Dundee 1773, sold Kinnaird and Inverdovat, which also belonged to Dr Walker, to John Berry of Wester Bogie, 1788.—*From the Original Charter in the possession of John Berry, Esquire of Tayfield and Inverdovat.* Kinnaird subsequently came into the possession of William Robertson, Town Clerk of Cupar, whose daughters sold it in 1799 to John Pitcairn, the grandfather of John Pitcairn, Esq., the present proprietor.

25. *The Wodmyln*, now the mains of Woodmiln, in the parish of Abdie, formerly the property of a branch of the family of Arnot. A portion of the walls of their mansion, which appears to have been a very unsubstantial structure, still stands. There is a large garden enclosed by high walls, and laid out in terraces, with a fine old yew tree in it, adjoining the ruins of the mansion house. Robert Arnot, a grandson of Arnot of Arnot, who was Captain of Stirling Castle and Comptroller of Scotland, A D. 1442, acquired the lands of Woodmiln from James IV. by Charter dated 6th March 1509. He fell with his Royal Master at the disastrous defeat of Flodden. The Arnots of Fernie and of Balcormo, of whom Hugo Arnot, the well known historical and antiquarian writer was descended, are sprung from Robert Arnot who acquired Woodmiln. In 1558 his grandson John succeeded to the estate, and his great grandson, also John, succeeded in 1606. The great grandson sold the estate to Sir John Arnot of Berswick, a descendant of another branch of the Arnots of Arnot. He was Provost of Edinburgh, and Treasurer Depute of Scotland A.D. 1604. John Arnot, merchant burgess of Edinburgh, was served heir to Sir John Arnot his grandfather, in the lands of Woodmilne, 28th February 1616.—*Fife Retours,* 257. His descendants continued in possession of the estate down to the beginning of the 18th century.

Sir Robert Arnot of Fernie, who was descended from the first branch of the Arnots of Woodmilne, married Margaret, daughter and heiress of Michael, 1st Lord Balfour of Burleigh, and by Royal Letters assumed that title on the death of his father-in-law. The Balfours of Fernie and Dunbog were descendants of this marriage. The representatives of the families of

Burleigh, Fernie, and Dunbog, joined the rising in favour of the Stuarts in 1715, and their estates were confiscated.

26. *The Frieland.* The lands of Lochend were formerly known by this name.—*Teind Court Records.*

27. *Inchery*, now *Inchrye*, formed part of the Earldom of Fife. On the 18th February 1526, James V. grants a charter under the Great Seal to this property, in favour of David Balfour of Inchery and his wife. This grant was renewed in 1541. In 1567 a charter was granted to David his son and heir (May 25). In 1594 a charter was granted by James VI. to David Balfour of Inschrie and his eldest son David, of the lands of Pallis of Clackmannan. In 1596 a charter was granted to David Balfour of Powhouse, and David Balfour his son, as heir of the lands of Inchry. In 1600 David Balfour of Incherie is described as ' heretable few firmorar and Immediat tennent thereof.'—*Act Scot. Par.* 1600. In 1628 John Spens was served heir to his father William Spens in Grange of Lindores, as heir to the lands of Inchery, described as within the Lordship and Stewartry of Fife. In 1683 Inchrye seems to have come into the possession of James Irvine, who is designed of Inchrey in the record of a baptism in Abdie church, of a daughter of William Balfour, the minister, on the 23d June of that year. Sir Michael Balfour of Denmylne and Johne Arnot are the other witnesses or sponsors. Woodmilne and Inchrye are now the property of the Right Rev. William Scot Wilson, Bishop of Glasgow.

28. *Loundoris*, now *Lindores*, formed part of the possessions of the Earl of Fife, who had a strong castle on the ridge overlooking the loch. ' As is evident,' says Sir James Balfour in his Topographical Notes, ' in aue donatioun of Donald Macduffs, Earll of Fyff, *Deo et St Mariae et Monachis de Lyndoris* (To God and St Mary and the Monks of Lyndoris) dated *ex arce nostra de Lochindore &c.* (at our castle of Lochindore).' ' Lindore,' he continues, ' is the Kingis property and a parcill of the patrimony of the ancient Earlls of Fyffe ; the teyndis, personage and viccarage of thir landis were given be Colban Earl of Fyffe to the Abbey of Lyndoris.' The Earldom of Fife, which fell to the Crown by the forfeiture of Murdoc, Duke of Albany, in 1425 (24 May) was annexed to the Crown by special Act of Parliament 4 August 1455. John of Ballone, who is subsequently named Balfour, obtained a grant of the lands of Ald Lindores ; and on the 10th October 1578, the following decision of the Lords of Council was given in his favour :—' The Lords ordanis th^t letters be writtin to the L^t of Fyfe charging him incontinent to devoide and Red John Gourlaw, Walt Smy^t, Jon methven, Alex^r Ballingaw, Thos Ballingaw, John Ballingaw, Robert wri^t and Alex^r Dysert furth of the lands of Ald Lundors gevin and assignit be our Soveraun lord to John of Ballone as is qteinit in his lrès

and that he keipe the said John undistrublit in the Joysing of the said lands ay and quhil the said psonis bring and schew before the lords sufficiat lres of tak of mar strength than the said John of Ballone now schewis.'—*Acta Dominorum*, p. 7. The tenants showed that they had a tack from Alexander Lesly, the King's Receiver, and they were allowed to remain in possession of the lands to the issue of their leases, the same as the king's other tenants in Fife. But they were decerned to remove at Whitsunday 1481.—*Ib.*, p. 19-50. How long the Balfours of Baldone retained possession of the lands of Ald Lindores does not appear, but in 1602 they were proprietors of Ballinblae and Nuthill.—*Fife Retours*, 115-122.

Sir James Balfour, in his Topographical Notes, says, that ' Lindore is the Heritage of James Macgil of Nether Rankelo quhose grandfather being Clerk Register had these landis for his good service from Andrew Earll of Rothes. The half of thir lands belonged reg Ja: 5 in anno 1530, to Alexander de Walloniis; they hold fewe, and is of the Kingis property.' A Charter of Confirmation was granted by Mary on 18th September 1569 to James M'Gill of Nether Rankelour and his spouse Jonet Adamson of the lands of Auld Lundors.—*Mag. Sig.* 32-379, M. 17. On the 19th May 1569, James VI. granted a Charter of Confirmation to the same lands in favour of Mr James M'Gill, Rankelour Nether, Clerk Register. Another charter to ' Auld Lundors' was granted by James VI. to Mr James M'Gill and Joanna Wemys his spouse, on 29 July 1587.—*Ib.*, 36-412. In the eighth generation from James M'Gill, the Clerk Register who acquired Lindores, the Honourable Charles Maitland, sixth son of the Earl of Lauderdale, married Margaret Dick, the heiress of Rankeillour and Lindores; she had succeeded in right of her mother, daughter of David M'Gill, who claimed the title of Viscount Oxfurd in 1734.—*Douglas Peerage, Oxfurd.* The Hon. Charles Maitland lived at Mugdrum for several years. At the outbreak of the American War of Independence he was appointed to the *Elizabeth* 74, and so greatly was he esteemed that upwards of forty young men belonging to Newburgh volunteered and went with him on that service. Admiral Maitland's younger son, Sir Frederick Lewis Maitland, born 1779, entered the navy and was on board his father's ship as a midshipman in Lord Howe's action off Ushant on the 1st June 1794. He was at the landing of the forces with Sir Ralph Abercromby in Egypt, and in many other engagements during the war. Napoleon Buonaparte delivered himself up to Captain Maitland on board the *Bellerophon* after his defeat at Waterloo. A narrative of the events connected with the Emperor's surrender was subsequently published by Captain Maitland. He retired for a few years from active service, and built a house which is beautifully situated, overlooking the Loch, on his ancestral property of Lindores. In

1838 he was appointed to the command of the fleet sent to China ; he died while on that service (1839), and was buried at Bombay. Captain Scott, the eldest son of Sir Walter Scott, was one of the pall-bearers at his funeral. A monument was raised to his memory, by public subscription, at a cost of £1500, and erected at Bombay, of which a bust of the Admiral forms a part. Auld Lindores, as it was formerly called, is now the property of Lewis Maitland, Esq., nephew of Sir Frederick Lewis Maitland. The other portion of the estate belongs to William Guild, Esq.

29. *The Denmill.* In a charter under the Great Seal, granted on the 29th September 1541, by James V. in favour of Patrick Balfour, heir-apparent, Denmiln is styled The King's Miln of Denmyln. After the disappearance of Sir Michael Balfour in 1709, he was succeeded in the estate and title by his son Sir Michael, who married Jane, daughter of Ross of Invernethy, by whom he had seven sons and three daughters.—*Abdie Register of Births.* The two eldest must have died before their father, as it is stated that he was succeeded by his third son John ; but he appears only to have succeeded to the title, for his father, Sir Michael, had assigned the lands of the barony of Denmiln to his creditors, as appears from the sasine recorded on 5th June 1750. Sir Michael did not long survive, as he was struck off the roll of freeholders in October following, with the word 'dead' marked against his name. After the death of Sir John without issue, the title, it is said, devolved on his next brother Patrick, who was baptised in Abdie Parish Church on the 4th December 1729. In the *North British Advertiser* of the 18th April 1846, the following advertisement appeared :—' Sir Patrick Balfour, deceased. Any person who can give information of the time of the death and place of burial of Sir Patrick Balfour of Denmill, North Britain, who is supposed to have died in England about six years ago, will receive adequate remuneration upon communicating the same to G. C. Meynell, Esq., 6 King's Bench Walk, Temple, London ; or to Messrs Smith & Kinnear, W.S., 35 Queen Street, Edinburgh.' If the Sir Patrick Balfour, who is supposed to have died in 1840 was the son of Sir Michael, who was born in 1729, he must have reached the improbable age of one hundred and seventeen. The probability is, that he must have died much earlier, or that his son succeeded to the barren title. Susanna Balfour, the youngest daughter of the last Sir Michael, baptised on 27th December 1738, married Robert Hamilton of Wishaw, who was entitled to succeed as sixth Lord Belhaven. Her son William made good his right in 1799, and became seventh Lord Belhaven. —*Douglas Peerage.* Through this connection the original portrait of Sir James Balfour, Lyon-King-of-Arms, now at Wishaw House, came into the possession of the Belhaven family.

The estate of Denmiln came into the possession of General Sir John Scott of Balcomie, by charter under the Great Seal, dated 6th August 1772. General Scott sold the freehold of Denmiln to Captain Thomas Rigg, late of the 26th Regiment, and of Wester Lumbenny and of Lochmill, to Captain Francis Stuart, late of the same regiment, to enable them to vote for the representative of the county in Parliament. Denmiln was sold by the Duchess of Portland, daughter of General Scott, to the ancestor of the present proprietor, Archibald A. Watt, Esq. of Denmiln. The castle, after it ceased to be the residence of the Balfours, was allowed to go to ruin. In the front wall of the steading of Denmiln there is a shield in stone, bearing the arms and initials of Sir Michael Balfour and of his wife Jean or Joanna Durham. It is surmounted by the motto, *Ditat Servata Fides.* The castle is now roofless, but the present proprietor has cleared out the ruins, and has put them in a becoming condition.

30. *The Parkhill.* Sir James Balfour, in his Topographical Notes, says : ' Betwixt the remaining shrubes of the forest of Ironsyde and Londors lyes parkhill. The Etomologie thereof being clear and conspicuous of itself, it is the inheritance of John Earl of Rothess, formerlie belonging to David, Erll of Huntingdone and Angus, as appears by ane donatione of his to the Abbot and Convent of Lyndores of a quarry of frie stone to build with, *e terris nostris de parkhill in Sylva de Ironsyd'* (from our lands of Parkhill in the wood of Ironside). James V. granted a feu-charter to John Leslie, Rector of Kinnore, brother-german of George, fourth Earl of Rothes, 1537. In 1540 James V. granted a charter of the same lands of Parkhill, and of the wood of Ironside, to John Leslie of Cleische and Eupham Moncrief, his spouse, 10th July 1542. John Leslie aided his nephew Norman, Master of Rothes, in the murder of Cardinal Beaton, for which his lands were forfeited, 14th August 1546. John Grant of Fruichy, who had obtained a charter of Parkhill for the conservation of the same, resigned them in favour of his beloved friend John Leslie of Parkhill, 8th August 1567. ' The relations and friends of Cardinal Beaton, in consideration of the repentance of John Leslie for the slaughter of the Cardinal their tender friend, forgave him the rankour of their wrath and deadly feud, with all actions civil or criminal, 3 July 1575.' John Leslie's daughter Euphan, married in 1572 Alexander Bruce of Earlshall. She probably died without issue, and having no direct male heir, John Leslie exchanged, in 1573, the lands of Parkhill with his nephew Andrew, Earl of Rothes, for a liferent lease for himself and a natural daughter, of the Mains of Rothes.—*Historical Records of the Family of Leslie,* Vol. II., p. 150–152. Parkhill is now the property of the Earl of Zetland.

31–36. The names of the places mentioned under these numbers are now obsolete. The Marie Croft seems to have lain near the precincts of the Abbey. In the Retour of Service of Sir Michael Balfour as heir to his father, 22d July 1675, Earneside-slack and Maries-craig-den occur as forming part of his possessions. Mariès Craig is the correct name of the craig now known as Mares Craig.

37. *The Newbruiche—passim.*

38. *The Grange* was the earliest possession of Lindores Abbey. Originally it consisted of at least the farm now called the Grange, and of Berryhoill, Ormiston, and the Hilton. In 1479 the monks let a fourth part of the town of the Grange (by this time much restricted in size) to Dionisius Chalmers and his son. On the 2d December 1526, John, Abbot of Lundoris, granted a charter in favour of John Blyth and his spouse of 3 acres of the lands of Grange; and to Ninian Blyth of 3 acres on the 19th March 1554, of 3 acres on 17th February 1558. In 1558 the Abbot granted a charter to John Wentoun of 8 oxgaits of the lands of Grange.— *Mugdrum Archives.* John Wentoun was succeeded by his son James, A.D. 1594.—*Fife Retours*, No. 1518. In 1657 Sir Robert Balfour of Denmiln was served heir to his grandfather, Sir Michael Balfour, in ' 8 oxingait of the lands of Graing of Lindores upon the north side of the town of Graing.' Also, in ' 3 aikers of the same lands called Keigisholl, Chapman-Croft and Eister and Wester Cunningares.'—*Fife Retours*, No. 877. The ' 8 oxingaits upon the north side of the town of Graing,' are evidently the farm now called North Grange, the property of Archibald A. Watt, Esq. of Denmiln.

38. *Berrieholl* (in the parish of Abdie). *Berry* and *Choille*, Gaelic, Wood. Alexander Ballingall had a Charter of Confirmation to the lands of Berrie-holl from Queen Mary on 31st May 1565.—*Reg. Mag. Sig.*, 31–534. In 1637 James Philip was served heir to his father in ' 8 bovates of the lands of Grange called Berriehoill.' In 1643 Alexander Johnston died possessed of another ' 8 bovates of the town of . Berriehoill in the Grange.' In 1672 Henry Philp succeeded, on the death of his uncle, Michael Philp of Newburgh, to the 8 bovates which belonged to him.—*Fife Retours*, 545, 637, 1117. Berryhoill, in common with most other properties in Fife and in Scotland generally, was much subdivided in the 17th century. Alexander Spence, writer in Edinburgh, bought the separate portions in 1671–4. He married Katherine Arnot, with consent of her grandfather, Mr James Cheape of Rossie, in 1686. In the south wall of Abdie old church there is a monument to the memory of Alexander Spence, surmounted by a crest, with a scroll on which a motto has been carved, and the initials A. S. K. A., with a hand grasping apparently two coulters and an ear of wheat. The stone is so much wasted that the inscription cannot

be read. Henry Spence was served heir to his father in 1713. In 1715 Henry conveyed two parts of Berryhoill to his brother William, chirurgeon in Dunkeld, and a few years afterwards the whole property was conveyed to George Paterson of Dunmuire, whose trustees sold it in 1742 to Alexander Spence, chirurgeon in Dunfermline, who resold it in 1763. After several changes, Berryhoill came into the possession of Major-General John Scott of Balcomie in 1774 ; his daughter, the Duchess of Portland, sold it in 1801 to John Arnot of Lumquhat, whose heirs sold it in 1817 to Henry Buist, the father of Andrew Walker Buist, Esq., the present proprietor.

38. *Ormistoun* (in the parish of Abdie) in 1564 was the property of James Philp, cousin to the Abbot Lundores, being so designated in a charter to the lands of the Quhyt Park and Park of Lundoris (now Mount Pleasant) of that date   In 1631 Ormiston belonged to Mr Henry Cheape ; he was succeeded by Mr James Cheape, designed of Ormiston, in 1644.— *Mugdrum Charters, and Abdie Session Records.*

Ormiston is now in the possession of George Buist, Esq.

38. *Hiltonhill* (in the parish of Abdie). In 1617 Mr Andrew Ayton, Advocate, received a charter to the lands of Halltounhill (now Hattonhill), Murierigs, and other lands in the Tenandry of Clunie from James VI., 2d December.—*Reg. Mag. Sig.*, 48, 305.

39. *Halhill* (in the parish of Collessie) ' belonged to Mr Henry Balnaves, Depute-Keeper of the Privy Seal. He gave the lands of Halhill to Sir James Melville, a son of the Laird of Raith, and with his posterity it continued till Charles II.'s reign, when Lord Melville (afterwards Earl) purchased it.'—Sibbald's *History of Fife*, p. 390.

Sir James Melville wrote an account of the transactions in which he was engaged in Queen Mary's reign. It has since been published under the title of *Memorials of his Own Life*, A.D. 1549–1593. There is a monument with a long inscription to his memory in Collessie churchyard, a copy of which is given in the *New Statistical Account of Collessie Parish.* Halhill is now the property of Lady Elizabeth Melville Cartwright.

40. *The Mylhill, Scheilles and Bowes*, were conveyed by Sir James Sandilands of Calder to his uncle, James Sandilands, by charter dated 17th May 1509. They are now the property of George Johnston, Esq. of Lathrisk.

41. *Newtoun of Cullesey* was conveyed by the same charter, as more fully stated below, also to James Sandilands. In the Records of the Burgh of Dysart, the following entry occurs :—' At the Newtown of Colessie and at Pitlair, 21st Octr. 1565. The whilk day Andrew Forester, minister at the Kirk of Dysart, made intimation to the persons following in

manner underwritten, of an assignation in his favour by the Abbot of Lindores, subscribed with his hand, under his seal of office, of certain sums of money and victuals which they ought and should pay to the Abbey of Lundores.'—*Notices of the Local Records of Dysart*, p. 32. Newton of Collessie now belongs to William Wallace, Esq.

42. *Pitlair.* · This property belonged in the 15th century to the Sandilands of Calder. In 1466 Sir James, eldest son of Sir John Sandilands of Calder, by his marriage with Margaret of ·Kynloch, daughter of John Kynloch of Crovy (Cruivie), acquired Pitlair, the Kirktown of Cullesey, with the mill and the lands of Pitlochy.—*Precept of Sasine (in Mugdrum Charter-Chest), dated at St Andrews, 4th June* 1466. The ancestor of John Kynloch of that ilk, had a charter to a mill and lands in the neighbourhood of Collessie in the reign of Alexander III. (1249-1285).—Sir Robert Sibbald's *History of Fife*, p. 390.

In a charter by James Sandelands of Calder, knight, also preserved in the archives of Mugdrum, he conveys to his uncle, James Sandelandis, his half of the lands of Cruwy, with the mansion-house thereof, the half of the lands of *Newtoun of Cullesey*, and the *Gaudwel, of Schelis*, of *Bowhous*, of Clesche and the lands of *Pitlair*, with the mill of Kirktoun Cullessy, of Mylhill of Pitlochy with the mill thereof ; and to the said James and Katrine Scot, his spouse, half of the lands of *Weddersbe*, reserving the third part of the said lands, except the half of the lands of *Widdersbe*, to Marion Forester, the granter's spouse, during the lifetime of Margaret Kar, Countess of Errole, and spouse of the late James Sandelandis, knight, the granter's grandfather. Dated at Edinburgh, 17th May 1509. Witnesses —John, Prior of St Andrews, William Scot of Balwery, Knight, Mr James Skrymgeour, and James Skrymgeour.

A precept of sasine under the Great Seal, in the reign of James V. (also preserved in the archives of Mugdrum), for infefting Mr Peter Sandelandis, Rector of Calder, as assignee to James Sandelandis, son and heir of the late James Sandelandis of Cruvy, brother of the said Mr Peter, in the lands of Pitlair, is dated at Edinburgh, 19th May 1539. The barony of Pitlair, which included the lands of Kirktown of Cullessie, Pitlochie, Pitlair, Drumclochope, and half of the lands of Weddersbie, Wodheid, Gadvane, Bowhous and Scheillis, continued in the possession of the Sandilands until Sir James Sandilands, created Lord Abercrombie in 1647, dissipated his whole estates in Fife, and sold them in 1649.—*Douglas Peerage, Wood's Ed.—Abercrombie; Lamont's Diary*, p. 13. Pitlair afterwards became much subdivided. In 1633, Janet Hardie was served heir to her father in the mill of Pitlair ; and the land adjacent to it. On the 31st May 1644, David Fyiff succeeded his father in a fourth part and half a fourth part, and to the right of pasturage on the barony of Pitlair.—*Fife Retours*, 494, 961.

43. *Daftmyln*, written Dafmyln in the oldest Rental, signifies the Ox-myln. *Damh* (pronounced Daff), being the Gaelic for Ox. Pitlair and Daff Mill belong to Miss Walker.

44. *Maristoun*—Mary's town, now corrupted to Merston, in all proba-bility named in honour of the Virgin. The property of David Maitland Makgill Crichton, Esq.

45. *Lawfield and Menysgrene.* Menegre is mentioned in the charter by Roger de Quinci, Earl of Winchester, to the monks of Lindores, 1306-1329. The name appears now to be obsolete. Lawfield is the property of F. L. Maitland Heriot, Esq. of Ramornie.

46. *Bellowmyln. Bealach*, Gaelic, a Pass or Gap. There is a story told that King James V. lost himself and found shelter for the night with the miller of Ballomiln, and that the King offered a reward to his host, and asked whether he would take the fourth part, or the eighth, or the sixteenth part of the land on which they stood. The miller, the story says, chose the eighth part, as to take the fourth would be cheating himself, and to take the sixteenth part would be too greedy.—*New Statistical Account, Fifeshire*, p. 29. This much is certain, that Ballomiln has for long been much subdivided. In 1562 the eighth part of the lands belonged to Margaret Wallace; a fourth part to John Turpie in 1607; an eighth to Turpie in 1610; and a fourth to Thomas Beaton in 1616.—*Fife Retours.* The great subdivision of property in the 16th and 17th centuries, arose from the want of outlet for the youth of the country in commercial enter-prise.—*Fife Retours*, 50, 180, 217, 258.

47. *Drumtennent* seems to have been an outfield or common to the pro-prietors of Ballomiln. The proprietors mentioned in the foregoing note had all a right of pasturage on it. In 1625 John Ayton of that ilk was served heir to his father 'in the lands of Drumtennand and the pendicle of the same called Hetherinch.' And in 1678 Jean Heriot, wife of Mr John Craig, Advocate, was served heir to her father in a quarter and an eighth part of Ballomiln, with a right to the *Sequelis* of Drumtennent.—*Fife Retours*, 365, 1166. Drumtennent now belongs to George Johnston, Esq. of Lathrisk.

48. *Kinloiche*, Gaelic *Kin*, the end or head of the Loch, anciently belonged to the De Quincys. Sibbald says: 'I have seen three original charters by the second Roger de Quinci, Comes de Wintoun, constabularius, to John of Kindeloche, of a miln and some lands about this place, about Alexander III.'s reign.'—*History of Fife*, p. 390. In 1582 William Scott of Abbotshall was served heir to his father in half the lands of Kinloche, and in 1590 Michael Balfour of Burlie succeeded to half the lands of

Kinloch as heir to his mother, Lady Margaret Balfour of Burlie. Subsequent to this date Kinloch appears to have been very much subdivided. In 1662 John Anderson succeeded as heir to his father Thomas, to the shady half of the sunny half of Kinloche, and in 1663 John Balfour succeeded to three eighth parts.—*Fife Retours*, 1475, 1494, 912, 937. Kinloch is now the property of John Boyd Kinnear, Esq., and of the Trustees of James Bogie.

49. *Rossie.* Rossan, Gaelic, a little jutting-point or headland. This property, Sibbald states, 'belonged in the reign of David I. to Sir Henry Rossey of that ilk, and in Malcolm IV.'s reign, anno 7, Sir Alexander of Rossey is forfaulted, and the lands are given to the Earl of Fife.'—P. 389. In the time of Robert, Duke of Albany, William de Lindesay granted an annual-rent of five merks to Eufamia de Lindesay, daughter of Alexander Lindesay of Glenesk, out of his two towns of Rossey in Fifeshire.— Robertson's *Index to Charters*, 166, 17. In 1569 Rossie had come into the possession of William Bonar, as we learn from a 'confirmation of a pension granted by Patrick, Commendator of Lindores, to Johne Bonar, son to umquhill William Bonar of Rossey.—*Presentation of Benefices*, 1569. Subsequently Rossie became the property of the family of 'the Cheaps of Mawhill, beside Kinross.'—Sibbald's *Fife*.

50. *Weddersbie.* As narrated under the head Pitlair (No. 42 of these Notes), Sir James Sandelandis of Calder conveyed by charter, in 1509, the half of the lands of Weddirsbe, otherwise called Wester Cullessy, to his uncle James Sandelandis. In 1567 Elizabeth Carnagie and her two sisters succeeded to half the lands of Weddersbie, as heirs to their mother Elizabeth Ramsay of Colluthie. In 1602 William Sandilands of St Monance came into possession of the other half on the death of his grandfather James Sandilands. In 1668 a portion of the lands of Weddersbie passed into the hands of James Arnot of Fernie. Sir Robert Sibbald, writing in 1710, says: 'To the north and to the east [west] of Kinloch is the barony of Weddersbie, the inheritance of Hamilton of Wishea in the west country, a learned antiquary. This was anciently the estate of the Kinlochs of that ilk.'—*History of Fife*, p. 390. Rossie and Weddersbie are now the property of George Johnston, Esq. of Lathrisk.

51. *Lumquhat.* John Ramsay obtained a charter from David II. (1329-1370) to the lands of Lumquhat, forfeited by Thomas Brechin.— Robertson's *Index to Charters*, 33-35. John Bonnar is named proprietor of Lumquhat in a charter under the Great Seal by James VI., A.D. 1592. In 1668 Lumquhat and the pendicles called Lochiehead, Downiehead, Cassindaill and Rattlingfuird, passed into the hands of Elizabeth Ranken on the death of her father Patrick Ranken of Lumquhat. In 1669 Lumquhat

became the property of Captain James Leslie, third son of Sir John Leslie of Newton, and grandson of Andrew, fourth Earl of Rothes. He married Mrs Mary Gibb, Lady Ormistown, on the 14th January 1703, and died in October 1705, leaving a son John, who had a son also John, who was served heir to his father 1728, whose son John was served heir to his grandfather 30th June 1771. He had a son John who was served heir to his father 2d February 1774. This John Leslie of Lumquhat was an officer in the 26th Regiment. He claimed the title of Lord Lindores, but, as stated in a previous page, his claim was rejected by the House of Lords.—*Historical Records of the Family of Leslie*, Vol. II., p. 197. In 1801 Lumquhat was the property of John Arnot. The rent of 'two pleuches of Lumquhat' is entered in the Rental of Lindores, *circa* 1580, as payable 'to the Queen's Grace's Chapel in Falkland, and to my Lord Angus' College in Abernethie.' There was an old castle at Lumquhat, which with unsparing Vandalism was demolished about twenty years ago for materials wherewith to erect farm buildings. Lumquhat belongs to Philp's Trustees, Kirkcaldy.

52. *Kilquhyss.* The prefix *Kil* is indicative of an ecclesiastical origin, and in all probability Kilwhiss was the site of an ancient chapel. There was a saint named Wissan, but nothing is known of his history. 'The Eglinton family had the right of patronage to the chaplainship of St Wissan, in the county of Ayr.—Bishop Forbes' *Kalendar of the Scottish Saints*, p. 463. Sir David Lyndsay of the Mount, in his poetical *Testament of Squyer Meldrum of the Bynnis*, puts the following sentiments into the dying squire's mouth :—

> Adew, my Lordis, I may na langer tarie,
>   My Lord Lindsay, adew abone all uther;
> I pray to God and to the Virgine Marie,
>   With your Ladie to live lang in the Struther;
>   Maister Patrik and young Normond your brother;
> With my ladeis, your sisteris, all adew!'

'Young Normond' here alluded to was the ancestor of the Lyndsays of Kilwhiss. 'Maister Patrik' was the Master of Lyndsay, afterwards sixth Lord Lindsay of the Byres, who bore such a prominent part in the events of Mary's reign, and whom his biographer Lord Lindsay, describes as 'the fiercest and most bigotted of the Lords of the Congregation, yet an honester man than most of his contemporaries.' It was he, while demanding and enjoying freedom of worship, that rushed armed to Holyrood Palace, threatening death to all who celebrated the Mass. 'Norman

Lyndsay of Kilwhiss died between 1574 and the 21st June 1587, leaving a son Patrick, who died in 1598. Patrick was succeeded by his son James, who was served heir to his grandfather Norman in 1627. James died in 1667, leaving two sons, James and Norman. James, the eldest son, was served heir to his father in 1669, and shortly afterwards sold Kilwhiss. No successor is known of these two brothers.'—*Lives of the Lindsays*, Vol. I., pp. 274, 276, 439.

53. *The Paroche of Auchtirmochtie.* The earliest mention we have of Auchtermuchty is in an account rendered by Walter of Cambhou (Cambo) of the Issues or Rents of the lands and tenements belonging to Duncan, Earl of Fife, on 20th November 1293. These lands had been put under the management of Walter of Cambhou by Edward I. at the time of Edward's attempted usurpation of Scotland. The reason assigned in the account for Edward's taking oversight of these lands was, that the Earl of Fife was under age and in his keeping. In the Extent or Rental of the lands handed over to the management of Walter of Cambhou, under the head 'Schyra de Stramigloke,' the following entries occur, which in the original are in Latin :—

'The part of the land of Utremukerty east of the burn x l. xiij$^{s.}$ iiij$^{d.}$

The mill of the same place, per annum, with Gervase's land, xiiij$^{l.}$ xiij$^{s.}$ iiij$^{d.}$

The Brewhouses of the same place per annum lxvj$^{s.}$ viij$^{d.}$

The xiiij Cottaries of the same place, xiiij$^{s.}$

The viij Gresmen of the same place, per annum iiij$^{s.}$

The land of the Muir of the same place per an. vi$^{s.}$ viij$^{d.}$

The Smith's Shop, vi$^{s.}$ viij$^{d.}$

In accounting for the rents, William of Cambhou charges 'for cutting turning, and carrying the hay on the meadow of Utermokerdy xxiij$^{s.}$ iiij^{d}, for which hay, he adds, ' I am owing.'—*Documents Illustrative of the History of Scotland*, Vol. I., p. 407–418.

The entries in the ' Rental and Accounts' of the Earldom of Fife are specially interesting in throwing light on the various grades of society in the end of the 13th century. The class denominated *Gresmen*, were tenants of cottages with no land attached, and derived their name from their being allowed to pasture such bestial as they possessed on the extensive common grass-lands at that period. The *Cotarii* were a class above these. We learn from the charter of the Abbey of Kelso that the cottars under the monks in 1290 occupied a cottage, and from one to nine acres of land each. —*See* p. 61. The low rent of the Gresmen's cottages, sixpence each, even taking the value of money at that time into account, shows that they were a class far below the cottars, and that their habitations must have been frail structures. The large rent paid for brewhouses, is another proof out of many, that ale was a common drink and the national beverage at that date; and the payment of wages for making hay shows that the employment of serfs was giving way, and free labourers employed. The *Extract* and *Accounts* from which these entries are taken, also throw light on the early history of other parts of the county which belonged to the Earl of Fife, and are well worthy the attention of local historians. The 'Extract' is ranged under the following heads:—'Coupresyre et Rathuly schyre, Schyra de Stramigloke, Schyra de Irat-lengre (*query* Lingo), Schyra de Ryrays.' Among the disbursements of the Factor, Walter of Cambhou, the following occurs:—

'For the repair of the houses of the Castle of Cupar, and of the hall of the manor of Rahulli liij$^{s.}$ j$^{d.}$'

'To the Constable of the Castle of Cupar for keeping the Castle per annum ciiij$^{s.}$'

'For the Hospital of Utrogenalle erected for pure charity, lxvj$^{s.}$ viij$^{d.}$'

The revenues of the Hospital of 'Utherogale,' which the Earls of Fife maintained for 'pure charity,' and which was specially available for the infirm in its immediate neighbourhood, were diverted to Trinity Hospital, Edinburgh, in 1462.—*Charters and Documents relating to Edinburgh*, 1143–1540; *Burgh Record Society*, p. 113. The old form of place-names which such an early Rental affords, throws light on their etymology. In the name *Rahulli* we have the origin of the modern Rathillet. *Rath* (as previously mentioned) signifies in Gaelic a circular fort, and *chuillin* a holly, the Fort of the Holly.— Joyce's *Irish Names of Places*, p. 294.

The young Earl of Fife, though he married the grand-daughter of Edward I., ultimately joined the cause of Bruce, and he was the first of the Barons who signed the letter to the Pope asserting the Independence of Scotland. There is some dubiety whether he or his son gave 'the church of Uchtermukedy and the lands which from of old belonged to it' to the Abbey of Lindores, as a thank-offering for his escape from the battle of Durham.—*Chartulary of Lindores*, pp. 43, 44. No mention appears to be made to whom the church of Auchtermuchty was dedicated, but the great annual Fair of the town, held on St Sear's day (the popular name of St Serf, who did so much for the early religious culture of the western districts of Fife), is convincing evidence that St Serf was the patron Saint of the town. The motto of Auchtermuchty Burgh Seal, *Dum Sero Spero*, seems, as is not uncommon in heraldic mottoes, a rhyming alliteration on the old saint's name. 'By the forfeiture of the Earldom of Fife in 1425, the town and lands of Auchtermuchty fell to the Crown, and either the whole or a portion of them came into the hands of the family of

Leslie. Leslie of Auchtermuchty was one of four commissioners from Queen Mary to Scotland, previous to her coming from France to take possession of the throne.—Tytler's *Hist. of Scot.*, Vol. III., p. 140. The lands of Auchtermuchty seem subsequently to have been much subdivided. In 1599 William Gilmour was served heir to his mother Euphemia Balcanquell, in the eighth part of the north quarter of the lands and town of Auchtermuchty. In 1620 John Arnott succeeded as heir to his father to an eighth part of forty-shilling land of the Bond-half. A forty-shilling land, of which so much was heard in connection with the electoral franchise, has been shown by Mr Cosmo Innes to be 104 acres.—*Lectures on Scotch Legal Antiq.*, p. 285. In 1632 Robert Maxwell succeeded to parts and portions of an eighth part of the Bond-half.—*Fife Retours*, No. 77, 302, 465. Numerous other entries occur in the Retours of similar subdivisions belonging to families whose names are still common in Auchtermuchty.

54. *Cotlandis and Marislands.* Cotlands is apparently the same as the Cotaries in the Rental of 1294; and Marislands (the Virgin Mary's Lands) is now corrupted to Maislands. In 1601 James Gilmour succeeded his father in half the lands of Marislands. In 1631 James Aytoun, brother-german of Mr Robert Aytoun of Inchderney, succeeded as heir to his uncle, Mr James Aytoun of Grange, to an eighth part of the Bond-half, and to half the lands of Marislands of Auchtermuchty and part of the other half. —*Fife Retours*, No. 107, 452.

55. *Gervisland* was in the direct possession of the Earl of Fife in 1293. In 1661 Mr James Robertson was served heir to his father Patrick Robertson, burgess of Edinburgh, in the east half of the lands of Jervesland of Auchtermuchty, extending to 2 merkland. Robert Stirk, as heir to his grandfather Richard Stirk, succeeded in 1661 to the west half of the same lands; and in 1681 Alexander Bayne, Bailie of Dingwall, succeeded as joint-heir of Mr John Bayne of Pitcairly in a 2 merkland of the east half of the Bond-half of Auchtermuchty called Jervese-lands.—*Fife Retours*, 96, 282, 1197.

56. *The Myres.* In 1628 John Paterson was served heir to his father, Michael Patersoun of the Myris, in the lands of the Myris, Over and Nether, of the lands of Auchtermuchty, and in that Outset called Dunschelt; also in the office of *Claviger* (key-bearer or macer) and serjeand-of-arms, with the sum of £10, 10s., as well as in the feu-fermes of the said land assigned as the fee of said office.—*Fife Retours*, No. 397. In all probability this official was originally the Macer of the Court of the Earls of Fife at their Castle of Falkland; an office of much higher dignity than it is now.

57. *Burnegrenis.* Name obsolete.

58. *Dempstertoun.* In the Records of Dysart the following notice of Strathmiglo (in the barony of which Dempstertown was included) occurs:— 'At the place of Strathmiglo, 10th Nov. 1561, the whilk day Sir David Kilgour, at the command of an honourable man, Sir William Scot of Balweary, Knight, produced the keys of the place and fortalice of Strathmiglo to Mr William Scott, fiar of Balweary, who received them in token of possession of these lands, and opened the doors thereof.'—*Notices from the Local Records of Dysart*, William Muir, pp. 26, 27. In 1579 James Scot was served heir to his father Sir William Scott of Balwerie, in the Barony of Stramiglow, comprehending among other lands those of Dempstertoun, the East and West Mills, Laingisland, Mugdrum, with the mill thereof and fishery in the water of Tay, and the right to the patronage of the Provostship and of the Prebendaries of the College of Stramiglow. Demperstoun, and other parts of the barony of Strathmiglo passed into the hands of the Balfours of Burghley. In 1665 John, Lord Balfour of Burghley, was served heir to his father Robert, Lord Balfour of Burghley, to the barony and town of Stramiglo, otherwise called Eglismartin. The name *Eaglais*, Gaelic for a church, is indicative of an origin in Celtic times, and the suffix shows that the church was dedicated to St Martin.—*Fife Retours*, 1456, 964.

59. *Redy.* In 1579 this property belonged to the Scots of Balwerie. In 1563 George Moncrief of Reidie was served heir to his father Andrew in the lands of Reidie and Layngswaird, utherways called the Waird of Reidie.—*Fife Retours*, No. 817.

60. *The paroche Kirk of Creiche* was dedicated to St Serf. *Bishop Forbes's Kalendar of Scottish Saints*, p. 447. The dedication of the Church of Criech to one of the Scottish saints is indicative of its being an early ecclesiastical settlement. In a Charter of Confirmation we have recorded a mortification or bequest 'made by Mr James Strauchen of certain annual rents to the Mary altar founded by him in the Kirk of Creichie, viz. an annual rent of 10 merks out of the lands of Meikle Berres (*query* Meikle Barnes) in Kincardine, of 4 merks out of Flemington, and of 8 merks out of the lands of Chappletoun both in Forfar; of 4 merks out of Easter Pitlour in Fyfe, of 5 merks out of the lands of Over Pratis; of 3 merks out of Middle Urquhart, alias Lassintoune, being 40 merk-land also in Fife, and of 20 shillings out of Wester Bonhard in Forfar in the Baronie of Kellie,' 24 Decem[b] *regnie regis* 26. *Chalmers M.S.*, p. 92. Unfortunately the record from which the foregoing is taken does not mention the name of the king in whose reign the charter was granted, and therefore the date cannot be fixed, neither does it specify that the altar was founded in Creich *in Fife;* but the fact that the properties from which the annual rents were drawn are

chiefly in Fife, and the neighbouring county of Forfar, may be held conclusive on that point. Besides, Criech in Fife is denominated *Crehy* in the Rental of the Earldom of Fife in 1293. In the old church of Creich there is a most elaborately carved tombstone bearing the arms of the families of Barclay and Douglas.—It must have originally been inlaid with brass, and was placed in the church to the memory of David Barclay, who died A.D. 1400, and to his wife Janet Douglas, who died 29th January 1421.—*New Statistical Account.* Laurence, official of Lindores Abbey, and one of the originators of the University of St Andrews, was Rector of Creich A.D. 1432. In 1493 Sir John Lyndsay, one of the witnesses to Lord Glammys' decision of the dispute between the convent of Lindores and the burgesses of Newburgh, is designated Vicar of Creich. The charge of appellation from Rector to Vicar shows that the Church of Creich had been bestowed on Lindores Abbey between the dates mentioned, but by whom does not appear; there being no record of the bestowal in the chartulary of the Abbey. In the year 1528 Mr David Seton of the family of Parbroath (of whom a notice appears in No. 62 of these Notes) is designated Vicar of Creich in a Writ of dispensation of a marriage in the parish of Balhelvy, of which he was ' persoune.'—*Antiquities of the Shires of Aberdeen and Banff*, Vol. III., p. 333. In a very early taxation of the churches of Fife, preserved in the Registrum de Dunfermelyn, p. 208, the following entry occurs :—' Ecc^a de Creych cum Caplla—XII. m^a. [marks.] This contemporary notice of a dependant chapel in the parish of Creich is confirmatory evidence of the correctness of the tradition mentioned by the Rev. Alexander Lawson in his valuable Statistical Account of the Parish, that an old barn at Parbroath (since demolished) was formerly a chapel. Creich church is not mentioned in Boaimund's Roll of Churches A.D. 1275 (*Statuta Ecclesiae Scoticanae*, pp. ccciv.-vi.) but the architectural features of the old church exhibit traces of considerable antiquity; in all probability it was erected in the 14th century.

61. *The town of Creich, and Castle*, derive importance from having been the property and residence of the Bethunes, a family of ancient lineage and of considerable influence in Scotland in the 16th century. ' David, son of John Bethune of Balfour, acquired the estate of Creich from a family of the name of Little or Liddel in 1502,' and his descendants held it for several generations. ' Janet Bethune, a daughter of the second Laird of Creich of that name, was married to Sir Walter Scott of Branxholm,' and is thus alluded to in ' The Lay of the Last Minstrel :'—

> ' Of noble race the Lady came,
> Her father was a clerk of fame
> Of Bethune's line of Picardie.'

Mary Bethune, another daughter of this house, was one of ' The Queen's four Maries,' so famed for their beauty and their connection with the un fortunate Mary Stuart.'—*Statistical Account of Creich*, p. 636. *Rev. James Campbell, M.A. Shores of Fife*, p. 93. A painting, said to be an original portrait of this lady, is in the possession of Admiral Bethune of Balfour. Creich Castle, the residence of the Bethunes, is now roofless, but the greater part of the walls are still standing, overgrown with ivy. The lands of Creich, described as *quondam pertinen. ad abbaciam de Lundoris*, came into possession of Thomas Anderson A.D. 1721. In 1760 they were acquired by Dr John Gillespie, ancestor of the present proprietor David Gillespie, Esq. of Mountquhanie.

62. *Parbroithe.* Anciently the property of the Ramsays, it passed by marriage, in the beginning of the 14th century, to a branch of the family of Seton. ' The first proprietor of Parbroath of the name of Seton was John, fourth son of the famous Alexander Seton, Governor of Berwick. He became proprietor of the lands of Parbroath by marrying Elizabeth Ramsay, heiress thereof.' *New Statistical Account, Parish of Creich.* The history of this alliance, and of the Setons of Parbroath, is thus quaintly related by Sir Richard Maitland in his ' Historie of the House of Seytoun.' ' King David II. gave to the said Sr Alexander the heretrix of Parbroth, callet Elizabeth Ramsay, dochter and air of Sr Nicl Ramsay, knycht; quhilk Elizabeth the said Sr Alexander gave in maryage to his sone callet Johne, as I sall efter schaw. This Sr Alexander deit in the latter [days] of the foresaid King David and was of grit age.' Alexander Seton of Parbroth was one of the counsellors of Lord Glamys in the dispute between the convent of Lindores and the burgesses of Newburgh in 1493-4 (*see* pp. 178-182). ' The fourt sone of Alexander Seytoun quha kepit Berwik, callet Johne, mareit the foresaid Elizabeth Ramsay, heretrix of Parbroth, quha bair to him ane sone callet Alexander; quhilk Alexander begat Sr Gilbert, knycht. This Sr Gilbert mareit Marioun Petcarne upon quhom he got fyve sonnis. The eldest callit Sr Alexander, knycht, quha succedit till his father; the second sone callit Williame, quha had also ane sone callit William that mareit Katharine Butlair, heretrix of Rumgavye; the thrid sone of the said Sr Gilbert, callet Johne, mareit Jouet Lauthrysk, heretrix of that Ilk. Of the quhilk Johne are descendit the Seytounis of Lauthrysk and Baubirny; the fourt sone calleit Maister David quha wes ane singular honest man and mareit all his elder brotheris dochteris, efter his deceiss, on landit men and payit thair tocheris, and coft ladyis of heritage to his brotheris sonnis.'

The old chronicler relates the following graphic incident in the life of Master David:—' In the tyme of King James the Ferd there was ane process laid aganis the baronnis, callit recognitionis. The Advocate at that tyme wes named Maister Richard Lausone and his assistant Maister James Henrysone. Maister David Seytoun in his defence of Lord Seytounis case said to the king, 'Schir, quhen our forbears gat yon landis at your maist nobill predecessouris [handis] for their trew service ; sumtyme gevand the blude of thair bodie, and sum tyme their lives in defence of this realme; at that tyme there wes nother Lau sone, nor Henry sone quha wald invent wayis to disheris the baronnis of Scotland.' The king seeing the warmth with which he made his defence said to him, ' Would you fight?' The old cleric, who was beyond the age when he had a right to challenge a decision by single combat, said that if the king would give permission he would fight his opponent. ' The kingis grace quha wes the maist nobil and humane prince in the warld smylit and leuch a little, and said na mair ;' admiring in his heart the nobility of the man who stood up so bravely for the rights of his kindred.

' This Maister David wes persoun of Fettercarne and Balhelvy ; and ane large man of bodie as was in his dayis, and stout thairwyth, the best lyk ageit man I ever saw. He levit quhill he was lxxx yeiris, undecrepit and did mony other actis wordy to be put in remembrance quhilk I omit for shortness. The fift sone callit Gilbert, ane Maister clerk, deit at Rome.'

' The said Sir Alexander, eldest sone to Sir Gilbert [and Marioun Pet-carne] mareit [circa 1540] Helen Murray dochter to the lard of Tuly-bardin, and gat on her one sone callit Alexander, quho deit befoir his father. This Alexander mareit Katherine, dochter to the Lord Lyndsay of the Byris, and gat upon hir tua sounis, the eldest callit Johne quha succedit to his gudschir, and was slane at Floudane, levand behind him na successouris of his body. Ane vther callit Andro quha succedit to the said Johne, his brother and levis presentlie. This Andro mareit —— Balfour, dochter to the lard of Burlie, and gat upon hir ane sone callit Gilbert quha was slane at the field of Pinkye, his father yet leiffand. This Gilbert mareit Mar-garet Leslie, dochter to the Erle of Rothos, on quhom he gat David appeir-and heir to his gudschir Andro. The rest of the successioun of the hous of Parbroth and the granis collateral of the samin, with their successioun and actis done by them, I refer to them that are descendit of the samin hous.'—*Maitland's Historie of the House of Seytoun.*

Sir Richard Maitland's account of the House of Parbroath only comes down to the year 1560, and none of 'the hous, or the granis collateral,' having left any account of the family behind them, we are left to glean their subsequent history from scattered scources. · David Seton was served heir to his grandfather in 1563.—*Fife Retours* 51. David Seton of Parbroath, who became Comptroller of Scotland, married Mary, daughter of Patrick sixth Lord Gray, *circa* 1590. In the next century, Margaret Seaton of the family of Parbroath, married Sir John Scrimgeour of Dudhope, who was created, Viscount Dudhope and Lord Scrimgeour by Charles I. in 1641. He was appointed by the same monarch Heritable Standard Bearer of Scotland, an honour which is held by the descendant of this marriage, Henry Scrimgeour Wedderburn of Birkhill. *Peerage of Scotland, Wood's* Ed., Vol. I., pp. 466, 671. Parbroath passed out of the hands of the Setons towards the end of the 17th century. The latest notice we have of the family is in Burke's 'Landed Gentry' (1850), where it is stated that 'Sir Walter Synnot of Ballymoyer, in the county of Armagh, Ireland, married in 1770 Jane, daughter of John Seton of Camberwell, Surrey, representative of the Setons of Parbroath.' In the year 1694, at which date the oldest volumes of the Parochial Registers of the parish of Creich begins, Parbroath formed part of the estate of Mr Andrew Baylie of the family of Carfin, in the west of Scotland. The house of Parbroath was a ruin at the beginning of the 18th century, when Sir Robert Sibbald published his History of Fife, and all that remains of the residue of a race who 'gave the blude of their bodie and their lives in defence of this realme,' is the half of an arch standing in the middle of a ploughed field. Parbroath (usually pronounced Petbroad) is now the property of Captain H. W. Hope.—On *Ainslie's Map of Fife*, published in 1774, the name is given, Pitbroad.

63. *Luthrey.* The Barony of Luthrie and Kinsliffe anciently belonged to Kinloch of Kinloch in Collessie parish. 'Not later than 1529 Sir David Lyndsay on his inauguration as Lyon King of Arms had assigned to him as his ordinary fee, four chalders and nine bolls of victual out of the King's Lands of Luthrie in Fife.'—*David Laing's Memoir of Lindsay. Poetical Works, Ed.* 1871. The estate of Luthrie, or at least a part of it, therefore belonged to the Crown in the beginning of the 16th century. On the death of Sir David Lindsay, Sir Robert Forman, who is designed of Luthrie, succeeded Lyndsay as Lyon King of Arms in 1555. 'According to a M.S. in the Advocates' Library, Forman was allowed his fee by Queen Mary out of the lands of Rathillet, being the King's property within the Stewartry of Fyffe. On the 18th of February 1594, John Forman, Rothesay Herald, was served heir in general to his father Domini Roberti Forman de Luchrie militis Leonis Regis Armorum.'—Seaton's *Law and Practice of Heraldry,* p. 481. Sir Robert and his descendants could only have possessed a part of Luthrie, as in 1549 the estate was much sub-divided. In 1549 a family of the name of Clark possessed the sixteenth part. In the 17th century, families of the names of Kinloche (possibly descendants of the ancient proprietors) and of Corbie, possessed each a sixteenth part; and one of the name of Barclett

a thirty-second part. Luthrie is now the property of the heirs of David Cook, and Upper Luthrie belongs to John Russell, Esq.

64. *Kinsleif*, now *Kinsleith*, correctly *Kinsleibh*, Gaelic signifying 'the End of the slope of the hill,' a name admirably descriptive. In 1616 this property belonged to David Barclay of Cullernie. The Barclays sold Easter Kinsleith in 1727 to the ancestor of the present proprietor George Cunningham Miller, Esq.

65. *Balmadyside.* *Bal-madadh*, Gaelic, the Town of the Wolf or Wild Dog. Robert III. confirmed a charter by Norman Leslie of Balnabriech to John Ramsay of Colluthye, to the lands of Balmadyside and Pittachop, blench to be holden of Leslie. This charter proceeds on a verdict pronounced at Glenduky, 5th July 1390, by the following jury—viz., Andrew de Ramsay of Redy, John of Kynnere, William of Berclay, John of Camera, Allan of Lochmalony, Walter of Ramsay, Maliseus of Kynnynmond, John of Kindelouch, William Stirk, William of Ferny, John of Ramsay, William of Lochmalony, Robert Lyel, Andrew of Camera and John of Arous.—Robertson's *Index to Charters*, 157, 27. Balmadyside reverted to the Leslies, for, on the 9th April 1613, John, Earl of Rothes, was served heir to his brother James, Master of Rothes in the barony of Ballinbriech and in the lands of Balmedysid and others.—*Fife Retours*, No. 1547. It now belongs to the heirs of Andrew Wallace.

66. *Wranghame*, in the parish of Kinnethmont.

67. *Fintray*, in the parish of Fintry, Aberdeenshire.

68. *Balmaw*, in the parish of Newtyle. The gift of Alexander, King of Scots, to the Abbey. Confirmed by David II., 20th September 1365.—*Lindores Chartulary*, p. 48.

68. *Newtyle.* A carucate of land in Newtile is mentioned in the Pope's Confirmation, A.D. 1198, as part of the possessions of Lindores Abbey. *Chartulary*, p. 40.

69. *Hylton* and *Mylton of Craigie*, in the parish of Dundee. The gift of Ysabella da Brous.—*Lindores Chatulary*, p. 14.

60. *Claypotts*, was conferred on Lindores Abbey previous to the grant of Balmaw by King Alexander.—*Lindores Chatulary*, p. 48. In 1678 Claypottis was the property of John Graham of Claverhouse, afterwards the famous Viscount Dundee; he succeeded to it as heir to his great-grandfather Sir William Graham.—*Forfar Retours*, No. 475.

71. *The barone of Mernis* by the annuales of Bervy. Inverbervy in the Mearns, formed part of the grant of William the Lion to his brother David, Earl of Huntingdon, Founder of Lindores.—*Fordun à Goodal*, Lib. ix., cap. xxvii.

72. *The Hauche.* The land on which Cullelo House is built, the property of John Cameron, Esq., was formerly known as 'The Haugh.'

73. *Woodheid.* The Abbot of Lindores conveyed the lands of Woodhead, described as the entire south half of the Wood of Lindores, to James M'Gill of Rankeillour, on the 23d June 1565. The charter of the Abbot was confirmed by Queen Mary. Woodhead belonged, in the end of the 16th century, to the Sandilands of St Monance. In 1668 James Arnot was served heir to his father, Sir James Arnot of Fernie, to Woodheid and Woodmilne.—*Fife Retours,* No. iii. 1050. Woodhead is now the property of Wm. S. Wilson, Bishop of Glasgow.

74. *Eistwood*—name now obsolete, part of the property of the Arnots of Woodmiln.

75. *The Brewhouse of the Grange.* The remains of brewing premises are still extant at the Grange, but they are of comparatively modern date, having been built out of the ruins of the Abbey about one hundred and fifty years ago, and therefore they are more modern than the brewhouse mentioned.

76. *Burgh maills and tennentis of Newbruiche.*

77. *The Annuellis of Sanctandrois.* There is no notice of these annual rents in any of the recorded charters of the Abbey.

78. *The Derach land of Creich.* Corrupted in ' The Court Roll of the Regallitie of Lundores 1695,' to ' the dowrie lands of Creich.' The term Dira-land and Dira-croft occurs in Kincardine and Aberdeenshires, and is understood to be the land, or croft, that pertained to the office of Toschach-derach, which Skene says ' was ane office, or jurisdiction, not unlike to ane Baillierie.'—*De verborum signific.* This word *Toshach-derach,* which we find imbedded in the parish of Creich, like the fragment of an ancient geological strata, Mr W. F. Skene, in his able dissertation on ' Tribe Communities in Scotland,' says, is derived from *Toisech,* Gaelic for Leader, and *Dior,* an old word signifying ' of or belonging to law,' and forms *Toiseach doracht,* the office of *Toiseach-dor,* or Coroner. This term is almost identical with the name given to the Coroner in the Isle of Man. ' In the Manks language that officer is named *Toshiagh Jioarey,* or chief man of the law.' Though the term Coroner has long ceased to be used in Scotland, there is, or was lately, a *rig* of land among the Burgh acres of Newburgh known as the Crowner's Rig. The smallness of the croft usually assigned to the Toiseach-derach, indicates that the office was of a subordinate kind. This is confirmed by a provision in the laws of William the Lion, in which ' a citation is directed to be made by the sergeant, or coroner or Tosordereh.'—*Historians of Scotland,* Vol. IV., pp. 458, 459. The office, in some instances, seems to have been hereditary.—*Miscell. Spald. Club,* Vol. IV., p. xxxiii. The Derachland of Creich cannot now be identified. In 1695, it belonged to the Laird of Balfour.

79. *The Luidging in Falkland.* In the older Rental this is named ' the Abbots Luidging in Falkland.'

80. *Clunie Eister.* Henry, Abbot of Lindores, conveyed the lands of Clunie Eister to George Orme, by charter dated 12th August 1520.—*Mug-drum Archives.* In 1672 they belonged to William Keir of Forret, who succeeded to them as heir to his father. In 1681 Alexander Bayne, Bailie of Dingwall in Ross-shire, succeeded to both the halves of Eister Clunie as joint-heir of Mr John Bayne of Pitcairlie, his uncle.—*Perth Retours*, 837-911. Easter Clunie is now the property of John Williamson, Esq.

81-85. *The Marie Croft*, named in honour of the Virgin, and the names of the other places mentioned under these numbers are now all obsolete, with the exception of Craigmylne, which formed part of the property of Sir Michael Balfour of Denmiln in 1652.—*Fife Retours*, 877.

86. *Innerraritie*, anciently *Inverquharity* (near Kirriemuir), where a fine old castle of the Ogilvies still stands.—*Jervise's Memorials of Angus and Mearns*, p. *17.

87-91. *Wistounis, hillend, Fyscherhill, Lytill Wistonis, Scottistone* and *Mylntoun*, and *Brewhouse of Wistonis*, are all in the parish of St Cyrus.

91. *The great Luidging in Perthe.* The monks of Lindores originally ac-quired their property in Perth from King William the Lion. By charter 1178-1214, he gave them ' one full toft in his Burgh of Perth.'—*Chartulary of Lindores*, p. 9.

Lindores Abbey and Lands adjoining. The lands of the Lordship of Lindores, as stated at p. 406, passed into the hands of John Bayne, Writer to the Signet, for advances made by him to Patrick, second Lord Lindores. From Mugdrum archives we learn that the sum advanced amounted to £5500 Scots. Through the aid of his relative John, Duke of Rothes, John, fourth Lord Lindores retained right to the Abbey itself, and the lands around it. His son David, fifth Lord Lindores, who died without issue, conveyed them on the 18th December 1718 to Dame Jane Leslie, Lady Newark. She, and her husband, Sir Alexander Anstruther, after a process of adjudi-cation, granted a disposition to the lands and lordship of Lindores, 20th April 1738, in favour of Sir Alexander Leslie, who assumed the title of Lord Lindores (*see* p. 407). Sir Alexander Leslie sold Lindores Abbey and lands, 20th July 1749 to Robert Laing, late minister of Newburgh, who sold them on the 30th January 1753 to Peter Hay of Leys, to whose de-scendant, Edmund Paterson Balfour Hay of Leys, the Abbey now belongs.

Mugdrum. The lands of Mugdrum formed no part of the property of the Abbacy of Lindores; but as they are now in the parish of Newburgh, having been disjoined from that of Abernethy, the following notes of their history are appended.

The first mention that we have of Mugdrum is in a charter by Laurence of Abernethy, of which the following is an abstract :—' Laurence, son of Orm of Abirnythy, etc. Know that we have given to God and to the church of St Thomas of Abirbrothoc the right of advocation to the church of Abirnythy with its pertinents, namely, the chapels of Dron, Dunbulcc, and of Eroyln ; with the lands of Belache [Ballo] and of Petenlouer, and half of the tithes of my estate ; the other half of which belongs to the *Keledei* of Abirnythy, and all the tithes of the territory of Abirnythy except those tithes which belong to the churches of Flisk and Cultra ; excepting also the tithes of my lordship of Abirnythy which the *Keledei* of Abirnythy have always held, *namely* of Mukedrum, Kerpul, Balebyrewelle, Ballecolly and of Invernythy from the east side of the burn, etc.'—Reeve's *Culdees of the British Islands*, p. 251. The terms used in this charter (habent et semper habere solebant), would seem to imply that the tithes of Mugdrum pertained to the Culdees of Abernethy from the first settlement of Christianity there. The foregoing charter was granted between A.D. 1188 and 1199.

The next mention that we have of Mugdrum is at an interval of nearly three hundred years ; in the record of an ' actioun & cause psewit' (before the Lords of Council, 12th January 1492) ' be the abbot & convent of Lundores, aganis George, erle of Rothes & Johne Covintre of Mukdrum, that is to say the said erle for the dampnage & scathis sustenit be the said abbot & qvent throw the making of a pretendit Recogniscioun upon the said lard of Mukdrumis landis of Mukdrum, in defraude & prejudice of the said abbot & qvent & als to shew ressonable cause why he deferris to lat the said landis to borch, etc. . . . . The Lords of Counsale decretts etc. that sen the said erle of rothes wald not qpere to show the said recogniscioun etc. It sal be lefull to the said John of Covintre to dispose upon the said landis of Mukdrum, or to the said abbot etc., to cause the samyn landis to be psit [prisit] for the soume of aucht skore of merks grantit awin to thaim be the said John Covintre etc.'—*Acta Dominorum Concilii*, p. 258.

On the 9th March 1510, William Scott of Balwery obtained a charter from James IV. to the lands of Mugdrum with the fishings, formerly reputed a tenandrie of Ballinbriech, then united in the barony of Strathmiglo.

William Scott gave Sasine of the lands of Muckdrum to George Orme, son of the deceased Stephen Orme (in all probability the same who acted as factor for Lindores Abbey in Flanders). George Orme also owned Clunie, as stated under Note, No. 80. Patrick, Lord Lundores, granted a charter to the same land on the 12th February 1575 in favour of David Orme. Mugdrum continued in the possession of the Ormes for a considerable period, and their succession was as follows :—Henry succeeded his father George in 1536, and in 1573 he conveyed them to his son James on his marriage. Helen and Catharine Orme were served heiresses to their brother James in 1581, they conveyed their respective shares of the lands to their uncle David Orme of Priorletham, who conveyed them in 1588 to Mr David Orme his eldest son.—*Mugdrum Charters.*

The Orme's of Mugdrum embraced the cause of Francis Stewart, Earl of Bothwell. In their complicity with this violent and reckless nobleman, they became involved in much trouble. He was a cousin of James VI., who treated him with much kindness, and bestowed favours upon him, which he requited by a series of violent attacks on the King. He and a band of accomplices beset the Palace of Holyrood in a violent and tumultuous manner, for which seven of those that were apprehended were hanged. ' In the same year, 1592, Bothwell, with armed adherents assailed Falkland when the King was there, and he was only repulsed by the peasantry of the neighbourhood rallying for the protection of the King. Bothwell's last and most formidable raid on the the royal household was in 1594, when he appeared suddenly at Leith with five hundred ruffians from the Border threatening Edinburgh.' Long before this, however, he and his accomplices were tried in absence, and condemned for high treason. These raids of Bothwell were productive of great uneasiness and disquiet, and the Magistrates of the ' Townis off the coist-syde had to find caution to appear before the King and Council, to ansuer to sic things as sal be inquirit of thame concerning the pairt-taking, etc., with Francis, sumtyme Erll Bothuill, etc., viz.—The magistrates of Kirkaldy, under the pane of 2000 merkis ; Kinghorne, 1000 merkis ; Dysart, 2000 pundis ; Pittinweyme, 1000 merkis ; Carraill, 500 pundis ; Sanct Androis, 2000 merkis ; Anstruther, 1000 pundis ; and Coupair 500 merkis.'

The estates and goods of those condemned (one of whom was David Orme of Mugdrum), were confiscated, and their persons doomed to underly the ' utter and last punishment appointit by the lawes of this realme.' The following proclamation was issued, April 13, 1594 :—*Apud Brunt-Iland,* against Capitane George Strang, Capitane Robert Melvill, Mr Jerome Lindsay, sone to Mr David L., minister, Mr John Murray, David Orme of Mugdrum, Mr Allane Orme and . . . Orme his brother, Robert Douglas sone naturell to Schir George D. and Patrik Clapene, brother to the Laird of Carslogy, his Maiesteis unnatural and disobedient subiectis, fugitive from his hienes lawis for thair tressonnable assisting, etc. Francis, sumtyme Erll Bothuill and utheris his accomplices, etc. ; and sum of thame for rasing bandis of men of weir, etc., for serving the saidis traitouris agaiuis his Maiestie. The lieges are therefoir discharged from furnishing them with ' meit, house, nor harbory,' etc.—Pitcairn's *Criminal Trials*, Vol. I., pp. 270-5, 309, 310.

Many of those implicated contrived to elude justice, but all were not so fortunate. Sir James Balfour of Denmyln records the following under the year 1594 :—' In Appryle this yeir Bothwell comes to Leith with 500 horse, and the King raises the toune of Edinburgh to apprehend him bot he fleies by the way of Dalkeith. Divers were hangit this yeire for resaitting and entertaining of him, as William Heggie 29 Appryle ; Allan Orme, brother to the Laird of Mugdrum, the 17 of September, James Gibson, James Cochrane the 24,' etc.—Balfour's *Annals*, Vol. I., p. 395. Bothwell, the author of all this misery, when last heard of in Scotland, was seen skulking near Perth with only two followers, and in utter destitution. He escaped to the continent, and died there in obscurity.—Tytler's *Hist. of Scotland*, Vol. IV., p. 231. Hill Burton's *History of Scotland*, Vol. IV., p. 50.

The sentence of confiscation against David Orme does not seem to have been carried out to the rigour, as Francis Orme, son of David Orme received a Charter of *Novodamus* to the lands of Mugdrum, on 27th November 1631, who conveyed them next day to Henry Cheap of Ormiston. In November 1631, Henry Cheap conveyed them to Stephen Orme of Halhill, who conveyed them, reserving his own liferent, to his eldest son George, on his marriage with Grizzel Spens 27th December 1634. George Orme sold Mugdrum to the Right Honourable Colonel Ludovic Leslie, brothergerman of Patrick, Lord Lundores, 20th February 1648. Colonel Leslie sold the estate to William Arnot, brother of the Laird of Woodmilne on 2d March 1663.

In 1647 Colonel Ludovic Leslie purchased from William Oliphant of Balgonie, ʻthe Insche callit the Reid Insche with the salmond fishings, etc., within the parochine and barony of Abernethie and Sheriffdom of Perth.' He sold this Island to William Arnot, along with Mugdrum ; and the two properties have ever since been conjoined. William Arnot married Jeane Cheape, daughter of Mr James Cheape of Ormiston, in 1663. These spouses conveyed Mugdrum and the Reid Inch to Harie Cheape, younger of Rossie, in 1684, who was succeeded by his son James in 1707. James Cheap sold them in 1718 to Richard Murray, merchant in Edinburgh, who conveyed them to Richard Oswald of Port Glasgow in 1723. Lord George Murray, as stated in a previous page, came into possession of Mugdrum and resided there. On the 15th May 1732, he granted a disposition to the community of Newburgh, affording them access to the Tay. Richard Oswald must have re-acquired Mugdrum and the Island, as on 12th February 1737, he conveyed them to Henry Barclay of Collernie, who on the same day, with consent of Alexander, Lord Lindores, conveyed them to Peter Hay, younger of Leys; in the possession of whose descendants they have ever since remained. There was, we learn from record, formerly an old castle at Mugdrum, but it has long since been destroyed, and no vestige of it remains.

At a subsequent date, however, Alexander Orme, Writer to the Signet, in all likelihood a descendant of the Ormes of Mugdrum, bought, in 1763, from Viscount Stormonth, the superiority, which entitled him to a voice in the election of a member of Parliament. Alexander Orme was succeeded in this *freehold* by his brother Dr David Orme, physician in London, in 1794, who sold it by public roup in the same year, and it was purchased for David Balfour Hay of Leys, then the proprietor of the lands of Mugdrum.

After the Ormes sold the lands of Mugdrum they bought 'The Haugh' betwixt Newburgh and the Tay. David Orme was one of the bailies of Newburgh. His son, Mr David, became minister of Newburgh, having been presented by Charles I., 8th June 1631. He was translated to Monimail, and died in 1684.

Mothel. Muthil Church, according to the Bull of Pope Innocent III. belonged to Lindores Abbey in 1198. There is no record to show how this ancient seat of the Culdees came into the possession of the Abbey, and there is no subsequent mention made of it in the Rentals which have come down to us. The probability is, that Easter Feddills and Bennie which pertained to the Abbey (*see* p. 433), and which were situated in what was originally the parish of Muthil, came through the grant confirmed in 1198. We extract the following regarding this ancient religious site from Dr Reeves' 'Culdees of the British Islands.' 'Concerning its [Muthil] foundation and early condition, history is silent. The veneration, indeed, entertained there in old times for St Patrick's Well and that of Struthill, with its adjacent chapel, reminds us of St Patrick's famous well at Struell, near Downpatrick, and may indicate some faint traces of Irish influence at a remote period.' Dr Reeves adds in a note, that '*Maothail*,' which is often in Ireland written *Moethail* is from the Gaelic *Maoth* soft, and signifies, 'spongy ground,' and not Mote-hill, as stated in the New Statistical Account, p. 175.

Inuerkeithing. Robert of Lundores, son of King William, the Lion, bestowed 'one full toft in the burgh of Inverketin' on the abbot and convent of Londoris. This grant was confirmed in 1291 by a Bull of Pope Nicolas IV.—*Antiq. of Aberdeen and Banffshires*, Vol. IV., p. 503.

Cumytun, in the diocese of Lincoln, was also confirmed to Lundoris by the same Bull. No other mention is made of these grants in the records of the Abbey.

No. V. p. 153.

(The reference at p. 149 should be No. VI. See p 489.)

Abstracts of Charters of Lindores Abbey.

The Chartulary of Lindores is preserved in the Advocates' Library. It consists of a small volume of 12mo size, and contains all the Charters that are printed in the first thirty-three pages of the Chartulary published by the Abbotsford Club. These have been copied without any regard to the order of date. The Chartulary is written in a small indistinct hand. At the end of the volume there are several memorandums, one of which is as follows :—

' Ye XVI. day of April four score vij. yeirs [*query* 1487] cherls . . warnit James betone, patrik leslie, and all to remowe from the lands of Vodriff befor thir witness Jhone Scott or Stewaird ; David hunter, Jhone philipe ; Alex^r balfour ; Gawin Adeson, Jhone Pitbladar.'

Besides the Charters contained in the manuscript volume mentioned, there are other ten in the printed Chartulary, of which the originals of three are preserved in the Advocates' Library, one of these is the Founda- tion Charter from the Denmylne collection. It is a beautiful specimen of penmanship, but the seals (one of which was that of the Founder, and another that of William the Lion) are all worn off.

The whole of the Charters are in Latin, but the following Abstracts are made in English, and are inserted in the order of their date, so far as can be ascertained. Those of numbers 28 and 29 are from an original copy preserved in the archives of Newburgh, and are interesting as con- taining the names of the monks and of the burgesses in the middle of the fifteenth century.

The preceding Rentals, show that many grants to the Abbey have not been recorded in the Chartulary, and that others had been alienated before the dissolution of the Monastery.

The numbers within brackets are those of the Chartulary printed by the Abbotsford Club.

No. 1. (I.) *Carta Fundationis Ecclesiæ et Monasterii de Londors in silvis de Ironside.* A.D. 1178-1198.

Earl David, brother of the King of Scotland. Know me to have founded the Abbacy of Londors of the order of Kelso, for the honor of God and of the blessed Virgin, and St Andrew the Apostle, and all the Saints ; for the welfare of the soul of King David my grandfather, of Earl Henry my father, and Ada my mother; of King Malcolm and King William my brothers, and Queen Armegarda and all my ancestors, and for the welfare of my own soul, and that of Matilda my spouse, of David my son, and of all my descendants ; and for the souls of my brothers and sisters : Granting and Confirming to the said Abbacy of Londors and the monks serving God there, in pure and perpetual charity, the Church of Londors and the land pertaining to the said Church as Master Thomas held the same; and the churches of Dunde, Fintrith and Inverurin, with the chapel of Munkegin; the churches of Durnach, Prame, Radmuriel, Inchemabanin, Culsamuel, and Kelalcmund, with the chapels, lands, and teinds, of the said churches, and all their pertinents, to the proper use and sustenance of the said monks; free from all service and exaction whatever. Witnesses, William, King of Scotland, John, bishop of Aberdeen, Ralph, bishop of Brechin, Osbert, abbot of Kelso, Henry, abbot of Aberbrudoc, Simon, archdeacon of Aberdeen, Robert, dean of Aberdeen, Walter, official, Mathew of Aberdeen, clerk to the King, David of Lindeseia, Walter Olifard, Robert Basset, Walkeline son of Stephan, William Wascelin, Galfrid of Watervile, Norman son of Malcom, constable of Innerurin, Henry of Beuile, Mathew the falconer, Simon Flamang, with many others.

Original Charter from Denmylne; Advocates' Library.

No. 2 (IL) *Bulla Papæ Innocentii III. de confirmatione privilegiorum*
19th *April* 1198.

Granting to Guido, abbot of Lundores, and his brethren, apostolic pro-tection, and confirming the privileges belonging to their Benedictine order, and also whatever possessions and goods they have received, or may in future receive, by the gift of pontiffs, the bounty of kings or princes, the offering of the faithful, or in any other lawful way; amongst which are reckoned the place itself, upon which the said monastery is built, granted by Earl David, brother of William, King of Scotland; the church of the town of Lundores, with its pertinents namely the chapels of Bundamer [Dundemor] and the lands pertaining to the foresaid church; the island called Redinche, and the fishings in Thay adjoining the said island ; the mill of Lundores, with all its multures, the church of Dunde, and the land belonging thereto ; and a toft in the burgh of Dunde free from all exac-tion and service ; and a carucate of land in the town of Neutile, and in the town of Pert ; the land called the island, beyond the moneth Fintreth ; the church of the said town with its pertinents in Garvich ; Lethgavel and Malind ; the church of Ritcheth with its chapels ; namely Inverurin and Munchegin ; the church of Duruah ; the churches of Prame, Rathmuriel, Inchemabanin, Culsamuel. In the diocese of Lincoln, the churches of Cuningroue and Wissenden. In the diocese of Stratheren, the churches of Mothel and Chelalcmund, with the chapels of the foresaid churches, together with the lands and teinds thereof ; and one full toft in the burgh of Inverurie. Given at the Lateran in the year of the Incarnation of our Lord M. CXCVIII.

No. 3 (21), *Carta Comitis David de quarrario.* A.D. 1178-1219.

Earl David, brother of the King of Scots. Know me to have given to my monks of Lundores, the privilege of taking stone from my quarry in Hyrneside, as much as they please for ever, for building their church, as well as all other edifices which shall be needful for them. Witnesses, William Wascelin, Walkeline, son of Stephen, Robert Basset, Nicholas of Aness, Walter Olifart, Philip the clerk, Henry of Nueriss and others.

No. 4 (4). *Carta Comitis David de Redinche.* A.D. 1178-1219.

Earl David, brother of the King. Know that we have given to God and to the church of St Mary and St Andrew of Lundores, and to the monks serving God there, the Island called the Redinche, and all the fishings in the Tay next to the said island, excepting only my *Jharam* [yair] at Colcrik. To be held in perpetual charity, in the same manner as the other lands which they hold and possess. Witnesses :—A   abbot of Dunfermline, Earl Duncan, Malise, Earl Fertheth, Malcolm, son of Earl Duncan, Walkelin, son of Stephen, R.   of Anos, Robert Basset, John of Wiltun, W. Oliphant, Ralph Cameis, etc.

No. 5 (6). *Rex Super toftis burgorum.* A.D. 1178-1214.

William, King of Scots, etc. Know me to have given to God and to the abbot of Lundores, and to the monks serving God there, one full toft in each of my burghs of Berevic, Strivelin, Karel, Pertht, Forfare, Munross and Aberdene. To be held in perpetual charity, Witnesses ; Earl David, my brother ; Hugh, my chancellor, William of Lindiss ; Robert of London, my son ; William of Hay; William of Sumervill ; Henry of Brade, marshal; Richard, son of Hugh. Given at Selechirche.

No. 6 (8). *Libertas Foreste de Fyntre.* A.D. 1216.

Alexander, King of Scots, etc. Know that we have conceded to the Abbot and Convent of Lundores that they should hold their whole wood in the fee of Fyntreth, in free forest ; straitly forbidding anyone from felling trees or hunting therein without licence from the said abbot and convent, under the penalty of ten pounds ; witnesses, Gilbert de Hay John de Vallis ; John of Hyrdmanstoun. Dated at Kingorne 20 May the second year of my reign.

No. 7 (5). *Piscaria in Tay.* A.D. 1189-1237.

David de Haya. Know me to have given by this present charter to God and to the church of St Mary and St Andrew of Lundores, etc., for the welfare of the souls of my father and mother, of my own soul, and those of my wives Ethina and Crua, and for the welfare of the souls of my brothers and sisters, my predecessors and successors, the third part of my draw-net fishing upon the sand-bank over against Colcrik, saving my stake-net fishings. Therefore I·will that the foresaid monks should hold the third part of my draw-net fishings on the sand-bank of Blasbannyn opposite Colcrick. To be held freely, etc. ; so that none of my successors should presume to exact from the said monks anything else but prayers for the welfare of the soul. Witnesses, Gilbert my son ; Robert de Hay ; Malcolm de Hay, my brothers Thomas Gy, Patrick the chaplain.

No. 8 (12) *Carta de Cragy.*

Ysabella of Brouss, etc. Know me to have given by this charter to God and to the church of St Mary and St Andrew of Lundores, etc., my messuage of Cragyn near Dundee, with the whole land pertaining to me in the town called Melneton, and in the town called Abrahe : To be held in perpetual charity for the sustenance of one monk, who shall celebrate mass for my soul, and the souls of my ancestors and successors for ever ; which the said monks granted to her at her petition. Witnesses, Sir William of Brechin, William of Loch, Hugh of Braumis, Michael of Muncur, knights, Albert of Dunde, Nicholas the son of Robert, Herin Coks, Norman of Castle, burgesses, with many others.

No. 9 (15). *Gregorius Episcopus Brechinensis. Circa* A.D. 1224.

Gregory, bishop of Brechin. Lest the pious gifts of the faithful should be disturbed, and walking in the footsteps of our predecessors Turpin, Radulf and Hugh we hold ratified that donation which they made to the abbot and monks of Lundoris, of the church of Dunde, with the chapels and lands belonging thereto ; conferring upon them also the full and free administration of all the revenues of the said church, and that they, on the demise of the vicar thereof, may lawfully present whomsoever they may think worthy of the cure of souls, assigning to him ten pounds sterling of yearly stipend, that he may minister competently and fitly in the church; he being answerable with regard to episcopal matters both to the bishop and his officials. Granting to the said abbot and convent liberty to plant schools wherever they please in the said town. That these things may remain firm and stable we have placed our seal to this present writing. Witnesses Sir G. abbot and convent of Abirbrothot, Sir W. abbot and convent of Scone, Sir Alexander, abbot of Cupar; Masters H. and H. of Norham and Munros, Andrew, chaplain of Brechin, M. prior of the Culdees of Brechin, and John, our clerk with many others.

No. 10 (16). *Confirmatio domini Pape Gregorii IX. ecclesie de Dunde.* 14 *Feb.* 1239.

Gregory, bishop, servant of the servants of God, confirms to the abbot and convent of Lundores the foregoing grant by the bishop of Brechin of the church of Dunde, and also the liberties and immunities from secular exactions granted by the Kings, earls, and barons of Scotland to the said abbot and convent. Given at the Lateran, the 16th Kalends of March (14 February) the 12th year of our pontificate.

No. 11 (7). *Admissio Willelmi de Mydford ad vicariam de Dunde.* A.D. 1252.

Albin, bishop of Brechin. Know, etc., when the abbot and convent of Lundoris presented William Mydford to the vicarage of the church of Dunde, we admitted him under reservation to us of the taxation of the said vicarage; and the monday before Lent in the year 1252 having been assigned to the said abbot and convent and the said master William, for making taxation. The said parties having appeared before us on the day fixed, and the revenues of the said church having been diligently considered by upright men, we ordain in name of the Father, Son, and Holy Spirit that the said vicar should receive the whole altarage in name of vicarage, rendering therefrom ten merks yearly at Easter to the said Abbot and convent. In testimony of this we have put our seal to these letters patent.

No. 12 (No. IV.) *Carta Willelmi de Brechin de terra ecclesie de Rathmuryel.* A.D. 1245.

William of Brechin. Know me for the love of God, and for the weal of my soul to have given to God and to the monastery of Lundoris, the land of the church of Rathmuryel which was perambulated, to the other Rathmuryel, the land of which is mine, and that the said land shall remain free of the said church of Rathmuryel, by the same marches which I had before the said perambulation, namely by the high-way which leads from the ford of Uri towards Leslyn. In witness whereof I have appended my seal. Witnesses Sir John de Haya, Sir William de Haya of Balcolmy, William de Haya, brother of Gilbert de Haya, Hugh of Bennis, Henry of Dunde-more, John Wyschard, Michael of Muncur, David of Louthre, my knights, and others. At Lundoris on the day after the festival of the Beheading of Saint John the Baptist. [29th August.]

> Erroneously dated 1345 in chartulary printed by the Abbotsford Club. Rathmuriel is the ancient name of Christ's Kirk.—*Antiq. of Aberdeen and Banff*, Vol. II., p. 625; Vol. IV., p. 501.

No. 13 (11). *Confirmacio domini Pape de Vicaria. Dunde* A.D. 1256.

Alexander, bishop, servant of the servants of God to the abbot and convent of Lundors. Your petition has shewn that the bishop of Brechin hath taxed the perpetual vicarage of the church of St Mary of Dunde, a suit-able portion being assigned to Master William, perpetual vicar thereof, and although the said vicar affirms that he was wronged by the taxation, yet as he did not prosecute his appeal within the legal time, as he might have done, we, believing that what was done by the Bishop was prudently done, in our fatherly solicitude confirm the said taxation and fortify it by the present writ. Given at the Lateran, 17th April, second year of our pontificate.

No. 14. (13) *Confirmatio Albini episcopi Brechinensis super vicaria de Dunde.* A.D. 1256.

Albin, bishop of Brechin. Know that when those religious men, the abbot and convent of Lundores, presented William of Mydford to the vicarage of the church of Dunde, we, under reservation of the taxation of the said vicarage, admitted the said William to the vicarage; and the revenues of the said church being fully considered, we have judicially de-cerned that the vicar shall receive the altarage in name of vicarage, on paying ten merks sterling at yearly Easter to the Abbot and convent; Master William having failed to pay though frequently warned and re-quired thereto by us and by the said Abbot and convent. The latter in consequence obtained letters of the apostolic See for adjudication to be made in the matter by the Prior of May and the Provost of the church of St Mary of St Andrews. The vicar, alleging that he could not be suit-ably supported on the stipend alloted to him, procured letters of the same See to the official of Aberdeen, but after he had proceeded a little with-drew, and the said Prior and Provost approved of our taxation and gave sentence accordingly. The vicar appealed to the abbot of Kynloss, but while his appeal was pending he, in the church of the Preaching friars of Perth, before the bishop of Dunblane and other prelates, amicably gave assent for the sake of peace, to our taxation of the foresaid vicarage, and to the payment of ten merks from the altarage of said church yearly; and for the payment of the arrears he bound himself by oath, submitting himself to the bishop of Dunblane and us with regard to the expenses incurred by the abbot and convent in the litigation; and the parties appearing before us in the chapter-house of Arbroath, and having carefully considered the matter, we ordain that the vicar shall pay to the abbot and convent fifty merks sterling as full satisfaction for the expenses incurred by them, the vicar submitting himself to them that they may do this as a special and courteous favour, the expenses having extended to a larger sum. In testimony we have placed our seals to the present writ, 20 September 1256.

No. 15 (14) *Bulla Pape Alexandri IV. ut Episcopus non Sequestrat ᵗfructus rectoris Ecclesie de Dunde, 11 Feb. 1257.*

Alexander, bishop, etc., to his beloved sons the abbot and convent of Lundores. Having signified to us that you possess the church of Dunde, and that a portion of the revenues of the church is assigned to the perpetual vicar for his maintenance, and for the payment of the episcopal dues and other burdens of the church, we strictly forbid the diocesan and archdeacon of Brechin from exacting any thing from the portion belonging to you or sequestrating the same. Given at the Lateran IV. Ides of February and of our pontificate the third year.

No. 16. (9) *Carta Libertas ᵗforeste de Lundoris, A.D. 1265.*

Alexander, king of Scots, etc. Know that we have conceded to the abbot and convent of Lundores that they may hold their whole wood, with the lands of Lundores in free forest. We prohibit any one from felling trees, or hunting in the said wood without licence of the said abbot and convent, under a penalty of ten pounds. Witnesses, Alexander Cumyn, Earl of Buchan, Justiciar of Scotland, William, Earl of Marr, chamberlain and Eustace of Tours. At Lundoris 14th March in the 16th year of our reign.

No. 17. (3) *Concessio domini Regis super libertate Novi burgi. A.D. 1266.*

A translation of this Charter, erecting the town of Newburgh into a burgh, is given at p. 142.

No. 18. (22) *Bulla Pape Nicholai de bonnetis utendis.* A.D. 1277-1294.

Nicholas, etc. To the abbot and convent of Lundores. It having been represented to us, that from a custom long observed in the monastery, some of you in the solemn festivals, while divine mysteries are being celebrated, are held standing clothed in albs and copes of silk bareheaded, and as the climate of Scotland is frigid, the cold has seized some of the monks, who have thereby contracted long-continued illness. Wherefore since divine worship is impaired by this cause, we, endeavouring to remove every thing by which the worship of the monastery is hindered, moved by your suppli- cations, grant indulgence by these presents, that as often as you are clothed for certain festivals and processions, you may use caps or bonnets suitable for your order in divine things, provided that in reading the Gospels, and in the elevation of the host, and in all other services, due reverence be observed. Given at Rome on the Ides of March in the second year of our pontificate.

No. 19. (10) *Declaratio dissencionis quondam habite inter Abbatem et Conventum de Lundoris et homines suos Novi burgi.* A.D. 1309.

Memorandum of the dissensions and controversy that had arisen be- tween the abbot and convent of Lundores on the one part, and the men of the New burgh of Lundores on the other part. The parties being con- vened before Sir Robert of Keth, marshal of Scotland, and Justiciar from the Forth to the mountains of Scotland, in the chapter-house of Lundores, on the Thursday before the feast of St Peter in cathedra [20 Feby.] in the year of Grace 1309. Sir Robert amicably requested from the men of the New burgh in form of law, their infeftment by which they claimed to use the privilege and liberty of the burgh, and that they should show cause why they had withheld for five years the fermes of the abbot and convent. Robert of Perth and William the baker sought and obtained leave to answer for all the neighbours of the New burgh: Having con- sulted with them, the two foresaid answered they held no infeftment of the abbot and convent, and that they were not accustomed to pay a ferme of one merk yearly for each brewhouse with an acre of land, which the abbot and convent demanded from them; nor would they consent to pay in future, unless it be found by inquest that the said abbot and convent were wont to receive the foresaid merk. That every suspicion might be removed, and their justice appear clearer than the light, the monks unani- mously consented to the making of said Inquest. Thereupon by command of the Lord Justiciar, certain barons, freeholders and other persons of Fyfe, worthy of trust, having been purged for the said inquest, and being present, Sir Robert Keth demanded of the foresaid men of the New Burgh if they would consent to all who were nominated to the said inquest, namely, John of Balfour, Thomas the Judge, Keth of Kynros, Michael Scot, Adam of Ramsay, Walter the Stewart, Malcolm of Balmeharg, Galfrid of Freslay, Patrick of Crambeth, William Cook, Patrick Scot, Alan Mair of Stradingloch, Maurice Scall, Patrick Fairhar, Nicolas son of Roger, William Syarpe, and John son of Nicholas ; they approved of all that were nominated excepting Adam Gray, alleging that he could not stand upon the said inquest, because he had been a servant to the abbot and convent, and was frequently employed by them ; upon which account he was excluded. The others having been sworn, and having consulted with deliberation, declared upon their oath, that from time immemorial the abbot and convent of Lundores received from each brewhouse with an acre of land in the said Newburgh one merk yearly, until those who were now in the said burgh withheld the said ferme for five years last past. All these things above written were done the day after Thursday, that is Friday, in the foresaid chapter-house of Lundores, the said abbot and convent with the foresaid men, being summoned, in presence of William, bishop of St Andrews, and of Thomas Ranulf, lord of the valley of Keth, and lieutenant for the time of the illustrious Prince of Scotland, from the Forth to Orkney, Sir Bernard, chancellor of Scotland, Master William of Eglishame, official of the Court of St Andrews, Sir Michael of Wemyss, knight, and John of Dondemore, whose seals, together with the seal of the said Sir Robert of Keth, justiciar, in token of perpetual testimony are appended to this Instrument.

No. 20. (III.) *Confirmatio Regis Roberti I. donacionis Rogeri de Quency.*
A.D. 1306–1329.

Robert, etc., Know that we confirm that donation which Roger de Quency, Earl of Wynton, Constable of Scotland made to God and the Church of St Mary of Lundores and to the monks serving God there, for the welfare of his soul, and the souls of his ancestors and successors, of two hundred cart loads of brushwood from their muir of Kindelouch annually, and the privilege of digging as many peats as they require for the use of their house in the peatery called Menegre, and that no other should dig peats in the same peatery without licence of the said monks, nor are they themselves to give, sell, alienate or convert the said peatery to any other purpose excepting the proper use of their house. Also one acre of land, to be assigned to them annually in length and breath adjacent to the place in which they shall dig peats, for drying the same ; and also one messuage next to the ford which is called Eschewyn on the east side in the field of Thoriston, containing two acres of land, to which they shall cause their brushwood and peats to be led ; also the common pasturage of the muir of Kindelouch for feeding of ten sheep and two cows for the benefit of the keeper of the said messuage, and the fuel which they shall lead thither, and the said monks and their men to have free passage with their oxen and waggons by the straight road towards the muir through the brushwood, and through the midst of the muir for peats, with common pasture in the said muir of Kindelouch for the oxen, when leading the foresaid fuel, from the time they begin to lead until the feast of the nativity of the Virgin yearly [8th September]. To be held by the said monks, and their successors of the said Earl and his heirs for ever.

No. 21. (V.) *Confirmacio Regis David Carte Duncani Comitis de Fyfe.* 31 *July* 1359.

David, etc., Know that we have inspected a charter which the deceased Duncan, Earl of Fyffe granted to the abbot and convent of Lundores, in these words. To all the faithful in Christ, etc., know that when we, and the rest of the nobles and magnates of the kingdom were destitute of human aid at the battle near Durham, and were in imminent peril of our lives, we vowed that if the prayers of the saints above, etc., for our deliverance from death, and from a miserable prison were heard, we would be-stow on the monastery of Lyndors, situated in our earldom, a benefit to endure for ever. Therefore for the honour of God, and the furtherance of divine worship there, and for the welfare of my soul and for the souls of my father and mother, and for the souls of my ancestors, etc., we give to God and to the Church of St Mary and St Andrew of Lundoris, and to the religious men serving God there, the right of patronage of the Church of Uchter-Mukedy which belonged to us and our ancestors. And we give this concession with the lands annexed of old to the said church to the present monks. To be held by them in perpetual charity. Given at the foresaid Abbey 17th March 1350. Witnesses, William, bishop of St Andrews, Sir John, Steward of Scotland, Regent of the Kingdom, Sir Robert Stewart his brother, Sir Thomas of Fawsyd, knight, Master Walter of Wardlaw, rector of the church of Erole, Sir Laurence Bell, provost of the collegiate church of Abernethy, Michael of Bottillero, Laurence of . . . , Thomas Sympill, Robert of . . , John our clerk, John Melvill and others. Which donation and concession we ratify and approve. At Dundee 31 July, 30th year of our Reign.

No. 22. (VI.) *Confirmacio Regis David carte David de Lyndesay de Cravford.*
A.D. 1365.

David, King of the Scots, etc. Know that we have seen a writing of
David de Lyndesay of Cravford, the tenor of which is as follows. David
de Lyndesay, Lord of Cravford for the welfare of my own soul and that of
the deceased Lady Marie my wife and the souls of my ancestors, etc.
Give to the abbot and convent of Londors, six stones of wax for maintaining a burning candle in the choir of the foresaid church at our sepulchre
daily at mass for my lady, and when for her, mass, matins and vespers,
and other solemnities are celebrated. I ordain the said six stones of wax
to be fully paid to the abbey at the feast of Pentecost, by the hand of
my bailie, or the tenant of Carny; for the maintenance of which wax I become bound in two merks due to me annually from the land of Pethfour,
near my land of Carny; and if the said two merks should not suffice, the
said wax shall be wholly forthcoming from my rents of Carny, under
penalty of one pound of wax to be paid after eight days, if I or my heirs
fail in the payment foresaid; and the monks of the said convent shall be
liable in the like penalty if they cease from keeping up the said candle, to
the maintenance whereof I and my heirs shall have power to compel them
by law, and to make satisfaction for the omission. Dated at the said abbey
19th November 1355. In witness, etc., we confirm, etc., at Lundores 3d
August the 36th year of our reign.

No. 23. (VII.) *Confirmacio* [*Carta*] *Regis David Carta Bertholomei de Loone.*
A.D. 1365.

David, King of Scots, etc. Know that for the welfare of our soul and
for the souls of our ancestors and successors Kings of Scotland, and also
for the welfare of the souls of Bertholomew of Loone and Philipa of
Moubray his spouse, daughter and heir of Philip of Moubray, knight, and
the souls of their ancestors and successors, and of all the faithful dead, we
have given to the abbot and convent of Londors and their successors serving
God there, the half of the lands of Easter Cragy in the barony of Barnbogall
and shire of Edinburgh; which lands were resigned by the said Bertholomew and his spouse before us and many nobles of the kingdom, for
infeftment thereof to be given to the foresaid monastery of Lundors: On
the condition that the monks celebrate one mass, on any day they choose,
before the altar of the blessed Michael in the foresaid church, for the welfare of all the souls foresaid. In witness, etc., At Lundors 30th August
the 36th year of our reign.

No. 24. (VIII.) *Confirmacio carte Regis Alexandri.* A.D. 1365.

David, King of Scots, etc. Know that we have seen a Charter of Alexander, King of Scots, the tenor whereof is as follows : Alexander, etc., know that we have granted that the abbot and convent of Londors shall have and hold all the lands which they have held from the first foundation of their house of Londors, with all their privileges and immunities. Wherefore we forbid anyone from disturbing this concession under pain of our displeasure. Witnesses, William, son of Alan, Steward, Justiciar of Scotland, William Olifer, Justiciar of Lothian, Bernard Fraser, Walter Byseth, John de Haya. At the Maidens Castle, 12th November in the 33d year of our reign. Which Charter we ratify and approve. And we will that the lands of Cragy of Milton, of Claypottis and Balmaw in which the said abbey was infeft before the grant of our predecessor be held by the same religious men free from all service. In witness, etc. At Dunde 20 September the 36th year of our reign.

No. 25 (IX.) *Confirmacio Regis Roberti III. carte David Aberkedor.* A.D. 1392.

Robert, King of Scots, etc. Know that we ratify the pledge made by William of angus, Abbot of Londors and the convent thereof to David of Abirkedor of seven merks of annual-rent due to the said monastery in the town of Dunde, namely, from the land of Patrick the butcher, and Michael of Mane, twenty shillings, from the land of Richard the clerk, twenty shillings, from the land of David of Abirkedor twenty shillings, from the land of the late Thomas Warderon, thirteen shillings and four pence, and from the land of the late Adam Bane, twenty shillings, and that for a certain sum of money for the sustentation of the said abbey, paid beforehand : To be held of the said monastery under reversion for forty merks sterling money of Scotland, payable in the church of St Mary of Dunde. We confirm the same, etc. Witnesses, Walter, bishop of St Andrews, Matthew, bishop of Glasgow, Robert, Earl of Fyf and Menteth, our brother, Archibald, Earl of Douglas, Lord of Galloway, our cousin, James, Earl of Douglas, Lord of Dalketh, Thomas of Erskine, our beloved cousins, knights, and Alexander de Cokburne of Langton, Keeper of our Great Seal. At Perth 23d March, the second year of our reign.

No. 26. (X.) *Donacio Isabelle de Douglas domine de Mar et de Garviache de Advocationis jure et patronatus ecclesie de Codilstane in la Mar.* A.D. 1402.

Isabella of Douglas, Lady of Mar, etc. Know that we in our pure widowhood, for the welfare of my soul and for the welfare of all my ancestors, etc., give to God, and to the monastery of St Mary and St Andrew of Lundores, and the monks serving God there, the right·of patronage and advocation to the church of Codilstane in Mar. In witness whereof we have appended our seal. At Kyndromy 8th November 1402.

No. 27. (17). *Saissina Regis Foreste de Irnside.* A.D. 1452.

James, King of Scots, To our beloved Alexander Napar, master of the Rolls, and David Berclay of Cullessin and our Sheriff of Fyfe, etc. Because we concede hereditarily to our beloved preachers, the venerable father in Christ and religious men, the abbot and convent of the monastery of Lundores, our lands of Parkhill, also the office of Forestry of our wood of Irnsyde, lying within the said lands, in the shire of Fyffe, as is more fully contained in our charter to the abbot and convent. We command that the said abbot and convent be infeft in said lands, and office, etc. Given under our Great Seal at Edinburgh 20th May, the 15th year of our reign.

No. 28-29. (1-2). *Abstract of Instrument on the Renewal by John Abbot of Lundors, of the rights and privileges of the Burgh of Newburgh, and of the Lands of the Burgh, narrating at length two Charters in favour of the Burgesses, dated 13th July 1457. Preserved in the charter chest of Newburgh.*

In the name of God, Amen. On the 13th day of July in the year one thousand four hundred and fifty-seven from the Incarnation of the Lord, according to the reckoning of the Scottish church, in the presence of the notary and witnesses underwritten, compeared personally a venerable father in Christ, John, abbot of the monastery of Saint Mary of Lundores, of the order of St Benedict, and diocese of St Andrews, with the convent of the same place, namely, Sir Thomas Waryne, Sir John of Arbrocht, Sir William Cultir, Sir Stephen of Kinghorn, Sir William Crammy, Sir Richard Bisset, supprior, Sir Gilbert Greynlaw, Sir John Cambas, Sir Andrew Allerdas, Sir William Dysert, Sir John Colsamuell; Sir James Roland, Sir George Boys, Sir James Lawerok, Sir John Ramsay, Sir William Halywell, Sir John of Balfour, Sir Thomas Culper, Sir Andrew Wintoun, Sir John Reyd, Sir John Westoun, Sir Andrew Cawerys, Sir Andrew Gray and Sir Patrick Snell, chapterly assembled on the one part, and the greater and more worthy portion of the community of Newburgh in Fyff on the other part, as at the hundredth day or term assigned by the foresaid Abbot and Convent to the said community, for the delivery and reception of certain letters and evidences, namely, of one concerning the new Infeftment of the said burgh, and the renovation of the privileges and liberties thereof, and of another in the form of an indented charter, of and upon the perpetual tack and demission at feu ferme of certain lands and pasturage. The which letters and evidences, written upon parchment, and sealed with the common seal of the foresaid monastery, having been found complete and sound in every part, were delivered by the said abbot to John Wyntoun, the notary there present, to be read and expounded in the vulgar tongue, which having been done, the said abbot and convent unanimously approved the said letters and evidences, and delivered them to these honest and prudent men, namely, Stephan Phylippe, and Henry of Kynglassi, bailies of the said burgh, in name of all the rest of their co-burgesses, inhabiting occupying or possessing the said burgh, namely, Master Thomas of Rosse, Thomas Laying, Master John Wintoun, John Joly, Angus of the Isles, John of Crysty, William Newman, John of Kynharde, James Lyndsay, John of Wemys, James Liston, David Grantuly, Richard of Kynglassy, James Foulfurde, John Emry, James Anderson, Alexander Bell, John Hughson, Andrew Lambert, Christian Bell, John Thomson, John Qwhiting, James Bane, William of Nes, Simon Colfhirde, Marion of Lundoris, Thomas of Kitchen, Nichola Bat, Alexander Blakburne, David Malcolmson, Walter of Ros, Michael of Machar, John Blak, John Glen, Andrew of Lundoris, Bertholomew Smyth, William Greenhorne, Sir Patrick Kirk, William Joly, the heirs of the deceased Robert of Kynharde, John Philippe, elder, John Rossy, John Wilson, Agnes of Balrame, William Ferny, Sir John Berclai, William Scharpe, Adam Sclater, the heirs of William Greynlaw, Henry of Bykirton, Mathew Quhiting, John Anderson, Laurence Ronald, Thomas Stob, John, son of the deceased Robert Stob, William Stob, Gilbert of Kinlocht, David Anderson, John Wilson, John Philippe younger, John Hawkarstoue, William Johnsone, Simon Bel, and John Davisone, and all their heirs and successors. The tenor of which letters or evidences is to this effect:—That whereas the charters and muniments of infeftments of the burgesses of Newburgh having been destroyed and taken away by wars, fire, or other hazards of this world, and therefore the said burgesses, by their continual supplications having unceasingly and unweariedly besought the said abbot and convent, as their Lords superior for a renewal of the Infeftment of the said burgh, and the remaking of their charters, the said superiors, at length listening to these requests, and considering them just and reasonable, unanimously judged that they should be granted, which accordingly they do hereby grant, conferring upon and confirming to their faithful burgesses, their heirs and successors, inhabiting, holding and possessing the said New Burgh, and who shall in all future times inhabit and possess the same, lawfully entering and to enter the said New Burgh, and all and sundry their tenements, as well fore as back, with all their just privileges, used and wont, purely and simply, as a free burgh, and market in the same, with free and full power of buying and selling victuals, wine, wax, cloths, linen and woollen, wool, flesh, fish, skins, hides, and of tanning these, and of fishing, brewing, making and choosing bailies, serjeants, and other officers whomsoever, of continuing, deposing, and electing another or others in their places each year, of holding courts, administering the burgal laws, passing reasonable statutes, duly punishing transgressors, and if need be banishing them, levying fines, setting forth, weighing and measuring goods of whatever kind, and of doing and exercising all other acts and offices pertaining by law and custom to the said burgh, proclaiming and holding annual fairs within the said burgh on Saint Katherine's day, levying, exacting and receiving escheats and fines therefrom and duly punishing delinquents, with all and sundry other liberties commodities and advantages pertaining by law or custom to the foresaid burgh, and which the granters themselves possess and are competent to grant, according to the tenor of the Charter granted by King Alexander to the said superiors and their successors over the said burgh, and preserved in the archives of the said monastery. To be held in free burgh, as freely and peaceably as any burgh of the like kind within the kingdom of Scotland, and a weekly market on every Tuesday of the year by the said burgesses and their heirs, etc., of the said abbot and convent and their successors in fee and heritage for ever, the said burgesses making due suit and homage to us and our successors at our three Head Courts during the year, and for the yearly payments of the *firmas burgales* [Burgh maills], namely, six shillings of current money for each rood or perch of land at the terms used and wont, reserving the itineraries, or Circuit Courts of justiciary and chamberlaincy in each year, together with the customs incident in the said burgh ; also that no stranger living without the said burgh, except lawful heirs, shall be received or admitted as a burgess unless the consent of the said superiors be expressly asked and obtained. Dated, and sealed with the common seal of the chapter, at the said monastery, 24 May 1457. The tenor also of the other letter in the form of an indented charter is to this effect : The said John, Abbot of Lundores, and convent thereof, unanimously grant to our beloved and faithful burgesses of New Burgh and their heirs, the land of Wodruff and the hill adjacent thereto on the south part of the said land of Wodruff, in the shire of Fife : To be held by the said burgesses, as the common land of the said New Burgh, of the granters and their successors in feu ferme heritably for ever, as freely as the granters and their predecessors held the same, by all its

H H

proper marches, beginning at the west end of the said New Burgh, and so ascending towards the south by the west side of the land of St Katharine, and by the west side of the wall of the Wood pertaining to the said monastery ; reserving to the granters, and their successors the right of taking turfs from the west side of the said wall for the building and repair thereof ; and ascending from the upper and west corner of said wall by a steep path, by certain stone marks, placed there for marches, as far as the great heap or cairn placed at the northeast corner or Horn at the foot of the Blakcarn hill, then turning to the west around the said hill, by the stone circle situated on the ridge of the said hill, which is vulgarly called the Ring of Blakcarn, as far as a certain spring which bursts up at the southern base of the said hill, and runs towards the south, and by the course of the water issuing from said spring as far as the burn of Lumbeny, and thence proceeding on the south and west parts by the outer marches of the lordships of Lumbeny, Mylcrage, Kerpule and Cluny, and on the north part by the southern boundaries of the granters lands of Brodlands as far as the west end of the said New Burgh, with all the privileges belonging to the said lands of Wodruff and the hill, Rendering therefor the common service used and wont, together with forty bolls of barley of the current measure, at the term of Pasche, reserving also to the granters and their successors, as much space of ground between the bounds of the gardens on the south part of the said New Burgh and the Wood of the Monastery, as shall be sufficient for the passage of a sledge or cart with peats or grain to be led to the granters. Also the said burgesses and their heirs shall grind all their grain growing on the lands which they hold of the granters and their successors, and also, what is purchased by those inhabiting the said New Burgh is only to be ground at the granters mill called Cragmyll, that is to say, mulcting wheat to the sixteenth grain, and malting-barley and oats to the twenty-first grain. In witness of all which, to that part of the indenture to remain with the granters, the seal of James, bishop of St Andrews procured by favour, together with the seal of the community of the said burgh, are appended by the said burgesses, in presence of these witnesses, master John Seras, Sir Hugh, vicar of Monymeyl, Alexander Kenedy, John of Monkreff, James Traill, Henry Stratoun, Walter Rwnen, with many others, and to that part of the indenture to remain perpetually with the foresaid burgesses their heirs and successors, the common seal of the chapter of the said monastery is appended 4th July 1457. After the reading, exposition in the vulgar tongue, delivery, and reception of the said letters and evidences, the said bailies together with the foresaid part of the community there present, immediately passed to the said burgh, having with them the said letters and evidences, and placed them in their archives for the sake of secure custody, and for the perpetual memory of the fact. Whereupon the said bailies, in name of the said community took instruments before these witnesses, Walter Rwnen, esquire, Master John Barbur, John Fogow, William of Kynross, burgess of Dysert, William Smyth, Patrick Baxter and John Lambert.'

The docquet of John Wyntone, Presbyter of the diocese of St Andrews, Notary Public, testifying to the accuracy of the Charter is appended ; with the motto, *Sit Laus Deo patri.*

No. 30 (20). *Litera Conventus de Lundoris de XL. solidis concessis per reverendum patrem, J. R. A. L.* A.D. 1474.

John, etc., Abbot of Lundores, etc. We make known that whereas from a remote period in the past, certain of our predecessors granted to any monk in the said monastery professed and in priests orders, the sum of two pounds scots, for the purchase and repair of their vestments, which sum was limited according to the means of the convent for the time, but now that the revenues thereof are more abundant, and considering that the regular worship of God ought to be furthered, we, moved by piety unitedly with our brethren of the convent, considering the sum of two pounds, now that everything has to be bought in a dear market, is inadequate for the maintenance of decent clothing and becoming dress of any of our brethren, unweariedly celebrating divine worship and devotedly ministering day and night. Remembering also that the mouth of the ox ought not to be muzzled while threshing, and that he who is elected to a place of trust should not be withheld of competent reward, and as saith the apostle, ' He that serveth at the altar ought to live by the altar.' Therefore we, with the advice, consent and order of Patrick, bishop of St Andrews our ordinary, at the time of his visitation have added other two pounds yearly to the present sum ; that thenceforth our brethren may walk in procession more fitly, raise the psalmody more sweetly, and read, sing, and perform all the divine offices, whether by day or night, more devoutly and with greater zeal, we ordain that the said four pounds be paid in ready counted money, at the feast of the Assumption three pounds, and at Martinmas in winter twenty shillings annually in all time coming. At our Monastery 18th May 1474. ·

No. 31 (19). *Copia assedacionis ville de Eglismagwll Georgio Muncrefe.* A.D. 1476.

Andrew, Abbot of Lundoris and the convent thereof, etc., have Let to our beloved George Muncrefe of Tybermolloke, our lands of Eglismagwll in the earldom of Stratherin, and shire of Perth with all the garbal teinds altarages and small teinds of the parish church thereof, also our mills of Eglismagwlle with their multures and pertinents, for the lifetime of the said George, entering thereto at the feast of Pentecost next, with the power of assigning or setting the same to his mother and brothers his minors and subtenants; namely labourers and husbandmen inferior in power to the said George, and to none others. Rendering to us and our successors forty merks Scots at Pentecost and Martinmas by equal portions; and four dozen of fat and well-fed capons, or else twelve pence for each at Christmas and Pasch, together with services used and wont; and if it should happen that there should be no cattle on the said lands to be taken and distrained for the fermes and capons foresaid, and that the said George and his tenants should be tardy in payment of them; in that case the said lands, etc., shall return to and be at our disposal, and this assedation shall cease to be of any force. In witness, etc., the common seal of the chapter is appended at our Monastery, 8th April 1476.

No. 32. *The Ÿollowing Abstract is from a Charter in the Register of the Great Seal* (Book VIII. No. 2). A.D. 1477.

It is not in the printed Chartulary.

David Spalding endows the altar of St Margaret and provides an annual-rent for the repair of the choir of the church of Dundee.

James III. King of Scots, etc. Know that we have confirmed a Charter by David Spalding, the tenor whereof is as follows: Know me, David Spalding, burges of Dunde to have given to God and to the abbot and convent of Lundores for the welfare of my soul, and the soul of Isabell my wife, etc., a tenement of land in the market street of Dunde, on the south side thereof, between the land of William Scrimgeour on the east, and the land of Walter of Abirkerdour on the west; also an annualrent of thirty shillings Scots, from the toft of the abbot and Convent of Abirbrothok, between the vennel commonly called Spalding's wynd on the west, and the land of the late Thomas Leis on the east. To be held in perpetual charity for payment yearly to the altar of St Margaret the Virgin, founded within the parish church of Dunde behind the high altar, of three pounds six shillings and eight pence, and twenty shillings for the repair of the choir of the said church. Dated at Dunde 6th July 1471; witnesses, Malcolm Duchir, one of the bailies of the said burgh, Robert Balmannoch, John Bell, clerk of the said burgh, and John Wentou, notary. Confirmed at Edinburgh 22d February 1476-7.

No. 33. *Charter by Andrew, Abbot of Lundores and the Convent to David Hathintoun.* A.D. 1478.

Andrew, by divine permission, Abbot of the Monastery of St Mary of Lundoris and the convent thereof, etc., know that we, considering the profit of our monastery, give, and by this present Charter have unanimously granted to our faithful servitor David Hathintown our quarrier, for grateful services to us byepast and depending on the like services in future, a rood of land in our burgh on the southside thereof, between the lands of the heirs of the late John Grenlaw on the west and our lands of the Sacristy of our monastery on the east, etc. Rendering thence to us and our successors yearly twelve pence Scots, together with services used and wont in burgh, etc. In testimony whereof, the common seal of our Chapter, at our Monastery 20th May 1478, is appended.

This Charter is preserved in the Charter-Chest of Newburgh; the seal is in excellent preservation. An engraving of it is given at page 185.

No. 34. (18). *Copia assedacionis facte Dionisio Cameris et Willelmo ejus filio de quarterio de Grangia.* A.D. 1479.

Andrew, Abbot of the Monastery of St Mary of Lundores and the convent, etc., have set to our beloved and special friends Dionisius Chalmers and William, his son and heir, for the whole time of their lives, one eighth part to each of them of our lands called the Grange, in the parish of Ebdy and shire of Fyffe, with power to admit other persons under them for cultivating and occupying the said lands, as they shall think expedient, provided that such persons be equal or inferior in authority, etc., to the foresaid Dionisius and William. Holding the said two eighth parts, etc. Rendering to us and our successors and officers £16, 13s. 4d. Scots, at the two usual terms of Pentecost and Martinmas; and one well-fed hog, failing which eight shillings at Easter, together with two dozen capons and two dozen hens yearly; failing which for each capon eight pence, and for each hen four pence Scots; with all other burdens and services used and wont. Reserving to us pasture for sixty wedders yearly. Also if it should please us to plant shrubberies and to cherish and keep up policies, we reserve to ourselves six acres of land where it will least hurt our fermorars, the other three quarters of the said town to be bound in future equally and proportionally for that purpose. Reserving further at our will and pleasure, the three tofts occupied by David Kernour, Andrew Hall and Symon of our Granary. If by the will of God one of the said fermorars dies before the other, the part of the tack which pertained to him shall immediately revert to us, and be at our disposal. The term of entry at Easter, etc. And if the said lands should happen to be undistrainable, etc., then in that case the said assedation shall revert to us and our successors, etc. In witness, etc., we have appended our Chapter Seal at our Monastery, 18 May A.D. 1479.

No. 35. *The following Abstract is from a Charter of Confirmation, under the Great Seal (Book 13, No. 416). A.D. 1500. It is not in the Chartulary.*

I John Oliphant of Dron, and lord of Pitcathly, by this Charter convey to Andrew, Abbot of Lundores and the convent thereof, for money paid to me, my half of the lands of Pitkathly, lying in the barony of Methven and shire of Perth. To be held of me and of my heirs, as lord superior, in feu and heritage for ever, for the payment of one penny Scots yearly in name of blench ferme if demanded. In witness whereof my seal is appended. At Perth on the ninth day of November A.D. 1500. Witnesses, David Setoun, rector of Fethirkarne, Master James Fentoun, treasurer of Dunkeld, Patrick Wellis, burgess of Perth, Sir John Lindesay, vicar of Creich and Andrew Eldar, presbyter and notary public. Confirmed under the Great Seal (by James IV.) at Edinburgh on the 6th November 1500.

Note.—Apparently by a clerical error the Confirmation is dated three days earlier than the original Charter.

No. 36. (24) *Obligacio Abbatis et Conventus de Lundoris Gilberto Menzes, etc. A.D. 1502.*

We, Andrew, Abbot of Lundores and the convent thereof hold ourselves firmly bound to these honourable and discreet men Gilbert Menzes, Robert Craig, William Suthas and Alexander Gray burgesses of Aberdeen in the sum of £283, 6s. 8d. Scots for payment of £100 Flemish money to our procurator Stephen Orme in Flanders or Zealand, between this date and the 10th August next. Which sum we Andrew, abbot and convent, etc., firmly bind ourselves to pay the said Gilbert, etc., at the terms under-written, namely the sum of 200 merks Scots on the 18th August next, and at Martinmas next or thereabout £75 Scots, the acquittance of our procurator for the full payment by the said Gilbert, etc., of the forewritten £100 Flemish money being first exhibited to us. And also at Easter next, or thereabout £75 Scots in full and complete payment of the foresaid £100 money of Flanders. Which sum of £283 Scots we firmly bind ourselves

PRECEPT OF SASINE SIGNED

CHARTER BY THOMAS RAITH V

SIGNED BY TH

De Vondoris et ejusdem loca quietant Dilectus Noster Mag
breys de Newbrught . . . .

- -

e presents meo et seriptuto Mannal dend M
julis Anno Dni millesimo quingent mo quadro qto

J. Johañes Abbas de Lundre

LUNDORES 29 APRIL 1544

as facts vicarius ecclie parochialis de Leslie & Auchtir In
provist et prelatacum consensu et assensu venerabilis In
Congregacon delecti tractatu et matura deliberacon

- -

ultimo predicto magistro primo Coram Jacobo Sclibers M
adq Domo — m coffirmacon huius Domus albis
nostre Thomas Scott

Thoma . . .   script

and our convent, and all our goods moveable and immoveable to pay at the terms written, without recourse of law. In witness, etc., we have appended the common seal of our Chapter at Lundores 13th May 1502.

No. 37 (23). *Obligatio Abbatis et Conventus de Lundoris of Andree Charters de Cuthilgurdi.* A.D. 1502.

We, Andrew, Abbot, etc., firmly hold ourselves bound to Andrew Charters of Cuthilgurdie in the sum of £60 Scots for the payment of £20 Flemish money by him to our factors in Flanders or Zealand, within six days after the showing of his obligation to him, or to his factors there. Which sum we, etc., firmly oblige ourselves to pay within forty days after the arrival of the acquittance of our Factors for the foresaid sum of twenty pounds. In like manner to Alex^r. Tyrie, burgess of Perth for £10 Flemish. And to Robert Clerk alias Vobster, also burgess of Perth for £10 Flemish, etc. At Lundoris 17 October 1502.

No. 38 (25). *Obligatio Abbatis et Conventus de Lundoris Johannes Quhitsum, burgensis.* A.D. 1502.

We, Henry, Abbot of Lundores, and the Convent thereof, etc., firmly hold ourselves bound to John Quhitsum, burgess of Perth, and his heirs and his assignees in the sum' of £105, 10s. 0d., Scots for £30, 3s. 4d. Flemish, and also for £10 Scots due by us to the said John for other payments made by him to our procurator Master Hugh Mertin, rector of Weym, etc. At Lundoris 20 March 1502-3.

No. 39. *Precept of Sasine by John, Abbot of Lundores.* A.D. 1544.

John, Abbot of Lundoris, and the convent, etc., to our beloved Mr Dionisius Chalmer and John Calvy bailies of our burgh of Newburgh, etc. Because we have given and of new have granted to our beloved Henry Philp, those three virgates of land lying on the southside of the king's highway in the said burgh, between the lands of Alan Myller on the west and George Rolland on the east, which were the property of Katharine Stob now in our hands through resignation by James Philp her procurator. We therefore command that the said Henry be put in possession of the said three virgates of land by the delivery of earth and stone, etc. Given under our signet and manual subscription at our Monastery of Lundoris, 29 April 1544. *Johannes Abbas de Lundoris. From the Charter Chest of Newburgh.* [*A fac-simile of part of this Precept is given.*]

No. 40. *Charter to the lands of Quhyte Park.* A.D. 1564.

John, Abbot of Lundors, and the Convent thereof, etc. Considering that the laws, and especially the acts of parliament of the Kingdom of Scotland, provide that all fertile lands within the said Kingdom should be set at feu-ferme, or perpetual tenancy [emphiteosim], that they may be rendered more fertile by the labour and industry of diligent husbandmen ; that lands not only unfruitful and untilled, but burdensome to us and to our place may yield to us advantage and yearly profit, and that we may be freed from the yearly payment of a salary for the keeping of the lands under-written, we have resolved to set the Wood, the two rabbit-warrens and the Quhyte Park, with teinds and pertinents included, at feu-ferme and perpetual tenacy, for a fixed yearly profit to be paid to us and our successors, and that the public welfare may be advanced by the assiduous labours of husbandmen. Upon which account and for money cheerfully paid and put into our hands by our beloved cousin James Philp of Ormestoun, and for his counsel and assistance rendered, and to be rendered to us, we give, grant, set and demit heritably at feu-ferme to the said James Philp and Margaret Forrett his spouse their heirs and assignees, etc., the said Wood, commonly called the park of Lundors, and the Quhyte Park, and the two rabbit-warrens, namely the west rabbit-warren within the bounds of the lands of Ormestoun, and the east rabbit-warren within the bounds of the lands of Grange, lying in our barony and regality of Lundors, within the shire of Fife : To be held of us and our successors in feu-ferme for ever, for the yearly payment of ten pounds, rendering also three suits at our three head courts to be held annually within our burgh of Newburcht, and they shall appear by themselves, or their procurators at our courts of chamberlainry, justiciary and circuit, if they are thereto required. And we John, Abbot, and the Convent appoint our beloved Stephen Orme one of the bailies of the burgh of Newburcht our bailie for the purpose of giving Sasine and heritable possession of the foresaid subjects to the said James Philip and Margaret Forret by delivery of earth and stone according to the usual custom. In witness whereof we have signed these presents and have appended the common Seal of our Chapter at the said Monastery of Lundors, 2 March 1564. Witnesses, Andrew, Earl of Rothes, Lord Leslie, Thomas Fleschour, Robert Williamson and John Paterson notaries public, with divers others, signed by John, Abbot of Lundors, James Carstairs, Robert Williamson, Andrew Freser, Patrick Galt, John Symmer, William Simpson, John Smijtht. JOHN PHILP, *Notary.*

From a certified copy belonging to David Laing, Esq., LL.D., Signet Library, Edinburgh.

No. VI. p. 148.

(The reference at p. 183 *should be No. VII. See p.* 401.)

The following are extracts from the Memoranda at the end of the Chartulary of Lindores Abbey. They are interesting as affording a glimpse of the furnishings of the Abbey, when it was occupied by the monks.

Memorandowme the yeyr of God Ane mi° V° et XXX yers deliverit To James Sympson.

Item iiij hayll claths for my lords bourd.

Item v ald elaths rewyne [riven] for my lords bourd.

Item vij hayll towellis at ij rewyne for my lords bourd.

Item xxxij hayll seruatours [table-napkins] for my lords bourd.

Item iiij cope-bourd claths.

Item ij gret elaths of fyne dorne work [Tournay work, damask table-cloths] wytht ij towels of ya samyne.

Item ij smaller claths of dorne werk wythout towells.

Item ane bassyng of silver wy^t ij law-ners [lavaturs ' vessels in which the monks washed before going to the refectory, or officiating priests before performing divine service.'—*Jameson's Dictionary.*]

Item ij pessis wytht ane coner.

Item ij Gowblats & ane salt falt.

Item xij Sylver spownis tharof the Granetre [the Granger] has ane.

Item ij payre of carwyng knyfs wytht ij forks of sylver.

Item in the chawmer nerrest the yet of the new houss iij bedds wy^t iij bostrs.

It. in the chawmer nerress the bourin iij bedds wy^t iij bostrs.

It. in the vicaris chawmer ij beddis wy^t bostrs.

It. in Mast^r W. chaumer ij beddis wy^t bostrs.

Item iiij bedds wy^t thar bostrs in the neddir chawmrs of the new houss.

Item xiij payre of hayll schets & ane brokyne payre.

Item xviij blancates & xij codis wy^t thar waris [codwares, pillowslips].

It. v codds of the supp^r [sup-prior].

Item xiiij arress works & wardours.

Item in ij lang set bourd claths.

It. deliuerit to James Symson twa pairs of new schets xij Septbr a° do^i xxxj°·

It. that samyn day to him four new towells.

It. to him a new burd clat for o^r burd & vi new purp^r anes.

It. ij schort set bourd elaths.

Item in ij couerings ane red ane o^r greyne batht ald.

Item in the ij chawmeris quhar my lord wess, four bedds vy^t thar boustrs & iiij blankates.

It. iiij half gallonis stoippis / xj q^{r}t stoippis iiij poynt stoppis. Item iiij gryt flawkonis and twa small of tyn. Item iiij waudit flawkonis thairf twa glass & ij laȳm [earthen-ware]. Item ane rownd flawkon of estland burd [wood from the east]. It. ane treyn stoup viz. a q^{r}t [wooden stoup].

John Chalmis compt of the geir he has in keippying in o^r chalm^r and wardrop xvij° Augt Do^i Mill° v^c xxx^o·

Item fyif banots w^t twa banot press.

It. ane albe maid for the kyrk. Item ane clair-schew [Gaelic, *clarseach*, a harp]. It. twa gryt boiss [casks or *graybeards*.] Item ane pair of carwyn knifis w^t ane caiss. Item thre gyltyn preikats v^t th^r caiss [holders for wax candles or tapers]. It. ane rostyn spreik. Item fowir galds of yryn for the hyngars of the bedds. . . . Item ane chaifer. Item ane fryin pan for the bed. Item twa pairs of thabills w^t thair men [chessboards]. Item thre panalls of carw^t werk. . . . Item xiiij bwig skyns [lambs-skins]. It. v qhyt cat skyns w^t diuerss furryngs of hwds and brok blak cla^t· Item twa haly walt^r fatts w^t cowfryngs gryt & small. Item twa bowss w^t hare & glw [gloves]. Item ix French halberts. It. vi Scotts halberts. It. x aksis [battle-axes]. It. ix gedward stawis [Jeddart— Jedburgh staves].

The memoranda from which the foregoing extracts have been taken, contain lists of many other articles of dress, such as ' mantils, hatts, blak howiss, soiks, taffite typpats, patonis [slippers], bwits [boots], schown [shoon],' etc. Also priestly vestments as skapulars, altar frontals, etc.

It is satisfactory to find in the foregoing memoranda, confirmatory evidence of the three carved oak panels (of which notice has been already taken, and of which an engraving is given at page 139), having belonged to Lindores Abbey. This evidence (which we overlooked in the previous notice), combined with the traditionary history of the panels is decisive on the point. These panels formed part of the collection of the late Mr Joseph Noel Paton of Dunfermline, and they are the only relics of the ancient furnishing of Lindores Abbey.

No. VII. p. 183.

Decreet Arbitral by Patrick Wellis, Provost of Perth, and others as to the disputes between the Abbot and Convent of Lundoris and the Bailies and Council and Community of Newburgh. Dated 6th Novr. 1501.

At Lundoris the sext day of the moneth of November in the yeir of God 1 ^{m.} v^{c.} and ane yeir, we Patrik of Wellis, pronest of Perth, James of Monthcreif and Andrew Bunsche Youngar, burges of the burgh of Perth, James Rollok, James Skrimgeour and master David Carale, burges of the burgh of Dunde, Charlis Ramsay and David Greig, burges of the burgh of Couper and master Johnne Andersoune, vicar of the kirk of Dunbulg, jugis arbittouris, consalouris, and amicable componitouris, commonly chosin betuix ane venerable fader in God, Andrew, Abbot of Lundoris, the convent of the samyn, and thar successouris, on the ta parte, and the baillies, counsale and comunite of the Newburgh besyd Lundoris, and thar successouris on the tothir parte, fornent the decisioun of the debaitis, questionis and contrauersiis movet betuix the saidis partiis, fornent the vsying of certane priuileges, fredomes and jurisdictions, as in taking of resignacionis within the said burgh, gewing of possessionis, creacioun of officiaris, resawing of burgess, ministracioun of Justice in Court, and fornent all maner of wtheris debaitis, questionis, contrauersiis, clames of landis, seruice or dewitcis, hurtis, displesour or wnkeyndnes standing betuix thame, to the day of the dait of this write, movet or to be movet eftir the tenour, forme and effecte of ane compromis maide in presens of ane noble and mychty lord Patrick, Lord Lyndesay of the biris and William Scot of Baluery, knycht, chaumerlanis of the regalite of Lundoris, in the chaumerlane aire of the saide regalite, haldin at day and place contenit in the said compromis instrumently maid, the saidis partiis being suorne and oblist in jugement to the effecte above writtin to abide at, wnderlie and fulfill our sentence, decrete, consale, and ordinance in the premiss, and we, in eliknes suorne to geive furtht our finale sentence, consale, decrete and ordinance efter our knawlege and conscience, in the saidis debatis, clames and contrauersiis the richtis, resonis, writtis, infeftmentis, documentis, munimentis, evidentis, instrumentis, and allegaciounis of baitht the saidis partiis befor ws pro ducit, red, herd, sene, wnderstandin and considerit, and we being all togidder weil and riplie avisit hawand Gode before E [eye], decretis, deli ueris, consalis and ordanis all in ane voice, bot ony discrepance in manner as efter followis, that is to say, that becaus that it is evidentlie vnder-

standin and knawin till ws, that the principal caus of the gret contencioun
of trouble betuix the saidis partiis, wes be the electioun of officiaris, and
inbringin of outmen within the said burgh, and making of thame nychtbouris and tenentis, be resaving of resignacionis and gewing possessionis
till the said outmen, quhilk is expres aganis thar infeftment, but licence
of the saidis abbot and convent, that tharfor, perpetualye in tym cuming,
we deliuer and ordanis that the electioun of the saidis officiaris, resignacionis and possessionis, and resaving of tenentis within the saide burgh,
and outmen to be nychtbouris proceid and haif passage in this maner, as
eftir followis for perpetuale tranquilite of pece to be hade betuix the saidis
partiis, that is to say, that upoun the principal consuetude day efter
Mychaelmes, at the chesing of the saidis officiaris, the said Abbot, convent
and thar successouris as superioris of the saide tovne of Newburgh, sall
haif full freedom, power and priuilegis to name and present to the ald
consall and nev of the said burgh, and men of craft being thar for the
tyme quhilkis is limit and ordanit be the act of parliament maid upoun the
election of officiaris in burrowis, four personis nychtbouris burges and in-
dwellaris within the said burgh quhilk salbe litis to the said office of bail-
yery, of the quhilkis four personis litis, the said ald counsale new and
craftsmen sall cheis tua to be bailies of the said burgh for that yeir, and
sua perpetualie till yeirlie indur, the quhilkis ballies sua chosin sall hald
court and plante, minister justice within the saide burgh, and sall haife
power to resauve and inter [enter] burges sonnis and dochteris that ar
airis to thar faderis and moderis heretagis, airschipis and fredomes of burgh,
be the assignacioun and cognicioun of hespe and staple, and als coniunct
infeftmentis and doweryis and all airis collaterale, that ar to be interit till
ony landis, or annuelis within the said burgh, to rais thar brenes of the
said abbot and conventis chapell, and to be seruit tharof, be ane inquest
before the saidis baillies, and saising to be gewin be the breif of saising be
the said ballies coniunctlie, or seueralie, to be direct to the said baillies, and
all alienacionis of all landis and annuel rentis that ar to be maid be nychtbour to nychtbour within the said burgh, to be resauit be the said ballies
and saising tharupoun be thame to be gewin, and all alienacionis that ar
to be maid be ony nychbour indueller in the said burgh till ony outman,
that thai resignacionis be maid in the handis of the said abbot and conuent,
as superioris of the said burgh and to be infeft be saidis abbot and conuent
as efferis, and possessioun to be gewin be thar precept of saising to be
direct to the said baillies tharapoun, and that the said abbotis chapell be
euer redy and opyn for the rasing of al maner of brenes perteining to the
said burgh, and in tymes cummyng that the said abbot and conuent and
thar successouris be ay redy to resane the said resignacionis, and direk-

ing of the said preceptis of saisiug tharupoun, and in elikwis that the saidis ballies counsale and communite in tyme cummyng resane nane ontman to be nychtbour and couburges within the said burgh, but speciale licence and consent of the said abbot and conuent, and thar successouris, askit and optenit, and for the gud and quiete, tranquilite and pece and sessing of pley in tymes to cum, we deliuer, consales and ordanis that the said abbot and conuent for thame and thar successouris ratify, appreive and conferme all alienacionis, possessionis, resauing of nychtbouris quhatsumeur maide and geivin in tymes bigane, and geve neid beis at the desir of party to geive new infeftmentis tharupoun, and ordanis thame peceablie to jois and brouk the samyn, pay and tharof to the said abbot and conuent thar dewiteis aucht and wont, and that the said ballies, counsale and communite quhen thai ar requirit to the kingis weris, sall pas in cumpany with the said abbotis ballie and remane wnder his baner all the tyme tharof, becaus thai haif maid sewte to the saidis abbot and conuent and haldis thar landis of hym in homage and seruice, and that the said baillies counsale and communite sall bring to the Cragmyll, pertenyng the said abbot and conuent, all thar cornes that growis to thame and that thai by and thar to grind the samyn and pay the multer tharof, that is to say the sexteind corne of quheit and the twenty-ane corne of bere malt and mele efter the forme of thare infeftment, and als we counsale the said abbot and conuent to superceid and continow the rasing and taking of all wnlawis and amerciamentis that ony of the said baillies, consale and communite has fallyn and are adjugiit in of tymes bygane owthir of justice airis, chaumerlane airis or othir courtis, wpoun thar gud and humble bering and nocht to be rasit without the awis [advice] of ws, or the mast parte of ws, and als becaus it is wndirstaudin till ws, that Syntoun of Kirkaldy has brocht and payit his money and coft fra the handis of Dauid Aldcorne and his spouse, the air of wmquhil Alexander Michelsoun, four roudis of land and four *s* [shillings] of annuell, liand in the Newburgh, and ane rude of land callit the well rude pertenit to Iosbell Wanis, we decret, deliueris, consalis and ordanis that the said abbot and conuent sall resane and inter [enter] the airis of the samyn, and thareftir resaue thar resignacionis and infeft the said Syntoun tharof, with Charter and saising in dew form as efferis, and als tueching all debatis, summondis, sentencis, denunciacionis that owthir of the partiis has apoun wtheris, owthir befor spirituale jugis or temporale, before the day of the dait of this present deliuerance, we suspend and decernis the samyn to be of nane awaile, force nor effect, and for ony clamis standing amang thame of debatis or iniuris that thai submit thame to amicable freyndis, tharupone or thane to be decidit befor the baillies of the said burgh in playn court, and gewe it sall happin the said abbay to waik [be vacant], or the said abbot to be absent the day of the said electioun, in that cais or cais the chaumerlane, gryntar [granator] or sallerar [cellarer] sal hawe sicklike power in the presenting of the said litis to the making of the said electioune as the said abbot and conuent, alsua, we deliuer and declaris that the blodewittis of the said burgh pertenis to the said abbot and conuent, and thar bailleis, and nocht to the said burgh, and as to the landis of Wodruf and Hill and all wthir profittis pertenyng to the said burgh, we ordaud that ilke nychtbour haife intrāes tharintill, siclike as thai had of befoir this contencioun and the hurt and distance or the cornis being tharupoune, the reformacioun tharof to be referrit to the said baillies or freyndis as said is, and as to the commoun gudis of the said burgh, we ordane it to be gaderit in tyme cummyng and put in the commoun kist, and yeirlie compt to be takin tharof be the communite, and the said kist till haife thre keyis, ane in the kepin of ane baillie, and tua to the mast famos personis of the said burgh to be chosin ycirlie be the [voice] of the samyn, in the quhilk kist the commoun sele, commoun [buk?] and commoun charteris sall remane and nocht to be openit without the awis of the communite, and als we ordand that the said communite stand in vnite, æfald kindnes and cherite that stud defferent in thar opinionis of befoir, and ilkane hartlie to remit and forgeive wtheris and tak wtheris be the handis, and alsua we deliver counsalis and with instance requiris the said abbot and conuent that thai remit and forgeive all rancour and displesour that ony of the saide communite all or parte has done or offendit till hyme or thame, and to resaue thame be the handis in hartlie kindnes, and to stand to thame ane gud Lord, and to stand to hyme leil and trew men seruindis and tenentis as thai suld to thar lorde, and the interpretacioun of this our deliverance, geive ony dowtis aperis, we reserue till ws alanerlie the samyn, and failyeing of ws to sicklike comburgess of the saidis burrowis, and geive the saidis baillies, counsale and communite of the said Newburgh thinkis expedient to have new infeftment, we ordand counsalis and deliueris, that the saidis abbot and conuent sall gewe thame ane new infeftment conforme to thar ald infeftment and this our deliuerance, and help thame to haif the solemniteis of law tharupoun, like as co 'firmacioun of the king and ordinar, and this our present deliuerance, consale, decrete and ordinance gewin, red and pronuncit in the saide abbay of Lundoris in the Ile of Sant Johnne the baptist, day and daite aboun exprimit, and for the mar securite the selis of ane parte of ws, togidder with the commoun selis of the saidis abbay and Newburgh ar to appensit.

Ita est Dauid Gregor prescriptus notarius publicus manu propria.

This Decreet Arbitral is preserved in the Charter Chest of Newburgh. Six tags are attached, but all the seals are worn off.

Patrick Wellis, Provost of Perth, died 4 July 1516. An endowment yielding £2, 13s. 4d. Scots yearly was made for the celebrating of his obit in the church of St John the Baptist, Perth.—*Book of Perth*, p. 74.

No. VIII. p. 189.

Rules of Chapmen.

Pedlars, or as they are named in Scotland, chapmen, were formerly united in Fraternities, similar to the Medieval Gilds. The rules of the 'Chapmen of Perthshire,' and the minutes of their transactions, from the year 1748 to 1815, have been preserved in a volume specially kept for the records of their proceedings. These rules bear out what has been said in the text, of the respectability and higher social position of the Craft in the last century.

The members of the Fraternity elected a Lord Principal, Lord Depute, a Treasurer, and Bailies of respective districts yearly. Admission to the Fraternity was called *Brothering*, and candidates for membership were required to produce 'a sufficient testimony of their carriage and conversation.' The Lord Principal, or, in his absence, the official who presided at their meetings (which were called courts), was addressed as 'My Lord,' and 'the middle place of the market' was alloted for his stall or *stand*. 'At the election of officials in Perth on the 10th July 1767 there were 52 members present. Among the offiee-bearers during a course of years appears Bailies for Errol, Scoon, Gartmore, Balquhidder, Dunblane, Callander, Down, Abernethy, Ochterarder, Comrie, Methven, Ochtergaven, Dunning, Lustylaw,[1] Blackford, and Monteith.'

The following, for which we are indebted to an interesting notice of the Fraternity to the 'Antiquarian Repository' of the *Perthshire Constitutional and Journal of November* 1873, are some of the Laws of the Craft:—

---

[1] This Fair, which has been discontinued for several years, was held on the top of the hill above Dron, far from any dwelling. There is a place bearing the same name—Lusie-law, in Derbyshire, where Danish names abound.

' *The breaking of the Sabath-day.*—That whosoever shall be found guilty of breaking the Sabath-day, either by traveling with their packs, or buying or seling (or any other way, except going to the Church), shall pay the sum of Five pounds Scotts.

For Wrong Measures.—That whosoever shall be found carrying wrong measures, such as weights and elnwands, shall pay Five pounds Scotts, and the said wrong weights or elnwands shall be broken in face of the whole Court.

Back-Biteing.—That whosoever shall speak evil of his neighbour, or give his gear an evil word, if it be made out against him, shall pay the sum of Three pounds Scotts.

Swearing.—That whosoever shall take the name of God in vain, or curse, or swear, or speak any idle or profane words, if it can be made out against him, shall pay Three pounds Scotts.

Theft and Lyeing.—That whosoever be proven a Theif, or a Lyar, shall be banished from our Court and Company, and all their goods confiscat and given to the Poor.

Wronging of any Person.—That whosoever shall wrong any man's house, or any person whatsomever, either by word or deed, in any place where he shall travel or happen to be, if it can be made out against him, shall pay Three pounds Scotts.

Drunkenness.—That whosoever shall be drunk in any place whatsomever, and misbehave himself, and trouble any company or person where he is, without a cause, and if it be proven against him shall pay Five pounds Scotts.

Playing or Gameing.—That whosoever shall play at cards or dice, or any other vitious game, and the same be proven against them, shall pay the sum of Three pounds Scotts.

Buying of Stollen Goods.—That whosoever shall be found buying of gold or silver veshil, or any other kind of mettles or goods whatsoever, that is stollen, if it be made out against him shall be lyable to pay according as the crime requires.

Contentious Wadgering.—That whosoever shall be found wadgering one with another, or gameing, if they wadger or play above sixpence at any moderate game, shall pay Twelve shillings Scotts.

Stubborn Persons.—That whosoever shall deny the price of any commodity to a comrade, they both being brothered, and will not help him to anything he stands in need of, if he can handsomely do it, not wronging himself, and will be so stubborn as not to help him, shall pay the sum of Four pounds Scotts.

Keeping Evil Company.—That whosoever shall be found drinking or keeping company with idle, profane, or debauched persons, if it be made out against them, shall pay the sum of Three pounds Scotts.

Manners or Breeding.—That whoever shall not carry themselves civilly in giveing obedience to their superiors, and who shall not be found keeping themselves neat and tight in their clothing, and combing their heads and washing their hands, and keeping themselves in clean linnens, like other honest men's bairns who take this occupation, and those who will not observe this at this occupatioun, let them betake themselves to another; and for ilk falyie shall be lyable to pay Twelve shillings Scotts.

Stands Marking.—That none offer to mark any Stands before sun riseing the day before the Market-day, and he who marks first is to mark ane deal length, which is three elns long; and none is to mark above an deal length for himself or any comrade with him; and this foresaid deal length is to be marked for my Lord's use, and that in the middle place of the market, and if it be neglected he is to take it where his pleasure is; and whoever is found marking more than is foresaid shall pay Twelve shillings Scotts.

Religion and Piety.—It is enacted for the farther propagating of Religion and Piety, that every brother Chapman shall have a Bible particularly for his own use, besides these he shall have for sale, and shall be obliged at the several Courts to bring along with him the said Bible, to be presented if required, under the penalty of Five pounds Scotts, and that those of the Brethren that cannot read be obliged to learn, at least to use their endeavours, under the aforesaid penalty.

Debates betwixt Brother Chapman.—It is enacted that in case any debate should fall out betwixt any of the Brethren of this Incorporation, in any Burgh or other place where they may happen to meet, that they presume not upon any account to enter their complaint to any Magistrate or other Judge, untill they first enter their grievances before my Lord, his Deput, or other members of the Incorporation having power to hold Courts, and get their sentiments thereupon; with certification that whoever contraveens this act shall be lyable in Six pounds Scotts for each transgression.'

This Rule is a relic of the old Law of the Burghs, by which traders in a Fair held ' *lot and cauyll,*' share and share or equal privileges with the Burghers, and could only be tried by their peers, and not by the Magistrates of the Town in which the Fair was held.—*Leges Burgorum,* No. LIV. See *antea,* p. 144.

No. IX., p. 133.

PATRICK, SECOND LORD LINDORES.

Charter of Feu-Ferme by King James VI. to Patrick Leslie, son of Patrick, Commendator of Lundores, of the possessions of the Abbey of Lundores, enumerated by name and rental, and erected into the Temporal Lordship and Barony of Lundores, with the Title, Honour, Order, and State of a Lord of Parliament, by the style of Lord Lundores, to the said Patrick Leslie and his heirs-male—A.D. 1600.

JACOBUS Dei Gratia Rex Scotorum . . . SCIATIS NOS . . . pro bono fideli et gratuito seruicio per nostrum domesticum seruitorem Patricium Commendatarium de Lundoiris et per fidelissimum et predilectum nostrum consanguineum et consiliarium Andream de Rothes comitem dominum Leslie, etc. eorumque familias et amicos nobis nostrisque predecessoribus impenso (ex dictorum Patricii et Andree de Rothes comitis largis et exorbitantibus sumptibus et expensis) DEDISSE . . . dilecto nostro Patricio Leslie filio dicti Patricii heredibusque suis masculis quibuscunque eorumque assignatis hereditarie Totam et integram maneriem de Lundoris ab antiquo vocatam monasterium et Abbacie Locum de Lundoris cum omnibus . . . domibus mansionibus edificiis et hortis eiusdem provt jacent et infra clausuram et dicte Abbacie precinctum situantur cum omnibus columbariis veridariis hortis sepibus officiorum domibus mansionibus . . . et iustis pertinentiis . . . NECNON dedisse . . . et in feudifirmam perpetuam dimississe . . . predicto Patricio Leslie heredibusque suis masculis suprascriptis eorumque assignatis quibuscunque hereditarie omnes terras et baroniam de Grange de Lundoris villas de Grange Berriehill Ormstonne Haltounhill Lumquhat Cluney Wodheid Southewood et Eistwood brasinam de Grange Clayis prata *lie Hauchis Hillok* Saltgers horreum et eiusdem hortos *bowbuttis* et Reidis Brodlandis Westwode cum cuniculariis manerium locis . . . piscationem super Aquam de Tay et libertatem cymbe vulgo *ane Yferrie boit* Saltinsche Reidinsche Kowinsche Saltgirs Reidhillok Park Litilhillok Inchis pomeria de Lundoris parvum pratum vocatum *Kingis medow* jacentem ab infimo de Parkhill ab occidente ad orientem burgum et villam de Newburghe domos tenementa hortos toftas croftas Dyikkcroft ac acras feudifirme firmas annuos redditus et eiusdem deuorias Durieland de Creichie toftam de Collessie toftam de Auld Lundoris toftam de Killoche toftam et brasinam de Auchtermuchtie . Craigend Craigmyle cum aridis multuris de Kynnaird *lie segis* et croftis eiusdem Kigishoill Maryscroft Cairtwaird Woodrooff Thriepland cum Monthe et Monasteri Almery crnik cum tiibus acris sub silua Terras ecclesiasticas de Ebdie Monkismos jacentem in Edinsmure cum . . . *lie Newland Vndland* . . . quinque tenementa terre infra ciuitatem nostram de Sanctandrois . . . magnum edifi cium ante et retro tenementum et hortum in villa de Falkland . . . annuum redditum quinquaginta trium solidorum quatuor denariorum de terris de Denmylne . . . octo solidorum de burgo Cupri in Fyiff . . . quinque solidorum et decem denariorum de Carraile . . . jacentia infra regalitatem de Lundoris et vicecomitatum de Fyiff Terras et baroniam de Feddellis Wester Feddellis Eister Feddellis molendinum de Feddellis Beny et Cathkin Eklismagirgill cum molendino eiusdem maneriei loco hortis pomeriis columbariis . . . magnum edificium in burgo nostro de Perth . . . Tenementum in Wattirgaitt . . . aliud tenementum in Wattirgaitt . . . Annuum redditum quadraginta solidorum de domo Roberti Blaikwood in Perthe quatuordecem solidorum de domo magistri Georgii Ruthven in Perthe . . . tredecem solidorum et quatuor denariorum de domo Johannis Rind in Perthe . . . quinque solidorum de domo Patricii Grant in Perthe . . . viginti sex solidorum et octo denariorum de terris de Pitfouri . . . septem solidorum de terris Jacobi Gild in Perthe . . . quatuor solidorum et quatuor denariorum de terris Joannis Drummond et Patricii Inglis in fine de Meilvennell . . . tredecim solidorum et quatuor denariorum de terris Roberti Cok pistoris . tredecim solidorum et quatuor denariorum de terris Dauidis Johnestoun jacentibus in Castell Gavill trium librarum sex solidorum et quatuor denariorum de Erlisdyikis . . . tredecem solidorum et quatuor denariorum de terris Andree Trumpet triginta solidorum de terris Oliueri Makesoune . . . octo decem solidorum de terris Gulielmi Lamb extra portam de Castellgavill . . . in dicto burgo de Perth infra dictam regalitatem et vicecomitatum nostrum de Perthe . . . Omnes terras de Balmaw Newtyle Hilend Hiltoune et Mylnetoune de Craigie Claypottis Ferrietoune cum albis et rubris piscationibus super aquam de Taye . . . terras de Ardoche terras ecclesiasticas de Dunde vel croftam terre vocatam *Vicaris Land* Abbatis horreum polentorum et hortum eiusdem in Dundie tenementum terre in Dundie in vico eiusdem vocato *Abbotiswynd* . . . aliud tenementum in dicto vico . . . peciam terre in dicto vico botham altaris Sancte Margarete in Dundie . . . tenementum et terram cum omnibus bothis et pertinentiis eiusdem capellanarie Sancte Margarete altaris aliud tenementum terre in Dundie . . . ab antiquo vocatum *le Vicaris Tenement* . . . annuum redditum trium librarum sex solidorum et octo denariorum de terris de Inuerraritie . . . infra regalitatem euisdem et vicecomitatum nostrum de Forfar. Omnes . . . terras de Halwistounis Hilend Fischerhill Litill Witstounes Nether Witstounes

Pittareis Pittargus Pittamous cum molendino astrictis multuris et brasina eiusdem Miltoune de Witstounes brasina de Witstounes Terras de Marcharie Scottistoune et terras officiarias cum rubris et albis piscationibus super mare et borealem aquam de Esk . annuum redditum de Bervie octo solidorum . . . jacentes in regalitate eiusdem infra vicecomitatum de Kincardin Omnes et singulas terras et baroniam de Wranghame terras de Craigtoune Kirkhill Mostoune Chrystiskirk Molendinum de Leslie terras ecclesiasticas de Auldleslie terras de Largie Newtoune Wranghame cum molendino et warda eiusdem Kirktoune de Culsalmount Pilquhyit Ledinghame et Williamstoun cum molendino et brasina eiusdem Malingsyid Flendiris Logydornocht cum brasina eiusdem Etherlik Kirktoune de Insche cum molendino et brasina eiusdem Kirktoune de Premna Tullymorgoune cum toftis croftis *lie outsettis* custumis seruitiis et singulis eorundem pertinentiis Terras ecclesiasticas de Kynnathmount Chrystiskirk Premna Insche Culsalmount Logydornocht Terras capellanarias de Garioche Terras et baroniam de Fintrie Haltoune Fintrie cum maneriei loco hortis pomeriis silva vocata Garvok et singulis suis pertinentiis Terras de Logyfintrie Fosterissait Wester Fintrie Langcruik Miltoune de Fintrie cum molendino terris molendinariis eiusdem Balbethin cum piscatione in Done Haddirweik Craigforthie Badiforie cum piscatione eiusdem in Done Monkegie et Westbynnes Kilmukis Tullycherie Westirdisblair Ester Disblair Cavillismilne Middil Disblair Smedyhous cum toftis croftis hortis et Smydiecroft Ailhouscroft cum prato vocato Insche derocroft brasinam de West Fintrie brasinam de Haltoune Fintrie toftam et croftam de Kilmukis salmonum piscationem super aquam de Done Domum cum hortulo et cymbe piscatione apud Futtey Annuos redditus de Balhagartie octo mercas . . . de Kellie decem mercas . . . de Inuerrurie viginti sex solidos et octo denarios Terras ecclesiasticas de Fintrie Inuerrurie et Monkegie que ad dictam Abbaciam de Lundoris perprius pertinuerunt jacentes in regalitate eiusdem infra vicecomitatum de Abirdene . . . Totum et integrum burgum baronie seu regalitatis et villam de Newburgh . . . cum potestate . . . tenendi liberum forum . . . hebdomatim die Sabbati wulgo *Setterday* . . . cum publico foro inibi tenendo annuatim . . . wulgo vocato *Sanct Kathernis Day* . . . Omnes et singulas ecclesias parochiales de Ebdie Auchtermuchtie Creiche Collessie Eglismagirgill Dundie Fintrie Innerrurie Monkegie Logydornoche Culsalmount Insche Kynnauchmount Christiskirk Auldleslie et Premna . . . unacum aduocatione donatione et jure patronatus . . . prefatarum ecclesiarum . . . Nos . . . EREXIMUS . . . rectoriam seu personagium in qualibet ecclesia predicta . . . pro quorum rectorum honesto et rationabili sustentatione . . . dedimus mansionem et glebam proprie pertinentes ad quamlibet dictarum ecclesiarum . . . necnon annua stipendia subscripta . . . soluenda . . . per prefatum Patricium Leslie

heredes suos et assignatos predictos annuatim in futurum de annuis deuoriis
decimarum garbalium et aliorum reddituum prenominatarum ecclesiarum . .
videlicet ministro seu rectori ecclesie parochialis de Ebdie . . . annuum stipen
dium sexdecem bollarum farine auenatice wulgo *teind ait meill* quatuor bollarum
decimalis ordei centum librarum monete cum minimis decimis vicarie totius
parochie de Ebdie . . . saluis tamen . . . prefato Patricio suisque heredibus pecunia agnis et lana dicte vicarie . . . Et lectori ecclesie de Newburgh qui erat magister scole grammaticalis dicti burgi eiusque successoribus quadraginta mercas monete regni nostri Item ministro seu rectori
ecclesie de Auchtermuchty eiusque successoribus sexdecem bollas farine
auenatice decimalis quatuor bollas ordei decimalis et centum libras monete
Item ministro seu rectori ecclesie parochialis de Creiche eiusque successoribus sexdecem bollas prefate farine quatuor bollas predicti ordei et
centum libras monete Item ministro seu rectori ecclesie parochialis de
Collessie sexdecem bollas predicte farine quatuor bollas ordei et centum
libras monete Item quia nulla vnquam erat functio ad ecclesiam de Eglismagirgill sed ab antiquo fuit capellanus qui cultum divinum in capella de
Eglismagirgill adminstrauit et inde est nulla ecclesia parochialis Nos IGITUR
. . . dedimus . . . potestatem et commissionem dicto Patricio Leslie suisque prescriptis lectorem in futurum ad dictam ecclesiam seu capellam nomi-
nandi et presentandi qui habebit in annuo stipendio quadraginta mercas
monete Item ministro seu rectori ecclesie parochialis de Dundie suisque
successoribus tricentas mercas monete Item ministro seu rectori ecclesie
parochialis de Fintrie eiusque sucessoribus centum libras monete cum minutis decimis vicariis dicte parochie . . . Item ministro seu rectori ecclesie
parochialis de Inuerrurie eiusque successoribus centum mercas monete cum
minutis decimis vicariis suprascriptis parochiarum de Inuerrurie et Monkegi
qui ideo curam ad ecclesiam de Monkegi imposterum seruire tenebuntur
quia ecclesia eiusdem est et fuit pendiculum tantum parochie de Inuerrurie
et eidem contigue jacet Item ministro seu rectori ecclesie parochialis de
Logydurnocht que inde transtulitur ad capellam de Garioche suisque successoribus centum mercas monete cum minutis decimis vicariis suprascriptis
dicte parochie Item ministro seu rectori ecclesie parochialis de Culsalmount
suisque successoribus centum mercas monete cum minutis decimis vicariis
prefate parochie Item ministro seu rectori ecclesie parochialis de Inscho
suisque successoribus octuaginta libras monete cum prefatis minutis decimis
dicti parochie Item ministro seu rectori ecclesie parochialis de Kynnath
mount suisque successoribus qui eam curam divinam ecclesie de Christiskirk seruire tenebuntur quia eadem est pendiculum tantum ecclesie parochialis de Kynnathmount centum mercas monete cum prefatis minutis decimis
vicariis parochiarum de Kynnathmount et Christiskirk Item ministro seu

rectori ecclesie parochialis de Auldleslie suisque successoribus centum mercas monete cum prefatis minutis decimis vicariis parochie eiusdem Item ministro seu rectori ecclesie parochialis de Premna suisque successoribus quadraginta libras monete et dictas minutas decimas parochie eiusdem INSUPER nos . . . creamus . . . prefatum maneriem seu manerei locum de Lundoris domos hortos et alia predicta . . . in vnum integrum et liberum temporale dominium et baroniam prefato Patricio Leslie heredibus suis masculis et assignatis predictis inde nuncupandum et in futurum nuncupaturum Dominium et Baroniam de Lundoris dantes et concedentes dicto Patricio Leslie suisque prescriptis titulum honorem ordinem et statum liberi Baronis et Domini nostri Parliamenti vocandi et intitulandi Dominos de Lundoris imperpetuum . . . TENENDA et habenda . . . de nobis et successoribus nostris in feudifirma hereditate baronia et regalite imperpetuum . . . REDDENDO inde annuatim . . . pro dicto maneriei loco . . . et pro omnibus prenominatis ecclesiis . . et pro dicto libero dominio . . . seruicium equitis aurati et vnum denarium monete . . . nomine alberfirme si petatur tantum Et pro dicto burgo de Newburgh . . . seruicium liberi burgi baroni et regalitatis cum quinque libris nomine annui redditus tantum Necnon soluendo annuatim nobis et successoribus nostris . . . pro villa et terris de Grange . . sexaginta octo libras monete . . . sexdecem denarios pro qualibet pultrea nonaginta sex pultrearum triginta duos denarios pro quolibet caponé sexaginta quatuor caponum cum pasturagio arreragio carreagio et debitis seruitiis vsitatis . . . Item pro villa et terras de Berriehoill . videlicet pro vno aratro eiusdem occupato per Alexandrum Johnestoun quinque libras duodecim solidos octo capones duodecim gallinas bollam ordei wulgo *multir beir* bollam farine auenatice wulgo *multir meill* . . . et pro reliquo dictarum terrarum et ville de Berriehill extendente ad tria aratra viginti quinque libras decem solidos monete Item pro villa et terris de Ormstoune quindecem libras duodecim solidos et octo denarios monete Pro villa et terris de Haltounhill quatuordecem libras octo solidos et octo denarios Pro villa et terras de Lumquhat decem libras septemdecem solidos et octo denarios Pro villa et terris de Cluney Eister sexdecem libras sex solidos et octo denarios Pro Wodheid Southwod et Eistwood sexdecem libras vitulum agnum octo · capones et duodecem pultreas Pro brasina de Grange septemdecem solidos Pro Clayis eiusdem includente Westmedow Hillok Saltgirs hortum horreum horrei *bowbuttis reiddis* et *hauchis* octodecem libras quindecem solidos et octo denarios Pro Brodlandis viginti octo libras Pro Westwood cum cuniculariis decem libras Pro piscatione super aquam de Tay cum libertate cymbe wulgo *ane ferriebott* Saltinsche Reidinsche Kowinsche Salgirs Reidhillok Park Litillhillok Insches cum pomeriis de Lundoris extra precinctum centum libras Pro parvo prato vocato *Kingis medow* jacente ad infimam partem de Park-

hill quadraginta solidos Pro Durieland de Creichie quadraginta solidos
Pro tofta· de Collessie quadraginta sex solidos Pro tofta de Auld Lundoiris octo solidos et octo denarios Pro tofta de Killoche decem soli_
dos sex gallinas duodecem equi onera wulgo *laidis* glebarum Pro tofta
et brasina de Auchtermuchtie viginti quatuor solidos pro horreis et hor_
reorum hortis eorundem Collessie Creiche et reliquarum toftarum pre-
dictarum sex solidos et octo denarios Pro Craigmylne et aridis multuris de
Kynnaird Segie et croftis eiusdem triginta nouem libras Pro Craigend et
Kigishoill quadraginta duos solidos Pro Cairtward duas bollas farine auenatice duas bollas ordei Pro Woodroof Threpland cum Monthe et Monasterii
quadraginta bollas ordei wulgo *furme beir* Pro Marycroft quadraginta duos
solidos Pro Almerycruik sex libras tresdecem solidos et quatuor denarios
Pro tribus acris terre sub silua quatuor libras et quatuor solidos Pro Croft-
dyik quinque libras quatuor solidos Pro terris ecclesiasticis de Ebdie quinquaginta tres solidos et quatuor denarios Pro quinque tenementis terre in
Sancto Andrea decem libras sexdecem solidos et octo denarios Pro tenemen-
to in Falkland quadraginta solidos cum seruicio vsitato et consueto Pro acris
de Newburghe vocatis *Hauche* quadraginta libras tredecem solidos et quatuor denarios Pro Monkismos cum omnibus suis priuilegiis quinquaginta
solidos Pro acris de Westmedow sub Newburghe quatuordecem libras
tredecem solidos et quatuor denarios Item pro dictis terris de Beny et
Cathkin in baronia de Feddellis decem libras tredecem solidos et quatuor
denarios Pro Wester Feddellis viginti sex libras sex solidos et octo denarios
viginti quatuor capones viginti quatuor pultreas quatuor petras butiri
Pro molendino de Feddellis octo libras sex capones sex gallinas .   Pro
Eister Feddellis viginti septem libras sexdecem denarios . . . Item pro
terris de Eglismagirgill cum maneriei loco hortis columbariis et molendino
eiusdem nonaginta octo marcas quatuor solidos et quatuor denarios cum
brasina et toftis eiusdem triginta solidos Pro tribus tenementis in Perthe
sexdecem libras sex solidos et octo denarios Item pro terris de Balmaw et
Newtyle in Angus septemdecem libras octo solidos triginta sex capones
. . . Pro terris de Hilend quadraginta quatuor solidos sex capones
Pro Hiltoune et Miltoune de Cragy Claypottis et Ferrietoune cum albis
piscationibus in aqua de Tay custumis deuoriis et seruitiis eorundem
triginta septem libras quadraginta octo capones Pro terris de Ardoche
sex libras tredecem solidos et quatuor denarios Pro terris ecclesiasticis
de Dundie siue crofta terre vocata terra vicaria quatuordecem solidos
Pro dictis omnibus tenementis in Dundie bothis et corundem pertinentiis
vnum et viginti libras Pro horreo vstrina et horto horrei vocato *Abottisbarne*
in Dundie septem solidos Item pro terris de Halwitstounes Hilend Fischerhill Littellwitstounes cum suis pertinentiis triginta quatuor libras quinde-

cem solidos et sex denarios duodecem capones triginta sex pultreas sex bollas avenarum wulgo *cane aittis* . . . Pro terris de Nether Witstounes Pitareis Pittargus Pittamons cum molendino Mylnetoune astrictis multuris et brasinis viginti novem libras duos solidos et octo denarios . . . Pro terris de Marcharie et Scottistoune cum terris officiariis rubris et albis piscationibus super mare et aquam borealem de Ask viginti duas libras septemdecem solidos et sex denarios Item pro terris de Craigtoune ex baronia de Wranghame tredecem libras sex solidos et octo denarios Pro terris de Kirkhill decem marcas et bollam auenarum wulgo *custome aittis* Pro Mostoun quadraginta solidos Item pro villa et terris de Chrystiskirk sexdecem libras quatuor solidos et octo denarios Item pro molendino de Leslie viginti sex solidos et octo denarios Pro terris ecclesiasticis de Auld Leslie sex solidos et octo denarios Pro terris de Largie tres libras sex solidos et octo denarios cum debito seruicio Pro Newtoune et Wranghame cum molendino et warda eiusdem sexaginta sex libras tredecem solidos et quatuor denarios Pro Kirktoune de Culsalmount octo libras quatuor solidos et sex denarios Pro Polquhit viginti quatuor libras quinque solidos quatuor denarios Pro Ledinghame et Williamstoune cum molendino et brasina quinquaginta quinque libras sex solidos octo denarios Pro Malingsyide viginti octo libras novem solidos et octo denarios pro Flendiris viginti quatuor libras sex solidos Pro Logydornocht et brasina eiusdem viginti libras octodecem solidos cum bolla auenarum wulgo *kane aittis* Pro Etherlik Kirktoune de Insche molendino et brasina eiusdem tredecem libras decem solidos Pro Kirktoune de Premna quatuor libras tredecem solidos et quatuor denarios Pro Tullymorgoune cum toftis croftis custumis et pertinentiis sexdecem libras cum arreagiis carreagiis custumis et debitis seruitiis . . . prenominatarum terrarum vsitatis et consuetis Pro terris ecclesiasticis de Kynnathmount Christiskirk Iusche Premna Culsalmount Logydornocht et terris capellanariis de Garioche viginti solidos Item pro Haltoune Fintrie cum maneriei loco hortis pomeriis silua de Garvok et eorundem pertinentiis Fosterissait Wester Fintrie Langcruik et singulis suis pertinentiis centum et viginti libras Pro terris de Logyfintrie octo libras Pro Mylnetoune de Fyntrie cum molendino et terris molendinariis eiusdem septem libras sex solidos et octo denarios Pro Balbithene cum piscatione in Done Heddirweik et Craigforthie viginti tres libras sex solidos octo denarios Pro Badiforrie et piscationibus in Done quinque libras septem solidos decem denarios Pro Monkegi et Westbynis novemdecem libras tredecem solidos quatuor denarios Pro Kilmukis viginti duas libras Pro Tullichery sex libras tredecem solidos quatuor denarios Pro Wester Disblair viginti quatuor libras Pro Eister Disblair et Cavillismylne et Middell Disblair quadraginta duas libras Pro Smedyhous toftis croftis hortis Smidycroft Ailhouscroft prato vocato Insche

Deracroft duabus brasinis de Fintrie et tofta de Kilmukis ac salmonum
piscatione in aqua de Done octo libras quinque solidos quatuor denarios Pro
domo hortulo et cymbe piscatione apud Futtey septem solidos cum arreagiis
carreagiis et debitis seruitiis vsitatis et consuetis omnium prenominatarum
terrarum Pro terris ecclesiasticis de Fintrey Inuerrurie et Monkegie septem
solidos et sex denarios Ac in augmentationem rentalis . . . sex solidos
et octo denarios . . Ac heredes et assignati dicti Patricii Leslie dupli-
cando feudifirmas deuorias primo anno cuiuslibet corum introitus ad dictas terras . . . NECNON . . . disponimus prefato Patricio Leslie heredibus
suis masculis et assignatis de dictis feudifirmis deuoriis et annuis redditibus
annuatim summam quingentarum mercarum monete regni nostri vnacum
viginti quatuor bollis ordei et duabus bollis farine auenatice cum omnibus et singulis dictis caponibus pultreis canis butiri casei et victualium
arreagiis carreagiis cum omnibus aliis seruiciis per presentes debitis . . .
IN CUIUS REI testimonium huic presenti carte nostre magnum sigillum nostrum apponi precepimus . . . Apud burgum nostrum de Perthe vltimo die
mensis Martii Anno Domini millesimo sexcentesimo et regni nostri tricesimo
tertio.—*Antiquities of the Shires of Aberdeen and Banff*, Vol. IV., pp. 504-513.
From the *Registrum Magni Sigilli*, lib. xlii. No. 189.

No. X.

' The Court Roll of the Regallitie of Lundors 1695.'

[*From Mugdrum Archives.*]

The Laird of Pitcur ffor the Lands of Witstoune.
The Toune & Lands off Logie durnoch & Brewhouse.
The Lands of Bedffurrow.
The Lands of Monkegie and Wester Barns.
The Lands off Logie fenton.
The Lands off the uther two Fentons belonging to the Earle of Murray.
The Mylne off Fenton.
Cluvers pleugh.
James Harvies halfe pleugh.
Mr W^m. Chalmers for his pleugh.
Tulliehamie.

Wester Disblair.

Easter Disblair and Milling Syde.

Midle Disblair.

Balbothie and Hedderwick.

Craige ffuthie.

Kilmucks.

The croft off Kilmucks.

The Croft off Fenton.

Stentoune & wranghame rothnay.

The Kirktoune off Colsamond and pulquat.

Lethame and Williamstoune.

Tullimorgame.

The Toune of Inch and Mylne.

Christs kirk Evlick & Brewstead of Inch.

The kirktoune of premna.

The Mylnetoune of Leslie.

The Lands off Craigtoune.

The Lands of Flenders.

Owkhill and mogtoune.

The Lands of Ballayarlie.

The Lands of Innerourie.

The Lands of Easter Fedalls.

The Lands of Wester Feddalls.

The Lands of Cromlick.

The mylne of Feddalls.

The toune & lands of Banie.

The Lands of Pitcairn.

The great Ludging in the wattergait pertaining to Andrew Rae.

The Ludging pertaining to Pat. Andersone.

The Ludging that pertained to Rob. Blackwood in the heugh geat head.

The Ludging p^taining to Pat. Grahame.

The booth & closs p^taining to Da. Sibbald.

The Ludging sometime p^taining to John Elder.

The Lands of Pitfour in the Carse.

The Lands of Witstoune Mylne.

The Lands of Scotstoune & mercarie.

The Lands of Arduch.

The Lands of Craigie ptaining to the Laird of Pittarrow

The Lands of Balnon [Balmaw] Newtyle & Temple bank.

The Claypotts & Ferritoune.

The mylnetoune of Cragie p^taining to Robert Clayhills.

The precinct of the Abbacie of Lundores & halfe marie croft and courtward nixt tharto.

The Reid inch and salt grass parke and year [yare] ptaining to the Earle of Rothes.

The Laird of Ballmedie for his Lands of Exmagirdle.

The Brewstead ptaining to John Levenox y^r.

The aires of Mr John Philp for the Lands of Hattoun hill, Ormestoune & intrest in the toune of Newbrough.

The Lands of Easter Cluney.

The Seud Croft in Collessie p^{t}aining to the Laird of Wishie.

John Williamson for his Brewstead in Kinloch.

James Maxwell for the seud croft in Aughtermughtie.

Rob. Maxwell y^r.

The Toune & Lands of Lumq^t and p^{t}ients tharto belonging.

The Laird of Rankillar for his Lands of Grange Woodhead & croft in Old Lundors.

Woodmylne for the bgr halfe of ye east wood ptaining to him.

Denmylne for his part of Grainge, Craigmylne.

Alex^r Spense for his Lands of Berriholl.

The Brewstead in Old Lundores.

Gavin Adamsone po^r thair.

The Laird of Balfour for the dowrie Lands of Creich.

Lord Burghlie for his Ludging in Falkland.

The Heretors in the Toune of Newburgh.

Mr William Grant.

John Wintoun for his Ten^t & Ruds.

John Anderson for his Rud.

Henry Beat for his Tenement & Rud thair.

Hellen Philp for the Tenement & Ruds lyferented be her.

Mr David Orme for his Tenent^s & Lands in Woodruff & Haugh.

John Tod for his tenement & Ruds, Lands of Woodruff & Haughs & Broadland.

John Freibairne for his Ten^t & Ruds.

Gavin Spense for his Ten^t & Ruds & Lands in Woodruff & haughs.

James Tod for his Ten^t & ruds and Lands in Woodruff.

Andrew Smith for his Ten^t & Ruds thair.

Richard Smith for his Ten^t and Rud.

John Litlejohn elder, bowar, for his Ten^t & Rud.

Robt Smith for his ten^t & Ruds.

John Litlejohn younger for his Ten^t & Ruds.

Patrick Scot for his Tenement & Ruds.

James Greinhill for his Ten^t & Ruds.
Robert Cairns for his Ten^{ts} & Ruds.
Alex^r· Ballingall for his aiker in the haugh.
John Fribarne for his Ten^t & Ruds.
John Marshall for his Ten^t & Rud.
Patrick Wmson for his Ten^t & Rud.
William Gray for his Ten^t & Rud.
John Hedderwick for his Ten^t & Rud.
John Ballingall for his Ten^t & Rud.
The aires of John Andersone.
David Ballingall for his Ten^t Ruds & Land.
Thomas Spence for his Tenement & Ruds & Woodruft Land.
Henry Tod for his Ten^t ruds & Woodruft Land.
Andrew Williamson for his Tenements & Ruds.
John Smart for his Tenment & Ruds.
The airs of James Smith.
John Small for his Ten^t & Rud.
James Wentone for his Ten^t & Ruds.
James Blyth for his Tenment & Ruds.
David Anderson for his Ten^t & Ruds.
John Halliburtone.
David Berwick.
David Biccartoune.
John Chrystie.
Robt^t· Blyth.
The aires of Andrew Williamsone.
Elspeth Young for her ten^{ts} & ruds Lyferented be her.
John Anderson, Wright for his Ten^t & Ruds.
John Bell for his Ten^t & Ruds.
James Blyth, Sailyor for his Ten^t & Ruds.
John Smart for Ten^t & Ruds.
John Ballingall elder for his Ten^t & Ruds.
Andrew Bruce for his.
Sames Blyth, wevar.
The aires of John Anderson.
John Blyth for his Ten^t & Ruds.
Robt· Wilsone for his Ten^t & Ruds.
John Lyall, elder for his Ten^t & ruds & land.
John Lyall younger for his Ten^t & lands & Ruds.
John Blyth for his Ten^t & Ruds & Woodruft Land.
Rob. Blyth for his Ten^t & Ruds.

Bessie Ballingall her Ten^t & Ruds.
The aires of John Ballingall.
John Gardner.
Robt Allan for his Ten^t & Ruds.
David Jacksone.
Robt. Blyth, Sailyer,
David Buist.
John Fribairne.
David drayburne.
James Young.
The aires of James Mathesone.
Henry Bussie his aires.
Henry Arnot for his Ten^t & Rud.
John Thomsone for his Ten^t & Ruds.
David Blyth earle.
The aires of William Andersone.
John Williamson for his Ten^t & Ruds.
David Spens for his Ten^t & Rud.
Andrew Rossie for his Ten^t & Ruds.
Robt. Dowie for his Ten^t & Ruds.
John Fairful for his Ten^t & Ruds.
The aires of Stephan Williamsone.
George More for his Ten^t & Ruds.
John Smith for his Ten^t & Ruds.
James Smith.
The aires of George Orome.
John Clew for his Ten^t & Ruds.
William Ballingall.
John Halliburtoune.
George Houdge.
William Halliburtoune.

No. XL, p. 178.

ABSTRACT OF THE CHARTERS PRESERVED IN THE CHARTER CHEST OF THE
BURGH OF NEWBURGH, TRANSLATED.

No. 1. *Charter by way of Indenture by the Bailies and Community of
Newburgh to John Vallange, burgess, of a piece of land belonging to
the Chapel of St Katherine.*   18th October 1470.

To all who shall see or hear this Charter by way of indenture, the
bailies and community of New Burgh, greeting in the Lord everlasting.
Know that we being specially assembled at the sound of the bell within
the chapel of St Katerine the Virgin of the said burgh, (after due consideration of the welfare of the community, and the honour and veneration of the foresaid virgin), have granted in perpetual feu-ferme, and by
this present Charter confirm, to John Vallange a piece of land belonging to
the said Chapel, given of old to the same by our predecessors, lying within
the said burgh, on the north side thereof, between the land of Stephen
Philpe on the west, and the foresaid chapel on the east : To be held, etc.
by the foresaid John Vallange, etc. in fee and heritage for ever : Rendering
therefor to us and our successors eight shillings Scots yearly for the
reparation of the foresaid chapel, and for maintaining a chaplain to celebrate divine service therein, and twelve pennies Scots to our lord, abbot of
Londoris, and the convent thereof, for borough mail, etc.   In witness whereof the common seal of the said burgh is appended to this indenture Charter,
and because the said John has not a seal of his own, the seal of the said
lord abbot is appended at his request, the 18 day of October 1470, before
these witnesses, Sir George Boys, subprior, Richard Lawsone, monks of
said monastery, and John Ramsay, Alexander Ramsay and John Porta
tyuys with many others.

The seals are entirely broken off.

No. 2. *Charter by John Wyntoun, presbyter of St Andrews and burgess of
Newburgh to his brother Thomas Wyntoun.*   25 May 1481.

To all that shall see or hear this Charter, John Wyntoun, presbyter
of St Andrews diocese and burgess of Newburgh, greeting in God everlasting.   Wit ye me, moved by natural affection for my kin and relations,
and very great love for them, and that after my decease they may share
of the goods God hath given me, whereby they may be more mindful of
the weal of my soul and may pray for it, and the souls of all the faithful

defunct, etc. to have granted to my well-beloved brother Thomas Wynton, also a burgess of Newburgh, my land and tenement lying within the said burgh on the north side thereof, between the lands of um- while Thomas Kynglassy son of the deceased Richard Kynglassy on the west, and the lands of Henry Lawsoun on the east, which lands I bought with my own money, and wholly built: To be held by the foresaid Thomas and his heirs lawfully begotten of his body, whom fail- ing by my nearest heirs whomsoever, of the lord abbot & convent of the monastery of St Mary of Lundoris in heritage for ever, etc : Reserving to me the frank-tenement thereof : Rendering therefor yearly five shillings Scots ; to wit two shillings for upholding of the lights and other orna- ments of the altar of St Katrine in the said burgh, & three shillings for distributing to the poor in bread by the hands of the possessors of the said tenement, at the sight and discretion of the chaplain of the said altar, as they shall answer to God : also three shillings to John Berclay, chap- lain, together with the burrow mails ; with service & free burgage of the said burgh, etc. Further it is my will that John Yunge & Christian his spouse should possess for all the days of their life that part of the land which they now occupy above the fruit trees, as far as the *herbarium* with the house which they now occupy, paying therefor the annual-rents above written, and after their decease to my brother as above. But the said Thomas & his heirs shall not waste the said land, nor burden it with any other annual-rent, nor sell, wadset, or alienate it, nor, from motives of piety mortmain it, under the pain of 20 lib. to be applied half to the fabric of the chapel of the said burgh, and half to the common purse of the said burgh. In witness whereof my proper seal is appended to this Charter the 25 May 1481. Witnesses, James Philpe, curate of the kirk of Ibdy, James Andrew, Henry Chawmer, Archibald Cannoth, James Philpe, John Atkyn, John Yunge, and John Wemyss, burgesses, with divers others.

No. 3. *Instrument of Sasine of Sir John Malcumsone, as procurator for the chaplain of the New Church of St Duthac, St Katerine, and St Mary Magdalene, of a certain land in the town of Newburgh.* 5 April 1508.

In the name of God amen. By this, etc., be it known to all men that in the year of our Lord 1508, on the 5 day of April, etc., personally past a venerable father, Andrew Caucris, pensionary of Lundoris, to a certain land lying within the said town of Newburcht, on the north side thereof, between the land of Thomas Philpe on the east, and the land of St Katrine on the west, and there by earth and stone resigned the said lands in the hands of Patrick Konle one of the bailies of the said burgh. Whereupon the said bailie gave seisin, state and heritable possession of the said land to Sir John Malcumsone, as procurator for a chaplain perpetually to minister in the new kirk to be built in the said burgh, for increase of the worship of God, and in honour of Saints Duthac, Katrine and St Mary Magdalene for ever: To be held in pure and perpetual alms. Done on the ground of said land, year day and month above said. Present, Archibald Carnow, Michael Andrew, James Moire, Stephen Orme, Sir Patrick Muir, and John Lawsoun, serjeand, with sundry others. *Follows docket by Barnard Marschel, notary.*

No. 4. *Instrument of Sasine of Sir John Malcumsome, in name of St Katherine of Newburgh, of two roods of land in the said Burgh.* 5 June 1508.

In the name of God amen: By this, etc., be it known, etc., that in the year of the Incarnation of the Lord 1508, on the fifth day of June, and 5th year of Pope Julius the Second, personally passed James Chawmer dwelling in Newburthg near Londoris; to two roods of land lying in the said new burgh on the south side thereof, between the land of the heirs of the late David Hadingtoun on the west, and the land of Robert Crychtoun on the east, and there by earth and stone, with consent of Thomas Chawmer his apparent heir, resigned the said two roods of land in the hands of Patrick Konle, one of the bailies of the said burgh, in favour of St Katherine, to pray for him, his heirs, successors, and ancestors, and for the souls of those to whom the said two roods shall belong; whereupon the said bailie gave state, sasine, and possession of the said two roods, with garden, etc., to St Katherine, and to Sir John Malcumsome in her name, as procurator of a chaplain, perpetually to minister in the new church of Newburgh: To be held in pure and perpetual alms. Done, etc., about four o'clock in the afternoon, of the day month and year above said: Present, Archibald Carnow, John Miller, Alexander Liele, John Syme, Sirs John Liel and Patrick Muir chaplains, with sundry others. *Follows docquet by Bernard Marshal, notary.*

No. 5. *Procuratory of Resignation by Michael Anderson and John Kawe, bailies of the burgh of Newburcht to James Philipe.* 26th February 1510, 11.

This Procuratory is in the vernacular, all the other Charters are in Latin.
Be it kend til al men be thir present lettres, us Michel Anderson and John Kawe, bailyeis of the burcht of Newburcht be west Londores, cunsel

and communite of the sammyn, to have maid, etc., our weil belovit nychbour our werray undoutit procurator and speciale erand berar, comittand to
him our ful power, etc., to pas to twa rudes of land lyand wythin the said
burcht upoun the south syd of the sammyn, betuix the land of Robert
Wychtoun at the est, and the land of umquhil David Heddingtoune at the
west, and thair, etc., be yird and stane, as ws of brucht is, in favouris of
Symoun Joly, to resing and give ouer to the said Symoun in excambion for four s̃. of annuale yearly, to be taue up be ws our successouris, etc., or chaplains of our kirk, etc., twa rudes of land lyaud
upoun the southt syd of the said brucht, betuix the land of Johnne Chaup-
man at the est, and the land of Schir Johne Malcumson at the west, etc.
In witness heirofe, etc., we has appensit our common seile, the twenty sext
day of the monetht of Februer, the yer of God ane thousand V^c. and ten
yeris befoir thir witnes, Sehir Johnne Malcumson, Johnne Burcht and
Schir Barnard Merschal, notar publice, with wthers divers.

No. 6. *Instrument of Sasine in favour of Sir John Malcumsone of an annual
rent of three shillings, from a tenement in the burgh of Newburgh.*
24 September 1511.

In the name of God amen. By this public Instrument, be it known to
all men, that in the year of God 1511, on the 24th of September .
personally compeared an honourable man, Archibald Carno, burgess of
Newburght, near Lundoris, and by delivery of one penny, resigned in the
hands of John Kawe, one of the bailies of the said burgh, three shillings of
annual-rent in favour of Sir John Malcumsone to be uplifted furth of his
tenement lying within the said burgh, on the south side thereof, between
the lands of umquhile Dionisius Caveris, on the east, and the land of
Michael Kynlocht on the west. Whereupon the said John Kawe, bailie
foresaid, gave heritable state and seisin thereof to the said Sir John
Malcumsone. Done at the Monastery of Londoris near the stone dial,
eleven o'clock forenoon or thereby. Present John Wemes & Andrew Lame
with sundry others. *Notary's docket by Barnard Marschale f̓llows.*

No. 7. *Instrument of Sasine of Sir John Malcumsone in an annual rent of
two shillings, from a tenement in Newburgh.* 17 October 1511.

In the name of God, etc., be it known to all men. That in the year of
our Lords incarnation 1511, on the 17 day of October, personally compeared in a fenced court held by David Culros, bailie of Newburgh, a pro-
vident woman, Jonet Kynnard, spouse of Archbald Carno; the said Archbald being removed out of court, she with her right hand extended above

the book, publicly swore by her great oath, that she was not coerced by her husband, but that of her own free will, etc., she renounced her right to an annual of two shillings furth of the tenement [lying as described in the preceding instrument]. And further freely consented to the alienation of whatsoever annual rents furth of the said land might be made by her said husband. Whereupon the said Archibald resigned the said annual rent in favour of Sir John Malcumsone. Which resignation the said David Culros, by delivery in his hands of one penny gave heritable possession of the said annual rent to Sir John Malcumsone to be uplifted for ever. Done at the said New Burgh, etc., witnesses John Kawe, Alexander Rawerd, John Lowfut, & Sir Laurence Lawsone, chaplain, with sundry others. *Follows docket by Barnard Marschell, notary.*

No. 8. *Instrument of Sasine of the image of St Katerine in an annual rent of five shillings.*   19 August 1513.

In the name of God, etc., be it known that in the year of our Lord's incarnation 1513, the 19th day of August, personally past a venerable man, Sir John Malcumsone, chaplain of the altar of St Dionisius, founded within the monastery of Londoris, to a certain tenement of Archbald Carno, lying within the toun of Newburgh, on the south side thereof, betwixt the land of Michael Kinlocht on the west, and the land of um-while Dionisius Caueris on the east, and in a fenced court held at the said tenement by John Kawe, bailie of the said burgh, by delivery of a penny, resigned in favour of the blessed virgin Katerine, and the chaplain minis-tering within her kirk, founded within the said burgh, for perpetual prayers to be made for him, his father, mother, and a venerable father Andrew Caueris, formerly Abbot of Lundoris, and founder of the said kirk, five shillings of annual rent to be uplifted furth of the said tenement, by the chaplain serving in the said kirk, to found prayers for the souls of his predecessors in all time coming, as he shall answer to the great judge of all. Whereupon the said bailie by laying of a penny in the hand of the image of St Katerine, then present; gave heritable possession, etc., to the said image in name of St Katerine ; and seised and infefted the said image, etc. Done at the said tenement. Present Patrick Kull, clerk of court, Richard Quhit, David Orme, John Ranaldsone, Thomas Bait, and David Culros, with sundry others. *Follows docket by Barnard Marschel, notary public.*

No. 9. *Testimonial of the Infeftment of Isobella Hadingtone or Mason, in a rood of land in the burgh of Newburgh.* 12 January 1518-19.

To all to whose knowledge the present letters shall come, Andrew Gyffart, one of the bailies of the burgh of Newburgh, by Londoris, greeting in God everlasting. Since it is a godly and praiseworthy thing to bear witness to truth, and especially in what lies upon me in my office, I make known to all of you, and bear witness that Isabella Hadingtone, *alias* Mason, presented to me a precept of Seisin of a venerable father in Christ, Henry, abbot of the monastery of Lundoris, and convent thereof, upon the ground of a rood of land; the tenor whereof is as follows :—

Henry, by permission of God, abbot of the monastery of Lundoris and convent thereof, to the bailies of our town of Newburght, greeting : Forasmuch as by inquest made by you and returned to our chancery, it is found that David Hadingtone, grandfather of Issobella Hadingtone, or Mason, bearer hereof died last vest & seized in a rood of land lying within the said burgh on the south side thereof, between the land of John Kynher on the east, and the land of Thomas Michelsone on the west; and that the said Issobella is nearest and lawful heir to umwhile David Hadingtone, her grandfather, and that she is of lawful age; and that it is held of us in chief. We therefore command & charge you, etc., to give state, seisin, & possession of the same to the said Issobella, according to the form and tenor of the old infeftment, etc. In witness whereof our signet, which we use in such cases, is affixed to these presents. At Lundoris 8 Oct. 1517

Having read which precept, I, the said Andrew Gyffart, gave and delivered to the said Issobella Hadingtone heritable possession of the said rood of land for evermore, etc. And this I make known and attest to all whom it effeirs. Done, etc., on the 12th of January 1518-19. In witness whereof, I have appended my proper seal to this present testimonial. *Follows attestation.*

No. 10. *Instrument of Sasine in favour of the bailies council and community of Newburgh of a rood of land in the said burgh.* 1 April 1522.

In the name of God Amen. By this public instrument be it known, etc., that in the year of our Lord's incarnation 1522, the first day of April, etc., personally compeared Issobella Hadintone before John Orme, one of the bailies of the burgh of Newburgh by Lundoris, upon the ground of a rood of land lyeing in the said burgh on the south side thereof between the lands of John Kinher on the east and the land of John Michelsone on the west, and there resigned for ever the said rood in favour of the bailies council and community of the said burgh and their successors, according to the tenor of the charter to be thereupon made by the said Issobella. The said bailie on the seventh day of the said month gave heritable possession thereof to James Ventone, another of the bailies of the said burgh, in name of the said town, community and councillors thereof. Done, etc. Present, Sir John Malcumsone, Sir John Cuyk, chaplains, Henry Lyall, Thomas Bait, John Kynlocht, James Chapman, John Stauns, Allan Kynlocht, Andrew Andersone, and John Isly, with sundry others. *Follows docket by Andrew Gyffart.*

No. 11. *Charter by Isobella Hadingtovne, to the bailies, council, and community of Newburght of a rood of land in the south side of the said burgh.* 12 April 1522.

To all who shall see or hear this charter, Wit ye me Issobella Hadingtoone, neither led by force or fraud, etc., to have sold, etc., to honorable men, James Wentone & Johne Horme, bailies of the burgh of Newburght by Lundoris, the councillors and community of the said burgh, and their successors, my rood of land lying [as in preceding instrument]. Reserving to me and my mother and the longer liver of us two, the Croft Ryg. To be held, etc., of the abbot & convent of Londoris in free burgage and feu ferme for ever, etc. Rendering therefor to me and my heirs nine shillings Scots; together with ten pennies to the altar of St John, situated within the monastery of Lundoris : also the burrow mail, etc.—In witness, etc., my seal is attached, at Newburgh the 12 day of April 1522. Witnesses Sir John Malcumson, Sir John Cuyk, chaplains; John Kynlocht, Henry Lyall, John Stauns, John Kynheir, Andrew Anderson, James Chapman, Thomás Bait, and Andrew Gyffart, notary public, with sundry others.

No. 12. *Instrument of Sasine of John Orme, as procurator of St Katerine and her church in the burgh of Newburgh, in a rood of land in the said burgh.* 15 January 1522–3.

In the name of God amen. By this instrument be it known, etc., that in the year of our Lord's incarnation 1522, on the 15 day of January, etc., personally compeared Alison Tod or Ymry, relict of umwhile John Tod, on the ground of a rood of land in Newburgh by Londoris, on the south side thereof, between the land of umwhile James Chavmer on the west, and the land of umwhile David Culros on the east, before John Calwy, one of the bailies of the said burgh; and there made oath, and swore upon the holy gospels, that not being coerced, etc., she with consent of Valter

Clemat her spouse, resigned her conjunct fee of the said rood for ever, in favour of James Tod, son of the said umwhile John Tod. Which resignation, being so made, the said bailie gave heritable possession of the said rood of land to the said James Tod, and seised him therein : which infeftment, being so made, the said James Tod resigned the said rood of land in favour of the blessed virgin, Katerine for ever, for the salvation of his own soul and the souls of his ancestors ; which resignation being so made, the said bailie, by delivery of earth and stone in the hands of John Orme, gave state, possession, and perpetual seisin of the same to him, as proeurator in name of St Katerine, and her kirk situated within the said burgh for ever ; conform to the charter of the said James Tod to be made thereupon. Done day, year, etc., abovesaid. Present Mr Thomas Pittillock, Schir Lavrence Lavsone, chaplains; James Litilihone, David Orme, John Ranaldson, James Bait, Michael Kynlocht, Andrew Andersone, Allan Kynlocht, Henry Chavmer, John Stauns, John Lovsone & Thomas Litilihone, serjeant, with sundry others. *Follows docket by Andrew Gyffart, notary public.*

No. 13. *Grant by James Tode, for the welfare of his soul and the souls of his father and mother, to God and all the saints, the blessed virgin Mary, and especially the blessed virgin Katharine and her church in the town of Newburcht, of a rood of land in the said burgh.* Dated 10th February 1522–3.

To all who shall see or hear this charter, James Tode greeting in the Lord everlasting, Wit ye me, etc. (having taken counsel with my friends & men of understanding), to have given for ever, for the weal of my soul, and the souls of my father and mother, in pure and perpetual alms, to God and all the saints, and the blessed virgin Mary, and especially the blessed virgin Katrine and her church founded within the town of Nevburght bewest Londoris, my rood of land lying in the said burgh on the south side thereof between the land of the late James Chawmer on the west, and the land of the late David Culros on the east. To be held, etc., of the abbot and convent of Londoris in fee and heritage for ever, in free burgage. The possessor of the said rood of land paying therefor yearly 5 s. Scots to the altar of St Ninian, established in the kirk of Ebde ; together with the borough mail due and wont. In witness whereof my seal is appended to this charter. At the foresaid burgh, the 10th day of February 1522, before these witnesses, Mr Thomas Pittillok, Sir John Cuyk, chaplains ; James Litilihonne, Michael Kynlocht, Dauid Gyb, John Stauus, with sundry others.

No. 14. *Instrument of Sasine of John Calwy, as procurator of the bailies and community of Newburght, in an annual rent of seven shillings payable from a rood of land in the said burgh.* 18 June 1526.

Jhesus Maria. In the name of God amen. By this public instrument be it known, etc., that in the year 1526, the 18th day of June, etc., personally compeared Issobella Hadyntone or Mason in presence of James Wentone, one of the bailies of the burgh of Nevburght by Londoris, on the ground of a rood of land lying in the said burgh on the south side thereof between the land of John Kynheir on the east, and the land of John Mechelson on the west, and there resigned and overgave from her and her heirs for ever, in the hands of the said bailie, an annual rent of seven shillings yearly to be uplifted furth of the said rood, in favour of the bailies councillors and community of the said burgh and their successors for ever. Whereupon the said bailie by delivery of a penny in the hands of John Calwy, elder, procurator for the said bailies, councillors and community gave and delivered to him as procurator foresaid, state seisin and heritable possession of the said annual rent of 7 shillings; and seised him therein. Done, etc., present Mr Thomas Pittillok, chaplain; James Litilihone, James Andrew, Henry Chaumer, John Ranaldsone, Dauid Orme, John Joly, Allan Kynlocht, Thomas Litilihone, and Michael Kynlocht, and also before all the scholars in the school, with sundry others. *Follows docket by Andrew Gyffart, notary public.*

No. 15. *Instrument of Sasine in favour of the bailies, council and community of Newburgh, of an annual rent of two shillings from a rood of land in the south of the said burgh.* 3 July 1526.

In the name of God amen. By this present instrument be it known to all men, that in the year 1526, the 3d day of July, etc., compeared Issobella Hadintone, or Mason, before a discreet man James Wentou, one of the bailies of the burgh of Nevburght by Londores, at the dwelling house of the said bailie, and there resigned in his hands an annual rent of two shillings to be uplifted out of a rood of land [same as last Instrument] in favour of the bailies councillors and community of the said burgh and their successors for ever. Whereupon the said bailies, past to the said rood of land, and there gave seisin of the said annual rent, to John Calwy elder procurator [as before]. Present James Chapman, John Joly, John Svane, John Lovsone, and John Stevinson, scholar with sundry others at school at the time. *Follows docket by Andrew Gyffart, notary public.*

No. 16. *Charter by Isobella Hadintone or Mason, to the bailies, council, and community of Newburgh, of an annual rent of nine shillings 'from a rood of land in the south of the said burgh.* 6 July 1526.

To all that shall see or hear this charter, Issobella Hadintone or Mason, Greeting in God everlasting. Wit ye me, etc., to have sold, and by title of pure vendition, alienated, etc., to James Venton, and Andrew Gyffart, bailies of the burgh of Nevburght by Londoris, council and community of the said burgh and their successors, an annual rent of nine shillings to be uplifted out of a rood of land on the south side of the said burgh [as before], for a certain sum of money paid to me by them. To be held etc., of the lord abbot & convent of Londoris in fee and heritage for ever. With full power to distrain the said rood of land, at their own hands for the said annual rent as often as need shall be, etc. In testimony whereof, my seal is appended to these presents, the 6th July, 1526, at the foresaid burgh, before these witnesses Sir John Cuyk, Sir John Lyall, chaplains, Sir Laurence Lovsone, Thomas Litilihon, Allan Kynlocht, Michael Kynlocht, John Gyffart, with sundry others.

No. 17. *Charter by Michael Tod, burgess of Nevbrough, to the bailies of Newbrough, patrons, and Sir John Richartson chaplain of St Katrines chapel, of two roods of land in the said burgh.* 20th June 1542.

To all who shall see or hear this charter, Michael Tod, burgess of the burgh of Nevbrough, son and heir of umwhile John Tod, burgess of the said burgh, greeting in God everlasting. Wit ye me not moved by fear, nor fallen into error, but of my own free-will (my own benefit being duly weighed), to have sold to the bailies, burgesses and community of the said burgh of Newbrough, patrons of the chaplaincy of St Katrine, founded by their predecessors within the new kirk of the said burgh, and to Sir John Richartson or Cuk, chaplain for the time being of the said chaplaincy, and his successors, those two roods of my land lying within the said burgh on the north side of the street thereof, between the land of umwhile Simon Kircaldy, and now the land of the chaplaincy of St Katrine, founded by the deceased Mr Henry Quhit, within the said church, on the east, and the land of the heirs of umwhile James Disert on the west, the common road at the south, and the stank between the hauch and yards of the said burgh on the north ; for a sum of money paid to me by them, and the said Sir John, in name of the church, for the said two roods of land : Which sum of money so paid to me by the bailies, council and community foresaid, for the sake of devotion, a venerable father in Christ, John, abbot of the monastery of Lundoris, gave for ever, and in pure and perpetual alms to the foresaid burgesses, etc., and to the said Sir John Cuk, chaplain for the time being of the said chaplaincy, in augmentation of the yearly stipend of the said chaplain, for prayers to be made for the souls of the founders of the said monastery, and for the souls of my father, mother, ancestors and successors, and all the faithful dead, etc. Whereof I hold me well content & paid, etc. To be held, etc., in pure and perpetual alms, and of the lords abbot and convent of the monastery of Lundoris, lords superior of the said burgh. Rendering therefor by the said Sir John and his successors, chaplains of the said chaplaincy, prayers and suffrages for the souls aforesaid ; and to the abbot and convent of Lundoris, the burrow mails used and wont. In witness whereof my seal is appended to this charter at the said burgh of Newbrough the 21st day of June 1542. Witnesses Masters Robert Lauson, John Philp, Sir Alexander Richartson, James Philp, Andrew Paige, James Symson and John Bennatt, with sundry others.

Michell Tod, witht my hand at the pen led witht Master Robert Lauson, notar public.

His seal is still attached.

No. 18. *Instrument of Sasine of Sir John Richartson, alias Cuk, for himself and his successors, chaplains of the chaplaincy St Katrine in the new church of Newburgh, in two roods of land in the said burgh.* 21 June 1542.

In the name of God amen. By this present instrument be it known to all men that in the year of our Lord's incarnation 1542 on the 21st day of June, etc, personally compeared a discreet man, Michael Tod, burgess of the burgh of Newburgh, and past to two roods of land [as in last charter] ; and there surrendered the said two roods in the hands of John Calwy one of the bailies of the said burgh. Whereupon the said bailie gave state, seisin, & possession of the said two roods to Andrew Ventoun one of the bailies of the said burgh in name of the bailies, burgesses, and communitie of the said burgh of Newburgh, patrons of the chaplaincy of St Katerine [as before], in name of the said chaplaincy, and in an augmentation of the stipend thereof made by Lord John, abbot, etc. Which being done, the foresaid Andrew Venton, as bailie of the said burgh, and in name of the bailies, burgesses, and community thereof, then for the most part present, anew resigned the said two roods in the hands of the said John Calwy ; which resignation being made, the said John Calwy gave state, seisin, and possession of the said two roods of land to Sir John Richartson or

Cuk, now chaplain of the said chaplaincy, founded [as before] according to the tenor of the charter of the said Michael Tod, thereupon made, and seised the said Sir John Richardson & his successors, chaplains, lawfully admitted to the said chaplaincy, for prayers to be made, etc. [as before] and for the soul of the said venerable father, John, now abbot of the said monastery, etc. Reserving the frank-tenement of the said two roods to Bessie Wentone mother of the said Michael Tod. Done on the ground of the said two roods. Present Sir Laurence Lauson, Andrew Orme, James Covyntre, chaplains; Thomas Litiliohne, Thomas Giffart, and Thomas Anderson laymen. *Follows docket by Robert Lausoune notary public.*

The *¾frank-tenement* reserved in the foregoing and previous charters, is defined by Jameson to be the ' The freehold ' of the tenement.

No. XII., p. 116.

REGALITY OF LINDORES.

In exercising the judicial powers conferred by the erection of the territories of the monastery into a Regality, the Abbot had either to act as judge himself, or appoint some one to act in his stead. From a Charter preserved in the Archives of Fernie Castle, we learn that David Barclay of Cullernie was appointed Bailie of that portion of the Regality lying in the Sheriffdom of Fife, and in Strathearn. In all probability authority over the remaining portion of the Regality in Aberdeenshire, was committed to some person resident in that neighbourhood, but no charter, or other evidence of such an appointment has appeared.

The following Assedation is wholly in the handwriting of the Abbot, and it bears his signet, which is simply the letters J. P. in Roman capitals, surmounted by the head of an abbot's crosier. These initials confirm the conclusion arrived at in the text, that the abbot's name was John Philp :—

' Be It kend till all men be thir present letteris Ws Ihone Abbot of Lundoris To haue maid constitut and ordanit and be thir present letteris makis constitutis and ordanis ane honorabill man and our belouit Dauid barclay of Cullarny our veray lauchfull and vndoutit bailye of all and sindry our landis of Eglismagull Newbrogh grange and vtheris our landis quhairto the said Dauidis his fader was bailye of befoir for all the days and termes of fyve yeiris His enteres thairto beginnand at the day and dait heirof Giffand grantand and committand to the said Dauid our bailye forsaid our

full fre and plane power generall and speciall commandment expres biding
and charge for ws and in our name and vpon our behalf bailye courtis of
our saidis landis ane or may to the tennentis and Inhabitantis thairof and
vtheris quhom it efferis to set begin afferme hald and continewals oft as
neid beis suttis to mak be callit absens to amerchiat trespassoris to punis
vnlaw amerchiamentis and eschettis of the saidis courtis to reis vplift and
to our ws apply and Inbring and for the samen gif neid be to poind and
distrenye at our command the tenentis and Inhabitantis of our saidis
landis befor quhatsumeuer Juge or Juges Spirituall or temporall thai be
attachit or arrestit to the preuilege and fredom of our saidis balye courtis
to replege reduce and agane bring caution of colereth[1] for Justice to be
ministret to parties complenand within terme of law to gif and find deputis
ane or ma vndir him be our adwis with clerk sargeand dempster and all
vther officiaris and memberis of court neidfull to mak creat ordane and
caus to be sworn with our consent and adwis And generalie all and sindry
thinkis[2] vtheris to do exers and wss that to the office of bailyalry in sic
caissis of law or consuetude is knawin to pertene And that we mycht do
thairin our self and we war personalie present affirme and stabill haldand
and fer to hald all and quhatsumeuer thingis our said bailye his deputtis
or officiaris in the premissis ledis to be don. Prouiding all ways that this
present assedation preiuge nocht our fewaris bot conforme to thair chartoris
quhilk we haue sett to tham And fer vsing and exersing of the quhilk office
of bailyary we haue gevin and grantit and be thir our letteris gevis and
grantis to the said David the some of tene merkis vsuall money of Scotland
to be pait to him yeirlie at twa vsuall termes in the yeir witsonday and
mertimes be equall portionis durand the space fersaid be ws our successoris
and chalmerlanis in our name present and to cum. Quhilk som we oblis
ws and our successoris to pay to him yeirlie dwring the said space of fyve
yeiris in feall[3] togidder with sic commodities proffitis and preuilegis as his

---

[1] Skene, in his De 'Verborum Significatione,' says of this term, 'Quhen ony
havand power or jurisdiction repledges ony man fra anuther man's court to his
awin court, he suld leif behind him in the Court fra the quhilk the replegiation
is maid, ane pledge or cautioner quha sal be bunden and oblished that he quha
vsis the replegiation, sal do justice within the year and daie in his awin Court,
to the parties complainand upon the person quha is repleged. Quhilk cautioner
left in the Court be him and behind him quha vsis the replegiation, is called
Culrach.' voce Colrach.

[2] Things.

[3] Jamieson, 'Dictionary of the Scottish Language,' defines 'Feall' to signify
salary or stipend.

predicessoris had for vsing of the samyn of befor. In witnes of the quhilk thing to thir our letteris of bailyarie subscribit with our hand our signet is affixit at ballinbie the xxviij day of August the yeir of God I^m v^c threscoir and thre yeiris befor thir witnes George Leslie in Hechem, Ihone Petcarne and Robert Wilyemson notar publik.

IOHNNE, Abbot of Lundoris.'

By a charter, executed by the Abbot and Convent at their monastery, on the 20th February 1563–64 (the original of which is preserved at Fernie Castle), they appointed David Barclay of Cullerny and his heirs male, whom failing, his nearest male heir, hereditary bailies over that portion of the Regality of Lindores situated in Fife and in Strathearn, whether in or beyond burgh. The Abbot and the brethren made this extended appointment, because of the valuable services rendered to them by David Barclay, and by his father and grandfather to their monastery in times past; they allowed him a salary of one hundred pounds Scots, and in security for due payment, they assigned the rents of their lands and mill of Eglismagrill, and of Cluny in Strathearn; also their lands of Haltone Hill, and of the eighth part of their lands of Grange, occupied by William Adeson. This charter was signed before James Leslie, rector of Rothes, Andrew Petcarne of Invernethy, George Leslie in Heitheme, James Calwy and Stephen Orme, burgesses of Newburgh, by 'Johannes, Abbas de Lundoris, &c., Jacobus Carstaris, Robertus Wilyemson, Johannes S . Willelmus Symson, Johannes Wobster, Johannes Smyth, Alexander Paterson, Thomas Wod, Andreas Fostar, Patricius Galt, Gilbertus Merschell.'

This charter was confirmed by Queen Mary at Dunbar, 26th April 1567.

It appears, however, from a mandate signed by James, Earl of Arran, who was appointed Regent on the death of James V., that the Barclays of Cullerny acted as bailies of the Regality of Lindores at an earlier period than the assedation granted by the Abbot and Convent in 1563. This mandate of the governor, which is preserved in the same archives, is endorsed, 'My Lord, Governor, Greeting,' and is as follows :—

GUBERNATOR.

'Baillie of the regalitie of Lundoris. It is oure will and for certane resonable caussis and considerationis moving ws we charge you that incon tinent eftir the sicht heirof ye freith and put furth of your handis Williame barclay and Dauid covintre alias Pottingar takin for the allegeit slauchteris of vmquhile Andro ballingall and thomas michelsoun and put thame to fredome swa that thai may be depeschit furth of this realme vnder the pane of tinsale of your office and warding of your persoun And ye sall nocht be callit nor accusit for putting of ye saidis personis to libertie nocht-withstandyng ony our writtingis maid or to be maid In the contrare nor Incurr ony skayth or danger in your persoun landis or gudis thairthrow in ony wis in tyme cuming ye keipand this writting for your warrand Sub-scriuit with our hand At Sanctandrois the last day of December The yeir of God I^m v^c xlv zeris

JAMES G.

The residences of the slaughtered men are not mentioned, but Ballingall and Michelson were common surnames in Newburgh at that period.

On the 15th December 1569, the Lords of Council gave decreet that Patrick Leslie, Commendator of the Abbey of Lundoris, should warrant to David Barclay of Cullerny the feu maills of the lands of Eglismagirdill, to the extent of 100 merks assigned to him for his bailie fee of the Abbacie of Lundoris.

Nearly half a century later, a Precept was issued by Patrick, Lord of Lundoris, for infefting Sir David Barclay of Cullerny as heir to David Barclay of Cullerny, his grandfather, in the office of Bailie of Lundoris and barony thereof in Fife, and Eglismagirdill in Stratherne, and all privileges and profits of the same. The seisin to be given within St Katherine's chapel, in the burgh of Newburgh. Dated at Monymeall, 18th December 1617.

The office of Bailie of Lindores was abolished, in common with all other hereditary jurisdictions, in the reign of George II.

No. XIII., p. 151.

Abstract of Charter by King James VI. in favour of the Burgesses of New-burgh, confirming their right to the lands of Wodriffe. 20 November 1593.

Jacobus, Dei gratia Rex Scotorum, etc. . . Sciatis nos quandam cartam donationis et dispositionis factam, datam et concessam per vene-rabilem in Christo patrem, quondam Joannem, abbatem monasterii nostri de Lundoris, pro seipso et ejusdem conventu, unacum consensu et assensu burgensibus novi burgi, suisque heredibus, de totis et integris terris, vocatis Woodriff et monte contigue. . . Tenendis de dictis monasterio et conventu suisque successoribus in feudifirma et hereditate; de mandato nostra visam, lectam et inspectam . . non rasam, non cancellatam, nec

in aliqua sui parte suspectam, ad plenam intellexisse, sub hac forma ;
Universis et singulis ad quorum notitias presens indentura per modum
carte et obligationis facta pervenerit, Joannes, permissione Divina, Abbas
Monasterii Sancte Marie de Lundoris, etc. [Here follows an exact copy
of the Charter to the lands of Wodrife and hill adjacent, as contained
in the Indenture between the Abbot and Convent of Lundoris and the
Burgesses of Newburgh, of 4 July 1457; but no reference whatever is
made to the Charter conferring the privileges of the Burgh; neither is
there any confirmation of these privileges given.] Quamquidem cartam,
etc. . . approbamus, ratificamus ac pro nobis et successoribus nostris
pro perpetuo, confirmamus. . . In cujus rei testimonium huic presenti
carte nostre magnum sigillum nostrum apponi precepimus. Testibus
predilectis nostris consanguineo et consilario, Joanne domino Hamilton
et Aberbrothok, Georgio comite Mariscallo domino Keith, etc., Joanne
domino Thirlestane cancellario nostro . Domino Ricardo Cockburne
juniore de Clerkingstoun, nostro secretario; Waltero, commendatario de
Blantyre . . Alexandro Hay de Eister Kennet, . . Domino Joanne
Cockburne de Ormiston, milite, Justiciarie clerico, et Magistro Willielmo
Scott de Grangemuir. . . Apud Halyrudhous vicesimo die mensis
Novembris, anno Domino millesimo quingentesimo nonagesimo tertio,
et Regni nostri vicesimo septimo.

Abstract of Charter by Charles I. to the Burgesses of Newburgh.
29 January 1631.

Carolus, Dei gratia Magnae Brittanniæ, etc. Sciatis nos . . dedisse
et hac præsenti carta nostra confirmasse . . dilectis nostris ballivis,
consulibus, burgensibus, inhabitantibus et communitati Burgi de Newburgh, et eorum successoribus, totum et integrum dictum Burgum et
omnia . . sua tenementa cum omnibus suis pertinentis, solitis et consuetis,
una cum annuis nundinis ejusdem, nuncupatis Sanct Kathrine's day et
hepdomadario foro . . die Saturni tenendo : cum custumis nundinarum et
hepdomadarii fori. Una cum plenaria facultate emendi et vendendi
victualia, etc. . . ballivos, seriandos ac alios officiarios quoscunque creandi,
etc. . . Et similiter totam et integram illam terram nuncupatam lie Wod
ruff et montem jacentem contigue ex parte australi dicte terre. . . Et
similiter ratificamus omnia et singula infeofamenta . . aliaque jura, titulos
quecunque facta et concessa per quemcunque abbatem de Lundoris .
vel per aliquem Dominum de Lundoris . . prefatis ballivis, etc., de Newbrughe . . de predicto burgo, tenementis eiusdem supra specificatis hepdo
madario foro, etc. . . preterea de novo dedimus . . prædictis Ballivis, etc.,

suisque successoribus, Totum et integrum predictum burgum, etc. . . . unacum dictis annuis nundinis ejusdem nuncupatis Sanct Kathrine's day et dicto hepdomadario foro infra dictum burgum hepdomadatim tenebatur . . die Veneris tenendo non obstante quod prius die Saturni . . Et cum plenaria libertate et privilegio creandi, eligendi, continuandi, et deponendi Balliuos, seriandos, etc. . . curias tenendi, leges burgales exercendi, statuta rationabilia concedendi, transgressores debite puniendi, et si opus fuerit eosdem expellendi, amerciamenta leuandi, mercemonia quecunque propinandi, librandi et mensurandi; et omnia alia et singula actus et officia, de jure et consuetudine dictum Burgum concerneutia faciendi et exercendi. Ac eeiam damus, etc. . . plenariam libertatem et licentiam crucem foralem, locum foralem et publicum forum die Veneris . . tenendi et habendi liberas nundinas . . in dicto Burgo singulis annis affuturis vigesimo quinto die mensis Novembris, nuncupato Sanct Katherine's day, per spatium duarum dierum duraturas, cum omnibus . . lie tollis, custumis, etc. . . ad liberum Burgum spectantibus. Necnon, cum privilegio proclamandi predictas nundinas infra dictum Burgum antedicta die . . delinquentes in eisdem puniendi . . cum omnibus . . libertatibus . . ad prædictum Burgum de jure vel consuetudine spectantibus. '. . Et similiter totam at integram praedictam illam terram nuncupatam lie Wodruffe, cum monte, etc. . . unacum omni jure, titulo, etc., que nos, predecessores, aut succéssores nostri habuimus, habemus, etc., ad predictum burgum, vel ad prefatas terras de Wodruffe . . ratione warde, nonintroitus, etc. . . Renunciando transferendo et extradonando eadem cum omni jure, lite et causa earundem pro nobis et nobis et nostris successoribus in favorem dictorum Ballivorum, Consulum et Communitatis predicti Burgi, . . Proviso quod tamen predicta Resignatio et hoc dictum nostrum. Infeofamentum . . nullo modo prejudicaverint particularibus infeofamentis . . predictis balliuis, consulibus et communitati dicti burgi de Newbrugh suisve predecessoribus . . de quibuscunque terris tenementis et annuis redditibus jacentibus in dicto burgo . . Necnon proviso quod predicta resignatio et hoc nostrum infeofamentum nullo modo prejudicaverint nominato Patricio, Domino Lundoris in aliquo jure quod ad burgales firmas et burgales rudas de Newbrugh, vel ad feudifirmas prefatarum terrarum de Wodruff et montis suprascripte neque

Infeofamento . . Joanni Calvie seniori in vitali reditu et Joanni Calvie juniori, etc. . . . de duabus partibus et dimidia parte prefatarum terrarum de Wodruff. . . Proviso etiam quod predictum nostrum infeofamentum ꞌnullo modo praejudicaverit. . . Domino Michaeli Balfour de Denmylne, militi heredibus suis nec assignatis in astrictione lie thirlage prefatarum terrarum ad molendinum, nuncupatum lie Craigmyln, more solito et consueto secundum sua jura et securitates ejusdem. Tenendum et habendum, prescriptum Burgum de Newburgh, etc. . . memoratis balliuis consulibus, et communitati dicti burgi suisque successoribus de nobis et dictis nostris successoribus in libero burgo, feodo et hereditate in perpetuum per omnes metas suas antiquas . . in domibus, edificiis, boscis, planis, moris, maresiis, viis, semitis, aquis, etc. . . cum curiis et carum exitibus, hiereyeldis, bludevitis, etc. . . cum communi pastura . . et cum omnibus et singulis suis libertatibus, etc. Reddendo prefati Ballivi, etc. . . pro toto et integro predicto Burgo, cum omnibus tenementis pertinentiis et privilegiis ejusdem prescriptis, summam quatuor librarum sexdecim soli- dorum et novem denariorum usualis monete dietl regni nostri tanquam antiquam firmam, cum summa duorum solidorum monete antedicte in augmentationem nostri rentalis plusquam prius persolverunt ad festum Pasce, nomine burgalis firme annuatim et pro custumis antedictis pre- fatarum nundinarum summam duorum solidorum ejusdem monete ad pre- dictum festum Pasce nomine feodifirme nec non reddendo annuatim pro predicta terra et monte triginta sex bollas tres firlotas et duas peccas ordei ad festum Pasce nomine feodifirme tantum. Etsi contingat praedictos burgenses dicti Burgi vel heredes suos deficere in solutione dictarum triginta sex bollarum, etc. . . obligant se, et omnia sua bona mobilia capienda, namanda et abducenda et si necesse fuerit vendenda, ad votum et voluntatem nostram et successorum nostrorum, sine licentia et judicio cujuscunque . . Insuper si contingat prefatos Burgenses deficere in solu- tione predicti erdei per tres terminos continuos, obligent se et heredes suos quod licitum erit nobis . . praefatas terres de Wodruff et montem . . in manibus nostris recognoscere appretiare et possidere, semper et donec praedictum ordeum una cum damnis, laboribus, expensis et interesse, quæ ob defectum solutionis ordei faciamus, vel sustineamus plenarie solu- tum fuerit. In cujus rei testimonium huic presenti Carte nostre magnum sigillum nostrum appendi precepimis: Testibus, Jacobo, Marchione de Hamilton, etc.; Willelmo Marriscalli domino Keith, etc.; Georgio, Vice- comite de Dupline domino Hay, nostro Cancellario; Thoma, Comite de Hadingtoun, domino Byning, etc., nostri secreti sigilli custode Willielmo Alexander de Menstre, nostro Secretario principali, Joanni Hamiltoun de Magdalens nostrorum rotulorum registri ac consilii clerico; Georgio Elphingstoun de Blythiswod, nostre Justiciarie clerico, et Joanne Scot de Scottistarvit, nostre Cancelarie directore, militibus; Apud Hali- rudhous, vigesimo nono die mensis Januarii, anno Domini millesimo sex- centesimo trigesimo primo, et anno regni nostri sexto.

No. XIV

LIST OF ABBOTS OF LINDORES;

In so far as they can be traced in record.

I. Guido, first Abbot. He governed the Abbey for twenty-eight years, and died on the 17th June 1219. He was succeeded by

II. John, a monk of the Abbey. How long he continued Abbot does not appear, but his name occurs as a witness in A.D. 1244.

III. Thomas, who is described as ' a man of great piety,' was Abbot in A.D. 1273. He died in that year, and was succeeded by

IV. John, the Prior, who died A.D. 1274, and was buried in Kelso Abbey.

V. Nicholas, the Cellarer. His name, as Abbot, appears as a witness to a charter in A.D. 1175.

VI. John, swore fealty to Edward I. at Lindores Abbey, A.D. 1291.

VII. Thomas, swore fealty to Edward, A.D. 1296.

VIII. Adam. His name appears as witness to Charters in A.D. 1331 and 1342.

IX. William of Angus. He was witness to a Charter in A.D. 1355, and attended a Parliament at Scone in A.D. 1538.

X. Roger appears as a witness in A.D. 1373 and 1382.

XI. John Steele, appears as witness, *circa* A.D. 1401–1407.

XII. James, of Rossey. His name appears as Abbot in A.D. 1443 and 1452.

XIII. John, granted renewal of Charter to the burgesses of Newburgh in A.D. 1457, and his name occurs as a witness in 1474.

XIV. Andrew Caveris, was a monk of the Abbey in A.D. 1457. He appears to have resigned office in A.D. 1503, and to have survived until A.D. 1508, as in that year he is named Pensionary of Lundores. During his tenure of office as Abbot, he was Master of work in Stirling. He entered on this duty on the 26th January 1496–7, receiving on his entry a payment of £106, 13s. 4d. for carrying on the work. He was succeeded in the Abbacy by

XV. Henry, in 1503. He accepted a coadjutor, John, in 1522, and was alive in the beginning of 1528-9.

XVI. John Philp, Abbot Henry's coadjutor and successor, appears to have held the Abbacy until A.D. 1566, when he resigned in favour of

XVII. John Leslie, Bishop of Ross, the last Abbot.

No. XV.

Altars in Lindores Abbey. Pp. 92, 192, 194, 195.

St Mary's.
St Michael's.
St Dionysius'.
St John's.

No. XVI.

Chaplains of St Katherine's Chapel, Newburgh.

John Berclay, A.D. 1481.
Sir John Malcumsone, A.D. 1508.
Mr Thomas Pittillock, A.D. 1523.
Sir Lawrence Lawson, A.D. 1523.
Sir John Lyall, or Liele, A.D. 1526.
Sir John Ritchartson or Cuyk, A.D. 1526–1542.

James Philpe, curate of Ibdy, A.D. 1481.

After the Reformation, the Rector of the Grammar School of Newburgh officiated as Reader in St Katherine's Chapel, and appears to have continued to do so, until Newburgh was disjoined from the parish of Abdie.

No. XVII.

IRNESIDE WOOD (see *antea*, pp. 86-90, 479). While these sheets are passing through the press, Mr Thomas Dickson, curator of the Historical Department of the Register House, Edinburgh, has most kindly furnished the author with the following notes connected with Irneside Wood:— In the account of the receiver of the rents of the Earldom of Fife, 13 April—3 August 1454 [Exchequer Roll, No. 217] there is a sum of forty-two shillings and sixpence allowed 'expensis in dolacione et quadracione octuagina peciarum meremii in Irnside ad fabricam domus de le stowe castri de Edinburgh.' That is, for felling and squaring eighty

L L

pieces of timber in Irnside wood, for the erecting of the stove house of the Castle of Edinburgh.

In the Lord Treasurer's Accounts, there are the following entries, relating to the making of wheels in Irnside wood, for the artillery of King James IV. preparatory to his raid into England, in support of the pretensions of Perkin Warbeck to the English throne.

' 1496. Item [the sext day of Februar], giffin to Thom Barkar, to pas to the wod of Irnside to tak the mesure of quhelis to wirk the irne grath to thaim, ... x. s.

' 1497. Item [xix Aprile], in Lundoris, to Thome Barkar, hupand the quhelis, for his owkis wage, ... xiiij$^{s.}$ iiij$^{d.}$

' Item [the sext day of Maii] gevin to Johne Mawar, elder, at the kingis command, for the quehelis making in Lundoris, iiij^{lib} x$^{s.}$

' Item, to Sande Davisone, on the xij day of Julij passand with the kingis lettrez to Disert, to Johne of Wynd for the about bringing of the quhelis fra Lundoris be seegait, ... xvi$^{d.}$'

The famous *Mons Meg* formed part of the train of artillery of this ill-advised expedition.—*Tytler's History of Scotland*, Vol. II., pp. 259, 264, 393.

No. XVIII.

CULLESSY (see *antea*, pp. 447, 452). In the accounts of the Receiver of the rents of the Earldom of Fife, 20 July 1451—13 April 1453, he takes credit for the payment of xxj$^{lb.}$ to the Lyon Herald out of the rents of Cullessy in these terms :—

' Et de firmis terrarum de Cullesy in manibus Heraldi Lioun nuncupati existentis per regem sibi assignatarum pro feodo suo de tribus terminis hujus compoti xxj^{li}.' [*Exchequer Roll*, No. 212.]

Alexander Nairne of Sandford, now St Fort, was Lyon King of Arms at this period.—*Seton's Law and Practice of Heraldry in Scotland*, p. 477.

The Chamberlain of Fife, in his account, 30 July 1477—6 July 1478, takes credit for the following payment :—

' Et de firmis viginti mercatarum terrarum de Murthocarny, in quarterio de Edin, concessis per dominum regem Marchmondo heraldo ad vitam xiij$^{li.}$ vj$^{s.}$ viij$^{d.}$ Et de firmis viginti mercatarum terrarum de Estir Culessy, similiter concessis per dominum regem Ross heraldo ad vitam, de dicto anno xiij$^{li.}$ vj$^{s.}$ viij.$^{d.}$, quarum literarum tenores registrantur in dorso rotuli presentis compoti.'—[*Exchequer Roll*, No. 274.]

A charter to the lands of 'Estir Culessy' was granted by James III. in favour of the Ross Herald for life, on the 26 January 1477-8. Mag. Sig. VIII. 58. On the 6th day of April 1494, James IV. assigned the lands of 'Cullessy,' which the former Ross Herald held, to the Marchmont Herald for life, in these terms:—

'Jacobus Dei gratia Rex Scotorum . . . Sciatis quod pro singulari fanore quam gerimus erga dilectum familiarem nostrum Marchmond heraldum ac pro suo fideli gratuito seruicio nobis impenso et impendendo dedimus . . eidem in feodo suo pro toto tempore vite sue totas et integras terras de Cullessy cum pertinentibus jacentes infra vice-comitatum nostrum de Fyff, quas quondam Ross heraldus de nobis in feodo suo prius habuit . . . Datum sub magno sigillo nostro apud Striuelin sexto dei mensis Aprilis et regni nostri sexto' [1494].—[*Exchequer Roll*, No. 304, *indorso*.]

The lands of Cullessy were let by royal authority, with consent of the Marchmont herald, to Walter Chapman, 18 December 1495.

In the account of the Chamberlain of Fife, for the period 9th August 1518—20th October 1521, there are the following payments:—

'Et quondam Leoni heraldo regi armorum qui solebat percipere annuatim viginti nnam marcas de firmis de Cullessy de primo anno compoti xiiij$^{li.}$ Et Marchmonde Heraldo percipiendi annuatim in feodo suo decem libras de terris de Murdocairny de annis compoti xxx$^{li.}$'—[*Exchequer Roll*, No. 365.]

Murdocairny, which is more than once mentioned in these notes, formed no part of the possessions of Lindores Abbey, and, therefore, it does not come within the range of its history; but the following letter is so quaintly expressed, that we have given it a place here:—

'James, be the Grace of God King of Scottis. Wit ye ws . . . havand consideratioune of the continewall labours and seruice done and to be done to ws, be oure louit familiar seruitour Johnne Meldrum alias Marchmond herald, and that his fee qubilk is the halfe of our landis of Murdocardny, extending yerelie to xx merkis, is sa litill that he may nocht remane to await upoun oure seruice and chargeis without the samyne be ekit . . . hes gevin . . . to the said Marchmond herald the soome of ten pundis vsuale money of oure realme, to be takin up yerely of the mayllis of that half of oure said landis of Murdocardny with the pertinents . . . during all the dayis of his life. . . . Gevin under our preve sele at Striueling, the xvj day of December, the yeir of God j^{m}v^{c}xxiij yeris, and of our regne the xj yere.'—[*Exchequer Roll*, No. 371, *indorso*.]

No. XIX.

THE CATHCARTS OF PITCAIRLIE.

The family of Cathcart acquired their surname from the lands of Cathcart, in the county of Renfrew. The first of the name that is mentioned in record is Rainald of Kethcart, who appears as a witness to a charter conveying the patronage of the church of Kethcart to the monastery of Paisley, A.D. 1178. William of Kethcart, and his son Alan, are witnesses to a charter in favour of the same monastery about 1199 or 1200. Alan was succeeded by his son William. Another William of Kethkirk swore fealty to Edward I. in 1296. To him succeeded Sir Alan, who espoused the cause of Bruce. He was one of a small but gallant company of horsemen under Edward Bruce, who attacked a body of cavalry more than ten times their number, and completely defeated them. Barbour, in relating this encounter in ' The Brus,' thus speaks of him :—

> A knight that there was in his rout,
> Worthy and wight, stalwart and stout,
> Courteous and fair, and of good fame :
> Sir Alan Cathcart was his name.'

The Cathcarts of Carbiston, now of Pitcairlie, are cadets of this family.

The following account, with slight abridgment, is from Paterson's ' History of the Counties of Ayr and Wigtoun' :—' The Cathcarts had a gift of the wardship of the lands of Carbiston [in the parish of Coylton, Ayrshire] during the reign of David II., in 1368. . . . The last male representative of this branch was William Cathcart of Carbiston, who is mentioned as one of the heirs of entail of John, fourth Lord Cathcart, of certain lands in Ayrshire. He died in 1547.' He was succeeded by his only surviving daughter and heiress, Janet, who married Alan Cathcart of Duchray, grandson of John, second Lord Cathcart, by Margaret, daughter of William Douglas of Drumlanrig.

ALAN CATHCART was succeeded by ' Allane Cathcart of Carbelstoun,' whose name appears in judicial records in 1576 and in 1585. The next of the family was

WILLIAM CATHCART of Carbiston. ' He married, 1st, Janet, one of the daughters and co-heiresses of Sir Robert Fairlie of that Ilk ; and, 2d, Margaret Lokhert. Besides John, his successor in Carbiston, he had a son James, who went to Germany, and for his merit was advanced to honourable offices. . . . He married the daughter and heiress of Balthasar Schemet, Schemet-Felt, chancellor to the Duke of Deux-Ponts, in Germany. He was master of the horse, and one of the councillors of the Duke, in which offices he continued till his death. He was solemnly interred in the great church of Heidelberg, where a noble monument was erected over him, with his arms, which (Nisbet, from whom this account is copied, says) 'I have seen on his seals, affixed to his missive-letters to his cousin, the present Laird of Carbiston.' His grandson, William Cathcart, was, at the time Nisbet wrote, one of the gentlemen of the bed-chamber to the Prince Palatine, and Duke of Deux-Ponts, and enjoyed his grandfather's estates in that country.'

JOHN CATHCART of Carbiston, the son of William, was succeeded by his son Robert, whose son, Francis Cathcart of Carbiston, is mentioned in records in 1643 and in 1659. Francis was succeeded by his son,

JAMES CATHCART of Carbiston, who married Magdalen, the eldest daughter of Sir James Rochead of Inverleith, Baronet, by whom he had two sons, Colonel James Cathcart, and Captain Thomas Cathcart; the latter of whom was killed in the Spanish wars. He was succeeded by his eldest son,

COLONEL JAMES CATHCART, who took the name of James Rochead Cathcart of Inverleith and Carbiston. He obtained a private Act of Parliament for selling one-fourth of the lands of Inverleith, and one-fourth of the lands of Darnchester, in Berwickshire, which had been entailed by his father. He died unmarried, and was succeeded by his grand-nephew,

JAMES TAYLOR CATHCART of Carbiston, 11th August 1760, in Carbiston, and other lands in Ayrshire, and in Pitcairlie in Fifeshire. He married Lucretia, the eldest daughter of Robert Colquhoun of St Christopher's and Santa Cruz. He joined the army, served in the 2d Dragoon Guards, died in 1795, and was succeeded by his son,

JAMES CATHCART, major in the 19th Dragoons. He was engaged in the storming of Bangalore and Seringapatam, and severely wounded in the battle of Assaye. He died unmarried, in 1810, and was succeeded by his brother,

ROBERT CATHCART, captain in the Royal Navy. In the battle of the Nile he served on board the 'Bellerophon,' as Fifth Lieutenant. His captain having been wounded early in the action, and the four senior lieutenants killed, he had the glory of continuing the contest with the 'L'Orient,' till that vessel blew up. For the bravery and skill displayed by him on this occasion, he received the approbation and thanks of Admiral Nelson, and was promoted to the rank of Master and Commander. In 1808, for a most gallant attack, in H.M. sloop 'Seagull,' against a vastly superior force in the Baltic, he was posted to the 'Ganymede.' In 1813, while in the 'Alexandria,' 32 guns, he gave chase for eighty hours (H.M. sloop 'Spitfire,' 18 guns, in company) to the American ship 'President,' 50 guns, Captain Rogers,—the latter only escaping by superiority of sailing. Captain Cathcart married, in 1814, Catherine Scrymgeour, daughter of Henry Scrymgeour Wedderburn of Wedderburn and Birkhill. He died in 1833, leaving no issue. He was succeeded by his brother,

TAYLOR CATHCART of Carbiston and Pitcairlie, many years resident in Jamaica. He married there in 1823, Frances, eldest daughter of George Moncy of Geneva and Kepp, by whom he had issue three sons and one daughter.

1. James Cathcart, Lieutenant 50th B.N.I., who died at Delhi 1850.
2. Robert Cathcart, who succeeded his father.
3. William Taylor Cathcart, Lieutenant Royal Artillery. Died at Portsmouth 1859; and one daughter,
1. Frances Cathcart.

Taylor Cathcart died in 1857, and was succeeded by

ROBERT CATHCART of Carbiston and Pitcairlie. He served in the 74th Highlanders in the Caffre war, 1852, for which he has a medal, and is a Deputy-Lieutenant of the county of Fife. He married, 1856, Agnes Baxter, eldest daughter and co-heiress of Henry Baxter of Idvies, Forfarshire, by whom he has issue :—

James Taylor Cathcart.
William Taylor Cathcart.
Alan Taylor Cathcart.

Arms, according to Nisbet :—' Azure, three cross crosslets fitchee, issuing out of as many crescents, argent, 2 and 1 ; and in the collar point a man's heart ensigned with an imperial crown, proper, as a maternal difference from other descendants of Cathcart.'

No. XX.

THE HAYS OF LEYS.

The traditionary account of the Hays of Leys is well known. It is told that a peasant, and his two sons, armed only with their plough-yokes, turned their countrymen, fleeing from an invading army of Danes, near

Luncarty, renewed the fight, and completely discomfited the invaders. That there is true history, mingled with legend, in this tradition, is probable. Ancient Norse Sagas show that the invasions of the Danes at that era (*circa* 980) were fierce and incessant, and it is quite likely that such an incident may have occurred. In the ' Volsunga Saga,' the following narration occurs : ' The storm abated, and on they fared till they came aland. . . . Then they let loose fire and sword, and slew men and burnt their abodes, and did waste all before them ; a great company of folk fled before the face of them to Lyngi, the king, and tell him that men of war are in the land, and are faring with such rage and fury that the like has never been heard of.

'So the king let send the war-message all throughout his realm, and has no wish to flee, but to summon to him all such as would give him aid. So he came against Sigurd with a great army, he and his brothers with him, and an exceeding fierce fight befell ; many a spear and many an arrow might men see there raised aloft, axes hard driven, shields cleft and byrnies torn, helmets were shivered, skulls split atwain, and many a man felled to the cold earth.'—(Pp. 56, 57.)

In the ' Orkneyinga Saga ' (p. 117) we read :—

> ' Half-a-dozen homesteads burning,
> Half-a-dozen households plundered ;
> This was Swein's work of a morning.'

It is not surprising that the memory of such fierce inroads as these, should hold their place in the traditions of the people, and that they should believe that the man who wrought a deliverance from them should be rewarded with a hawk's-flight of land for his heroism. Such grants were not uncommon, at a time when much of the land of the country was lying waste. Robert Browning thus describes a similar grant :

> ' Take this   .   .   .   .
> Plant the same on the garden ground to grow ;
> Run thence an hour in a straight line and stop :
> Describe a circle round (for central point).
>   .   .   .   .
> The length of that hour's run ; I give it thee—
>   .   .   .   .
> The whole to be thy children's heritage.' [1]

---

[1] *The Ring and the Book*, Vol. IV., p. 183.

Daniel Wilson, in his 'Prehistoric Annals of Scotland,'[1] says, 'The Saxum Falconis,' or 'Hawk Stane,' at St Madocs, Perthshire, which stands on the marches of what is known to have been the ancient possessions of the Hays of Errol, . . is referred to by Bœce as existing in his day (1500), and as having been set up immediately after the defeat of the Danes at the battle of Luncarty. The victory is ascribed, according to a well-known tradition—still commemorated in the armorial bearings of the Hays—by the timely interference of the Scottish peasant and his two sons: ' Sone aftir ane counsal was set at Scone, in the quhilk Hay and his sonnis war maid nobil, and doted for thair singular virtew proven in this field with sundry landis to sustain their estait. It is said that he askit fra the king certane landis liand betwix Tay and Arole, and gat as meikil thairof as ane Falcon flew of ane mannis hand, or scho lichtit. This falcon flew to ane toune four milis fra Dunde, called Rosse, and lichtit on ane stane, quhilk is yet callit the Falcon Stane; and sa he gat al the landis betwix Tay and Arole six milis of lenth and four of breid; quhilk landis ar yet inhabit be his posterite.'[2]

Such is the traditionary account of the origin of the family of the Hays of Errol, from whom the Hays of Leys are sprung; but, unfortunately, the narrative of Bœce is unsupported by any other testimony, either in record or in history: it rests solely on his own authority, no trace of it being found either in Fordun, or Wyntoun, our earliest historians.[3] The first mention that we have, in writing, of any of the name of Hay in Scotland, is in the twelfth century, and the form of the name indicates that the family are of Norman extraction. 'In Normandy there were lands and a lordship denominated Haye [of which La Haye Saint (the Holy Hedge), and Ter la Haye, on the field of Waterloo, are memorable instances]; and in the roll of those who accompanied William the Conqueror into England, le Sieur de la Haye is expressly mentioned.'[4]

William de Haya, who settled in Lothian in the end of the twelfth century, had the office of Pincerna Domini Regis during the reigns of Malcolm IV. and William the Lion; and from him are descended the Hays of Errol, Leys, Melginch, and Kinnoul. The following account of the family of Leys is abridged from an ' Historical Account,' drawn up from records either published, or in possession of the family, and printed in 1832 for private distribution :—

[1] Ed. 1851, p. 94.
[2] Bellenden's *Bœce* b. XI., Chap. VIII.
[3] Hill Burton's *History of Scotland*, Vol. I., p. 364. First Edition. Anderson's *Genealogy and Surnames*, pp. 91, 92.

I. WILLIAM DE HAYA married Juliana de Soulis, daughter of Ranulph de Soulis, Lord of Liddesdale. He died about 1170, leaving two sons:
1. William de Haya.
2. Robert de Haya, ancestor of the Tweeddale family.

II. SIR WILLIAM DE HAYA, the eldest son, obtained from William the Lion, the manor of Herol, now Errol, between 1178 and 1188, for the services of two soldiers. He married Eva de Petenalin. By her he had six sons ·—
1. David de Haya, who succeeded him.
2. William de Haya, who granted to the Abbey of Couper, for the welfare of his own soul, of his wife Ada, of his father, and of his mother, all the lands he had obtained in the Carse from his brother David de Haya.
3. John de Haya, who is designed of Ardnaughton, in a donation made by him to Couper Abbey, for the welfare of the soul of the deceased Juliana de Lascelles his wife. This grant is witnessed by Gilbert de Haya, his nephew, ancestor of the Hays of Naughton, in Fife.
4. Thomas de Haya, made a donation to Couper Abbey, for the welfare of the souls of King William, of his father, of his mother, and of Ada his wife.
5. Robert de Haya.
6. Malcolm de Haya.
    These two latter are witnesses to the grant to Couper Abbey, by their brother David de Haya, of the fishing and the hermitage referred to at page 70.

III. DAVID DE HAYA succeeded his father in the lands of Herol. He married Helen, daughter of Gilbert, Earl of Strathearn, by whom he had two sons :—
1. Gilbert de Haya, from whom are descended the Earls of Errol.
2. William de Haya, the youngest son, is the ancestor of the Hays of Leys.

I. WILLIAM DE HAYA received, on the 7th June 1235, from his brother, Gilbert de Haya of Errol, two carucates of land, called Leys, for faithful counsel and services willingly rendered by him in times past.
    William de Haya, the first of Leys, was succeeded by his

II. SON, who was succeeded by his son.

III. EDMUND DE HAYA of Leys.   He obtained a lease for thirty years, of
the lands of Balgarvie, from the Abbot of Scone, in favour of himself, and his
son William. 'This lease, like all deeds of the time, was extended in Latin.
But there were provisions of great importance to the tenant, a layman and
country gentleman; and for his benefit a clerkly hand has gone over the
deed, and interlined over each phrase of special consequence to the tenant
its equivalent in the vernacular.' [1] A fac-simile of the original lease, exhibiting the interlineations, is given in the second volume of ' The National
Manuscripts of Scotland,' No. XIX.   These interlineations are specially
interesting; as, with the exception of one or two isolated words, they are
the earliest instance of the vernacular that we have in record; and unless
the song given by Wyntoun, in his ' Cronykil,' on the death of Alexander
III., is a copy of a song written at the time (which is probable), the
glosses in the lease in favour of the Laird of Leys, is the earliest example
of the Scottish language that we possess.   Edmund de Haya of Leys
espoused the cause of Bruce, and distinguished himself in the contest for
independence.   He was succeeded by his son,

IV. WILLIAM DE HAYA del Leys, joint-lessee of Balgarvie.   He was
Sheriff of Inverness-shire 1292-6.   He was succeeded by his

V. SON, who was succeeded by his

VI. SON.   This latter was succeeded by his son,

VII. EDMUND HAY of Leys.   He had a Charter of Confirmation in 1451,
from his ' cousin' William, Earl of Errol, of the lands granted to his ancestor in 1235; which charter completely establishes his being the lineal
heir-male of William de Haya, first of Leys.   He had two sons :—
    1. Edmund, who succeeded his father
    2. Peter Hay of Melginch, from whom are descended the Hays of
        Pitfour, Seggieden, and the Earls of Kinnoul.

VIII. EDMUND HAY of Leys had seisin of Leys 1496.   He had four
sons (the eldest of whom died before his father).   He was succeeded by
his second son,

IX. PATRICK HAY of Leys, 1497.   He married Elizabeth Moncrieff,
daughter of John Moncrieff of Moncrieff, by whom he had a son,

---

[1] Cosmo Innes's *Scotland in the Middle Ages*, p. 254.

X. EDMUND HAY of Leys. He married Elizabeth Durham, 1522, by whom he had two sons; the eldest,

XI. PATRICK HAY of Leys, succeeded his father. He left only one daughter, Margaret Hay, who, as heir of line, renounced her succession to the lands of Leys. He was succeeded in the estate by his nephew,

XII. GEORGE HAY of Leys, heir male. He had only one son,

XIII. JOHN HAY of Leys, who succeeded him, and also his uncle Edmund Hay, in Nether Leys, 1549–1584. He left two sons. George, the youngest, was parson of Turriff 1585. The eldest,

XIV. PETER HAY of Leys, succeeded his father 1586. He had an only son,

XV. PETER HAY of Leys, styled in a sasine to the lands of Leys, 'an honourable youth,' 1611. He conveyed, in 1644, the lands of Leys to his eldest son,

XVI. PETER HAY of Leys, on the marriage of the latter with Joan Gray, daughter of John Gray of Ballygerno, by whom he had one son Peter, and a daughter, Mary, who married James Balfour of Randerstone. He was succeeded by his only son,

XVII. PETER HAY of Leys, who received a grant of the lands of Leys from his father, upon his marriage in 1671 with Catherine Blair, daughter and heiress of James Blair of Newbigging; by whom he had issue three sons and five daughters, of whom George Hay Balfour was the eldest. The second son died young; the third, James Hay, merchant, Dundee, was born 1694, and is named in an instrument of resignation by David Hay Balfour of Leys, 10 June 1758; he married and had issue, and his descendants were resident in 1832, when the 'Historical Account of the Hays of Leys' was drawn up.

XVIII. GEORGE HAY BALFOUR of Leys, born 1682, succeeded his father in 1712; he married Mary Balfour, his cousin-german, only daughter of James Balfour of Randerston, and by his marriage with her, acquired the estate of Randerston. The issue by this marriage was one son and four daughters :—

Peter Hay, born **1717**, who succeeded his father.

Mary Hay, died young.

Catherine Hay, born **1733**, married George Clephane of Carslogie.

Mary Hay, born **1727**, married Sir Robert Gordon of Gordonstown.

Elizabeth Hay, born **1729**, married —— Sinclair, Esq.

XIX. PETER HAY of Leys, only son of George Hay Balfour of Leys. He bought the lands and house of Mugdrum 1737 (*see antea*, page 465), where his descendants have resided ever since, and he bought Lindores Abbey, with the lands around it, 1753 (*see antea*, page 462). He married Elizabeth Scott, daughter of David Scott of Scotstarvit, **1737**, by whom he had issue two sons and eight daughters :—

David Hay Balfour, who succeeded his father.

John Hay Balfour, who became his brother's heir.

Lucy Hay and Mary Hay, both died young.

Lindsay Hay, born **1743**, married John Dalziel of Lingo, and had issue

Elizabeth Hay, married Peter Stewart of Collarnie, and had issue

Lucy Hay, born **1785**, married Patrick Moncrieff of Reidie, eldest son of Colonel George Moncrieff of Reidie, and Mrs Helen Skene, and had issue

Petty Hay and Janet Hay, twins; in consequence of the death of their father previous to their birth, Robert Hay, merchant, Dundee, cousin-german, became sponsor. They both died young.

XX. DAVID HAY BALFOUR of Leys and Randerston, was served heir to his father, Peter Hay of Leys, in the lands of Leys, and to his great-grandfather, James Balfour of Randerston, 1757. He was succeeded, **1759**, by his brother,

XXI. JOHN HAY BALFOUR of Leys and Randerston, married Catherine Moncrieff, daughter of Colonel George Moncrieff of Reidie, **1777**. He died at Bath **1791**, and was buried in the Abbey Church there, in which there is a monument to his memory. By his marriage he had two sons and one daughter :—

1. David Balfour Hay, his successor.

2. Captain Peter Hay of the 18th Light Dragoons. He served with distinction in the Peninsula, in the expedition under Sir John Moore. He died unmarried in **1846**, and was buried in Newburgh Church.

1. Jane Hay, the only daughter of John Hay Balfour of Leys,

married James Paterson of Carpow. She survived her husband, and died in September 1865, aged 87. By her marriage she had three sons and five daughters :—

1 and 2. James and John, both died young.

3. Peter Hay Paterson, succeeded his father in the estate of Carpow. He married, in 1848, the Honourable Marianne Oliphant Murray, youngest daughter of Alexander, eighth Lord Elibank. He died on 23d June 1865. His widow died on the 6th September 1873. By their marriage they had issue two sons and three daughters :—

    1. Edmund de Haya Paterson.

    2. Peter Hay Paterson.

    1. Marianne Hay Paterson.

    2. Jane Hay Paterson, died in infancy.

    3. Charlotte Emily de Haya Paterson.

1. Catherine Paterson, who married Sir William Dunbar, Bart. of Mochrum, and has issue two sons :—

    1. Uthred James Hay Dunbar.

    2. William Cospatrick Dunbar.

2. Elizabeth Oliphant Paterson, died unmarried.

3. Margaret Drummond Paterson.

4. Helen Skene Paterson.

5. Jane Hay Paterson, who married the Honourable John Rollo, second son of John, eighth Lord Rollo of Duncrub, and has issue three sons and one daughter ·—

    1. John Harry Rollo.

    2. James Arthur Rollo.

    3. Robert William Rollo.

    1. Martha Hay Rollo.

XXII. DAVID BALFOUR HAY of Leys and Randerston, who succeeded his father, was a Captain in the 26th Light Dragoons, having joined the army in 1797. Captain Hay served in the expedition to Holland in 1799, and for his gallant conduct in one of the engagements of the campaign, honourable testimony was awarded to him in the 'London Gazette' at the time. He was much beloved by those under him ; and it is said that he owed his safety to his servant carrying him off the field, when nearly exhansted by loss of blood, from a wound he received in battle. The estate descended to him through unbroken descent of heirs-male, from the 7th June 1235, and the line of heirs-male only became extinct on his death, on the 21st August 1868. He died in the 89th year of his age, and was buried in Newburgh Church. He was succeeded in the estate of Leys and Randerston by Edmund de Haya Paterson, eldest son of his nephew, Peter Hay Paterson of Carpow, now

XXII. Edmund Paterson Balfour Hay, present proprietor.

The arms of the Hays of Leys are three escutcheon gules and ermine; their crest being a countryman holding the yoke of a plough over his shoulder, with the motto *Primus E. Stirpe*, in allusion to their being the immediate younger branch of the family of Hay of Errol.

No. XXI.

LIVINGSTONES, EARLS OF NEWBURGH, AND THEIR ANCIENT SEAT OF KINNAIRD.

The patent creating the earldom of Newburgh does not specify from which Newburgh the title is derived. Sir James Livingstone of Kynnaird, the first Earl, had no connection with Newburgh-Fife, either by birth or territory. He was grandson of Robert, second son of Sir John Livingstone of Callendar, and his properties of Kynnaird and Flacraig, from which the inferior titles are taken, are in the parish of Kynnaird, on the opposite side of the Tay. Neither does he appear to have had any connection with Newburgh on Ithan, in Aberdeenshire. In absence of any written evidence, the circumstance of Newburgh-on-Tay, in Fifeshire, being distinctly seen from the old castle of Kynnaird, seems to show that it was from the latter that the title was derived.

The property of Kynnaird, which now belongs to Sir Patrick Murray Threipland, Baronet, of Fingask, belonged for centuries to the Kynnairds of that Ilk. On the 26th March 1618, John Kynnaird, elder, and Margaret Ogilvie his spouse, with consent of their son, sold the whole barony of Kynnaird to John Livingstone, gentleman of the bed-chamber to King James VI. This included the superiority of half the lands of Nauchtone, and of that of Inverdovate, and the patronage of the chapel of St Thomas of Seymylne, in Fife. On the 12th June 1622, Mr John Livingstone (then Sir John Livingstone), and Dame Janet Sprokestoune, his spouse, was infeft in the barony of Kynnaird. Their son, Sir James Livingstone of Kynnaird, was served heir to his father in the barony, on the 28th February 1629, including the superiorities and patronage mentioned.[1]

I. SIR JAMES LIVINGSTONE became one of the gentlemen of the bedchamber to Charles I. He died in 1670. By his wife, Lady Catherine Howard, daughter of the second Earl of Suffolk, he had one son, Charles, who succeeded him.

The political troubles of the first Earl of Newburgh involved him in pecuniary difficulties, which compelled him to grant several wadsetts on his estate. After the death of the Earl, Sir Patrick Murray Threipland of Fingask, out of friendship, arising from the ties of neighbourhood and the devoted attachment of the two families to the House of Stuart, bought up the various *wadsetts*, or mortgages, and ultimately, after an interval of many years, purchased (14 June 1686) the whole barony from Charles, the second Earl. The Earl of Newburgh was so satisfied with the disinterestedness of Sir Patrick, that in one of his letters he says—' When at Windsor, I mentioned to the King [James VII.] the handsome manner you had behaved to me. His Majesty replied, " I am glad to find that Sir Patrick Threipland is as honest as I know him to be loyal." '

II. CHARLES, second Earl of Newburgh, married Frances, granddaughter of George, Earl of Cardigan. He died in 1694, leaving an only child,

III. CHARLOTTE MARIA, Countess of Newburgh, who, after possessing the title sixty-one years, died 4th August 1755. She married, first, Thomas, eldest son of Hugh, Lord Clifford of Chudleigh, by whom she had two daughters :—

    1. Lady Frances Clifford, who married William Middleton, Yorkshire.
    2. Lady Anne Clifford, who married, in 1739, Sir James Joseph Mahony, Count Mahoni, a Lieutenant-General in Naples, and from whom the present Countess of Newburgh is descended. The Countess married, secondly, 1724, the Hon. Charles Radcliffe, third son of Francis Lord Radcliffe, by whom she had three sons and four daughters :—
    1. James Bartholomew Radcliffe.
    2. James Clement Radcliffe, a general officer in the French service, who died 18th May 1788.
    3. Charles Radcliffe.

---

[1] Perth Retours, Nos. 21-23, 237-375; Fife, 406.

1. Charlotte, died 1800.
2. Barbara, died at Cambray, 1769.
3. Thomasina, died before 1769.
4. Mary, married Francis Eyre of Hassop, in Derbyshire; died 1798.

The Hon. Charles Radcliffe, and his brother James, Earl of Derwentwater, took part in the rising of 1715. They were both taken prisoners, and condemned for high treason. The Earl was beheaded 24th February 1716, and his great and beautiful estates forfeited; but his brother contrived to escape, and fled to France, where he married the Countess of Newburgh. On the next attempt of the Stuarts to regain the throne, in which Charles Radcliffe joined, he was not so fortunate: he was taken prisoner, when on the passage to Scotland with supplies for Prince Charles, and landed at Deal. He was committed to the Tower, and beheaded on Tower Hill, on the 8th December 1746, in terms of his former sentence. On the death of his nephew, John, Lord Radcliffe, Charles Radcliffe assumed the title of Lord Derwentwater; his coffin, therefore, bore the following inscription:—' Carolus Radcliffe, Comes de Derwentwater, decollatus die 8vo December 1746, ætatis 53, requiescat in pace.'

In 1749, his son, James Bartholomew Radcliffe, Lord Kynnaird, made a representation to his Majesty, beseeching him to extend his grace and favour, by granting an allowance out of the Derwentwater estates, to his mother, the Countess of Newburgh, and his surviving brothers and sisters, the children of the Hon. Charles Radcliffe; humbly representing that if no relief is granted, they will be destitute after his mother's death. This application was so far successful, that £30,000 was allotted them; the residue of the vast ancestral estates of the family being devoted to the support of Greenwich Hospital.

IV. James Bartholomew Radcliffe Livingstone, third Earl of Newburgh, was born at Vincennes, in France, 23d April 1725. He was, therefore, only twenty years old when he was taken prisoner on his way to Scotland with his father. He married Barbara, only daughter and heiress of Anthony Kemp of Slindon, Sussex, and died there on 2d January 1786, leaving a daughter, who died unmarried, and a son,

V. Anthony James Radcliffe Livingstone, fourth Earl of Newburgh, born in 1767. In 1788, he obtained, on petition from Parliament, £2500 yearly to himself and his heirs male of his body, out of the Derwentwater estates. He died on the 29th November 1814, without issue. On his death, the title was assumed by Francis Eyre of Hassop,

Derbyshire, and Walworth Castle, Northamptonshire, son of Mary Radcliffe, daughter of Charlotte Maria, Countess of Newburgh, by her second
marriage. He died 23d October 1827, and was succeeded by his elder
son, Thomas, who assumed the title of Earl of Newburgh. He married, in
1817, Lady Margaret Kennedy, daughter of the Earl of Cassilis, but left
no issue. Thomas was succeeded by his brother Francis, called the
seventh Earl of Newburgh, who died unmarried in 1852. His sister,
Mary Dorothea, immediately assumed the title of Countess of Newburgh.
She married Colonel Charles Leslie of Balquhain, Aberdeenshire, 21st July
1836, and died 22d November 1853. After her death, the title was
claimed by Maria Cecilia, Princess Giustiniani, Marchioness Dowager Bandini, of the Roman States. She proved that she was the great-grand-
daughter of Lady Anne Clifford, second daughter of Charlotte Maria,
first Countess of Newburgh, by her first husband. The House of Lords
sustained her claim on the 29th July 1858, and found that the assumption
of the title by Francis Eyre, and his descendants, was an usurpation. The
Princess Giustiniani, and second Countess of Newburgh in her own right,
was born on 5th February 1796. Her eldest son, Sigismund Nicholas,
Marquis Bandini and Viscount Kynnaird, was born 30th June 1818, and
has issue two sons and three daughters. The present Countess of Newburgh and Viscount Kynnaird and his children were all naturalised as
British subjects by Act of Parliament in 1857.

Arms of the Livingstones, Earls of Newburgh.—Argent in a bend
between three gilly flowers, gules, an anchor of the first, all within a double
tressure, vert. CREST.—A Moor's head proper, banded gules and argent,
with pendants, argent, at his ears. SUPPORTERS.—Dexter, a wild man,
wreathed round his loins with oak, vert proper. Sinister, a dapple-grey
horse, bridled and saddled, gules. MOTTO.—*Si je puis.*

SIR PATRICK THREIPLAND (who purchased Kynnaird from the second
Earl of Newburgh), and his descendants, were so closely linked with the
same cause for which the Livingstones suffered, that any notice of Kinnaird would be incomplete without a brief outline of their history.

Sir Patrick, when Provost of Perth, was made a Knight Bachelor by
Charles II. in 1674, and a Baronet of Nova Scotia by James VII. in 1687.
His attachment to the cause of James brought him under suspicion at the
Revolution, and he was seized by order of the Convention of Estates
that met in Edinburgh in 1689, and dragged to Stirling Castle, where he
died in a few days. Sir David, his only son, was among the first to join
the Earl of Mar's standard in 1715. After the dispersion of Mar's forces,
Sir David lurked about under the name of Mr Hume, and after many

M M

hairbreadth escapes, had the good fortune to reach two French frigates in the Orkneys, which conveyed him and a number of other gentlemen to Gottenburg, in Sweden. Sir David was attainted by Act of Parliament in 1716, and his estates forfeited. The Government sold all the forfeited properties to ' The York Building Company for raising the Thames Water to London.' That Company granted leases of the property they had thus acquired. Sir Alexander Lindsay of Evelick, Drummond of Megginch, and Crawford of Inchmartine, obtained a lease of Fingask and Kinnaird in 1716-17, which they immediately subset to Lady Threipland, Sir David's wife, so that by the friendly intervention of the neighbours named, Lady Threipland and her daughters never had to quit the family mansion and estates. After an exile of about four years, Sir David was permitted to return from abroad, and to reside at Fingask. He married Elizabeth, daughter of Sir James Ramsay of Bamff, in 1688, by whom he had seven sons and three daughters; and, secondly, in 1707, Dame Catharine Smythe of Barnhill, by whom he had two sons and four daughters. His youngest son, Stuart, who was born prematurely in 1715, while soldiers were in Fingask Castle searching for his father, received his Christian name from his mother's devotion to the cause for which his father was suffering. Stuart Threipland followed the profession of medicine, and in 1737 was one of eight original members of the Royal Medical Society of Edinburgh when it was formally constituted. He graduated in Edinburgh in 1742, and was admitted a Fellow of the Royal College of Physicians in 1744.

When Prince Charles Stuart landed in 1745, Sir David Threipland's devotion to the old cause burst out afresh, and at the age of seventy-nine he prepared to join the Prince; but while in the act of drawing on his jack-boots, preparatory to mounting his steed, he was seized with a paralytic stroke, of which he died. His eldest son David was killed at the battle of Preston, and another son at Culloden. His youngest and only surviving son, then Sir Stuart, gave up his professional career in Edinburgh, and joined the Prince. He shared in all the fortunes of the expedition. After the defeat at Culloden, he wandered for months among the mountains, with the Prince and his other followers; often sleeping among the heather on the open hill-side. At length he contrived to reach Edinburgh, and eventually London, to which latter place he travelled in the friendly company of William Gordon, a bookseller of Edinburgh, disguised as his apprentice. Sir Stuart immediately left for Ronen, where he joined a party of similar exiles, among whom were William Hamilton of Bangour; Andrew Lumisden, who subsequently became private secretary to Prince Charles; Robert, afterwards Sir Robert Strange, the celebrated engraver; Sir James Stewart of Coltness, and others. The whole estates of the family were again forfeited. Sir Stuart availed himself of the Act of Indemnity, and after an exile of three or four years, returned to his native country. On his return, Sir Stuart resumed practice as a physician. In 1753 he married Janet, eldest daughter of David Sinclair of Southdon, in Caithness; and, secondly, in 1761, Janet Murray of Henryland and Toftingall, of the same county, by whom he had one son and four daughters. Though latterly independent of professional income, Sir Stuart continued to practise as a physician; and in the end of 1766, he was elected President of the Royal College of Physicians, Edinburgh.[1] The York Building Company failed in 1783-4, and the forfeited estates they had bought were sold by their creditors. Sir Stuart bought back Fingask and Kinnaird; but not having sufficient means to pay for the whole of the lands, he sold Kinnaird Castle and a portion of the lands to Mr Richardson of Pitfour. Sir Stuart died in 1805, at the age of eighty-nine. He was stately in his demeanour, of refined and cultivated tastes, and was a zealous patron both of the useful and fine arts. His sufferings for the cause, for which he had adventured so much, did not make him forsake his political principles. To the very last, the dignified old man dedicated his first glass of wine, after dinner, to ' The Land o' Cakes, and the right *Steward* to deal them.' His descendants preserve, with pious care, memorials of his taste in Fingask Castle, and have also the richest and most interesting collection of Jacobite relics to be found in Scotland, the value of which is enhanced by the undoubted genuineness of every relic preserved.

Sir Stuart was succeeded by his eldest son, Sir Patrick Murray Threipland, fourth baronet. When George IV. visited Scotland in 1822, Sir Patrick presented a petition to the King, praying for the restoration of the title which his father and grandfather had forfeited. His petition was granted, and a bill was introduced into Parliament, whereby, in 1826, the attainder was reversed, and the title restored. Sir Patrick married Jessie Murray, daughter of William Scott Kerr of Chatto, Roxburghshire, by whom he had one son and three daughters. He died in 1837, and his only son, Sir Patrick Murray Threipland, fifth and present baronet, repurchased, at a great sacrifice, in 1853, the castle and estate of Kinnaird. He was four years old at the date of his grandfather, Sir Stuart's, death, and he lives to tell that he has conversed with one who fought at Culloden, and attended Prince Charles Stuart in the greater portion of his wanderings after that fatal defeat.[2]

---

[1] Prof. Maclagan's Inaugural Address, *Edinburgh Medical Journal*, January 1875.
[2] Sir Patrick Murray Threipland's MS. Notes.

No. XXII.

THE GEOLOGY OF THE PARISH OF NEWBURGH AND NEIGHBOURHOOD.

The Reverend John Anderson, D.D., from whose published writings' the following extracts are taken, was a native of Newburgh. His father, John Anderson, was, for a long series of years, one of the magistates of the burgh; and his mother, Margaret Stuart, was a sister of the Rev. Dr Thomas Stuart, minister of the parish of Newburgh. Dr Anderson, who received his education at the parish school, and at St Andrews and Edinburgh Universities, was ordained minister of the parish of Dunbarney in 1821. In 1833 he was chosen by the congregation to be the minister of his native parish. He devoted much of his leisure to the study of the then comparatively new science of Geology, and from time to time published (besides others) the works from which the following notices of the geology of the district are extracted. Dr Anderson died at Nice, whither he had gone, in the autumn of 1863, for the benefit of his health, on the 16th March 1864. He was interred in the burying-ground attached to the old chapel of the Church of England there, and a tombstone marks his grave.

' The county of Fife, of which the parish of Newburgh forms the north-west extremity, may be regarded, in a geological view, as one of the most interesting in the whole island,—rich in organic remains, and in all those important facts which belong to the carboniferous era. Although the parish of Newburgh partakes of few or none of its distinguishing characteristics, one or two observations may be permitted on the materials in its immediate neighbourhood, from which the relative position of its own may be best ascertained, and in which some interesting and valuable facts recently brought to light, may be stated. Immediately on the east, along the margin of the Tay, the old red sandstone appears, on which there rests a bed of limestone; and corresponding to this, on the opposite side of the river, a similar bed is to be found in the property of Murie. Not far from the limestone, and nearer to Newburgh, there is a bed of calmstone with vegetable impressions, and the flowering portion, in considerable numbers, of what Dr Fleming considers a *Scirpus*. It lies immediately under clinkstone trap; and although the junction cannot be traced with regard to the sand and limestones, its position is unquestionably that of an upper member of the series. A similar bed, with identically the same impressions, occurs near the mouth of the river in the parish of Arbroath. The parish of Abernethy, on the west, likewise displays sections of the old red sandstone; and at a very elevated position, on the very summit of the Ochils, a conglomerate bed of limestone may be observed. Near the church of Dron, a clayslate or calmstone, similar to that on the east of Newburgh, occurs in the same relative position to the stratified and amorphous rocks, but without, as far as has yet been observed, vegetable impressions. Intermediate between what has now been described, rises the parish of Newburgh, in one unbroken undulating mass of trap, the lower portion, immediately above the town, being a fine-grained porphyritic greenstone; that in the higher ridges approaches to a compact feldspar; and on the property of Pitcairlie, beds of trap tuffa may be traced. In the small veins which occur abundantly in the greenstone, may be observed crystals of quartz, carbonate of lime, barytes, and olivine; the feldspar rocks contain nodules of claystone and jaspery agates, the latter very numerous, and approaching in character and beauty to the Mocha-stone. The parks or table-land of Mugdrum is an accumulation of the *debris* of the old red sandstone and other gravelly matter, of great depth, and furnishes, in a geological point of view, some interesting problems as to the causes of its accumulation at this particular spot. Peat occurs immediately on the south, where the surface dips considerably, forming the bed of a loch, which has been lately drained, and in the low fields of Pitcairlie there is abundance of the same material.

' Along the sides and summits of the hills, boulders of the primitive rocks, granite, gneiss, quartz, mica-slate, with garnets and primitive greenstone, occur in the greatest abundance, and many of them of the most unwieldy dimensions. Towards their base, and skirting the southern boundary of the valley, there are various accumulations of a fine dark-red sand, containing rolled masses from a few inches to one foot in diameter, which belong, for the most part, to the secondary rocks. The materials, in both cases, have evidently been brought from the west; and, considering that the heaviest boulders occupy the most elevated position, are we not warranted to infer the existence of two separate currents, of unequal magnitude and of different ages, as the agents of transportation? This remark applies to several of the adjacent parishes, where similar appearances may be observed.

' A well, which was opened lately here, on the sloping bank beneath the town, exhibits the following interesting beds, and affords the geologist an excellent illustration of the *alluvium* formation in this quarter. It is thirty feet in depth, and intersects four distinct deposits. The first of these, about five feet thick, is a rich alluvial clay, common to all the low lands in the district; a bed of peat succeeds, composed of the usual materials which are found in that substance, with the addition of branches of the *Alnus glutinosa* and *Corylus avellana*, and many minute seeds, belonging, apparently, from their angular shape, to the Carex tribe of plants. This bed is about two feet thick, and belongs to the great deposit which extends throughout Strathearn and the lower basin of the Tay. Under the peat is a deposit of two and a half feet thick, of extremely fine sand, of a light-blue colour, and very unctuous in its character; it contains a considerable quantity of magnesia, which may be derived from the decompo-

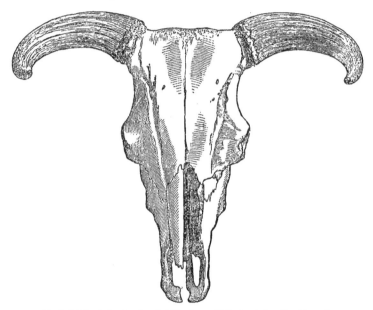

Skull of *Bos primigenius*, found at Mugdrum, 27¾ inches in length. See p. 2.

sition of steatite, so abundant in the greenstone in the neighbourhood. But what is most remarkable here is the fact, that this matter is confined entirely to this single bed, not a particle of which is to be found in the superincumbent peat, or in the underlying stratum. What peculiar agency has produced this? The lowest bed of the series, the depth of which is unknown, is a plastic clay, or *till*, containing boulders of the secondary rocks, mixed up with the *debris* of the old red sandstone. The surface of the ground here is about forty feet above the level of the Tay; and the geologist will naturally inquire, whether it occupied the same level, or what was its condition, during the formation of the above-mentioned deposits?

' The soil in the upper part of the parish, though generally of little depth, is of great fertility. It mostly consists of either a loose black loam, or of a more compact ferruginous mould. Here the entire property of Pit-cairlie, through an intelligent and enterprising tenantry, has been brought into the highest state of cultivation, and marks itself out to the traveller among the Ochils as an insulated spot of singular beauty and fertility. The soil on the north-east of the town, where the ground is low and flat, consists of the richest clay, not inferior to the best portions of the Carse of Gowrie.'—*Statistical Account of Fifeshire*, 1845, pp. 59-61.

In addition to the foregoing, we quote the following passages from the more recent writings of Dr Anderson :—

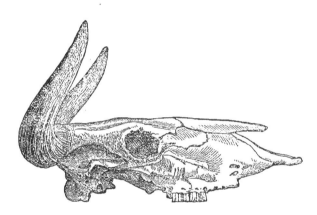

Side view of Skull of *Bos primigenius*, found at Mugdrum.

' The cuttings of the Edinburgh and Perth Railway [now the North British Railway] give excellent sections of the various minerals of the county, from the grey sandstone to the uppermost coverings of the coal-field. Entering Fifeshire from the west, your course lies deep among the detritus of the various members of the old red series. At the Newburgh station, and under the cliffs of Clachard, the grey sandstone and cornstone may be observed—the latter is regularly stratified; the former is em-braced among the igneous rocks, broken, isolated, and inclined at every possible degree of the horizon. Clachard-craig itself has been stirred to its foundations; the huge mass rests on highly-inclined beds of the grey sandstone; the black transverse dyke of basalt, a few hundred yards on the west, may be conjectured to have been the instrument of upheaval, as in fancy we can discern, in the half-raised, half-suspended position of the rock, the enormous pressure required for its elevation.'—*The Course of Creation*, p. 137. 1850.

No. XXIII.

LIST OF PLANTS GROWING IN THE NEIGHBOURHOOD OF NEWBURGH.

CLASS I.—DICOTYLEDONS.

RANUNCULACEÆ.—Anemone nemorosa, L., *Wood Anemone;* Lochmill hill, east side. Ranunculus aquatilis, L., *Common Water Crowfoot;* Lochmill and Loch-Lindores. R. heterophyllus, and R. circinatus, *Rigid-leaved Water Crowfoot;* Loch-Lindores. R. Ficaria, L., *Lesser Celandine;* Abbeyburn. R. acris, L., in pastures frequent. R. repens, L., *Creeping Crowfoot;* a troublesome weed in pastures. Caltha palustris, L., *Common Marsh Marygold;* Lindores Pow, Tay below Mugdrum. Helleborus viridis, L., *Green Hellebore;* Lindores Abbey.

BERBERIDACEÆ.—Berberis vulgaris, L., *Common Barberry;* Lindores Abbey.

NYMPHŒACEÆ.—Nymphæa alba, L., *Great White Water-Lily;* west end of Lochmill, and Black Loch. Nuphar lutea, Sm., *Common Yellow Water-Lily;* Lochmill and Loch-Lindores.

PAPAVARACEÆ.—Papaver Argemone, L., *Long prickly-headed Poppy;* The Mair's Craig. P. dubium, L., *Long Smooth-headed Poppy; Ib.* P. Rhæas L., *Common Red Poppy;* cornfields.

FUMARIACEÆ.—Fumaria officinalis, L., *Common Fumitory;* common in highly-cultivated fields and gardens.

CRUCIFERÆ.—Cheiranthus cheiri, L., *Common Wall-flower;* Abbey walls. Arabis hirsuta, Br., *Hairy Rock Cress;* The Mair's Craig. Cardamine pratensis, L., *Common Bitter Cress,* or *Lady's Smock;* Loch-Lindores, Pow, etc. Nasturtium officinale, Br., *Common Watercress;* Ninewells Burn. Draba verna, L., *Whitlow-grass;* Wall tops, Lindores. Capsella Bursa Pastoris, D. C., *Common Shepherd's Purse;* cornfields, Wodriffe. Sinapis arvensis, L., *Wild Mustard; Ib.*

RESEDACEÆ.—Reseda Luteola, L., *Common Dyer's Rocket;* The Mair's Craig. R. lutea, L., *Wild Mignonette;* roadside between Mugdrum and Carpow.

CISTACEÆ.—Helianthemum vulgare, *Rock Rose;* Ormiston hill, The Mair's Craig.

VIOLACEÆ.—Viola odorata, L., *Sweet Violet;* Ballinbriech Castle grounds. V. canina, L., *Dog Violet;* Ormiston hill. V. arvensis, *Pansy,* or *Heart's Ease;* The Mair's Craig.

DROSERACEÆ.—Drosera rotundifolia, L., *Round-leaved Sun-dew;* Lochmill hill, west.

PARNASSIEÆ.—Parnassia palustris, L., *Grass of Parnassus;* near Butter well.

POLYGALACEÆ.—Polygala vulgaris, L., *Common Milkwort;* Ormiston hill, abundant.

CARYOPHYLLACEÆ.—Dianthus deltoides, L., *Maiden Pink;* The Mair's Craig. Saponaria officinalis, L., *Common Soapwort;* observed once at Knock-Murdo, Pitcairly. Silene inflata, Sm., *Bladder Campion;* The Mair's Craig. Lychnis Flos-Cuculi, L., *Ragged Robin;* Lindores, Pow-side, etc. L. vespertina, *White Campion;* frequent. L. diurna, *Red Campion;* near Craigmill. Agrostemma Githago, L., *Corn Cockle;* cornfields, too abundant. Sagina subulata, *Awl-shaped Pearl-wort;* The Mair's Craig. S. procumbens, *procumbent Pearl-wort; Ib.* Stellaria holostea, L., *Greater Stitchwort;* Barony-road, Lochmill-den. S. glauca, *Glaucous Marsh Stitchwort;* Loch-Lindores. S. graminea, L., *Lesser Stitchwort;* Lecturer's Inch, Loch-Lindores. Spergula arvensis, *Spurry;* The Mair's Craig. Cerastium triviale, *Narrow-leaved Mouse-ear Chickweed;* a weed in cultivated ground.

LINACEÆ.—Linum catharticum, L., *Purging Flax;* Ormiston hill (gathered for medicinal purposes).

MALVACEÆ.—Malva sylvestris, L., *Common Mallow;* Abbey. M. moschata, *Musk Mallow; Ib.* M. rotundifolia, *Dwarf Mallow;* near Glenburnie.

HYPERICACEÆ.—Hypericum perforatum, *common perforated St John's Wort;* The Mair's Craig. H. humifusum, *trailing St John's Wort;* Ormiston hill. H. pulchrum, *small upright St John's Wort;* Abbot's Seat, The Mair's Craig.

GERANIACEÆ.—Geranium sanguineum, *bloody Crane's-bill;* Fincraig. G. pratense, *blue Meadow Crane's-bill;* Loch-Lindores, Black Loch, with white flowers near Kinnaird Doo'-cot. G. lucidum, *shining Crane's-bill;* east end of Lochmill, side of burn, (Lindores Abbey introduced). G. Robertianum, *Herb Robert,* or *Poor Robin;* hedges, common. G. molle, *Dove's-foot Crane's-bill;* pastures, common. G. dissectum, *Jagged-leaved Crane's-bill;* Ormiston hill. G. columbinum, *long-stalked Crane's-bill;* The Mair's Craig.

OXALIDACEÆ.—Oxalis Ascetosella, *Common Wood-sorrel;* Blackcairn wood, etc.

LEGUMINOSÆ.—Ulex Europæus, *common Whin;* Ormiston hill. Genista

Anglica, or *Petty Whin*, grows on the common at Ladybank, but it is fast being extirpated. Sarothamnus scoparius, *Common Broom;* Loch mill hills. Ononis arvensis, *Rest-harrow;* Wodriffe road, Fincraig. Anthyllus Vulneraria, *Lady's Fingers;* The Mair's Craig, Fincraig. Trifolium arvense, *Hare's-foot Trefoil;* The Mair's Craig. T. procumbens, *Hop Trefoil; Ib.* T. repens, *Dutch Clover;* Ormiston hill. Lotus corniculatus, *Common Bird's-foot Trefoil; Ib.* L. major, *Narrow-leaved Bird's-foot Trefoil;* Loch-Lindores. Ornithopus perpusillus, *Common Bird's-foot;* Clachard. Vicia cracca, *Tufted Vetch.* Hedges. Lathyrus pratensis, *Meadow Vetchling;* Loch-Lindores, Fincraig. Orobus tuberosus, *Bitter Vetch;* Monkswell.

ROSACEÆ.—Prunus spinosa, L., *Sloe,* or *Blackthorn;* Fincraig, etc. P. Cerasus, L., *Morello,* or *Wild Cherry;* near Ballinbriech Castle. (Prunus Padus, or *Bird Cherry*, grows in Glenfarg, near the Bein Inn.) Spiræa Ulmaria, *Queen of the Meadow;* Loch-Lindores and Pow-side. Geum urbanum, *Common Avens;* Abbey burn. G. rivale, *Water Avens;* Lochmill, west end. Fragaria vesca, *Wood Strawberry;* Woodmill wood. Potentilla anserina, *Silver-weed;* road-side near East Toll, etc. P. argentea, *Hoary Cinque-foil;* The Mair's Craig. P. reptans, *creeping Cinque-foil;* river-side, Ballinbriech. P. Tormentilla, *Tormentil;* Ormiston hill. P. Fragariastrum, *Barren Strawberry;* roadside near Denmiln. Alchemilla vulgaris, *common Lady's Mantle;* Ninewells Burn. Rosa spinosissima, *Scotch Rose;* The Mair's Craig. R. tomentosa, *downy-leaved Rose; Ib.* R. rubiginosa, *true Sweet-Briar;* bank near Ballinbriech. R. canina (*var.*), *Dog-Rose; Ib.* Cratægus oxyacantha, L., *Hawthorn;* stray plants common.

ONAGRACEÆ. — Epilobium parviflorum, *small-flowered hairy Willow-herb;* Abbey burn. E. montanum, *broad-leaved Willow-herb;* Fincraig. E. palustre, *Marsh Willow-herb;* Abbey burn.

HALORAGACEÆ.—Myriophyllum spicatum, *Spiked Water-Milfoil;* Loch-Lindores.

LYTHRACEÆ.—Lythrum Salicaria, *spiked, Purple Loose-strife;* Loch-Lindores.

CRASSULACEÆ.—Sempervivum tectorum, *House-leek,* or *Fouat;* Hatton-hill. Sedum Telephium, *Live-long,* or *Orpine;* Loch-Lindores, Wodriffe Road. S. reflexum, *Crooked Yellow Stonecrop;* Abbey, formerly abundant on Denmiln orchard wall. Sedum acre, *Biting Stonecrop;* The Mair's Craig.

SAXIFRAGACEÆ.—Saxifraga granulata, *white Meadow Saxifrage; Ib.*, and Clachard.

UMBELLIFERÆ.—Hydrocotyle vulgaris, *Marsh Pennywort;* Loch-Lindores. Sanicula Europæa, *Wood Sanicle;* Abbey. Cicuta virosa, *Cowbane;* formerly in Lindores Loch; supposed to be now covered up by the railway embankment. It was known in the neighbourhood as *Deathen*, and cattle are said to have been poisoned by eating it. Ægopodium Podograria, *Gout-Weed*, or *Bishop-Weed;* common in this neighbourhood; a troublesome weed. Bunium flexuosum, *Earth-nut*, known as *Lusie-arnut;* hill pastures, Wester Lumbenny. Æthusa Cynapium, L., *Fool's Parsley;* a weed in cultivated ground. Heracleum Sphondylium, L., *Cow-Parsnip;* waste places, common. Scandix Pecten, *Venus's Comb;* cornfields. Chærophyllum temulentum, *Rough Chervil;* The Mair's Craig. Myrrhis odorata, *Sweet Cicely*, better known as *Myrrh* in this neighbourhood; around the old site of Easter Lumbenny. Daucus Carota, *wild Carrot;* foot of Clachard.

ARALIACEÆ.—Hedera Helix, *common Ivy;* ruins of Lindores Abbey, Fincraig.

CAPRIFOLIACEÆ.—Sambucus nigra, *Common Elder*, or *Bour-tree;* Abbey burnside. Lonicera Periclymenum, *Common Honeysuckle;* Fincraig, South Caldron, Lochmill, Ballinbriech.

RUBIACEÆ.—Galium verum, *yellow Bed-straw;* Ormiston hill. G. Saxatile, *smooth Heath Bed-straw; Ib.* G. palustre, *white Water Bed-straw;* Loch-Lindores. G. aparine, *Goose-grass;* Abbey burnside. Asperula odorata, *sweet Woodruff;* Fincraig. Sherardia arvensis, *blue Sherardia*, or *Field Madder;* The Mair's Craig.

VALERIANACEÆ.—Valeriana officinalis, *great wild Valerian;* river-bank near Ballinbriech, and Den at west end of Lochmill.

DIPSACEÆ.—Dipsacus sylvestris, *wild Teasel;* once observed in Mugdrum woods; grows in Glenfarg. Knautia arvensis, *Field Knautia;* The Mair's Craig. Scabiosa succisa, *Devil's-bit Scabious;* Fincraig, and roadsides.

COMPOSITÆ.—Tragopogon pratensis, *yellow Goat's-beard;* Parkhill Inches. Hypochæris radicata, *Long-rooted Cat's-ear;* Loch-Lindores. Lactuca virosa, *strong-scented Lettuce;* Abbey. Sonchus oleraceus, L., *Common annual Sow-Thistle;* a weed on cultivated ground. Leontodon Taraxacum *common Dandelion;* waste places. Hieracium pilosella, L., *common Mouse-ear Hawk-weed*; Ormiston hill. Arctium Lappa, *common Burdock;* Abbey burnside. Carduus palustris, *Marsh Plume-Thistle;* Loch-Lindores. C. lanceolatus, L., *Spear Plume-Thistle;* waysides. Centaurea Cyanus, *Blue-Bottle, Blawart*; Mair's Craig. Bidens cernua, *Nodding Bur-Marigold;* Loch-Lindores. Tanacetum vulgare, *Tansy;* Lindores Abbey. Artemisia vulgare, *Mugwort, Wormwood;* Wodriffe road. Artennaria dioica, *Mountain Everlasting;* Ormiston hill. Petasites vulgare, *Butter-bur;* Abbey burn. Tussilago Farfara, *Colts-foot; Ib.* Aster Tripolium, *Sea Starwort;* near Ballinbriech. Senecio vulgaris, L., *Groundsel;*

a weed on cultivated ground. S. sylvaticus, *Mountain Groundsel;* The Mair's Craig. Filago minima, *least Filago; Ib.* S. Jacobea, *Ragweed, Weebow;* common. S. Aquaticus, *Marsh-Ragweed;* Loch-Lindores and Pow. Doronicum Pardalianches, *Great Leopard's-Bane;* near Ballinbriech Castle, and Mugdrum. Bellis perennis, *Daisy, Gowan;* abundant. Chrysanthemum Leucanthemum, *Great White Ox-eye;* railway slopes. Anthemis arvensis, *Corn Chamomile;* Mary's Craig. Achillea Ptarmica, *Sneezewort;* Loch-Lindores. A. millefolium, *Milfoil;* Wodriffe road.

CAMPANULACEÆ.—Campanula rotundifolia, *Harebell;* Ormiston hill, abundant, Abdie churchyard. C. latifolia, *Giant Bell-flower;* once observed at Black Loch.

ERICACEÆ.—Vaccinium Myrtillus, *Blaeberry;* Blackcairn, Lochmill Woods. (V. Oxycoccos, L. *Cranberry,* grows in bogs near Pitmenzie.) Erica Tetralix, *Cross-leaved Heath;* Lochmill hill westward. E. cinerea, *fine-leaved Heath;* White Craig, etc. Calluna vulgaris, *common Ling,* Lochmill hill. Pyrola rotundifolia, *round-leaved Wintergreen;* Wood, near Butterwell; Weddersby Wood, near Black-loch.

GENTIANEÆ.—Gentiana campestris, *Field Gentian;* Abbot's-Seat, and north summit of Fincraig. Menyanthes trifoliata, *Marsh-Trefoil; Bogbean;* Loch Lindores, Lochmill.

CONVOLVULACEÆ.—Convolvulus arvensis, *small Bindweed;* Wodriffe fields, near Ninewells. C. Soldanella, *Seaside Bindweed;* river side, near Ballinbriech.

BORAGINEÆ.—Echium vulgare, *Viper's Bugloss;* Wodriffe. Lithospermum arvense, *Corn Gromwell;* fields near Ninewells. Myosotis palustris, *Forget-me-not;* river side, east from *Shore.* M. cæspitosa, *tufted water Scorpion Grass;* Loch Lindores. Lycopsis arvensis, *small Bugloss;* the Mair's Craig. Symphytum officinale, *Comfrey;* Burnside, and near Denmiln.

SOLANACEÆ.—Hyoscyamus niger, *Henbane;* Lindores Abbey-orchard. Solanum Dulcamara, *Woody Night-shade;* mouth of burn Invernethy.

SCROPHULARIACEÆ. —Veronica serpyllifolia, *Thyme-leaved Speedwell.* Ormiston hill. V. scutellata, *Marsh-Speedwell;* Loch Lindores. V. Beccabunga, *Brooklime, Ib.* and Ninewells Burn. V. Chamædrys, *Germander Speedwell;* Ormiston hill. V. hederifolia, *Ivy-leaved Speedwell.* Fields. Bartsia Odontites, *Red Bartsia;* field above Monkswell, How-Kavell. Euphrasia officinalis, *Eye-bright;* Ormiston hill. Rhinanthus Crista-Galli, *common Yellow-rattle;* the Mair's Craig, Fincraig. Pedicularis palustris, *Marsh Lousewort;* Loch Lindores. Mimulus luteus, *common Mimulus;* shores of the Tay above Mugdrum. Scrophularia nodosa, *knotted Figwort;* foot of Clachard. S. vernalis, *yellow Figwort;* Abbey. Digitalis purpurea, *Folk's-glove, Dead-men's-bells;* Ormiston hill. Linaria Cymbalaria, *Ivy-leaved Toad-flax;* Lindores Abbey, introduced. L. vulgaris, *yellow Toad-flax;* Fincraig. Verbascum Thapsus, *Great Mullein;* Ballinbriech, Abbey (one plant 6½ feet in height, 1873). V. Lychnitis, *White Mullein;* Abbey, Denmiln orchard wall, and wall at Burnside.

LABIATÆ.—Mentha aquatica, *Water-Mint;* west end of Lochmill. Thymus Serpyllum, *wild Thyme;* Ormiston hill. Origanum vulgare, *Marjoram;* foot of Fincraig. Teucrium Scorodonia, *Wood Germander; Ib.* Ajuga reptans, *common Bugle;* Lochmill burn, west. Galeopsis Tetrahit, *Common Hemp-nettle;* the Mair's Craig. Lamium purpureum, L. Red Dead Nettle; a weed in cultivated ground. L. amplexicaule L. *Henbit Nettle;* a common weed. Stachys sylvatica, *Hedge Wound-wort;* Abbey. S. palustris, *Marsh Woundwort;* Loch Lindores. Nepeta Glechoma. *Ground-Ivy;* Clachard. Prunella vulgaris, *Common Self-heal;* common. Scutellaria galericulata, *Common Skull-cap;* observed once in Lindores Burn, below Eel-house.

LENTIBULARIACEÆ.—Pinguicula vulgaris, *Common Butterwort;* Ninewells, and near Butterwell.

PRIMULACEÆ.—Primula vulgaris, *Primrose;* Ballinbriech, Fincraig. P. elatior, *Oxlip;* Glenfarg. P. veris, *Cowslip; Ib.* Glaux maritima, *Sea-Milkwort;* Ballinbriech. Trientalis Europœa, *Chickweed Winter-green;* the nearest *habitat* is the wood above Gattaway. Lysimachia nemorum, *Wood Loose-strife;* Glenfarg. Anagallis arvensis, *Scarlet Pimpernel;* fields, North-Grange and Ormiston.

PLANTAGINACEÆ.—Plantago major, *Plantain;* roadsides. P. lanceolata, *Ribwort;* pastures frequent. P. maritima, *Seaside Plantain;* riverside, above Ballinbriech. Littorella lacustris, *Plantain Shoreweed;* Loch Lindores, Lochmill.

CHENOPODIACEÆ.—Chenopodium album, *White Goosefoot;* the Mair's Craig. C. Bonus Henricus, *Good King Henry.*

SCLERANTHACEÆ.—Scleranthus annuus, *Knawel;* Mary's Craig.

POLYGONACEÆ.—Polygonum viviparum, *Alpine Bistort;* Lochmill hill. P. aviculare, L. *Common Knot-grass;* roadsides. P. convolvulus. L. *climbing Buckwheat;* cornfields. P. amphibium, *Buckwheat;* Loch Lindores, Lochmill. Rumex ascetosella, *Sheep's Sorrel;* the Mair's Craig.

EUPHORBACEÆ.—Mercurialis perennis, *Dog's Mercury;* foot of Fincraig. Euphorbia helioscopia, L. *Sun Spurge;* a garden weed.

URTICACEÆ.—Urtica urens, L. *Small Nettle;* a weed in fields and gardens. U. dioica L. *Great Nettle;* waste places. Parietaria diffusus, *Pellitory of the Wall* walls of Lindores Abbey.

CANNABINEÆ.—Humulus Lupulus, Hop (male plant); Abbey, burnside.

BETULACEÆ.—Betula alba, *common Birch;* foot of Clachard—sprung up since the cutting for the railway. Aluus glutinosa, *Common Alder;* Maw Inch, Lindores.

CLASS II.—MONOCOTYLEDONS.

ORCHIDACEÆ.—Orchis mascula, *early purple Orchis;* Woodmill wood. O. maculata, spotted Orchis; woods. Habenaria viridis, *green Habenaria;* Ormiston hill.

IRIDACEÆ.—Iris Pseud-acorus, *Yellow Water Iris* or *Flag;* Lindores Loch, Steel's Den.

AMARYLLIDACEÆ.—Galanthus nivalis, Snowdrop; Ballinbriech.

LILIACEÆ.—Agraphis nutans, *Wild Hyacinth;* Fincraig. Allium ursi-num, *Ramsons* or *Broad-leaved Garlick;* Lindores Abbey.

JUNCACEÆ.—Juncus effusus, *Soft Rush;* Lindores Loch. J. conglo meratus L. *Common Rush;* on undrained land. J. bufonius L. *Toad Rush,* common. J. Gerardi, round-fruited Rush; beach near Ballinbreich Castle. Luzula sylvatica, Great Wood Rush; foot of White Craig. L. campestris, *Field Wood-rush;* in pastures common.

ALISMACEÆ. — Alisma Plantago, *Great Water Plantain;* Lindores, Lochmill.

TYPHACEÆ.—Typha angustifolia, *Lesser Reed Mace;* Lindores Loch.

LEMNACEÆ.—Lemna minor, *Lesser Duck-weed;* Lindores Pow.

NAIADACEÆ.—Potamogeton plantagineus, *Plantain-leaved Pond-weed;* Loch Lindores. P. crispus, Curly Pond-weed; *Ib.*

CYPERACEÆ.—Eriophorum angustifolium, *Narrow-leaved Cotton-grass;* Lochmill hill. Eleocharis palustris, *Spike Rush:* Loch Lindores.

GRAMINEÆ.—Anthoxanthum odoratum, Sweet-scented Vernal-grass; Fincraig. Nardus stricta, Mat-grass; Blackcairn. Alopecurus pratensis, *Meadow Fox-tail grass;* Ormiston hill. A. geniculatus, *Floating Fox-tail grass;* Loch Lindores. Phleum pratense, *Cat's-tail* or *Timothy-grass;* Ormiston hill. Aira cœspitosa, *Tufted Hair-grass;* foot of White Craig, Lindores. Holcus lanatus, *Meadow Soft-grass;* Ormiston hill. Arrhena-therium avenaceum, *Oat-like grass;* Loch Lindores. Glycera aquatica, *Reed Meadow-grass; Ib.* G. fluitans, *Floating M.; Ib.* Kœleria cristata, *Crested K.;* Mary's Craig. Briza media, *Quaking-grass;* Ormiston hill. Poa aquatica L. *Reed Meadow-grass;* Marshy shores of the Tay. Cyno-surus cristatus, *crested Dog's-Tail grass;* Nine-wells burn. Phragmitis communis, *Common Reed;* Mugdrum Island, Lindores Pow. Triticum repens, L. *Wheat-grass;* road sides.

CLASS III.—ACOTYLEDONS OR CRYPTOGRAMS.

FILICES.—Polypodium vulgare, *Common Polypody;* Mary's Craig, Blackcairn. P. Dryopteris, *Oak Fern, tender three-branched Polypody,* among *debris* at foot of White Craig. Aspidium Filix mas, *Male Fern.* Ring of Blackcairn. A. Oreopteris, *Heath Shield Fern;* Ormiston hill. Asplenium Ruta muraria, *Wall-rue Spleenwort;* old walls, abundant. A. Trichomanes, *Maidenhair Spleenwort;* the Mair's Craig. Scolopendrium vulgare, *Common Hart's-Tongue;* Abbey walls. Pteris aquilina, *Common Bracken;* Ormiston hill. Blechnum boreale, *Northern Hard Fern;* west end of Lochmill.

LYCOPODIACEÆ.—Lycopodium clavatum, *Common Club-moss;* Loch mill hill.

EQUISETACEÆ.—Equisetum fluviatile *great Water Horse-tail;* Lochmill. E. arvense, *Corn Horse-tail;* cornfields. E. limosum, smooth Naked Horse-tail; Loch Lindores. E. sylvaticum, *branched Wood Horse-tail;* Lochmill woods.

ALGÆ.—Rivularia species; occurs in such profusion in some parts of Loch Lindores, as to make the water have a thickened discoloured appearance.

Moulding of door-way leading from the Cloister-garth to the nave of Lindores Abbey church.

INDEX.